# Standing Before Us

## Unitarian Universalist Women and Social Reform, 1776–1936

**Dorothy May Emerson, Editor**

**June Edwards and Helene Knox, Contributing Editors**

✦ ✦ ✦

For Tamara,
In appreciation for teaching us to color outside the lines without making a mess of the vision.
With affection,
the Ministerial Fellowship Committee

April 2000
Chicago

**Skinner House Books**
**Boston**

Published by Skinner House Books, an imprint of the Unitarian Universalist Association, 25 Beacon Street, Boston, MA 02108-2800.

Printed in Canada.

ISBN 1-55896-380-4

04 03 02 01 00 99
10 9 8 7 6 5 4 3 2 1

**Library of Congress Cataloging-in-Publication Data**

Standing before us : Unitarian Universalist women and social reform, 1776–1936 / by Dorothy May Emerson, editor ; June Edwards and Helene Knox, section editors ; with biographical sketches by more than 30 authors.

p. cm.

Includes bibliographical references and index.

ISBN 1-55896-380-4

1. Church and social problems—Unitarian Universalist churches. I. Emerson, Dorothy May, 1943– . II. Edwards, June. III. Knox, Helene.

BX9856.S73 1999

261.8'088'281—dc21 99-32908

CIP

**Text Credits:**

"The Opening Doors" by Olympia Brown, Olympia Brown Papers. Reprinted by permission of the Schlesinger Library, Radcliffe College.

Selected letters from the Judith Sargent Murray Papers. Reprinted by permission of the Mississippi Department of Archives and History.

Selected quotations from the diary of Amy Morris Bradley, Amy Morris Bradley Papers. Reprinted by permission of the Special Collections Library, Duke University.

Handwritten notes by Susan B. Anthony, Folder 23, Susan B. Anthony Collection. Schlesinger Library, Radcliffe College. Reprinted by permission of Mary Anthony Coughlin and the Schlesinger Library.

"Obedience to the Heavenly Vision," Sermon notes. Mary Safford Papers. Reprinted by permission of the State Historical Society of Iowa.

# Contents

✦ ✦ ✦

Contents

# Preface

✦ ✦ ✦

*Standing Before Us* brings together writings of women who were leaders in movements for social reform and took part in the liberal religious movements of Unitarianism and Universalism. These women put their religious principles into action by responding to the needs of the world they lived in. Despite all odds, they found the means to move their world toward justice.

Today, the lives and words of these women empower those of us who continue that struggle. We can learn from both their successes and their failures, from both their rich insights and their limited views. Upon hearing their stories—and thus coming to know the women who stand before us in this great project of re-forming the world—we can be inspired by their vision and take heart in their perseverance. Making this connection with the past may help us realize that we are part of a living stream of witnesses who believe that it is up to us to make the world a better place for all.

This anthology spans the period in the United States from the signing of the Declaration of Independence to the mid 1930s. Although most of the authors are from the United States, Canadian and British women are included as well. Canadian women often participated directly in U.S. reform efforts and eventually founded similar reform organizations in Canada. British women were concerned with many of the same issues, and their writings both influenced and reflected what was happening in North America. Viewing all these women's writings as a whole, we begin to understand the international character of movements for social reform.

## Organization

The first section, Call to Reform, introduces the concept of social reform as it was understood by women who were leaders in various reform movements. Their writings indicate areas of reform of particular concern to liberal religious women and suggest some of the unique contributions of Unitarian and Universalist women.

The second section, The Search for Education, considers the struggle for access to education as an essential foundation for other reforms. Universalist and Unitarian women were able to provide significant leadership in education reform because they were often educated by their families long before the practice of educating daughters became common in society.

The third section, The Struggle for Racial Justice, begins by examining the abolitionist movement and continues with a look at efforts following the Civil War to establish a just society for people of all races. Because working to end slavery taught many women how to organize effectively for social change, this reform movement prepared the way for those that followed. Unitarian and Universalist women were among those in the forefront of the antislavery struggle from the beginning.

The fourth section, Reform in Religion, explores religious ideas and theology as well as the practice of religion and the changing structures and goals of churches. The writings in this section demonstrate ways women influenced future developments in both Universalism and Unitarianism.

Each piece of historical writing is preceded by a brief statement introducing its author and indicating its context and significance both in the author's life and in the time in which it was written. A Biographical Sketch of the author follows the first appearance in the anthology of writing by that author.

## Biographical Sketches

An important aspect of this project has been the involvement of many people in recovering and sharing Unitarian Universalist women's history. In addition to the women who served as section editors, a broad range of people were invited to submit biographical sketches of the women whose writings appear in this anthology. The authors of these sketches have a clear sense of connection with the woman or women of the past about whom they have written. Their participation in this project demonstrates the strong relationship people today feel with these Universalist and Unitarian women who stand before us in the struggle for social justice.

The bibliographical information provided for each author varies depending on what materials were available. For some women, only a few resources were discovered; all of those are listed. For women who wrote and published extensively and about whom much has been written, only those resources related to their selections in the anthology are listed. In a few cases, incomplete information is given because that is all that was available. If you have additional information and/or corrections to these listings, please forward them to the Unitarian Universalist Women's Heritage Society, 2 Elm Street, Malden, MA 02148. Or contact us via email at uuwhs@aol.com.

## Notes on Language and Style

One of the important principles of historical analysis is the need to understand people from the past in the context of their own times. As a committed practitioner of gender-inclusive language, I have had to come to terms with the need to present these texts in their original format, even though by today's standards, some of the language seems sexist. A few of these women from history seemed to have understood that the words *man, mankind,* and *brothers* do not generally include women; however, most were quite comfortable with the then-common understanding of these words as gender inclusive.

To some individuals, revising these original texts to make them more palatable to current standards for inclusive language would give a false impression. Nevertheless, when using these selections for worship or inspirational readings, I generally do change the language to be inclusive on the assumption that had these women participated in the contemporary dialogue on inclusive language, they would have changed the way they expressed themselves, as many of us have done. When quoting these sources in changed format, I simply include the term *adapted* following the listing of the source.

The use of language that seems more traditionally Christian than is common in today's Unitarian Universalism may lead to confusion. It is important to realize that references to *Jesus, Christ, Father, Lord,* and so on were part of the ordinary religious language of the time within the liberal religious community. This language does not mean that these writers were orthodox, as we understand the term today.

Many of the texts printed here include antiquated words regarding race, such as *colored* and *negro,* as well as statements that could be considered racist by today's standards. The section editors agreed to retain the words originally used by the authors. When reading these passages, it is important to note the historical context. Although white women who worked for abolition and racial justice at times expressed sentiments that were undoubtedly racist, their work remains an important part of the struggle for racial justice.

Another dilemma that arises, particularly in the Biographical Sketches and introductions to readings, concerns what name is used to refer to a woman once her full name has been given. The traditional academic style is to refer to a person by her or his surname. A feminist objection to this practice when used to refer to a woman is that this name is often either her husband's or her father's name. Citing a woman's surname becomes particularly confusing if she did some of her work before marriage and other work after marriage or if she married more than once. One alternative is to use the woman's first name or the name she preferred to be called during her life. However, this practice has been criticized as trivializing women, since men are generally referred to by their surnames. In this anthology, the editors have decided to let each author choose her or his own style.

Other conventions used throughout this text deserve to be mentioned here, as well. Since our goal is to provide a glimpse into the thoughts and feelings of Universalist and Unitarian women of the past, rather than an exhaustive analysis of their ideas, we have chosen to excerpt longer writings to make them accessible and hopefully to whet your appetite to read more. When long writings are extensively excerpted, we have used ✦ ✦ ✦ to indicate that a paragraph or more has been omitted. The conventional ellipsis (i.e., . . .) is used to indicate brief omissions within paragraphs. Although historical fidelity is very important, in some instances we have used modern punctuation and spelling and divided long passages into paragraphs to improve the readability of the text.

## Looking to the Future

The areas of reform presented in this anthology spill over into each other and into other areas of reform that developed during the one hundred sixty years spanned by these writings. After the Civil War, women who had worked to end slavery turned their attention to the fundamental issues of human freedom and opportunity, including women's suffrage. Women concerned with the corrosive effect of alcohol on families poured their energies into settlement houses, educational institutes, special homes, and shelters for women. To protect their families and to improve the quality of life in their communities, women became involved in sanitation and health reforms. Others provided leadership in economic development and social welfare, the rights of workers, and the development of unions. The women's club movement originated as a way to provide continuing education and empowerment for women and to make women's voices heard on public and political issues. The suffrage movement often broke through male resistance on a city-by-city basis, as women gained the right to vote on school issues; many Unitarian and Universalist women found their first positions of public power by serving on school boards. Women were actively involved in efforts to improve the treatment of prisoners and people who were mentally ill. And women led a variety of efforts to promote world peace.

These important issues of reform are barely touched on in this anthology, although Universalist and Unitarian women actively participated in all of them. Moreover, the fifty women whose writings are included in this anthology are only a few of those who participated in the development of these movements toward justice. We hope to expand this initial core of reform women and writings in future volumes to demonstrate the broad impact that Universalist and Unitarian women have had on our lives today.

For too long, our understanding of religious and social history has been limited by a focus on the lives and work of men. In the liberal religious traditions of Universalism and Unitarianism, women were often the ones to activate and demonstrate the values of their faith, such as freedom, tolerance, acceptance of diversity, and individual rights. They translated liberal theology into real work to promote justice in the world and, at the same time, struggled with inequities in their own religious institutions.

We still confront many of the same issues faced by our foremothers. By engaging with these women of the past, we hope to empower and inspire today's women and men to continue the work of creating a world of justice and peace for all.

*Dorothy May Emerson*
Editor

# The Past, the Present, and the Future

*We sometimes speak as if the past were over and done with: "That's past; that's out of date; that's ended." Yet try to obliterate in your thought all that is past. It is impossible, of course, because in so doing we obliterate ourselves. Without the help of what we call the past we could not live at all.*

✦ ✦ ✦

*The past, instead of being done with, is, then, the real fiber of the world as we know it. Just as the food we eat nourishes us till it becomes what we* act with, *so the past is always what we* think with.

✦ ✦ ✦

*The present . . . is what we make of it, and its size is exactly that size which our hands are capable of grasping.*

✦ ✦ ✦

*Our future is in our power—not, indeed, what happens to us, but what we* do *with what happens to us.*

✦ ✦ ✦

*How can we best meet an unknown future? Three things seem to be essential: resolve, resource, discipline.*

✦ ✦ ✦

*Our own future may be spiritually and physically . . . rough, wild, [and] complicated. . . . To meet its uncertainties we need to know what to do in woods where we have lost our life-way and in whirlpools that break to pieces our cherished hopes.*

—ELLA LYMAN CABOT[1]

# Standing Before Us

*Chorus:*

Standing before us, making us strong
Lending their wisdom to help us along
Sharing a vision, sharing a dream
Touching our thoughts, touching our lives
Like a deep flowing stream.

✦ ✦ ✦

These are the women who throughout the decades
Have led us and helped us to know
Where we have come from and where we are going,
The women who've helped us to grow.

✦ ✦ ✦

These are the women who joined in the struggle,
Angry and gentle and wise.
These are the women who called us to action,
Who called us to open our eyes.

✦ ✦ ✦

These are the women who nurtured our spirits,
The ones on whom we could depend.
These are the women who gave us courage,
Our mentors, our sisters, our friends.

✦ ✦ ✦

These are a few of the women who led us.
We know there have been many more.
We name but a few, yet we honor them all,
These women who went on before.

—CAROLE ETZLER EAGLEHEART[1]

# Call to Reform

## by Dorothy May Emerson

✦ ✦ ✦

THESE WRITINGS DOCUMENT the awakening of women to the need for social reform. In some cases, the women are struggling to define their voices in the face of a long tradition of silence. They are fighting for air, trying to figure out how to be alive and free in a world that wants to keep them under control. Liberal religious ideas of individual worth and dignity both inspire them and confirm their inspiration to move beyond their traditional roles and call for reform—for themselves and their world. Those of us who have created this anthology contend that among the important factors leading women to acknowledge the need for reform and begin to take an active role in its promotion was their involvement with the liberal religious ideas of Unitarianism and Universalism and the networks of people who embraced them.

One of the major goals of this anthology is to present for the first time a resource that draws together some of the characteristic Unitarian and Universalist women's writings on social reform. This section introduces the idea of social reform and offers insight into the way Unitarian and Universalist women understood their roles as agents of change in their various contexts. These selections span a period of 131 years, from 1776 to 1907. The sixteen Universalist and Unitarian women who wrote these selections are from the United States, Canada, and Great Britain. They represent a range of social and economic classes, racial backgrounds, levels of education, and life struggles and achievements. We hope this initial collection will pique the curiosity of scholars and others interested in women's and liberal religious history and encourage further study of the origins of reform within the Universalist and Unitarian traditions.

The foundational ideas of both these religious movements were developing in the United States at the time of the first writings in this volume. Both movements had roots and separate histories in England, although both were considered nonconforming religions. Unitarianism became the religion of the New England intelligentsia, and thus, for the first part of the nineteenth century, it was considered the religion of the educated establishment, especially in urban areas. Universalism, which was more of a populist movement, appealed to the emerging merchant class, working class, and people in more rural areas; however, there were many well-educated people among them, and the Universalists had many urban churches as well.

Although both religious movements were multilayered and arose in response to a variety of theological issues and concerns, each can be characterized by its primary challenge to orthodox Christianity, as described in its name. The characteristic Unitarian challenge was the assertion of the unity of God, as opposed to the idea of the trinity. The characteristic Universalist challenge was the declaration of universal salvation, as opposed to the Calvinist idea of salvation only for the elect. What these movements had in common was faith in freedom, reason, tolerance, and an affirmation of human responsibility. Both traditions featured an openness to alternative understandings of truth, a resistance to creeds, and a focus on the importance of action in this world, as contrasted with life after death. Although historical differences were among the impediments keeping Unitarians and Universalists apart, these two liberal religious movements joined in 1961 to form the Unitarian Universalist Association.

According to *Webster's Collegiate Dictionary* (10th ed.), the word *reform* means "1. to put or change into an improved form or condition; 2. to amend or improve by change of form or removal of faults or abuses; 3. to put an end to (an evil) by enforcing or introducing a better course of action." Unitarianism and Universalism are generally viewed as reform movements within Christianity because both sought to remove what they saw as faults and abuses in Christian doctrine.

Some of the women who participated in these movements may have felt they were outside the mainstream. Perhaps this factor alone encouraged them to question other norms of the day and consider the need to improve conditions they found abusive, such as how women were treated by law and by custom. Such individual observations were transformed into social movements when women shared their ideas with one another through personal dialogue and correspondence, through friendship and social connections, and eventually in organized meetings. When women gathered in groups to challenge the evils of female subjugation, they sought to formulate better ways of doing things and to introduce a course of action to change both custom and law.

Once these women recognized a need for reform, they did not sit idly by and wait for things to change. They took action. In many different forms, they expressed their concerns about the way things were and their visions for a better tomorrow. They wrote letters to one another, full of conviction and encouragement. They wrote essays, stories, and poems for denominational and popular journals of the day. They wrote books. They organized meetings and conventions and took to the public platform, speaking out for the rights of various groups of disenfranchised people. They organized clubs and raised money for causes. They lobbied the government. In sum, they made certain their voices were heard and did not rest until the changes they sought finally were made.

Previous studies of the social reform movements of the nineteenth and early twentieth centuries have viewed the roots of reform as arising from the evangelical Christian tradition, often demonstrating connections with the Second Great Awakening,[1] a series of revivals that swept much of the United States beginning in the early 1800s and reaching its peak in the 1820s and 1830s. (The First Great Awakening occurred in the 1730s and 1740s.) According to this view, the impetus for reform arose from the demands of evangelical ministers to apply Christian moral values to public life.

Among the popular literature of the time, there was significant discussion about what modern historians have called "the cult of true womanhood" or "the cult of domesticity."[2] This social ethic viewed women as holding a central position in the creation of successful homes and families. Women's special roles and abilities as homemakers, educators, and nurturers were believed to give them a place of honor in the culture designated the *woman's sphere.* Although most evangelical preachers did not intend to suggest that women should move out of their traditional roles, the effect of drawing attention to social problems ultimately led women more and more into the public arena and away from a singular focus on family life. Some reformers viewed this as an extension of women's domestic responsibilities, while others ultimately challenged the norm of separate spheres altogether.

Those who were inspired primarily by evangelical preaching turned to what was called *moral reform.* The first emphasis of this movement was on eliminating prostitution. Female Moral Reform societies began forming in the 1820s, particularly in Massachusetts and New York. Their goals were to reform prostitutes by helping them develop self-respect, to identify and make public the men who patronized them, and to bring up both boys and girls to uphold chastity before marriage and fidelity in marriage.[3] In England, a similar movement among women emerged in 1835 and was flourishing by the 1860s; it also was inspired by evangelical preaching against sexual immorality. Although the movement for moral reform focused on individual morality, it heightened awareness of the double standard that then existed in judging men's versus women's sexual behavior. Recognition of this double standard also helped focus attention on the need to work specifically for women's rights.[4]

Although some liberal religious women became involved in social change through moral reform, more often their entry point was through participation in the antislavery, temperance, or peace movements or through involvement in efforts to gain education for women. The Civil War created opportunities for women to serve their country and gain valuable organizational and work experience, although they had to fight for acceptance in these roles. Later, the establishment of women's clubs inspired intellectual development and prepared women for the sustained struggle for voting and other legal rights. One of the significant areas of reform for liberal religious women was the reform of religion itself. Even within their liberal traditions, women challenged narrowly defined norms and worked to change their institutions to include more opportunities and eventually equality for women.

A few studies of the origins of social reform have pointed to sources beyond evangelical religion that may have inspired reform in political and economic realms. In one analysis, women are identified as challenging the male-dominated world directly. In another, women are seen as working with men to change the social structure, allowing for the emergence of the middle class.[5]

Several studies consider the possible influence of liberal religion on the emergence of an independent reform movement in the United States that focused on abolition and women's rights;[6] however, these studies do not go into any depth as to precisely what those influences might have been in terms of beliefs and practices. Nancy Cott suggests that what may have precipitated some women and not others "to cross the boundaries from 'woman's sphere' to 'woman's rights'" may have been "escape from conventional evangelical Protestantism—whether through Quakerism, Unitarianism, radical sectarianism, or 'deconversion.'" She defines *deconversion* as "ideological disengagement from the convincing power of evangelical Protestantism (or inability to accept the whole of it.)"[7] Both Unitarianism and Universalism were significant forces in challenging traditional evangelical Protestantism, undoubtedly leading to the deconversion of many people.

One issue that inspired deconversion for a number of women was the fact that the orthodox theology that dominated most protestant Christian churches at the time considered all those who were unbaptized to be damned to hell for eternity, even babies and young children. A number of women (and undoubtedly some men, as well) could not accept this idea and began to question other tenets of orthodoxy. Universalism, in particular, offered a clear alternative to this orthodox belief.

British historians have been more specific in naming the influence of Unitarianism on social reform movements there.[8] Christine Bolt explains the active participation of many Unitarians in reform movements as "a means of gaining the social respectability that their small numbers and early political disabilities would otherwise have denied them."[9] Duncan Crow suggests that "Unitarianism and other nonconformist beliefs had the liberating effect of making those young women with any spark of initiative more ready to struggle for a measure of independence."[10]

Olive Banks credits Unitarians with keeping the feminist-sounding doctrines of the Enlightenment alive and identifies the superior education given to girls in Unitarian families (along with the effect of growing up in homes with a tradition of reform) as factors contributing both to the responsiveness of Unitarians to the doctrine of women's rights and to the large number of early reformers who came from this religious tradition. She suggests that although Unitarians were active in reform movements in the United States, they participated more as individuals than as a movement, perhaps partly because Americans viewed Unitarianism as being more prestigious, which deflated its radical activist mindset.[11]

American historians are likely to identify writers who were Universalists as among the first to speak and write about women's rights but generally fail to identify their religious affiliation. Some commonly given examples of Universalist trailblazing are Dr. Benjamin Rush's declaration in 1787 that the principles of equality of the newly established republic should apply to women's education and Judith Sargent Murray's essays calling for women's equality, first published in 1790.[12] Interestingly, these same historians regularly credit the Quakers as leaders in reform and list numerous references to Quakers in their indexes, while omitting any references to either Universalists or Unitarians. Although Anne Firor Scott identifies Universalists as the religious group "most accepting of activist women," next to the Quakers, she generally fails to name the religious affiliations of the women activists she presents, unless they are Quakers. One dramatic example of this exclusion occurs in her account of five of the leaders in the Sanitary Commission during the Civil War. Two were Unitarians, two were Universalists, and one was a Quaker, but only the Quaker affiliation is named.[13]

When challenged concerning this tendency to identify Quaker but not other religious affiliations, one of the compilers of a listing of women in the suffrage movement at the National Women's History Project responded that *Quaker* is considered a historic identification, whereas *Unitarian Universalists* are today known as radicals, perhaps causing the connection with historical women to be misunderstood. The two denominations also are frequently confused, so that Universalist women are sometimes identified as Unitarian, the better known of the two traditions.[14]

It is time to set the record straight: to identify these women with Unitarianism and Universalism, to begin to explore the influence of their beliefs on their work for reform, and to acknowledge that these two liberal religious traditions contributed many women to the reform movements, despite their relatively small numbers in relation to the general population. The fact that Universalist and Unitarian women were among the first and most consistent to work for women's rights and for reform in a variety of fields is something historians can agree on. This anthology is intended as a beginning step in the exploration of why this is so.

Unitarian Universalists today continue to be known for their activism in working for social justice. These historical women and their writings provide a link between the present and the past while locating the origins of social reform within liberal religion. In some cases, these women and their writings are well known; some were widely circulated at the time and had a strong influence on the reforms they advocated. Other writings were and remain less well known, perhaps only influencing a small circle or revealing a voice that was nearly silenced. All reflect an emerging awareness of the need for change. Whether it is a communication among a network of friends or a speech from a famous platform, these words represent an unbroken tradition that deserves to be recognized today as a link with the real historical past. Each writer articulated her vision of life as it should be and called to her constituency and beyond to re-form the world to guarantee justice and promote peace for all.

# We Are Determined to Foment a Rebellion

## Letter to Mercy Otis Warren, 1776

*This section, Call to Reform, begins with a letter from Abigail Smith Adams to Mercy Otis Warren. Both women were early unitarians before there was an official Unitarian church in the United States. They also shared a concern that the new government of the republic should provide equity for women.*

ABIGAIL SMITH ADAMS (1744–1818) *was a lady of letters, a farmer, a patriot of the American Revolution, and First Lady of the United States. Writing just before the signing of the Declaration of Independence, she expressed to her friend her frustration at the negative response she had received from her husband, John Adams (later the second president of the United States), when she asked him to make sure the laws for the new country be based on "just and liberal principles" that would apply to women as well as men. When he scoffed at her request, she threatened to foment "a Rebellion" if the rights of women were ignored.*

See the Biographical Sketch on pages 8–12.

Braintree, Massachusetts, April 27, 1776

To Mercy Otis Warren,

He [Mr. Adams] is very saucy to me, in return for a list of female grievances which I transmitted to him. I think I will get you to join me in a petition to Congress. I thought it was very probable our wise statesmen would erect a new government and form a new code of laws. I ventured to speak a word in behalf of our sex who are rather hardly dealt with by the laws of England which gives such unlimited power to the husband to use his wife ill. I requested that our legislators would consider our case and as all men of delicacy and sentiment are averse to exercising the power they possess, yet as there is a natural propensity in human nature to domination I thought the most generous plan was to put it out of the power of the arbitrary and tyranick to injure us with impunity by establishing some laws in our favor upon just and liberal principles.

I believe I even threatened fomenting a Rebellion in case we were not considered and assured him we would not hold ourselves bound by any laws in which we had neither a voice nor representation.

In return he tells me he cannot but laugh at my extraordinary code of laws that he had heard their struggle had loosened the bonds of government, that children and apprentices were disobedient, that schools and colleges were grown turbulent, that Indians slighted their guardians and Negroes grew insolent to their Masters. But my letter was the first intimation that another Tribe more numerous and powerful than all the rest were grown discontented. This is rather too coarse a compliment, he adds, but that I am so saucy he won't blot it out.

So I have helped the sex abundantly, but I will tell him I have only been making trial of the disinterestedness of his virtue [and] when weighed in the balance have found it wanting.

It would be bad policy to grant us greater power say they since under all the disadvantage we labor we have the ascendancy over their hearts

"And charm by accepting,
by submitting sway."

## ✦ *Biographical Sketch*

**Born:** *November 11, 1744, Weymouth, Massachusetts*

**Died:** *October 28, 1818, Braintree (now Quincy), Massachusetts*

**Buried:** *In the crypt under the United First Parish Church (Unitarian), Quincy, Massachusetts*

Resourceful, competent, self-sufficient, willful, opinionated, witty, and vivacious, Abigail Adams is one of our most remarkable foremothers. Remembered chiefly as the wife of John Adams, second president of the United States, and the mother of John Quincy Adams, fifth president, she left a voluminous correspondence whose keen intelligence shows her to be a formidable force in her own right. Through her letters, she reveals a dedication to principle, a commitment to rights for women and people of color, a fierce partisanship to her husband's (and her family's) interests, an irreverent sense of humor, and an absolute sincerity.

Born in the parsonage of the First (Congregational) Church of Weymouth to the Reverend William Smith and Elizabeth Quincy, Abigail was raised simply and without pretension, in spite of the fact that her relatives, especially on her mother's side, were among the leading Puritan families of their time. To her great regret, she received no formal schooling, although she certainly benefited from the many books and lively conversation in the parsonage. Her lack of education later embarrassed her, as she was very self-conscious of her inability to spell or punctuate properly as well as of her inability to speak or read French. Even so, Abigail would become a devoted reader of history and an astute judge of its impact upon her own time.

Received into the Congregational church in 1759 at age fourteen, Abigail first met John Adams that same year. By 1762, he and Abigail were exchanging love letters that are so frankly affectionate and full of mischievous humor that it is hard to remember the authors are of the most revered Puritan stock.

Abigail Smith and John Adams were married in 1764, when he was twenty-nine and she almost twenty. Their marriage, one of history's great partnerships, was also one of its great love stories. Rather than resent his wife's abilities to manage a farm and raise a family without him (during his long absences on the nation's business), John took considerable pride in her accomplishments. He jokingly told her that she was so successful in budgeting, planting, managing staff, regulating livestock, buying provisions, and nursing and educating their children that the neighbors would surely remark on how much better things seemed to be in his absence.

After accompanying her husband on diplomatic missions to France and England from 1783–1788, Abigail was glad to return to the Adams farm in Braintree. As she wrote to Thomas Jefferson, she preferred her farm to "the court of St. James, where I seldom meet with characters so inoffensive as my Hens and chickings, or minds so well improved as my garden."[15]

A visit below the Mason-Dixon line solidified Abigail's conviction, passionately shared by her husband, that slavery was not only evil but a threat to the American democratic experiment. Both believed in offering opportunities of education and advancement to African Americans and had little use for the Southern slavery accommodationists. At one point, Abigail wrote that she doubted the distinguished Virginians in the corridors of power had quite the "passion for Liberty" they claimed to have, since they were used to "depriving their fellow Creatures" of freedom.[16]

Just before John's inauguration as president, Abigail wrote to him regarding a black servant boy who had come to her requesting the opportunity to go to school and to learn to write. When she enrolled the boy in a local evening school, one of the neighbors came to her to report serious objections of some unnamed "others" to the presence of the black boy in the school. Abigail swiftly responded that the boy is "a Freeman as much as any of the young Men and merely because his Face is Black, is he to be denied instruction? How is he to be qualified to procure a livelihood? . . . I have not thought it any disgrace to my self to take him into my parlor and teach him both to read and write."[17] Her firm response to this neighbor apparently put an end to the complaints.

In an often-quoted letter to her husband, written just before the signing of the Declaration of Independence, Abigail spoke up for more opportunities for women. Although she did not insist on full enfranchisement for women, she warned of the consequences of ignoring women:

> *Remember the Ladies, and be more generous and favorable to them than your ancestors. Do not put such unlimited power into the hands of the Husbands. Remember all Men would be tyrants if they could. If particular care and attention is not paid to the Ladies we are determined to foment a Rebellion and will not hold ourselves bound by any Laws in which we have no voice or Representation.*[18]

A fervent advocate of education for women and for married women's property rights, Abigail was determined that women should be recognized for their intellectual capabilities; for their ability to shoulder responsibilities for managing household, family, and financial affairs; and for their capacity to morally guide and influence the lives of their children and husbands. She believed women should be seen as more than decorous companions to their husbands, willing to submit to laws clearly not in their own best interest.

Disturbingly, both Abigail and John Adams supported the Alien and Sedition Acts during Adams's single term in the presidency. Designed to put a stop to virulent criticism of the president of the United States, this controversial set of laws prosecuted those who attacked the policies of John Adams for sedition and possibly treason.

As First Lady, Abigail showed her usual good cheer and refusal to wallow in self-pity. The White House was a cavernous structure so cold and damp that fires had to be kept lit constantly in those rooms that were to be at all habitable. Abigail set up a laundry in one of the great rooms and spanned clotheslines across its vast space.

Both Abigail and John Adams were active members of the First Parish Church in Quincy, which was already Unitarian in theology by the 1750s, even though the official founding of the American Unitarian Association would not take place until 1825.[19] Abigail's theology is clearly stated in her letters. To her son, John Quincy, she wrote: "I acknowledge myself a unitarian—Believing that the Father alone, is the supreme God, and that Jesus Christ derived his Being, and all his powers and honors from the Father."[20] Her conviction was clear, as she explained later: "There is not any reasoning which can convince me, contrary to my senses, that three is one, and one three." To her daughter-in-law, Louisa, she confessed: "True religion is from the Heart, between Man and his creator, and not the imposition of Man or Creeds and tests."[21]

After leaving public life in 1800, both John and Abigail enjoyed a productive retirement at their homestead in Braintree. The parents of four children, they took pleasure in the rise of their son John Quincy Adams to prominence, first as a U.S. senator, then as minister to Russia, and finally in 1817 as James Monroe's secretary of state. They worried about the errant ways of their sons Thomas and Charles and were concerned about their beloved daughter Nabby's profligate and spendthrift husband. On the whole, however, they took much pleasure in their family, prospering farm, and community.

Abigail fell ill with typhus (also described as a nervous or bilary fever) early in October 1818 and died several weeks later.

*Biographical Sketch by* LAURIE CARTER NOBLE

## ✦ Writings of Abigail Adams

Adams, Charles Francis, ed. *Letters of Mrs. Adams.* Boston: C. C. Little & J. Brown, 1840.

Butterfield, L. H., ed. *The Adams Papers: Adams Family Correspondence.* 2 vols. New York: Atheneum, 1963.

Butterfield, L. H., Marc Friedlaender, and Mary-Jo Kline, eds. *The Book of Abigail and John: Selected Letters of the Adams Family, 1762–1784.* Cambridge, MA: Harvard University Press, 1975.

Cappon, Lester J., ed. *The Adams-Jefferson Letters.* Chapel Hill: University of North Carolina Press, 1988.

## ✦ Biographical Resources

Akers, Charles W. *Abigail Adams, An American Woman.* Boston: Little, Brown, 1980.

Levin, Phyllis Lee. *Abigail Adams.* New York: St. Martin's Press, 1987.

Nagel, Paul C. *The Adams Women: Abigail and Louisa Adams, Their Sisters and Daughters.* New York: Oxford University Press, 1987.

Whitney, Janet. *Abigail Adams.* Boston: Little, Brown, 1947.

## ✦ Archives

Most of Abigail Adams's correspondence is in the Adams Papers at the Massachusetts Historical Society in Boston and has been published on microfilm. The Warren-Adams Letters (Collections, vols. LXXII–LXXIII) document her friendship with Mercy Otis Warren.

# The Times That Try Men's Souls

## Response to Pastoral Letter, 1837

MARIA WESTON CHAPMAN (1806–1885), *a key organizer of the abolitionist movement in Boston, worked closely with William Lloyd Garrison and edited* The Liberator, *the mouthpiece of the Massachusetts Anti-Slavery Society. She was also a founder of the Boston Female Anti-Slavery Society. A member of the Federal Street Church in Boston, she was a close friend of William Ellery Channing, one of the early founders of Unitarianism in the United States. She challenged him to speak out against slavery.*

*When the orthodox Congregational ministers of Massachusetts issued a pastoral letter in 1837 to warn of potential dangers to the female character caused by speaking in public, Maria Weston Chapman chose humor for her response. Her Unitarian background is evident in her incisive theological insight and analytical ability to separate Christian principles from the patriarchal domination of women.*

See the Biographical Sketch on pages 15–18.

Confusion has seized us, and all things go wrong,
The women have leaped from "their spheres,"
And instead of fixed stars, shoot as comets along,
And are setting the world by the ears!
In courses erratic they're wheeling through space,
In brainless confusion and meaningless chase.

In vain do our knowing ones try to compute
Their return to the orbit designed;
They're glanced at a moment then onward they shoot,
And are neither "to hold nor to bind";
So freely they move in their chosen elipse,
The "Lords of Creation" do fear an eclipse.

They've taken a notion to speak for themselves,
And are wielding the tongue and the pen;
They've mounted the rostrum; the termagant elves,
And—oh horrid!—are talking to men!

With faces unblanched in our presence they come
    To harangue us, they say, in behalf of the dumb.

They insist on their right to petition and pray,
    That St. Paul, in Corinthians, has given them rules
For appearing in public; despite what they say
    Whom we've trained to instruct them in schools;
But vain such instructions, if women may scan
    And quote texts of Scripture to favor their plan.

Our grandmothers' learning consisted of yore
    In spreading their generous boards;
In twisting the distaff, or mopping the floor,
    And *obeying the will of their lords,*
Now, misses may reason, and think, and debate,
    Til unquestioned submission is quite out of date.

Our clergy have preached on the sin and the shame
    Of women, when out of "her sphere,"
And labored *divinely* to ruin her fame,
    And shorten this horrid career;
But for spiritual guidance no longer they look
    To Fulsom, or Winslow, or learned Parson Cook.

Our wise men have tried to exorcise in vain
    The turbulent spirits abroad;
As well might we deal with the fetterless main,
    Or conquer ethereal essence with sword;
Like the devils of Milton, they rise from each blow,
    With spirit unbroken, insulting the foe.

Our patriot fathers, of eloquent fame,
    Waged war against tangible forms;
Aye, *their* foes were man—and if ours were the same,
    *We* might speedily quiet their storms;
But, ah! their descendents enjoy not such bliss—
    The assumptions of Britain were nothing like this.

Could we but array all our foes in the field,
    We'd teach these usurpers of power
That their bodily safety demands they should yield,
    And in the presence of manhood should cower;
But, alas! for our tethered and impotent state,
    Chained by notions of knighthood—we can but debate.

Oh! shade of the prophet Mahomet, arise!
    Place woman again in "her sphere,"
And teach that her soul was not born for the skies,
    But to flutter a brief moment here.
The doctrine of Jesus, as preached up by Paul,
    If embraced in its spirit, will ruin us all.

(signed) *The Lords of Creation*

## ✦ *Biographical Sketch*

**Born:** *July 25, 1806, Weymouth, Massachusetts*

**Died:** *July 12, 1885, Weymouth, Massachusetts, age 78*

**Buried:** *Weymouth, Massachusetts*

Maria Weston Chapman was the oldest of the five Weston sisters of Weymouth, all of whom became active in the antislavery struggle. She was educated in London under the best of circumstances for a woman in that day and returned to London in 1828 to become principal of Ebeneezer Bailey's Young Ladies' High School.

In 1830, Maria married Henry G. Chapman, who was an abolitionist like his parents. All were supporters of the Massachusetts Anti-Slavery Society, led by William Lloyd Garrison. Both Maria and Henry were members of Federal Street Church (today, Arlington Street Church) in Boston, where William Ellery Channing was minister. Within two years, she and twelve other women had founded the Boston Female Anti-Slavery Society, a *separate* society, since there was strong resistance to women "moving out of their sphere" in work on the public platform, and public and political organization. (She also became editor of their Annual Report, *Right and Wrong in Boston.*) It was regarded as unfeminine, even immoral, and certainly totally inappropriate for a woman to speak before mixed (female and male) audiences in that day. Maria Weston Chapman was in full possession of all the social graces her privileged, influential background could provide. Historian Louis Filler describes her as "vibrant and arresting."[22] Thus, she quickly became known for her abolitionist convictions, speeches, and activities and received extensive personal and public abuse from Boston society.

Maria and her sisters were all teachers and educators and worked on behalf of education for Boston's free black people, never a popular cause, although Boston was more progressive than most of the North.

The Chapman home became a daily meeting place and place of refuge for the local abolitionist community, which was despised and openly denounced almost everywhere in Boston. Abolitionists from all over New England gathered there for conversation and planning.

It was natural that Maria Weston Chapman would become chief lieutenant to the Massachusetts Anti-Slavery Society, often taking on editorial responsibilities for *The Liberator* when Garrison was away and fielding the many questions and demands that flowed through its offices in those heady days. Garrison was a defender of women's initiative and leadership, and the so-called woman issue became one of the causes that split up the American antislavery movement. Chapman also helped edit the periodical of the New England Non-Resistant Society, *The Non Resistant.*

When the Grimke sisters made their controversial tour of the North, often speaking in and around Boston, the Massachusetts Association of Congregational Ministers issued a pastoral letter to all associated clergy in the commonwealth, noting that some women were speaking to indiscriminate audiences of men and women and otherwise moving beyond their God-ordained sphere. Proper believers were counseled to avoid them and under no circumstances to imitate them, praying to God to remove this scourge from God's chosen Israel.[23] Maria Weston Chapman, needless to say, ignored the counsel, and the infant American Unitarian Association did not make the mistake of counseling a like silence. Too many Unitarian women already had found their voices. In fact, Chapman introduced Angelina Grimke over a howling mob in Philadelphia in 1838.[24]

Beginning in 1834, Maria Weston Chapman, with her sisters and others, organized huge antislavery fairs to raise money for antislavery societies; these popular fairs were attended by large numbers of folk, many of whom were not particularly supportive of the antislavery cause. The annual fair of the Massachusetts Anti-Slavery Society was the group's primary fundraiser. Maria Weston Chapman also edited *The Liberty Bell,* a well-illustrated annual gift book of articles and poetry from New England's leading liberal citizens and others from as far away as England's Harriet Martineau.[25]

Maria Weston Chapman is particularly remembered for the words she spoke in 1835 when Garrison was mobbed while attempting to address a Boston interracial meeting of women concerned with black education. When Boston Mayor Theodore Lyman urged the women to disperse in light of the immediate threat of violence, Chapman, tall and quietly forceful, said in the midst of the large volatile mob: "If this is to be the last bulwark of freedom, we may as well die here as anywhere."[26] The women adjourned and quietly marched through the angry crowd to the Chapman house to finish the meeting.

With others, Maria Chapman assisted in lawsuits to free enslaved women, labored in the perennial antislavery petition movement, and organized the first women's Anti-Slavery Convention in New York. In 1840, she was elected to the Executive Committee of the American Anti-Slavery Society in New York. She and Wendell Phillips are listed as secretaries to the famous New York meetings at which William Lloyd Garrison's declaration of "No Union With Slaveholders" was approved, driving moderate antislavery forces to create a competing national organization.[27] Chapman soon became coeditor of the *National Anti-Slavery Standard.*

After her husband died in 1842, Maria Weston Chapman took her children to Paris for their education, not returning to the United States until 1855. During these years abroad, she continued to be an active contributor to the antislavery cause and its publications. Maria Weston Chapman's writing was crisp and clean, relatively unadorned for that age. Garrison published a volume of her songs and hymns, and she frequently contributed poetry and stories to *The Liberator* and *The Liberty Bell.* In one of her stories, she recounted a litany of proslavery, white-supremacist arguments she had heard from a distinguished Harvard professor. She "meekly inquired whether, if the three million blacks could be suddenly turned white, we would venture to present a single one of these considerations for keeping [blacks] in slavery." She went on to note: "An ignorant, unthinking vulgar prejudice is, in fact, the American's only ally in the war which his mistaken notions of political and pecuniary interest lead him to wage against liberty."[28]

With the end of the Civil War, many Americans, including old antislavery advocates, turned their backs on the needs of African Americans in the South. Maria Weston Chapman was not one of them. She immediately joined supporters of both of the old rival antislavery societies in support of the Tappans' Fortress Monroe and later of the Port Royal Experiment in South Carolina, directed by fellow Unitarian Laura Towne.[29] Writing in wonderment, Chapman noted: "From the high historic point of view, was ever progress so swift? But thirty years from the start, and you are organizing the leading slave state in Freedom."[30]

Maria Weston Chapman was not active in most women's rights issues except indirectly. Like her friend Lydia Maria Child,[31] she avoided direct competition with men, and "in their appeals to other women, [they] advocated the moral pressures available to daughters, wives, mothers, and sisters, rather than a battle for the vote."[32] Even so, her life was a testament to women's rights

The British Unitarian author Harriet Martineau, entranced by Chapman's classic beauty and personal force of character, was a supporter and friend. Chapman, returning the respect, turned her talents to publishing an American version of the much-enhanced two-volume edition of Martineau's *Autobiography* in 1877.

Maria Weston Chapman was an extraordinary woman who found and exercised her rights. She was a critical force in the development of American antislavery thought and action.

*Biographical Sketch by* DAVID JOHNSON

## ✦ Writings of Maria Weston Chapman

*Autobiography of Harriet Martineau, with Memorials by Maria Weston Chapman.* London: Elder, 1877.

"How Can I Help to Abolish Slavery? or, Counsels to the Newly Converted." *Anti-Slavery Tracts* 14 (1855): 7–9.

Poems and articles in *The Liberty Bell.* Boston: Annual volumes, 1850s.

Songs and hymns in *Songs of the Free and Hymns of Christian Freedom.* Boston: Isaac Knapp, 1836.

*Ten Years of Experience.* Boston: O. Johnson, 1842.

## ✦ Biographical Resources

Cole, Phyllis. *Woman Questions: Emerson, Fuller, and New England Reform.* Proceedings of Massachusetts Historical Society Conference, Boston, 1997.

Filler, Louis. *The Crusade against Slavery.* New York: Harper Torchbooks, 1960.

Lutz, Alma. "Maria Weston Chapman." In *Notable American Women,* edited by Edward T. James et al. Cambridge: Belknap Press, 1971.

*There is no serious biography of Maria Weston Chapman. Details of her life are found in antislavery histories, her voluminous correspondence, and biographies of her friends.*

SARAH CARTER EDGARTON [MAYO]

# A Thought on Female Culture

## Article in *The Universalist and Ladies' Repository,* December 1841

*One of the instruments for the developing discussion of the role and status of women was a Universalist literary journal. Seven years before the publication of this article, the editor had added the words* Ladies' Repository *to the journal's name,* The Universalist, *to "advocate the rights of* FEMALES, *and earnestly contend for* FEMALE *education."*[33]

SARAH CARTER EDGARTON [MAYO] (1819–1848) *was a popular poet and frequent contributor to Universalist journals. She also wrote children's books and served as editor of the Universalist women's journal,* Rose of Sharon. *In her essay "A Thought on Female Culture," she struggled with the question and implications of the equality of women. After some deliberation, she concluded that for women to be true companions of men, they must have access to equal education and opportunities for intellectual development. She went on to affirm that not all women needed to be married but should have the option of "an independent existence."*

*Her support for women's equality reflected her Universalist theological belief in the goodness of God and the inherent worth and dignity of God's creation. Her argument for women as whole beings was careful and gentle and as apt today as it was in 1841.*

See the Biographical Sketch on pages 21–23.

I think woman greatly misjudges her own happiness in making it depend so entirely upon the chances of her fortune, and the gratification of her affections. She is too much inclined to the belief that she is a *dependent* creature—that she cannot make herself and her fortunes. I would not inculcate the absurd doctrine of physical independence, nor ground my arguments on the supposition that woman can render herself indifferent to exterior circumstances. But that same good Being who has given to the minutest insect some instrument of self-preservation, sent not into this world the most beautiful creation of his hands to be the sport of circumstance and the victim of feeling.

I am not intending at this time, nor in this place, to give full expression to the opinions that are gaining daily strength in my mind, respecting the proper culture and discipline of the female character. It seems to be a prevalent idea that something is wrong either in the education or in the position of woman. Her *rights* are discussed, her sphere disputed, her very privileges seem to be subjects of doubt and inquiry. One claims for her a place in the halls of legislation, in the pulpit, the lecture-room, and at the polls. He would see her clad, like Joan of Arc, in the iron panoply of war—with helm on her head, and shield at her heart. Another, not less devoted to her happiness, would make her, like the Lares, a household divinity, presiding at the hearth-stone—the mother of children, the tender nurse, the frugal housewife, and—nothing more.

I think these contending advocates for the sex are both at fault in making exterior condition the source of female influence and happiness. If woman's mind and heart are right, it is not of essential importance whether their operations are in private, and upon her household, or whether they take a more open and bustling sphere of duty. The most she wants is a character, a power, an independence. Not that independence which erects "Liberty-poles" and shouts "Freedom!" from the forum; but the calm, still, holy consciousness of mental and moral power; the elevation and strength which is born of knowledge, of thought, and of just self-reliance.

The education which will fit woman to be the companion of man in intellect, as well as in feeling, will not subtract, in the minutest degree, from those qualities which render her lovely in domestic life. Indeed, can any woman be so valuable to a husband as one who is capable of sharing the confidence of his *mind* as well as his heart? She is but half-wedded who cannot enter into the intellectual sympathies of her companion. It is only when he *feels,* that she is his wife; when he *thinks,* she is alone.

And then, again, woman is not necessarily born for marriage. She has the birthright of an independent existence; and to this birthright she owes reverence as to a holy gift. Her motto should be *"Equal to either fortune"*—and at all times let her remember that though it may be *expedient* for her to marry, it is her *privilege* to be single. I hope, in another place and at another time, to give a clearer and better expression to these opinions. I wish to exhibit woman as she can be, rather than as she is—a being of noble capacities and powers, educated to be useful, having individual resources, unfailing self-reliance, and a knowledge of happiness not subject to exterior contingencies. In a word, as the poet has beautifully described her—

> "A being breathing thoughtful breath,
> A traveler between life and death;
> With reason firm, and temperate will,
> Endurance, foresight, strength and skill;
> A *perfect woman,* nobly planned,
> To warn, to comfort, and command."

## ✦ *Biographical Sketch*

**Born:** *March 17, 1819, Shirley, Massachusetts*

**Died:** *July 9, 1848, Gloucester, Massachusetts, age 29*

**Buried:** *Shirley, Massachusetts*

Throughout her short life of twenty-nine years, Sarah Edgarton saw herself as a professional writer. She wrote poetry, essays, and novels that reflected her love of nature, education, and religion. She was an ardent Universalist who shared editorship of *The Universalist and Ladies' Repository* with noted Universalist writer Henry Bacon. As she wrote to a friend in one of her many letters to those who shared her interest in intuitive religion, "We are rich because we love and are beloved. What more do we ask?"[34]

Sarah grew up in Shirley Village, Massachusetts, a rural factory town west of Boston. She was the tenth of fifteen children (four of whom died in infancy) and was closest throughout life to her brother John. Her parents, Joseph and Mehitable, were Universalists, and Sarah profited from frequent visits by stimulating individuals as well as from her father's extensive library. With her brother John and friends Starr King and Julia Scott, she delighted in intellectual discussions. By the time she was seventeen, she was already sending her writing to *The Universalist and Ladies' Repository.* She excelled in all subjects and continued to study throughout her life. In addition to translating German and French Romantic prose, she read a wide array of nature poets, such as William Wordsworth and Lord Byron, and philosophical writers, including Thomas Carlyle, Ralph Waldo Emerson, and William Ellery Channing.

In 1840, Sarah and her parents traveled to the Universalist convention in Auburn, New York. From there, she began an extensive tour of New York State, recording her impressions in a detailed journal. Many of her descriptions were sent as letters to *The Universalist and Ladies' Repository,* and today these entries offer us much historical insight into life in upstate New York at the time.

In 1846, Sarah married Universalist minister A. D. Mayo from Amherst. They lived in Gloucester, where she gave birth to their first daughter, Caroline Frances, known as Carrie. Because Sarah's husband was never healthy, most of her writings appeared before their marriage.

All of Sarah Edgarton's writings reflected her Universalist sentiments and her love of nature. She opposed the doctrinaire theological treatises of Calvinism and declared her beliefs in the spirit within, which could be experienced through both the contemplation of nature and an inward focus. She endorsed the Cult of True Womanhood, but while emphasizing the moral virtues and power of women in the domestic sphere, she also emphasized that women should be educated as intellectuals as well as for domestic duties. In "A Thought on Female Culture," written in 1841, seven years *before* the first women's rights convention in Seneca Falls, she asserted that women should be treated equally, whether they led a single or married life.

Sarah Edgarton Mayo wrote prolifically, primarily for income that would help her and her family lead a more secure life. Most contemporary critics declare her domestic fiction *Annette Lee, The Palfreys,* and its sequel *Ellen Clifford* rather one dimensional, but according to B. Susan Brown, Mayo's most profound thoughts and original language appear in her letters, essays, entries in *The Universalist,* and some of her poems. Brown praises her annual *Rose of Sharon,* first published in 1839, as one of her best works. It was a compendium of works by many of her friends, primarily women. One of her poems ends as follows:

> I paced the beach like some sleep-walking child,
> wrapt in a dream of beauty and of awe;
> Were they ideal visions that beguiled?
> Was it my eye, or but my *soul* that saw?[35]

*Biographical Sketch by* SUSAN SWAN

## ✦ Writings of Sarah Carter Edgarton [Mayo]

*Ellen Clifford; or the Genius of Reform.* Boston: A. Tompkins and B. B. Mussey, 1838.

*The Fables of Flora.* Lowell: Merrill and Straw, 1844.

*The Floral Fortune-Teller; a Game for the Season of Flowers.* Boston: A. Tompkins, 1846.

*The Palfreys, a Tale by a Lady.* Boston: A. Tompkins, 1838.

*Poetry of Woman.* Boston: A. Tompkins and B. B. Mussey, 1841.

*Selections from the Writings of Miss Sarah C. Edgarton Mayo: With a Memoir by Her Husband.* Boston: A. Tompkins, 1849.

## ✦ Biographical Resources

Brown, B. Susan. "The Spark Within, the Flame Without: Two Universalist 'Scribblers' of the Nineteenth Century." Term paper, Harvard Divinity School, 1985.

Gemmill, Eva H. S. "Sarah Edgarton Mayo: More Than a 'Sweet Singer of God's Unbounded Love.'" Occasional Paper #12. Malden, MA: Unitarian Universalist Women's Heritage Society, 1996.

Goodwin, Joan W. "The Ladies' Repository: A Sisterhood of Universalists." Occasional Paper #19. Malden, MA: Unitarian Universalist Women's Heritage Society, 1998.

Hanson, Eliza R. *Our Women Workers.* Chicago: Star and Covenant, 1882.

## MARGARET FULLER

# In Behalf of Woman

### From *Woman in the Nineteenth Century*, 1845

MARGARET FULLER (1810–1850) *was an author, critic, teacher, and revolutionary thinker. One of the few women to participate actively in the Transcendentalist movement, she served as the first editor of the Transcendentalist journal* The Dial. *To encourage women to think for themselves and to learn to express their opinions publicly, she held a series of Conversations for women.*

*In 1843, she published an essay in* The Dial *entitled "The Great Lawsuit: Man versus Men, Woman versus Women." Two years later, she expanded it to become her second book,* Woman in the Nineteenth Century. *This book had an important and lasting effect on the empowerment of women and became a sort of "bible" for the incipient movement for women's rights.*[36] *The excerpts that follow indicate the core of her argument for women's equality. Her combination of Transcendentalist/Unitarian spirituality with practical agitation proved electrifying and inspiring to those who gathered in 1848 in Seneca Falls, New York, at the first women's rights convention.*

See the Biographical Sketch on pages 27–29.

It should be remarked that, as the principle of Liberty is better understood, and more nobly interpreted, a broader protest is made in behalf of Woman. As men become aware that few men have had a fair chance, they are inclined to say that no women have had a fair chance. The French Revolution, that strangely disguised angel, bore witness in favor of Woman, but interpreted her claims no less ignorantly than those of Man. Its idea of happiness did not rise beyond outward enjoyment, unobstructed by the tyranny of others. The title it gave was "citoyen" and "citoyenne"; and it is not unimportant to Woman that even this species of equality was awarded her. Before, she could be condemned to perish on the scaffold for treason, not as a citizen, but as a subject. The right with which this title then invested a human being was that of bloodshed and license. The Goddess of Liberty was impure. . . . Yet truth was prophesied in the ravings of that hideous fever, caused by long ignorance and abuse. Europe is conning a valued lesson from the blood-stained page. The same tendencies, further unfolded, will bear good fruit in this country.

✦ ✦ ✦

As to men's representing women fairly at present, while we hear from men who owe to their wives not only all that is comfortable or graceful, but all that is wise, in the arrangement of their lives, the frequent remark "You cannot reason with a woman,"—when from those of delicacy, nobleness and poetic culture, falls the contemptuous phrase "women and children," and that in no light sally of the hour, but in works intended to give a permanent statement of the best experiences,—when not one man, in the million, shall I say? no, not in the hundred million, can rise above the belief that Woman was made *for Man,*—when such traits as these are daily forced upon the attention, can we feel that Man will always do justice to the interests of Woman? Can we think that he takes a sufficiently discerning and religious view of her office and destiny *ever* to do her justice, except when prompted by sentiment,—accidentally or transiently, that is, for the sentiment will vary according to the relations in which he is placed? The lover, the poet, the artist, are likely to view her nobly. The father and the philosopher have some chance of liberality; the man of the world, the legislator for expediency, none.

Under these circumstances, without attaching importance, in themselves, to the changes demanded by the champions of Woman, we hail them as signs of the times. We would have every arbitrary barrier thrown down. We would have every path laid open to Woman as freely as to Man. Were this done, and a slight temporary fermentation allowed to subside, we should see crystallizations more pure and of more various beauty. We believe the divine energy would pervade nature to a degree unknown in the history of former ages, and that no discordant collision, but a ravishing harmony of the spheres, would ensue.

Yet, then and only then will mankind be ripe for this, when inward and outward freedom for Woman as much as for Man shall be acknowledged as a *right,* not yielded as a concession. As the friend of the negro assumes that one man cannot by right hold another in bondage, so should the friend of Woman assume that Man cannot by right lay even well-meant restrictions on Woman. If the negro be a soul, if the woman be a soul, apparelled in flesh, to one Master only are they accountable. There is but one law for souls, and, if there is to be an interpreter of it, he must come not as man, or son of man, but as son of God.

✦ ✦ ✦

The late Dr. Channing, whose enlarged and tender and religious nature shared every onward impulse of his time, though his thoughts followed his wishes with a deliberative caution which belonged to his habits and temperament, was greatly interested in these expectations for women. His own treatment of them was absolutely and thoroughly religious. He regarded them as souls, each of which had a destiny of its own, incalculable to other minds, and whose leading it must follow, guided by the light of a private conscience. He had sentiment, delicacy, kindness, taste; but they were all pervaded and ruled by this one thought, that all beings had souls, and must vindicate their own inheritance. Thus all beings were treated by him with an equal, and sweet, though solemn, courtesy. The young and unknown, the woman and the child, all felt themselves regarded with an infinite expectation, from which there was no reaction to vulgar prejudice. He demanded of all he met, to use his favorite phrase, "Great truths."

✦ ✦ ✦

I believe that, at present, women are the best helpers of one another.

Let them think; let them act; till they know what they need.

We only ask of men to remove arbitrary barriers. Some would like to do more. But I believe it needs that Woman show herself in her native dignity, to teach them how to aid her; their minds are so encumbered by tradition. . . .

If you ask me what offices they may fill, I reply—any. I do not care what case you put; let them be sea-captains, if you will. I do not doubt there are women well fitted for such an office, and, if so, I should be . . . glad to see them in it. . . .

I think women need, especially at this juncture, a much greater range of occupation than they have, to rouse their latent powers. A party of travellers lately visited a lonely hut on a mountain. There they found an old woman, who told them she and her husband had lived there forty years. "Why," they said, "did you choose so barren a spot?" She "did not know; *it was the man's notion.*" And, during forty years, she had been content to act, without knowing why, upon "the man's notion." I would not have it so.

## ✦ *Biographical Sketch*

**Born:** *May 23, 1810, Cambridge, Massachusetts*

**Died:** *July 19, 1850, off Fire Island, New York, age 40*

**Buried:** *Memorial Marker, Mount Auburn Cemetery, Cambridge, Massachusetts*

Margaret Fuller was a leading nineteenth-century literary and social critic who campaigned for women's rights and equal education. She was also an ardent Transcendentalist and the founding editor of the Transcendentalist periodical *The Dial.*

She was born to Unitarian parents in Cambridge, Massachusetts, in 1810. Her father was a liberal politician and a supporter of equality for women. He educated his precocious daughter at home for several years, instilling in her principles of independent thought and moral courage, which he derived from his own beliefs and study of Greek and Latin writers. Fuller reached adulthood as a formidably intelligent, socially eccentric young woman who was either intensely disliked or intensely admired but who could not be ignored. First as a teacher and later as a literary and social critic, she won the respect of the male intellectual establishment by sheer force of mind and personality.

In the 1830s and 1840s, Fuller became one of the leaders of Boston's young Unitarian (soon-to-be Transcendentalist) circle, a group that included James Freeman Clarke, William Henry Channing, Theodore Parker, George Ripley, and Ralph Waldo Emerson. With the aging Reverend William Ellery Channing, she read German philosophy and theology. Through their discussions, her own emerging convictions began to take shape—on religion, social issues, and the status of women.

In 1843, with James Freeman Clarke and his sister Sarah, Fuller toured what was then the western American frontier. She wrote *Summer on the Lakes,* a book that preserves a picture of the newly arrived European and Yankee settlers of Illinois and Wisconsin and the destitute survivors of the native tribes they had displaced.

Since conversation was a key activity of the Transcendentalists and Fuller took a particular interest in encouraging women to express themselves rationally and articulately on challenging subjects, she conceived a plan to offer a series of Conversations for eminent women in the Boston area. These gatherings, most of which took place in Elizabeth Peabody's[37] foreign language bookstore in Boston during 1839 and 1840, also provided Fuller with some financial support. Participants discussed such topics as mythology, art, ethics, education, faith, health, women's rights, and the lives and ideas of great men and women.

Out of her experience as leader of these all-female Conversations, Fuller wrote the first major feminist book in the United States, *Woman in the Nineteenth Century,* in 1845. It called for legal, social, political, educational, and vocational equality, based on religious faith in the equality of all souls before God. In the same year, she joined Horace Greeley's liberal *New York Tribune,* becoming one of two significant American literary critics of the day (with Edgar Allan Poe) and commenting on abolition, prison reform, treatment of people who are insane, and other social issues. In 1846, she sailed to Europe as foreign correspondent for the *Tribune.* She observed the social unrest there and the enormous problems of the poor. In Rome in 1847, she decided to remain in Italy and join the revolutionary cause. Her *Tribune* letters gave her American readers a close view of the brief life of the infant Roman Republic.

Meanwhile, Fuller had fallen in love with a young Italian nobleman, Giovanni Ossoli, and had borne their child. In 1850, now married and in danger of arrest by the authorities because of their participation in the Italian freedom struggle, Margaret Fuller sailed for the United States with her husband and child. Their ship was wrecked in a hurricane off Long Island, and all three were killed.

*Biographical Sketch by* PAULA BLANCHARD

## ✦ Writings of Margaret Fuller

*At Home and Abroad.* Edited by Arthur B. Fuller. Boston: Crosby, Nichols, 1856.

*Life Without and Life Within.* Edited by Arthur B. Fuller. Boston: Brown, Taggard, and Chase, 1860. Reprint, Gregg Press, n.d.

*Memoirs of Margaret Fuller Ossoli.* Edited by Ralph Waldo Emerson, William Henry Channing, and James Freeman Clarke. 2 vols. Boston: Phillips, Sampson, 1852. Reprint, New York: Burt Franklin, 1972.

*Papers on Literature and Art.* New York: n.p., 1846. Reprint, New York: AMS Press, 1976.

*Summer on the Lakes.* Boston: Greeley and McElrath, 1845.

*Woman in the Nineteenth Century.* Edited by Arthur B. Fuller. Boston: Charles C. Little and James Brown, 1844. Reprint, New York: Norton, 1871.

## ✦ Biographical Resources

Blanchard, Paula. *Margaret Fuller: From Transcendentalism to Revolution.* Reading, MA: Addison-Wesley, 1987.

Capper, Charles. *Margaret Fuller: The Private Years.* New York: Oxford University Press, 1992.

Chevigny, Bell Gale. *The Woman and the Myth: Margaret Fuller's Life and Writings.* New York: Feminist Press, 1976.

Dall, Caroline W. H. *Margaret Fuller and Her Friends.* Boston: Roberts Bros., 1895.

Deiss, Joseph Jay. *The Roman Years of Margaret Fuller.* New York: Crowell, 1969.

Miller, Perry. *Margaret Fuller, American Romantic: A Selection from Her Writings and Correspondence.* New York: Anchor Books, 1963.

Myerson, Joel. *Margaret Fuller: A Descriptive Bibliography.* Pittsburgh: University of Pittsburgh Press, 1978.

Rossi, Alice S. "The Making of a Cosmopolitan Humanist: Margaret Fuller." In *The Feminist Papers, from Adams to de Beauvoir,* 144–158. New York: Columbia University Press, 1973.

Von Mehren, Joan. *Minerva and the Muse: A Life of Margaret Fuller.* Amherst: University of Massachusetts, 1994.

## LUCY STONE

# To Labor for the Elevation of My Sex

### Letter to Her Mother, Hannah Stone, 1846

LUCY STONE (1818–1893) *has been called "the morning star of the woman's movement" because she was the first major public lecturer for women's rights. She became a Unitarian after she discovered the Congregational church of her youth would not allow her to vote in its proceedings. A moving force behind the women's suffrage movement, she founded and edited its weekly newspaper,* The Woman's Journal. *Lucy Stone also was the first woman from Massachusetts to graduate from college. She wrote this letter to her mother during her last year at Oberlin, explaining her decision to become a public lecturer for the Anti-Slavery Society, which she described as her calling.*

See the Biographical Sketch on pages 31–34.

I know, Mother, you feel badly about the plans I have proposed to myself, and that you would prefer to have me take some other course, if I could in conscience. Yet, Mother, I know you too well to suppose that you would wish me to turn away from what I think is my duty, and go all my days in opposition to my convictions of right, lashed by a reproaching conscience.

I surely would not be a public speaker if I sought a life of ease, for it will be a most laborious one; nor would I do it for the sake of honor, for I know that I will be disesteemed, nay, even hated, by some who are now my friends, or who profess to be. Nor would I do it if I sought wealth, because I could secure it with far more ease and worldly honor by being a teacher. But, Mother, the gold that perishes in the using, the honor that comes from men, the ease or indolence which eats out the energy of the soul, are not the objects at which I aim. If I would be true to myself, true to my Heavenly Father, I must be actuated by high and holy principles, and pursue that course of conduct which, to me, appears best calculated to promote the highest good of the world. Because I know that I shall suffer, shall I for this, like Lot's wife, turn back? No, Mother, if in this hour of the world's need I should refuse to lend my aid, however small it may be, I should have no right to think myself a Christian, and I should forever despise Lucy Stone. If, while I hear the wild shriek of the slave mother robbed of her little ones, or the muffled groan of the daughter spoiled of her virtue, I do not open my mouth for the dumb, am I not guilty? Or should I go, as you said, from house to house to do it, when I could tell so many more in less time, if they should be gathered in one place? You would not object, or think it wrong, for a man to plead the cause of the suffering and the outcast; and surely the moral character of the act is not changed because it is done by a woman. . . .

But, Mother, there are no trials so great as they suffer who neglect or refuse to do what they believe is their duty. I expect to plead not for the slave only, but for suffering humanity everywhere. *Especially do I mean to labor for the elevation of my sex.* But I will not speak further upon this subject at this time, only to ask that you will not withold your consent from my doing anything that I think is my duty to do. You will not, will you, Mother?

## ✦ *Biographical Sketch*

**Born:** *August 13, 1818, West Brookfield, Massachusetts*

**Died:** *October 18, 1893, Dorchester, Massachusetts, age 75*

**Buried:** *Forest Hills Cemetery, Boston, Massachusetts; the first person to be cremated in Massachusetts*

In her time, Lucy Stone was one of the best-known leaders of the early movement for women's rights and suffrage. She was uncompromising in her belief that women had not only a right to share in the governance of the nation but a duty to do so. She passionately believed that women had rights to education and to meaningful work. She believed that women, like men, deserved the chance to develop themselves, their talents, their opinions, and their skills.

With great tenacity, Lucy Stone carved out a life for herself. She was the fifth of eight children of Francis and Hannah Stone. Hannah Stone believed strongly in education, so Lucy and her siblings attended primary school regularly. Like her older brothers, Lucy decided she wanted to go to college, but unlike her brothers, her father refused to pay for her education. At age fifteen, she went to work as a schoolteacher. She taught and saved for nearly ten years before entering Oberlin College in 1843, the only college in the United States open to women at that time.

At Oberlin, Stone studied classics, philosophy, languages, and mathematics. She became life-long friends with another young woman student, Antoinette Brown (Blackwell), who was later to become the first woman ordained a Congregationalist minister and Stone's sister-in-law. Stone formed a women's rhetoric and debating club when she learned that women were not allowed to enroll in the regular public-speaking classes.

While at Oberlin, Stone's values and beliefs were shaped in profound ways. She had been raised in the orthodox Congregational church in West Brookfield. Required to attend religious services and prayer meetings at Oberlin presided over by Charles Finney, the "hell-fire and brimstone" preacher of the Second Great Awakening, Stone grew more and more disillusioned with the church of her upbringing. She declared herself Unitarian and remained dedicated to Unitarian principles until her death. In order to earn money, she taught school to a class of fugitive slaves and freedmen. And while Stone taught her students to read, they taught her, from their firsthand experience, about the evils of slavery. Her passionate commitment to the abolitionist movement began at that time and continued throughout her life as dedication to the ongoing struggle for human rights for African Americans.

Lucy Stone graduated in 1847, the first Massachusetts woman to earn a bachelor of arts degree, and came home to West Brookfield determined to make a career as a lecturer on abolition and women's rights. She gave her first public speech, entitled "The Province of Women," in October 1847 at the Evangelical Congregational Church in Gardner, Massachusetts, where her older brother, Bowman, was minister.

Stone proved to be a powerful, charismatic speaker and quickly rose to prominence in the women's rights and abolition movements in New England. Her name headed the list of eighty-nine women and men who signed the call for the first National Woman's Rights Convention in Worcester in 1850, and she organized the second National Woman's Rights Convention in 1851. It was also at this time that she began her association with Elizabeth Cady Stanton and Susan B. Anthony.[38]

By 1854, Stone's fame as an orator was widespread, and she traveled the United States by train, stagecoach, and horse-drawn carriage, speaking on women's rights and abolition. Addressing every state legislature in the country, she attempted to persuade them to broaden suffrage to include women and to amend state laws that denied women rights. Stone understood the power of organizing at the community level. In the small towns and cities where she lectured, she organized small education and action committees to continue the work for women's rights. She also created pamphlets that instructed women how to petition their state legislatures and local governments.

In 1855, Lucy Stone married Henry Blackwell, the brother of Dr. Elizabeth Blackwell,[39] the first woman physician in the United States. Stone kept her own name after marriage, and she and Blackwell drew up a "marriage protest," which expressed their outrage about women's lack of legal or property rights in marriage. They read this protest during their wedding ceremony, which was conducted by a Unitarian minister.

Their daughter, Alice Stone Blackwell, was born in 1857. Due to their financial need, as well as to her own determination not to stop working, Stone continued touring and lecturing throughout her pregnancy and soon after the baby was born.

In the years immediately following the Civil War, the rift that had been growing between Lucy Stone and Elizabeth Cady Stanton and Susan B. Anthony over the direction of the women's rights movement reached an impasse. Unlike Stanton and Anthony, Stone had remained staunchly and publicly committed to full enfranchisement for African Americans, even if it meant securing rights for blacks before women. Thus, she supported passage of the Fifteenth Amendment, which guaranteed newly freed black males the right to vote but did not extend suffrage to white or black women. Stone also opposed Stanton and Anthony's plan to urge passage of a women's suffrage amendment to the federal Constitution, preferring instead to work for suffrage laws on a state-by-state basis.

Stone organized the American Woman Suffrage Association in 1869. Its purpose was to gain the vote for women by state action and through amendments to state constitutions. An unfortunate rivalry developed between this organization and the Stanton/Anthony–led National Suffrage Woman Association, dissipating the drive toward a suffrage amendment. Twenty years later, Stone was instrumental in forging an agreement enabling the two separate organizations to reconnect, forming the National American Woman Suffrage Association.

Lucy Stone and Henry Blackwell founded the weekly paper *The Woman's Journal* to support and publicize the policies and activities initially of the American Woman Suffrage Association and then of the movement as a whole. Stone and Blackwell and later their daughter Alice edited *The Woman's Journal* for forty-seven years.

After a long life of great struggle and great accomplishments on behalf of the rights of women, Lucy Stone died in 1893 at her home in Dorchester, Massachusetts. Her last audible words—"Make the world better!"—encouraged her daughter to continue the work. Stone had advised her family against holding a public funeral, saying that not enough people would come to fill a church; however, she left the decision up to them. Not only did some 1,100 people fill the Church of the Disciples (Unitarian) in Boston for her funeral, but hours beforehand, people gathered and stood silently in the street to bid this great woman farewell.

*Biographical Sketch by* ELEA KEMLER

## ✦ Writings of Lucy Stone

Numerous letters. In *Friends and Sisters: Letters Between Lucy Stone and Antoinette Brown Blackwell, 1846–1893,* edited by Carol Lasser and Marlene Merrill. Urbana: University of Illinois Press, 1987.

"Protest Against the Laws of Marriage, May 1, 1855." In *History of Woman Suffrage,* edited by Elizabeth Cady Stanton, Susan B. Anthony, and Matilda J. Gage. Vol. 1, 260–261. New York: Fowler and Wells, 1881.

Speech at National Woman's Rights Convention, Cincinnati, Ohio, 1855. In *History of Woman Suffrage,* edited by Elizabeth Cady Stanton, Susan B. Anthony, and Matilda J. Gage. Vol. 1, 165–167. New York: Fowler and Wells, 1881.

## ✦ Biographical Resources

Blackwell, Alice Stone. *Lucy Stone: Pioneer of Women's Rights.* Boston: Little, Brown, 1930.

Hays, Elinor Rice. *Morning Star: A Biography of Lucy Stone, 1818–1893.* New York: Harcourt, Brace & World, 1961.

Kerr, Andrea Moore. *Lucy Stone: Speaking Out for Equality.* New Brunswick: Rutgers University Press, 1992.

# Male and Female Created He Them

## Speech to Akron Women's Rights Convention, Ohio, May 1851

FRANCES DANA BARKER GAGE (1808–1884) *was an author, poet, editor, and lecturer who advocated abolition, temperance, and women's suffrage, which she called one great "triune cause."*

*In the 1850s, women's rights conventions became a frequent occurrence across the United States. Women quickly learned that meeting to strategize and to demand their rights had important public impact and also provided them with experience in public discourse and organizing for change. Frances Gage was chosen to preside at the second Ohio women's rights convention, held at the Universalist church in Akron in 1851, which was one of the first run entirely by women. In her opening remarks to the convention, she spoke eloquently, although she claimed never to have attended a regular business meeting before. As a Universalist, she turned to the Bible and recalled the story of creation that gave dominion to male and female together. She called for woman to "act for herself" and to "create a revolution without armies, without bloodshed," that would ultimately change the world for the better.*

See the Biographical Sketch on pages 38–41.

Permit me to draw a comparison between the situation of our forefathers in the wilderness, without even so much as a bridle-path through its dark depths, and our present position. The old land of moral, social, and political privilege seems too narrow for our wants; its soil answers not to our growing, and we feel that we see clearly a better country that we might inhabit. But there are mountains of established law and custom to overcome; a wilderness of prejudice to be subdued; a powerful foe of selfishness and self-interest to overthrow; wild beasts of pride, envy, malice, and hate to destroy. But for the sake of our children and our children's children, we have entered upon the work, hoping and praying that we may be guided by wisdom, sustained by love, and led and cheered by the earnest hope of doing good.

I shall enter into no labored argument to prove that woman does not occupy the position in society to which her capacity justly entitles her. The rights of mankind emanate from their natural wants and emotions. Are not the natural wants and emotions of humanity common to, and shared equally by, both sexes? Does man hunger and thirst, suffer cold and heat more than woman? Does he love and hate, hope and fear, joy and sorrow more than woman? Does his heart thrill with a deeper pleasure in doing good? Can his soul writhe in more bitter agony under the consciousness of evil or wrong? Is the sunshine more glorious, the air more quiet, the sounds or harmony more soothing, the perfume of flowers more exquisite, or forms of beauty more soul-satisfying to his senses than to hers? To all these interrogatories every one will answer, No!

Where then did man get the authority that he now claims over one half of humanity? From what power the vested right to place woman—his partner, his companion, his helpmate in life—in an inferior position? Came it from nature? Nature made woman his superior when she made her his mother; his equal when she fitted her to hold the sacred position of wife. Does he draw his authority from God, from the language of holy writ? No! For it says that "Male and female created he *them,* and gave *them* dominion." Does he claim it under law of the land? Did woman meet with him in council and voluntarily give up all her claim to be her own lawmaker? Or did the majesty of might place this power in his hands? The power of the strong over the weak makes man the master! Yes, there, and there only, does he gain his authority.

In the dark ages of the past, when ignorance, superstition, and bigotry held rule in the world, might made the law. But the undertone, the still small voice of Justice, Love, and Mercy, have ever been heard, pleading the cause of humanity, pleading for truth and right; and their low, soft tones of harmony have softened the lion heart of might, and, little by little, he has yielded as the centuries rolled on; and man, as well as woman, has been the gainer by every concession. We will ask him to yield still; to allow the voice of woman to be heard; to let her take the position which her wants and emotions seem to require; to let her enjoy her natural rights. Do not answer that woman's position is now all her natural wants and emotions require. Our meeting here together this day proves the contrary; proves that we have aspirations that are not met. Will it be answered that we are factious, discontented spirits, striving to disturb the public order, and tear up the old fastnesses of society? So it was said of Jesus Christ and His followers, when they taught peace on earth and good-will to men. So it was said of our forefathers in the great struggle for freedom. So it has been said of every reformer that has ever started out the car of progress on a new and untried track.

We fear not man as an enemy. He is our friend, our brother. Let woman speak for herself, and she will be heard. Let her claim with a calm and determined, yet loving spirit, her place, and it will be given her. I pour out no harsh invectives against the present order of things—against our fathers, husbands, and brothers; they do as they have been taught; they feel as society bids them; they act as the law requires. Woman must act for herself.

Oh, if all women could be impressed with the importance of their own action, and with one united voice, speak out in their own behalf, in behalf of humanity, they could create a revolution without armies, without bloodshed, that would do more to ameliorate the condition of mankind, to purify, elevate, ennoble humanity, than all that has been done by reformers in the last century.

✦ ✦ ✦

# One Hundred Years Hence

## Hymn Text, 1852

FRANCES DANA BARKER GAGE (1808–1884) *composed the text of "One Hundred Years Hence" for John W. Hutchinson, a member of the famous singing family from New Hampshire, who wrote an original tune to go with it. First sung at the women's rights convention held in the Universalist church in Akron, Ohio, in 1852, it was recommended as "a very desirable song for the Conservatives who pray for a procrastination of the Millennial Day." It was noted that the words were "composed by that long tried, and earnest advocate of human progress, and the rights of the family of man,* AUNT FANNIE GAGE.*"*[40] *The song has been revived recently in Unitarian Universalist circles, sung to the tune St. Denio 11.11.11.11.*[41] *Fannie Gage's faith in the future is both charming and a poignant reminder of the work that remains for us to do today.*

See the Biographical Sketch on pages 38–41.

One hundred years hence, what a change will be made
In politics, morals, religion and trade,
In statesmen who wrangle or ride on the fence,
These things will be altered a hundred years hence.

Our laws then will be uncompulsory rules,
Our prisons converted to national schools,
The pleasure of sinning 'tis all a pretense,
And people will find that, a hundred years hence.

All cheating and fraud will be laid on the shelf,
Men will not get drunk, nor be bound up in self,
But all live together, good neighbors and friends,
As Christian folks ought to, a hundred years hence.

Then woman, man's partner, man's equal shall stand,
While beauty and harmony govern the land,
To think for oneself will be no offense,
The world will be thinking, a hundred years hence.

Oppression and war will be heard of no more
Nor blood of a slave leave his print on our shore,
Conventions will then be a useless expense,
For we'll go free-suffrage a hundred years hence.

Instead of speech-making to satisfy wrong,
We'll all join the chorus to sing Freedom's song;
And if the Millenium is not a pretense,
We'll all be good brothers a hundred years hence.

## ✦ *Biographical Sketch*

**Born:** *October 12, 1808, Union, Ohio*

**Died:** *November 10, 1884, Greenwich, Connecticut*

**Buried:** *Greenwich, Connecticut*

Frances Dana Gage—social reformer, writer, and public speaker—dedicated her life to reform work directed toward women's rights, temperance, and racial justice. She was a member of the Universalist church for many years but left it when she felt it lagged behind the reform movements she sponsored. As a reformer, she had a keen understanding of the interrelatedness of oppressions. In her own words: "Temperance, freedom, justice to the negro, justice to women, are all parts of one great whole, one mighty temple whose builder and maker is God."[42]

Frances grew up in a pioneer family. Her father was an early settler and farmer in Marietta, Ohio, and her mother was from a Massachusetts family with a long tradition of reform interests. Frances had little opportunity for formal education, but in her large family of ten, she learned early to speak up for her rights. When she was twenty-one, she married James Gage, an ardent abolitionist. They raised eight children, while she continued to work for social justice.

In 1850, Frances Gage organized a petition drive, gaining 8,000 signatures supporting suffrage for women and African Americans for the Second Ohio Constitutional Convention of 1850. She was elected president of the Ohio Women's Rights Conventions in 1851, 1852, and 1853. As president, she refused to let men speak, ruling "out of order" anyone who tried. As the chroniclers of the suffrage movement observed: "For the first time in the world's history, men learned how it felt to sit in silence when questions in which they were interested were under discussion."[43] It was at this convention that Sojourner Truth gave her famous "Ain't I a Woman?" speech, which Gage recorded for posterity. Also in 1853, Gage was nationally recognized by her election as vice president of the National Women's Rights Association. By 1854, she was known as the only woman to speak in the South for women's rights. In 1857, she campaigned until the state legislature passed Ohio's first Married Woman's Property Rights Law in 1861. She inspired people throughout the Midwest with her commitment to human rights.

During this time, Gage also spoke out and worked for temperance and abolition. She organized the first Woman's Temperance Society and spoke at the 1853 World's Temperance Convention in New York. She also wrote many antislavery and temperance articles, although at times these two reform agendas were in conflict. Two temperance publications, one in Missouri and one in Ohio, refused to continue publishing her work because she insisted on commenting on the evils of slavery.

During the Civil War, with four sons fighting on the Union side, Gage could not remain at home in Ohio. In 1862, she and her daughter Mary traveled to the Sea Islands of South Carolina, where she was responsible for five hundred former slaves on Parris Island under General Rufus Saxon, as part of the Port Royal project.[44] This work involved caring for the sick, finding decent housing and clothing, teaching reading and writing, and doing whatever else she thought necessary to provide for these people.

In 1863, Frances Gage had to return home to Ohio to care for her sick and dying husband. Upon returning from another trip south later that year, she resolved to convey to Northern audiences the dramatic story of conditions among the former slaves, speaking to soldiers' aid societies in Pennsylvania, New York, Ohio, and Illinois. In 1864, she volunteered as an agent for the Western Sanitary Commission, traveling up and down the Mississippi giving packages, caring for the sick and wounded, and doing whatever she could to ease the suffering. The so-called colored hospitals benefited greatly from her work to improve conditions and provide supplies. Through her efforts, the Freedman's Bureau was added to the Mississippi Valley Sanitary and Freedmen's Fair, which raised money for the Union soldiers and freed slaves.

Frances Gage suffered a stroke in 1867, but she continued to write. As "Aunt Fanny," she wrote children's stories, articles on home and garden, and poems in many publications. After her stroke, this remarkable woman published a book of poems and five novels.

Gage died in November 1888. Clara Barton wrote of her: "sainted citizen . . . the friend of the bondsman and oppressed, who knew no sect, sex, race or color, but toiled on for freedom and humanity . . . the grandest of them all—whose sleeping dust is an honor to Ohio."[45]

*Biographical Sketch by* PAULA COPESTICK

## ✦ Writings of Frances Dana Barker Gage

"Autobiography." *Woman's Journal,* 31 March 1883.
*Elsie Magoon, or The Old Still-House in the Hollow: A Tale of the Past.* Philadelphia: Lippincott, 1867.
*Gertie's Sacrifice.* New York: John Ross, 1871.
*Poems.* Philadelphia: Lippincott, 1867.
*Six Mitten Books.* 6 vols. New York: W. L. Allison, 1876 ff.
*Steps Upward: A Temperance Tale.* Utica, NY: Temperance Patriot Office, 1870.

Numerous articles in *Anti-Slavery Bugle* (1851–1856), *Anti-Slavery Standard* (1859–1865), Cleveland, Ohio, *Daily Herald* (1852–1854), Columbus, Ohio, *Field Notes* (1861), *Ladies' Repository* (1864–1874), *Lily,* Marietta, Ohio, *Republican* (1851), Ohio, *Cultivator* (1850–1861), *Ohio Farmer* (1861, 1864–1865), *Ohio Magazine* (1908), *Saturday Visitor, Western Literary Magazine* (1908), *Woman's Journal* (1883–1884).

## ✦ Biographical Resources

Barker, Elizabeth F. *Barker Geneology.* n.p. 1927.
Brockett, L. P., and Mary C. Vaughan. *Woman's Work in the Civil War: A Record of Heroism, Patriotism and Patience.* Philadelphia: Zeigler, McCurdy, 1867. Reprinted as *Women at War.* Stamford, CT: Longmeadow Press, 1993.

Cantrell, Edna Pearl. "'Temperance, Justice to the Negro, Justice to Women': Frances D. Gage and the 'Triune Cause'." Master's thesis, College of Arts and Sciences, Ohio University, 1987.

Coggeshall, William T. *The Poets and Poetry of the West: With Biographical and Geographical Notes.* Columbus, OH: Follett, Foster, 1860.

Gagel, Diane VanSkiver. *Ohio Women Unite: The Salem Convention of 1850.* Columbus: Ohio Historical Society, 1976.

Hanson, Eliza R. *Our Women Workers.* Chicago: Star and Covenant, 1882.

Holtzman, Clara. "Frances Dana Gage." Master's thesis, Ohio State University, 1931.

O'Conner, Lillian. *Pioneer Women Orators: Rhetoric in the Antebellum Reform Movement.* New York: Columbia University Press, 1954.

Pierce, Edward L. *The Freedman of Port Royal, South Carolina.* New York: Rebellion Record, 1863.

Stanton, Elizabeth Cady et al. *History of Woman Suffrage.* Vols. 1 & 2. New York: Fowler and Wells, 1881.

# Woman's Rights and Wrongs

## Notes for Speech, 1854

SUSAN B. ANTHONY (1820–1906), *perhaps the best-known advocate for women's suffrage, began her public career working for temperance. Although she was raised as a Quaker (and is often identified as such), she and her family joined the Unitarian church in Rochester, New York, when their Quaker meeting refused to take a stand against slavery. She was among the first to confront the inequity of not allowing women to mix with men or speak at men's temperance meetings. In February 1853, she gave a powerful speech to the New York Women's State Temperance Society, drawing over three thousand listeners, in which she called for women to organize statewide temperance societies. But she would soon learn that women had neither the financial resources nor the leisure time to achieve this kind of organization.*

*In the following speech (taken from her papers of 1854), Susan B. Anthony refers to a comment made by a Unitarian minister, the Reverend Thomas Wentworth Higginson, who was a strong advocate for women's rights. As president of the 1852 Whole World Temperance Convention, Higginson had addressed the convention saying, "This is not a Woman's Rights Convention, but simply a convention in which* Woman is not wronged." *It is not clear where or when the following speech was delivered, although Susan B. Anthony recorded in her diary giving a Temperance Society lecture on April 6, 1854. This may have been that speech. The wrongs that were on her mind when she wrote this, however, were those dealing with wage inequities and other financial restrictions on women, which kept them poor and dependent on men. This speech paved the way for her famous "True Woman" speech of 1857.*

See the Biographical Sketch on pages 49–53.

Friends, when we come before you to advocate the Cause popularly termed "Woman's Rights," we simply ask that *Woman is not wronged.*

We ask for her justice & equality—not favor & superiority—the rights and privileges her humanity charters to her equally with man, not arbitrary powers & selfish dominion. We ask for her the removal of the many customs & laws that prevent the full exercise of all her God given powers, the entire freedom of thought, word & action, that *man* claims for himself. . . . Yes, in this last half of the 19th Century, we ask that Woman shall have free access to every possible means of improvement necessary to the full development of both body & soul. . . .

We are not ignorant of the fact that great fears are entertained on all sides, lest the enlargement of woman's area of freedom—the granting to her perfect liberty to decide for herself what is proper, of what improper for her to do, or not to do—will have the effect to take from her feminine nature, & in its stead, give to her that of the masculine.

But if God has really given to woman a nature essentially dissimilar to that of man's, then will all the outward circumstances of education, avocation & profession fail to produce a similarity. . . .

If it be true, that to Woman is given the empire of the affections, while to man is given that of the intellect, to govern & direct, you may educate them as you will, alike or unlike, side by side, or entirely apart, & still each spirit will assume none other than its God-ordained sphere.

If to educate woman side by side with man, to discipline her mind equally with his in the study of Logic, the Languages, & Mathematics, Theology, Law & Medicine, does produce a change in what have hitherto been thought the *essential* elements of her womanhood, if she thereby becomes strong like the *oak,* capable in intense intellectual efforts, in their results like those of Man, & ceases to live wholly in the affections, what then is the inference to be drawn? Why of course none other than that the difference is not of God's ordaining—but the result of false education & conventionalisms.

Therefore, whether we believe in the mental dissimilarity of the sexes or otherwise, we have before us but the one work to do, that of giving to every human being the fullest possible liberty to develop his or her spirit just in accordance with its own promptings.

But without waiting to settle this vexed question as to the precise points of resemblance or dissimilarity in the mental constitutions of Man & Woman, allow me to say that I feel fully assured that woman will be woman still, be her position what it may. Whether she be Mother, wife, daughter, sister, teacher, seamstress, domestic; President, Legislator, Judge, Juror, Lawyer, Doctor, Minister, still will she be Woman.

Is Queen Victoria any the less the wife, the mother, the woman, that she wields the sceptre of the British Empire, on whose broad domain the sun is said never to set?

When we read of the heroic Joan of Arc, she who went forth to fight the battles of her country, and do we not feel that she was woman still?

✦ ✦ ✦

Are Drs. Elizabeth Blackwell,[46] Harriot K. Hunt,[47] Lydia F. Fowler, Gleason & Scores, yea hundreds of other noble women working in womanly dignity, as they skillfully minister to the sick & the suffering? Are they any the less pure chaste & kindly affectioned, that they have sat side by side with men in the medical lecture room, that they have been members of the same dissecting classes?

Is my esteemed friend Antoinette B. Brown, any the less lovely, modest & womanly, that sabbath after sabbath takes her place in the Pulpit, & speaks to the people the truths of what God has made her Soul the Medium?

Are the Quaker women, who, ever since the organization of that religious society, have not only been eligible to the officers of Minister & Elder, but have quite as frequently occupied them, & quite as honorably discharged the duties pertaining to them? Are the Quaker women, I ask you, any less decorous in their manner, less affectionate in their natures, or less Christian in their daily lives, than are the women of other religious societies, who have ever been taught that "Women should keep silence in the churches"?

✦ ✦ ✦

Are the few young women who are now setting type in several of the printing offices of our large cities, for 5, 8 & 10 dollars per week, any the less feminine, any the less virtuous even than when stitching with their needles from early dawn late into the night for a scanty pittance scarce sufficient to keep body & soul together?

✦ ✦ ✦

If in the few instances named, woman's engaging in what are usually considered masculine employments & professions has failed to rob her of the essential elements of her womanhood, why longer entertain or doubt, as to the fixedness, the unchangeableness or the God-implanted instincts of her nature?

Call these exceptions if you will, what do exceptions prove, but that the many may be like them, if they but bring into equal exercise like powers & like will?

True womanhood, like true manhood, desires continuous progress; and the woman who is content to be just what her mother was, & seeks no higher culture of the soul, than that attained by the preceding generation, is wanting, sadly wanting, the noblest instincts of humanity.

✦ ✦ ✦

I have great faith in the everlasting principles of *truth* & *right:* and firmly believe that to establish them among men, is to secure that blessed state of society, that makes a heaven of earth.

Wherever there is a wrong, rest assured no ill can follow its removal. If I prove to you that existing customs & laws are crushing & degrading to the noblest instincts of womanhood, may you have the courage to labor for their immediate overthrow—the courage "to do the right though the heavens fall."

To Woman has hitherto been assigned but three of the industrial avocations—viz. those of sewing, teaching & domestic service. And even in these, man stands as a competitor, & thrusts himself into the most honorary & lucrative departments.

The man "tailor" is paid from $10 to $15 for making a coat, while the woman, possessed of equal skill gets only $2, $3, or $5. . . .

The first class work is usually made to order. The young gent says to the merchant I want this coat *well made;* let not a woman set stitch to it—he's willing to pay liberally. At the appointed time he calls for his coat—puts it on, surveys himself in the mirror, exclaims, what an admirable fit! What a beautiful finish, no woman can make a coat like this,—indeed *I* would not wear a coat made by a woman. Could that pompous fraction of manhood, but take a peak into an adjoining work shop, he might there see, seated on the bench, the very woman who had not only "set every stitch," but put every finishing touch of the iron to that admirable coat—the woman who, perchance receives $4 out of the $10 or $15 lavishly paid for the superior skills of Man.

✦ ✦ ✦

The man teacher, in both our public & private schools, receives a salary of $600, $1,000 or $1,500 per year, while the woman possessed of equal, perchance better qualifications, both by nature and education, is paid but $200 or $400. In this profession, as in that of the needle, man is careful to secure to himself the most honorary & lucrative positions. . . .

✦ ✦ ✦

Here at the north, we hear much talk of the "dignity of labor;" and yet it is ever at the loss of taste, that the woman eats the bread of patient industry. She may sew, cook & teach; and perform the most menial offices of the household, provided she does all these things for the comfort & benefit of husband or son, father or brother, quietly receiving in return, such of the necessaries or luxuries of life as masculinity sees fit to proffer, all this, & the world will applaud.

But paid labor is a reproach to womanhood—the world looks with pity on any & every woman whose necessities compel her to go forth & get to herself a support by the labor of her hands. The world seems to have adopted the idea that only misfortune or misconduct can drive woman from the intimacy of home. It gives her no credit for innate love of independence & freedom.

Why is it that woman's industrial position is ever that of the subordinate? Why is it that the public is willing to pay man twice & three times the sum for the performance of a certain amount of labor than it does to woman? To me the reason is obvious—it is the direct result of the legislation of our country. . . .

But I am not here to complain that man does not give to woman a bigger share of the proceeds of his well-paid labor—No! far be it for me. I ask only that every human being, without regard to sex, shall be left free to choose their occupation; that labor shall be as honorable to woman as man & that the quantity and quality of work done, not sex, shall regulate the price of labor.

✦ ✦ ✦

Does it cost the widow any less to support her little ones than it did the father? Can she pay house rent, purchase bread and fuel, & clothe & educate her children for any less money than could her husband when living? Or if she owns a little house & garden spot, will her tax thereon be less than if owned by a man? Most certainly not! And yet she has all these expenses to meet, with less than *one half* the wages earned by her husband.

And how is it with the young woman, who is thrown upon self-support? Does it cost her any less to clothe & educate herself than it does a young man?

✦ ✦ ✦

Is the expense of *educating* a young woman any less than that of a young man? To the contrary, it is an established fact that the tuition of young ladies seminaries & boarding school is higher than that of high schools, colleges & universities for young men—for this, there are two prominent causes: 1st all the institutions of the higher grades, for young men, are endowed by state appropriations & individual contributions—the interest of these endowments paying the salaries of the professors—while not a school for young women has ever had an appropriation from the public treasury—all female seminaries & boarding schools must not only pay their incidental expenses out of their tuition bills, but also the salaries of their teachers & professors; 2nd all the branches deemed necessary for the young men to be pursued at the college or university are reckoned in the course, & require no extra pay—while at the fashionable ladies school, all of what are termed the ornamental branches . . . all these are extra branches, for which must be paid $5, $10, $20 & $40 per term above the ordinary tuition fee.

✦ ✦ ✦

This assertion then, that the expenses of life to woman are less than to man, proves false. And even if it were true, there would still be no justice in the principle that bases the price paid for labor on any condition or circumstance save that of the amount done.

It is not a few women, only, who are compelled to depend upon the labor of their own heads & hands for daily bread. Go from house to house through any rural district, & see if there be not many even there, who either by sewing, teaching or domestic service, gain their own livelihood: then add to these actual workers the hundreds & thousands, who sigh for some employment, that may give to them a pecuniary independence, that shall enable them to cease to be burdens on the family estate, who sigh over woman's lot, that of remaining useless members of society, without the means even of developing their own souls, or contributing to the happiness of their fellows, except it be at the will & the pleasure of Father, guardian or Husband.

✦ ✦ ✦

I have often had the wives & daughters of rich farmers, merchants, mechanics & manufacturers say to me, "My soul is deeply interested in this or that good cause, but my husband or my father gives no thought to it, & will not give me the means to help it on. Could I but get some sort of work to do, I would toil incessantly, that I might obtain the wherewithal to gratify my heart's desire, in forwarding what seems to me the true & the right."

But, say you, no man worthy the sacred name of husband & Father will ever withhold from his wife or daughter of any necessary or reasonable desire. "Aye, there's the rub." Man is ever the umpire—twixt necessary & unnecessary, reasonable & unreasonable—he, alone, may draw the line.

✦ ✦ ✦

In all this I do not blame man. Educated in the belief that he earns all the money, how can he but feel it is his right to control it?

An independent purse will give independent action to woman, no less than man. But what can these women do? . . . They can do nothing . . . unless they have the courage to face a false public sentiment & engage in some business beyond the narrow limits of "woman's sphere" and as but few women, any more than men, are born to be martyrs, the large majority will spend their lives in vain regrets.

Then visit the by-streets & narrow lanes of our large cities & see what vast numbers of women are forced to depend entirely on their own earnings for a support—the worse than widowed wives of drunkards, the worse than orphan daughters of drunkards—are all found here, huddled together in damp cellars & rickety garrets.

✦ ✦ ✦

And more heart sickening still, picture to yourselves the widowed wife & mother with fifteen shillings a week—to rent a room, feed, warm & clothe herself, & one, two, three or more helpless children; & then marvel if you can, that with grim want thus staring her in the face, her little ones crying for bread & shivering around her fireless hearth, she yields herself a victim to the spoiler, sells her virtue to the highest bidder, that she may eke out her scanty subsistences, that she may dry the tears of her wretched babes. Turn not coldly away from these fallen ones—they are our Sisters still. Be ours the nobler work, to create a public sentiment, that shall open wide to woman the doors of all our mechanic shops, stores & offices, & bid her go in & work side by side with her brother man, paying to her equal wages for equal service rendered, & we shall have done more to relieve the suffering, & save the lost, than all the Moral Reform Societies, Sisters of Charity, Homes for the Friendless & the thousands of other benevolent institutions that now act as ministering angels to these hapless victims of poverty & vice.

It is honest employment & just compensation, not monied charity, that a vast majority of those whom we are accustomed to look as hopelessly degraded, as lost to all virtue, ask at the hands of the truly benevolent.

It is in vain that our pious church women distribute religious tracts & Bibles among the poor & vicious of either sex, so long as they are suffering from cold & hunger, with no possible means to supply their wants, except by a resort to vice & crime. Why will they longer refuse to learn of Jesus, who, with true philosophy, first fed the multitude, & then ministered to them in spiritual things?

## ✦ *Biographical Sketch*

**Born:** *February 15, 1820, Adams, Massachusetts*

**Died:** *March 13, 1906, Rochester, New York, age 86*

**Buried:** *Mount Hope Cemetery, Rochester, New York*

For fifty years, Susan B. Anthony was the central figure in the first organized movement for women's rights. She inspired and sustained the suffragists through countless defeats toward "that right protective of all other rights,"[48] the right to vote.

During her Quaker childhood in Adams, Massachusetts, and eastern New York, Susan Anthony enjoyed a secure and industrious family life. That changed when the failure of Daniel Anthony's textile mills forced the family to move to western New York for a new beginning on a small farm near Rochester. Susan joined them in 1849 after ten years of teaching. Having scrimped to help pay the family debts on a salary one-fourth that of her male colleagues, she felt keenly the lack of opportunities and the social and legal strictures that pushed women into crippling dependency. She had received offers of marriage and there would be more, but she would always choose independence.

Anthony left teaching to run the family farm, which became the meeting place of antislavery workers on Sunday afternoons. William Lloyd Garrison and Wendell Phillips were visitors, as was Frederick Douglass; all became lifelong friends of Anthony's and powerful allies of the suffrage movement. Daniel Anthony's heart was in the abolitionist movement, but the Society of Friends disapproved of these secular and political actions. Gradually, the Anthonys, along with several other liberal Quaker families, attached themselves to Rochester's First Unitarian Society, where abolitionists were rampant.

In that church in 1848, Lucy and Daniel Anthony and their youngest daughter, Mary, attended the first Woman's Rights Convention when it reconvened in Rochester from Seneca Falls. When Susan Anthony arrived the next year, she joined her family in the church and was an active member of the congregation for more than fifty years. Her ties to the Society of Friends were not severed, but Rochester's First Unitarian became her church home. In 1853, her minister, the Reverend William Henry Channing, already known as a women's rights activist, encouraged and assisted her first steps as a political leader. Within that circle, she would always find encouragement and support. In 1893, following a church anniversary celebration and rededication, Susan B. and Mary Anthony signed the membership book.

By 1853, Anthony had joined Lucy Stone,[49] Antoinette Brown Blackwell, Amelia Bloomer, Ernestine Rose, Lucretia Mott, and Elizabeth Cady Stanton in the leadership of the National Woman's Rights Society. The dynamic friendship of Anthony and Stanton, a philosophical and political partnership, drove the movement for forty years.

From 1854 to 1860, Anthony initiated, managed, and financed door-to-door petition and speaker campaigns across New York State, demanding that women have equal rights to child custody, property, earnings, and the ballot. She began running statewide antislavery campaigns in 1856, repeatedly facing down hostile mobs. Emotion ran too high for written speeches; so from then on, Anthony spoke or lectured spontaneously. Consequently, few of her reportedly powerful speeches were saved.

In 1859, Anthony started a Free Church in Rochester, based on the ideas of Theodore Parker. The church was short lived, but Anthony continued to bring speakers such as Ralph Waldo Emerson and Charlotte Perkins Gilman[50] to Rochester and often to the pulpit of the Unitarian church. She also sponsored protests against capital punishment and John Brown's execution and secretly aided Harriet Tubman with supplies for fugitive slaves.

The movement for women's suffrage split following the Civil War, when Republicans dropped the goal of universal suffrage and focused on seeking voting rights for black men only. Anthony and Stanton, still proclaiming equal rights for all, began publishing a suffrage paper,

*The Revolution.* In 1869, they founded the National Woman Suffrage Association, which continued the struggle (later merging with the American Woman Suffrage Association) for fifty-one years to the day of victory.

Anthony spent the next thirty-five years building the suffrage movement, constantly traveling, organizing, lecturing, supporting state and local campaigns across the United States, raising money, lobbying and holding conventions. In 1872–1873, she was arrested and tried for voting illegally in an attempt to reach the Supreme Court with women's claims. During the 1880s, Anthony helped write three volumes of the *History of Woman Suffrage,* based largely on material she had saved. She also launched the International Council of Women to advance women's status around the world. In the 1890s, Anthony moved the headquarters for the combined National American Woman Suffrage Association to her home in Rochester. This decade brought the first great victories when Wyoming, Colorado, Utah, and Idaho granted women full voting rights.

Although Susan B. Anthony died in 1906, her work continued. In 1920, her chosen successor, Carrie Chapman Catt, guided the organization through the final passage and ratification of the Nineteenth Amendment to the Constitution of the United States, granting women the right to vote. This momentous legislation was justly known as the Susan B. Anthony Amendment.

From the beginning, religion loomed large in the life of the women's rights and suffrage movements. Conservative churchmen denounced these women as destroyers of social and religious order, while Stanton, Matilda Joslyn Gage, and others denounced organized religion for the degradation and enslavement of women. Anthony tried to steer the suffragists through the controversies and avoid mortal damage. In addition, she constantly pushed for women's rights organizations to have broader appeal while keeping them open to freedom of thought. She did not want to alienate conventional women, many of whom saw the movement as belonging to the ultrists and either disgraceful or unimportant to them.

Yet even Anthony could be provoked. In one letter, she advises patience with the "dear religious bigots."[51] And on hearing a college president preach a sermon slanderous and insulting to women, Anthony stood on her pew and furiously announced that he "ought to be spanked!"[52]

Without question, her beliefs were radical for her day. In her own words:[53]

> "Of the before and after I know absolutely nothing, and have very little desire and less time to question or to study. I know this seems very material to you, and yet to me it is wholly spiritual, for it is giving time and study rather to making things better in the *between,* which is really all we can influence."
>
> "Work and worship are one with me."
>
> "Pray with your ballots!"
>
> "Failure is impossible."

*Biographical Sketch by* COLLEEN HURST

## ✦ Writings of Susan B. Anthony

*History of Woman Suffrage,* Vol. 1–3. Edited by Elizabeth Cady Stanton, Susan B. Anthony, and Matilda Joslyn Gage. New York: Fowler & Wells, 1881–86. Vol. 4, edited by Susan B. Anthony and Ida Husted Harper, Rochester, NY: Susan B. Anthony, 1902. [Vol. 5 and 6, edited by Ida Husted Harper, 1922.] All six volumes reprinted, New York: Arno, 1969.

*The Revolution,* edited by Elizabeth Cady Stanton and Parker Pillsbury, owned, published, and written in part by Susan B. Anthony. New York, 1868–69.

## ✦ Biographical Resources

Anthony, Katherine. *Susan B. Anthony: Her Personal History and Her Era.* New York: Doubleday, 1954.

Barry, Kathleen. *Susan B. Anthony: A Biography of a Singular Feminist.* New York: Doubleday, 1988.

Dorr, Rheta Childe. *Susan B. Anthony, The Woman Who Changed the Mind of a Nation.* New York: Frederick A. Stokes, 1928.

DuBois, Ellen Carol, ed. *The Elizabeth Cady Stanton–Susan B. Anthony Reader: Correspondence, Writings, Speeches.* Rev. ed. Boston: Northeastern University Press, 1992.

Edwards, G. Thomas. *Sowing Good Seeds: The Northwest Suffrage Campaigns of Susan B. Anthony.* Portland: Oregon Historical Society, 1990.

Flexnor, Eleanor. *Century of Struggle: The Woman's Rights Movement in the United States.* Cambridge: Harvard University Press, 1959.

Gordon, Ann D., ed. *The Selected Papers of Elizabeth Cady Stanton and Susan B. Anthony, In The School of Anti-Slavery, 1840–1866.* Vol. 1. New Brunswick, NJ: Rutgers University Press, 1997 [first of 6 projected volumes].
Harper, Ida Husted. *Life and Work of Susan B Anthony.* Vol. 1–3. Indianapolis: Hollenbeck, 1898, 1908. Reprint, Salem, NH: Ayer, 1983.
Harper, Judith. *Susan B. Anthony: A Biographical Companion.* Santa Barbara, CA: ABC-CLIO, 1999.
Kendall, Martha E. *Susan B. Anthony, Voice for Women's Voting Rights.* Springfield, NJ: Enslow Publishers, 1997.
Lutz, Alma. *Susan B. Anthony, Rebel, Crusader, Humanitarian.* Boston: Beacon Press, 1959.
Sherr, Lynn. *Failure Is Impossible: Susan B. Anthony in Her Own Words.* New York: Times Books, 1995.
Weisberg, Barbara. *Susan B. Anthony.* New York: Chelsea House, 1988.

## ✦ Archives

Huntington Library, San Marino, CA
Library of Congress, Washington, DC
New York Public Library, New York, NY
Schlesinger Library, Radcliffe College, Cambridge, MA
Sophia Smith Collection, Smith College, Northampton, MA
University of Rochester, Library of Rare Books & Manuscripts, Rochester, NY

# Disappointment Is the Lot of Woman

## Speech to National Woman's Rights Convention, Cincinnati, Ohio, 1855

*Inspired by the first women's rights convention in Seneca Falls, New York, in 1848, other similar conventions were held in many locations across the United States, many of them drawing national leaders to their platforms. One of these was the National Woman's Rights Convention in Cincinnati, Ohio, in 1855. This selection is* LUCY STONE'S (1818–1983) *extemporaneous response to a previous convention speaker who had dismissed the emerging movement for women's rights as being promoted only by "a few disappointed women." Lucy Stone demonstrated her skill as a public debater by turning a negative argument into a rationale for social change.*

See the Biographical Sketch on pages 31–34.

The last speaker alluded to this movement as being that of a few disappointed women. From the first years to which my memory stretches, I have been a disappointed woman. When, with my brothers, I reached forth after the sources of knowledge, I was reproved with "It isn't fit for you; it doesn't belong to women." Then there was but one college in the world where women were admitted, and that was in Brazil. I would have found my way there, but by the time I was prepared to go, one was opened in the young State of Ohio—the first in the United States where women and negroes could enjoy opportunities with white men. I was disappointed when I came to seek a profession worthy an immortal being—every employment was closed to me, except those of the teacher, the seamstress, and the housekeeper. In education, in marriage, in religion, in everything, disappointment is the lot of woman. It shall be the business of my life to deepen this disappointment in every woman's heart until she bows down to it no longer. I wish that women, instead of being walking show-cases, instead of begging of their fathers and brothers the latest and gayest new bonnet, would ask of them their rights.

The question of Woman's Rights is a practical one. The notion has prevailed that it was only an ephemeral idea; that it was but women claiming the right to smoke cigars in the streets, and to frequent barrooms. Others have supposed it a question of comparative intellect; others still, of sphere. Too much has already been said and written about woman's sphere. Trace all the doctrines to their source and they will be found to have no basis except in the usages and prejudices of the age. This is seen in the fact that what is tolerated in woman in one country is not tolerated in another. . . . Wendell Phillips says, "The best and greatest thing one is capable of doing, that is his sphere." I have confidence in the Father to believe that when He gives us the capacity to do anything He does not make a blunder. Leave women, then, to find their sphere. And do not tell us before we are born even, that our province is to cook dinners, darn stockings, and sew on buttons. We are told woman has all the rights she wants; and even women, I am ashamed to say, tell us so. They mistake the politeness of men for rights—seats while men stand in this hall to-night, and their adultations; but these are mere courtesies. We want rights. The flour merchant, the house-builder, and the postman charge us no less on account of our sex; but when we endeavor to earn money to pay all these, then, indeed, we find the difference. Man, if he have energy, may hew out for himself a path where no mortal has ever trod, held back by nothing but what is in himself; the world is all before him, where to choose; and we are glad for you, brothers, men, that it is so. But the same society that drives forth the young man, keeps woman at home—a dependent—working little cats on worsted, and little dogs on punctured paper; but if she goes heartily and bravely to give herself to some worthy purpose, she is out of her sphere and she loses caste. Women working in tailor shops are paid one-third as much as men. Someone in Philadelphia has stated that women make fine shirts for twelve and a half cents apiece; that no woman can make more than nine a week, and the sum thus earned, after deducting rent, fuel, etc., leaves her just three and a half cents a day for bread. Is it a wonder that women are driven to prostitution? Female teachers in New York are paid fifty dollars a year, and for every such situation there are five hundred applications. I know not what you believe of God, but I believe He gave yearning and longings to be filled, and that He did not mean all our time should be devoted to feeding and clothing the body. The present condition of woman causes a horrible perversion of the marriage relation. It is asked of a lady, "Has she married well?" "Oh, yes, her husband is rich." Woman must marry for a home, and you men are the sufferers by this; for a woman who loathes you may marry you because you have the means to get money which she can not have. But when woman can enter the lists with you and make money for herself, she will marry you only for deep and earnest affection.

I am detaining you too long, many of you standing, that I ought to apologize, but women have been wronged so long that I may wrong you a little. . . . I have seen a woman at manual labor turning out chair-legs in a cabinet-shop, with a dress short enough not to drag in the shavings. I wish other women would imitate her in this. It made her hands harder and broader, it is true, but I think a hand with a dollar and a quarter a day in it, better than one with a crossed ninepence. . . . The widening of woman's sphere is to improve her lot. Let us do it, and if the world scoff, let it scoff—if it sneer, let it sneer—but we will go on emulating the example of the sisters Grimke and Abby Kelley. When they first lectured against slavery they were not listened to as respectfully as you listen to us. So the first female physician meets many difficulties, but to the next the path will be made easy.

Lucretia Mott has been a preacher for years; her right to do so is not questioned among Friends. But when Antoinette Brown felt that she was commanded to preach, and to arrest the progress of thousands that were on the road to hell; why, when she applied for ordination they acted as though they had rather the whole world should go to hell, than that Antoinette Brown should be allowed to tell them how to keep out of it.

✦ ✦ ✦

# Protest Against the Laws of Marriage

## Protest Read at Wedding Ceremony, May 1, 1855

LUCY STONE (1818–1893) *had not intended to get married. However, Henry Browne Blackwell wooed her with a copy of Plato and long letters on equal rights for women. He also participated in many women's suffrage meetings, often as the only man present. When Lucy and Henry decided to marry, Henry suggested that they draw up a "Protest Against the Laws of Marriage" to be read at their wedding on*

*May 1, 1855. Their statement received wide publicity through Unitarian minister Thomas Wentworth Higginson, who performed their ceremony and then had the protest published and distributed with his endorsement.*

*Lucy Stone decided to keep her own name after marriage, upon discovering there was no law forbidding it. For many years, women who followed this practice were called "Lucy Stoners."*

See the Biographical Sketch on pages 31–34.

While acknowledging our mutual affection by publicly assuming the relationship of husband and wife, yet in justice to ourselves and a great principle, we deem it a duty to declare that this act on our part implies no sanction of, nor promise of voluntary obedience to such of the present laws of marriage, as refuse to recognize the wife as an independent, rational being, while they confer upon the husband an injurious and unnatural superiority, investing him with legal powers which no honorable man would exercise, and which no man should possess. We protest especially against the laws which give to the husband:

1. The custody of the wife's person.
2. The exclusive control and guardianship of their children.
3. The sole ownership of her personal, and use of her real estate, unless previously settled upon her, or placed in the hands of trustees, as in the case of minors, lunatics, and idiots.
4. The absolute right to the product of her industry.
5. Also against laws which give to the widower so much larger and more permanent an interest in the property of his deceased wife, than they give to the widow in that of the deceased husband.
6. Finally, against the whole system by which "the legal existence of the wife is suspended during marriage," so that in most States, she neither has a legal part in the choice of her residence, nor can she make a will, nor sue or be sued in her own name, nor inherit property.

We believe that personal independence and equal human rights can never be forfeited, except for crime; that marriage should be an equal and permanent partnership, and so recognized by law; that until it is so recognized, married partners should provide against the radical injustice of present laws, by every means in their power.

We believe that where domestic difficulties arise, no appeal should be made to legal tribunals under existing laws, but that all difficulties should be submitted to the equitable adjustment of arbitrators mutually chosen.

Thus reverencing law, we enter our protest against rules and customs which are unworthy of the name, since they violate justice, the essence of law.

(Signed)

*Henry B. Blackwell,*
*Lucy Stone*

# Reasons for the Enfranchisement of Women

## Paper Read at National Association for the Promotion of Social Science, October 1866

BARBARA LEIGH SMITH BODICHON (1827–1891) *was one of the first organizers for British women's rights, calling for reform in the mid-nineteenth century, particularly of marriage laws and voting rights. She grew up in a radical Unitarian family and learned early on to work for social change. An artist, writer, educator, and philanthropist, she worked throughout her life for equal rights for women.*

*Among her organizational affiliations was membership in the National Association for the Promotion of Social Science, an organization unique for featuring women as committee members and conference presenters. In her 1866 presentation to this group, entitled "Reasons for the Enfranchisement of Women," she provided a logical rationale for women to vote. She argued for full citizenship for women, since they could not be fairly represented by men, as evidenced by the lack of attention to women's needs in the system then in operation. This paper was reprinted as a pamphlet in 1869 and distributed widely as one of the major tracts in support of women's suffrage. An 1872 edition was printed and circulated by the National Society for Woman Suffrage.*

See the Biographical Sketch on pages 64–68.

That a respectable, orderly, independent body in the state should have no voice, and no influence recognized by the law, in the election of the representatives of the people, while they are otherwise acknowledged as responsible citizens, are eligible for many public offices, and required to pay all taxes, is an anomaly which seems to require some explanation, and the reasons alleged in its defense are curious and interesting to examine. It is not, however, my present purpose to controvert the various objections which have been brought forward against the extension of the suffrage to women. Passing over what may be called the negative side of the question, I propose to take it up at a more advanced stage, and assuming that the measure is unobjectionable, I shall endeavor to show that it is positively desirable.

✦ ✦ ✦

There are now a very considerable number of open-minded, unprejudiced people who see no particular reason why women should not have votes, if they want them, but, they ask, what would be the good of it? What is there that women want which male legislators are not willing to give? And here let me say at the outset that the advocates of this measure are very far from accusing men of deliberate unfairness to women. It is not as a means of extorting justice from unwilling legislators that the franchise is claimed for women. In so far as the claim is made with any special reference to class interests at all, it is simply on the general ground that under a representative government, any class which is not represented is likely to be neglected. Proverbially, what is out of sight is out of mind, and the theory that women, as such, are bound to keep out of sight finds its most emphatic expression in the denial of the right to vote. The direct results are probably less injurious than those which are indirect, but that a want of due consideration for the interests of women is apparent in our legislation could very easily be shown. To give evidence in detail would be a long and an invidious task. I will mention one instance only, that of the educational endowments all over the country. Very few people would now maintain that the education of boys is more important to the State than that of girls. But as a matter of fact, girls have but a very small share in educational endowments. Many of the old foundations have been reformed by Parliament, but the desirableness of providing with equal care for girls and boys has very seldom been recognized. In the administration of charities generally, the same tendency prevails to postpone the claims of women to those of men.

Among instances of hardship traceable directly to exclusion from the franchise and to no other cause may be mentioned the unwillingness of landlords to accept women as tenants. Two large farmers in Suffolk inform me that this is not an uncommon case. They mention one estate on which seven widows have been ejected, who, if they had had votes, would have been continued as tenants.

✦ ✦ ✦

All women who [are] heads of a business or a household fulfill the duties of a man in the same position. Their task is often a hard one, and everything which helps to sustain their self-respect, and to give them consideration and importance in the eyes of others, is likely to lessen their difficulties and make them happier and stronger for the battle of life. The very fact that, though householders and taxpayers, they have not equal privileges with male householders and taxpayers is in itself a *deconsideration,* which seems to me invidious and useless. It casts a kind of slur on the value of their opinions, and I may remark in passing that what is treated as of no value is apt to grow valueless. Citizenship is an honor, and not to have the full rights of a citizen is a want of honor. Inconspicuously it may be, but by a subtle and sure process, those, who without their own consent and without sufficient reason, are debarred from full participation in the rights and duties of a citizen lose more or less of social consideration and esteem.

These arguments, founded on consideration of justice and mercy to a large and important class, might, in a civilized country and in the absence of strong reasons to the contrary, be deemed amply sufficient to justify the measure proposed. There remain to be considered those aspects of the question which affect the general community. And, among all the reasons for giving women votes, the one which appears to me the strongest is that of the influence it might be expected to have in increasing public spirit. Patriotism, a healthy, lively, intelligent interest in everything which concerns the nation to which we belong, and an unselfish devotedness to the public service—these are the qualities which make a people great and happy; these are the virtues which ought to be most sedulously cultivated in all classes of the community. And I know no better means at this present time, of counteracting the tendency to prefer narrow private ends to the public good, than this of giving to all women, duly qualified, a direct and conscious participation in political affairs. Give some women votes, and it will tend to make all women think seriously of the concerns of the nation at large, and their interest having once been fairly roused, they will take pains, by reading and by consultation with persons better informed than themselves, to form sound opinions. As it is, women of the middle class occupy themselves but little with anything beyond their own family circle. They do not consider it any concern of theirs if poor men and women are ill-nursed in workhouse infirmaries and poor children ill-taught in workhouse schools. If the roads are bad, the drains neglected, the water poisoned, they think it is all very wrong, but it does not occur to them that it is their duty to get it put right. These farmer-women and business-women have honest, sensible minds and much practical experience, but they do not bring their good sense to bear upon public affairs, because they think it is men's business, not theirs, to look after such things. It is this belief—so narrowing and deadening in its influence—that the exercise of the franchise would tend to dissipate. The mere fact of being called upon to enforce an opinion by a vote would have an immediate effect in awakening a healthy sense of responsibility. There is no reason why these women should not take an active interest in all the social questions—education, public health, prison discipline, the poor laws, and the rest—which occupy Parliament, and they would be much more likely to do so if they felt that they had importance in the eyes of Members of Parliament and could claim a hearing for their opinions.

Besides these women of business, there are ladies of property, whose more active participation in public affairs would be beneficial both to themselves and the community generally. The want of stimulus to energetic action is much felt by women of the higher classes. It is agreed that they ought not to be idle, but what they ought to do is not so clear. Reading, music and drawing, needlework, and charity are their usual employments. Reading, without a purpose, does not come to much. Music and drawing and needlework are most commonly regarded chiefly as amusements intended to fill up time. We have left, as the serious duty of independent and unmarried women, the care of the poor in all its branches, including visiting the sick and the aged and ministering to their wants, looking after the schools, and in every possible way giving help wherever help is needed. Now education, the relief of the destitute, and the health of the people, are among the most important and difficult matters which occupy the minds of statesmen, and if it is admitted that women of leisure and culture are bound to contribute their part towards the solution of these great questions, it is evident that every means of making their cooperation enlightened and vigorous should be sought for. They have special opportunities of observing the operation of many of the laws. They know, for example, for they see before their eyes, the practical working of the law of settlement—of the laws relating to the dwellings of the poor—and many others, and the experience which peculiarly qualifies them to form a judgment on these matters ought not to be thrown away. We all know that we have already a goodly body of rich, influential working-women, whose opinions on the social and political questions of the day are well worth listening to. In almost every parish, there are, happily for England, such women. Now everything should be done to give these valuable members of the community a solid social standing. If they are wanted, and there can be no doubt that they are, in all departments of social work, their position in the work should be as dignified and honorable as it is possible to make it. Rich unmarried women have many opportunities of benefiting the community, which are not within reach of a married woman, absorbed by the care of her husband and children. Everything, I say again, should be done to encourage this most important and increasing class, to take their place in the army of workers for the common good, and all the forces we can bring to bear for this end are of incalculable value. For by bringing women into hearty cooperation with men, we gain the benefit not only of their work but of their intelligent sympathy. Public spirit is like fire: A feeble spark of it may be fanned into a flame, or it may very easily be put out. And the result of teaching women that they have nothing to do with politics is that their influence goes towards extinguishing the unselfish interest—never too strong—which men are disposed to take in public affairs.

Let each member of the House of Commons consider, in a spirit of true scientific inquiry, all the properly qualified women of his acquaintance, and he will see no reason why the single ladies and the widows among his own family and friends should not form as sensible opinions on the merits of candidates as the voters who returned him to Parliament. When we find among the disfranchised such names as those of Mrs. Somerville, Harriet Martineau,[54] Miss Burdett Coutts, Florence Nightingale, Mary Carpenter,[55] Louisa Twining, Miss Marsh, and many others scarcely inferior to these in intellectual and moral worth, we cannot but desire, for the elevation and dignity of the Parliamentary system, to add them to the number of electors.

✦ ✦ ✦

The extension proposed would interfere with no vested interests. It would involve no change in the principles on which our Government is based, but would rather make our Constitution more consistent with itself. Conservatives have a right to claim it as a Conservative measure. Liberals are bound to ask for it as a necessary part of radical reform. There is no reason for identifying it with any class or party in the State, and it is, in fact, impossible to predict what influence it might have on party politics. The question is simply of a special legal disability, which must, sooner or later, be removed.

It was said by Lord Derby, in his speech on entering upon the office of Prime Minister last Session, in reference to Reform—that "there were theoretical anomalies in our present system which it was desirable, if possible, to correct; that there were classes of persons excluded from the franchise who had a fair claim and title, upon the ground of their fitness to exercise the privilege of electors; and that there was a very large class whom the particular qualifications of the Act of 1832 excluded." I venture to submit that the exclusion of female freeholders and householders from the franchise is an anomaly which it is very desirable, and not impossible, to correct; that there is no class of persons having a fairer claim and title upon the ground of their fitness to exercise the privileges of electors; and that whatever may be deemed expedient with regard to other classes, this class, at any rate, should not be excluded by the particular qualifications of the Reform Act of the future.

## ✦ *Biographical Sketch*

**Born:** *April 8, 1827, Watlington in Sussex, England*

**Died:** *June 11, 1891, age 64*

**Buried:** *Brightling Churchyard, Sussex, England*

Barbara Leigh Smith Bodichon publicized the fact that women forfeited many rights when they agreed to marry under common law, and she initiated the first committee formed to equalize rights for British women. She also organized the presentation of a substantial petition for women's suffrage to Parliament. An artist, she was co-founder of a British feminist journal and co-planner of Girton College for women.

The oldest of five children, Barbara was seven when her mother died. Her parents had never married. She grew up in a family known for its political radicalism. Her grandfather, William Smith, was a Unitarian dissenter who sympathized with independence for the American colonies and relinquished property holdings in Savannah, Georgia. Elected to Parliament in 1837, her father campaigned against the Corn Laws and consequent high grain prices.

The Smith children were taught at home and encouraged to listen to political and literary discussions in the drawing room. Politicians, political refugees, and authors were frequent guests. When Barbara and her sisters came of age, each received an "independence" of three hundred pounds a year from their father, an arrangement usually made only for sons. This enabled Barbara to engage in the activities she chose and to support the worthwhile efforts of others.

Striving to overcome the lack of provision for training women artists, Barbara Smith and other aspirants shared the expenses of Eliza Fox's cooperative art classes for women, starting in the late 1840s. In 1849, Smith attended the nonsectarian Bedford College for Women opened by Elizabeth Jesser Reid, a Unitarian philanthropist. She received class instruction in drawing as well as private instruction. Women were not yet admitted to the Royal Academy School and had difficulty exhibiting their works, so Smith organized a petition drive to change this situation. She later studied with water colorist John Valery and painter William Holman Hunt, Sr.

Smith and her friend Bessie Rayner Parkes sought out and supported Dr. Elizabeth Blackwell,[56] who was socially isolated in London while continuing her medical education to become the first woman doctor. They introduced Blackwell to a lively literary and social circle, and Smith's father helped finance Blackwell's clinic in New York City.

In 1854, Barbara Smith was given title to the charity school she had attended as a girl and reopened it as The Portman Hall School. She studied new approaches to teaching and made the school coeducational, mixing students of varied social classes and religious backgrounds. Her school taught students to value investigation rather than rote learning, and inspirational readings were used to illustrate moral rather than sectarian points. There was no corporal punishment. Smith operated the school for a decade and then closed it to direct her resources to developing women's concerns.

At the same time, Smith grew concerned that the holdings of wealthy women were secured in costly premarital agreements by trusteeship or by the Courts of Equity but that most women lost all property to their husbands and rights to any of their own income under common law. She published a pamphlet, "The Brief Summary in Plain Language of the Most Important Laws Concerning Women," which caused a sensation. Its popularity raised hopes that significant changes of these laws might accompany the general updating of statutes then being promoted.

In 1856, Smith coordinated the first committee of women to work to secure their own rights. They wrote a petition in which the absorption of married women's wages by their husbands was compared to slavery. They presented the petition to Parliament with over 24,000 signatures (eventually there were 60,000), requesting changes in the Married Women's Property Acts. As a result, Parliament made the process of divorce for women slightly easier and granted control of their own income to separated married women.

During 1855, Smith considered a free-love arrangement with the married John Chapman, editor of the *Westminster Review,* and then traveled to Rome for a change of scene. In autumn 1856, she began a lengthy stay in Algeria, where she published a pamphlet, "Women and Work," that acknowledged "the 'economic' importance of women in the home." She urged initiative, training, and acceptance for women beyond the options of "marry-stitch-die or do worse."[57]

While in Algeria, Smith met Dr. Eugene Bodichon, who was active in the campaign to end slavery there. They married in the Little Portland Unitarian chapel in London in July 1857, after promising to continue to follow their own interests and filing an agreement to that effect in the Courts of Equity. During their honeymoon trip to the United States and Canada, Barbara Smith Bodichon sketched in the New Orleans, Savannah, Cincinnati, Toronto, and Montreal areas. She visited many schools and churches (including those of slaves) and spoke of slavery and women's issues with Lucretia Mott in Philadelphia. Bodichon painted in Sarah Clarke's studio and heard Theodore Parker in Boston: "He prayed to the Creator, the infinite Mother of us all (always using Mother instead of Father in this prayer). It was the prayer of all I ever heard in my life which was the truest to my individual soul."[58]

In 1858, Bodichon founded *The Englishwoman's Journal* with Bessie Rayner Parkes, who became its editor. The *Journal*'s home in Langham Place became a gathering place for women, gained a significant circulation for almost a decade, and led to development of the Society for the Promotion for the Employment of Women, a training school, the Victoria Press, and other periodicals. Bodichon is considered the model for her friend George Eliot's title character of Romola.

Bodichon was a founder of the Portfolio Club, which held meetings for at least a decade for women to display literary and artistic work. She also founded and contributed regularly to the Society of Female Artists. In 1857, she was invited by Dante Gabriel Rossetti to contribute to the Exhibition of English Art in America, and thirteen of her works were displayed in eastern U.S. cities. Her sketches of the South were shown in Washington, D.C. In 1859 and 1861, Bodichon had shows at the French gallery in London, featuring some of her Algerian landscapes.

Bodichon campaigned for John Stuart Mill's election to Parliament in 1865; she had read his *Political Economy* in 1849 as applicable to women and appreciated his work on articles about women's rights with

Harriet Taylor. Bodichon also became co-planner with Emily Davies of Hitchins College in 1873. It was the first institution to insist that qualified women be given the same university education as men and pass the same examinations in the same amount of time. It became Girton College, for which she was a major fundraiser and counselor.

In 1877, an illness left Bodichon partially paralyzed. After some recovery, she journeyed to Algeria to see her husband during his illness in the early 1880s. After his death in 1885, she was able to continue some artwork and night classes for area children and young adults. Bodichon signed yet another suffrage petition in 1891, the year she died. A portrait of her by Emily Mary Osborn hangs at Girton College.

*Biographical Sketch by* IRENE BAROS-JOHNSON

## ✦ Writings of Barbara Leigh Smith Bodichon

*An American Diary, 1857–1858.* Edited by Joseph W. Reed, Jr. London: Routledge & Kegan Paul, 1972.

*A Brief Summary in Plain Language of the Most Important Laws of England Concerning Women.* London: Holyoke, 1854; 1856; London: Trubner, 1869.

*Objections to the Enfranchisement of Women Considered.* London: J. Bale, 1866.

*Reasons for the Enfranchisement of Women.* London: J. Bale, 1866.

*Women and Work.* London: Bosworth & Harrison, 1857; New York: C. S. Francis, 1859.

### Selected Articles in the *English Woman's Journal*

"Algiers: First Impressions" 6 (September 1860): 21–32.

"An American School" 2 (November 1858): 198–200.

"Cleopatra's Daughter, St. Marciana, Mama Marabout and Other Algerian Women" 10 (February 1863): 404–416.

"Middle Class Schools for Girls" 6 (November 1860): 166–177.

"Of Those Who Are the Property of Others and of the Great Power that Holds Others as Property [American slaveholding]" 10 (February 1863): 370–381.

"Slave Preaching" 5 (March 1860): 87–94.

"Slavery in America" (with Eugene Bodichon) 2 (October 1858): 94–100.

### Other Selected Articles

"Australian Forests and African Deserts," *Pall Mall Magazine* (1868).

"Authorities and Precedents for Giving the Suffrage to Qualified Women," *Englishwoman's Review of Social and Industrial Questions* 1 (January 1867): 63–75.

"A Conversation on the Enfranchisement of Female Freeholders and Householders," *Englishwoman's Review of Social and Industrial Questions* 4 (April 1873): 105–111.

"A Dull Life," *MacMillan's Magazine* 16 (May 1867): 47.

## ✦ Artworks

Some of Barbara Leigh Smith Bodichon's 200 artworks are displayed at Hastings Art Gallery and Girton College.

## ✦ Biographical Resources

Bradbrook, Muriel Clara. "Barbara Bodichon, George Eliot and the Limits of Feminism." Bryce Memorial Lecture, Somerville College, Oxford, 6 March 1975.

Burton, Hester. *Barbara Bodichon.* London: Constable, 1949.

Chadwick, Whitney. *Women, Art and Society.* London: Thames & Hudson, 1990.

Cherry, Deborah. *Painting Women: Victorian Women Artists.* London: Routledge, 1993.

Herstein, Sheila R. *A Mid-Victorian Feminist, Barbara Leigh Smith Bodichon.* New Haven: Yale University Press, 1985.

Kinzer, Bruce L., Ann P. Robinson, and John M. Robson. *A Moralist In and Out of Parliament: John Stuart Mill at Westminster 1865–1868.* Toronto: University of Toronto Press, 1992.

Lacey, Candida Ann. *Barbara Leigh Smith Bodichon and the Langham Place Group.* New York: Routledge & Kegan Paul, 1987.

Marsh, J., and P. G. Nunn. *Women Artists and the Pre-Raphaelite Movement.* London: Virago, 1989.

Matthews, Jacquie. "Barbara Bodichon: Integrity in Diversity (1827–1891)." In *Feminist Theorists,* edited by Dale Spender. New York: Pantheon Books, 1983.

Perry, Kate. *Barbara Leigh Smith Bodichon, 1827–1891.* Cambridge: Girton College, 1991.

Reed, Joseph W., Jr., ed. "Barbara Leigh Smith Bodichon." In *An American Diary, 1858.* London: Routledge and Kegan Paul, 1972.

# What Do Women Want of a Club?

## Speech to Woman's Club of New York (Sorosis), 1869

ALICE CARY (1820–1871) *was a writer of poems, short stories, novels, and local color sketches about life in rural Ohio, where she grew up. She and her sister Phoebe worked and lived together most of their lives. Deeply religious, they continued in their family's Universalist tradition, which was expressed through their concern for the welfare of others, their belief in the need for the economic independence of women, and their support for abolition and women's rights.*

*By the late 1860s, the women's club movement in England, Canada, and the United States had expanded from local groups advocating specific reform causes to larger organizations addressing broader purposes, such as women's educational development and community improvement. These clubs provided women with opportunities to improve their education, develop their ability to read and discuss literature and current political issues, and form alliances that encouraged them to make connections beyond their own social and economic class.*[59] *One of the first of these clubs was formed in New York City in 1869 and later became known as Sorosis.*

*Although Alice Cary was basically a quiet, nonassertive woman, she accepted the invitation to become the first president of this pioneer women's club. Speaking at the founding meeting in 1869, she made light of men's objections to women's associations and established the rationale for such groups as "an honest, earnest, and unostentatious effort toward broader culture and nobler life." She claimed that the fact that men seemed to be threatened by women's associations was a clear indication of women's power and should motivate women to organize and work together for the common good. This is her only known public speech.*

See the Biographical Sketch on pages 72–74.

Ladies,—As it will not be expected of me to make speeches very often, hereafter, I think I may presume on your indulgence if I take advantage of this one opportunity. Permit me, then, in the first place, to thank you for the honor you have done me in assigning to me the

President's chair. Why I should have been chosen, when there are so many among you greatly more competent to fill the position, I am at a loss to understand; unless, indeed, it be owing to the fact that I am to most of you a stranger, and your imaginations have clothed me with qualities not my due. This you would soon discover for yourselves; I mention it only to bespeak your forbearance, though in this regard, I ventured almost to anticipate your lenity, inasmuch as you all know how untrained to business habits, how ignorant of rules, and how unused to executive management most women are.

If I take my seat, therefore, without confidence, it is not without the hope of attaining, through your generous kindness and encouragement, to better things. "A Woman's Club! Who ever heard of the like! What do women want of a Club? Have you any aims or objects?" These are questions which have been propounded to me day after day, since this project was set afoot—by gentlemen, of course. And I have answered that, in our humble way, we were striving to imitate their example. You have your exclusive clubs, I have said, and why should not we have ours? What is so promotive of your interests cannot be detrimental to us; and that you find these reunions helpful to yourselves, and beneficial to society, we cannot doubt.

You, gentlemen, profess to be our representatives, to represent us better than we could possibly represent ourselves; therefore, we argue, it cannot be that you are attracted by grand rooms, fine furniture, luxurious dinners and suppers, expensive wines and cigars, the bandying of poor jests, or the excitement of the gaming table. Such dishonoring suspicions as these are not to be entertained for a moment.

Of our own knowledge, I have said, we are not able to determine what special agencies you employ for your advantage and ours in your deliberative assemblies, for it has not been thought best for our interests that we should even sit at your tables, much less to share your councils; and doubtless, therefore, in our blindness and ignorance, we have made some pitiful mistakes.

In the first place, we have "tipped the teapot." This is a hard saying, the head and front of the charges brought against us, and we cannot but acknowledge its justice and its force; we are, in fact, weighed down with shame and humiliation, and impelled, while we are about it, to make full and free confession of all our wild and guilty fantasies. We have, then, to begin at the beginning, proposed the inculcation of deeper and broader ideas among women, proposed to teach them to think for themselves, and get their opinions at first hand, not so much because it is their right as because it is their duty. We have also proposed to open out new avenues of employment to women, to make them less dependent and less burdensome, to lift them out of unwomanly self-distrust and disqualifying diffidence, into womanly self-respect and self-knowledge; to teach each one to make all work honorable by doing the share that falls to her, or that she may work out to herself agreeably to her own special aptitude, cheerfully and faithfully, not going down to it, but bringing it up to her. We have proposed to enter our protest against all idle gossip, against all demoralizing and wicked waste of time; also against the follies and tyrannies of fashion, against all external impositions and disabilities; in short, against each and every thing that opposes the full development and use of the faculties conferred upon us by our Creator.

We have proposed to lessen the antagonisms existing at present between men and women, by the use of every rightful means in our power; by standing upon our divine warranty, and saying and doing what we are able to say and to do, without asking leave, and without suffering hindrance: not for the exclusive good of our own sex, for we hold that there is no exclusive and no separate good; what injures my brother injures me, and what injures me injures him, if he could but be made to know it; it injures him, whether or not he is made to know it. Such, I have said, are some of our objects and aims. We do not pretend, as yet, to have carefully digested plans and clearly defined courses. We are as children feeling our way in the dark, for it must be remembered that it is not yet half a century since the free schools, even in the most enlightened portions of our country, were first opened to girls. How, then, should you expect of us the fullness of wisdom which you for whole centuries have been gathering from schools, colleges, and the exclusive knowledge and management of affairs?

We admit our short-comings, but we do feel, gentlemen, that in spite of them, an honest, earnest, and unostentatious effort toward broader culture and nobler life is entitled to a heartier and more sympathetic recognition than we have as yet received from you anywhere; even our representatives here at home, the leaders of the New York press, have failed in that magnanimity which we have been accustomed to attribute to them.

If we could have foreseen the sneers and sarcasms with which we have been met, they of themselves would have constituted all-sufficient reasons for the establishment of this Woman's Club; as it is, they have established a strong impulse towards its continuance and final perpetuity. But, ladies, these sneers and sarcasms are, after all, but so many acknowledgments of our power and should and will stimulate us to braver assertion, to more persistent effort toward thorough and harmonious organization; and concert and harmony are all that we need to make this enterprise, ultimately, a great power for good. Indeed, with such women as have already enrolled their names on our list, I, for my part, cannot believe failure possible.

Some of us cannot hope to see great results, for our feet are already on the downhill side of life; the shadows are the lengthening behind us and gathering before us, and ere long they will meet and close, and the places that have known us, know us no more. But if, when our poor work is done, any of those who come after us shall find in it some hint of usefulness toward nobler lives and better and more enduring work, we, for ourselves, rest content.

## ✦ *Biographical Sketch*

**Born:** *April 26, 1820, Hamilton County, Ohio*

**Died:** *February 12, 1871, New York City, age 50*

**Buried:** *Greenwood Cemetery, Brooklyn, New York*

Alice Cary, along with her sister, Phoebe, achieved a respected literary reputation and reigned over a notable literary salon in New York City. In addition, both Cary sisters worked for reforms in racial justice and women's rights and explored the spiritualist movement together.

Alice was born near Cincinnati to farming parents who had deep roots in New England reform movements and were newly converted to Universalism. Of the family's seven daughters and two sons, Alice was the fourth child and Phoebe, the sixth. The children were devoted to their family and their Universalist religion, and they loved exploring nature around the farm. Their adored mother died in 1835, and they were then raised by a stepmother who did not encourage their passions for reading and writing. In fact, life was so stressful with their new stepmother that their father left the children with the old house and built a new one on the farm for his wife and himself.

Farm work was arduous, and the Cary children's schooling was irregular and hampered further by a tiny home library. Yet by the age of fourteen, both Alice and Phoebe had had poems published. Horace Greeley visited the family in 1849 and encouraged the sisters in their writing; he would write a tribute to them in 1873. Other supporters were Edgar Allan Poe and John Greenleaf Whittier. Whittier praised Alice's "Pictures of Memory" and later wrote an ode to her called "The Singer."

The sisters' first collection, appearing in 1850, was *Poems of Alice and Phoebe Cary,* for which they received $100. That same year, they traveled to New York City and Boston, visiting writers and observing the eastern literary scene. Alice decided to establish residence as a writer in New York City, and Phoebe joined her the next year. They began a series of Sunday evening gatherings that attracted a wide assembly of artists and other notables.

Alice was always the more prolific writer and thus sought after by the leading periodicals of her day. In 1852, she published *Clovernook Papers,* which would eventually be expanded to three volumes of short stories. In them, she vividly described country life in Ohio, its people and the natural world around them. Other novels—*Hagar, A Story of To-day; Married, Not Mated;* and *The Bishop's Son*—appeared in the 1850s and 1860s. Alice wrote easily and was a very popular poet, producing five books of poetry in her lifetime. Her themes continued to address nature and the deep spiritual values found in the rural life she knew so well.

Alice was involved to some extent in reforms of the day. She revered the nineteenth century's "true woman" role at home, yet she also believed in removing the barriers that hindered women from reaching self-fulfillment. In 1869, she became the first president of the famed women's club Sorosis.

Unfortunately, Alice inherited her mother's ill health, and she spent the end of her life still writing but much weakened by tuberculosis. Phoebe nursed her yet died the same year, 1871.

*Biographical Sketch by* SUSAN SWAN

## ✦ Writings of Alice Cary

*The Bishop's Son.* New York: G. W. Carleton, 1867.
*The Clovernook Children.* New York: John W. Lovell, 1855.

*Clovernook, or Recollections of Our Neighborhood in the West.* New York: John W. Lovell, 1852.
*Hagar, a Story of Today.* New York: Redfield, 1852.
*Married, Not Mated, or How They Lived at Woodside and Throcharorton Hall.* New York: Derby and Jackson, 1856.
*Pictures of Country Life.* New York: Derby and Jackson, 1859.

Clemmer, Mary, ed. *The Poetical Works of Alice and Phoebe Cary.* Household Edition. Boston: Houghton, Mifflin, 1882. (Clemmer compiled all of the sisters' poems found in separate books into a single volume, organized under each author's name.)

## ✦ Biographical Resources

Clemmer, Mary. "A Memorial of Alice and Phoebe Cary." In *The Poetical Works of Alice and Phoebe Cary,* edited by Mary Clemmer. Boston: Houghton, Mifflin, 1882.
Greeley, Horace. "Alice and Phoebe Cary." In *Eminent Women of the Age,* edited by James Parton et al. Hartford, CT: S. M. Betts, 1869.

# The Century of the Woman Movement

## From Speech to Toronto Women's Literary Club, 1878

EMILY HOWARD JENNINGS STOWE (1831–1903) *was the first woman to become a physician in Canada. A member of the First Unitarian Congregation in Toronto, she was also a pioneer for women's rights in education and a leader in the Canadian women's suffrage movement. In her 1878 speech to the Toronto Women's Literary Club, she asserted that if women were "swayed by fear of opprobium, of unpopularity, of the unfashionableness of women reading and thinking for themselves," they were clearly unfit for membership. Despite resistance, women persisted in forming clubs, holding regular meetings, and learning, through their organizations, to make changes in their own lives, in their local communities, and in the larger society in which they were becoming a more significant force.*

See the Biographical Sketch on pages 76–77.

To know what is right, and to pursue it independently of public opinion or of censure, is a high characteristic, and one that we should individually strive to attain. To be swayed by fear of opprobrium, of unpopularity, of the unfashionableness of women reading and thinking for themselves, is to be unfitted for membership in a club like ours. . . . Every effort that has ever been made for the amelioration or advancement of any class has been decried or tabooed as unpopular. It is a hard matter to get out of the old ruts and, in some soil, hard to make new furrows. But the nineteenth century is eminently an age of progress, and it is preeminently the century that is marked by the woman movement. In all periods there have been able women who have done honor to their sex; but never in any preceding century have women united in a common sisterhood to work for the common cause of freedom—freedom from the bonds of ignorance that enslave alike body and soul.

## ✦ *Biographical Sketch*

**Born:** *May 1, 1831, Norwich, Upper Canada*

**Died:** *April 30, 1903, Toronto, Ontario, age 71*

Emily Howard Jennings Stowe was a respected reformer in Canadian women's struggles for equal rights and education. She was the oldest of six girls born to a strong Quaker family. Her mother encouraged Emily's education, both in domestic duties and in academics. Emily attended and then taught in local schools and later became the first woman principal in the Canadian school system.

She married John Stowe, a Methodist laypreacher and carpenter, in 1856, and they had three children. John soon was diagnosed with tuberculosis, however, and Emily was left to support her family while he was convalescing. Teaching did not pay enough, she decided, and to pay her bills, she began the study of medicine with the hope of becoming a women's physician.

Undeterred by being refused admission to the Toronto medical school, Stowe enrolled at the New York City Medical College for Women and graduated in 1867. She soon established a thriving practice, despite the public hostility shown to her as a woman doctor. The Ontario Medical Act denied her a license, however, as the law forbade certification to anyone who had studied abroad. Dr. Stowe was not allowed to sit in on certificate-qualifying lectures at the Toronto School of Medicine until 1870. Even then, the treatment of her was so offensive that she did not follow through with the licensing exam until 1880.

Stowe's husband, John, now recovered from his illness, decided to become a dentist, and with his wife's support, he earned the degree. The couple established a joint practice, and they worked together for several years.

In 1888, Emily Stowe became a founding member of the Toronto Women's Literary Club, a reform group that lobbied for legislation that would improve the social and economic lives of women. The issues embraced by their campaigns ranged from better factory conditions for women to a Canadian Married Women's Property Act to women's admission to universities. In 1883, the group formally dedicated themselves to working for suffrage. In that regard, Stowe traveled to Washington, D.C., with Susan B. Anthony[60] to attend the International Council of Women. Stowe then became president of the newly expanded Canadian Suffrage Organization. In addition, she also began to campaign for other social justice reforms in the prison, labor, education, and banking systems.

John Stowe died in 1891, and two years later, Emily Stowe had to discontinue her medical practice after an accident disabled her. She retired and spent her last days gardening at her island retreat home. She died in Toronto in 1903. At her instruction, her body was cremated so as not to pollute the earth.

Dr. Stowe was a member of the First Unitarian Church in Toronto, and the minister of this congregation performed her memorial service. In Stowe's obituary, the Toronto *Saturday Night* wrote: "Canada could not lose a more remarkable daughter. Progressive, aggressive and liberal, in medicine, politics and religion, her life stands as an inspiration for all women who may come after her, and was a help and guide to thousands of her contemporaries."

*Biographical Sketch by* SUSAN SWAN

## ✦ Writings of Emily Howard Jennings Stowe

### Archives

Stowe Gullen Collection at Pratt Library, Victoria University, Toronto
Stowe-Gullen at Wilfred Laurier University, Waterloo, Ontario

## ✦ Biographical Resources

Killoran, M. Maureen. *Dr. Emily Howard Stowe: A Most Remarkable Daughter.* Occasional Paper #1. Malden, MA: Unitarian Universalist Women's Heritage Society, June 1992.

Ray, Jane. *Emily Stowe.* Ontario: Fitzhenry and Whiteside, 1978.

# Uplifting the Sphere of Woman's Life

## From *Massachusetts in the Woman Suffrage Movement,* 1881

HARRIET JANE HANSON ROBINSON (1825–1911) *began working in the mills of Lowell, Massachusetts, at age ten. At age eleven, she led a protest for worker's rights. Her career as a writer began when she contributed a poem to the* Lowell Offering, *the first magazine produced entirely by women. She became a Universalist, then married a Unitarian, and later in life renounced organized religion. Her activism as an abolitionist and suffragist led her to become an important chronicler of various reform movements. In her 1881 book on women's suffrage in Massachusetts, she evaluated the progress women had made toward full citizenship throughout the United States and particularly in New England. Her sense of excitement in being part of a major societal change is clearly apparent in her writing.*

See the Biographical Sketch on pages 80–84.

A thousand little streams have helped to swell the tide which has uplifted the sphere of woman's life.

✦ ✦ ✦

Never, in the history of civilization, has woman held the political, legal or social position that she does in Massachusetts today! New avenues of employment for her capacity are constantly being opened, and in every department of public trust to which she has been promoted, she has shown her ability. In this first hour of woman's triumph, it only remains for her to keep what she has gained and use faithfully the new privileges which have come into her life.

Being a woman, or because she is a woman, is no longer any reason why she cannot do the thing for which she is best fitted. There should be no shrinking, from timidity or love of ease, when she is called upon to fill a public position or to express her opinions by ballot at the polls. Home duties, ever sacred and nearest the true woman's heart, will be better and more wisely performed if assisted by the knowledge and experience which contact with life and public affairs cannot fail to give. The fact is already patent that it is not so much "more life and fuller" that we want, for women, but that more women are needed for the wider life and the responsible positions waiting for them.

Trained leaders are needed—women strong of purpose, who are willing to confront the public as presiding officers, or as public speakers, and to guide wisely the large masses of their sex who have not yet learned to think for themselves. They have too long been led in flocks, like sheep; the time has come for better leadership.

More educated women doctors are needed; more lawyers, preachers, professors and teachers in the higher grades of schools and in laboratories. More women are called for who will be willing to sacrifice their time and their domestic ease and serve without compensation on School Committee boards.* It is a noted fact that, especially in the towns of the State, there cannot be found enough educated women who are willing to have their names used as candidates for this office.

More plucky women who understand the law and know how to use the newly-acquired "inalienable right of all American citizens" are needed to go to the assessor's office, to the caucus, and to the polls. More women are needed in the "fourth estate,"—not only as novelists, story-tellers, or journalists but also as writers on ethical, moral, and social questions, as dramatists, and as the biographers of their own sex. Historians are needed, who shall give the record of nations and events from the woman's standpoint and include in the story of a people that which is often ignored,—the part taken by their sex in the occurrences of the times. Historians also are needed who will expose to public execration the woman side in the horrors of war and who will give to future generations a fairer estimate of the character of the sex of which God has made one-half the human race than has come down to us through the Hindu, the Greek, the Roman, and sometimes the Christian literature.

To sum up the progress of the woman movement in all parts of the civilized world, it is well to begin with the record of its advance in our own country. Massachusetts is by no means ahead in the march of this great reform. Other states in the Union have more than kept pace with

*In 1874, the New England Women's Club projected the movement by which women were first elected on the School Committee of Boston, and it also prepared the petition to be sent to the Massachusetts Legislature of 1879, the result of which was the passage of the law allowing women to vote for School Committees.

her, and many of them have made laws to improve the legal and social condition of woman. School Suffrage laws have been enacted in New Hampshire, Vermont,* Connecticut, New York, Colorado, Nebraska, Minnesota, Oregon, Kansas, Michigan, and Arizona Territory.

Constitutional amendments giving women the right of suffrage have just been passed by the Legislatures of Oregon, Nebraska, and Indiana. These proposed amendments cannot become a part of the constitution until they are submitted to the men voters of the State for their ratification. In Nebraska the Suffragists are very active, and in order to enlighten the men who will be called upon to vote upon the matter in 1883, they have started a *Western Woman's Journal,* whose motto is "An aristocracy of sex is repugnant to a republic."

✦ ✦ ✦

The most hopeful sign of the continued success of this great reform is found in the fact that the women themselves, of all nations, are getting ready to work for their own emancipation from the bondage of centuries. The women are "up in America, and they are already past their first sleep in Persia." For them the hour has indeed struck, the morning light has dawned, and they are forever awakened to freedom and to independence.

## ✦ *Biographical Sketch*

**Born:** *February 8, 1825, Boston, Massachusetts*

**Died:** *December 22, 1911, Malden, Massachusetts, age 87*

**Buried:** *Sleepy Hollow Cemetery, Concord, Massachusetts*

Though descended from solid pioneer stock, the Hanson family was far from prosperous, and the death of Harriet's father when she was six left them nearly destitute. In 1832, they moved to Lowell, where Harriet's mother found work as the matron of a factory-owned boarding house for mill workers, and Harriet herself, age eleven, found employment as a bobbin doffer.

*By a law passed Dec. 18th, 1880, the women of Vermont are eligible for the office of superintendent of schools, and of town or city clerk. In March, 1881, Miss Electa F. Smith was chosen city clerk in Vergennes, Vermont, and a great many of the towns elected women for school superintendants.

A year later, the company cut back on wages for older workers, and they organized a *turn out,* the term then used for a strike. Harriet impulsively led out her younger companions too, which set the course for her life as an activist. Although Harriet was proud of what she did, there were dire consequences for the family. Her mother lost her job at the company boarding house because she was unable to prevent the actions of her daughter. After some time of hardship, Harriet's mother was able to find another boarding house to run.

Although mill jobs required long hours of work, they provided a few benefits. Legislation required that the mills provide some education for the workers, and Harriet took full advantage of it. In addition, there were periods between tasks at the mill during which she could read, and the new library offered plenty of books. Most of the mill girls were interested in self-improvement, and Harriet joined the classes in drawing, dancing, languages, and other subjects. There were endless literary and political discussions.

At age fifteen, during the religious revival of 1840, Harriet converted to Universalism and was officially excommunicated from the Congregational church in 1842. Many years later, she became an Episcopalian.

The mill girls published a monthly magazine called the *Lowell Offering,* in which their poetry, stories, and articles appeared. One of Harriet's poems caught the attention of William Stevens Robinson, the young editor of the *Lowell Courier.* They were married on November 30, 1848. Although he was rather shy on a personal level, William Robinson was politically and socially radical, and his writings were always witty, progressive, and challenging.

With the arrival of four children (one of whom died at age five of typhoid fever), Harriet settled into the domestic role, although she continued to edit William's writing. His columns under the name *Warrington* attracted like-minded people, and their home became a meeting place for antislavery activists. He published *The Lowell American,* one of the first free-soil papers, from 1849 to 1854. Harriet joined the sewing circle of the local women's antislavery society.

The Robinson family lived in Concord from 1854 to 1857, and Ralph Waldo Emerson and Henry David Thoreau and their families were neighbors. Unfortunately, William's outspokenness also made enemies, and he had difficulty finding steady employment. However, in 1862, he was elected clerk of the Massachusetts House of Representatives, and this position brought considerable stability, even prominence, to the family.

After the Civil War, both William and Harriet became advocates for women's suffrage. Their daughter, Harriet Lucy Robinson Shattuck (called Hattie), joined them in this struggle. When William died in 1876, mother and daughter continued to write, speak, and organize for the cause. They formed the National Woman Suffrage Association of Massachusetts, a local chapter of Susan B. Anthony's effort. Harriet also helped Julia Ward Howe[61] organize the New England Women's Club and served on the first board of directors of the General Federation of Women's Clubs.

Harriet was a handsome woman with dark hair and eyes and a very firm, strong jaw. Her presence on the platform was striking, and she was determined to present herself as a devoted wife and mother as well as a tough contender for women's rights. She considered herself a self-made woman and was justly proud of this fact.

The Massachusetts legislature passed a law in 1879 that permitted women to vote for their towns' school committees. Hattie was the first to register, and Harriet soon followed. Even Harriet's mother, Harriet Browne Hanson, registered but decided that, at age eighty-five, she was not strong enough to brave the public derision she would have to face if she were to go out openly to the polling place. Together, Harriet and Hattie mobilized fifty women who summoned the necessary courage to cast their votes.

Harriet published *Massachusetts in the Woman Suffrage Movement* in 1879. Seven years later, this work became a chapter in the monumental *History of Woman Suffrage.* Harriet petitioned Congress for the removal of her "political disabilities" and went to Washington in 1882 to speak before a special Senate committee.

Harriet's only novel, *Captain Mary Miller* (1887), which she later rewrote as a play, dramatized the issues of women's rights. It was the story of a woman who took over the helm of a ship when the male captain became ill. Captain Mary then studied and became officially licensed to handle captain's responsibilities over the strenuous objections of the ship's owner. Hattie played the title role in the original production of this play.

Two years later, Harriet published a book-length poem entitled *The New Pandora* (1889). Although an important statement of Harriet's convictions about women's place in society, this work is less skillful than her other writings. It portrays Pandora as the bringer of beauty, civilization, and hope to the world. One can hear Harriet in Pandora's lines:

> That I am a woman doth not define my scope
> Sex cannot limit the immortal mind.
> We are ourselves, with individual souls,
> Still struggling onward toward the infinite.

*Loom and Spindle* (1898, reprinted in 1976) was perhaps Harriet's most important work. It is an expansion of a previous account, *Early Factory Labor in New England* (1883), in which she added personal notes and anecdotes as well as analysis of the social hierarchy of Lowell. This work stands as a powerful description of the life of the mill workers and as a detailed record of a particular historical era, a unique one in the labor movement. Harriet was adept at capturing the distinct personality types who came to work there—the women who had been viewed as burdens in the homes they lived in but who became independent and even proud of themselves with the wages they earned at the factories. Harriet's focus is perhaps a bit too optimistic, as she says little about the darker side of mill life, including the exploitation it involved.

In her later years, Harriet was frequently asked to lecture to various groups about her mill experiences and the changes that occurred in the lives of women at that time. Her working-class background gave a broader perspective on the reform movements she served, in contrast to the intellectual approaches of many of her co-workers. She died in her Malden home at the age of eighty-seven.

*Biographical Sketch by* DOROTHY BOROUSH

## ✦ Writings of Harriet Jane Hanson Robinson

*Captain Mary Miller.* Boston: W. H. Baker, 1887.

*Early Factory Labor in New England.* Boston: Wright and Potter, 1883.

*Loom and Spindle; or Life Among the Early Mill Girls.* Boston: T. Y. Crowell, 1898. Reprint, Kailua, HA: Press Pacifica, 1976.

*Massachusetts in the Woman Suffrage Movement.* Boston: Roberts Brothers, 1881.

*The New Pandora.* New York: G. P. Putnam, 1889.

"*Warrington*" *Pen-Portraits.* Boston: Lee and Shepard, 1877.

## ✦ Biographical Resources

Eisler, Benita, ed. *The Lowell Offering: Writings by New England Mill Women 1840–1845.* New York: J. B. Lippincott, 1977.

Foner, P. S. *The Factory Girls.* Urbana: University of Illinois, 1977.

Josephson, Hannah G. *The Golden Threads: New England's Mill Girls and Magnates.* New York: Duell, Sloan, and Pearce, 1949. Reprint, New York: Russell & Russell, 1967.

Maniero, Lina, ed. *American Women Writers.* Vol. 3. New York: Frederick Ungar, 1981.

Merk, L. "Massachusetts and the Woman-Suffrage Movement." Ph.D. diss., Radcliffe College, 1961.

Rothman, E. "Harriet Hanson Robinson: A Search for Satisfaction in the Nineteenth Century Woman Suffrage Movement." Ph.D. diss., Radcliffe College, 1973.

Selden, Bernice. *The Mill Girls.* New York: Athenaeum, 1983.

# Woman as a Citizen of the State

## From Lecture "To an Audience of Ladies," London, 1881

FRANCES POWER COBBE (1822–1906), *founder of the Society for the Protection of Animals Liable to Vivisection, was a successful journalist, lecturer, and social reformer in England. As an adult, she associated with many Unitarians and together with her lifelong friend, sculptor Mary Lloyd, joined the Little Portland Street Chapel, a Unitarian church where James Martineau, noted Unitarian theologian, served as minister.*

*In 1891, Frances Cobbe delivered a course of lectures concerning women's duties to herself, her family, her community, and as a citizen of the state. By moving systematically outward in her analysis, she was able to apply traditional concepts of women's responsibility to promote virtue in the home as rationale for women's participation in public life. She particularly admonished women of the upper classes to seek influence in public affairs to bring justice to poor and oppressed women. This series of lectures,* The Duties of Women, *became her most popular book on both sides of the Atlantic and was a recommended reading by American suffragists.*

See the Biographical Sketch on pages 91–94.

The share which women have hitherto been permitted to take in the public affairs of nations has singularly oscillated. Our sex always seems to be in the zenith or at the nadir, on the throne or nowhere, at the goal or out of the running. There have been two or three dozen great female rulers in universal history; and the proportion of able and prosperous sovereigns among them, compared to the proportion of similarly able and prosperous monarchs among the many hundreds of kings, is a most astonishing fact.

✦ ✦ ✦

Historians, when they deign to notice this curious preponderance of ability among female rulers, have been wont to explain it in a way delightfully soothing to masculine pride. They say that a queen is well guided by her male ministers, while a king is too often misguided by bad female favorites. I will only remark that the power of *choosing* able ministers is the very first qualification of a sovereign, and that, unluckily for the theory, a great number of the most prosperous queens kept the reins tightly in their own hands and employed secretaries rather than ministers. On the other hand, a king who chooses bad favorites, and allows himself to be guided by them, appears to exhibit the very worst and most mischievous weakness which could beset a sovereign.

Again, beside the great queens, we find all down the stream of history, when a nation has been involved in extreme peril, it has happened that some woman—some Jael or Judith or Esther, some Maid of Saragossa or of Orleans—steps forth and saves the situation; and she has been duly lauded for her heroism to the skies, though occasionally left by her chivalrous countrymen to be burned at the stake.

But between these heights of royalty and heroism and the abasement of political nonentity, there seems to be no *mezzo termine* for our unfortunate sex. *Public spirit* is a quality which we are not encouraged to cultivate; and it is almost by a figure of speech that I have spoken of our duties as Citizens of the State. The dignity of citizenship (as understood by the old Romans, for example) certainly included more than *our* particular privilege; namely, that of paying all the taxes without possessing any corresponding rights! It has been assumed that not only should a woman's charity begin at home but stop there; or, at the most, make the round of the parish under the direction of the parson, distributing tracts and soup tickets.

But, at last, womanly charity and public spirit have broken their bonds. An immense breach was made in the invisible hedges wherewith our mothers and grandmothers were surrounded within the memory of many of us, when Miss Nightingale and the late regretted Mary Stanley went out to the Crimea to nurse the soldiers. Mary Carpenter[62] also, of blessed memory, managed by sheer dint of volition . . . to force so many legislative reforms through Parliament and cut such a quantity of masculine red tape, that MP's and heads of Departments began to recognize women's ideas as things which might actually deserve attention . . . Then came the school-board election and representation, by far the greatest bound forward our cause has made. Who would have thought, my dear *contemporaries* here present—who would have thought, when you and I were young, that we should live to see the day when elections of women, for what is practically a great Civil Parliament, should be going on now all over England, and everywhere with such extraordinary and triumphant success that the newspapers complain peevishly of the useless waste of votes in showing how determined the electors are to return female candidates! The possession of votes for municipal elections and the occasional election of women . . . as Guardians of the Poor are also vast strides in the direction of public usefulness for women. Further, as the safeguard and basis of the whole movement, we have the enormous improvement, I might call it revolution, which has been made of late years in the education of women,—fitting them to undertake all their tasks on equal terms with men.

By their aid, at last the education of women has been pushed so far that it became impossible longer to refuse to recognize its success by university degrees; and henceforth women may stand not only *actually* (as they have sometimes done before) but *admittedly* on a level, as regards knowledge, with men.

Having gained so great a vantage ground on our upward way, it can, I think, only depend on women themselves how far their entrance into public and political life shall proceed. . . .

Be it our part, my friends, I implore you, to aid with all our power of example and voice to show that liberty *now,* for the women of England, shall . . . be the nurse of purest virtue for us. And let us, as the needful beginning of such a true liberation, take uttermost precaution that we adopt no habits, assume no freedoms, which, even if they might be safe for ourselves individually, might be unsafe for other women. Better to forego for a time some of the privileges which our sex shall hereafter enjoy than imperil by any laxity, any want of caution and wisdom now, the whole character of this great reformation.

We now turn directly to consider how stands the Duty of Women in England as regards entrance into public life and development of public spirit. What ought we to do at present, as concerns all public work wherein it is possible for us to obtain a share?

The question seems to answer itself in its mere statement. We are bound to do *all* we can to promote the virtue and happiness of our fellow-men and women, and *therefore* we must accept and seize every instrument of power, every vote, every influence which we can obtain, to enable us to promote virtue and happiness.

✦ ✦ ✦

When one of us women sees a wrong needing to be righted, or a good to be achieved, or a truth to be taught, or a misery to be relieved, we wish for wealth, for influence, for the tongue of an orator, or the pen of a poet to achieve our object. These are holy wishes, sacred longings of our heart, which come to us in life's best hours and in the presence of God. And why are not we also to wish and strive to be allowed to place our hands on that vast machinery whereby, in a constitutional realm, the great work of the world is carried on, and which achieves by its enormous power tenfold either the good or the harm which any individual can reach, which may be turned to good or turned to harm, according to the hands which touch it? In almost every case, it is only by legislation (as you all know) that the *roots* of great evils can be touched at all and that the social diseases of pauperism and vice and crime can be brought within hope of cure. Women, with the tenderest hearts and best intentions, go on laboring all their lifetimes often in merely pruning the offshoots of these evil roots, in striving to allay and abate the symptoms of the disease. But the nobler and much more truly philanthropic work of plucking up the roots, or curing the disease, they have been forced to leave to men.

You will still judge from these remarks the ground on which, as a matter of *duty,* I place the demand for woman's political emancipation. I think we are bound to seek it, in the first place, as a *means,* a very great means, *of doing good,* fulfilling our Social Duty of contributing to the virtue and happiness of mankind, advancing the kingdom of God. . . . In a government like ours, where the basis of representation is so immensely extensive, the whole business of legislation is carried on *by pressure*—the pressure of each represented class and party to get its grievances redressed, to make its interests prevail. The nonrepresented classes necessarily go to the wall, not by mere willful neglect on the part of either ministers or members of Parliament, but because they must attend to their constituents first, and to their pressure (they would lose their places and seats, if they did not); and the time for attending to the non-represented people, amid the hurry and bustle of the session, never arises. To be *one of a represented class* is a very much greater thing in England than merely to drop a paper into a ballot box. It means to be able to *insist* upon attention to the wants of that class and to all other matters of public importance which may be deemed deserving of attention. It is one of the sore grievances of women in particular that, not possessing representation, the measures which concern them are forever postponed to the bills promoted by the represented classes (e.g., the Married Woman's Property Bill was, if I mistake not, six times set down for reading in one session in vain, the House being counted out on every occasion).

Thus, in asking for the Parliamentary franchise we are asking, as I understand it, for the power to influence legislation generally; and in every other land of franchise, municipal, parochial, or otherwise, for similar power to bring our sense of justice and righteousness to bear on public affairs. To achieve so great an end, we ought all to be willing to incur trouble and labor and the loss of that privacy we some of us so highly value, with the ridicule and obloquy of silly men and sillier women.

✦ ✦ ✦

I have often thought how strange it is that men can at one and the same moment cheerfully consign our sex to lives either of narrowest toil or senseless luxury and vanity and then sneer at the smallness of our aims, the pettiness of our thoughts, the puerility of our conversation! Are we, then, made of different stuff, that the *régime* which would make Hercules pusillanimous and effeminate should make us courageous and noble-minded?

But there is a special reason why we women of the upper classes in England should at this time stir ourselves to obtain influence in public affairs. That reason is the miserable oppressions, the bitter griefs, the cruel wrongs our sister women are doomed to suffer, and which might be relieved and righted by better legislation. I have explained just now how every underrepresented class in a constitutional country *must* be neglected by ministers and members of Parliament; and, in the case of women, there are such enormous arrears of bad laws regarding them lying over from far-off times of barbarism, and needing now to be revised, that this difficulty of obtaining attention to our concerns is a double cruelty. Instead of needing no legislation because their interests are so well cared for (as some senators have audaciously asserted), I boldly affirm that there is no class of men in England who could not better, and with less consequent injustice, forego the franchise than women.

There are thousands of poor women who suffer the worst of these wrongs,—some who are placed legally at the mercy of savage husbands, or who are driven by misery and ill-paid, hopeless labor into the Dead Sea of vice, and some, of a little higher class, whose children are torn from their arms, perhaps to satisfy a dead or a living husband's religious fanaticism. These most piteously wronged of all God's creatures are breaking their hearts day by day and year by year all around us; no *man* much understanding their woes; no *man* having leisure to seek their remedy. And can *we* sit patiently by, and know all these things, and long to relieve all this agony and stop all these wrongs, and yet accept contentedly as a beautiful dispensation—not of God, but of man—the law which leaves us tongue-tied and hand-bound, unable to throw the weight of one poor vote into the scale of justice and mercy? Can we think our wretched drawing-room dignities and courtesies, and the smiles and approval of a swarm of fops and fools, worth preserving at the cost of the knowledge that we *might* do something to lift up this load, and do it *not?*

Needless, I hope, it is to add that we must come to these public duties, whenever we may be permitted to fulfill them, in the most conscientious and disinterested spirit, and determined to perform them excellently well. Approaching them from the side I have indicated, this can scarcely fail to be the case; and we must all bear in mind that for a long time to come every step women take in the field of politics will be watched by not unnaturally prejudiced spectators of the innovation, and that to show either indifference toward the acquirement of new powers, or misuse or neglect of those we already possess, cannot fail to be recorded in damning characters against our whole movement.

Practically, I think that every woman who has any margin of time or money to spare should adopt some one public interest, some philanthropic under-taking, or some social agitation of reform, and give to that cause whatever time and work she may be able to afford; thus completing her life by adding to her private duties the noble effort to advance God's Kingdom beyond the bounds of her home. Remember, pray, that I say emphatically "*adding* to her private duties," not *subtracting* from them. I should think it a most grievous and deplorable error to neglect any private duties already incurred for the sake of new public duties subsequently adopted. But, in truth, though we read of "Mrs. Jellybys" in novels, I have failed yet to find, in a pretty large experience of real life, a single case in which a woman who exercised public spirit, even to the extent of self-devotion, was not *also* an admirable and conscientious daughter, wife, mother, or mistress of a household. This spectre of the female politician, who abandons her family to neglect for the sake of passing bills in Parliament, is just as complete an illusion of the masculine brain as the older spectre whom Sydney Smith laid by a joke,—the woman who would "forsake an infant for a quadratic equation."

✦ ✦ ✦

We are, many of us, in these days wandering far and wide in despairing search for some bread of life whereby we may sustain our souls, some *Holy Grail* wherein we may drink salvation from doubt and sin. It may be a long, long quest ere we find it; but one thing is ready to our hands. It is *duty.* Let us turn to that in simple fidelity, and labor to act up to our own highest ideal, to *be* the very best and purest and truest we know how, and to *do* around us every work of love which our hands and hearts may reach. When we have lived and labored like this, then, I believe, that the light will come to us, as to many another doubting soul; and it will prove true once more that "they who do God's will shall know of his doctrine," and they who strive to advance his kingdom here will gain faith in another divine realm beyond the dark river, where Virtue shall ascend into Holiness, and Duty be transfigured into Joy.

## ✦ *Biographical Sketch*

**Born:** *December 4, 1822, Dublin, Ireland*

**Died:** *April 5, 1904, age 82*

**Buried:** *Llanelltyd, Wales, next to Mary Lloyd*

Frances Power Cobbe was a successful literary and journalistic writer and early advocate for women's rights. Her articles on wife battering prompted changes in law. She also promoted equal education and expanded vocational opportunities for women. She was part of Barbara Leigh Smith Bodichon's Langham Place Group.[63] Well known as a liberal religious writer, Frances Cobbe edited the British edition of Theodore Parker's *Collected Works.* She spent the last three decades of her life leading the antivivisection campaign.

Frances grew up as the youngest of the five children of Charles Cobbe and Frances Conway. After being raised by a series of governesses, Frances was sent to a prestigious finishing school in Bristol. As a young woman, she taught at a local school twice a week and assisted in local communities during the great famine. Her mother died when Frances was twenty-five, which left her to run the household.

Frances Cobbe's first book, *The Theory of Intuitive Morals,* was inspired by Immanuel Kant's *Metaphysics of Ethics.* Printed anonymously to spare her father embarrassment, it received positive reviews as a significant first work. Theodore Parker advocated republication in the

United States. Later religious works included *Broken Lights* (1864) and *Dawning Lights* (1868) as well as a book of liberal religious prayers. Her essay of introduction to the London edition of Parker's *Works* was so popular that it was published as a booklet.

Searching for a way to contribute to society, Cobbe became the assistant to educator Mary Carpenter[64] through Unitarians Harriet St. Leger and Lady Noel Byron. After becoming disillusioned with Carpenter's severe lifestyle and philosophy for educating the deprived and retrieving delinquent youth, Cobbe served as a workhouse visitor in Bristol. She wrote articles promoting positive policies in these fields.

Cobbe's father died when she was thirty-five, at which point she obtained employment as Italian correspondent to the *Daily News.* While she was in Italy, mutual friends introduced Cobbe to sculptor Mary Lloyd, with whom she continued to live after returning to England. They purchased a house in South Kensington and became members of the Little Portland Street Chapel, where James Martineau was the minister.

Cobbe wrote material for a dozen monthly and quarterly publications. Preferring not to do book reviews, she included observations on current books in thematic essays. She became a lead columnist for seven years for the London *Echo,* a half-penny paper, and later wrote regularly for the *Standard,* presenting topics of humor and ethical interest. Cobbe credited her pursuit of women's rights to her 1859 meeting with American Unitarian minister Samuel J. May. In 1862, she was ridiculed after she advocated opening university examinations to women in a paper to the Social Science Congress.

A decade later (1878), Cobbe's pamphlet "Wife Torture" proposed that wife battering be made grounds for legal separation. In addition, Cobbe proposed that custody of children be routinely granted to mothers rather than fathers, as was then customary. Her campaign influenced passage of the Matrimonial Causes Act of 1878.

Because of such articles, Cobbe was invited to participate in women's rights and suffrage activity by Unitarian Barbara Leigh Smith Bodichon. In July 1867, Cobbe chaired the first meeting of the organization, which became the London National Society for Women's Suffrage. She worked on the Married Women's Property Committee and served on the Committee of the Society for Promoting the Return of Women as Poor Law Guardians.

*The Duties of Women,* Cobbe's 1881 series of lectures, became her most popular book and was recommended by American suffragists. As a result of her writing and activism, Cobbe was voted an honorary membership in Sorosis, a New York women's club. She argued that women's suffrage was a way to extend women's compassion and meet their societal responsibilities.

Cobbe was also a founder of the Society for the Protection of Animals Liable to Vivisection, known as the Victoria Street Society, and served as its secretary until 1884. Her articles on this topic were some of the first to address the moral ramifications of the torture of animals for medical research and training.

In 1884, a legacy bestowed by a contributor to her antivivisection work enabled Cobbe to retire to Emily Lloyd's family home in Wales. There, the two women continued to be well known for their stimulating hospitality. Cobbe and Lloyd both worked on Cobbe's biography. Lloyd's death in 1898 left Cobbe with an ongoing sense of loneliness. In 1902, for her eightieth birthday, Frances Power Cobbe received a congratulatory annuity for her strenuous philanthropic activity and the high moral purpose of her life, an honor which was covered by twenty newspapers.

*Biographical Sketch by* IRENE BAROS-JOHNSON

## ✦ Writings of Frances Power Cobbe


*Alone to the Alone: Prayers for Theists, by Several Contributors.* 2nd ed. London: Williams and Norgate, 1872.

*Broken Lights. An Inquiry into the Present Condition & Future Prospects of Religious Faith.* Boston: J. E. Tilton, 1864.

*Cities of the Past.* London: Longham, 1864.

"Criminals, Idiots, Women and Minors. Is the Classification Sound? A Discussion of the Laws Concerning the Property of Married Women." *Fraser's Magazine* (1868).

*Dawning Lights. An Inquiry Concerning the Secular Results of the New Reformation.* London: Edward T. Whitfield, 1868.

*The Duties of Women: A Course of Lectures.* London: William and Norgate, 1881.

*Essays on the Pursuits of Women.* London: Emily Faithful, 1863.

*Italics. Brief Notes on Politics, People and Places in Italy in 1864.* London: Trubner, 1864.

*The Life of Frances Power Cobbe by Herself.* London: Richard Bentley, 1894.

*The Theory of Intuitive Morals.* London: Longman, 1855.

"What Shall We Do with Our Old Maids?" *Fraser's Magazine* (November 1862).

## ✦ Biographical Resources

Banks, Olive. *The Biographical Dictionary of British Feminists 1800–1930.* New York: New York University Press, 1985.

Bauer, Carol, and Lawrence Ritt. "'A Husband Is a Beating Animal'—Frances Power Cobbe Confronts the Wife-Abuse Problem in Victorian England." *International Journal of Women's Studies* 6 (1983): 99–118.

Crawford, Anne, et al. *The Europa Biographical Dictionary of British Women.* Detroit, MI: Gale Research, 1983.

French, Richard D. *Anti-Vivisection and Medical Science in Victorian England.* Princeton: Princeton University Press, 1975.

Lacey, Candida Ann. *Barbara Leigh Smith Bodichon and the Langham Place Group.* New York: Routledge & Kegan Paul, 1987.

Levine, Philippa. *Victorian Feminism 1850–1900.* Tallahassee, FL: State University Press, 1987.

# The Woman's Christian Temperance Union and the Colored Woman

## Article in *African Methodist Episcopal Church Review*, July 1888

*Nineteenth-century African American women were part of the same social changes faced by white women. One of the best-known black reform leaders was* FRANCES ELLEN WATKINS HARPER (1825–1911), *who worked tirelessly for abolition, temperance, and suffrage while also pursuing a literary career as a poet and novelist. Although she wrote Sunday school materials for the African Methodist Episcopal church, she was a member of the Unitarian church in Philadelphia.*

*In her 1888 article on the participation of African American women in the temperance movement, she revealed some of the dynamics that persist even today as people of different racial and ethnic groups struggle to find common ground. She wrote of the "twin evils of slavery and intemperance" and demonstrated their negative effects on the lives of women of all races. However, she confessed that when she first learned of the women's organizational work in progress to address these problems, she was not certain the participation of women of color would be welcome. And when she did become involved, she was asked to direct the "work among colored people." Although she recognized that progress toward racial harmony and cooperation was slow, she saw the work of temperance as one place where women of different races could learn to work together for a common cause.*

See the Biographical Sketch on pages 102–105.

A woman sat beneath the shadow of her home, while the dark waves of intemperance dashed against human hearts and hearthstones, but there came an hour when she found that she could do something else besides wring her hands and weep over the ravages of the liquor traffic, which had darkened so many lives and desolated so many homes. Where the enemy spreads his snares for the feet of the unwary, inexperienced and tempted, she, too, could go and strive to stay the tide of ruin which was sending its floods of sorrow, shame and death to the habitations of men, and 1873 witnessed the strange and wondrous sight of the Woman's Crusade, when the mother-heart was roused up in defense of the home and all that the home held dearest. A Divine impulse seemed to fan into sudden flame and touch with living fire earnest hearts, which rose up to meet the great occasion. Lips that had been silent in the prayer meeting were loosened to take part in the wonderful uprising. Saloons were visited, hardships encountered, insults, violence, and even imprisonment endured by women, brave to suffer and strong to endure. Thousands of saloon visits were made, many were closed. Grand enthusiasms were aroused, moral earnestness awakened, and a fire kindled whose beacon lights still stream o'er the gloomy track of our monster evil. Victor Hugo has spoken of the nineteenth century as being woman's era, and among the most noticeable epochs in this era is the uprising of women against the twin evils of slavery and intemperance, which had foisted themselves like leeches upon the civilization of the present age. In the great antislavery conflict women had borne a part, but after the storm cloud of battle had rolled away, it was found that an enemy, old and strong and deceptive, was warring against the best interests of society; not simply an enemy to one race, but an enemy to all races—an enemy that had entrenched itself in the strongholds of appetite and avarice and was upheld by fashion, custom and legislation. To dislodge this enemy, to put prohibition not simply on the statute book but in the heart and conscience of a nation, embracing within itself such heterogeneous masses, is no child's play nor the work of a few short moons. Men who were subjects in their own country and legislated for by others become citizens here, with the power to help legislate for native-born Americans. Hundreds of thousands of new citizens have been translated from the old oligarchy of slavery into the new commonwealth of freedom and are numerically strong enough to hold the balance of power in a number of the States and sway its legislators for good or evil. With all these conditions, something more is needed than grand enthusiasms lighting up a few consecrated lives with hallowed brightness. We need patient, persevering, Christly endeavor, a consecration of the moral earnestness, spiritual power and numerical strength of the nation to grapple with this evil and accomplish its overthrow.

After the knowledge and experience gained by the crusade, women, instead of letting all their pure enthusiasms become dissipated by expending in feeling what they should utilize in action, came together and formed the Woman's Christian Temperance Union. From Miss Willard we learn that women who had been crusading all winter called conventions for consultation in respective States and that several organizations, called Temperance Leagues, were formed. Another step was the confederation of the States into the National Christian Temperance Union. A circular, aided by an extensive circulation through the press, was sent out to women in different parts of the country, and a convention was called, which met in Cleveland in November, 1874, to which sixteen States responded. A plan of work was adopted, financial arrangements made, and the publishing of an organ resolved upon. Mrs. Whittemyer, of Philadelphia, was elected President, and Miss Willard, of Illinois, Corresponding Secretary. This Union has increased in numbers and territory until at its last convention it embraced thirty-seven States and Territories. For years I knew very little of its proceedings and was not sure that colored comradeship was very desirable, but having attended a local Union in Philadelphia, I was asked to join and acceded to the request and was made city and afterwards State Superintendent of work among colored people. Since then, for several years I have held the position of National Superintendent of work among the colored people of the North. When I became National Superintendent there were no colored women on the Executive Committee or Board of Superintendents. Now there are two colored women on the Executive Committee and two on the Board of Superintendents. As a matter of course the colored question has come into this work as it has into the Sons of Temperance, Good Templars, and elsewhere. Some of the members of different Unions have met the question in a liberal and Christian manner; others have not seemed to have so fully outgrown the old shards and shells of the past as to make the distinction between Christian affiliation and social equality, but still the leaven of more liberal sentiments has been at work in the Union and produced some hopeful results.

One of the pleasantest remembrances of my connection with the Woman's Christian Temperance Union was the kind and hospitable reception I met in the Missouri State Convention and the memorable words of their President, Mrs. Hoffman, who declared that the color-line was eliminated. A Superintendent was chosen at that meeting for colored work in the State, at whose home in St. Louis the National Superintendent was for some time a guest. The State Superintendent said in one of the meetings to the colored sisters, "You can come with us, or you can go by yourselves." There was self-reliance and ability enough among them to form a Union of their own, which was named after the National Superintendent. Our work is divided into about forty departments, and among them they chose several lines of work and had departments for parlor meetings, juvenile and evangelistic work, all of which have been in working order. The Union held meetings in Methodist and Baptist churches and opened in the African Methodist Episcopal Church an industrial school for children, which increased in size until from about a dozen children at the beginning, it closed with about one hundred and fifty, as I understand. Some of the Unions, in their outlook upon society, found that there was no orphan asylum for colored children, except among the Catholics, and took the initiative for founding an asylum for colored children, and in a short time were successful in raising several hundred dollars for that purpose. This Union has, I have been informed, gathered into its association seventeen school teachers, and I think comprises some of the best brain and heart of the race in the city. From West Virginia a lady informs the National Superintendent that her Union has invited the colored sisters to join with them and adds, "Praise God, from whom all blessings flow." In a number of places where there are local Unions in the North, the doors have been opened to colored women, but in the farther South separate State Unions have been formed. Southern white women, it may be, fail to make in their minds the discrimination between social equality and Christian affiliation. Social equality, if I rightly understand the term, is the outgrowth of social affinities and social conditions and may be based on talent, ability or wealth, on either or all of these conditions. Christian affiliation is the union of Christians to do Christly work and to help build up the kingdom of Christ amid the sin and misery of the world, under the spiritual leadership of the Lord Jesus Christ. At our last National Convention two States were represented by colored representatives. The colored President of an Alabama Union represented a Union composed of white and colored people and is called No. 2, instead of Colored Union, as it was not composed entirely of colored people, and in making its advent into the National Union brought, as I was informed, more than twice the amount of State dues which was paid by the white Alabama Union, No. 1. The question of admission into the White Ribbon Army was brought before the National President, through a card sent from Atlanta. Twenty-three women had formed a Union and had written to the National Superintendent of colored work in the North asking in reference to their admission and if black sheep must climb up some other way to tell them how. I showed the card to Miss Willard, who gave it as her opinion "that the National could not make laws for a State. If the colored women of Georgia will meet and form a Woman's Christian Temperance Union for the State, it is my opinion that their officers and delegates will have the same representation in the National." The President of the Second Alabama was received and recognized in the National as a member of the Executive Committee and had a place, as I was informed, on the Committee of Resolutions. Believing, as I do, in human solidarity, I hold that the Woman's Christian Temperance Union has in its hands one of the grandest opportunities that God ever pressed into the hands of the womanhood of any country. Its conflict is not the contest of a social club but a moral warfare for an imperiled civilization. Whether or not the members of the farther South will subordinate the spirit of caste to the spirit of Christ, time will show. Once between them and the Negro were vast disparities, which have been melting and disappearing. The war obliterated the disparity between freedom and slavery. The civil law blotted out the difference between disfranchisement and manhood suffrage. Schools have sprung up like wells in the desert dust, bringing the races nearer together on the intellectual plane, while as a participant in the wealth of society the colored man has, I believe, in some instances, left his former master behind in the race for wealth. With these old landmarks going and gone, one relic remains from the dead past, "our social customs." In clinging to them let them remember that the most ignorant, vicious, and degraded voter outranks, politically, the purest, best, and most cultured woman in the South, and learn to look at the question of Christian affiliation on this subject, not in the shadow of the fashion of this world that fadeth away, but in the light of the face of Jesus Christ. And can any one despise the least of Christ's brethren without despising Him? Is there any path that the slave once trod that Jesus did not tread before him and leave luminous with the light of His steps? Was the Negro bought and sold? Christ was sold for thirty pieces of silver. Has he been poor? "The birds had nests, the foxes had holes, but the Son of man had nowhere to lay His head." Were they beaten in the house of bondage? They took Jesus and scourged Him. Have they occupied a low social position? "He made himself of no reputation, and was numbered with the transgressors." Despised and trodden under foot? He was despised and rejected of men; spit upon by the rabble, crucified between thieves, and died as died Rome's meanest criminal slave. Oh, my brothers and sisters, if God chastens every son whom He receiveth, let your past history be a stimulus for the future. Join with the great army who are on the side of our God and His Christ. Let your homes be the best places where you may plant your batteries against the rum traffic. Teach your children to hate intoxicating drinks with a deadly hatred. Though scorn may curl her haughty lip and fashion gather up her dainty robes from social contact, if your lives are in harmony with God and Christly sympathy with man, you belong to the highest nobility in God's universe. Learn to fight the battle for God and man as athletes armed for a glorious strife, encompassed about with a cloud of witnesses who are in sympathy with the highest and holiest endeavors.

✦ ✦ ✦

# Woman's Political Future

## Speech to World's Congress of Representative Women, Chicago, 1893

*One of the watershed events of the late nineteenth century was the World's Fair and Columbian Exposition held in Chicago in 1893. A number of important conferences were held there, bringing together diverse people from around the world to consider the crucial issues of the day. (Speeches from two of these assemblies are found elsewhere in this anthology.[65]) In her address to the World's Congress of Representative Women,* FRANCES ELLEN WATKINS HARPER (1825–1911) *challenged American women to seize the opportunity at hand "to create a healthy public sentiment; to demand justice, simple justice, as the right of every race." Her words beg women today to continue to secure her still unfulfilled vision that one day "Eden would spring up in our path, and Paradise be around our way."*

See the Biographical Sketch on pages 102–105.

If before sin had cast its deepest shadows or sorrow had distilled its bitterest tears, it was true that it was not good for man to be alone, it is no less true, since the shadows have deepened and life's sorrows have increased, that the world has need of all the spiritual aid that woman can give for the social advancement and moral development of the human race. The tendency of the present age, with its restlessness, religious upheavals, failures, blunders, and crimes, is toward broader freedom, an increase of knowledge, the emancipation of thought, and a recognition of the brotherhood of man; in this movement woman, as a companion of man, must be a sharer. So close is the bond between man and woman that you cannot raise one without lifting the other. The world cannot move without woman's sharing in the movement, and to help give a right impetus to that movement is woman's highest privilege.

✦ ✦ ✦

Today women hold in their hands influence and opportunity, and with these they have already opened doors which have been closed to others. By opening doors of labor woman has become a rival claimant for at least some of the wealth monopolized by her stronger brother. In the home she is the priestess, in society the queen, in literature she is a power, in legislative halls law-makers have responded to her appeals, and for her sake have humanized and liberalized their laws. The press has felt the impress of her hand. In the pews of the church she constitutes the majority; the pulpit has welcomed her, and in the school she has the blessed privilege of teaching children and youth. To her is apparently coming the added responsibility of political power; and what she now possesses should only be the means of preparing her to use the coming power for the glory of God and the good of mankind; for power without righteousness is one of the most dangerous forces in the world.

✦ ✦ ✦

O women of America! Into your hands God has pressed one of the sublimest opportunities that ever came into the hands of the women of any race or people. It is yours to create a healthy public sentiment; to demand justice, simple justice, as the right of every race; to brand with everlasting infamy the lawless and brutal cowardice that lynches, burns, and tortures your own countrymen.

To grapple with the evils which threaten to undermine the strength of the nation and to lay magazines of powder under the cribs of future generations is no child's play.

Let the hearts of the women of the world respond to the song of the herald angels of peace on earth and goodwill to men. Let them throb as one heart unified by the grand and holy purpose of uplifting the human race, and humanity will breathe freer, and the world grow brighter. With such a purpose Eden would spring up in our path, and Paradise be around our way.

## ✦ *Biographical Sketch*

**Born:** *September 24, 1825, Baltimore, Maryland*

**Died:** *February 22, 1911, Philadelphia, Pennsylvania, age 85*

**Buried:** *Eden Cemetery, Philadelphia, Pennsylvannia*

Frances Ellen Watkins Harper was an anomaly in her lifetime. She achieved financial independence and nationwide acclaim as a lecturer, writer, and social activist in the nineteenth century, an era when such opportunities were not usually available to American women of any race.

Born in 1825 to free African American parents in Baltimore, Maryland, Frances Watkins suffered the loss of her mother at age three. An enlightened uncle took charge of her formal education and strongly influenced her early intellectual development. At a time when it was considered a crime to teach a slave to read and write, her free status allowed her to pursue her education. Around age fourteen, she secured employment with a white family. In their home, she was given access to their library and read widely.

Frances Watkins formed a lifelong friendship with William Still, an ex-slave who taught himself to read and write. In 1847, he became secretary of the Pennsylvania Abolition Society, one of many antislavery societies formed by black people. In 1859, after John Brown's failed raid on Harper's Ferry, Watkins spent two weeks with Brown's wife while he was on trial.

Other details about Watkins's life during this period are scant. She continued to lecture and teach during and after the war, becoming one of the first female lecturers, black or white, hired by abolitionist associations to speak to and represent antislavery organizations around the country. In addition to donating generous portions of her income to other abolitionists, she never charged black people for her lectures. Watkins married Fenton Harper in 1860 and lived with him until his death in 1864. They had one daughter, and during her marriage, she limited her activism to her immediate locale of Virginia.

The emancipation of slaves kindled the possibility of voting rights for blacks and women. Frances Watkins Harper and her contemporaries campaigned tirelessly for women's right to vote. She also worked with the Women's Christian Temperance Union for almost a decade and served as its national superintendent of the black division for ten years (1878–1888). An excerpt from her temperance speech to the Women's Congress was reprinted in the January 1878 issue of the *English Woman's Review.*

Harper's literary works were prolific and very popular. She supported herself through the sale of her books, selling over fifty thousand copies, which was remarkable for this era. One of the most widely read American poets of the nineteenth century, she published over 120 poems in eleven volumes between 1854 and 1901. Her essays, speeches, and poems appeared regularly in all the prominent African American periodicals. Harper's passionate energy was directed toward several movements: abolitionism, race advancement and equality, women's and children's rights, Christian morality, and temperance.

While Harper's education and breeding helped develop middle-class white audiences for her literary talents, she was also able to write significant protest literature in the black liberation tradition. She argued for self-help and self-advancement of the race, and much of her poetry addressed subjects of oppression, religion, and the social and moral reform of black people. She used her influence and position to argue in support of civil rights for black people, women, and children.

Harper was one of the first black women known to publish a short story, *The Two Offers,* in 1859, and to publish a novel, *Iola Leroy,* in 1892. Though she was a political writer, her decision to use the romance novel to communicate her messages of racial pride and service to the race reflected the limited options available to women, despite their talents. *Iola Leroy* portrays "race" issues, and the chief character boldly embraces her black roots despite having white features that could help her pass into the more privileged world of white society. Iola's sense of "race loyalty" causes her to reject the trappings of the white world and struggle for her race.

Harper's life represented some of the earliest strains of black women's womanism and feminism. As part of the womanist tradition, she broke many social norms that restricted women in the eighteenth and nineteenth centuries. For instance, she often traveled by herself during her continuous lectures for the Anti-Slavery Society of Maine and others. She also spoke to audiences that were mixed both in terms of race and gender, something quite unusual at the time. As a married woman, she campaigned for women's financial independence and marriage equity issues.

Harper never seemed to view herself as less capable than her male peers and colleagues. Her female characters Iola and Janette in *Iola Leroy* and *The Two Offers* are liberated women. Janette gains personal as well as economic independence as a successful though unmarried career woman.[66] Her female characters are centrally placed in each novel and short story, and the plots depict the lives of women and their realities as prominent, with males playing secondary roles.

Frances Harper's deep concern for the plight of black people, witnessed during her travels throughout the United States, provided continued impetus for her work. She worked at the Bethel African Methodist Association, although she was a member of the First Unitarian Church of Philadelphia. Her strong Christian beliefs were consistently projected in all her work. In *Iola Leroy,* the main character, Iola, states her most admired Old Testament characters are Moses and Nehemiah because they are willing to put aside their own advantages in order to benefit their race and country.

In her later years, Harper was an activist for a renewed morality within her race. She organized Sunday schools, lectured on temperance issues, and helped found the National Association of Colored Women.

*Biographical Sketch by* QIYAMAH RAHMAN

## ✦ Writings of Frances Ellen Watkins Harper

*A Brighter Coming Day: A Frances Ellen Watkins Harper Reader.* Edited by Frances Smith Foster. New York: Feminist Press, City University of New York, 1990.

*Complete Poems of Frances E.W. Harper.* Edited by Maryemma Graham. New York: Oxford University Press, 1988.

*Iola Leroy, or Shadows Uplifted.* Boston: Beacon Press, 1994.

*Minnie's Sacrifice; Sowing and Reaping; Trial and Triumph: Three Rediscovered Novels.* Boston: Beacon Press, 1990.

## ✦ Biographical Resources

Braxton, Joanne M., and Andree Nicola McLaughlin, ed. *Wild Women in the Whirlwind: African-American Culture and the Contemporary Literary Renaissance.* New Brunswick, NJ: Rutgers University Press, 1990.

Brown, Halli Q. *Homespun Heroines and Other Women of Distinction.* New York: Oxford University Press, 1988.

*Ebony Pictorial History of Black America: Vol. 1, African Past to the Civil War.* Nashville, TN: Johnson, 1971.

Flexner, Eleanor. *Century of Struggle: The Woman's Rights Movement in the United States.* Cambridge, MA: Belknap Press, 1959.

Gates, Henry L., Jr., ed. *Three Classic African-American Novels.* New York: Random House, 1990.

Morsbach, Mabel. *The Negro in American Life.* New York: Harcourt, Brace and World, 1961.

Sterling, Dorothy, ed. *We Are Your Sisters: Black Women in the Nineteenth Century.* New York: W. W. Norton, 1984.

Washington, Mary Helen. *Invented Lives: Narratives of Black Women 1860–1960.* New York: Doubleday, 1987.

ANNA CARPENTER GARLIN SPENCER

# Advantages and Dangers of Organization

## Speech to World's Congress of Representative Women, Chicago, 1893

ANNA CARPENTER GARLIN SPENCER (1851–1931) *was a Unitarian minister, a spokesperson for the Ethical Culture movement, and the first woman to become a professor at Meadville Theological School, where she taught sociology and ethics. A nationally known lecturer and author, she addressed many women's groups and wrote frequent articles for several national magazines on such topics as the difficulties of married women wage earners, the frustrations of talented women, the problems of unmarried and older women, as well as prostitution, divorce, and suffrage.*

*In her address to the World's Congress of Representative Women, Anna Garlin Spencer struck a critical note concerning the relationship between the individual and society. She commended the development of women's organizations as evidence of woman's growing awareness of her "right and duty to interpret her own nature and grow according to the law written in her own being." Yet she raised the question of whether it was time for women to join with men in organizations to continue the work of improving society together.*

See the Biographical Sketch on pages 113–116.

I know no better exercise for man or woman capable of real thought than the study of this problem which we may phrase briefly thus: What is the just and true relation of the individual to the social organism? . . .

I will speak more particularly of the voluntary organization of women. What is its history, what its growth and tendency, what its advantages, what its dangers?

In the first place, let us distinctly recognize one fact, for herein lies the kernel of the matter, namely, the history of the voluntary organization of women in every department of thought and action begins with the self-consciousness and self-assertion of woman's individuality. So long as women were universally considered by themselves, as well as by men, nothing but the attaches, wards, and subordinates of the masculine half of creation, women never dreamed of cooperation with each other upon any line either of resistance to tyranny, or self-improvement, or of philanthropic effort. In religion, which contained in the ancient world all germs of growth, so long as it was doubtful whether woman had a soul of her own to save, no woman dreamed of uniting, even in the most subdued and modest form, in helping to save other's souls.

✦ ✦ ✦

The call of the Christian religion to each soul of man or woman, of bond or free, to work out its own salvation, was womanhood's Declaration of Independence, for our inherited civilization at least. Therefore, we may say that sense of individuality in woman which is the only patent of her cooperative power in modern life, was born when she learned that her soul was her own. At first, and for long generations, she knew nothing of aught save purely religious applications of that truth. She had no refuge from oppression in family or state but the martyr's death or the devotee's renunciation. But gradually, very slowly, the soul that owns itself has come to believe that it has right to some freedom of growth and expression. At first the growth of women in these directions was strictly along the line of the newly awakened individualism. The great persons among the mass of women lifted themselves to freedom and power. And the practical result has been that the individualism, which once awoke the few women to revolt for their own sakes, has now touched with stimulating power the multitude of women to organization for personal development and world service.

And just as soon as the main body of womanhood began to sense the freedom and opportunity which the specially endowed had procured for them, the principle of voluntary organization began to permeate all departments of woman's thought and work. So today, to take a leap in history, what have we? We have the general benevolence of women organized for independent, or well-nigh independent, action, so far as man's control is concerned. We have the intellectual craving of women organized in clubs of women, in collegiate alumnae associations from women's colleges. We have the desire for full freedom among women organized in woman suffrage associations and leagues and in special combinations for securing juster laws. We have the protective power of women organized in friendly societies to succor young and exposed women seeking work in strange places; in associations which aim to guard those solitary children and women whom god has not set in families; in industrial and educational unions which aim to surround the less favored feminine life of great cities with the dignity, the power, the uplifting self-respect which the best and strongest womanhood displays; and we have the moral conservatism of women organized. We have the wonderful Women's Christian Temperance Union, with its temperance center and its ever-widening circumference of purification and moral growth in almost all directions of woman's power. And last, we have the new movement which, like the charity organizations, aims to make a synthesis of those analyzed specialties. We have the movement toward a national and international conference of women which shall leave each smallest club and most insignificant association free to do its work in its own way but link all together in an army where weakness shall gather strength, ignorance shall gather wisdom, bigotry shall gather tolerance, and selfish exclusion shall gather world sympathy, by the elbow touch of a common aim to grow freely toward goodness and truth and give generously what is received from the universe to the world's poorer souls and bodies. I look upon this latest movement among women . . . as the finest flower of woman's special organization.

✦ ✦ ✦

When woman found herself, when she began to learn that she was a person and not merely a passive conveyor of personality from generation to generation, she began to see also two other things; not clearly at first, but little by little has her sight come in these two great lines. The first thing woman began to see was that, being a person as man is a person, being herself an individual and not merely a purveyor to the individuality of men, she had both a right and a duty to interpret her own nature and grow according to the law written in her own being. This meant freedom to learn for herself, freedom to outline her own powers and uses. This meant again resistance to such crippling laws and conditions as forbade free expansion. This meant again, do you not see, the joining together of such isolated women as had come to self-knowledge and self-respecting love of freedom, in order that these crippling laws and conditions might be more successfully resisted, and these opportunities for growth and self-development might be increased, as single effort was powerless to increase them. You can have no *esprit de corps* among slaves who are slaves in spirit. It is only when they are united in a common impulse toward freedom that they can depend upon one another for support. So long as they look for personal advantage in slavery, they are treacherous and know no loyalty save to their masters. So of women, until they had come to a time when they looked not to manhood for reflected power and conferred privilege, but to their own womanhood for patent of their own nobility, they could not work together.

✦ ✦ ✦

The first joining of hands of gifted women for mutual improvement was along religious lines and generally within church bonds. But when the neighborhood meeting grew to the city club, the local church gathering to the county conference, and these both grew again to the state or national association, women's organization also enlarged. Nor will we forget the second insight which came to woman with awakening individuality. Not only did it become increasingly clear to her that, being a person as man is a person, she had a right and duty to interpret her own nature and grow according to the law of her own being, but it became also increasingly clear to her that, being a person like and yet different from man, she had a right and a duty of world service which she alone could fitly discover and fulfill. Hence, hand in hand from the first, the organizations of women for self-development and for others helping have climbed the road toward freedom and power. With some leaders, the master impulse has been justice; with others, the master impulse has been duty. With some, the watchword has been rights; with others, the watchword has been service. With some, the call has been "Make the most of yourself." With others, the cry has been . . . "Linger not by the hearth fire in selfish comfort . . . Give, oh woman, of your own store. . . ."

It is true that the aims and methods of women thinkers and workers have deepened and widened with the growth among them in power of organization. . . . The advantages of organization among women are patent beyond all cavil. The isolation of woman when she was a fragment, or a "relict," [widow] must have been, beyond all present understanding, terrible and dwarfing. The mind of a feminine Shakespeare, the moral devotion of a feminine Savonarola, the heart of a feminine St. John, must have been smothered in such loneliness and misunderstanding as marked the lot of all exceptional women in the older time. We feel but thrills of pity and indignation when we read of the saintly dignified Quaker maiden, Abby Kelley, being dragged out of a meeting feet foremost because she lifted up a woman's voice for the slave. We think with shame of the lonely Harriot K. Hunt[67] and Elizabeth Blackwell[68] seeking in vain so long, the one in Boston, the other in London, for a respectable house to shelter them, because they, being women, determined to be also doctors. But those who had learned to speak and to do, and who were no longer in spiritual bonds, these were those glorious and not unhappy martyrs who wear the crown while yet the pang is sharp!

✦ ✦ ✦

Today, not only the exceptional but the common woman can do, without greatly daring, almost her full pleasure. Today a cord of helpfulness, formed of a great-hearted and clean-handed womanhood encircles, almost without break, the least of women's needs and desires. . . . In face of such facts, it almost seems ungracious to speak of the dangers of organization connected with women and their work.

✦ ✦ ✦

The first danger is of woman's organization. The second danger is of women's organization.

The first, then, of woman's organization.

✦ ✦ ✦

Women's clubs . . . and associations for mutual improvement are increasing very fast and do not move in the least in the direction of seeking vital union with existing men's clubs for the same object or in the line of greater hospitality to harassed and busy men, who are not progressive enough to have clubs of their own! Now the expression of any misgiving lest this tendency create an extreme sex feeling on the part of women is met with one invariable answer, viz.: that only a few women have the courage and ability to command equal recognition for their word and work among men and that the great majority, even of progressive, cultivated, earnest women, need the separate drill by themselves for many years before they can take a balanced part in the associated effort of men and women. All very true. Yet it is not the whole truth. Women in clubs and associations, when they compare themselves with men, select for comparison only the best-drilled men, professional men, master specialists. But take men and women in America as a whole, and the women are better educated and more drilled in the understanding and discussion of everything but technical, political, and financial questions than are men. . . . The proof of this is in the fact that her old age is generally richer than his in all that makes life happy and helpful—in the fact that she, oftener than he, finds elevating work for intellectual and moral ends when the drudgery of personal cares is lifted. In how many families the men live only for business; the women do all the higher spiritual work! How many husbands let their wives represent the entire family interest in education, in philanthropy, and in religion and perhaps cannot help it, so voraciously do business demands devour the whole man.

But if this tendency of the average husband and father to be absorbed in financial specialties until taste for general culture becomes obsolete; and for the average wife and mother, with widening opportunities and freedom, to become more and more generally cultured; if this tendency increases I say, a gulf will be fixed between women and all but professional and learned men which will be as hurtful to both as the older forms of sex separation. I hate to see this tendency divide as often as it does today. I should fear its extreme as a social menace. Therefore, I believe that the average woman has learned the delight and value of women's work with women, for women; the exceptional women should make haste to assume their places as human beings, with men, in associated effort for highest ends. It is time that the most clear-eyed women should cease to spend themselves chiefly in women's things and should press wider open the doors now ajar which lead to channels of high commerce of mind and heart transcending sex limits.

And lest a new caste of sex, in which women shall show themselves the selfish superiors, shall be created, I think it high time that women whose husbands are too busy to make, or too ignorant to enjoy, literary and philanthropic clubs should patiently, sweetly, charmingly woo their other halves to the delights they themselves feed upon!

Next, the danger of women's organization.

Did we not agree that sense of individuality preceded power of associated effort in the growth of womanhood?

Then is it not equally clear that in the individual woman all healthful development must follow the self-same order? Is it not clear that until a woman has some understanding of her own nature, its worth, its use, its social power, its supreme obligations, she can gain nothing vital by associated life with others? Mind, I do not say the ignorant woman must grow wise before she belongs to a club seeking wisdom. On the contrary, in the associated scheme she may gain far more, and sooner learn to give as she gains, than in any separate study. But this I do say, the ignorant woman must know her ignorance and long to grow wise before she can gain anything but a foolish, make-believe knowledge from the brightest club.

Mind, I do not say the religious woman must first outgrow her selfishness before she can join with profit a society for philanthropic effort. But this I do say, the selfish woman must sense her selfishness and long to grow nobler before she can gain much but self-righteousness even from the communion of saints.

Mind, I do not say the woman, stung by some personal injustice to a new apprehension of sex wrongs, must first learn impartial and abstract justice before she can usefully work with other women for equal rights. But this I do say, the woman who does not sense her union to what has been and what shall be, and long to understand it, can never gain true breadth of view even from the sages of woman's leadership.

Today the organization of woman's effort in thought and action has reached a position of such dignity, such power, such charm, such helpfulness that small-natured, pretentious, vain, and selfish women see its advantages and seek to share them in some form or other. And the chief danger of it all lies just here, that on the one side the leaders will be "leveled down" as the membership is leveled up, and a half-growth only be secured; and on the other hand that pride of form, devotion to the letter of woman's association, shall kill its spirit. Look at the question as it relates to religion and charity, the first specialties of woman's associated effort. An item from a society journal which I clipped not long ago will illustrate my thought. In the column of "Correspondence" the question is asked, "How may I, a stranger in New York, with ample means, but with no first-class letters of introduction, best acquire social standing?" The response was this: "Hire an eligible sitting in a church frequented by people of high social influence, join two or three popular charitable associations managed by society women, subscribe liberally to their work, and get elected if possible on their boards of directors." Comment on this seems unnecessary, but I wonder if any of us fully realize how degraded from its high uses a church and a charitable organization must become if a majority of its membership considered it only in the light of a ladder to social distinction.

✦ ✦ ✦

Beware of the danger in charitable club-life if it makes you contented only with giving in the mass to the mass. No woman is ennobled by such effort. What is wanted for all true growth for the individual woman as for the sex is the awakening to self-knowledge, the stimulation to personal study and work. And herein lies one of the great gifts of the Woman Suffrage Association to woman's growth. By its very nature, so broadly inclusive and so sharply logical is it, the woman suffrage demand has been debarred an easy popularity. It has never had any social distinction to care for, any personal ambition to serve which might not be more easily and quickly attained from other sources. Always has its emphasis been strongest of all the organizations of women upon the full and free development and expression of the individual. And in it men and women have always worked side by side.

Beware of the danger in associated demand for rights and privileges if it leads you to forget personal duty toward your inferior, in nature or circumstances, in the abstract demand for equality of rights. No woman grows in individual justice by "resolutions," or even by most strenuous and wise labors which base themselves on that virtue, unless her homage and service to the universal principle constantly leads her to practice it downward as well as demand it upward.

I have known a woman visit "slums" with benevolence and beat down the wages of her children's governess. I have known a woman gloat over a fine essay at a club and neglect the simplest rules of intellectual development in her own life and family. I have known a woman to spend unceasing devotion in defending and establishing abstract principles of justice who never stopped to inquire if the money on which she lived was unstained by oppression or if the labor she exacted from her servants was righteously compensated.

But say you all, I am sure, just here, such women are not made worse by the associated effort; they have only not yet pulled themselves up to their own standard. Yes, true; but a subtle danger to character, unknown to the isolated woman, lies in these modern associations, the danger that we pretend to be what we are not, that we think ourselves leading in the march of progress when we are only tagging on because the crowd attracts us.

The "Time Spirit" speaketh these words, I repeat, Individual Development, Associated Effort.

## ✦ *Biographical Sketch*

**Born:** *April 17, 1851, Attleboro, Massachusetts*

**Died:** *February 12, 1931, New York City, age 79*

**Buried:** *Swan Point Cemetery, Providence, Rhode Island*

Anna Garlin was a lively, diminutive person with a vivacious manner and a warm smile. One friend described her as "no bigger than a half-pint of cider."[69] At seventeen, she was a girl of unusual charm with unmistakable dignity, poise, and authority. It was then that she began the teaching career that would dominate her life work and also joined the staff of the *Providence Journal* as a reporter.

Forebears on both sides of Anna Garlin's family were robust pioneers, sea captains, early settlers in New England, and fighters in the Revolutionary War. Anna attended public schools in Providence, Rhode Island, but was also educated privately by tutors. At the age of nine, she became convinced that she had a religious calling, and at twelve, she wrote to the Richmond Street Congregational Church in Providence requesting membership. She was accepted and thus took the first step in her religious journey.

Anna Garlin's own ethical and intellectual growth took her into more and more liberal theological positions. In her midtwenties, she joined and soon became an officer of the National Free Religious Association. On August 15, 1878, she married the Reverend William H. Spencer, a Unitarian minister, and then settled in Haverhill, Massachusetts. She worked with him in ministries at Haverhill and Florence, Massachusetts, and in Troy, New York.

An important development in the Spencers' lives occurred in 1889, when James Eddy died in Providence. He was a philosopher and writer who amassed a considerable fortune as an importer of art and artifacts from Europe and Asia. He left a bequest "for religious and moral purposes" to be administered at Bell Street Chapel, a family house of worship he had erected to assist in the administration of the bequest. Together, Anna Spencer and the trustees established the Religious Society of Bell Street Chapel.

Eventually, Anna Spencer was asked to serve as minister of the chapel and was ordained there in 1891, the first woman ordained to the ministry in Rhode Island. Five denominations were represented at her ordination: Universalist, Unitarian, Baptist, Congregational, and Swedenborgian. Although she was physically small, she had a powerful speaking voice that she cultivated, lecturing frequently on various subjects of the liberal agenda. This speaking experience served her well in the pulpit. She organized various programs of social concern for the Providence community and became active in both the women's suffrage and temperance movements. In 1902, pleading exhaustion, she tendered her resignation, which was accepted with great regret.

Although she continued to preach in liberal churches for the rest of her life, Spencer's major focus shifted to teaching and particularly to the teaching of social hygiene. From 1903 to 1913, she was associate director and staff lecturer of the New York School of Philanthropy, which became the New York School of Social Work. In addition, she lectured at the University of Wisconsin from 1908 to 1911 on social services and the social aspects of education. In the summers of those years, she directed the summer School of Ethics for the American Ethical Union. She served as director of the Institute of Municipal and Social Service in Milwaukee, Wisconsin, in 1910 and 1911.

For five years (1913–1918), Spencer was Hackley Professor of Sociology and Ethics at the Theological School, Meadville, Pennsylvania, now Meadville/Lombard Theological School of Chicago. In 1920, at the age of sixty-nine, she joined the staff of the Teacher's College at Columbia University and spent the last years of her life lecturing and teaching courses for social workers there. Her teaching methods were practical as well as theoretical. She pioneered what would now be called *field placement,* and her students told vivid stories of being taken to jails and poorhouses; to New York's facility for the care of children with mental retardation, aswarm with flies; to houses of prostitution; and to slum areas.

Spencer was the only woman in charge of a section at the Columbian Exposition in Chicago in 1893. She chaired the section on The Care of Dependent, Neglected and Wayward Children of the International Congress of Charities and Corrections. She spoke at the general sessions, preached at the concluding Sunday morning worship service, and was involved with organizing the exhibits. At the time of her death in 1931, she left unfinished the task of organizing new exhibits for the Chicago World's Fair of 1932.

A strong voice for all women's issues, Spencer was active in the National American Women Suffrage Association, the Women's Council of the USA, and the National Institute of Social Sciences. She opposed the Women's Suffrage Association's support of U.S. entry into World War I and challenged adoption of "The Star-Spangled Banner" as the national anthem because of its warlike setting. After the war, Spencer was a charter member of the Women's International League for Peace and Freedom and served at one time as its president. (Her vice president was Eleanor Roosevelt.)

Anna Garlin Spencer was a frequent contributor to various magazines and other publications. Her articles appeared in the *American Journal of Sociology,* the *International Journal of Ethics, Forum, Survey,* the *Ladies' Home Journal, Harpers,* and the *Christian Register,* among others. Her analysis of the structure and dynamics of the family was one of her most important contributions. She emphasized the family as the basic unit of the democratic society and saw it as the critical element in teaching democratic ideals to the coming generations. A family that was not democratic in its dynamics could not fulfill its responsibilities to the country. Equality between the sexes was crucial.

Anna Garlin Spencer was the principal speaker at a luncheon honoring her close friend Jane Addams, founder of Hull House in Chicago. Two weeks later, Spencer suffered a heart attack and died while attending a dinner at the League of Nations Association. Her funeral was held at the West Side Unitarian Church in New York, and a memorial service was conducted at the Ethical Culture Society.

In an interview conducted when she was seventy-six, Spencer declared that her dearest wish was to have at least ten more years to devote to the work she was doing. She was aware, however, that her dreams would not see completion during her lifetime.

*Biographical Sketch by* DOROTHY BOROUSH

## ✦ Writings of Anna Carpenter Garlin Spencer

*The Family and Its Members.* Philadelphia: J. B. Lippincott, 1923.

*The History of the Bell Street Chapel Movement.* Providence, RI: Privately published, 1903.

*James Eddy, Biographical Sketch, Memorial Service, Selected Thoughts.* Providence, RI: Privately published, 1889.

*Orders of Service for Public Worship.* Providence, RI: The Compiler, 1896.

*The Thoughts on Religion and Morality of James Eddy.* Providence, RI: Privately published, 1891.

*Women's Share in Social Culture.* New York: Mitchell Kennerley, 1912.

## ✦ Biographical Resources

Adler, Mrs. Felix. "Anna Garlin Spencer, A Memorial Tribute." *The Standard* 17 (March 1931).

"Anna Garlin Spencer, 1851–1931." *Journal of Social Hygiene* 17 (March 1931).

Helvie, Clara Cook. "Unitarian Women Ministers." Bound typescript presented to the Historical Society of the American Unitarian Association, 1928.

Kirkland, Winifred and Frances. *Girls Who Became Leaders.* New York: Ray Long & Richard R. Smith, 1932.

Peebles, Linda Olson. "Anna Garlin Spencer: 'The Three-Fold Path of Life.'" Occasional Paper #9. Malden, MA: Unitarian Universalist Women's Heritage Society, 1995.

Sikes, Tanya C. "Balancing the Vocational Divide: Anna Garlin Spencer on Women, Work, and Family." Occasional Paper #8. Malden, MA: Unitarian Universalist Women's Heritage Society, 1995.

# What Women Can Do in Uniting the Culture and Religious Forces of Society

## Speech to First American Congress of Liberal Religious Societies, Chicago, May 1894

CAROLINE JULIA BARTLETT [CRANE] (1858–1935) *was a Unitarian minister and civic reformer. She and other members of the so-called Iowa Sisterhood pioneered the concept of the full-service church, with facilities and programs to meet a wide variety of personal, educational, and social needs.*[70] *Later in life, she entered the new field of urban sanitation, instituting a program of meat inspection in Michigan slaughterhouses and designing legislation to ensure standards of sanitation.*

*In her 1894 address at the first American Congress of Liberal Religious Societies, she chided the planners of the congress for having invited her to speak about what women could do "in uniting the culture and religious forces of society" while omitting any talk of what men could do. Her challenge to the male leadership of the congress for women to be recognized as equal participants "in the light of consistency with the avowed principles of this congress" is reminiscent of confrontations that still occur today in both religious and secular organizations.*

See the Biographical Sketch on pages 127–130.

When a child, I sometimes amused myself, foolishly enough, by repeating some familiar word or name over and over, until it was emptied of all real significance and became filled with some curious and perhaps uncanny meaning which its mere sound suggested to my fancy. Some such foolishness, I think, the world is now practicing upon the word "woman," until the appellation that but just now conveyed an idea familiar enough to the world has become the symbol for a great unknown quantity—unknown, but not unknowable, if the world can help it. From her obscurity as a seldom commented upon member of the genus homo, she has been suddenly evoked by the spirit of the nineteenth century which discovered her and invited everywhere to define herself sharply against the background of the regnant sex; and it may be confessed that she has responded with no undue coyness or reluctance. However, many women had ventured to hope that the Great Divide has been reached and over-passed in that Columbian[71] year and that woman might now be permitted to descend from the dizzy and arid heights of self-consciousness into a somewhat less conspicuous but more fruitful area of existence. But no! this most notable assembly, the child of that Parliament of Religions, demands to know "what women can do in uniting the culture and moral forces of society."

Having been requested to open the discussion of this matter, I study the question carefully—both the question and its relation to the rest of the program. Does it imply a recognition of woman as an actual or possible coordinate factor with man in uniting the culture and religious forces of society? Does it imply even more? for indeed I cannot find anywhere upon the program a question concerning what man can do to these ends. Now far be it from women to take advantage of the modesty of these gentlemen (who so kindly arranged the program without demanding their assistance) by exploiting the actual or possible achievements of women. What can women do in uniting the culture and religious forces of society? The gentlemen were doubtless thinking of woman's efforts to unite the moral culture of women and men under a single, identical standard. Yet will we not boast until our efforts give surer signal of success. They are thinking that women as mothers contribute more influence than do men as fathers to ennoble, and thus to unify, the minds and hearts of each successive generation of children. We reply: Perhaps men may do quite as much when they awaken to their full share of parental responsibility. They are thinking of that great uniting social force, our true "National Guard," the women public school teachers of America. We say: There is no statutory bar against men assuming more of the honorable tasks (and less of the honorary emoluments) of public education. They are thinking of what women in the club life are doing to stimulate thought and action in currents that sweep away the barriers of sect and unite on the great sea of ideas and ideals that all well-intentioned people hold in common. We say: Gentlemen, do not be discouraged; you have a few clubs for serious purposes even now! They are thinking of that vast field of organized and personally administered philanthropies by which women are *leading* the world towards that practical solidarity of human interests which the world most needs. We reply: If men seldom yet give themselves, it is something that they freely give their money; and there are a few men in Chicago, even now, patterning after Miss Addams and the Hull House! Take heart! In all these lines you may do as much as anyone, when once you decide to share more equally with woman the burdens and privileges of nurturing, teaching, comforting, nursing, repairing, sympathizing that bring one near the heart of the world.

But it is just possible that such words of sisterly encouragement are ill bestowed. A second scanning of the program suggests that our brothers are not, after all, unduly depressed concerning their importance. In an *American* Congress of Free Religious Societies, occupying three full days, it would not seem, on second thought, that fifteen or twenty minutes given to woman to discuss, not the subject in hand, to be sure, but to discuss herself (with a few minutes allowed another woman to mention any omitted fact concerning the sex),—it would not seem that this is giving undue prominence to woman's part in this great and prophetic movement—not, at least, when we recall, with some difficulty, a mental shock, that this is an *American* Congress of *Liberal* Religions called into being by men and women, and that call eloquent of a belief "in the great law and life of love," and "a desire for a nearer and more helpful fellowship in the social, educational, industrial, moral and religious thought and work of the world."

The proposed nearer and more helpful fellowship in the thought and work of humanity is thus inaugurated by assigning one half of humanity to the pleasant and placating task of talking about itself for a few minutes before beginning the discussion of the subject for which the convention is called—after which that one half of humanity has no part nor recognition whatever in this council for uniting the culture and religious forces of the world. ("In the world, but not of the world," as it were.) I ask pardon. The ladies are permitted to give a reception in honor of the Congress and to provide suitable refreshment for those who have gallantly and quite cheerfully borne the toils of thought and debate for them.

Now to be serious (and I have meant to be serious, but the question presents difficulties, you see), I hope no one supposes we take it as an intended slight from the brethren. I am sure they never thought of such a thing—that it is a perfectly involuntary and artless revelation of a state of mind. While they were busy arranging this magnificent program for discussing social, educational, industrial, moral, and religious fellowship "of the most inclusive kind," they were quite unconscious of our existence. After it was all completed, somebody looked down and said: "Why, there are some women here! They can do something—let's see—society!—that's it! Let them prattle about it, and then we will give them some good advice as to just how they shall begin."

And, gentlemen, we shall be glad, when the question comes to general discussion, if you will kindly tell us how we are to begin to do the work it is needful we should do with you, if the proportions of this program truly indicate your expectations of us.

If I have indicated in a word some of the work which women are doing and shall do to unite the culture and moral forces of different classes and grades of society, surely enough has been said upon this subject when the great problem remains—namely, *the union of the culture and religious forces of the two coordinate halves of society, men and women.*

And be it understood, I make no special plea for woman. She may and does suffer from the divorce. But she is no longer asleep to her needs nor her defects. She is started on the road to progress at last, and she knows her goal. She, in touch with human service in the home, the school, the slum, the hospital, the world at large, leads a more interior life than you; she can evolve her soul's freedom and destiny alone, if she must. It will be imperfect, not roundly human, for the lack of you; but it will not be so imperfect as your expression of religion made without her help. Because: she is the mother, not merely physical but spiritual, of humanity,—she mothers humanity, and what she sees in this child of hers, she keeps and ponders in her heart.

I would not boast. Indeed, I must admit whether I would or not, that men have thus far led the world in thought and action. Reasons can justly be assigned for this which do not imply woman's necessary and continued inferiority in influence here. But even were it true (which I will neither admit nor stop to argue) that men always will lead in thought and action, how does this touch our problem? In all the past of theology, men have been at the front, have led the church *militant,* have conducted the great controversies, made the great schisms, formulated the creeds, hunted and impaled the heretics, set the standards, and done the *preaching* of the world. Meanwhile, woman, thus relieved, has had some time to do the practicing. And let me ask, in passing, have you ever observed that where anyone names the qualities of the ideal church, . . . they are precisely the qualities attributed to the ideal woman? Does not this suggest a hitherto unutilized means of bringing both nearer the ideal?

But now, what have the church and the world profited by this excessive division of function to which I have alluded? I will not speak of the moral effects, further than to affirm that this alienation of men and women along the higher lines of thought and life has been the chief producer of that pernicious double standard which has robbed manhood of one set of virtues and womanhood of another. Pass this by, but here we have, as the product of man's intellect, all the cruel and inhuman and separatist creeds, to combat and to disintegrate which has been a great part of the life work of all the liberal religious societies here assembled; to surmount which is the gigantic task proposed by this Congress. "Salt," said the little boy, "is what makes potatoes taste bad when you don't put any on." Womanhood, I say, is what makes religion hard and inhuman when she hasn't any voice in it.

Calvinism is faultlessly logical. "Faultlessly logical"—what more would you? O, for a mighty rising of womanhood in that hour, to declare the forgotten wisdom of the ancients, that the true seat of the intellect is in the heart!

Do not misunderstand me. I repudiate that popular antithesis of man as a reasoning and woman as an emotional being. Both reason and emotion are *human* qualities, and the man or woman who is radically deficient in either is not a well-rounded human being. If there be a sex difference, I say it is a difference of proportion and emphasis; and if it be (as I believe it is) characteristic of women that they are inclined to worship a throbbing ideal rather than a lifeless formula, by that token should they be respected and valued in a religious conference whose initial and central utterance is belief "in the great law and life of *love*."

✦ ✦ ✦

But why must we choose between two phases of human development that are by nature not mutually exclusive but mutually complementary? *This*, this is the solemn truth: that we never yet once have had, and that we never will have, a *natural* religion, a religion of *humanity*, till the two co-ordinate elements of humanity mingle to create it. Men and women may separately struggle free from many of the errors of the past, but neither sex can ever rise above its innate incapacity to express in terms of itself the whole of the humanity of which it is but half.

✦ ✦ ✦

[There is the story of the] little girl who, being asked to define the word "epistle," said she wasn't sure, but she thought it was the feminine of "apostle." . . . I want to be at least an epistle among these apostles of free religion—an epistle begging favor to be read in the light of consistency with the avowed principles of this congress.

And this is the inevitable postscript appended to this "so long epistle which I have written with mine own hand." If it be time for the various branches of liberalism to quit outlining themselves severally against each other and against the background of Orthodoxy and to set at some united constructive work for the world, is it not time for men and women as human beings to do the same? What can women do thus to unite the culture and religious forces of society? They can refuse longer to talk of themselves and their achievements and possibilities (as I had determined to refuse in this case until I thought of a few things I would really like to say). They can resolutely labor to make mere sex-distinctions as obsolete to the spirit and work of a congress like this, as are the terms Unitarian, Universalist, Jew—all swallowed up and forgotten in the task set, the ideal striven for by the common humanity in us all when touched by the Divine brooding in all and over all.

Shall man execute this long delayed justice? or shall it be that woman must, at least, sadly assert her own discredited divine prerogative, take up that crown of *human*-hood, and crown herself?

But men and women are natural allies. This artificial separation in the higher provinces of life is based on false principles which it is the glory of this congress to transcend. And thus, out of the logic and out of the spirit of this congress, there will come, as I hope and also believe, that better day—infinitely better for us all—when there shall be no Jew nor Gentile, Greek nor barbarian, male nor female but all shall be *one* in the renaissance of that Christ-spirit which even now dawns upon an expectant world.

✦ ✦ ✦

# The Individual Factor in Social Regeneration

## Speech to Biennial Meeting, General Federation of Women's Clubs, Louisville, Kentucky, May 1896

*Speaking to the General Federation of Women's Clubs in Louisville, Kentucky in 1896,* CAROLINE JULIA BARTLETT [CRANE] (1858–1935) *took a thoughtful look at the long process of social change and made recommendations women might well take to heart today to pace them-*

*selves and avoid becoming frustrated in their own work for social justice. She reminded her audience that "we need to be born again into the inheritance of our own powers and possibilities, before we can greatly assist in the regeneration of society." Her address was reprinted in the* New Unity, *one of the official publications of the American Congress of Liberal Religious Societies.*

See the Biographical Sketch on pages 127–130.

Walking is defined as a process of falling and recovering one's self. All progress involves this problem of moving equilibrium.

The most extraordinary phenomenon of today is woman's progress along lines of associated activity. The most hopeful feature of this is the awakened conscience of womanhood toward those conditions which indicate the need of social regeneration and her prompt addressing herself to its apparent task.

If, in choosing to speak today upon the individual factor in social regeneration, I seem to slight or undervalue the power of associated efforts to that end, it is only in the seeming. It is because I am convinced that progressive women need to be reminded of this difficulty ever besetting progress, namely—the difficulty of moving equilibrium. That we are moving needs no demonstration. That we are duly maintaining equilibrium is indispensable to continued progress. Lest I seem to be climbing upon the judgment seat, let me say that I believe myself to have erred in the respect named as much as most awakened and eager women. It is an experience to be regretted but not one necessarily disqualifying the sufferer for giving testimony.

Let us turn for a moment to the conditions out of which the era of women's associated activity began. We know well the former isolation of women upon the intellectual and imaginative side of their nature; the unquiet yearning to realize self-expression and to help the human needs of others to their fulfillment; the spasmodic sense of power which sunk back into self-distrust because of the loneliness—the not knowing of the hundreds of thousands of other hearts that burned with the same heaven-given fire. And then, women found one another, and so discovered each herself—and dared! And it was good—the best! We could say it was worth waiting for, did not there rise before us the ghosts of starved lives that perished ere we reached the Promised Land.

But it is good for us. We would have it better, would we not? for those who shall come after. Then let us take heed as we run that we do not fall by a too headlong hand-to-hand forced march which leaves to the individual woman no time to pick and choose her way—to sit down by the roadside, if she will, and rest.

That is, I believe the peril which threatens us today—an excessive reaction from the old. Natural? Yes, as all unnatural things are in the last analysis, natural; but to be resisted by all the wisdom and patience and self-control of which we can possess ourselves.

There is danger that an outlet may become a drain; that the associated life of women shall make inroads upon the associated life of man and woman and child; that a woman may turn mind and body out of house and home and into committee rooms and clubs and congresses; that manifold charities may leave small room for charity; entertainment for hospitality; symposiums for study; church work for religion: that the only class under heaven totally bereft of leisure shall be the leisure class.

✦ ✦ ✦

I am not unmindful for one moment of the vastness and the importance of the results achieved by women's associated efforts. As I sat here yesterday and listened to the reported work of such organizations as the Chicago Women's Club and a score of others that are doing God's work in the world, a spasm of remorse seized me that I contemplated the utterance to-day of any word which might seem to the undiscerning an abatement of the praise and honor justly due them. But then, I recalled one member of my acquaintance who, when urgently pressed to take the chairmanship of an important committee for some work of civic reform, said, with a sigh of genuine resignation: "Well, yes; I'm chairman of so many committees now that one, more or less, does not matter." And remembering this, I took courage for my jeremiad.

. . . [If] every woman who feels the life being literally sapped out of her by the incessant and cruel demands made by the exigencies of organized philanthropy, would *stop* and *drop* all that she must in order to live her life serenely and completely, the Kingdom of Heaven would draw nearer to us by a great bound. If need be, drop it all—but in the name of everything that is good, let us recall the fact that social regeneration isn't a medicine entirely for the "other person"; that there is a time-honored maxim which runs: "Physician, heal thyself," and that if we have not the Kingdom of Heaven within us, we need to be born again into the inheritance of our own proper powers and possibilities before we can greatly assist in the regeneration of society.

Why is it so hard for us to do as little as we ought? Because we are caught in the flood-tide of remorseless activity which is the complement of long-enforced stagnation. Because the inertia of motion is as much a law as the inertia of rest, and we are started. Because many of us, I fear, are unable to join in that hymn of Jean Ingelow's,—

> "I am glad to think
> I am not bound to make the world go right,"

having well-defined convictions to the contrary!

And that isn't wholly bad. Nay, infinitely better than the state of mind which sings it, not in humility, but in lazy complacency. But do we not need to curb our superabounding inclination to put an active hand to "*what*soever things are pure and lovely and of good report?" We are bidden to "think on these things," but that doesn't necessarily involve the formation of a stock company in behalf of each and every-one. And, if we do this, we will not "think on them" so much nor so finely. Charles Darwin bemoaned the fact that his intense devotion to natural science robbed him utterly of that sense of the grand and beautiful in nature which was a prominent characteristic of his youth. There is peril of losing the charity that suffereth long and is kind, that vaunteth not itself and is not puffed up, in the new kind of charity that begins not at home but in the committee room and ends on the rostrum and in the newspapers.

Would it not be good, ladies, for each of us to ask ourselves a few searching questions? "Am I attending to my own regeneration? Am I being as good a woman as I can in my interior life? Am I living out my own days as one should who claims to have a passion for righteousness, and to be working to help establish righteousness, and to be working to help establish righteousness in the earth? If I am hurried, feverish, cross, is it not time that I declare myself an officious person, and drop some of this self-assumed burden, till I can go on my way rejoicing?"

✦ ✦ ✦

The conditions which we today deplore owe their existence chiefly to the unnatural separation of the classes. Edward Everett Hale has well said that college settlements are a great step toward the solution of social difficulties but that family settlements would be a far greater. The time will surely come when whole families, repenting themselves that they have withdrawn into the select regions and away from the toiling and suffering masses, will, like prodigals of life's substance, return to their brothers who are living like swine upon husks, crying, "I have sinned before heaven and against thee!"

But what can the woman do who cannot transport her family? She can partly annihilate space by the spirit of sincere personal love and care; and I solemnly believe that if every woman who yearns to help would patiently make friends with some one family, near or far, bereft of work or comfort or encouragement, and patiently strive to lead her household with her, it would be supremely worth while—yea, if in order to do it, the club rosters which had known her name should know it no more forever!

And then, to come nearer home.

✦ ✦ ✦

[Why not] ask ourselves about some of the plain, good folks of our acquaintance, to whom an evening in our home and at our board would be a taste of heaven? Something, too, about the young men and young women who have no place on earth to go and yet must and will go some place. Aren't we content to help decent people? Do we rather yearn to snatch the half-charred brand from the burning? Of course, we want to help decent people! Then, let us ask ourselves some questions that will show us better how; and the brand-snatching business won't be so pressing.

And our house-helpers and those who make our clothes. Mrs. Makely was enthusiastic over little Miss Camp because she sewed "so cheap!" Do we ever thoughtlessly purchase garments at prices that are starvation or heart-break or ruin to some poor woman who makes them? . . .

"If one is a faithful, careful, high-minded woman, wife, mother, relative, friend, hostess, mistress, she won't have time for associated work?" Then let it go, if this be true. But it isn't true. She won't have time for the Civic Federation Monday and the Free Kindergarten Tuesday and the Summer Schools Wednesday and the New Hospital Thursday and the Country Week Friday and the Sewing School Saturday. But then she won't have to go to bed Sunday to escape hysteria! She will have time for some one, at least, of these things, and she and her home will be the better for her participation therein. And she will have some time for such invaluable intellectual help as the club gives, too. And what she does in the way of associated effort will be genuine, wholesome—

reflecting and enlarging her personality. And she will bring to these councils sweet reasonableness and a weight of well-rounded character.

I know there are women who live thus—who make their clubs and other associations a means to an end—not the end itself. It is only needful that we all do this, and then the real beneficence of association will demonstrate itself anew. Let us henceforth refuse to be swept along by the power of numbers, after the wholesome initial impulse has died away. Let us do this *because* we believe in association and would not witness its suicide.

The call today to women is *to live their own lives more abundantly.* We've only one life to live—here—and we are each of us one of those in whom God wants to see his image perfected. "In union there is strength"? Yes, but it is not the union of the bundle of dry sticks we want but the union of the separate live twigs upon the common tree. The appeal in behalf of woman is, now, not so much to man as to the woman herself,—to give herself

> . . . "space to burgeon out of all
> Within her . . . make herself her own,
> To give or keep, to live and learn and be
> All that not harms distinctive womanhood."

## ✦ *Biographical Sketch*

**Born:** *August 17, 1858, Hudson, Wisconsin*

**Died:** *March 24, 1935, Kalamazoo, Michigan, age 76*

**Buried:** *Ashes in Mountain Home Cemetery, Kalamazoo, Michigan*

Caroline Bartlett Crane was a popular Unitarian minister who successfully combined community welfare activities with her church work. Known as Carrie in her youth, she was the only daughter of Dr. Lorenzo Dow Bartlett, a steamboat captain turned physician and inventor, and Julia A. Brown.

Early on, Bartlett questioned the concepts of eternal damnation and the Christian focus on the crucifixion. After hearing the Iowa Unitarian Reverend Oscar Clute allay her fears about her unorthodox ideas in one of his speeches, she decided to become a Unitarian minister. Her father objected to his daughter's entering this all-male profession, but she persisted by developing skills she knew would be of use someday in the pulpit. She received support for her dream of becoming a minister from two older friends, Mary Safford and Eleanor Gordon, who were to become key members of the Iowa Sisterhood.[72]

The Bartlett family moved to Illinois, and it was there, at Carthage College, that Caroline Bartlett earned her B.A. and M.A. degrees. She then began to find other paths to reach her goal of ministry, turning to teaching and then to journalism. She first published in the *Minneapolis Tribune* in 1883; three years later, she went on to land the city editor's job at the Oshkosh, Wisconsin, *City Times.* As a journalist, she interviewed a number of suffragists whom she met at the 1885 National Woman Suffrage Association in Minneapolis. She became close to Susan B. Anthony, Anna Howard Shaw, and Lucy Stone.[73] She credited her newspaper experience with teaching her how to write effective prose and involving her in the real world, as opposed to the idealized world of the pulpit.

In 1887, having gained independence and confidence from her journalist career and support from her new feminist friends, Bartlett now felt she was ready to formally prepare for Unitarian ordination. With direction from the Oscar Clute, she embarked on a course of self-study, writing out her answers to key theological questions to send to Clute and to Jenkin Lloyd Jones for their critiques. In the fall of 1887, Bartlett was welcomed as a ministerial colleague by Mary Safford and others at a meeting of the Iowa Unitarian Association in Des Moines. Bartlett's first parish was in Sioux Falls, South Dakota, where she worked with and then succeeded Eliza Tupper Wilkes, the energetic minister who had founded the congregation there. Bartlett helped expand the church's membership and build a new building. She also actively encouraged use of the church for community activities.

In 1889, Bartlett accepted a call to the First Unitarian Church in Kalamazoo, Michigan, where she was ordained that fall. Once again, she increased membership, encouraged a focus on social involvement, and built a new building, this time in the center of the city. The new facility was dedicated in 1894 and renamed the People's Church, affirming its mission to reach out to the wider community. It was designed to be a center of community activities, with a great beehive fireplace in the corner of the sanctuary, reflecting the vision of the church as a home.

While always a successful preacher, Bartlett was most appreciated for her public activities. She led efforts to establish the first public kindergarten in the newly built People's Church and to initiate domestic science and other kinds of education for women. She reached out especially to African Americans in her neighborhood.

Bartlett married one of her parishoners, Dr. Augustus Warren Crane, on New Year's Eve, 1896. Crane was ten years younger than Bartlett and a devoted follower. They would eventually adopt two children, but the new Mrs. Crane was not to stay in one career or situation for long. She went on to a Grand Rapids church in 1901 and then became interested in urban sanitation and the study of the new field of sociology in Chicago. When she finally returned to Kalamazoo in 1903, it was as a meat inspector of Michigan slaughterhouses. She worked successfully for more civic control of city sanitation inspections, and by 1916, she had become famous for her knowledge and activism around this issue. In 1924, she designed a prize-winning home that would allow a mother to care for her children in a central, step-saving location. The house, called Everyman's House, was one of many municipal improvements that earned her the nickname of "America's Housekeeper."[74]

Throughout her life, Caroline Bartlett Crane enjoyed publicizing her works and views. She was always a sought-after speaker and made sure that the press covered her activities. She was a believer in practical religion, which, when combined with science, would improve the conditions of American cities. She believed that "sociology must be essentially Christian" if it were to be of use.[75]

*Biographical Sketch by* SUSAN SWAN

## ✦ Writings of Caroline Bartlett Crane

*Business Versus the Home.* New York: National American Woman Suffrage Association, 1915.

"The Church and Poverty." *Old & New* 6 (October 1897).

"Every Day Religion: or Studies in Good Citizenship." *Old & New* 6 (September 1897).

*Everyman's House.* Garden City, NY: Doubleday, Page, 1925.

"The Individual Factor in Social Regeneration." *The New Unity* 34, new series 3 (6 August 1896): 382–384.

"Is God Responsible?" Young Men's Union, People's Church, Kalamazoo, MI, 1898.

"Life's Challenge." People's Church, Kalamazoo, MI, 1898.

*Report on a Campaign to Awaken Public Interest in the Sanitary and Sociologic Problems in the State of Minnesota.* St. Paul: Volkszweitung, 1911.

"A Temperance Message from the Church to Young Men." Unitarian Temperance Society, Boston, 1894.

"What of a Day?" Boston: James West, September 1895.

"What Women Can Do in Uniting the Culture and Religious Forces of Society." Address given at First American Congress of Liberal Religious Societies, Chicago, May 1894. In *Proceedings of the First American Congress of Liberal Religious Societies, Chicago,* May 22–25, 1894, 18–21.

## ✦ Biographical Resources

Hitchings, Catherine, ed. *Universalist and Unitarian Women Ministers.* 2nd ed. Boston: Unitarian Universalist Historical Society, 1985.

Loehr, Davidson. "Introductory Remarks to 'Life's Challenge,' 1898 Sermon by Carolyn Bartlett Crane." Kalamazoo, MI: People's Church, 1989.

Richard, O'Ryan. *A Just Verdict: The Life of Caroline Bartlett Crane.* Kalamazoo, MI: New Issues, 1994.

Rynbrandt, Linda J. *Caroline Bartlett Crane and Progressive Reform: Social Housekeeping as Sociology.* New York: Garland, 1999.

Tucker, Cynthia Grant. *Prophetic Sisterhood.* Boston: Beacon Press, 1990.

# Our Mission to Save by Culture

## Article in *Old & New,* September 1900

ELEANOR ELIZABETH GORDON (1852–1942) *was one of the central members of a group of Unitarian ministers in the Midwest known as the* Iowa Sisterhood.[76] *A Unitarian minister for thirty-three years, she worked throughout her life for women's rights on both state and national levels. She and her close friend and sister minister, Mary Safford, served for many years as editors of* Old & New, *a missionary magazine published by the Iowa Unitarian Association.*

*The first selection included here is an essay in which she articulated her view of the role of the liberal church in the title: "Our Mission to Save by Culture." In her view, the responsibility of religion extended beyond traditional boundaries and into all aspects of community life. She wrote: "Our work is mapped out for us. Our ideal is clear before us—to make truth, goodness and beauty the supreme things in the world." However, she realized that this could only be done by a slow process of educating children, inspiring young men and women, and making religion applicable to all aspects of life, not something that is practiced in isolation from the practical realities of daily life.*

See the Biographical Sketch on pages 139–142.

Without criticizing the work of other organizations, with no suggestions as to what may be or as to what may not be their work, it seems to me our duty is plain. Our work is mapped out for us. Our ideal is clear before us—to make truth, goodness and beauty the supreme things in the world by the slow process of education, by the slow process of line upon line, precept upon precept, by training the children, by inspiring young men and women, by making religion the one *real* thing in the world, by making the religious life the all-inclusive life. Shall I make this still more concrete? Shall I speak still more plainly? I recently visited a village for Sunday services. As I went from the station I was compelled to make my way through cigarette smoking, tobacco spitting, and a crowd of uncouth-looking men and boys on the platform. There was evidence of thrift in the village on every hand, but everything was hopelessly, drearily dull and homely.

I was in the place two days and the following is the substance of many conversations held with different residents:

"Why do you not have a Village Improvement Society and cut these weeds and sprinkle the streets and plant trees and improve the yards and do many things to make the place more attractive?" "There is no one to be interested or take the lead." "How many ministers in the place?" "Four." "Why cannot they do it?" "Oh, they wouldn't; that isn't religious work." "Have you a humane society?" "No." "Do you not need one?" "Yes—very much." "Why do not the churches unite for this work?" "Oh, they wouldn't think that religious work." "Have you a literary club, or debating club, or a reading room, or anything to make life beautiful or interesting to the boys and girls?"—and I thought with a shudder of the boys I had seen on the station platform. "*No, there is no one to take the lead* in such things. Our teachers are too young." "What do your ministers do?" "They preach sermons and lead the prayer meetings." "What do they preach about ?" "Doctrines. The Methodist is a mighty good hand to show that the Baptists and Presbyterians are wrong and the others do about the same." "What do you do at prayer meetings?" "Why, pray, of course."

Four church buildings, each one homelier than the others, four ministers, four Sunday schools, four prayer meetings, and the emphasis in one and all on certain little narrow interpretations of certain texts of the Bible! Nothing from one week's end to another that made for life in the highest, broadest sense of the word. Everything that makes life beautiful, rich, pure, humane, left out. Art and literature a dead letter. Poetry an unknown tongue. Kindness and mercy only dimly hinted. Grace and refinement of speech or bearing utterly neglected.

This village, added to or subtracted from, is your problem and mine. Not the slums of the city, not the desperately wicked or abandoned,—although they may be found in places such as these,—are so much for your consideration.

These people had plenty to eat, lived in comfortable homes, the tyranny of trusts or the evil of unjust discrimination did not much affect their lives; but think you not that they hungered and thirsted not for the bread and water of life? The Liberal minister that will go into such a place as this and unite with the men and women who are waiting for such a leader to make life there beautiful, good and true; to make life pure, refined, humane; to reveal the inspiration of art, the marvel of music, the glory of literature; to lift men and women into the atmosphere of a rational religion and noble ethics—such a minister is doing the noblest work that can be given to a child of God to do.

It may have been a religious act for Rachel Winslow to renounce forever the artist's life and dedicate her voice to the cause of the poor, but that religious impulse is dwarfing and in so far not to be trusted that would confine the voice of the trained singer to the singing of gospel hymns at revival meetings. The great masters of music and poetry have their message too for the sorrowful of earth. To sing "Follow Me" or some other simple religious music, and by the singing to move men and women to resolve to be better and do better, is religious work; but the artist who sings the compositions of the great masters to an audience of cultivated people may be doing a far more beautiful thing. In the one audience, as in the other, there may be aching hearts needing comfort, stolid souls that need to be awakened, deeper feelings that need to be stirred. It depends upon the motive with which one sings whether it is religious work or not. The voice may sing "Oh to be nothing, nothing" at a revival meeting and the heart may be filled with arrogance and self-conceit.

To win for ourselves and to win for others, in so far as one soul can win for another, the life that is true, good and beautiful—this is our ideal. And whence our inspiration? All the truth that the past has won, in bibles, books of science, history, we will search for the word of God, test what we find, claiming to be this word by your own experience and hold fast to that which seemeth true. All the goodness of the past, the devotion of the humble as well as the exalted, the earnestness of the ignorant as well as that of the learned, all that made for noble living, for brave daring, is for our heritage. All that is fair of form or face,—the music of childhood and of birds and of artists, the color of sunset sky and painted canvas, the revelation of poem and tale,—from one and all we shall draw our inspiration until our hearts give glad recognition that "all truth when fully realized is beautiful, that all beauty when fully realized is good, and all goodness, when fully recognized, is both truthful and beautiful."

Is this a hard saying? Would some of us choose the easier way? Do we still question our strength and wisdom? One thing, and one only, we need to remember and we are strong again—from whence our strength? A great artist once stood before the masterpiece of the great genius of his age and whom he could never hope to equal or even rival. And yet the beautiful creation before him only elevated his feeling, for he saw realized there those conceptions which had floated before him dim and unsubstantial.

In every line and touch he felt a spirit immeasurably superior to his own and yet kindred. As he looked upon the great picture before him he exclaimed with dignified humility, "And I too am a painter!"

Is not this our spirit as we stand before the great responsibilities of our work? We pass in review the history of humanity. We trace step by step the steady gain of the true, the good, and the beautiful. Our hearts thrill in response to the brave deeds of the past, throb with exultation as we learn more of the devotion of patriot, of the heroism of reformer and martyr, more of the earnestness of saint, prophet, and poet.

As we read of what they did we know that we cannot win what they succeeded in winning; and yet, in the presence of their success and proud achievement, in dignified humility we recognize our kinship and each can say, "I too am a human soul. I too am a child of God. I too am an heir of all that has been won. I stand in the long line of succession and claim as my own all that I am worthy to have to hold."

✦ ✦ ✦

# The Worth of Sympathy

## Sermon in *Old & New,* June 1907

*In her sermon "The Worth of Sympathy," published in 1907 in* Old & New, ELEANOR ELIZABETH GORDON (1852–1942) *demonstrated the importance of sympathy as a guiding principle in all situations. She defined* sympathy *as the ability "to put ourselves in another's place, in so far as we understand his [sic] temptations, his needs, his habit of mind." By describing a typical situation in which a group of people who set out to help another group did so with a condescending attitude, she demonstrated how efforts at reform fail unless people have the "spirit of love" in their hearts. She stressed the necessity of applying the principles of reform in daily life, in all our encounters with each person we meet.*

See the Biographical Sketch on pages 139–142.

"Rejoice with them that rejoice and weep with them that weep."
—Romans, 12:15

The word sympathy taken literally means to "suffer with." Common usage, to a certain extent, justifies this meaning of the word. When we speak of offering our sympathy to anyone we usually mean that some misfortune has happened to him and we are trying to be kind in his hour of need.

But I prefer to give a broader meaning to the word, to use it in its philosophic sense. I choose Professor Bain's definition rather than the one warranted by the derivation of the work.

"Sympathy," says professor Bain, "is to enter into the feelings of another and to act them out as if they were our own."

"To enter into the feelings of another." Just what does that mean?

As I understand it these words mean this: If I have suffered defeat in the battle of life; if I am lonely or sad, you are to forget for the time being your own good fortune and to feel with me, striving to show me that my sorrow is your sorrow and my grief your grief. But it also means that if you are happy over some good fortune that the year has brought to you, I am to forget that I have failed where you have succeeded and enter into your joy so heartily that no suggestion will come to you that your joy is not my own. The first is not so difficult. It is easy for kind-hearted people to forget for the moment their own pleasure while they enter into the sorrow of another, but it is hard, very hard, to forget our own pain and sense of loss while we enter freely and fully into the triumphs and joys of another. But these words mean more than this. They mean that we are to understand the feelings of others. They mean that in judging the act or word of anyone we are to try to see from his standpoint. I do not mean that we are to change our opinions or try to alter our convictions—far from that—we need not, often cannot, have any sympathy with certain conclusions, but we may have sympathy—that is, we may understand—the feeling that prompts the conclusion. To illustrate what I mean:

You are a radical in thought. Inheritance, training, inclination, all lead that way. If you are narrow in your outlook upon life, if you are inclined to be dogmatic, you have nothing but words of scorn for your conservative neighbor. But if on the other hand you are broad in your sympathies, if you really seek to enter into the feelings of others, you remember that your neighbor has had other training, other inheritance than yours; you remember that his mental constitution is different from yours, and, although you are a radical still, you have the same consideration for his thought that you expect him to have for yours.

Although a radical still, you do not forget that views different from yours are not necessarily inconsistent with good morals and good manners.

A certain amount of knowledge and experience is necessary to broad sympathies. Ignorance is always cramped and narrow. I do not mean knowledge that comes from books alone, but the knowledge that comes from wide reading, much observation and manifold experience. It is usually supposed that travel widens one's outlook and deepens one's sympathy. In a measure this is true, but one may travel around the world and see only what he wants to see. He may travel with all his prejudices close at hand and measure everything by his own little rule of good and bad.

If we have no imagination, if we are unable to put ourselves in the place of the one we are judging, then it matters little whether we go abroad or live in our own little house. Our world is bounded by our own petty desires and ambitions.

✦ ✦ ✦

Knowledge, experience, imagination, yes, we need all of these if we are to have generous sympathies, but more than all we need to care more for people. Love sharpens the understanding and quickens the perceptions. We love to talk of human fellowship in our Unitarian churches, but I wonder sometimes if we have found its real essence, that certain something that makes us feel that we are of one family and leads us to say with the Latin poet that nothing that is human is uninteresting to us.

When we really care for people we do not have to make ourselves interested in them. When we really care their joy is ours, their longings, triumphs, are ours.

Admitting the beauty of this human sympathy of what practical use is it?

This sympathy can be cultivated, but it cannot be pretended. There must be the real interest in human welfare, the real love of all things human, or it will not ring true.

✦ ✦ ✦

Human helpfulness depends upon sympathy. Just in so far as we are able to put ourselves in another's place, in so far as we understand his temptations, his needs, his habit of mind, in so far as we know him, just in so far are able to be of service to him. How quickly we turn away from sympathy that is mingled with criticism. How quickly the most stupid of us will notice the judging spirit. How instinctively we draw back and put up the bars of reserve when we feel that back of the sympathetic word is the feeling that would say: "I told you so." "You should have known better." "I am sorry for you, but you could have helped it." How often we fail in what we want to do because we cannot divorce from our word and manner the judging spirit. It may be in the discussion of some intellectual topic where we had hoped to change the thought of a friend, or it may be in social life where we had hoped to bring a better atmosphere, whatever it may be that we hope to do, we fail because we come with the critical rather than the sympathetic spirit.

Have you not often noticed this lack of sympathy on the part of those who have made their way in the world—self-made men and women? One would think that their own hard struggle would make them gentle and sympathetic with those who are contending against hard conditions, but often this is not the case. Such people excuse themselves by saying: "We had no help. No one cared about us," forgetting that all may not have their physical strength, their power of endurance, or strong will.

Much earnest work in philanthropy fails for the same reason. Not long ago in a city not a thousand miles from Des Moines, ten young women organized themselves into a band of King's Daughters. They chose for their work the helping of the cash girls in a certain large department store of their city. They appointed an evening for the first meeting, but no cash girls were there; again and again they attempted to have a meeting, but the little girls would not come. I was interested to know why they had failed and asked some of them about it. It took but a moment's conversation to reveal the secret. These young women were earnest and perfectly honest in their desire to be of service, but they were working entirely from a sense of duty; there was no joy, no delight, in the work. They had no real interest in the little girls who were contending against such odds in the battle of life. They had a sort of grim, half-impatient desire to do something for the helping of the world about them—more because they were ashamed not to do something than because they were really interested. They condescended, reached down, patronized, and each sturdy little cash girl refused to be helped in that way. Not long after I was standing in the same store and overheard two little girls talking.

"Are you going tonight?" said one. "Going where?" said the other. "Going to the club for shop girls?" "No," said the first, and her voice showed great scorn. "No, I ain't going to be done good to."

Think what might have been done for both the young women and the little girls—for the young women needed the little cash girls as much as the little cash girls needed them. Think of what might have been done for both and was not done because the spirit of love was lacking.

Sociologists tell us that society is an organism, that socially speaking there is no such thing as an individual, that we are so related that together we must rise or fall. This is the science of the question. So far all students of economies and sociology are agreed, but what this principle means in religion and ethics is not readily believed, or rather not so readily worked out. Why? Because we have not yet learned how to rejoice with those that rejoice and weep with those that weep.

We claim to be true democrats. We pray, "Our Father who art in heaven," we talk glibly of human brotherhood and sisterhood and yet we go about well protected with all sorts of reserves of manner and words. I realized this not long ago while waiting in a railway station. It was hot and dusty and we had to wait many hours. The room was full of tired, impatient people. We were not satisfied with our environment and so we tried to make it as bad as possible. No one thought of being cheery or agreeable. There were many fretful children, but no one made the slightest attempt to amuse them. Each withdrew into the most impenetrable reserve. After a while a boy came in with pond-lilies for sale. This made a slight diversion, for most people care for flowers, but the severe-looking man in the corner and the sour-looking woman near him paid no attention. The man took more than his share of the seat, and the sour-looking woman would not move her bundles. After a while when the effect of the flowers had worn away and everyone was again looking cross, a young man took from his pocket a small French-harp or mouth organ and began to play softly for the amusement of one of the fretful babies. The tune soon wandered into "Home, Sweet Home." The music was touching and sweet and at last a common bond of sympathy was found. We all had homes of some sort. Each one was either going home or going away from home. Each face softened. Tears came into some of the tired eyes. The cross-looking man moved away from the arm of the seat where he had been crowding a meek little woman. The sour-looking woman moved her bundles, giving the one next her more room and offered some candy to a baby nearby. An indescribable hush and peace stole into the hot, dusty room. It seemed cooler, and we remembered that our wait was nearly over and it had not been so bad after all. We began to talk to each other, to laugh and joke about the heat. We were friends, united by the one common bond of sympathy—the love of home. Strange, was it not, that it took a whole afternoon to find one bond of sympathy among a room full of tired people all needing to be cheered and comforted.

As I went on my way that night, I thought over the sermon of the afternoon. Life is full of waiting for most of us. The trains that are to bear us away to happiness came slowly and in some cases never come at all. There are long forenoons, dreary afternoons, lonesome evenings. It cannot be otherwise in a world where each must carve out his own character and work out his own salvation. But how much cheerier would be these waitings, how much beauty and inspiration would come into them if we would help more to bear each other's burdens. If our eyes were quick to see, our ears to hear, our hearts to feel. If we really tried to understand each other.

Professor DuBois writes the whole story when he says:

> "Herein lies the tragedy of the age, not that men are poor,—
> All men know something of poverty;
> Not that men are wicked, who is good?
> Not that men are ignorant, what is truth?
> Nay, but that men know so little of each other."

## ✦ *Biographical Sketch*

**Born:** *October 1, 1852, Hamilton, Illinois*

**Died:** *January 6, 1942, Keokuk, Iowa, age 89*

**Buried:** *Hamilton, Illinois*

Eleanor Elizabeth Gordon was the oldest of six children. Because of her mother's poor health and her father's enlistment in the Union army, Gordon took over much of the management of family and household at an early age.

Gordon's mother was Free Will Baptist and her father's family Unitarian. Her uncle William was a "radical Unitarian"; her aunt Caroline a "Channing Unitarian"; and her uncle James a Spiritualist. Her childhood was filled with religious discussions, and thus Gordon was exposed to a variety of religious ideas at a young age. After listening to these discussions, she decided her uncle William was right. Despite the eclectic mix of religious ideas represented in her extended family and discussed in her home, her immediate family attended first the Free Will Baptist church and then the Presbyterian.[77] Although she listened carefully to sermons, she was indifferent to the teachings and dared challenge the Sunday school teacher. The young Gordon expressed "'utter indifference' to the specters of hellfire and damnation—which she doused in waves of laughter."[78]

From the time she was a young girl, Gordon read widely. Along with her friend and later colleague Mary Safford, she explored the works of Benjamin Franklin, Thomas Jefferson, and Thomas Paine and Unitarians William Ellery Channing, Ralph Waldo Emerson, and Theodore Parker. Emerson's appeal "to scholars not to hoard their book learning but to use it to make the world better . . . set up [Gordon's] life's agenda,"[79] and the idea that education is of little value if not put to the proper use appears frequently throughout Gordon's sermons.

Gordon began her professional life as an educator, returning to Illinois to teach after a year's study at the University of Iowa (1873–1874). Although she dreamed of earning a formal degree, from this point on Gordon studied independently, with the exception of a semester studying religion at Cornell University in 1889.

In the mid 1870s, Eleanor Gordon and Mary Safford pledged to spend their lives spreading liberal religion as a team. Safford had dreamed of being a minister from the time she was a little girl and now announced her intention to become a Unitarian minister. Gordon was appointed assistant principal and teacher at the high school in Centerville, Iowa, in 1875. She continued to feel that her call was to teaching, not preaching, and agreed to serve Safford and the church as a lay partner.

The first of many churches Gordon and Safford were to found or organize, together and individually, grew out of the Hawthorne Literary Society, which Safford started in their hometown of Hamilton, Illinois. The society sponsored weekly debates and brought in guest lecturers. Unitarian minister Oscar Clute, from Keokuk, Iowa, just across the river, was one of the most popular speakers. The success of Clute's lectures, along with his personal instruction to them on the ministry, inspired Gordon and Safford to start a Unitarian church in Hamilton in 1878. Safford served as minister of the new church, with Gordon assisting.

In 1880, impressed by the vitality of the Hamilton church, where Sunday attendance averaged around 150 and lectures and plays were held during the week, Jenkin Lloyd Jones, Secretary of the Western Unitarian Conference, asked Safford to move to Humboldt, Iowa, to serve as minister to a group that had recently built a church. Humboldt was also in need of a high school principal, so Gordon accompanied Safford to Iowa.

Gordon and Safford remained in Humboldt for five years. During those years, Gordon found herself fulfilling, at times, many if not all of the duties of parish minister—preaching, "running a church school, preparing worship services, helping oversee clubs and church sociables, and making parish calls."[80] When Safford was called to a church in Sioux City in 1885, Gordon accompanied her with the understanding that she would serve as parish assistant and when the church was sufficiently steady, she would be given time off to attend theological school. Gordon never did find both the money and the right opportunity to go back to school for a formal theological education. In spite of this, however, she began her preparation for ordained ministry in Sioux City. Jenkin Lloyd Jones oversaw her theological education, suggesting a semester at Cornell to finish areas she could not do independently.

Eleanor Gordon was ordained at Sioux City in 1889, with the Reverend Marion Murdoch[81] giving her ordination sermon. Gordon remained in Sioux City until 1896. At that time, she felt she needed some space and independence and went to Iowa City to take a pastorate of her own, although she and Safford continued to work and live together periodically after that. Over the next twenty-two years, Gordon served churches in Burlington, Iowa; Fargo, North Dakota; Des Moines, Iowa (with Mary Safford); and Orlando, Florida.

In addition to her pastorates, Gordon served as field secretary for the State Unitarian Conference of Iowa for three years and for ten years filled the office of secretary of that conference—"an office important to the life and vigor of the missionary projects of Iowa."[82] For many years, Gordon wrote for and edited *Old & New*, the paper of the Iowa Conference. She was also one of the early suffrage leaders in Iowa, once serving as vice president of the Iowa Equal Suffrage Association.

Eleanor Gordon retired from the parish ministry in 1918. She continued to be active in church affairs and women's issues until her death in 1942.

*Biographical Sketch by* LISA DOEGE

## ✦ Writings of Eleanor Elizabeth Gordon

"Character Is Destiny." *Old & New* 15 (September 1907).
"The Consumers' League." *Old & New* 9 (November 1900).
"Giving What We Have: A Christmas Sermon." *Old & New* 10 (December 1901).
"The Glory of the Imperfect." *Old & New* 12 (February 1904).
"Lessons Learnt from the War." *Old & New* 6 (July 1897).

"A Little Bit of a Long Story." Autobiography typescript. Iowa State Historical Society, Iowa City, Iowa, 1934.

"Our Mission to Save by Culture." *Old & New* 9 (September 1900).

"Why Young Women Do Not Go to Church." *Old & New* 13 (October 1905).

"The Woman Minister." *Unity* 88 (20 October 1921).

"The Worth of Sympathy." *Old & New* 15 (July 1907).

## ✦ Biographical Resources

Helvie, Clara Cook. *Unitarian Women Ministers.* Bound typescript, presented to the Historical Society of the American Unitarian Association, 1928.

Hitchings, Catherine F. *Universalist and Unitarian Women Ministers. The Journal of the Universalist Historical Society* 10 (1975).

Tucker, Cynthia Grant. *Prophetic Sisterhood: Liberal Women Ministers of the Frontier.* Boston: Beacon Press, 1990.

# The Search for Education

## by June Edwards

✦ ✦ ✦

FOR CENTURIES, FEMALES SUFFERED from the pronouncements of philosophers and other so-called learned men that they were inferior in intelligence, reasoning, and morality and were useful mainly for bearing children, doing domestic chores, and serving men. These views were often based on biblical assertions, such as "[The man] is the image and glory of God: but the woman is the glory of the man" (I Corinthians 11:7) and "It is a shame for women to speak in the church" (I Corinthians 14:35). Men were told to give honor to their wives "as unto the weaker vessel" (I Peter 3:7), and wives were ordered to "submit yourselves unto your own husbands" (Ephesians 5:22).

These biases were further validated by the influential French writer Jean-Jacques Rousseau. In his novel *Émile* (1762), a story that sets forth the ideal education for a well-to-do French boy, he created a companion named Sophy who exemplified the perfect woman. In explaining the "natural" differences between men and women, Rousseau stated: "The man should be strong and active; the woman should be weak and passive; the one must have both the power and the will; it is enough that the other should offer little resistance. . . . Woman is especially made for man's delight." According to Rousseau, it followed that the education of females must also be different—namely "planned in relation to man. To be pleasing in his sight, to win his respect and love, to train him in childhood, to tend him in manhood, to counsel and console, to make his life pleasant and happy, these are the duties of woman for all time, and this is what she should be taught while she is young."[1]

With the 1770s political revolutions in the United States and France came protests against such opinions, assertions about the strong intellectual ability of females, and demands for equal education as a basic human right. The women who wrote essays and books on these topics were often highly influenced by the Enlightenment belief in reason as the primary, if not the sole, determiner of what is ethical and good.

Such Unitarians as Mary Wollstonecraft, Harriet Martineau, and Margaret Fuller and Universalist Judith Sargent Murray had great faith in the power of education to elevate all persons, but especially females, to their rightful place as autonomous individuals, free to develop their individuality and choose their own destiny, no matter what the circumstances of their birth. Women in England, North America, and elsewhere, they felt, were being held hostage by a white male tyranny, buttressed by orthodox religious dogma and institutions, that proclaimed them to be inferior beings, capable of only superficial thinking and suited only for sexual duties and domestic labor. These women saw education as a major source of enlightenment and power, and being forbidden access to it was viewed as the means of keeping females, much like the working class in Europe and the slaves in the United States in subjugation.

The writings of the women at the forefront of the demand for education were in stark contrast to those of male scientists, such as George Romanes, a naturalist and friend of Charles Darwin. In *Descent of Man* (1887), Romanes stated: "Seeing that the average brain-weight of women is about five ounces less than that of men, on merely anatomical grounds we should be prepared to expect a marked inferiority of intellectual power in the former." Basing his proof on evolution, he asserted that no matter how much education a female would receive, "It must take many centuries for heredity to produce the missing five ounces of the female brain."[2]

The women theorists, on the other hand, argued that no differences existed between males and females with regard to mental capacities. The apparent weaknesses in the thought processes of adult women were not due to innate deficiencies but to lack of opportunities to acquire knowledge, train their mental faculties, and expand their skills beyond domesticity. Some women pressed for an identical education for boys and girls, while others believed that the existing schools were poorly suited for either sex. Females would be better served by having their own quality academic institutions specially designed for their needs and learning styles.

These ideas were met with scorn and derision on both sides of the Atlantic. In addition to their unorthodox views, some of the women's unconventional lifestyles caused them to be viewed as domineering, unfeminine, unsexed, pitiful creatures. Wollstonecraft, for example, was denounced by Horace Walpole as a "hyena in petticoats."[3] An *intellectual woman* (often considered an oxymoron) became a derogatory phrase used to dismiss females who had the audacity to believe they were rational, thinking beings equal to males. Nevertheless, the writings of these women influenced social reformers in both England and North America and helped advance the cause of female education and liberation.

In the next decades, those who continued the movement believed that education not only would equalize the intellectual capacities of males and females and release women from legal and social constraints but also would be the catalyst for making the world progressively better. The ability to reason, accompanied by free inquiry and wide reading, would lead directly to reforms of all kinds. Since vice, corruption, poverty, and oppression stemmed largely from ignorance and superstition, access to knowledge would be the salvation of society.[4]

Industrialization had brought middle-class women greater prosperity, labor-saving devices, more leisure time, and an increase in what sociologist Barbara Welter labeled "the cult of true womanhood."[5] It also created a separation between home duties and economic contributions as husbands left home each day for employment in factories and offices. Whereas colonial women had clearly contributed financially by helping with farm work or the family business, this new separation of what was considered men's work and women's work, plus the stereotype of what a woman should be, decreased the value given to household responsibilities and those who performed them.

The image of a "true woman" was a replica of Sophy, Rousseau's fictional ideal of perfection: pure, pious, submissive, and domestic. She was also fragile, both physically and emotionally, and had no reason to cultivate her mental capacities (or so she was told). She especially needed to be protected from the dirty world of politics. Her major contribution, besides domestic skills, was her superior moral sense, which was best used to raise good children and temper the vices and excesses of the men in her life. For instance, Catharine Beecher, a noted educator who established two academic schools for girls and several teacher-training institutions, also wrote immensely popular books urging women to treat family and home care as a serious, sacred profession requiring practical skills, dedication, knowledge, and hard work. Concerned about the ill health of middle- and upper-class women due to lack of exercise and poor nutrition, as well as the irrelevance of much school curricula, Beecher wrote in an early work, *Treatise on Domestic Economy* (1841): "The physical and domestic education of daughters should occupy the principal attention of mothers. . . . Much less time should be given to school and much more to domestic employments, especially in the wealthier classes."[6] She also believed that the moral center of society was the home and that if women were gentle and unassuming they would have influence over men and thus power in the larger world.

Kept from the stimulation of education and the larger society—their accomplishments undervalued and their health damaged by poor nutrition and repeated pregnancies (which too frequently resulted in miscarriages or stillbirths)—some women retreated into invalidism as perhaps a way of avoiding the sexual demands of their husbands and the physical and psychological stresses of child care. They fainted easily, aged quickly, and often died during childbirth or while their young children were still small. A major factor in the physical weakness of many middle- and upper-class women was the fashion of wearing tight corsets, which constricted the natural development of women's bodies to the point of causing broken ribs and damaging internal organs.[7]

Male physicians and educators asserted, however, that the female mind and body were too delicate for the strain of intellectual studies. Not only was education a waste of time for persons so mentally limited that they could not benefit from it, but a girl's reproductive system made her psychologically unstable. In fact, too much learning would even lead to mental retardation.

Particularly damaging statements came from retired Harvard Medical School professor Dr. Edward Clarke. Distressed that females were enrolling in colleges and demanding entrance into medical and divinity schools, he wrote in *Sex in Education* (1873) that women's "female apparatus" would be endangered if they used up their "limited energy" on academic studies. It was true that females could do advanced learning, as evidenced by the several Vassar College students he studied, but they would not be able to "retain uninjured health and a future secure from neuralgia, uterine disease, hysteria, and other derangements of the nervous system."[8] Young women had the obligation not to improve their minds but to protect their bodies in order to perform their biological role as childbearers. This pronouncement thus gave scientific credence to the traditional belief that females did not have the strength, endurance, or need for educational pursuits.

To counter this type of thinking and to improve the health of women and their children, especially teenage daughters, Unitarian Elizabeth Blackwell used her knowledge, writing abilities, and speaking skills to educate the public about nutrition, sanitation, hygiene, disease prevention, and physical exercise. She and others, such as Elizabeth Peabody, threw their energies into establishing schools for extended age groups, breaking legal and societal barriers for females, and opening doors for women's entrance into such traditionally male professions as medicine, college teaching, and school administration. These women challenged the biases and practices of men by working outside mainstream institutions and with a nontraditional clientele: the very young, teenage girls, and adult women.

Not only did these educators believe in the intellectual potential of their students, but they used radical teaching methods that were unique and highly effective. In contrast to the often rigid, pedantic instruction found in traditional male institutions, female teachers focused on student engagement, problem solving, cooperation, hands-on activities, creativity, and open-ended research as well as in-depth studies of subject matters. Other women, such as Margaret Fuller and Fannie Barrier Williams, provided invaluable opportunities for adult women to meet for mutual support, to expand their knowledge on a wide variety of topics, and to challenge the biases and barriers that kept women from obtaining the same rights and benefits as men.

Though the contributions of each woman cited in this section were different, their personalities and experiences had many similarities. Foremost was their belief in the equal intelligence and abilities of females and males, the right to the same quality of education for both, and equal access to career opportunities. By sheer determination and sometimes through self-direction, they obtained an outstanding education for themselves and pursued nontraditional goals, despite both official and social prejudices that kept most women in the home and out of the public eye. These women reformers also possessed amazing self-confidence and courage, which kept them moving forward in the face of hostility and disappointment. In addition, they opened schools, shared knowledge, served as role models and mentors, and unselfishly helped make the way a little easier for the women who followed.

However, they used different strategies to justify their arguments for educating girls and women. The point was sometimes made that knowledge would make women better wives, mothers, and homemakers. Citing the need to know about good nutrition, health care, childrearing, economics, and household responsibilities, the aim was not only to improve the quality of lives for females and their families but to raise the status of so-called women's work in the eyes of society by tying it to education. Others decried this goal, believing it fostered inferior instruction for females, the establishment of special schools with a limited curriculum and less-qualified teachers, and a continued dearth of desirable careers beyond teaching and homemaking. Moreover, as Mary Rice Livermore pointed out, family welfare should not be solely women's responsibility but should be of equal concern to men.

All the writers in this section, however, stressed the importance of developing the mind for its own sake. Whether the knowledge gained was useful for domestic affairs or paid employment was less important than the joy provided by intellectual stimulation. Women had achieved less in society over the centuries not because they were inferior in intelligence and abilities but because they had been barred from educational institutions, treated from a young age as inferior to their brothers, and given few opportunities for self-growth. If males and females received equal education, whether together or separately, they would soon be equal in society.

From hindsight, we can see the simplism of that theory. Though improvements have been made and more opportunities have become available for women, both social and psychological forces have mitigated against equal treatment, even in coeducational classrooms.[9] Once out of school, even the highest-achieving females are still often confronted with closed doors and "glass ceilings" that block their advancement. Childrearing and household duties continue to fall more heavily on mothers than fathers, even when both have full-time professional careers. Education alone, without parallel changes in other aspects of society, cannot bring about true equality between the sexes.

Nevertheless, the courageous, determined Unitarian and Universalist writers included in this section made great contributions toward the advancement of education for girls and women. Bolstered by their liberal religious convictions, they championed the female intellect, established schools, organized for educational and civil rights purposes, and tore down roadblocks to traditional male professions. Such endeavors paved the way for many others in their time, as well as ours, to have high aspirations and reach previously unattainable goals.

# On the Equality of the Sexes

## Article in *Massachusetts Magazine,* 1790

JUDITH SARGENT STEVENS MURRAY (1751–1820) *wrote one of the earliest published statements on women's rights. With her husband, John Murray, a minister who shared his wife's beliefs and encouraged her writing, Judith Sargent Murray helped establish the Universalist denomination in North America.*

*In the following article, published in March and April 1790 but written eleven years earlier, Judith Sargent Murray, using the pseudonym* Constantia, *presented a radical challenge to the belief that male minds are inherently superior. She claimed that difference in educational opportunities was the cause of many women's deficiencies in reasoning and judgment. Largely self-educated, she had acquired an impressive amount of knowledge through sheer determination but championed the rights of females to have the same instruction and access to information as their brothers.*

See the Biographical Sketch on pages 156–159.

To the Editors of the Massachusetts Magazine,

Gentlemen, The following essay is yielded to the patronage of candor. —If it hath been anticipated, the testimony of many respectable persons, who saw it in manuscript as early as the year 1779, can obviate the imputation of plagiarism.

That minds are not alike, full well I know,
This truth each day's experience will show;
To heights surprising some great spirits soar,
With inborn strength mysterious depths explore;
Their eager gaze surveys the path of light,
Confest it stood to Newton's piercing sight.
Deep science, like a bashful maid retires,
And but the *ardent* breast her worth inspires;
By perseverance the coy fair is won.
And Genius, led by Study, wears the crown.

But some there are who wish not to improve,
Who never can the path of knowledge love,
Whose souls almost with the dull body one,
With anxious care each mental pleasure shun;
Weak is the level'd, enervated mind,
And but while here to vegetate design'd.
The torpid spirit mingling with its clod,
Can scarcely boast its origin from God;
Stupidly dull—they move progressing on—
They eat, and drink, and all their work is done.
While others, emulous of sweet applause,
Industrious seek for each event a cause,
Tracing the Hidden Springs whence knowledge flows,
Which nature all in beauteous order shows.
Yet cannot I their sentiments imbibe,
Who this distinction to the sex ascribe,
As if a woman's form must needs enroll,
A weak, a servile, an inferior soul;
And that the guise of man must still proclaim,
Greatness of mind, and him, to be the same:
Yet as the hours revolve fair proofs arise,
Which the bright wreath of growing fame supplies;
And in past times some men have *sunk* so *low,*
That female records nothing *less* can show.
But imbecility is still confin'd,
And by the lordly sex to us consign'd;
They rob us of the power t'improve,
And then declare we only trifles love;
Yet haste the era, when the world shall know,
That such distinctions only dwell below;
The soul unfetter'd, to no sex confin'd,
Was for the abodes of cloudless day design'd.
Mean time we emulate their manly fires,
Though erudition all their thoughts inspires,
Yet nature with equality imparts,
And *noble passions,* swell e'en *female hearts.*

✦ ✦ ✦

Is it upon mature consideration we adopt the idea that nature is thus partial in her distributions? Is it indeed a fact that she hath yielded to one half of the human species so unquestionable a mental superiority?

I know that to both sexes elevated understandings, and the reverse, are common. But suffer me to ask, in what the minds of females are so notoriously deficient, or unequal. May the intellectual powers be ranged under their four heads—imagination, reason, memory and judgment?

The province of imagination hath long since been surrendered up to us, and we have been crowned undoubted sovereigns of the regions of fancy. Invention is perhaps the most arduous effort of the mind; this branch of imagination hath been particularly ceded to us, and we have been time out of mind invested with that creative faculty. Observe the variety of fashions (here I bar the contemptuous smile) which distinguish and adorn the female world; how continually are they changing. . . . Now what a playfulness, what an exuberance of fancy, what strength of inventive imagination, doth this continual variation discover?

✦ ✦ ✦

Are we deficient in reason? We can only reason from what we know, and if opportunity of acquiring knowledge hath been denied us, the inferiority of our sex cannot fairly be deduced from thence.

Memory, I believe, will be allowed us in common, since every one's experience must testify that a loquacious old woman is as frequently met with as a communicative old man; their subjects are alike drawn from the fund of other times, and the transactions of their youth, or of maturer life, entertain, or perhaps fatigue you, in the evening of their lives. . . .

Yet it may be questioned, from what doth this superiority, in thus determining faculty of the soul, proceed. May we not trace its source in the difference of education and continued advantages? Will it be said that the judgment of a male of two years old is more sage than that of a female of the same age? I believe the reverse is generally observed to be true.

But from that period what partiality! How is the one exalted and the other depressed by the contrary modes of education which are adopted! The one is taught to aspire, and the other is early confined and limited. As their years increase, the sister must be wholly domesticated, while the brother is led by the hand through all the flowery paths of science. Grant that their minds are by nature equal, yet who shall wonder at the apparent superiority, if indeed custom becomes second nature; nay if it taketh the place of nature and that it doth the experience of each day will evince. At length arrived at womanhood, the uncultivated fair one feels a void, which the employments allotted her are by no means capable of filling. What can she do? To books she may not apply; or if she doth, *to those of the novel kind,* lest she merit the appellation of *a learned lady?* . . . Meantime, she herself is most unhappy; she feels the want of a cultivated mind. Is she single, she in vain seeks to fill up time from sexual employments or amusements. Is she united to a person whose soul nature made equal to her own, education hath set him so far above her that in those entertainments which are productive of such rational felicity, she is not qualified to accompany him. She experiences a mortifying consciousness of inferiority, which embitters every enjoyment. Doth the person to whom her adverse fate hath consigned her possess a mind incapable of improvement, she is equally wretched, in being so closely connected with an individual whom she cannot but despise. Now, was she permitted the same instructors as her brother . . . for the employment of a rational mind an ample field would be opened. In astronomy she might catch a glimpse of the immensity of the Deity, and thence she would form amazing conceptions of the august and supreme Intelligence. In geography she would admire Jehovah in the midst of his benevolence, thus adapting this globe to the various wants and amusements of its inhabitants. In natural philosophy she would adore the infinite majesty of heaven, clothed in condescension; and as she traversed the reptile world, she would hail the goodness of a creating God.

✦ ✦ ✦

Every requisite in female economy is easily attained; and, . . . when once attained, they require no further *mental attention.* Nay, while we are pursuing the needle or the superintendency of the family, . . . our minds are at full liberty for reflection; that imagination may exert itself in full vigor; and that if a just foundation early laid, our ideas will then be worthy of rational beings. If we were industrious we might easily find time to arrange them upon paper, or should avocations press too hard for such an indulgence, the hours allotted for conversation would at least become more refined and rational. . . . Is it reasonable that a candidate for immortality, for the joys of heaven, an intelligent being, who is to spend an eternity in contemplating the works of Deity, should at present be so degraded, as to be allowed no other ideas, than those which are suggested by the mechanism of a pudding, or the sewing of the seams of a garment? . . .

Yes, ye lordly, ye haughty sex, our souls are by nature *equal* to yours; the same breath of God animates, enlivens, and invigorates us; and that we are not fallen lower than yourselves, let those witness who have greatly towered above the various discouragements by which they have been so heavily oppressed; . . . from the commencement of time to the present day, there hath been as many females, as males, who, by the *mere force of natural powers,* have merited the crown of applause; who, *thus unassisted,* have seized the wreath of fame.

✦ ✦ ✦

The exquisite delicacy of the female mind proclaimeth the exactness of its texture, while its nice sense of honor announceth its innate, its native grandeur. And indeed, in one respect, the preeminence seems to be tacitly allowed us, for after an education which limits and confines, and employments and recreations which naturally tend to enervate the body, and debilitate the mind; after we have from early youth been adorned with ribbons and other gewgaws, dressed out like the ancient victims previous to a sacrifice, being taught by the care of our parents in collecting the most showy materials that the ornamenting of our exterior ought to be the principal object of our attention; after, I say, fifteen years thus spent, we are introduced into the world, amid the united adulation of every beholder.

Praise is sweet to the soul; we are immediately intoxicated by large draughts of flattery, which being plentifully administered, is to the pride of our hearts the most acceptable incense. It is expected that with the other sex we should commence immediate war and that we should triumph over the machinations of the most artful. We must be constantly on our guard; prudence and discretion must be our characteristics; and we must rise superior to, and obtain a complete victory over those who have been long adding to the native strength of their minds, by an unremitted study of men and books, and who have, moreover, conceived from the loose characters which they have seen portrayed in the extensive variety of their reading, a most contemptible opinion of the sex. Thus unequal, we are notwithstanding forced to the combat, and the infamy which is consequent upon the smallest deviation in our conduct, proclaims the high idea which we formed of our native strength; and thus, indirectly at least, is the preference acknowledged to be our due.

And if we are allowed an equality of acquirements, let serious studies equally employ our minds, and we will bid our souls arise to equal strength. We will meet upon even ground the despot man; we will rush with alacrity to the combat, and, crowned by success, we shall then answer the exalted expectations which are formed. Though sensibility, soft compassion, and gentle commiseration are inmates in the female bosom, yet against every deep laid art, altogether fearless of the event, we will set them in array; for assuredly the wreath of victory will encircle the spotless brow. If we meet an equal, a sensible friend, we will reward him with the hand of amity, and through life we will be assiduous to promote his happiness. . . .

*Constantia*

✦ ✦ ✦

*By way of supplement to the foregoing pages, I subjoin the following extract from a letter wrote to a friend in the December of 1780.*[10]

And now assist me, O thou genius of my sex, while I undertake the arduous task of endeavouring to combat that vulgar, that almost universal error, which hath, it seems enlisted even Mr. P— under its banners. The superiority of your sex hath, I grant, been time out of mind esteemed a truth incontrovertible; in consequence of which persuasion, every plan of education hath been calculated to establish this favorite tenet. . . . I mean to bend the whole of my artillery against those supposed proofs, which you have from thence provided, and from which you have formed an entrenchment *apparently* so invulnerable.

And first, to begin with our great progenitors; but here, suffer me to promise, that it is for mental strength I mean to contend, for with respect to animal powers, I yield them undisputed to that sex, which enjoys them in common with the lion, the tiger, and many other beasts of prey. . . .

Well, but the woman was first in the transgression. Strange how blind *self love* renders you men; were you not wholly absorbed in a partial admiration of your own abilities, you would long since have acknowledged the force of what I am now going to urge. It is true some ignoramuses have absurdly enough informed us that the beauteous fair of paradise was seduced from her obedience by a malignant demon in *the guise of a baleful serpent;* but we, who are better informed, know that the fallen spirit presented himself to her view, *a shining angel still;* for thus, saith the critics in the Hebrew tongue, ought the word to be rendered. Let us examine her motive—Hark! The seraph declares that she shall attain a perfection of knowledge; for is there aught which is not comprehended under one or other of the terms *good* and *evil.*

It doth not appear that she was governed by any one sensual appetite but merely by a desire of adorning her mind; a laudable ambition fired her soul, and a thirst for knowledge impelled the predilection so fatal in its consequences. Adam could not plead the same deception; assuredly he was not deceived; nor ought we to admire his superiour strength, or wonder at his sagacity, when we so often confess that example is much more influential than precept. His gentle partner stood before him, a melancholy instance of the direful effects of disobedience; he saw her not possessed of that wisdom which she had fondly hoped to obtain, but he beheld the once blooming female, disrobed of that innocence, which had heretofore rendered her so lovely. To him then deception became impossible, as he had proof positive of the fallacy of the argument, which the deceiver had suggested. What then could be his inducement to burst the barriers and to fly directly in the face of that command, which *immediately* from the mouth of Deity *he* had received, since, I say, he could not plead the fascinating stimulus, the accumulation of knowledge, as indisputable conviction was so visibly portrayed before him.

What mighty cause impelled him to sacrifice myriads of beings yet unborn, and by one impious act, which he saw would be productive of such fatal effect, entail undistinguished ruin upon a race of beings, which he was yet to produce? Blush, ye vaunters of fortitude; ye boasters of resolution; ye haughty lords of creation; blush when ye remember that he was influenced by no other motive than a bare pusillanimous attachment to a woman! by sentiments so exquisitely soft, that all his sons have, from that period, when they have designed to degrade them, described as highly feminine. Thus it should see, that all the arts of the grand deceiver . . . were requisite to mislead our general mother, while the father of mankind forfeited his own, and relinquished the happiness of posterity, merely in compliance with the blandishments of a female.

✦ ✦ ✦

Lastly, let us turn our eyes to man in the aggregate. He is manifested as the figure of strength, but that we may not regard him as anything more than a figure, his soul is formed in no sort superior, but every way equal to the mind of her, when in the emblem of weakness, and whom he calls the gentle companion of his better days.

## ✦ *Biographical Sketch*

**Born:** *May 5, 1751, Gloucester, Massachusetts*[11]

**Died:** *July 6, 1820, Natchez, Mississippi, age 69*

**Buried:** *Natchez, Mississippi, on what was then the Fatherland Plantation*

Judith Sargent Murray was the beloved daughter and oldest child of prosperous and influential sea merchant Winthrop Sargent and his accomplished wife, Judith Robinson Saunders Sargent. The Sargents were politically active, first in the American colonies and then in the new nation, and assumed many positions of leadership. Their self-confidence and boldness were not just relegated to the male members of the family, however; they defined Judith's character, as well. Her parents' early adherence to the new Universalist faith affected her profoundly.

Judith Sargent Murray's contributions to early Universalist theology place her in the ranks of Universalism's most original thinkers. Her feminism and her Universalism are intimately linked. Her first published writing, a Universalist catechism (1782), gives early evidence of why she is considered one of North America's first feminist thinkers. Her philosophy is revealed clearly in this comment from a letter written in 1778: "A universalist, your heart cannot but dilate, and your affections widen, until the divine expansion, like the ambient atmosphere, encircles every form, that is acted upon by an immortal spirit."[12]

As the daughter of a merchant-class family, Judith was taught rudimentary reading and writing skills by a woman she called her "ill taught Preceptress." But watching her brother, Winthrop, study to enter Harvard College with a skilled tutor, she felt keenly the difference in their education and how males and females were prepared for life. But perhaps being denied a formal education actually allowed Judith greater freedom to expand her intellectual capabilities. Encouraged by the Universalist views of her family and their enlightened thinking, Judith turned to the family library where, on her own, she developed her literacy and intellectual skills far beyond what was expected.

At age eighteen, Judith married sea merchant John Stevens. At twenty-one, she took in her husband's two orphaned nieces—the first of many young people whose education and moral development she would oversee.

By her early twenties, Judith knew she wanted a public voice, because she had ideas about what kind of country the United States could become. Using assumed names to conceal her identity, she began publishing poems and essays that tackled the political issues of the Revolutionary era. Writing as *Constantia,* she urged equal educational opportunities for girls in her 1784 essay "Desultory Thoughts upon the Utility of Encouraging a Degree of Self-Complacency, Especially in Female Bosoms" and encouraged women to have greater self-respect.

The Sargent family actively supported Universalist ideas, and when English-born Universalist preacher John Murray arrived in the American colonies, he was invited by the Sargents to visit Gloucester. In 1774, he made Gloucester his home, and the Sargent family helped him establish the first American Universalist church there.

Judith's first husband died in 1781; she married John Murray in 1788. They had two children—Fitz Winthrop, who died in childbirth, and Julia Maria, who survived. Judith's writing flourished during her marriage to John Murray. Her most important series of political essays addressed female equality, federalism, revolution, and more. Using the name *The Gleaner,* these essays were published beginning in 1792 in *Massachusetts Magazine.* In 1794, the Murrays moved to Boston, where John had agreed to serve as pastor to Boston's Universalist church the previous year. There, Judith found more outlets for her literary pursuits. She continued with her essays and poetry but also wrote two plays on gender and class issues—*The Medium, or Virtue Triumphant* and *The Traveller Returned.* Both plays were performed in Boston, and Judith became the first American playwright to be so honored.

In 1798, with the family income declining and her daughter's future to consider, Judith decided to publish in book form her Gleaner essays. She added a few new works and produced a three-volume set of books she sold by advance subscription to some of the leading thinkers and political figures of her time. Today, *The Gleaner* is considered a fine example of post-Revolutionary thought on religion, politics, and morality, recognizing the value of all life—that women, as well as men, must have access to education and economic independence for America to become a just society. Her social activism and writing consistently reflected her Universalist belief in the connectedness of humankind. Also in *The Gleaner,* Judith (who had been using such pseudonyms as *Constantia, Honora Martesia, Mr. Vigilius,* and *The Reaper*) revealed her identity to her readers and forever established herself among the most prominent of contemporary American authors.

In 1803, her role in progressive thinking on female education established, Judith agreed to help Judith Saunders (a cousin) and Clementine Beach start a female academy in nearby Dorchester. In 1807, Judith wrote her third play, *The African,* which was performed in Boston. To date, no copy has been found.

John Murray was paralyzed by a stroke in 1809. While his mind remained alert, his care became one of Judith's main concerns. She was raising her daughter as well, overseeing her education and that of numerous nieces and nephews who lived in the Murray home or boarded at nearby preparatory schools or Harvard College. (One of these students was Adam Louis Bingaman, whom Julia Maria would eventually marry.) In 1812, in the midst of an approaching war, Judith edited and published John Murray's *Letters and Sketches of Sermons,* and the following year, she welcomed her first grandchild, Charlotte.

When John Murray died in 1815, Judith was urged to finish the autobiography he had been writing for many years. She did so, adding an introduction, and *The Life of John Murray* was published in 1816. Sadly, because Judith, not John, completed the work he had stopped writing in 1774, there are no words from him to describe their mutually supportive relationship or her contribution to early Universalism. In 1818, Judith and Julia Maria moved to Natchez, Mississippi, taking up residence with Julia Maria's husband. Judith died there in 1820, followed by her granddaughter, and then her daughter two years later. There are no living direct descendants.

Today, Judith Sargent Murray's legacy lies not just in her published writings, which have recently found a new audience, but in her twenty letterbooks, discovered in 1984 by Unitarian Universalist minister Gordon Gibson. These books, containing copies of Judith's outgoing correspondence from ages fourteen to sixty-seven (1765–1818), form a unique document in American history. They bring to light a woman of creative genius who was at the forefront of the development of Universalism. Hers was an important prophetic voice whose words are still relevant today.

*Biographical Sketch by* MARIANNE DUNLOP and BONNIE HURD SMITH

## ✦ Writings of Judith Sargent Murray

*From Gloucester to Philadelphia in 1790: Observations, Anecdotes and Thoughts from the Letters of Judith Sargent Murray.* Edited by and with biographical introduction by Bonnie Hurd Smith. Gloucester, MA: Judith Sargent Murray Society and The Curious Traveller Press, 1998.

*The Gleaner: A Miscellaneous Production.* 3 vols. Boston: I. Thomas and E. T. Andrews, 1798; Schenectady, NY: Union College Press, 1992.

*Judith Sargent Murray: Her First 100 Letters.* Introduction and transcription by Marianne Dunlop. Foreword by Bonnie Smith. Gloucester, MA: Sargent House Museum, 1995.

*Records of the Life of the Rev. John Murray, Written by Himself, with a Continuation by Mrs. Judith Sargent Murray.* Boston: Francis and Munroe, 1816; Boston: Marsh, Capen and Lyon, 1832.

*The Selected Writings of Judith Sargent Murray.* Edited by Sharon M. Harris. New York: Oxford University Press, 1995.

*Some Deductions from the System Promulgated in the Page of Divine Revelation: Ranged in the Order and Form of a Catechism.* Portsmouth, NH: n.p., 1782. Reprinted with an introduction by Bonnie Hurd Smith (Cambridge, MA: Judith Sargent Murray Society, 1999).

## ✦ Biographical Resources

Dunlop, Marianne. *Judith Sargent Murray (1751–1820): Champion of Social Justice.* Gloucester, MA: Sargent House Museum, 1993.

Dykeman, Therese Boos, ed. *American Women Philosophers 1630–1930: Six Exemplary Thinkers.* Lewiston, NY: Edwin Mellen, 1993.

Gibson, Gordon. "The Rediscovery of Judith Sargent Murray." *Not Hell, But Hope: The John Murray Distinguished Lectures, 1987–1991,* edited by Charles Howe. Lankota, NJ: Murray Grove Association, 1991.

Howe, Charles A. *The Larger Faith: A History of Universalism in America.* Boston: Skinner House Books, 1993.

Kerber, Linda K. *Women of the Republic: Intellect and Ideology in Revolutionary America.* New York: W. W. Norton, 1986.

McElroy, Lori Jenkins, ed. *Women's Voices: A Documentary History of Women in America.* New York: Gale Research, 1997.

Moynihan, Ruth Barnes, Cynthia Russett, and Laurie Crumpacker, eds. *Second to None: A Documentary History of American Women.* Lincoln: University of Nebraska Press, 1993.

Norton, Mary Beth. *Liberty's Daughters: The Revolutionary Experience of American Women, 1750–1800.* New York: HarperCollins, 1980.

Smith, Bonnie, ed. *Judith Sargent Murray—Philosopher, Writer, and Champion of Social Justice: Proceedings of a Conference Held May 1, 1993, Independent Christian Church.* Gloucester, MA: Sargent House Museum, 1994.

## ✦ Archives

The original manuscripts of the Judith Sargent Murray Papers, consisting of twenty letterbooks, are located at the Mississippi Department of Archives and History, where the microfilm may be purchased. Direct inquiries to:

Curator of Manuscripts, Archives & Library Division
Mississippi Department of Archives & History
P.O. Box 571, Jackson, MI 39205-0571

# Thoughts on the Education of Women

## From *A Vindication of the Rights of Woman,* 1792

MARY WOLLSTONECRAFT (1759–1797) *was an educator and writer, active in Unitarian circles in England in the late eighteenth century. The book that made her famous,* A Vindication of the Rights of Woman, *was published two years after Judith Sargent Murray's essay "On Equality of the Sexes."*[13] *It was an aggressive response to French statesman Talleyrand's "Report on Public Instruction," in which he recommended that French schools exclude girls, who, he believed, needed only to learn domestic skills at home. Mary Wollstonecraft argued that females should be intellectually cultivated; freed from the confinements of dress, manners, and domesticity; and encouraged to be independent thinkers and achievers. Though vilified by conservatives and the general public for her unconventional ideas and lifestyle, her writings influenced social reformers in both England and North America and helped advance the cause of women's education and liberation.*

See the Biographical Sketch on pages 165–168.

After considering the historic page, and viewing the living world with anxious solicitude, the most melancholy emotions of sorrowful indignation have depressed my spirits, and I have sighed when obliged to confess that either nature has made a great difference between man and man or that the civilization which has hitherto taken place in the world has been very partial. I have turned over various books written on the subject of education and patiently observed the conduct of parents and the management of schools; but what has been the result?—a profound conviction that the neglected education of my fellow-creatures is the grand source of the misery I deplore; and that women, in particular, are rendered weak and wretched by a variety of concurring causes, originating from one hasty conclusion. The conduct and manners of women, in fact, evidently prove that their minds are not in a healthy state; for, like the flowers which are planted in too rich a soil, strength and usefulness are sacrificed to beauty; and the flaunting leaves, after having pleased a fastidious eye, fade, disregarded on the stalk, long before the season when they ought to have arrived at maturity.—One cause of this barren blooming I attribute to a false system of education, gathered from the books written on this subject by men who, considering females rather as women than human creatures, have been more anxious to make them alluring mistresses than affectionate wives and rational mothers; and the understanding of the sex has been so bubbled by this specious homage that the civilized women of the present century, with a few exceptions, are only anxious to inspire love, when they ought to cherish a nobler ambition and by their abilities and virtues exact respect.

✦ ✦ ✦

The education of women has, of late, been more attended to than formerly; yet they are still reckoned a frivolous sex and ridiculed or pitied by the writers who endeavor by satire or instruction to improve them. It is acknowledged that they spend many of the first years of their lives in acquiring a smattering of accomplishments; meanwhile strength of body and mind are sacrificed to libertine notions of beauty, to the desire of establishing themselves,—the only way women can rise in the world,—by marriage. And this desire making mere animals of them, when they marry they act as such children may be expected to act;—they dress; they paint, and nickname God's creatures.—Surely these weak beings are only fit for a seraglio!—Can they be expected to govern a family with judgment, or take care of the poor babes whom they bring into the world?

If then it can be fairly deduced from the present conduct of the sex, from the prevalent fondness for pleasure which takes the place of ambition and those nobler passions that open and enlarge the soul; that the instruction which women have hitherto received has only tended, with the constitution of civil society, to render them insignificant objects of desire—mere propagators of fools!—if it can be proved that in aiming to accomplish them, without cultivating their understandings, they are taken out of their sphere of duties and made ridiculous and useless when the short-lived bloom of beauty is over. I presume that *rational* men will excuse me for endeavoring to persuade them to become more masculine and respectable.

Indeed the word masculine is only a bugbear; there is little reason to fear that women will acquire too much courage or fortitude; for their apparent inferiority with respect to bodily strength must render them in some degree dependent on men in the various relations of life; but why should it be increased by prejudices that give a sex to virtue and confound simple truths with sensual reveries?

✦ ✦ ✦

## The Prevailing Opinion of Sexual Character Discussed

To account for, and excuse the tyranny of man, many ingenious arguments have been brought forward to prove that the two sexes, in the acquirement of virtue, ought to aim at attaining a very different character: or, to speak explicitly, women are not allowed to have sufficient strength of mind to acquire what really deserves the name of virtue. Yet it should seem, allowing them to have souls, that there is but one way appointed by Providence to lead *mankind* to either virtue or happiness.

If then women are not a swarm of ephemeron triflers, why should they be kept in ignorance under the specious name of innocence? Men complain, and with reason, of the follies and caprices of our sex when they do not keenly satirize our headstrong passions and groveling vices.—Behold, I should answer, the natural effect of ignorance! The mind will ever be unstable that has only prejudices to rest on, and the current will run with destructive fury when there are no barriers to break its force. Women are told from their infancy, and taught by the example of their mothers, that a little knowledge of human weakness, justly termed cunning, softness of temper, *outward* obedience, and scrupulous attention to a puerile kind of propriety, will obtain for them the protection of man; and should they be beautiful, everything else is needless, for, at least, twenty years of their lives.

✦ ✦ ✦

The most perfect education, in my opinion, is such an exercise of the understanding as is best calculated to strengthen the body and form the heart. Or, in other words, to enable the individual to attain such habits of virtue as will render it independent. In fact, it is a farce to call any being virtuous whose virtues do not result from the exercise of its own reason. This was Rousseau's opinion respecting men: I extend it to women and confidently assert that they have been drawn out of their sphere by false refinement and not by an endeavor to acquire masculine qualities. Still the regal homage which they receive is so intoxicating that till the manners of the times are changed and formed on more reasonable principles, it may be impossible to convince them that the illegitimate power, which they obtain, by degrading themselves is a curse and that they must return to nature and equality, if they wish to secure the placid satisfaction that unsophisticated affections impart. But for this epoch we must wait—wait, perhaps, till kings and nobles, enlightened by reason, and preferring the real dignity of man to childish state, throw off their gaudy hereditary trappings: and if then women do not resign the arbitrary power of beauty—they will prove that they have *less* mind than man.

✦ ✦ ✦

I have, probably, had an opportunity of observing more girls in their infancy than J. J. Rousseau—I can recollect my own feelings, and I have looked steadily around me; yet, so far from coinciding with him in opinion respecting the first dawn of the female character, I will venture to affirm that a girl whose spirits have not been damped by inactivity, or innocence tainted by false shame, will always be a romp, and the doll will never excite attention unless confinement allows her no alternative. Girls and boys, in short, would play harmlessly together, if the distinction of sex was not inculcated long before nature makes any difference—I will go further and affirm, as an indisputable fact, that most of the women in the circle of my observation who have acted like rational creatures, or shown any rigor of intellect, have accidentally been allowed to run wild—as some of the elegant formers of the fair sex would insinuate.

✦ ✦ ✦

## On National Education

Let an enlightened nation then try what effect reason would have to bring [women] back to nature and their duty; and allowing them to share the advantages of education and government with man, see whether they will become better, as they grow wiser and become free. They cannot be injured by the experiment; for it is not in the power of man to render them more insignificant than they are at present.

To render this practicable, day schools, for particular ages, should be established by government, in which boys and girls might be educated together. The school for the younger children, from five to nine years of age, ought to be absolutely free and open to all classes. A sufficient number of masters should also be chosen by a select committee in each parish, to whom any complaint of negligence, &c. might be made, if signed by six of the children's parents.

✦ ✦ ✦

To prevent any of the distinctions of vanity, [the children] should be dressed alike, and all obliged to submit to the same discipline, or leave the school. The school-room ought to be surrounded by a large piece of ground, in which the children might be usefully exercised, for at this age they should not be confined to any sedentary employment for more than an hour at a time. But these relaxations might all be rendered a part of elementary education, for many things improve and amuse the senses, when introduced as a kind of show, to the principles of which, dryly laid down, children would turn a deaf ear. For instance, botany, mechanics, and astronomy. Reading, writing, arithmetic, natural history, and some simple experiments in natural philosophy might fill up the day; but these pursuits should never encroach on gymnastic plays in the open air. The elements of religion, history, the history of man, and politics might also be taught by conversations, in the socratic form.

After the age of nine, girls and boys, intended for domestic employments or mechanical trades, ought to be removed to other schools and receive instruction in some measure appropriated to the destination of each individual, the two sexes being still together in the morning; but in the afternoon, the girls should attend a school, where plain work, mantua making, millinery, &c. would be their employment.

The young people of superior abilities, or fortune, might now be taught, in another school, the dead and living languages, the elements of science, and continue the study of history and politics, on a more extensive scale, which would not exclude polite literature.

Girls and boys still together? I hear some readers ask: yes. And I should not fear any other consequence than that some early attachment might take place; which, whilst it had the best effect on the moral character of the young people might not perfectly agree with the views of the parents, for it will be a long time, I fear, before the world will be so far enlightened that parents, only anxious to render their children virtuous, shall allow them to choose companions for life themselves.

✦ ✦ ✦

In public schools women, to guard against the errors of ignorance, should be taught the elements of anatomy and medicine, not only to enable them to take proper care of their own health but to make them rational nurses of their infants, parents, and husbands; for the bills of mortality [lists of those who have died] are swelled by the blunders of self-willed old women, who give nostrums of their own without knowing any thing of the human frame. It is likewise proper only in a domestic view to make women acquainted with the anatomy of the mind by allowing the sexes to associate together in every pursuit; and by leading them to observe the progress of the human understanding in the improvement of the sciences and arts; never forgetting the science of morality or the study of the political history of mankind.

✦ ✦ ✦

Besides, by the exercise of their bodies and minds women would acquire that mental activity so necessary in the maternal character, united with the fortitude that distinguishes steadiness of conduct from the obstinate perverseness of weakness. For it is dangerous to advise the indolent to be steady, because they instantly become rigorous and to save themselves trouble, punish with severity faults that the patient fortitude of reason might have prevented.

But fortitude presupposes strength of mind; and is strength of mind to be acquired by indolent acquiescence? by asking advice instead of exerting the judgment? by obeying through fear, instead of practicing the forbearance, which we all stand in need of ourselves?—The conclusion which I wish to draw is obvious; make women rational creatures, and free citizens, and they will quickly become good wives, and mothers; that is—if men do not neglect the duties of husbands and fathers.

## ✦ *Biographical Sketch*

**Born:** *April 1759, London, England*

**Died:** *September 10, 1797, Somers, Town, England; age 38*

**Buried:** *Old St. Pancras Churchyard, Somers Town, England; remains moved to Bournemouth in 1851*

Two hundred years after her death, Mary Wollstonecraft's life and work remain striking testimony to woman's struggle to gain economic and social justice while achieving some degree of harmony in personal life.

A fascinating and paradoxical woman, Mary Wollstonecraft was branded a "whore" and an "unsex'd female" by her critics during her lifetime and lauded as a brilliant thinker and author by her many admirers.

The controversy about Wollstonecraft's character and lifestyle as a woman in the eighteenth century resonate in the contemporary age. On one hand a tireless advocate for female intellectual, domestic, and political emancipation, she was also an obsessive lover—twice appealing to married men who rejected her offer to join their families as a live-in mistress. It is also ironic that Wollstonecraft, the famous author of the powerful polemic *A Vindication of the Rights of Woman,* twice attempted suicide after having been spurned by lovers. These inconsistencies reveal Wollstonecraft's painfully real embodiment of the plight of women in her era.

Born in London in April 1759, Wollstonecraft was the second of seven children and the daughter of a domineering, philandering, alcoholic father and a subservient mother. Her early years of emotional and economic deprivation in this unhappy family impressed upon her the evils of poverty and the troubling nature of the institution of marriage, which she later either vilified or idealized in her own writings.

When she was sixteen, Wollstonecraft formed an intense attachment to a girl named Fanny Blood, whose own family was even poorer and more pitiable than the Wollstonecrafts. This passionate friendship fulfilled Wollstonecraft's need for love and intimacy, and her connection to her friend continued even after Fanny's death from consumption in 1785. Wollstonecraft, who was present during Blood's last days in Portugal, named her own first daughter Fanny. Her grief at the loss of this dear companion is evident even in her last completed book, *Letters Written during a Short Residence in Sweden, Norway and Denmark.*

Wollstonecraft spent her early professional life in several of the roles to which women were then limited: teacher, governess, and companion. She struggled as the exhausted teacher of a small school, governess under an officious female employer, and paid companion to a wealthy and demanding elderly woman. Along with these respectable but severely limiting positions, Wollstonecraft added the additional burden of assigning herself primary caretaker to her own and Fanny Blood's family.

Intellectual salvation came to Wollstonecraft through the events of the late eighteenth century, especially the French Revolution. In her essay *A Vindication of the Rights of Men* (a reply to Edmund Burke's conservative argument against the revolution), Wollstonecraft passionately defended the endless potential of human reason to improve and eventually perfect human nature. These convictions were a direct result of Wollstonecraft's allegiance to the Unitarian Christianity she embraced in objection to the pessimistic, Calvinist view of humanity preached by the orthodoxy of her day.

Wollstonecraft found mutually supportive companionship with successful author and rationalist William Godwin, whom she married after becoming pregnant with his child. On August 30, 1797, she bore the daughter who became Mary Shelley, the famous author of *Frankenstein.* Eleven days later, Mary Wollstonecraft died from an infection following childbirth. Though she was only thirty-eight years old, she left a remarkable intellectual and literary legacy that still greatly informs and inspires feminist thought.

*Biographical Sketch by* VICTORIA WEINSTEIN

## ✦ Writings of Mary Wollstonecraft

*Letters Written During a Short Residence in Sweden, Norway and Denmark.* London: Joseph Johnson, 1796; Lincoln: University of Nebraska Press, 1976.

*Mary, A Fiction.* London: Joseph Johnson, 1788; Reprint, New York: Garland, 1974.

*Original Stories from Real Life: With Conversations Calculated to Regulate the Affections and Form the Mind to Truth and Goodness.* London: Joseph Johnson, 1788.

*Thoughts on the Education of Daughters: With Reflections on Female Conduct, in the More Important Duties of Life.* London: Joseph Johnson, 1787; Reprint, New York: Garland, 1974.

*A Vindication of the Rights of Men, in a Letter to the Right Honorable Edmund Burke.* London: Joseph Johnson, 1790; Reprint, Scholar's Facsimile and Reprints, 1960.

*A Vindication of the Rights of Woman with Strictures on Political and Moral Subjects.* London: Joseph Johnson, 1792; New York: W. W. Norton, 1975.

*The Wrongs of Woman: or, Maria.* New York: Oxford University Press, 1976 (or as *Maria or the Wrongs of Woman,* W. W. Norton, 1975).

## ✦ Biographical Resources

Falco, Maria J., ed. *Feminist Interpretations of Mary Wollstonecraft.* University Park: Pennsylvania State University Press, 1996.

Ingpen, Roger, ed. *The Love Letters of Mary Wollstonecraft to Gilbert Imlay, with a Prefatory Memoir.* London: Hutchison, 1908.

Kurtz, Benjamin P., and Carrie C. Autrey, eds. *Four New Letters of Mary Wollstonecraft and Helen Maria Williams.* Berkeley: University of California Press, 1937.

Sunstein, Emily W. *A Different Face: The Life of Mary Wollstonecraft.* New York: Harper & Row, 1975.

Todd, Janet. *A Wollstonecraft Anthology.* New York: Columbia University Press, 1990.

Tomalin, Claire. *The Life and Death of Mary Wollstonecraft.* London: Penguin Books, 1992.

Wardle, Ralph M., ed. *Godwin and Mary: Letters of William Godwin and Mary Wollstonecraft.* Lawrence: University of Kansas Press, 1966.

———. *Collected Letters of Mary Wollstonecraft.* Ithaca, NY: Cornell University Press, 1979.

# On Female Education

## From Article in *Monthly Repository,* 1823

HARRIET MARTINEAU (1802–1876), *a radical British Unitarian, was a prolific writer on a wide range of topics. Her astute, sometimes acerbic comments about the social realities she observed both at home and during her two-year trip across the United States brought both praise and condemnation. An independent, somewhat eccentric intellectual, she became instantly famous with her first book,* Illustrations of Political Economy, *which made her self-supporting. Her major life efforts were devoted to the cause of equal rights and educational opportunities for women. In this article, writing under the pseudonym* Discipulus, *she called for a full program of academic studies for girls, arguing that females were as intelligent and capable as males.*

See the Biographical Sketch on pages 174–178.

Norwich, November, 1822

In discussing the subject of Female Education, it is not so much my object to inquire whether the natural powers of women be equal to those of men as to show the expediency of giving proper scope and employment to the powers which they do possess. It may be as well, notwithstanding, to inquire whether the difference be as great as is generally supposed between the mental structure of men and of women.

Doubtless the formation of the mind must depend in a great degree on the structure of the body. From this cause the strength of mind observable in men is supposed to arise; and the delicacy of the female mind is thought to be in agreement with the bodily frame. But it is impossible to ascertain how much may depend on early education; nor can we solve our doubts on this head by turning our view to savage countries, where, if the bodily strength be nearly equal in the two sexes, their minds are alike sunk in ignorance and darkness. In our own country, we find that as long as the studies of children of both sexes continue the same, the progress they make is equal. After the rudiments of knowledge have been obtained, in the cultivated ranks of society (of which alone I mean to speak), the boy goes on continually increasing his stock of information, it being his only employment to store and exercise his mind for future years; while the girl is probably confined to low pursuits, her aspirings after knowledge are subdued, she is taught to believe that solid information is unbecoming her sex, almost her whole time is expended on light accomplishments, and thus before she is sensible of her powers, they are checked in their growth; chained down to mean objects, to rise no more; and when the natural consequences of this mode of treatment arise, all mankind agree that the abilities of women are far inferior to those of men. But in the few instances where a contrary mode of treatment has been pursued, where fair play has been given to the faculties, even without much assistance, what has almost invariably been the result? Has it not been evident that the female mind, though in many respects differently constituted from that of man, may be well brought into comparison with his? If she wants his enterprising spirit, the deficiency is made up by perseverance in what she does undertake; for his ambition, she has a thirst for knowledge; and for his ready perception, she has unwearied application.

It is proof sufficient to my mind, that there is no natural deficiency of power, that, unless proper objects are supplied to women to employ their faculties, their energies are exerted improperly. Some aim they must have, and if no good one is presented to them, they must seek for a bad one.

✦ ✦ ✦

I wish to imply by what I have said not that great stores of information are as necessary to women as to men but that as much care should be taken of the formation of their minds. Their attainments cannot in general be so great, because they have their own appropriate duties and peculiar employments, the neglect of which nothing can excuse; but I contend that these duties will be better performed if the powers be rationally employed. If the whole mind be exercised and strengthened, it will bring more vigor to the performance of its duties in any particular province.

The first great objection which is made to enlightening the female mind is that if engaged in the pursuit of knowledge, women neglect their appropriate duties and peculiar employments.

2nd. That the greatest advances that the female mind can make in knowledge must still fall far short of the attainments of the other sex.

3rd. That the vanity so universally ascribed to the sex is apt to be inflated by any degree of proficiency in knowledge and that women therefore become forgetful of the subordinate station assigned them by law, natural and divine.

To the first objection I answer that such a pursuit of knowledge as shall lead women to neglect their peculiar duties is not that cultivation of mind for the utility of which I am contending. But these duties may be well performed without engaging the whole time and attention. If "great thoughts constitute great minds," what can be expected from a woman whose whole intellect is employed on the trifling cares and comparatively mean occupations, to which the advocates for female ignorance would condemn her? These cares and these occupations were allotted to women to enable them to smooth our way through life; they were designed as a means to this end and should never be pursued as the end itself. The knowledge of these necessary acts is so easily acquired, and they are so easily performed, that an active mind will feel a dismal vacuity, a craving after something nobler and better to employ the thoughts in the intervals of idleness which must occur when these calls of duty are answered, and if nothing nobler and better is presented to it, it will waste its energies in the pursuit of folly, if not of vice, and thus continually perpetuate the faults of the sex.

Some will perhaps say, "If household occupations are insufficient to exercise the mind, the wide field of charity is open to the employment of its energies." It is so. But how inefficient is benevolence when not directed by knowledge! And how comparatively faint will be the exertions in the cause when the views are bounded, the motives narrow and even selfish (for ignorance is the mother of selfishness), and charity pursued more as a present employment, than with the desire of doing permanent good to the objects of this shallow benevolence! How different is this from the charity of an enlightened mind, of a mind which, enlarged by knowledge, can comprehend extensive views, can design not only the present relief of misery, but can look forward to the permanent improvement of its kind; which, understanding the workings of the mind and able to profit by the experience of others, can choose the best means for the attainment of certain ends, and thus by uniting knowledge and judgment with benevolence can make its efforts doubly efficient!

✦ ✦ ✦

If we consider woman as the guardian and instructress of infancy, her claims to cultivation of mind become doubly urgent. It is evident that if the soul of the teacher is narrow and contracted, that of the pupil cannot be enlarged. If we consider that the first years of childhood exert an influence over the whole future life, we cannot be too careful to preserve our children from the effects of ignorance and prejudice on their young minds. It has been frequently and justly observed that almost all men, remarkable for talents or virtue, have had excellent mothers, to the early influence of whose noble qualities the future superiority of their children was mainly to be ascribed. If this be true, what might not be hoped from the labors of a race of enlightened mothers, who would early impress on their children's minds lessons of piety and wisdom, and who would make the first sentiments of their souls noble and enlarged, who would take in at one comprehensive view all that was to be done to render them what they ought to be, and who would render their first instruction subservient to the objects to be afterwards pursued! If such were to be the foundation of character, what might not the super-structure be!

It may be said that many minds have been great, capable of conceiving and executing noble designs, without any advantages of education. It is certainly true, but these minds have been too aspiring to be chained down by the fetters of ignorance; they have become great in spite of disadvantages and not in consequence of them; and had their powers been cultivated, their efforts would probably have been better directed and doubly successful. . . .

With respect to the second objection, viz. that the greatest advances which the female mind can make in knowledge must fall far short of the attainments of the other sex,—I allow that the acquirements of women can seldom equal those of men, and it is not desirable that they should. I do not wish to excite a spirit of rivalry between the sexes; I do not desire that many females should seek for fame as authors. I only wish that their powers should be so employed that they should not be obliged to seek amusements beneath them and injurious to them. I wish them to be companions to men, instead of playthings or servants, one of which an ignorant woman must commonly be. If they are called to be wives, a sensible mind is an essential qualification for the domestic character; if they remain single, liberal pursuits are absolutely necessary to preserve them from the faults so generally attributed to that state, and so justly and inevitably, while the mind is buried in darkness. . . .

With respect to the third objection, viz., that the vanity so universally ascribed to the sex is apt to be inflated by any degree of proficiency in knowledge and that women, therefore, become forgetful of the subordinate stature assigned them by law, natural and divine: the most important part of education, the implanting of religious principles, must be in part neglected if the share of knowledge which women may appropriate should be suffered to inflate their vanity or excite feelings of pride. Christian humility should be one of the first requisites in female education, and till it is attained every acquirement of every kind will become a cause of self-exultation, and those accomplishments which are the most rare, will of course be looked upon with the most self-complacency. But if the taste for knowledge were more generally infused; and if proficiency in the attainments I have mentioned were more common, there would be much less pedantry than there is at present; for when acquirements of this kind are no longer remarkable, they cease to afford a subject for pride. I suppose, when knowledge was rare among men, many of those who had made some proficiency were as pedantic as the blue stockings of the present day. As the spread of information extended there was less cause for conceit, and the case would be the same with the female sex. This is a fact, which is proved from year to year, for female education is rapidly improving, and the odious pedantry to which it at first gave rise is less observable and will, ere long, I hope, be more a name than a reality. . . .

When woman is allowed to claim her privileges as an intellectual being, the folly, the frivolity, and all the mean vices and faults which have hitherto been the reproach of the sex will gradually disappear. As she finds nobler objects presented to her grasp, and that her rank in the scale of being is elevated, she will engraft the vigorous qualities of the mind of man on her own blooming virtues and insinuate into his mind those softer graces and milder beauties, which will smooth the ruggedness of his character.

Surely this is the natural state of things, and to this perfection will they arrive, if the improvement of the female mind proceeds with the same rapidity which we have now reason to anticipate. . . .

I cannot better conclude than with the hope that . . . examples of what may be done may excite a noble emulation . . . [and] a conviction of the value of the female mind, as shall overcome our long-cherished prejudices and induce us to give our earnest endeavors to the promotion of woman's best interests.

*Discipulus*

## ✦ *Biographical Sketch*

**Born:** *June 12, 1802, Norwich, England*
**Died:** *June 27, 1876, Ambleside, England, age 74*
**Buried:** *Birmingham, England*

Prolific as a didactic writer of nearly two thousand articles and other writings, Harriet Martineau promoted women's education and rights, popularized economic theory, and publicized the American abolitionist movement. She was also known for travel writings that reflected her religiously liberal perspectives. Seeing her task as a devotion to truth, she moved from the confines of the Unitarian circles of her early career to expound necessarianism, mesmerism, and positivism.

Born the sixth of eight children, Harriet Martineau remembered her childhood as distressing. Malnourished and lacking the senses of smell and taste, she had hypersensitivities and anxieties, a somber preoccupation with her imperfections, and a sense that her mother was unappreciative of her. She remembered crying daily and as an adolescent thought of committing suicide so that she could join God. Her increasingly poor hearing from the age of twelve was only slowly acknowledged by her family. Despite her deafness, she did not use an ear horn until her late twenties.

Both her father and mother were Unitarians who believed that all of their children should receive a comprehensive education. During early years, Harriet was tutored, but also teased, by older siblings. She attended the schools of the Reverend Isaac Perry, a recent convert to Unitarianism, and an aunt in Bristol, who gave her the affection she had not received from her mother. She developed a passion for translation of classic and modern languages. In 1821, when her beloved younger brother, James, went away to college, he suggested that she write to alleviate the loneliness caused by his departure.

Martineau's first published article, "Female Writers on Practical Divinity," appeared in the Unitarian *Monthly Repository* in 1822. The next year, in "On Female Education," she asserted, under a male pseudonym, that intellectual differences between the sexes were the result of educational disparity. Justifying improved education as a continuation of the improvement brought by Christianity, she maintained that marital companionship and child development would benefit when women used their potential, without disturbing their subordination or necessary domestic functions. Martineau submitted three essays anonymously to a contest, addressing why Catholics, Jews, and Moslems should become Unitarian, and all three won. In the five years beginning with 1826, she contributed over one hundred reviews, articles, and poems to the *Monthly Repository.*

Martineau's father died in 1826, and her intended husband suffered a breakdown. She never again considered marriage. Collapse of the family business in 1829 necessitated that she sew for income, ask remuneration for her writing, and live in London. Although she had trouble finding a publisher, Martineau was motivated to write on economics after reading Jane Marcet's popularization of political economy. Following a pattern derived from the work of James Mill, her weekly articles advocating the ideas of Adam Smith, Thomas Robert Malthus, and David Ricardo were immensely popular, selling up to ten thousand copies each. Reflecting Joseph Priestley's and David Hartley's philosophy of necessarianism, she cites "natural laws" operating throughout the universe, with inevitable consequences and without interference from random will, human or divine. In over two years of installments, only one article (which dared to broach birth control) was attacked as unfeminine. Reprinted in bound volumes, her *Illustrations of Political Economy* was read by the upper classes, including Princess Victoria.

Harriet Martineau was a literary celebrity when she visited the United States from 1834 to 1836. She frequently accepted hospitality from Unitarian ministers, including William Ellery Channing in Boston, William Henry Furness in Philadelphia, and Samuel Gilman in Charleston. She was also welcomed by established Unitarian writer Catharine Maria Sedgewick and aspiring writers Harriet Beecher and Margaret Fuller[14] (who introduced her to Ralph Waldo Emerson).

Written on the sea voyage to the United States, *How to Observe Morals and Manners* is regarded as an early attempt at sociological systemization. With this theoretical framework, she wrote *Society in America,* published in 1837, an assessment of whether the new society lived up to its democratic principles.

Although one of her political economy stories, "Demerara," critically portrayed slavery, Martineau was hospitably treated in the South. Martineau's supportive comments at an antislavery meeting she attended with Charles and Eliza Cabot Follen,[15] however, led to her being threatened and socially shunned during the second half of her American journey. Martineau's books on the United States and her article "The Martyr Age in the United States," which appeared in the *Westmin-*

*ster Review* and was reprinted as a pamphlet, introduced the British public to the struggles of the American abolitionist movement in 1838. She was one of the first to analogize women's situation with slavery. Ninety of her letters appeared in New York's abolitionist newspaper, *The National Anti-Slavery Standard.*

Throughout her life, Martineau managed to translate her experiences into writings that caught the public interest. A painful illness (from an ovarian cyst) in the 1840s became *Life in the Sick-Room.* Contact with mesmerists (hypnotists) became "Letters on Mesmerism," published in *The Athenaeum* in 1844. Her trip to the Middle East prompted her to consider similarities in the development of religions and led to *Letters of Man's Social Nature and Development,* which revealed her criticisms of organized religion and the clergy and contained her declaration of atheism. This was read with horror by Unitarians and people of more traditional religious beliefs.

Martineau's political concerns motivated other writings. She published *Dawn Island* in 1845 as a fundraiser for the Anti-Corn Law League, which aimed to rectify unfairness to farmers and the poor. And because of her own negative childhood experience, she urged parents to be sensitive to the emotional and developmental needs of children as individuals in *Household Economy* (1849). Because she thought she was dying, she completed her candid, spiritual *Autobiography,* using many letters demanded back from friends and then destroyed. It was not issued until after her death in 1877, edited by Maria Weston Chapman,[16] a Boston abolitionist correspondent, who added eulogies.

Martineau wrote leading articles, reviews, obituaries, and other pieces for the liberal *Daily News* for fourteen years. Appearing several times a week, these commentaries on current political events and societal trends were often reprinted in other newspapers. Topics included education for women, changes in divorce and property laws regarding women, nursing and medical careers for women, and women's suffrage.

Harriet Martineau died of bronchitis in 1876. She wrote her own obituary, which was published by the *Daily News.* As biographer Susan Hoecher-Drysdale concludes, to the extent possible without the vote, Harriet Martineau "wished to be part of the debates and events of her time."[17]

*Biographical Sketch by* IRENE BAROS-JOHNSON

## ✦ Writings of Harriet Martineau

*Autobiography, with Memorials by Maria Weston Chapman.* London: Elder, 1877.

*Dawn Island: A Tale.* Manchester, England: J. Gadsby, 1845.

*The Essential Faith of the Universal Church: Deduced from the Sacred Records.* London: Unitarian Association, 1831.

*The Faith as Unfolded by Many Prophets.* London: Unitarian Association, 1832.

"On Female Education." *Monthly Repository* 18 (1823): 77–81.

"Female Industry." *Edinburgh Review* 109 (April 1859): 151–173.

"Female Writers of Practical Divinity." *Monthly Repository* 17 (October 1822): 593–596.

*Forest and Game-Law Tales.* London: Edward Moxon, 1845–1846.

"Freedom or Slavery?" *Household Words* 9 (1854): 537–542.

*The Hour and the Man: An Historical Romance.* London: Cassell, 1841.

*Household Education.* London: Edward Moxon, c. 1848.

*How to Observe Morals and Manners.* London: Charles Knight, 1838.

*Illustrations of Political Economy.* 9 vols. London: Charles Fox, 1832–1834.

*Letters on Mesmerism.* London: Edward Moxon, 1845.

*Letters on the Law of Man's Social Nature and Development.* With Henry G. Atkinson. London: John Chapman, 1851.

*Life in the Sick-Room: Essays by an Invalid.* London: Edward Moxon, 1844.

*The "Manifest Destiny" of the American Union.* New York: American Anti-Slavery Society, 1857.

*The Martyr Age of the United States.* New York: S. W. Benedict, 1839.

*My Servant Rachel: A Tale.* London: Houlston, 1838.

*Principle and Practice; or the Orphan Family.* Wellington, England: Houlston, 1827.

*Providence as Manifested through Israel: An Essay . . . Issued by the British and Foreign Unitarian Association and Addressed to the Jews.* London: British and Foreign Unitarian Association, 1831.

*Retrospect of Western Travel.* London: Saunders & Olney, 1838.

*Society in America.* London: Saunders & Olney, 1837.

## ✦ Biographical Resources

Arbuckle, Elisabeth Sanders, ed. *Harriet Martineau's Letters to Fanny Wedgwood.* Stanford, CA: Stanford University Press, 1983.

Banks, Olive. *The Biographical Dictionary of British Feminists.* New York: New York University Press, 1985.

Fielding, K. J., and Anne Smith. "Hard Times and the Factory Controversy: Dickens vs. Harriet Martineau." *Nineteenth Century Fiction* 24 (1970): 404–427.

Halbersleben, Karen I. *Women's Participation in the British Antislavery Movement 1824–1865.* Lewiston, NY: Edwin Mellon, 1993.

Hoecher-Drysdale, Susan. *Harriet Martineau: First Woman Sociologist.* Oxford: Berg, 1992.

Kelley, Mary, ed. *The Power of Her Sympathy: The Autobiography and Journal of Catharine Maria Sedgwick.* Boston: Massachusetts Historical Society, 1993.

Myers, Mitzi. "Unmothered Daughter and Radical Reformer: Harriet Martineau's Career." In *The Lost Tradition: Mothers and Daughters in Literature,* edited by Cathy Davidson and E. M. Broner. New York: Frederick Unger, 1980.

Pichanick, Valerie Kossew. *Harriet Martineau: The Woman and Her Work, 1802–76.* Ann Arbor: University of Michigan Press, 1980.

Rivlin, Joseph B. *Harriet Martineau, a Bibliography of her Separately Printed Works.* New York: New York Public Library, 1937.

Sanders, Valerie. *Harriet Martineau: Selected Letters.* Oxford: Clarendon Press, 1990.

———. "The Most Manlike Woman in Three Kingdoms: Harriet Martineau and the Brownings." *Browning Society Notes* 9 (1979): 9–13.

———. *Reason over Passion: Harriet Martineau and the Victorian Novel.* Sussex, England: Harvester Press, 1986.

Webb, R. K. *Harriet Martineau: A Radical Victorian.* New York: Columbia University Press, 1960.

Weiner, Gaby. "Harriet Martineau: A Reassessment (1802–1876)." In *Feminist Theorists,* edited by Dale Spender. New York: Pantheon Books, 1983.

Yates, Gayle Graham. *Harriet Martineau on Women.* New Brunswick, NJ: Rutgers University Press, 1985.

# School Teaching

## Journal Entry, Spring 1837

MARGARET FULLER (1810–1850), *a Unitarian and a Transcendentalist, was one of the best-educated, most influential women of her time. In her desire to be self-supporting, she initially chose teaching as a way to use her mind and talents, since other occupations were closed to females. She first worked in the experimental school in Boston run by A. Bronson Alcott, also a Unitarian and the father of Louisa May Alcott, and then became head of Greene Street School in Providence, Rhode Island, in the spring of 1837.*

*In the following selection, Margaret Fuller outlined her educational philosophy and approach to teaching, particularly as it applied to younger children. Students liked and respected her, for she utilized techniques and exhibited an attitude that would be termed* progressive education *in the twentieth century. She was particularly enthusiastic about the efforts to train teachers for the new common schools then being established throughout the United States.*

See the Biographical Sketch on pages 27–29.

The new institution of which I am to be "Lady Superior" was dedicated last Saturday. People talk to me of the good I am to do; but the last fortnight has been so occupied in the task of arranging many scholars of various ages and unequal training that I cannot yet realize this new era.

The gulf is vast, wider than I could have conceived possible, between me and my pupils; but the sight of such deplorable ignorance, such absolute burial of the best powers, as I find in some instances, makes me comprehend, better than before, how such a man as Mr. Alcott could devote his life to renovate elementary education. I have pleasant feelings when I see that a new world has already been opened to them.

Nothing of the vulgar feeling towards teachers, too often to be observed in schools, exists towards me. The pupils seem to reverence my tastes and opinions in all things; they are docile, decorous, and try hard to please; they are in awe of my displeasure but delighted whenever permitted to associate with me on familiar terms. As I treat them like ladies, they are anxious to prove that they deserve to be so treated.

There is room here for a great move in the cause of education, and if I could resolve on devoting five or six years to this school, a good work might, doubtless, be done. Plans are becoming complete in my mind, ways and means continually offer, and, so far as I have tried them, they succeed. I am left almost as much at liberty as if no other person was concerned. Some sixty scholars are more or less under my care, and many of them begin to walk in the new paths pointed out. General activity of mind, accuracy in processes, constant looking for principles, and search after the good and the beautiful are the habits I strive to develop.

I will write a short record of the last day at school. For a week past I have given the classes in philosophy, rhetoric, history, poetry, and moral science, short lectures on the true objects of study, with advice as to their future course; and today, after recitation, I expressed my gratification that the minds of so many had been opened to the love of good and beauty.

Then came the time for last words. First, I called into the recitation room the boys who had been under my care. They are nearly all interesting and have showed a chivalric feeling in their treatment of me. People talk of women not being able to govern boys; but I have always found it a very easy task. He must be a coarse boy, indeed, who, when addressed in a resolute, yet gentle, manner by a lady will not try to merit her esteem. These boys have always rivaled one another in respectful behavior. I spoke a few appropriate words to each, mentioning his peculiar errors and good deeds, mingling some advice with more love, which will, I hope, make it remembered. We took a sweet farewell. With the younger girls I had a similar interview.

Then I summoned the elder girls, who have been my especial charge. I reminded them of the ignorance in which some of them were found and showed them how all my efforts had necessarily been directed to stimulating their minds,—leaving undone much which, under other circumstances, would have been deemed indispensable. I thanked them for the favorable opinion of my government which they had so generally expressed but specified three instances in which I had been unjust. I thanked them, also, for the moral beauty of their conduct, bore witness that an appeal to conscience had never failed, and told them of my happiness in having the faith thus confirmed that young persons can be best guided by addressing their highest nature. I declared my consciousness of having combined, not only in speech but in heart, tolerance and delicate regard for the convictions of their parents, with fidelity to my own, frankly uttered. I assured them of my true friendship, proved by my never having cajoled or caressed them into good. Every word of praise had been earned; all my influence over them was rooted in reality; I had never softened nor palliated their faults; I had appealed not to their weakness but to their strength; I had offered to them, always, the loftiest motives and had made every other end subordinate to that of spiritual growth. With a heartfelt blessing, I dismissed them; but none stirred, and we all sat for some moments, weeping. Then I went round the circle and bade each, separately, farewell.

✦ ✦ ✦

# Conversations

## From Letters, Autumn 1839

*Greatly admired for the brilliance of her writing and speeches, in 1839* MARGARET FULLER (1810–1850) *launched a series of Conversations usually held in Elizabeth Peabody's foreign language bookstore in Boston.*[18] *These gatherings were a means of providing education to adult women. Tickets were sold, and the participants were expected to prepare for the sessions and engage in discussions. In her letters, reprinted in her* Memoirs, *Margaret Fuller set forth her rationale for holding the Conversations—to help women develop their abilities to think critically and overcome their reticence to speak in public—and her plan for the topics to be discussed. Later, she commented with some surprise and obvious delight on the success of her efforts.*

See the Biographical Sketch on pages 27–29.

### To Sophia Dana Ripley

My dear friend:—The advantages of a weekly meeting for conversation, might be great enough to repay the trouble of attendance, if they consisted only in supplying a point of union to well-educated and thinking women, in a city which, with great pretensions to mental refinement, boasts, at present, nothing of the kind, and where I have heard many, of mature age, wish for some such means of stimulus and cheer, and those younger, for a place where they could state their doubts and difficulties, with a hope of gaining aid from the experience or aspirations of others. And, if my office were only to suggest topics, which would lead to conversation of a better order than is usual at social meetings, and to turn back the current when digressing into personalities or commonplaces, so that what is valuable in the experience of each might be brought to bear upon all, I should think the object not unworthy of the effort.

But my ambition goes much further. It is to pass in review the departments of thought and knowledge and endeavor to place them in due relation to one another in our minds. To systematize thought, and give a precision and clearness in which our sex are so deficient, chiefly, I think, because they have so few inducements to test and classify what they receive. To ascertain what pursuits are best suited to us, in our time and state of society, and how we may make best use of our means for building up the life of thought upon the life of action.

Could a circle be assembled in earnest, desirous to answer the questions—What were we born to do? and how shall we do it?—which so few ever propose to themselves till their best years are gone by, I should think the undertaking a noble one, and, if my resources should prove sufficient to make me its moving spring, I should be willing to give to it a large portion of those coming years, which will, as I hope, be my best. I look upon it with no blind enthusiasm, nor unlimited faith, but with a confidence that I have attained a distinct perception of means, which, if there are persons competent to direct them, can supply a great want and promote really high objects. So far as I have tried them yet, they have met with success so much beyond my hopes, that my faith will not easily be shaken nor my earnestness chilled. Should I, however, be disappointed in Boston, I could hardly hope that such a plan could be brought to bear on general society in any other city of the United States. But I do not fear, if a good beginning can be made. I am confident that twenty persons cannot be brought together from better motives than vanity or pedantry, to talk upon such subjects as we propose, without finding in themselves great deficiencies, which they will be very desirous to supply.

Should the enterprise fail, it will be either from incompetence in me or that sort of vanity in them which wears the garb of modesty. On the first of these points, I need not speak. I cannot be supposed to have felt so much the wants of others, without feeling my own still more deeply. And, from the depth of this feeling, and the earnestness it gave, such power as I have yet exerted has come. Of course, those who are inclined to meet me feel a confidence in me and should they be disappointed, I shall regret it not solely or most on my own account. I have not given my gauge without measuring my capacity to sustain defeat. For the other, I know it is very hard to lay aside the shelter of vague generalities, the art of coterie criticism, and the "delicate disdains" of *good society,* and fearlessly meet the light, even though it flow from the sun of truth. Yet, as without such generous courage, nothing of value can be learned or done, I hope to see many capable of it; willing that others should think their sayings crude, shallow, or tasteless, if, by such unpleasant means, they may attain real health and vigor, which need no aid from rouge or candlelight to brave the light of the world.

Since I saw you, I have been told of persons who are desirous to join the class, "if only they need not talk." I am so sure that the success of the whole depends on conversation being general that I do not wish any one to come who does not intend, if possible, to take an active part. No one will be forced, but those who do not talk will not derive the same advantages with those who openly state their impressions and can consent to have it known that they learn by blundering, as is the destiny of man here below. And general silence, or side talks, would paralyze me. I should feel coarse and misplaced, were I to harangue over-much. In former instances, I have been able to make it easy and even pleasant, to twenty-five out of thirty, to bear their part, to question, to define, to state, and examine opinions. If I could not do as much now, I should consider myself as unsuccessful, and should withdraw. But I shall expect communication to be effected by degrees and to do a great deal myself at the first meetings. My method has been to open a subject—for instance, Poetry, as expressed in–

External Nature;
The life of man;
Literature;
The fine arts;

or, the history of a nation to be studied in–

Its religious and civil institutions;
Its literature and arts;
The characters of its great men;

and, after as good a general statement as I know how to make, select a branch of the subject, and lead others to give their thoughts upon it.

When they have not been successful in verbal utterance of their thoughts, I have asked them to attempt it in writing. At the next meeting, I would read these "skarts[19] of pen and ink" aloud and canvass their adequacy, without mentioning the names of the writers. I found this less necessary, as I proceeded, and my companions attained greater command both of thought and language; but for a time it was useful and may be now. Great advantage in point of discipline may be derived from even this limited use of the pen.

I do not wish, at present, to pledge myself to any course of subjects. Generally, I may say, they will be such as literature and the arts present in endless profusion. Should a class be brought together, I should wish, first to ascertain our common ground, and, in the course of a few meetings, should see whether it be practicable to follow out the design in my mind, which, as yet, would look too grand on paper.

Let us see whether there will be any organ, before noting down the music to which it may give breath.

✦ ✦ ✦

## To Ralph Waldo Emerson

My class is prosperous. I was so fortunate as to rouse, at once, the tone of simple earnestness, which can scarcely, when once awakened, cease to vibrate. All seem in a glow and quite as receptive as I wish. They question and examine, yet follow leadings; and thoughts, not opinions, have ruled the hour every time. There are about twenty-five members, and every one, I believe, full of interest. The first time, ten took part in the conversation; the last, still more. Mrs. — came out in a way that surprised me. She seems to have shaken off a wonderful number of films. She showed pure vision, sweet sincerity, and much talent. Mrs. — keeps us in good order, and takes care that Christianity and morality are not forgotten. The first day's topic was the genealogy of heaven and earth; then the Will, (Jupiter); the Understanding (Mercury); the second day's, the celestial inspiration of genius, perception and transmission of divine law, (Apollo); the terrene inspiration; the impassioned abandonment of genius, (Bacchus). Of the thunderbolt, the caduceus, the ray, and the grape, having disposed as well as might be, we came to the wave, and the seashell it molds to Beauty, and Love her parent and her child.

I assure you, there is more Greek than Bostonian spoken at the meetings; and we may have pure honey of Hymettus to give you yet.

✦ ✦ ✦

### To Another Friend

The circle I meet interests me. So even devoutly thoughtful seems their spirit, that, from the very first, I took my proper place and never had the feeling I dreaded, of display, of a paid Corinne. I feel as I would, truly a teacher and a guide. All are intelligent; five or six have talent. But I am never driven home for ammunition; never put to any expense; never truly called out. What I have is always enough; though I feel how superficially I am treating my subject.

✦ ✦ ✦

# Profession of Teaching

## From Column in the *New York Tribune,* September 30, 1845

*After the publication of several major books,* MARGARET FULLER'S (1810–1850) *reputation as a writer and significance as a thinker grew beyond her Boston-area audience. In 1844, she accepted an invitation from Horace Greeley to come to New York as literary critic for the* New York Tribune. *In her columns, she continued to raise questions about the role of women similar to those she had examined earlier in* Woman in the Nineteenth Century, *but her focus here was on practical, rather than theoretical, issues. As a columnist, she tied her ideas to events of the day.*

*The following selection was written in response to the gathering in city hall of several hundred women engaged in the sewing trade to form the Ladies' Industrial Association.*[20] *Margaret Fuller argued that it was evident that, despite the rhetoric about women remaining in "their sphere," many women worked outside the home out of necessity. She called for opening various professions to women, particularly teaching and nursing.*

See the Biographical Sketch on pages 27–29.

The other profession is that of teacher, for which women are peculiarly adapted by their nature, superiority in tact, quickness of sympathy, gentleness, patience, and a clear and animated manner in narration or description. To form a good teacher, should be added to this, sincere modesty combined with firmness, liberal views, with a power and will to liberalize them still further, a good method, and habits of exact and thorough investigation. In the two last requisites women are generally deficient, but there are now many shining examples to prove that if they are immethodical and superficial as teachers, it is because it is the custom so to teach them, and that when aware of these faults, they can and will correct them.

The profession is of itself an excellent one for the improvement of the teacher during that interim between youth and maturity when the mind needs testing, tempering, and to review and rearrange the knowledge it has acquired. The natural method of doing this for one's self is to attempt teaching others; those years also are the best of the practical teacher. The teacher should be near the pupil, both in years and feelings; no oracle but the eldest brother or sister of the pupil. More experience and years form the lecturer and director of studies but injure the powers as to familiar teaching.

These are just the years of leisure in the lives even of those women who are to enter the domestic sphere, and this calling most of all compatible with a constant progress as to qualifications for that.

Viewing the matter thus, it may be well seen that we should hail with joy the assurance that sixty thousand *female* teachers are wanted, and more likely to be, and that a plan is projected which looks wise, liberal, and generous, to afford the means, to those whose hearts answer to this high calling, of obeying their dictates.

The plan is to have Cincinnati as a central point, where teachers shall be for a short time received, examined, and prepared for their duties. By mutual agreement and cooperation of the various sects, funds are to be raised and teachers provided, according to the wants and tendencies of the various locations now destitute. What is to be done for them centrally is for suitable persons to examine into the various kinds of fitness, communicate some general views whose value has been tested, and counsel adapted to the difficulties and advantages of their new positions. The central committee are to have the charge of raising funds, and finding teachers, and places where teachers are wanted.

The passage of thoughts, teachers, and funds will be from East to West—the course of sunlight upon this earth.

The plan is offered as the most extensive and pliant means of doing a good and preventing ill to this nation, by means of a national education, whose normal school shall have an invariable object in the search after truth and the diffusion of the means of knowledge, while its form shall be plastic according to the wants of the time. This normal school promises to have good effects, for it proposes worthy aims through simple means, and the motive for its formation and support seems to be disinterested philanthropy.

It promises to eschew the bitter spirit of sectarianism and proselytism, else we, for one party, could have nothing to do with it. Men, no doubt, have oftentimes been kept from absolute famine by the wheat with which such tares are mingled; but we believe the time is come when a purer and more generous food is to be offered to the people at large. We believe the aim of all education to be to rouse the mind to action, show it the means of discipline and of information; then leave it free, with God, Conscience, and the love of Truth, for its guardians and teachers. Woe be to those who sacrifice these aims of universal and eternal value to the propagation of a set of opinions!

# Household Education

## From *Household Education,* 1848

*Twenty-five years after writing "On Female Education"* (see pp. 169–173), HARRIET MARTINEAU (1802–1876) *continued to argue that girls were capable of handling the same academic studies as boys and should be given that opportunity for the same reason: "to improve the quality of their minds." If "women are made for domestic duties," they would perform them much better if they were educated. And those who do not marry need to prepare themselves for employment and self-sufficiency. In either case, a woman should develop all her faculties and not be shut out "from any study she is capable of pursuing."*

See the Biographical Sketch on pages 174–178.

I mention girls, as well as boys, confident that every person able to see the right, and courageous enough to utter it, will sanction what I say. I must declare that on no subject is more nonsense talked (as it seems to me) than on that of female education, when restriction is advocated. In works otherwise really good, we find it taken for granted that girls are not to learn the dead languages and mathematics, because they are not to exercise professions where these attainments are wanted; and a little further on we find it said that the chief reason for boys and young men studying these things is to improve the quality of their minds. I suppose none of us will doubt that everything possible should be done to improve the quality of the mind of every human being. If it is said that the female brain is incapable of studies of an abstract nature, that is not true: for there are many instances of women who have been good mathematicians and good classical scholars. The plea is indeed nonsense on the face of it; for the brain which will learn French will learn Greek; the brain which enjoys arithmetic is capable of mathematics. If it is said that women are light-minded and superficial, the obvious answer is that their minds should be more carefully sobered by grave studies and the acquisition of exact knowledge. If it is said that their vocation in life does not require these kinds of knowledge, that is giving up the main plea for the pursuit of them by boys; that it improves the quality of their minds. If it is said that such studies unfit women for their proper occupations, that again is untrue. Men do not attend the less to their professional business, their counting house or their shop, for having their minds enlarged and enriched and their faculties strengthened by sound and various knowledge; nor do women on that account neglect the workbasket, the market, the dairy, and the kitchen. If it be true that women are made for these domestic occupations, then of course they will be fond of them. They will be so fond of what comes most naturally to them that no book-study (if really not congenial to their minds) will draw them off from their homely duties. For my part, I have no hesitation whatever in saying that the most ignorant women I have known have been the worst housekeepers; and that the most learned women I have known have been among the best, wherever they have been early taught and trained to household business, as every women ought to be. A woman of superior mind knows better than an ignorant one what to require of her servants, how to deal with tradespeople, and how to economize time: She is more clear-sighted about the best ways of doing things; has a richer mind with which to animate all about her, and to solace her own spirit in the midst of her labors. If nobody doubts the difference in pleasantness of having to do with a silly and narrow-minded woman and with one who is intelligent and enlightened, it must be clear that the more intelligence and enlightenment there is, the better.

✦ ✦ ✦

As for women not wanting learning, or superior intellectual training, that is more than any one should undertake to say in our day. In former times, it was understood that every woman (except domestic servants) was maintained by her father, brother, or husband; but it is not so now. The footing of women is changed, and it will change more. Formerly, every woman was destined to be married; and it was almost a matter of course that she would be: so that the only occupation thought of for a woman was keeping her husband's house and being a wife and mother. It is not so now. From a variety of causes, there is less and less marriage among the middle classes of our country; and much of the marriage that there is does not take place till middle life. A multitude of women have to maintain themselves who would never have dreamed of such a thing a hundred years ago. This is not the place for a discussion whether this is a good thing for women or a bad one; or for a lamentation that the occupations by which women might maintain themselves are so few; and of those few, so many engrossed by men. This is not the place for a speculation as to whether women are to grow into a condition of self-maintenance and their dependence for support upon father, brother, and husband to become only occasional. With these considerations, interesting as they are, we have no business at this moment. What we have to think of is the necessity,—in all justice, in all honor, in all humanity, in all prudence,—that every girl's faculties should be made the most of, as carefully as boys'. While so many women are no longer sheltered, and protected, and supported in safety from the world (as people used to say), every woman ought to be fitted to take care of herself. Every woman ought to have that justice done to her faculties that she may possess herself in all the strength and clearness of an exercised and enlightened mind and may have at command, for her subsistence, as much intellectual power and as many resources as education can furnish her with. Let us hear nothing of her being shut out, because she is a woman, from any study she is capable of pursuing: and if one kind of cultivation is more carefully attended to than another, let it be the discipline and exercise of the reasoning faculties. From the simplest rules of arithmetic let her go on, as her brother does, as far into the depths of science, and up to the heights of philosophy as her powers and opportunities permit; and it will certainly be found that the more she becomes a reasoning creature, the more reasonable, disciplined, and docile she will be: the more she knows of the value of knowledge and of all other things, the more diligent she will be, the more sensible of duty, the more interested in occupations, the more womanly. This is only coming round to the points we started from; that every human being is to be made as perfect as possible: and that this must be done through the most complete development of all the faculties.

# Criticism of the Physical Education of Girls

## Lecture Given in New York, 1851

ELIZABETH BLACKWELL (1821–1910), *who was born in England and returned there to complete her career, was the first woman in the United States to graduate from a medical college. She was part of the notable Unitarian family that included Lucy Stone and Antoinette Brown Blackwell,*[21] *both of whom married her brothers.*

*Dr. Blackwell was initially unable to establish a medical practice because of prejudice in the mid 1800s against female physicians. To launch her career, she used her talent for teaching, developed in her younger days, and delivered a series of lectures to adolescent girls and their mothers. These lectures were both praised and criticized for their forthright talk on physical fitness and sexuality and were later published as* The Laws of Life, with Special Reference to the Physical Education of Girls *(1852). Dr. Blackwell also lambasted public schools for their irrelevant curricula and poor teaching methods as well as their inattention to children's growing bodies. Instead of current practices, she advocated outdoor exercise, loose clothing, nutritional meals, independent thought, nonconformist actions, and useful studies—all radical ideas for the time.*

See the Biographical Sketch on pages 195–198.

Let us consider first our system of school education, which embraces the most important period of youthful life. The large majority of children enter school about the age of 7 years—they leave at the age of 16. Now this period embraces, you will remember, all those remarkable changes of bodily organization which occur, from the establishment of second dentition to the attainment of puberty—a period of rapid growth—when the body is enlarging its range of action for the powers already established, and acquiring new functions of immense importance to the individual and to the race and when consequently the body makes incessant demands upon the vital energy, and requires the most favorable circumstances to perform its work well.

✦ ✦ ✦

Now what do we do, at this period of special physical growth? We completely ignore the body; we substitute mental for physical training; we entirely change the order of nature, and oppose the most formidable obstacles to the *proper* growth of the body.

For, to ensure this proper growth, the appropriate nourishment of every physical function must be supplied in abundance. Thus a constant supply of fresh air is essential, and large amounts of *exercise* in the open air, with plenty of simple nourishing food; the body never grows so well as in the companionship of the trees and flowers and streams of a healthy country district.

The great object of the child's life is school—pure intellectual training. The best part of every day, generally from 9 to 3, is spent in the schoolroom, where the mind is forced to long and *unnatural* exercise; and in order to meet the tasks imposed upon it, it must either rouse itself to a constant exertion, that would be difficult for an adult, or it must rest contented with half misunderstanding its studies and learn by rote; a habit which is injurious to the best qualities of the mind. . . . [It is] quite impossible to keep the atmosphere of schoolrooms fit for human lungs to inhale; it is difficult in summertime, with all the windows open, to maintain an entirely pure air where so many human bodies are congregated for hours together; but during a greater part of the year, the windows must be shut—for several months the rooms must be artificially heated, generally with stoves, and often red-hot. . . . The atmosphere is laden with human exhalations and becomes a slow poison to those who breathe it. . . . [T]he blood is unable to supply the normal stimulus to the brain, and the child is forced to make more difficult efforts to perform its studies well. . . . A playground is very seldom connected with the school; once or twice during the six or seven hours of schooltime, the child may go down for five minutes into the yard—there may be half an hour's intermission in the middle of the day—but there is no provision for amusement; the children are exhausted by the morning's efforts, they lounge about and eat their luncheon, and are not, for the most part, inclined to take bodily exercise.

There is another serious evil; . . . it is the injurious position in which a great part of the time is passed, leaning over the desks in study or writing. This position is exceedingly mischievous: the chest, which should expand freely to receive the air, to strengthen its muscles and grow, is cramped and contracted by this stooping attitude, and the pressure against the desk; the shoulders, which should be thrown back at an equal level, are thus drawn forwards, and the right one thrown upward by the action of the arm in writing, often retains this position, and we have the narrow chest and crooked shoulders so commonly seen in schoolgirls. The seats are hard, generally without backs; the body is wearied by a constrained position, exhausted by mental efforts; the muscles of the back cannot maintain with vigor the upright position; they seek to relieve themselves of the weight of the head and back by awkward attitudes—leaning on one side, resting on the desk, curving the back. This effort continued day after day weakens the muscles, often distorts the spine, and produces other bodily deformities—for it must ever be borne in mind, that they are the *young*, not adults that we are educating—growing bodies, soft and pliable, that give way to undue pressure and cannot resist evil influences with the power of older years.

✦ ✦ ✦

The instruction given at school is almost purely intellectual; the senses receive little regular training: their power is used in very moderate degree to aid the mind—yet they are the first teachers of the young. Grammar, history, definition, composition call for simple intellectual exertion—the natural sciences are very slenderly illustrated by sensible examples, and the poor engravings in the text books are often the only illustration they receive. The most abstruse subjects, that tax the attention of the strongest mental powers, are presented as studies for the young; girls of 13 or 15 are called upon to ponder the problems of *mental and moral philosophy*, to demonstrate the *propositions of Euclid*, to understand the refinements of *rhetoric and logic*—admirable studies, truly, but they are the food of mature minds, not suitable to children. . . . If the object be mental discipline, there is no surer way of defeating such an object than to attempt to give the mind a superficial view of a subject too difficult for it to grasp—to confuse it with a multitude of disconnected studies—to hurry it from subject to subject, so that the simple studies more suited to the young mind, are imperfectly acquired and soon forgotten. Thus the greater part of the time devoted to the so-called cultivation of the intellect is really wasted.

✦ ✦ ✦

The teacher is not to blame for this wretched system of cramming. He is compelled to present as formidable an array of knowledge to be acquired at his school as his neighbors do; and most patiently and earnestly he may strive to aid his pupils in the acquisition. The evil is in the system itself, which substitutes names for things; which fails to recognize the necessity of adapting the kind of instruction to the quality of the mind. This formidable array of names and superficial amount of instruction is required by the community, and he is compelled to meet the demand; this system is radically wrong—no effort of the teacher can make it right. . . .

We have not yet spoken of the accomplishments! accomplishments to be acquired with great labor, to a superficial extent, and laid aside directly the serious duties of life commence. French, Latin, Italian, perhaps Spanish, German, and Greek—I believe Hebrew is not introduced in this country—vocal and instrumental music, piano, harp, guitar, drawing, painting, and various kinds of fancy work, swell the increasing list. Now many of these pursuits are beautiful and useful in themselves and would refine and elevate life if acquired at the *right time,* in the *right way.* But as studied at present, added on to the burdens of the young school-girl, their acquisition is not simply useless; they consume much time, and thereby become highly injurious, by increasing still further the efforts of the mind and preventing the slightest attention being given to the necessities of the body. . . .

Perhaps the child is sent out to take a walk on her return from school; but what is there attractive or invigorating in a walk through our streets? Can there be a more melancholy spectacle than a boarding school of girls taking their afternoon walk? There is no vigor in their step, no pleasure in their eye; the fresh air is certainly good for their lungs, but the unattractive exercise is of most questionable benefit.

There is little that is interesting to young girls in walking out without an object; they cannot play in the streets; their dress would be inconvenient; the mud and the carts, and the passengers, would prevent it. Children playing in the streets are nuisances; though some may watch with pleasure the lively movements of a group of boys, who have taken possession of a slippery pavement with their sleighs and skates and though we would not for one moment dislodge them from their only playground—still they are out of place—and the unfitness should be still more striking, if the players were a group of girls, for there is an ideal of beauty in womanhood which may not be neglected, and our natural perception of fitness is always more outraged by coarse arrangements for girls than for boys.

✦ ✦ ✦

In the ordinary school-hours, the child remains for seven hours without any proper meal, for the luncheon taken to school is often hastily put up or consists of some improper article; the pickles and candy that children frequently carry to school with them are hardly more wholesome than the chalk, India rubber, and slate pencils, that they chew in such large quantities.

Thus under the combined influences of confinement and close air, of unsuitable food, and injudicious mental excitement, the school days pass; under such influences the child changes from a girl into a woman; such is the foundation laid for the important duties of adult life!

If we were to sit down and carefully plan a system of education which should injure the body, produce a premature and imperfect development of its powers, weaken the mind and prepare the individual for future *uselessness,* we could hardly by any ingenuity construct a system more admirably calculated to produce these terrible results. . . . [By the girls'] very conformity to rules, by striving to please their teachers and parents and maintain an honorable position—they fall completely into the snare and sin against nature, in exact proportion to their obedience to society!

## ✦ *Biographical Sketch*

**Born:** *February 3, 1821, Bristol, England*

**Died:** *May 31, 1910, Hastings, England, age 89*

**Buried:** *Kilmun, Scotland*

Elizabeth Blackwell was born in England and spent her last forty years there. She is, however, best known for her educational contributions in the United States as well as being the country's first female physician.

Elizabeth's family emigrated to the United States when she was eleven. Her father, a well-to-do owner of a sugar refinery in Bristol, was highly respected for his integrity but also attacked for being a Dissenter (an unpopular religious minority). Though an academic education was considered unneeded and wrong for girls, Samuel Blackwell encouraged his daughters to read, write, and study the classics along with their brothers, who were also barred from schools because of their religious beliefs. When the factory burned and hard times hit, the Blackwells sailed for the United States to start a new sugar business in New York and later in Cincinnati. Her father died suddenly when Elizabeth was seventeen, leaving his widow, nine children, and many debts.

Elizabeth turned to teaching—first in her home, then in Kentucky, and later in the Carolinas, where she saw firsthand the brutality of slavery. Returning to Ohio, she joined the abolitionist movement as well as the Cincinnati Unitarian church, whose eloquent minister, William Henry Channing, was the nephew of Boston's leading preacher, William Ellery Channing. Reared in an environment of liberal religious beliefs, all of the Blackwell children became independent thinkers and social and political activists. Elizabeth's brother Samuel married Antoinette Brown, the first woman ordained as minister, and her brother Henry married Lucy Stone,[22] a leader in the women's rights movement.

A few years later, a dying female friend suggested to Elizabeth that she become a physician. Realizing the comfort a woman doctor would be to female patients, she determined to pursue this profession, despite the fact that women were barred from all medical schools in North America. She borrowed books from a few male doctors who supported her goal, attended lectures, and engaged in a long independent study program. She was turned down by eight medical schools because of her sex, until in 1847 the male students at Geneva College in New York (now Hobart and William Smith) voted, as a lark, to accept her. Despite the faculty's reservations, Elizabeth Blackwell proved to be a superior student and graduated with top honors, the first woman in the modern world to earn a medical degree.

Elizabeth then went to Paris to become a surgeon, but a tragic event changed her path. She lost an eye due to a severe infection caught from a patient. Undaunted, she turned her attention and energy to the prevention of disease through education about health, sanitation, and the human body. One of her most valued friends at the time was a young Englishwoman, Florence Nightingale, who was then attempting to change nursing from a disreputable activity into a respectable, admired career. Nightingale convinced her physician friend that careful sanitation should be a primary means of saving lives.

In 1851, Elizabeth returned to the United States, where she again faced harsh prejudice toward female doctors. With few patients and no hospital that would accept her, she advertised in a newspaper a series of six lectures on bodily hygiene and sex education. These were later compiled into a book, *The Laws of Life in Reference to the Physical Education of Girls.* She was an effective public speaker and, at a time when the words *sex* and *body* were considered offensive and taboo, her courageous talks caused a sensation.

With the help of friends, mostly Quakers, Elizabeth opened a free clinic in one of the worst slums of New York City, largely populated by recent, indigent immigrants. In contrast to the prevailing use by doctors of bleeding, leeching, opium, and stomach purging for problems during pregnancy, she advocated exercise, nutrition, sunlight, soap and water, fresh air, lighter clothing, and no drugs.

With her younger sister Emily Blackwell and Marie Zakrzewska, both of whom had recently graduated from the Medical College of Cleveland, Elizabeth opened the New York Infirmary for Indigent Women and Children in 1857. Staffed entirely by women, it was endorsed by several prominent male physicians, who risked their reputations by encouraging this venture. The New York Infirmary was one of the first to incorporate regular sanitation procedures, which greatly reduced the number of mother and infant deaths during childbirth. Later, a nurses' training school was established, the first in the United States. The school became a major supplier of nurses for clinics and hospitals treating wounded soldiers during the Civil War.

In 1868, the women opened the Woman's Medical College of the New York Infirmary in order to give females the same medical courses offered to males at other institutions, with additional emphasis on hygiene and disease prevention. A sanitary visitor was hired to go into homes in slum areas and teach women the need for and methods of ventilation, cleanliness, nutrition, and economics. Also on the staff was the first black woman in history to earn a medical degree, Dr. Rebecca Cole.

When she was nearing fifty, Elizabeth Blackwell left the New York institutions in the capable hands of her sister Emily and returned to her native England. For the next forty years, she gave lectures, helped women enter science professions, fought prostitution, promoted health and hygiene, helped establish the London School of Medicine for Women, and was a professor of gynecology there for thirty-two years. She published numerous books and articles, including the autobiographical sketches called *Pioneer Work in Opening the Medical Profession for Women,* co-authored with Emily Blackwell.

Elizabeth Blackwell never married, but early in her career, she unofficially adopted a seven-year-old orphan named Kitty Barry, who remained her life-long companion, helper, and friend. A fall late in life disabled Elizabeth physically, but her mind and pen remained active until she died at the age of eighty-nine. She and Kitty are both buried in their favorite vacation spot in Kilmun, Scotland.

*Biographical Sketch by* JUNE EDWARDS

## ✦ Writings of Elizabeth Blackwell

*Counsel to Parents on the Moral Education of Their Children in Relation to Sex, under Medical and Social Aspects.* London: Hatchards, 1879; New York: Brentano, 1879; London: George Bell, 1913.

*The Human Element in Sex.* London: J. and D. C. Churchill, 1894.

*The Influence of Women in the Profession of Medicine.* London: George Bell, 1889.

*The Laws of Life, in Reference to the Physical Education of Girls.* New York: Putnam, 1852.

*Pioneer Work in Opening the Medical Profession to Women.* With Dr. Emily Blackwell. London: Longmans, 1895; New York: Dutton, 1895; London: Everyman's Library, 1914.

*Wrong and Right Methods of Dealing with Social Evil.* London: D. Williams, 1883.

## ✦ Biographical Resources

Hays, Elinor Rice. *Those Extraordinary Blackwells.* New York: Harcourt, Brace and World, 1967.

McFerran, Ann. *Elizabeth Blackwell: First Woman Doctor.* New York: Grossett and Dunlap, 1966.

Whittier, Isabel. *Dr. Elizabeth Blackwell: The First Woman Doctor.* Brunswick, ME: Brunswick, 1961.

Wilson, Dorothy Clarke. *Lone Woman: The Story of Elizabeth Blackwell, the First Woman Doctor.* Boston: Little, Brown, 1970.

HARRIOT KEZIA HUNT

# From Educator to Physician

## From *Fifty Years Social, Including Twenty Years Professional Life,* 1856

HARRIOT KEZIA HUNT (1805–1875), *raised in a Universalist family in Boston, was the first woman to practice medicine in the United States, albeit without formal medical training. In 1827, she and her sister Sarah opened a successful school for girls in their parents' home, which not only afforded Harriot great satisfaction at the time but served as excellent preparation for her later medical studies. Sarah's debilitating illness led her sister to trade teaching for doctoring, skills that were later united in her efforts to educate women and girls about sanitation and disease prevention. These excerpts from Harriot Hunt's autobiography begin with her assertion that it is necessary to educate girls for real work and go on to detail the story of her own transition from educator to physician.*

See the Biographical Sketch on pages 204–207.

I have a purpose here, I cherish a hope to arouse public thought respecting the position of our young women after they have left school. Their parents—many of them—are in only moderate circumstances. They have toiled early and late to procure the education of their daughters; and, if they were truly parents, they should desire to see some worthy result follow that education, to see it practically applied to the business of life. Alas! what is the truth on this subject? Girls are educated,—for what? They are sedulously trained—for what? For nothing but marriage! They are early taught to consider what are their chances and attractions for the market! I say the market—for I have no more scruple in applying this term to the state of society with regard to women than I have in applying it to the marts where any other purchasable article is bought and sold. . . . Now I see no possible reason why young women, unless they are absolutely needed in the domestic circle,—and even then, self-reliance should be taught them,—should not be trained to some healthful, remunerative employment. To say nothing of its beneficial effects on their own character, or of the independent position it would give them in society, such employment would often enable them to sustain their parents by their own earnings, when the chances and changes of life have brought reverses to the home, and to gladden the declining years of those parents with comforts, too often wanting now. Daughters would then be capable of rendering assistance, as well as sons. Within my own knowledge, fathers with families of daughters lament the loss of a son because "girls are so expensive!" Think of it! This constant keeping back our sex from an early, active participation in the duties of life has been the means of throwing upon many a father with a family of daughters, a burden he was utterly unable to bear.

He has given them money, hardly earned by toilsome and anxious hours—perhaps a creditor needed it;—but they must appear well at the party—they must make their market! Hard-working, kindhearted, but injudicious mothers are hid away in the kitchen, that silly daughters may be flauntingly dressed in the parlor, thrumming tunes without a touch of melody for the entertainment of Mr. Bombastes! How many of these cases are around us? They are heartless deceptions and outrages on womanhood. Too many of these poor children marry and return to their parents broken-hearted through the failure of their husbands (many of whom never had anything to fail on) or penniless widows with children who sorrowfully increase their care in old age. Such heart-histories appeal powerfully to our sympathies, while they rouse our indignation at the degradation and uselessness of our sex. . . .

May it not be affirmed that the prevalent custom of educating young women only for marriage, and not for the duties and responsibilities consequent on marriage—only for appendages and dead weights to husbands—of bringing them up without an occupation, profession, or employment, and thus leaving them dependent on anybody but themselves is an enormous evil and an unpardonable sin. In the name of my sex, a protest should be issued against the fashionable education fathers and mothers give their daughters, encouraging them to acquire those peacock accomplishments, those shallow charms of conversation, and those personal airs, manners, and graces which they are pleased to term "attractions," in order that they may catch the fancy of some wealthy simpleton or arrant knave and so win a husband! It is educating their daughters for what is not marriage in any worthy sense of that word. Yes, their protest, earnest, solemn, touching, should be entered against the custom of bringing up young women who are to become wives and mothers without a knowledge of those domestic duties and responsibilities, which alone can fit them to live true to those relations, without those solid intellectual attainments and spiritual graces, by which they are to educate their children and hallow the atmosphere of home; and without those "attractions," enduring when youth and beauty are gone, which can alone win and keep for them the respect and love of any sensible, upright, and noble man, worthy the name of husband! Against the wrong done to young women, who may never enter the marriage state, by giving them no trade, occupation, or profession, and thus leaving them to idleness, dependence, helplessness, and temptation. Let every girl see to it that she has the means of her own support. . . . It *must* soon be seen that bringing up daughters for nothing but marriage mingles poison in the cup of domestic life, is traitorous to the virtue of both sexes, for neither suffers alone, is adverse to happiness, to the development of conscience and to religion, and introduces to the dwellings of wretchedness and despair. The result of this degradation is pride, intemperance, licentiousness—nay, every vice, misery, and degradation. When labor becomes honorable and elevating, when we realize that labor is the charm to stay this fiend, and the pride from which it had its origin and sustenance, dies at the awakening of the sense of our relation to human kind, and our responsibility to God. Then will every woman prepare herself for useful occupation and follow it. Then will man see that industrial avenues are open to women, that they can follow any business or profession for which they are qualified without being exposed to contemptible insults which are heaped upon those who have independence enough to step out of the beaten track.

✦ ✦ ✦

These admonitions are from one who has labored, yes, and dearly loved to labor! The felt necessities of my soul urged me to open for myself some path of usefulness. As our house was large for so small a family, my parents gave me a pleasant chamber overlooking the broad blue ocean, and there I opened a school and became a teacher. My own school days were fresh upon me; the surroundings were favorable; I was in the neighborhood of my whole life; our social circle was of the highest respectability; all these were advantages. But hidden within—far away from the little world without, that wondered at my enterprise—was my own consciousness of its importance. My father's hospitable nature, added to the depression of business, and his own ill health for a few years before, had made it a duty for me to act. Was it not noble in those parents who had sheltered, loved, and breathed prayers on their children, that when the time came for the eldest (who had ever been loved because she was the eldest) to act, they gladly, cheerfully, encouraged and sustained her? I feel now a thrill of gratitude for my home—yes, and of deep responsibility to my parents; and during my professional life, when some people have marveled, I have felt depressed by my consciousness of the unworthiness of the response that life has made to home influences so excellent. The secret of whatever has been worthiest in my existence is in my home. My first independent movement—my school—was blessed by my parents. The pleasant room was soon alive with happy childhood, and I tried to profit by the wise fact that had led me along in leading others. The ninth of April, 1827, found me in my schoolroom with eight pupils, and when the following October came, I had twenty-three!

Our domestic life lost none of its joys by my stated daily avocation. That avocation but widened our sympathies; it gave us better opportunities to meet the parents of the children on a higher plane. It also opened to me a rich experience in social life. Many of my former schoolmates at this time had no graver employment than muslin work. Of course, we were still on visiting terms, though I had lost some caste by becoming useful. I was struck at an early period by the selfish, contemptible indolence they indulged in, as by the lamentable ennui it occasioned. Living on their parents, like parasites, most of them dwindled away and became uninteresting to me. A chasm had yawned between our friendships, for I was at work—they were at play. Our lives had nothing in common. My school was a grand use to me for it not only called out gratitude to my parents for the advantages they had given me but also for the delight and enthusiasm with which I pursued the occupation. I was an enigma to those who had once been schoolgirls with me. They knew not the magic of usefulness. They often told me—boastingly!—they had "nothing to do," they had "all their time!" Soon, marriages of convenience, of position, some of true affection were entered upon; but even in view of the latter, I often had reason for the queries, "Why so much indifference to these holy relations? Why so little continued interest in intellectual pursuits?" One would have thought that these last would still be prosecuted for the pleasure they afford, to say nothing of the power they bestow on a mother in relation to her children. One would naturally suppose that being loved and loving would be a healthy stimulus to mental growth and freshness; but nevertheless my married schoolmates and friends—too many of them—sank down into a monotonous half-life. I often pondered on these things, as one does over a puzzling sum. It was not until my medical life opened to me that I perceived causes which are poisoning womanhood, inducing physical diseases, and beclouding even the perceptions of duty.

✦ ✦ ✦

My school was commenced in April, 1827, and in 1833, a change passed over my life: a new call for *consideration* was heard—a loud one too. My sister's health was the point in our family, the nucleus around which all our desires clustered. We asked—we looked—we wondered! Is there no permanent hope? No balm in Gilead? In the fullness of time we were answered.

On the thirtieth of June, 1833, I saw a physician, Mrs. Mott, who, with her husband, had come to Boston to establish themselves in practice:—they were English people. I had called on her the day before, but she could not see me. I remember vividly my conversation with her: her sympathizing manner, as I unfolded my sister's case, was comfort to me; and after hearing me patiently, she said she thought my sister could be cured. We were open to all sorts of opposition for even thinking of such a thing as employing "a quack!" But we were weary and tired out with "regulars"; and it did not occur to us that to die under regular practice, and with medical etiquette, was better than any other way. Affection works out her sums by different rules. Even conversing with a new mind awakened hope; and it is often in this way, rather than by a change of treatment, that invalids are benefited. . . .

On Monday, July 1st, Mrs. Mott and her husband came to our home in Fleet Street. They pronounced the case consumption and took it, expressing much sympathy for us and evidently attracted to the invalid. Here was my first thought of woman as a physician; and yet this was but a partial exhibition, for her husband was at her side, giving to her position some gloss of what the world calls propriety, and you felt his power as well as hers.

✦ ✦ ✦

My sister's health commenced improving. Her hope was healthfully stimulated; new influences were doing good work for her. . . . This was new life for us. Our home was once more brightened, gladdened, and cheered. . . . An attachment sprang up between us and them; and in September they made me an offer to come to their residence, and write for them. . . . So I left my school and adventured on a new life.

When I was not occupied in writing, I passed my time at home. My daily joy at getting there was only excelled by my sister's gaining in strength and being able to come to Dr. Mott's house and see me; for she gradually recovered!

✦ ✦ ✦

My daily duties kept me in Mrs. Mott's business room. My letter-writing to patients for her kept thought active, and the sympathy I had given to my sister, I now gave to every sufferer. Several advised me to study for the profession—saying that it would always be useful to me—it would enable me to meet physicians or take care of myself, if need be. It wanted not a word, a hint, for within me was now the consciousness that it was to be! My problem was now solved, my foreshadowing realized, my intuition ultimated, and my individualism aroused to obey the mentors who had for so many years been preparing me to meet this destiny. In waking hours, in reveries, and in dreams, pictures had been painted on the mind's "mysterious far away"; and now the lenses were given through which they could be viewed. A vague and indistinct idea had now taken a form. Hopes and fears were equally balanced and uses and activities seen in a new light. Diligence renewed her claim, and hope beckoned on. I needed no stimulus but the *successful* practice of Doctor and Mrs. Mott.

## ✦ *Biographical Sketch*

**Born:** *November 9, 1805, Boston, Massachusetts*

**Died:** *January 2, 1875, Boston, Massachusetts, age 69*

**Buried:** *Mount Auburn Cemetery, Cambridge, Massachusetts*

Long before women were accepted into medical schools in the United States and elsewhere in the world, Harriot Kezia Hunt practiced medicine in Boston. In addition to her pioneering medical practice, Hunt was a strong advocate for public health education, women's rights, and the abolition of slavery.

Harriot Hunt, born in Boston in 1805, was the first child of Joab and Kezia (Wentworth) Hunt, who were both descendants of old New England families. Harriot's father was a ship's joiner and navigator, and her mother was a well-read woman who loved politics. The fourth and final member of the family, Sarah, was born three years after Harriot's birth.

Harriot Hunt believed that her happy childhood was the key to her subsequent happy and productive life. In her autobiography, *Glances and Glimpses,* she argues emphatically that children who are received into the world by parents who truly want them have one birthright while those who are not welcome and are raised grudgingly have another. Throughout her career, Harriot Hunt advocated strong family life as a factor in the health and well-being of individuals.

Harriot's mother had been raised an Episcopalian and her father, a Congregationalist. As adults, however, they became enthusiastic Universalists and raised their daughters in a liberal religious tradition. The Hunt daughters were educated in local private schools taught by neighborhood women and were encouraged to read widely.

In 1827, at age twenty-two, Harriot started a home school of her own. Initially, she had only a handful of children, but enrollment rapidly grew. Although her father died shortly after the school opened, her mother remained supportive and her sister Sarah helped out as well. Harriot ran the school until the early 1830s, when Sarah became seriously ill.

For three years, Sarah was unsuccessfully treated by conventional doctors using common methods such as leeches, blisters, mercurial ointments, prussic acid, and calomel. Desperate to help her sister, Harriot sought out a British couple, the Motts, who had recently come to Boston and were practicing alternative health methods regarded as quackery at the time. Mrs. Mott, assisted by her husband, determined that Sarah had a tubercular illness and began treatment. Sarah recovered fully, which inspired Harriot to close her school and begin training with the Motts. Sarah joined her. The sisters studied avidly, and in 1835, they opened their own practice.

The methods employed by the Hunts sound modern to our ears. They emphasized prevention, with attention to hygiene, exercise, rest, diet, and good nursing. And they listened carefully and sympathetically to their patients. This attention to the mental health of patients reflected the Hunts' understanding, based on experience, that psychological state has a significant impact on physical health.

In 1840, Sarah married and withdrew from medical practice. Harriot continued and over the next several years took her teaching and medical talents out into the public domain. In 1843, she organized the Ladies Physiological Society in Charlestown—a group of patients and friends who gathered for her talks on human physiology, good hygiene, and appropriate health practices.

Harriot's mother died in 1847, leaving her with a profound sense of loss but strengthening her commitment to her profession and to working harder for the cause of women. In a daring effort, she wrote to Dr. Oliver Wendell Holmes, dean of the Harvard Medical School, and asked to attend lectures there. Holmes wanted to grant her request, but the Harvard board rejected it.

Other women were also trying to obtain medical training in other places at this time, provoking a great deal of controversy. How could women, with their delicate temperaments, tolerate blatant discussions of physiology and surgery and bodily functions? How could men and women be in the same room together, listening to discourses on the human body?

Harriot took Harvard's rejection in stride and went on with her work, bringing her lectures on health to working-class areas of Boston. The problems facing women—including restricted education, poor pay for labor, and limited work opportunities—became increasingly apparent to her. When the first national woman's rights convention was held in October 1850 in Worcester, Massachusetts, she attended. There she met like-minded women who supported and encouraged her. She began to travel and speak more widely, advocating health education, rights for women, and the abolition of slavery.

Later that year, Harriot reapplied to Harvard Medical School. This time, permission to attend lectures was granted, but the students reacted with such intense, highly publicized protests that Harriot gave up the effort. Public response, however, was generally supportive of her, and the publicity surrounding her reception by Harvard students may have had a strengthening impact on the women's movement. One direct effect was that the Female Medical College of Philadelphia awarded Harriot an honorary degree in 1853.

Harriot continued her medical practice for two more decades until her death from Bright's disease in 1875. Her educational and reform efforts continued as well. During that time, she helped found a school of design for women in Boston to improve women's employment options.

Harriot Hunt's grave is marked by a statue of the goddess Hygeia, which she had earlier commissioned by the black sculptor Edmonia Lewis. The inscription reads simply, "Harriot Kezia Hunt. For forty years a physician in Boston. She hath done what she could."

*Biographical Sketch by* MARILYN CARROLL WILSON

## ✦ Writings of Harriot Kezia Hunt

*Glances and Glimpses; or Fifty Years Social, Including Twenty Years Professional Life.* Boston: John P. Jewett, 1856.

## ✦ Biographical Resources

Bonner, Thomas Neville. *To the Ends of the Earth, Women's Search for Education in Medicine.* Cambridge: Harvard University Press, 1992.

*Dictionary of American Biography, Comprehensive Index.* New York: Charles Scribner's Sons, 1996.

*Eminent Women of the Age.* Hartford, CT: S. M. Betts, 1968.

James, Edward T., ed. *Notable American Women, 1607–1950.* Cambridge: Belknap Press of Harvard University, 1974.

Shore, Eleanor G., and Miles F. Shore. "Vita, Harriot Kezia Hunt." *Harvard Magazine* 98 (September–October 1995): 54.

Whitman, Alden, ed. *American Reformers.* New York: H. W. Wilson, 1985.

# The Educational Rights of Women

## From *The College, the Market, and the Court,* 1859

CAROLINE WELLS HEALEY DALL (1822–1912) *was a well-known proponent of equal rights who worked independently of the major women's organizations of her day and broadened the fight beyond suffrage to include economics, education, and other issues that affected women's welfare. She was influenced at an early age by the Boston Unitarians and Transcendentalists. Between 1858 and 1862, Caroline Dall delivered a series of lectures in Boston, which were published in 1867 as* The College, the Market, and the Court. *This widely read book had a strong impact on the social reform movements of the day. The following selection is from her first lecture, "The Christian Demand and the Public Opinion."*

See the Biographical Sketch on pages 212–215.

Some time since, we laid down this proposition: "A man's right to education—that is, to the education or drawing-out of all the faculties God has given him—involve the right to a choice of vocation; that is, to a choice of the end to which those faculties shall be trained. The choice of vocation involves the right and duty of protecting that vocation; that is, the right of deciding how far it shall be taxed, in how many ways legislative action shall be allowed to control it; in one word, the right to the elective franchise."

This statement we made in the broadest way; applying it to the present condition of women and intending to show that, the moment society conceded the right to education, it conceded the whole question, unless this logic could be disputed.

Men of high standing have been found to question a position seemingly so impregnable but only on the ground that republicanism is itself a failure and that it is quite time that Massachusetts should insist upon a property qualification for voters.

In this State, so remarkable for its intelligence and mechanical skill—a State which has sent regiment after regiment to the battlefield, armed by the college, rather than the court—in this State, one somewhat eminent voice has been heard to whisper that *men* have not this right to education; that the lower classes in this country are fatally injured by the advantages offered them; that they would be happier, more contented, and more useful if left to take their chance or compelled to pay for the reading and writing which their employers, in some kinds, might require.

We need not be sorry that these objections are so stated. They are a fair sample of all the objections that obtain against the legal emancipation of *woman,* an emancipation which Christ himself intended and prophesied—speaking always of his kingdom as one in which no distinctions of sex should either be needed or recognized. Push any objector to the wall, and he will be compelled to shift his attitude. He says nothing more about women but shields himself under the old autocratic pretension that man, collectively taken, has *no* right to life, liberty, or the pursuit of happiness; that republicanism itself is a failure.

Our hearts need not sink in view of this assertion, apparently sustained by a civil war that fixes the suspicious eyes of autocratic Europe in sullen suspense. A republic whose foundations were laid in usurpation could not expect to stand, till it had, with its own right arm, struck off its "feet of clay." It is not freedom which fails but slavery.

The course of the world is not retrograde. Massachusetts will not call a convention to insist upon a property qualification for voters, neither will she close her schoolhouses nor forswear her ancient faith. The time shall yet come when she shall free herself from reproach and fulfill the prophetic promise of her republicanism by generous endowment for her women and the open recognition of their citizenship.

It is not our purpose, however, to dwell upon facilities of school education. More conservative speakers will plead, eloquently as we could wish, in that behalf; and suggestions on other topics need to be made.

We have already said that the educational rights of women are simply those of all human beings—namely, "the right to be taught all common branches of learning, a sufficient use of the needle, and any higher branches, for which they shall evince either taste or inclination; the right to have colleges, schools of law, theology, and medicine open to them; the right of access to all scientific and literary collections, to anatomical preparations, historical records, and rare manuscripts."

And we do not make this claim with any particular theory as to woman's powers or possibilities. She may be equal to man or inferior to him. She may fail in rhetoric and succeed in mathematics. She may be able to bear fewer hours of study. She may insist on more protracted labor. What we claim is that no one knows, as yet, what women are or what they can do—least of all, those who have been wedded for years to that low standard of womanly achievement, which classical study tends to sustain. Because we do not know, because experiment is necessary, we claim that all educational institutions should be kept open for her; that she should be encouraged to avail herself of these, according to her own inclination; and that, so far as possible, she should pursue her studies, and test her powers, in company with man. We do not wish her to follow *any* dictation; not ours, nor another's. We ask for her a freedom she has never yet had. There is, between the sexes, a law of incessant, reciprocal action, of which God avails himself in the constitution of the family when he permits brothers and sisters to nestle about one hearthstone. Its ministration is essential to the best educational results. Our own educational institutions should rest upon this divine basis. In educating the sexes together under fatherly and motherly supervision, we avail ourselves of the highest example; and the result will be a simplicity, modesty, and purity of character, not so easy to attain when general abstinence from each other's society makes the occasions of reunion a period of harmful excitement. Out of it would come a quick perception of mutual proprieties, delicate attention to manly and womanly habits, refinement of feeling, grace of manner, and a thoroughly symmetrical development. If the objections which are urged against this—the divine fashion of training men and women to the duties of life—were well founded, they would have been felt long ago in those district schools, attended by both sexes, which are the pride of New England. The classes recently opened by the Lowell Institute, under the control of the Institute of Technology, are an effort in the right direction, for which we cannot be too grateful. Heretofore, every attempt to give advanced instruction to women has failed. Did a woman select the most accomplished instructor of men, and pay him the highest fee, she could not secure thorough tuition. He taught her without conscience in the higher branches; for he took it upon himself to assume that she would never put them to practical use. He treated her desire for such instruction as a caprice, though she might have shown her appreciation by the distinct bias of her life. We claim for women a share of the opportunities offered to men, because we believe that they will never be thoroughly taught until they are taught at the same time and in the same classes.

The most mischievous errors are perpetuated by drawing masculine and feminine lines in theory at the outset. The God-given impulse of sex, if left in complete freedom, will establish, in time, certain distinctions for itself; but these distinctions should never be pressed on any individual soul. Whether man or woman, each should be left free to choose its own methods of development.

✦ ✦ ✦

Let us pass over that portion of our statement which hints at vocation and confine ourselves, for the present, to that part of it which looks to an unrestricted mental culture. Nowhere is this systematically denied to women. It is quite common to hear people say, "There is no need to press that subject. Education in New England is free to women. In Bangor, Portsmouth, Newburyport, and Boston, they are better Latin scholars than the men. Nothing can set this stream back: turn and labor elsewhere."

We have shown to how very small an extent this statement is true. If it were true of the mere means of education, education itself is not won for woman till it brings to her precisely the same blessings that it bears to the feet of man; till it gives her honor, respect, and bread; till position becomes the rightful inheritance of capacity and social influence follows a knowledge of mathematics and the languages. Our deficiency in the last stages of the culture offered to our women made a strong impression on a late Russian traveler.

"Is that the best you can do?" said Mr. Kapnist, when he came out of the Mason Street Normal School for Girls. "It is very poor. In Russia, we should do better. At Cambridge, you have eminent men in every kind,—Agassiz, Gray, Peirce. Why do they not lecture to these women? In Russia, they would go everywhere—speak to both sexes. At a certain age, recitation is the very poorest way of imparting knowledge."

To all adult minds, lectures convey instruction more happily than recitation; and, when men and women are taught together, the lecture system is valuable, because it permits the mind to appropriate its own nutriment and does not oppress the faculties with uncongenial food.

## ✦ *Biographical Sketch*

**Born:** *June 22, 1822, Boston, Massachusetts*
**Died:** *December 17, 1912, Washington, DC, age 90*
**Buried:** *Mount Auburn Cemetery, Cambridge, Massachusetts*

Caroline Healey Dall was one of the most effective promoters of independence for women in the nineteenth-century United States. She campaigned for gender equity on all fronts: women's suffrage, women's education, women's economic opportunities, and married women's rights.

Caroline Wells Healey was provided with an excellent private education by her wealthy, self-made father. She attempted to fulfill his high expectations by writing childhood novels, publishing translations before she was thirteen, and contributing short homilies to the *Christian Register,* a Unitarian journal. Her early association with the Boston-area Transcendentalists provided nontraditional role models and helped set her life's course on a track of idealism and independence. At age twelve, she was a member of Ralph Waldo Emerson's lecture audience; at age eighteen, she came under the influence of the prominent educator Elizabeth Palmer Peabody, who arranged for her to attend Margaret Fuller's Conversations in 1841.[23] Fuller became her inspiration to campaign for women's rights issues.

Another figure crucial in Caroline Healey's spiritual and intellectual development was Theodore Parker, the Unitarian preacher, reformer, and Transcendentalist. Reared a Unitarian in Boston's West Church, she was eighteen when she first heard the firebrand Parker preach and she wrote in her journal: "His sermon startled me, waked me up into admiration and dread."[24]

When her father faced financial ruin in 1842, Caroline Healey became a teacher in a school for young ladies in the Georgetown area of Washington, DC. There, she met a visiting Unitarian minister, Charles Henry Appleton Dall, a recent graduate of Harvard Divinity School. Their marriage in 1844, though happy for several years, was a mismatch. He was unable to hold a pulpit for long and, following an illness of "brain fever," began behaving erratically and inexplicably toward his wife. After several wrenching months, she wrote in her journal that she now felt toward him as she would for a sick child. To her amazement, Charles Dall decided to become a missionary in India, where he died more than thirty years later. Left in the United States with two small children and inadequate support from her husband, Caroline Dall turned to writing, lecturing, occasional teaching, and intermittent charity from her father for livelihood. She also intensified her participation in reform activities.

From the mid 1840s, Dall was associated with the abolitionists. In 1849, she also became active in the women's rights movement, which would be her main sphere for the next quarter century. She made speeches at conventions in Boston and New York, delivered public lectures, addressed a committee of the Massachusetts legislature, and served as co-editor with Paulina Wright Davis of the country's first feminist journal, *The Una.*

In her time, Dall was a reformer of national stature, a powerful advocate for women's issues, and the author of numerous books. Her best-known and most influential was *The College, the Market, and the Court; or, Woman's Relation to Education, Labor, and Law* (1867). Whereas many first-wave feminists focused exclusively on suffrage, Dall recognized that crucial battles were to be fought in other arenas as well, such as the marketplace and education.

In her books, Dall urged the expansion of higher education for women, including their admission to medical schools. On the economic front, she argued that women's labor should be valued at the same rate as men's. She portrayed sympathetically the lot of prostitutes, whose only choices were often "death or dishonor." She encouraged women of means to become entrepreneurs, suggested an early version of the temporary employment agency, and looked forward to a (somewhat romanticized) era of dual-career couples. Dall also pointed out how unfairly English common law (on which most state laws were based) treated women in matters of divorce and property rights. Her plea for the franchise and full equality of women in education, labor, and law was based on her Unitarian belief in the worth of all human souls and the duty to develop one's God-given faculties.

Unfortunately (or maybe fortunately, in terms of her broad scope and productivity), Dall did not get along with other female leaders and was excluded from membership in suffragist Lucy Stone's New England Women's Club, formed in 1868. As a result, she was to work independently of organized women's groups. Carrie Chapman Catt, writing in the early twentieth century, regretted that someone who contributed so greatly to the women's movement in earlier times had been nearly forgotten. In her day, however, Dall was highly regarded as a pioneer by a generation of women whose lives and opportunities were enhanced by her lectures and writings. Her chief contribution was to provide a theoretical foundation (with more specific applications than Margaret Fuller provided) for the women's movement in the United States. In recognition of her work, she received an honorary doctor of laws degree from Alfred University in 1877.

Continually crossing swords with other leaders of the women's movement, Dall began devoting her energies to the American Social Science Association, which she helped found, serving as its director and vice president for thirty-five years. The organization worked especially for improvements in prison conditions, better treatment of people who are mentally ill, public health, and education. Active also in religious activities, she served as Sunday school superintendent in James Freeman Clarke's Church of the Disciples and occasionally filled Unitarian pulpits in the Boston area.

In 1878, Caroline Dall moved to Washington, DC, to be near her son, an eminent naturalist at the Smithsonian Institution, and she lived there her remaining years. Active nearly until her death in 1912, she continued to write, pursue reform work, and conduct classes for women.

*Biographical Sketch by* HELEN R. DEESE

## ✦ Writings of Caroline Healey Dall

*"Alongside": Being Notes Suggested by "A New England Boyhood" of Doctor Edward Everett Hale.* Boston: Thomas Todd, 1900.

*The College, the Market, and the Court; or Woman's Relation to Education, Labor, and Law.* Boston: Lee and Shepard, 1867.

*Historical Pictures Retouched: A Volume of Miscellanies.* Boston: Walker, Wise, 1860.

*Margaret and Her Friends; or Ten Conversations with Margaret Fuller.* Boston: Roberts Brothers, 1895.

*Transcendentalism in New England: A Lecture.* Boston: Roberts Brothers, 1897.

## ✦ Biographical Resources

Conrad, Susan Phinney. *Perish the Thought: Intellectual Women in Romantic America, 1830–1860.* New York: Oxford University Press, 1976.

Deese, Helen R. "Alcott's Conversations on the Transcendentalists: The Record of Caroline Dall." *American Literature* 60 (March 1988): 17–25.

———. "Caroline H. Dall: Recorder of the Boston Intellectual Scene." *Documentary Editing* 12 (December 1990): 86.

———. "A Liberal Education: Caroline Healey Dall and Emerson." In *Emersonian Circles: Essays in Honor of Joel Myerson,* edited by Wesley T. Mott and Robert Burkholder, 237–260. Rochester, NY: Rochester University Press, 1996.

———. "A New England Women's Network: Elizabeth Palmer Peabody, Caroline Healey Dall, and Delia S. Bacon." *Legacy: A Journal of American Women Writers* 8 (Fall 1991): 77–91.

———. "Tending the 'Sacred Fires': Theodore Parker and Caroline Healey Dall." *Proceedings of the Unitarian Universalist Historical Society* 33 (1995): 22–36.

Goodman, Gary Sue. "'All About Me Forgotten': The Education of Caroline Healey Dall (1822–1912)" (Ph.D. dissertation, Stanford University, 1987). Ann Arbor, MI: University Microfilms.

Leach, William. *True Love and Perfect Union: The Feminist Reform of Sex and Society.* New York: Basic Books, 1980.

Welter, Barbara. "The Merchant's Daughter: A Tale from Life." *New England Quarterly* 42 (1969): 3–22.

# Thoughts on Kindergarten Education

## From *Guide to the Kindergarten and Intermediate Class,* 1860

ELIZABETH PALMER PEABODY (1804–1894) *is best known today as the founder of the kindergarten movement in the United States. She was recognized in her time as a leading intellectual in New England, a prominent Transcendentalist, an educator par excellence, and a writer of numerous books and articles on education and other social issues. Her circle of friends included Unitarian ministers William Ellery Channing and Theodore Parker; Bronson Alcott, in whose experimental school she taught; Margaret Fuller; and her brothers-in-law Horace Mann and Nathaniel Hawthorne. The foreign language bookstore Peabody owned for ten years was a frequent meeting place for Margaret Fuller's Conversations and other Transcendentalist gatherings.*[25]

*Elizabeth Peabody became involved with early education in her late fifties after reading the work of German educator Friedrich Froebel. In 1860, with her sister Mary Mann, she opened in Boston the first English-speaking kindergarten in the United States and wrote* Guide to the Kindergarten and Intermediate Class *(1860) followed by* Moral Culture of Infancy, and Kindergarten Guide *(1863, with Mary Mann). Both books expressed in detail her beliefs about the divine nature of children and the role of the teacher in helping them develop naturally, according to their own inner needs, desires, talents, and time clock.*

See the Biographical Sketch on pages 221–224.

*Kindergarten* means a garden of children, and Froebel, the inventor of it, or rather, as he would prefer to express it, *the discoverer of the method of Nature,* meant to symbolize by the name the spirit and plan of treatment. How does the gardener treat his plants? He studies their individual natures and puts them into such circumstances of soil and atmosphere as enable them to grow, flower, and bring forth fruit—also to renew their manifestation year after year. He does not expect to succeed unless he learns all their wants, and the circumstances in which these wants will be supplied, and all their possibilities of beauty and use, and the means of giving them opportunity to be perfected. On the other hand, while he knows that they must not be forced against their individual natures, he does not leave them to grow wild but prunes redundancies, removes destructive worms and bugs from their leaves and stems and weeds from their vicinity—carefully watching to learn what peculiar insects affect what particular plants and how the former can be destroyed without injuring the vitality of the latter. After all the most careful gardener can do, he knows that the form of the plant is predetermined in the germ or seed and that the inward tendency must concur with a multitude of influences. . . .

In the kindergarten, *children* are treated on an analogous plan. It presupposes gardeners of the mind, who are quite aware that they have as little power to override the characteristic individuality of a child, or to predetermine this characteristic, as the gardener of plants to say that a lily shall be a rose. But notwithstanding this limitation on one side, and the necessity for a concurrence of the Spirit on the other—which is more independent of our modification than the remote sun—yet they must feel responsible, after all, for the perfection of the development, in so far as removing every impediment, preserving every condition, and pruning every redundance.

✦ ✦ ✦

The indispensable thing now is a sufficient society of children. It is only in the society of equals that the social instinct can be gratified and come into equilibrium with the instinct of self-preservation. Self-love, and love of others, are equally natural; and before reason is developed, and the proper spiritual life begins, sweet and beautiful childhood may bloom out and imparadise our mortal life. Let us only give the social instinct of children its fair chance. For this purpose, a few will not do. The children of one family are not enough and do not come along fast enough. A large company should be gathered out of many families. It will be found that the little things are at once taken out of themselves and become interested in each other. In the variety, affinities develop themselves very prettily, and the rough points of rampant individualities wear off. We have seen a highly-gifted child, who, at home, was—to use a vulgar, but expressive word—pesky and odious, with the exacting demands of a powerful but untrained mind and heart become "sweet as roses" spontaneously, amidst the rebound of a large, well-ordered, and carefully watched child society.

✦ ✦ ✦

But let us not be misunderstood. We are not of those who think that children, in any condition whatever, will inevitably develop into beauty and goodness. Human nature tends to revolve in a vicious circle around the idiosyncrasy; and children must have over them, in the person of a wise and careful teacher, a power which shall deal with them as God deals with the mature, presenting the claims of sympathy and truth whenever they presumptuously or unconsciously fall into selfishness. We have the best conditions of moral culture in a company large enough for the exacting disposition of the solitary child to be balanced by the claims made by others on the common stock of enjoyment—there being a reasonable oversight of older persons, wide-awake to anticipate, prevent, and adjust the rival pretensions which must always arise where there are finite beings with infinite desires, while Reason . . . is yet undeveloped.

✦ ✦ ✦

It was Froebel's wisdom to accept the natural activity of childhood as a hint of the Divine Providence and to utilize its spontaneous play for education. And it is this which takes away from his system that element of baneful antagonism which school discipline is so apt to excite and which it is such a misfortune should ever be excited between the young and old. Nothing is worse for the soul, at any period of life, than to be put upon self-defense; for humility is the condition of the growth of mind as well as morals and ensures that natural self-respect shall not degenerate into a petty willfulness and self-assertion. The divine impulse of activity in children should not be directly opposed but accepted and guided into beautiful production, according to the laws of creative order, which the adult has studied out in nature and genially presents in *playing* with the child.

But such playing is a great art and founded on the deepest science of nature, within and without; and therefore Froebel never established a Kindergarten without previously preparing kindergartners [kindergarten teachers] by a normal training, which his faithful disciples have scrupulously kept up. . . . Hundreds of pupils of these normal classes have proved that any fairly gifted, well-educated, genial-tempered young woman who will devote a reasonable time to training for it can become a competent kindergartner.

Nothing short of this will do; for none of the manuals which have been written to guide already trained experts can supply the place of the living teacher. Written words will not describe the fine gradations of the work or give an idea of the conversation which is to be constantly had with the children. It would be less absurd to suppose that a person could learn to make watches by reading a description of the manufacture in an encyclopedia than to suppose a person could learn to educate children by mere formulas.

Indeed, it is *infinitely* less absurd. For a child is not finite mass to be molded, or a blank paper to be written upon at another's will. It is a living subject whose own cooperation—or at least willingness—is to be conciliated and made instrumental to the end in view. Would a Cremona violin be put into the hands of a person ignorant of music, to be tuned and made to discourse divine harmonies? . . . Looking at children's first schools, it would seem that anybody is thought skillful enough to begin a child's education. It takes a long apprenticeship to learn to play on the instrument with seven strings, in order to bring out music. But it is stupidly thought that anybody can play on the greater instrument, whose strings thrill with pleasure or pain, and discourse good or evil, as they are touched wisely or unwisely!

✦ ✦ ✦

Childish play has all the main characteristics of art, inasmuch as it is the endeavor to "conform the shows of things to the desires of the mind"—Bacon's definition of poetry. A child at play is histrionic. He personates characters, with costume and mimic gesture. He also undertakes to represent whatever thing interests his mind by embodiment of it in outward form. . . . Everybody conversant with children knows how easily they will "make believe," as they call it, all these different forms, out of any materials whatever; and are most amused, when the materials to be transformed by their personifying and symbolizing fancy are few, for so much do children enjoy the exercise of imagination that they find it more amusing to have simple forms, which they can "make believe"—first to be one thing and then another—than to have elaborately carved columns, and such like materials, for building. There is nothing in life more charming to a spectator than to see this shaping fancy of children, making everything of nothing and scorning the bounds of probability and even of possibility.

✦ ✦ ✦

[In what is called religious education,] teachers often do great harm, with the best intentions, to finely strung moral organizations. Encouragement to good should altogether predominate over warning and fault finding. It is often better, instead of blaming a child for shortcoming or even wrongdoing, to pity and sympathize and, in a hopeful voice, speak of it as something which the child did not mean to do, or at least was sorry for as soon as done; suggesting at the same time, perhaps, how it can be avoided another time. Above all things, an invariable rule in moral education is not to throw a child upon self-defense. The movement towards defending one's self and making excuses is worse than almost any act of overt wrong. Let the teacher always appear as the friend who is saving or helping the child out of evil, rather than as the accuser, judge, or executioner.

✦ ✦ ✦

I now come to Object Lessons, which should begin simultaneously with all the above exercises; for mental exercises are not only compatible with physical health but necessary to it. The brain is not to be overstrained in childhood, but it is to be used. Where it is left to itself, and remains uncultivated, it shrinks, and that is disease. A child is not able to direct its own attention; it needs the help of the adult in the unfolding of the mind, no less than in the care of its body. . . .

The new method of education gives a gradual series of exercises, continuing the method of Nature. It cultivates the senses by giving them the work of discriminating colors, sounds, &c; sharpens perception by leading children to describe accurately the objects immediately around them.

Objects themselves, rather than the verbal descriptions of objects, are presented to them. The only way to make words expressive and intelligible is to associate them sensibly with the objects to which they relate. Children must be taught to translate things into words before they can translate words into things. Words are secondary in nature; yet much teaching seems to proceed on the principle that these are primary, and so they become mere counters, and children are brought to hating study, and the discourse of teachers, instead of thirsting for them. To look at objects of nature and art, and state their colors, forms, and properties of various kinds, is no painful strain upon the mind. It is just what children spontaneously do when they are first learning to talk. It is a continuation of learning to talk. The object teacher confines the child's attention to one thing, till all that is obvious about it is described; and then asks questions, bringing out much that children, left to themselves, would overlook, suggesting words when necessary, to enable them to give an account of what they see. It is the action of the mind upon real things, together with clothing perceptions in words, which really cultivates; while it is not the painful strain upon the brain which the study of a book is.

✦ ✦ ✦

I am desirous to make a strong impression on this point, because, to many persons, I find object-teaching seems the opposite of teaching. They say that to play with things does not give habits of study. They think that to commit to memory a page of description about a wild duck, for instance, is better than to have the wild duck to look at, leading the child to talk about it, describe it, and inquire into its ways and haunts! They do not see that this study of the things themselves exercises the perception, and picturesque memory, which is probably immortal, certainly perennial, while the written description only exercises the verbal memory. Verbal memory is not to be despised; but it is a consequence and should never be the substitute for picturesque memory. It is the picturesque memory only which is creative.

✦ ✦ ✦

The secret of power and success is *gradualism.* Any child can learn anything, if time and opportunity is given to go step by step. Then learning becomes as easy and agreeable as eating and drinking. Every degree of knowledge, also, must be practically used as soon as attained. It then becomes a power: makes the child a power in nature; and prepares him, when his spirit shall come into union with the God of Nature, and Father of Human Spirits, to become a power over Nature.

## ✦ *Biographical Sketch*

**Born:** *May 16, 1804, Billerica, Massachusetts*

**Died:** *January 3, 1894, Jamaica Plain, Massachusetts, age 90*

**Buried:** *Sleepy Hollow Cemetery, Concord, Massachusetts*

Greatly esteemed in the 1800s as part of the intellectual elite of Boston, a member of the Transcendentalist inner circle, a prolific writer, and a leading educator, Elizabeth Palmer Peabody is best known today as the person responsible for establishing the kindergarten movement in the United States.

Until her involvement with kindergartens, many of Peabody's educational methods were modeled on those used by her mother, who ran a successful, rigorous girls' school in her home to supplement her father's low income from dentistry. This school, the only one the three daughters attended, nourished the girls' creative abilities and self-esteem, while the three sons were subjected to the harsh, conforming discipline of a typical boys' school.

Peabody was a precocious student. By the time she was in her teens, she was teaching at her mother's school in Salem. In her lifetime, she mastered ten languages and had a good grasp of theology, history, and literature. She translated works from German, French, and Italian; gave lectures on ancient history; and opened a series of schools that established her reputation in Boston as a leading progressive educator.

Peabody's bonds with Unitarian minister William Ellery Channing were strong. He guided her reading in Transcendentalism in the 1820s and 1830s, and she later recorded his sermons. In 1834, she met Bronson Alcott. His Pennsylvania school had closed, and Peabody offered to help him establish a new school based on Transcendentalist ideas then current in Boston. Out of this association came a journal, *Record of a School,* which publicized Alcott's philosophy and projects.

Peabody was a serious scholar of religion and saw it as an essential part of education. She was drawn first to liberal Unitarianism and then to Transcendentalism, both of which stressed the goodness of humans, respect for nature, the responsibility to improve life on Earth, and the divine nature of each inner soul. For ten years, the foreign language bookstore she owned in Boston was a meeting place for such persons as Ralph Waldo Emerson, Henry David Thoreau, Margaret Fuller,[26] Horace Mann (husband of her sister Mary), Nathaniel Hawthorne (husband of her sister Sophia), and Theodore Parker. The bookstore also became a gathering place for leading women of the time, serving as the site for an important series of meetings for women referred to as Conversations.

In her late fifties, Peabody was introduced to German educator Friedrich Froebel's ideas on early childhood education.[27] She found them compatible with her own beliefs and is credited with opening the first English-speaking kindergarten in the United States in Boston in 1860. She spent the next thirty years establishing many such schools, training teachers, giving talks, and writing numerous articles and books on kindergarten theory and practices.

Central to the Froebel/Peabody philosophy was the belief that teachers should help children grow naturally, according to each one's internal divine plan. As gardeners cultivate flowers according to what each needs for full bloom, so teachers must nurture children to become whatever they were created to be. "True education," said Peabody, "shall lead out the imprisoned spirit."[28] Teachers were to treat children gently and courteously at all times, believing in their essential goodness, guiding their growth but respecting their will, and leading them to self-discipline and determination through play and other self-initiated activities.

The kindergarten curriculum included arts, crafts, nature studies, science exploration, singing, dancing, conversation, and reflection—but not reading and writing, which inhibited children's creativity and imagination when taught too soon. The emphasis was on children achieving success, learning through experimenting, appreciating nature, appreciating the individuality in themselves and all humans, and finding joy in working and playing together.

Peabody continued to champion new causes into her old age, as reflected by her books of the 1880s. In 1886, she published reflections on her friendship with artist Washington Allston together with her collected essays from *The Dial* and *Aesthetic Papers.*

Although not an original philosopher of education, Elizabeth Peabody did as much or more than any other American in her time to turn new knowledge and theory on child growth and development into successful practice. Through her efforts, creative, spirit-freeing, and humane teaching methods, in both private and public schools, were encouraged and education for countless children was vastly improved.

*Biographical Sketch by* JUNE EDWARDS

## ✦ Writings of Elizabeth Peabody

*Guide to the Kindergarten and Intermediate Class.* New York: Schermerhorn, 1860; Rev. ed. New York: E. Steiger, 1877.

*Kindergarten Messenger.* Edited by Elizabeth P. Peabody (May 1873 to December 1875 and January–December 1877). Merged with the *New England Journal of Education.*

*Lectures in the Training School for Kindergartners.* New York: D. C. Heath, 1886.

*Moral Culture of Infancy and Kindergarten Guide.* With Mary Mann. Boston: H.E.O.P. Burnham, 1863; Rev. ed. Cambridge, 1869; New York: J. W. Schermerhorn, 1876; Reprint, New York: Arno Press and The New York Times, 1969.

"A Plea for Froebel's Kindergarten as the First Grade of Primary Education." In *Last Evening with Allston and Other Papers,* 331–342. Boston: D. Lothrop, 1886.

*Record of a School.* Boston: J. Monroe, 1835. Reprint, New York: Arno Press and The New York Times, 1969.

*Reminiscences of Rev. Wm. Ellery Channing. D.D.* Boston: Roberts Brothers, 1880.

## ✦ Biographical Resources

Baylor, Ruth M. *Elizabeth Palmer Peabody, Kindergarten Pioneer.* Philadelphia: University of Pennsylvania Press, 1965.

Edwards, June. "The Unitarian Influence on Elizabeth Peabody and American Kindergartens." Occasional Paper #13. Malden, MA: Unitarian Universalist Women's Heritage Society, 1996.

Ronda, Bruce, ed. *Letters of Elizabeth Palmer Peabody, American Renaissance Woman.* Middletown, CT: Wesleyan University Press, 1984.

Tharp, Louise Hall. *The Peabody Sisters of Salem.* Boston: Little, Brown, 1950.

MARY CARPENTER

# The Education of Workhouse Girls

## Paper Read Before Social Science Association, 1862

MARY CARPENTER (1807–1877), *the daughter of a Unitarian minister and teacher, opened the first reformatory school for girls in England and later another one for boys. She not only worked to improve the living conditions, health, and treatment of poor children, she also argued, in the following selections from her paper entitled "The Education of Pauper Girls," that the government should provide good schools to allow such children to rise out of squalid, depressing environments. To protect indigent girls from futures in adult workhouses and prisons, they especially deserved to be taught by kind, loving teachers who would help them overcome their feelings of inferiority and encourage them to become successful in society.*

See the Biographical Sketch on pages 229–232.

The education of the female sex is one of the most important problems of the present day. If, at *all* times, it is essential to the well-being of the human race that those to whom is committed its early nurture should be duly prepared and educated for those important duties, at the present day, when female emigration is pointed to, on the one hand, as the only means of relieving society of an enormous and unprofitable surplus of female labor; and on the other, we are warned that untrained and helpless women are as little wanting at the Antipodes as here, it is especially evident that women, in order to do their true life's work in any station, in any part of the globe, *must be educated.*

But for this simple proposition to be practically adopted by the country, we must wait at least for another generation to pass and only hope that all the mistakes of this present one—all the difficulties and trials consequent on them, all the lessons which have been given by the experienced, and forgotten as soon as received by the thoughtless—that all these may have had some small due effect; we can only hope that when we are gone our words may be remembered. But with respect to the girls who are the subject of this paper, we need not wait for them or their parents or friends to be convinced that our views are sound and ought to be carried out. *They,* the next generation, the mothers of the one that follows, are in our hands, the hands of society, to be trained as the most enlightened educationists of the day may deem best. We see enormous evils round us which we cannot remedy, we behold multitudes of young girls springing up in our midst to misery and ruin, and we cannot stretch out a helping hand to save them, for they have low, ignorant parents, who know nothing and care little about their daughters' true education. Some, perchance, have sunk so low, and been so ill-trained, that the law interferes and takes them out of the hands of their parents; and we stand on this bad foundation to raise a good superstructure in a reformatory. But the workhouse girls are our own charge; *we* have the sole responsibility of them; the Government is not sparing in its allowance to their teachers, devoting some 30,000 pounds annually that workhouse children may be well trained. The parents cannot interfere. There is no criminal taint to be washed out. We have every opportunity in our hands of rearing up another generation of wives and mothers, far better than the present, or of preparing a better race of female emigrants to our colonies, and *we are NOT doing it.* Whether we ask commissioners on education, or inspectors, or visitors of workhouses, or governors of jails, we shall have the same mournful answer from all. However they may differ in other matters, they will agree in this—that bad as is the education and training usually given to boys in ordinary workhouse schools, the girls receive one even less calculated to fit them for the duties of life; and the exceptions to this general experience will only be where there has been some special influence exerted to counteract the evils of the system. . . .

We use the term *pauper* girls because it is the common one to designate the class before us; but we would wish to see it altered. Children ought never to be considered as paupers; they have committed no act of their own which should degrade them. Children *must* always be dependent on others for their support; nature assigns to the parent the support of them, society discharges to the child a duty which the parent cannot, or does not perform. All human beings in a free and Christian country should be regarded as entering the world free and unstained by any acts of others—all equal in the sight of the Creator. We must divest ourselves therefore of the idea that a child, because in a workhouse, is less *entitled* to care than the highest in the land.

✦ ✦ ✦

We are not to think of them as a number of pauper children who must be taken care of at as little expense as possible but as young girls who, when grown to womanhood, will be the bane or blessing of the next generation and whom we must prepare for their part in life to the best of our ability, as fulfilling a solemn duty.

✦ ✦ ✦

All girls then, from the time they leave the infant school until within a year of their being likely to go out to service, should be placed in schools not too large to admit of a distinct family feeling and family management. Nor should these schools be mere subdivisions according to age, learning, etc., of a large number. If it *is* necessary to congregate many in one locality, let them be divided (as is done with full success at Lancaster U.S.) into genuine family homes, where the different ages and varieties of temper of the girls may prevent the injurious monotony; where there may be real home duties which even the youngest may learn to perform, and where home affections may be cherished. With such an arrangement all the separate homes might unite in one common schoolroom, and thus all the advantages of economy and superior classification be obtained. The size of these homes may vary from twenty to thirty but should not exceed forty girls. After the girls have gone through this ordinary home and school training, it would be highly desirable that they should be placed where they can obtain more special training for their future work in life—in separate homes, where they should have somewhat more liberty and have more preparation for the particular mode of life they are intended for. Mrs. Way has admirably carried out this plan in her Brockham Home for Workhouse Girls of about fourteen years of age. In some districts homes connected with factory work might be valuable, but they should still exercise a parental tutelage over the girls. In all cases where the girls are actually put out to earn their own living, a friendly interest in them should still be maintained; and there should be a home to which they can return during temporary loss of employment as in Miss Twining's Industrial Home. These prove that girls must still feel that they have friends, that they are not uncared for, that there are those who grieve when they do wrong, and rejoice at their successful career.

Such, I believe is a brief statement of what ought to be the education of workhouse girls. I need not say that it is *not* of this character in our country. There are doubtless some few and exceptional cases where the country workhouse under the management of some benevolent and judicious guardians, aided by lady visitors, becomes a true home. But these exceptions only prove the rule. Even in well managed workhouse schools, quite separated from the adult paupers, the girls look listless and in a very inferior condition to the boys: this I have myself observed; nor, if the principles here laid down are admitted, is it at all difficult to assign the reason for this. If there is any connection between the workhouse for adult paupers and that for children, none can tell what contamination is the consequence; what influences are imbibed, even by young children, who are placed for care with female paupers, it may be of the lowest character. A pauper element is infused into them from earliest childhood—an element devoid of all that is good or would defend from evil in the female sex. Hence the appalling fact which was revealed in a recent Parliamentary return, that during the ten years ending 31 December 1860, 1,736 young girls returned to the workhouse—being double the number of boys; and 1,896 returned not from misconduct but to become a burden on the country. In January 1859, there were (as stated in the Poor Law Report, p. 189) 12,353 illegitimate pauper children. This awful fact speaks for itself. Are we going to rear up these twelve thousand infants as we reared their mothers? and as we reared the multitudes of wretched girls who did not return to the workhouse but found their way to penitentiaries and jails? Such facts ought to be widely known by the country, and then we believe that the country would demand an *entire alteration* of the whole system. No palliatives will avail to cure a system which is based on an entirely false principle. No home feeling can exist in any institution in which voluntary Christian effort does not infuse some of that love which was appointed by the Creator to be the very atmosphere of childhood. No guardians appointed to administer poors' rates ought ever to manage schools for the children. No men, however wise and good, ought to superintend institutions for young girls. The children ought all to be separated from adult paupers and begin life anew, free from reproach; and the management of them should be committed to benevolent and enlightened women, under whose direct control all officials should be placed.

We shall be told that it will be impossible to find voluntary workers among the female sex who will undertake so enormous a work as that of managing schools for all the pauper girls in the country. A similar difficulty was made ten years ago, when we, the voluntary workers, asked the Government to give into our care the criminal children, who were becoming an increasing burden to the country in gaols. The Government gave us the needed authority and pecuniary aid, and there has been no lack of managers or teachers adapted to the work. Women have been making a rapid advance during the last ten years in the power of working for themselves and others. Numbers of ladies have already devoted themselves to workhouse visiting and will doubtless be ready to take the less painful and difficult work of managing the schools.

Now, such a change in the present order of things may be effected, I stated in a paper read before another section of this Association last year, entitled "What shall we do with our pauper children?" I also stated it in my evidence before the Poor Law Committee last year. It does not fall within the province of the present paper to discuss it; but only, after considering the principles of the education of pauper girls, to express the strong conviction that this cannot be carried out efficiently, either as regards the country or the children, except by voluntary benevolent and Christian agencies, combined, as in the case of schools for juvenile delinquents, with inspection and pecuniary aid from the Government.

## ✦ *Biographical Sketch*

**Born:** *April 3, 1807, in Exeter, England*

**Died:** *June 14, 1877, in Bristol, England, age 70*

**Buried:** *Arno's Vale Cemetery, Bristol, England*

Mary Carpenter was concerned about society's neglect of poor children and campaigned for laws and policies assuring that society would take responsibility for them and provide for their basic education. In addition, she believed in the possibility of reclaiming delinquent children through caring supervision and instructive reformatories, instead of retributive prison sentences.

The oldest daughter of Unitarian minister Lant Carpenter, Mary Carpenter was given an exceptional education for a woman, including the classics and sciences, in her father's school in Bristol. She was a private governess for two years. When her father's health forced him to close his school in 1829, Mary joined her mother, Anna Penn Carpenter, and sister Anna in running a girl's school to maintain the family's income. This monetary security enabled her father to pursue social concerns as an integral part of his ministry until his death in 1840. Though interested in theology during that period, Mary did not find her interest welcomed. When the Unitarians convened in Bristol, she and other women were not allowed to attend the sessions but were expected to assist with hospitality.

In 1831, Mary Carpenter began two decades as superintendent of the afternoon Sunday school. Influenced by her father's Christian message and by sermons of American Unitarians William Ellery Channing and Joseph Tuckerman, Mary Carpenter extended Lewin Mead Meeting's ministry to poorer members of the community, prompted by conditions she saw while visiting students' families. In 1835, she founded a visiting society to reach more severely deprived children and served as its secretary for two decades. In 1838, she began preparatory work to promote a ministry to the poor, starting a school for so-called ragged children in 1846 to coincide with the August 1 anniversary of Britain's freeing of slaves.

Mary Carpenter was an early advocate of providing nutritious meals for poor children to enable normal physical development and an extended attention span. Increasingly, she found occasions to write or speak about the conditions of children, interspersing her comments with portrayals of existing conditions, specific cases of neglected children, and effects of positive intervention. She promoted a family-modeled environment of caring structure and increasing levels of trust. She thought deprived urban youth needed to experience being children, including the beneficial effects of natural scenery and other educational excursions.

Mary Carpenter founded Red Lodge in Park Row, a reformatory for girls, in 1854. She was assisted for a time by Frances Power Cobbe,[29] but Cobbe left after finding Mary's lifestyle too severe. Red Lodge was expanded through contributions by Unitarian philanthropist Lady Noel Byron. After Mary's mother died, Lady Byron fostered her living next door to the Red Lodge complex in a house that became a promotion for girls training for domestic service. With Lady Byron's death in 1856, Mary received a legacy that enabled her to buy the house, along with a small stipend.

Concern for the antislavery cause in the United States prompted Mary's support, which included gathering contributions for boxes sent to the Boston Anti-Slavery Christmas bazaars, over which her sister assumed responsibility. Mary Carpenter met major abolitionist speakers, including Frederick Douglass and William Lloyd Garrison, and she invited an escaped slave to speak with her classes. Concerned that former students should have a meeting house for continued self-cultivation, she established a workmen's hall in 1863. Mary then closed the ragged school and opened an industrial day feeding program.

Her book *Our Convicts,* published in 1864, encouraged a societal sense of responsibility for convicted criminals. It was well received by notable critic Harriet Martineau[30] and widely read. Income from the sale of the book provided funds to educate Mary's informally adopted daughter and allowed her to accept invitations to travel in pursuit of her reform interests.

Mary Carpenter published *Last Days in England of the Rajah Rammohun Roy* in 1866, after having contact with Indian students coming to England to be educated and take civil service exams. She became concerned about the circumscribed educational opportunities afforded Indian women and felt called to go to India. After her return to England in 1868, she wrote a popularly received book, *Six Months in India,* which prompted an invitation from Queen Victoria. Mary returned to India three more times (in 1868, 1869, and 1875) to initiate schools to train women to teach others. Unfortunately, this project had extremely limited results. She wrote a report to the governor general and made a number of addresses in England describing conditions in India's prisons and the need to institute reformatories.

Travel to North America in 1873 showed that Mary Carpenter's theology was dated, but her experience with varied delinquent and criminal populations was illuminating. She spoke privately in Boston and publicly in New York, Hartford, and Newark. She also pursued her interest in the education of former slaves, to which she had faithfully contributed. Frederick Douglass introduced her address at Howard University in Washington, DC, and Henry Whitney Bellows accompanied her to a graduation at Hampton Institute in Virginia. Visiting her brother in Montreal, Mary inspected prisons there and informed the governor that they were the worst she had ever seen. She also visited First Nation communities.

Though invited to support women's suffrage by John Stuart Mill in the 1860s, Mary refused, finding not enough need for it herself and becoming concerned that her support would damage her effectiveness in reformatory and educational concerns. At the end of her life, Mary Carpenter wholeheartedly opposed the Contagious Diseases Acts, which made women vulnerable to forced medical examination as prostitutes, and she supported women's entrance to medical school in an 1870s petition. She also finally signed a petition for women's suffrage.

*Biographical Sketch by* IRENE BAROS-JOHNSON

## ✦ Writings of Mary Carpenter

*An Address on Prison Discipline and Juvenile Reformatories.* Calcutta, India: W. Jones, 1876.

*The Duty of Society to the Criminal Classes.* Address delivered in the Church of the Messiah, Montreal, Sunday, July 6, 1873. Montreal: D. Rose, 1873.

*Female Life in Prison.* London: Low, 1868.
*Red Lodge Girl's Reformatory School, Bristol: It's History, Principles, and Working.* Bristol, England: n.p., 1875.
*Juvenile Delinquents, Their Condition and Treatment.* London: W. and F. G. Cash, 1853.
*The Last Days in England of the Rajah Rammohun Roy.* London: Trubner, 1866.
*Memoir of Joseph Tuckerman, D.D., of Boston.* London: Christian Tract Society, 1849.
*Morning and Evening Meditation, with Prayers, for Every Day in a Month.* 5th ed. (with additions). London: Longmans, Green, 1868.
*On Reformatory and Industrial Schools for India.* Paper read at the Congress of the Social Science Association, Glasgow, Scotland, October 1874.
*Our Convicts.* London: Longman, Green, Longman, Roberts and Green, 1864.
*Prison Discipline and Juvenile Reformatories.* Calcutta, India: n.p., 1876.
*Ragged Schools, Their Principles and Modes of Operation.* London: Partridge and Oakley, 1850.
*Reformatory Schools: For the Children of the Perishing and Dangerous Classes and for Juvenile Offenders.* London: C. Gilpin, 1851.
*Six Months in India.* London: n.p., 1868.
*Voices of the Spirit and Spirit Pictures.* Bristol, England: Arrowsmith, 1877.
*What Shall We Do with Our Pauper Children?* Paper read at the Social Science Association, Dublin, Ireland, 1861.
*The Work of School Boards for the Neglected and Destitute Children.* Paper read in the education section of the Congress of the Social Science Association, Leeds, England, October, 1871. Bristol, England: Arrowsmith, 1871.

## ✦ Biographical Resources

Carpenter, J. Estlin. *The Life and Work of Mary Carpenter.* London: Macmillan, 1879.
Carpenter, William Benjamin. *Sketch of the Life and Work of Mary Carpenter.* Bristol, England: Arrowsmith, 1877.
Lavan, Spencer. *Unitarians and India: A Study in Encounter and Response.* Chicago: Exploration Press, 1991.
Manton, J. *Mary Carpenter and the Children of the Streets.* London: Heinemann, 1976.
Saywers, Ruby J. *Mary Carpenter of Bristol.* Bristol, England: Bristol University, 1964.
Schupf, Harriet. "Mary Carpenter." *Victorian Studies* 17 (1974): 301–317.
Taylor, Clare. *British and American Abolitionists.* Edinburgh: Edinburgh University Press, 1974.
Wells, Gannett, Mrs. "A Memorial Chapter, Mary Carpenter." *Unitarian Review* 8 (August 1987): 173.

# What Shall We Do with Our Daughters?

## Lecture Delivered over 800 Times, 1868–1895

MARY ASHTON RICE LIVERMORE (1820–1905) *like many educated, young, single American women of her time, began her career as a governess, but after marriage to Universalist minister Daniel Livermore, she turned her talents to social reform in a variety of areas. An outstanding organizer, she was well known for her work with the Western Sanitary Commission during the Civil War. She also wrote numerous articles for her husband's denominational newspaper and edited the paper in his absence. A national leader in the suffrage movement as well, Mary Livermore devoted her energies after the war to editing the* Woman's Journal *and giving public speeches, where she again excelled.*

*Over the years, she gave thousands of lectures on women's rights, temperance, equal education, and other causes. Her most frequently requested talk was "What Shall We Do with Our Daughters?" in which she pleaded for educating females in an academic curriculum as demanding as that given any male.*

See the Biographical Sketch on pages 240–242.

It is more than fifty years since Margaret Fuller, standing, as she said, "in the sunny noon of life," wrote a little book, which she launched on the current of thought and society. It was entitled "Woman in the Nineteenth Century"; and as the truths it proclaimed and the reforms it advocated were far in advance of public acceptance, its appearance was the signal for an immediate widespread newspaper controversy that raged with great violence. I was young then, and as I took the book from the hands of the bookseller, wondering what the contents of the thin little volume could be to provoke so wordy a strife, I opened at the first page. My attention was immediately arrested, and a train of thought started by the two mottoes at the head of the opening chapter,—one underneath the other, one contradicting the other.

The first was an old-time adage, endorsed by Shakespeare, believed in by the world, and quoted in that day very generally. It is not yet entirely obsolete. “Frailty, thy name is Woman.” Underneath it, and unlike it, was the other, “The Earth waits for her Queen.” The first described woman as she has been understood in the past; as she has masqueraded in history; as she has figured in literature; as she has, in a certain sense, existed. The other prophesied of that grander type of woman, towards which today the whole sex is moving,—consciously or unconsciously, willingly or unwillingly,—because the current sets that way, and there is no escape from it.

✦ ✦ ✦

Born and bred for generations under . . . conditions of hindrance, it has not been possible for women to rise much above the arbitrary standards of inferiority persistently set before them. Here and there through the ages, some woman, endowed with phenomenal force of character, has towered above the mediocrity of her sex, hinting at the qualities imprisoned in the feminine nature. It is not strange that these instances have been rare; it is strange, indeed, that women have held their own during these ages of degradation.

✦ ✦ ✦

A great wave is lifting [women] to higher levels. The leadership of the world is being taken from the hands of the brutal and low, and the race is making its way to a higher ideal than once it knew. It is the evolution of this tendency that is lifting women out of their subject condition, that is emancipating them from the seclusion of the past, and adding to the sum total of the world’s worth and wisdom by giving to them the cultivation human beings need. The demand for their education,—technical and industrial, as well as intellectual,—and for their civil and political rights, is being urged each year by an increasing host and with more emphatic utterance.

The doors of colleges, professional schools, and universities, closed against them for ages, are opening to them. They are invited to pursue the same courses of study as their brothers and are graduated with the same diplomas. Trades, businesses, remunerative vocations, and learned professions seek them; and even the laws, which are the last to feel the change in public opinion,—usually dragging a whole generation behind,—even these are being annually revised and amended, and then they fail to keep abreast of the advancing civilization.

✦ ✦ ✦

As I listen to the debates that attend their progress, and weigh the prophecies of evil always inspired by a growing reform, as I hear the clash of the scientific raid upon women by the small pseudo-scientists of the day,—who weigh their brains and measure their bones to prove their inferiority to men,—my thoughts turn to the young women of the present time. "What shall we do with our daughters?" is really the sum and substance of what, in popular phrase, is called "the woman question."

✦ ✦ ✦

It is for our young women that the great changes of the time promise the most; it is for our daughters,—the fair, bright girls who are the charm of society and the delight of home; the sources of infinite comfort to fathers and mothers, and the sources of great anxiety also. What shall we do with them,—and what shall they do with and for themselves?

✦ ✦ ✦

The changed conditions of life which our young women confront compel greater care and thought on the part of those charged with their education than has heretofore been deemed necessary. They are to be weighted with larger duties and to assume heavier responsibilities; for the days of tutelage seem to be ended for civilized women, and they are to think and act for themselves.

Let no one, therefore, say this question of the training of our daughters is a small question. No question can be small that relates to half the human race. The training of boys is not more important than that of girls. . . . Men are today confessing their need of the aid of women by appointing them on school committees, boards of charities, as prison commissioners, physicians to insane asylums, positions which they cannot worthily fill without preparation.

Therefore, not only for their own sakes but for the sake of the human family, of which women make one-half, should we look carefully to the training of our daughters. Nature has so constituted us that the sexes act and react upon each other, making every "woman's cause" a man's cause and every man's cause a woman's cause. . . . And they are the foes of the race, albeit not always intentional, who set themselves against the removal of woman's disabilities, shut in their faces the doors of education or opportunity, or deny them any but the smallest and most incomplete training. For it is true that "who educates a woman educates a race."

Good health is a great prerequisite of successful or happy living. To live worthily or happily, to accomplish much for one's self or others when suffering much from pain and disease, is attended with difficulty. . . . Therefore I would give to "our daughters" a good physical education.

We shall by-and-by come to recognize the right of every child to be well born,—sound in body, with inherited tendencies towards mental and moral health. . . . When shall an enlightened public sentiment demand that those who seek of God the gift of little children shall make themselves worthy the gift, by healthful and noble living, practical acquaintance with prenatal laws of being, and all that relates to the hereditary transmission of qualities.

If we would give to our daughters a good physiological training, we must attend carefully to their dress. The dress of women at the present time is about as unhygienic as it well can be. And many of our girls are made the victims of disease and weakness for life, through the evils of the dress they wear from birth. The causes of their invalidism are sought in hard study, coeducation, too much exercise, or lack of rest and quiet in certain periods when nature demands it. All the while the medical attendant is silent concerning the "glove-fitting," steel-clasped corset; the heavy, dragging skirts, the bands engirding the body, and the pinching, distorting boot. These will account for much of the feebleness of women and girls; for they exhaust energy, make freedom of movement a painful impossibility, and frequently shipwreck our young daughter before she gets out of port.

✦ ✦ ✦

The prevailing French boots made for women, and exhibited in the shop windows, are painfully suggestive. Pointed and elongated, they prophesy cramped and atrophied toes; while the high and narrow heel that slides down under the instep throws the whole body into an unnatural position in walking, creating diseases which are difficult of cure. . . .

While the clothing of our daughters should not deform the figure nor injure the health, it need be neither inelegant nor inartistic. No particular style of dress can be recommended, but each one should choose what is most becoming and appropriate in fashion and material. With sacred regard to the laws of health, and without too large expenditure of time and money, every woman should aim to present an attractive exterior to her friends and the world. So, indeed, should every man; for it is the duty of all human beings to be as beautiful as possible.

✦ ✦ ✦

Food, sleep, exercise, and other matters demand attention when one is entrusted with the education of girls. American children, unlike those which we see abroad, generally sit at table with their parents, eat the same food, keep the same late hours, and share with them the excitement of evening guests, evening meetings and lectures, and the dissipation of theatres, operas, balls, and receptions. This is unwise indulgence. Children require simple food, early hours for retiring, and abundance of sleep, as well as freedom from social and religious excitements.

✦ ✦ ✦

It is hardly necessary that anything should be said in advocacy of the higher intellectual education of our daughters. For the question of woman's collegiate education is practically settled; and it is almost as easy today for a woman to obtain the highest university education as it is for a man.

But no phase of the great movement for the advancement of women has progressed so slowly as that which demands their technical and industrial training. To be sure, the last fifty years, which have brought great changes to the women of America, have largely increased the number of remunerative employments they are permitted to enter. When Harriet Martineau visited America in 1840, she found but seven employments open to women. At the present time, . . . there are about three hundred and fifty industrial occupations open to women.

And yet it is true, however, that women have received very little special industrial training to fit them for the work they are doing or for a higher kind of work which will give them better pay. . . .

I cannot leave this topic of women's industrial training without speaking of our culpability in neglecting to give our daughters some knowledge of business affairs. With utter indifference on our part, they are allowed to grow to womanhood unfamiliar with the most ordinary forms of business transactions,—how to make out bills and to give receipts; how to draw bank-checks; how to make notes, and what are the cautions to be observed concerning them; what is the best method of transmitting funds to a distance, whether by postal orders or bank drafts; what are safe rates of interest; how to purchase a life annuity, or effect an insurance on life or property, and so on.

If property is to pass into their possession, our daughters certainly need to know much more than this, that they may be able to manage it with wisdom or even to retain it securely. They need to know what are the elements of financial security; what may be considered safe investments; how to rent, improve, or sell property; what margin of property above the amount of the loan should be required, when it is made on real estate; what constitutes a valid title to property; what cautions are to be observed concerning mortgages; what are the property rights of married women in the states of their residence, with other like information.

We talk much of preparing our daughters to be good wives, mothers, and home-makers. Do we systematically attempt this? Do we conduct the education of girls with this object? Do we not trust almost entirely to natural instinct and aptitude, which, in the woman, is incomparably strong in the direction of wifehood, motherhood, and the home? For the mighty reason that the majority of women will always, while the world stands, be wives, mothers, and mistresses of homes, they should receive the largest, completest, and most thorough training. It is not possible to state this too strongly; for these positions are the most important that woman can occupy. Education, religion, human affection, and civil law, all should conspire to aid her in these departments, to do the best work of which she is capable.

The very highest function of woman is to raise and train the family; it is the very highest function of man also. Indeed, civilization has but this end in view,—the perpetuation and improvement of the race. The establishment of homes, the rearing of families, the founding of schools and colleges, the planting of institutions, the maintaining of governments, all are but means to this end. . . .

The duties of the mother begin long before her child comes into life,—ay, and the duties of the father also. She needs to know all that science can teach of the prenatal laws of being and of the laws of heredity. Her acquaintance with physiology should not be the superficial knowledge, given in the ordinary school or college even. It should be a thorough exposition of the mysteries of her own physical being, with a clear statement of the hygienic laws she must obey, if she would grow into healthy, enduring, glorious womanhood. She should be taught the laws of ventilation and nutrition; what constitutes healthful food; the care of infancy; the nursing of the sick; and in what that vigilant and scrupulous cleanliness consists, which almost prohibits certain forms of disease from passing under one's roof. Intelligence, system, economy, industry, patience, good nature, firmness, good health, a fine moral sense, all these are called into action. So is a knowledge of cooking, laundry work, how to make and repair clothing, together with the other industries of domestic life, even when one has means to employ servants to perform this work; for a woman cannot tell when she is well served, unless she knows what good work is. It requires a very high order of woman to be a good wife, mother, and housekeeper; and she who makes a success in these departments possesses such a combination of admirable qualities, both mental and moral, that, with proper training, she might make a success in almost any department.

We should never forgot that moral and religious training underlies and permeates all other training when it is wisely and judiciously given. . . .

Let our sons and daughters be taught that they are children of God, so divine in ancestry, so royal of parentage, that they must carry themselves nobly and not consent to meanness, low, selfish lives, and vice. Let them be taught that to love God is to love whatever is good and just and true; and that loving brothers, sisters, schoolmates, and humanity as a whole is also loving God, since God is our common Father, and "we are all brethren."

They should be trained to regard earthly life as the first school of the soul, where there are lessons to be learned, tasks to be mastered, hardships to be borne, and where God's divinest agent of help is often hindrance; and that only as we learn well the lessons given us here may we expect to go joyfully forward to that higher school to which we shall be promoted, where the tasks will be nobler, the lessons grander, the outlook broader, and where life will be on a loftier plane. While the coldness of skepticism seems to be creeping over the age,—mainly, I believe, because of its great immersion in materialism of life and activity,—it is possible to train children to such a far-reaching, telescopic religious vision that they will overlook all fogs and mists of doubt. The low fears and dismaying presages that weigh down so many souls will be dispelled by the clear atmosphere in which they will dwell; and with hearts throbbing evenly with the heart of God, they will say confidently, "Because He lives, I shall live also."

## ✦ *Biographical Sketch*

**Born:** *December 19, 1820, Boston, Massachusetts*
**Died:** *May 23, 1905, Melrose, Massachusetts, age 85*
**Buried:** *Wyoming Cemetery, Melrose, Massachusetts*

Although Mary Ashton Rice Livermore is not as well known today as some of her nineteenth-century contemporaries, she was popular with the public in her own time for her energetic involvement with many reform movements of the day. Born the fourth of six children to a deeply religious Boston family, she initially accepted her family's stern Calvinist faith. However, her parents also believed in education for females, and Mary received the best schooling available for girls at the time. She excelled, graduated at age fourteen with honors, and began a teaching career.

When her younger sister died before being "saved," Mary anguished over the girl's eternal damnation. To counteract her depression, she took a job as a governess on a Virginia plantation but was appalled by the brutality toward the slaves. After three years, she returned to Massachusetts, an ardent abolitionist. She soon met a young Universalist minister, Daniel P. Livermore, who convinced her of a different kind of religion, in which all souls are saved by a loving, forgiving God. The two were married in 1845, had three children (one of whom died from illness), and devoted their lives to the principles of Universalism.

In 1857, the family moved to Chicago, where Mary Livermore's most noted work began. Besides using her intellectual abilities to write numerous articles and helping her husband edit *The New Covenant,* a Universalist paper, she became cohead in 1862 of the Midwest branch of the Sanitary Commission, which was responsible for all military hospitals in that area. Through her genius at fundraising and organizing, she ensured that vital supplies for the wounded (such as food, medicine, and surgical dressings), were provided throughout the Civil War. Meanwhile, she also did volunteer work for the Chicago Home of the Friendless, helped found the Home for Aged Women and the Hospital for Women and Children, and joined the temperance movement.

After the war, Livermore turned her energy to voting rights for women. In 1868, she became the founding president of the Illinois Woman Suffrage Association and established its newspaper, the *Agita-*

*tor.* The next year, she—along with Julia Ward Howe and Lucy Stone[31]—formed the American Women's Suffrage Association. When her family moved back to Massachusetts the following year, Livermore became editor of the organization's publication, *Woman's Journal.*

Mary Livermore's popularity grew even stronger when she joined the lecture circuit, delivering thousands of animated speeches for over two decades on women's rights, temperance, education, and many other social issues. In addition, she was the first president of the Association for the Advancement of Women, the president of the Women's Christian Temperance Union (WCTU) in Massachusetts for ten years, president of the American Woman Suffrage Association for three years, and an organizer of the General Federation of Women's Clubs. Livermore was also involved in prison reform and many other civil and welfare issues of the day.

Mary Livermore's first book, *Pen Pictures,* was published in 1863. Her most popular lecture, "What Shall We Do with Our Daughters?" (which she delivered over eight hundred times) appeared in print in 1883. Four years later, her memoirs of the Civil War, *My Story of the War,* became a bestseller. In 1893, she co-edited, with Frances Willard, a book of biographical sketches of women activists called *A Woman of the Century,* which included sketches of many Unitarians and Universalists.

At age seventy-five, Livermore finally retired from lecturing, celebrated her fiftieth wedding anniversary, and helped found the Women's Education and Industrial Union. Her autobiography, *The Story of My Life,* appeared in 1897. She died at age eighty-five in 1905, six years after her beloved husband.

*Biographical Sketch by* JUNE EDWARDS

## ✦ Writings of Mary Ashton Rice Livermore


*My Story of the War.* Hartford, CT: A.D. Worthington, 1889.

*Pen Pictures: or Sketches from Domestic Life.* Chicago: Griggs, 1862.

*The Story of My Life: Or the Sunshine and Shadow of Seventy Years.* Hartford, CT: Worthington, 1899.

*The Two Families, and the Duty That Lies Nearest: Prize Stories.* Boston: A. Tompkins, 1848.

*What Shall We Do with Our Daughters?, Superfluous Women, and Other Lectures.* Boston: Lee and Shepard, 1883; Reprint, New York: Garland, 1987.

*A Woman of the Century.* With Frances E. Willard. New York: Charles Wells Moulton, 1893; Reprint, Detroit: Gale Research, 1967.

"Woman's Work in the Temperance Reform." National Temperance Convention, Saratoga, NY, July 15, 1891.

*Women's View of Divorce.* New York: n.p., 1890. (Orig. pub. North American Review, 1890)

## ✦ Biographical Resources

Howe, Charles A. "Daniel and Mary Livermore: The Biography of a Marriage." *Proceedings of the Unitarian Universalist Historical Society* 19 (1982–83): 14–35.

Kennedy, Patricia Scileppi, and Gloria Hartmann O'Shields. *We Shall Be Heard: Women Speakers in America.* Dubuque, IA: Kendall/Hunt, 1983.

O'Connell, Daniel S. "The Outcome of This Faith: How Universalism Changed History in the Person of Mary Ashton Livermore." Occasional Paper #7. Malden, MA: Unitarian Universalist Women's Heritage Society, 1995.

Phelps, Elizabeth Stuart. "Mary A. Livermore." In *Our Famous Women,* 386–414. Hartford, CT: A. D. Worthington, 1884.

# Spiritual Aspects of Early Childhood Education

## From Lectures Delivered in Boston, 1872–1882

ELIZABETH PALMER PEABODY'S (1804–1894) *lectures on kindergarten education summarized her major work in this field. She stressed the spiritual nature of early childhood education, the inherent worth of each child, and the divine nature of the calling to be a teacher. She recognized the mutual nature of all education—that teachers and students must be open to learning from each other. Her commitment to the education of all people made her one of the foremost educators of the nineteenth century. The lectures were assembled and published in 1886 as* Lectures in Training Schools for Kindergartners *(that is, kindergarten teachers). The following selection contains excerpts from three of these lectures.*

See the Biographical Sketch on pages 221–224.

Froebel's method is a radical change of direction. It changes the educator's point of view. Instead of looking down upon the child, the kindergartner must clear her mind of all foregone arbitrary conclusions and humbly look up to the innocent soul, which in its turn sees nothing but the face of the Father in heaven—(for thus Christ explains children's being "of the kingdom of heaven"). This is difficult for her to do, because—not seldom—a shadow has fallen on the original innocence of the children confided to her care from those human beings in relation to them, who have not done for them what every human being needs by reason of the essential dependence of individuals upon their race.

✦ ✦ ✦

We are always either educating or hindering the development of our fellow creatures; we are always being uplifted or being dragged down by our fellow creatures. Education is always mutual. The child teaches his parents (as Goethe has said) what his parents omitted to teach him. Every child is a new thought of God, whose individuality is significant and interesting to others, though it is his own limitation; and to appreciate a child's individuality is the advantage the teacher gets in exchange for the general laws which he leads the child to appreciate. It is this variety of individuals that makes the work of education fascinating and takes from it all wearisome monotony. Those persons who feel that education is wearisome work have not learned the secret of it. I have never seen a good kindergartner who was not as fond of the work as a painter of his painting, a sculptor of his modeling. Teachers who are not conscious of learning from their pupils may be pretty sure they teach them very little.

✦ ✦ ✦

I would like to speak with some comprehensiveness and particularity on the subject of religious nurture. Mark me, I say religious *nurture,* not religious teaching. The religion that integrates human education is not to be taught. . . . Every individual child is a momentum of God's creativeness which the human Providence of education must take as its *datum.*

✦ ✦ ✦

Children must believe in themselves as a preliminary to believing in God. Let them with things create order; and you will have influence with them in proportion to their feeling that you respect their free will and divine in a genial way what they want; and this you can do if you inform yourself of what is *universal* in human desire, keeping your eyes open to what modifications *their* individuality suggests; and it is your cognizance of these individualities which makes your part of the enjoyment. If there are no two leaves alike, much more are there no two human individuals precisely alike, and human intercourse is made refreshing by these various individualities playing over the surface of the universal race-consciousness. If you respect the individuality of a child and let it have fair play, you gain its confidence. Nothing is so delightful as to feel oneself understood. It is much more delightful than to be admired. But to give a child's individuality fair play in a company of children, you must open children's eyes to one another's individualities, and you will find that if you suggest their respecting each other's rights in the plays, there is something within them that will justify you. . . .

The religious nurture which Froebel proposes therefore consists simply in so living with children as to preserve their primeval joy by tenderly and reverently respecting it, as that human instinct prompts which is in the highest power in the mother. Sympathetic tenderness is the first of all means for moral culture. The child's faith in *God* must be cherished into self-reliance. There is a self-distrust that is really a distrust of *God,* and no harm we can do a child is so great as to lead it to doubt its own spontaneity. The common religious teacher—even a conscientious mother—sometimes does this and, so far from nurturing the child's conscious union with *God,* starts a morbid self-consciousness, the opposite of religious peace. . . .

I do not think it right or wise to suggest to little children that *their* wrongdoings, which are more weaknesses than presumptions, are *sins against God.* Children can comprehend their relations to each other, and the violation of each other's rights to happiness, and can be easily led to sympathize with the pain or inconvenience of those they make suffer, which touches their sense of justice and generosity; they can appreciate wrong and its consequences to their equals and to themselves in the *present life.* But *God* is too great to be injured by them; and to bring *God* to their imagination as personally angry with them, overwhelms thought, and annihilates all sense of responsibility, with all self-respect. . . . The naughty child, at his worse, needs only to think of *God* as sorry for him, and "waiting to be gracious," like the father of the prodigal son.

✦ ✦ ✦

What I insist upon is that a child should never be left to doubt but should always be helped to feel *sure* that *God* is loving him better than he loves himself; is sorry far more than angry with him when he has done wrong, and therefore it is that He will not let him succeed in doing wrong, but has so arranged things that the wrong always gets checked; that *God* is especially good precisely because He "makes the ways of the transgressor hard." Never let the Infinite Power appear to the naughty child's imagination as punishing but only as encouraging, inspiring, helping!

# The Higher Education of Women

## Article in *The Repository,* February 1874

OLYMPIA BROWN (1835–1926), *a Universalist who is credited with being the first woman ordained by full denominational authority,*[32] *also gained fame through her leadership role in the campaigns for women's suffrage and temperance. She wrote many articles on social issues for her husband's newspaper and other periodicals and eventually resigned from parish ministry to devote her full attention to the fight for women's rights.*

*In the following article, published in a Universalist journal, Olympia Brown advocated higher education for women with the best instruction available, not the usual modified course for the female mind. Young women, she argued, are capable of comprehending all subjects, and the larger their experience, the better suited they will be for whatever position or duty they are called to undertake.*

See the Biographical Sketch on pages 251–255.

Among the subjects proposed for consideration at the recent Woman's Congress was "The Higher Education of Women," a subject which embraces all that we seek for woman. For education, in its largest sense, means not merely the curriculum of the schools, the jargon of science, or the refinements of literature; it is something more than the memorizing of facts and dates, names and terms. It means rather the exact training of every faculty, and that full development of all the powers, which shall fit one for largest usefulness in the world.

*Higher* education looks to the supremacy of all that is noblest and best in human nature; it means that quickening of the moral sense, that opening of the spiritual eye, which makes one not merely an efficient worker in the business of the world but one of the immortals, a companion of the angels. In the higher education of women we seek that which shall make them noble characters.

At the present day too many women, even of good culture, confound character with reputation and think it of little consequence what they really are, if they can only manage to make a fair show before the world.

Now there is a very broad distinction to be made between character and reputation. Character is what God thinks of us; reputation is what men say about us. A good character is the result of years of discipline and experience, of watchfulness and self-denial; a good reputation is often gained by a single lucky chance or may be attained by the intrigues and management of a charlatan or a hypocrite. Sometimes by the misjudgment of the multitude, or a false public opinion, an act in itself bad will gain for the doer a good reputation; and the same action which gives a bad reputation at one period may be chief cause of one's glory at another.

Reputation is ever changing; it is one thing today, another thing tomorrow. Dependent upon the caprice of a fickle multitude, a word, a hint, sometimes even a look is sufficient to destroy it. But character is a treasure beyond the reach of the world; it abides through all time and change; it is ours after this world with its transient excitements shall have passed away; it must be the chief source of our power and peace here as well as of our hopes for the hereafter.

✦ ✦ ✦

A good character is composite in its nature; it is made up of a combination of tastes, aspirations, virtues, gained by the experience of a lifetime all bound together in one. . . .

[A] noble character is formed not of a single trickling rill, pure and bright though it may be, but of many qualities combined. That energy which takes its rise among the rough and rugged experiences of primitive society and ever presses on, gathering new life with every trial, that frugality born of want, that integrity which is nurtured in the exact world of business, that sweet charity begotten of a large knowledge of human frailty, that gentle trustfulness, acquired by basking in the sunshine of Christian love—all these and many more are the tributary streams which unite to form the noble Christian character; which shall be earnest and efficient in the work of the world, bearing the burdens of life without complaining itself a thing of beauty, lending blessedness to every scene until at last it mingles itself with that ocean of truth and love, the heart of God.

We seek for women the higher education which shall give them such a composite, many-sided, symmetrical Christian character; an education which shall give them the executive ability of the business man, the intellectual acumen of the scholar, the comprehensive thought of the philosopher, the prophetic vision of the seer, and all adorned and glorified by those Christian graces, faith, hope, and charity.

It remains for us to consider the kind of education which will secure to women those qualities which most ennoble human character.

There are three sources of education—instruction, experience, and inspiration; and woman wants them all in their largest, fullest sense. She wants the best instruction which the age affords. Too long men have stingily doled out to us broken bits of knowledge, half-truths and make-believes. We have been fed these many years with crumbs from the rich man's table; it is time that we go home and sit with Abraham in the sunshine of eternal truth. If our colleges have been made repositories of the richest learning of the time, if there are garnered there the choicest stores of knowledge, the fullest libraries, the most complete cabinets, the most learned men, surely there woman ought to go and enrich herself by vast treasures of that knowledge which in all the ages of the past has made men wise and strong. Let her sit at the feet of the sages and refresh her mind with the knowledge of the wisest; let her hold converse with the poets and lift her soul into companionship with the purest spirits of all times. Let her accept no modified course, prepared with special reference to the female mind. Let her turn with contempt from the female seminary, that miserable farce with which women have been cheated by a semblance of learning without the reality, and demand all the instruction, in all departments of learning, that is given to men. Let the standard be fixed as high as may be, women must come up to the mark. . . .

Does anybody tell us that these things are not possible to the woman, that her strength of body and power of mind are insufficient to grasp the most profound subjects? I answer, this is not a matter of speculation, it is a demonstrated fact that women are capable, both physically and mentally, of most severe study and largest attainments. The names of illustrious women, who in spite of the fetters imposed upon the sex, have, in different periods of the world, achieved the highest things in learning, rebuke the falsehood. The testimony of the most experienced educators of our day bears witness to woman's ability. President Angell, of the Michigan University, says, "And I say with all frankness that in all departments of study the young ladies had fully held their own, to say the least, and no less in the higher mathematics than in the departments of literature, they have shown the same variety of aptitude, the same variety of skill that the young men have." In speaking of their physical endurance, he says, "Any lady who can endure the draft that modern dress and modern society make upon her can certainly endure any college course so far as physical endurance is concerned. I am simply here to bear testimony in the plainest way to what our experience has shown. I have made it an object of particular examination and scrutiny, and I am thoroughly convinced that there is no danger which need be considered worthy of mention, for any young woman, in tolerably good health, in pursuing the regular course prescribed; nor has it actually been the case that they have been impaired in health by the course." Other testimonials might be brought to the same effect, although perhaps there is no other man of so high authority who has had the same opportunity to judge. But every day's experience is testing and revealing woman's ability, and with larger opportunity her powers are more fully demonstrated. Why then should woman be content with partial study and superficial attainments? The whole world is her own; there is no subject worthy the attention of mortals which she may not study, no profound secret of nature which she may not investigate, no height in the heavens to which she may not aspire. As of old wisdom was represented by goddess Minerva, so still let woman's name stand for all that is excellent in learning. But the most complete and thorough instruction can avail little if it not be matured, assimilated, and formed into character by the routine of daily experience. Until then it is chaotic, formless and useless, like the red-hot molten iron before it has been run in molds or hammered into useful implements.

Woman must from the streams of knowledge, which come seething from the brains of the wise, forge for herself an armor in which to do battle with the world. There can be for her no great victories without conflict. He is no true soldier who expects to bear off the honors, while he sits on cushioned chairs in luxurious parlors and simply reads books of military tactics. He only is worthy of the name of soldier, who has been the hero of an hundred fights, whose noble scars bear witness of his valor on the field of battle, and whose muscles have been trained to endurance by long and perilous marches and the strict discipline of the camp. So woman must earn her title to valuable attainments, not by merely memorizing bits of information but by brave and faithful service on the world's great battlefield.

Just that experience in the business of the world, which develops character in men, women need to make them self-reliant, brave, and true. . . . [It] is only by an experience in the great world of business that woman's knowledge can be ripened and her character matured. If boys after leaving school went home to be supported and devoted themselves to needlework and novels, we should look for no noble manhood, and only when girls cease to do this and seek some business of life whereby to independently support themselves and benefit society can we look for the truest womanhood. But, says some objector, women will no longer be angels when brought in contact with the rude world. Alas! The United States of America in 1874 is not a favorable place for angels, nor are the men of the nineteenth century suitable companions for them. An angel in American society at the present time would be sadly out of place and very uncomfortable.

✦ ✦ ✦

[T]his is the great argument in favor of the enfranchisement of women; it is not so much the repealing of wicked laws, or the establishment of justice, although these are important, as it is that women should gain that self-respect and independence which is the characteristic of the free. Not till women share in the responsibilities, and enjoy the privileges of the enfranchised citizen, can it be expected that they will gain the highest excellence.

Freedom and responsibility have in all times been thought essential conditions of mental growth in men; they are not less essential to the development of women. Nor does this larger life militate at all against those duties which are peculiar to women. The position of wife and mother will be far better filled by one whose mind is enlarged by a great knowledge of affairs, and whose character is matured by the discipline of life, than by one whose sympathies and whose knowledge extends no farther than the half dozen or more rooms which she calls her home.

✦ ✦ ✦

And then woman wants the education of inspiration. It is a grand thing to have a mind well stored with richest learning; it is a better thing to have a character which has been developed, strengthened, and ripened by the actual experiences of life; but grander and higher than all is the education which comes from communion with God. When the soul comes to the throne of grace and with earnest seeking, looks to God for the truth, not content with a mere passing wish or an aspiration, but with intensest prayer and longing, it agonizes to enter into the realm of truth, then the will of the Lord is revealed, and his wondrous goodness is made known. Suddenly, sometimes, the soul beholds a vision of truth and beauty, the common daily task is transfigured, the world seems full of heavenly harmonies. . . .

✦ ✦ ✦

When learning, experience, and inspiration shall have combined to develop woman's character, then the objects of the higher education will have been attained in the realization of the power and beauty of a true womanhood. . . .

## ✦ *Biographical Sketch*

**Born:** *January 5, 1835, Prairie Ronde, Michigan*

**Died:** *October 23, 1926, Baltimore, Maryland, age 91*

**Buried:** *Mound Cemetery, Racine, Wisconsin*

Universalist minister Olympia Brown is generally recognized as the first woman to receive full ministerial status in an American denomination.[33] In addition to her church work, she was an active women's rights supporter.

Born on a farm in Michigan to Universalist parents who had recently moved there from Vermont, Olympia was the oldest of four children. An aunt and uncle who lived nearby were abolitionists who ran an Underground Railroad station in their Michigan home. Her mother was a strong believer in education for girls, so her father built a schoolhouse for area children, many of whom were poor immigrants. Eventually, as a teenager, Olympia rode her horse to the town school, where, to her dismay, she first met a sexual barrier: Female students were not allowed to give speeches.

Olympia loved to study and wanted to go to college, but no colleges of the day admitted women. A few years later, she enrolled in the new all-female college in Mount Holyoke, Massachusetts. Appalled by the strict rules and Calvinist religion preached there, however, she moved the following year to the more liberal Antioch College in Yellow Springs, Ohio, which had been founded as a coeducational institution and imposed no religious dogma. Antioch's president, Horace Mann, was a Unitarian and the father of the common school movement that established free schools for boys and girls of all social (though not all racial) groups.

While at Antioch, Olympia invited the Reverend Antoinette Brown (not related) to speak. Inspired by both the Reverend Brown's presence and her sermon, Olympia decided to become a minister. With considerable persistence, she managed to convince St. Lawrence University's theological school to admit her in 1861, even though its president ardently tried to dissuade her from coming. Her fellow ministerial students ridiculed her for her petite size and small voice. Admitting women to the ministry at that time was thought to set a dangerous precedent, since they could bring down the cost of preaching. Interestingly, Olympia Brown's graduation from St. Lawrence University's theological school in 1863 is now regarded as a source of great pride. On the centennial of her graduation and ordination, a plaque was unveiled in honor of this formidable woman and her achievements. It reads: "The flame of her spirit still burns today."

In 1864, the newly ordained Reverend Brown was called to serve the Universalist church in Weymouth Landing, Massachusetts, where she met her future husband, John Henry Willis. Six years later, she accepted a call to a larger Universalist church in Bridgeport, Connecticut. She and Willis were married there in 1873. He fully supported her chosen career, and they agreed to have her continue to use her birth name. Throughout a long and loving marriage, they admired and respected one another. A man of principle and courage, Willis took great pride in his wife's accomplishments and in her commitment to human rights and social justice. Even when her work took her away from home, sometimes for extended periods, Willis encouraged Olympia to pursue the path that she felt she must.

While in New England, Olympia Brown became active in the women's rights movement, making friends with Lucy Stone, Susan B. Anthony,[34] and other leaders. At Stone's invitation, Olympia took a leave of absence from the Weymouth church to campaign for equal rights in Kansas for four months, having been assured that all arrangements for a speaking tour had been made for her. When she arrived in the state, it became evident that no arrangements for either lodging or transportation had been made. Most of the time, she had to make her own speaking arrangements, as well. She often addressed crowds that were openly hostile. Nevertheless, undaunted, resourceful, and determined to succeed, she delivered more than three hundred speeches. In spite of the fact that only one-third of the voting population (all male, of course) approved the amendment, she was not discouraged. Susan B. Anthony wrote her an admiring letter in gratitude for her efforts, telling her that her work was a glorious triumph, regardless of the final vote tally.

In 1868, when she was in her forties, Olympia Brown and her family moved to Racine, Wisconsin, where she served as minister of the Universalist Church of the Good Shepherd for nine years. Her husband, a strong supporter of women's rights, was editor and publisher of the town newspaper.

At the age of fifty-three, when her children were almost grown, Olympia Brown decided to leave parish ministry to launch full time into her second career as a leader in the women's rights movement. Three years earlier, she had been elected vice president of the National Woman Suffrage Association and also became president of the Wisconsin Woman Suffrage Association. She later was a founder of the Federal Suffrage Association and served as its president from 1903 to 1920, when the Nineteenth Amendment was finally passed.

After three decades in the Midwest, ministering and fighting for equal rights for women, Olympia Brown moved to Baltimore in 1914 to be near her daughter but kept her Racine home, where she spent summers. It was this daughter, Gwendolyn Brown Willis, who preserved much of her mother's correspondence, sermons, and writings and encouraged her to write her autobiography. Although a gifted and prolific writer, Olympia Brown found herself a less than fascinating topic. She finally produced a brief sketch of her life but essentially was so uninterested in the project that she left it for her daughter to complete following her death. As she told her daughter, she would much rather actively try to right wrongs in the present than sit still and reconstruct the past.

Although in her eighties, Olympia Brown took to the streets with the re-energized women's suffrage movement, under the leadership of Alice Paul, from 1913 until success in 1919. Whether marching in front of the White House in freezing February weather to protest Woodrow Wilson's turning his back on women's suffrage or publicly burning his speeches in Lafayette Park, Olympia Brown was relentless. She had worked tirelessly for suffrage since 1866 and was one of the few early organizers to live long enough to see passage of the amendment for which so many had struggled for so long. She voted in her first election at age eighty-five.

At the time of her death, the *Baltimore Sun* perfectly captured the independence, fearlessness, and passionate commitment to justice of the Reverend Olympia Brown by stating: "Perhaps no phase of her life better exemplified her vitality and intellectual independence than the mental discomfort she succeeded in arousing, between her eightieth and ninetieth birthdays, among conservatively minded Baltimoreans."[35] An active member of the American Civil Liberties Union, the Women's International League for Peace and Freedom, and the militant National Woman's Party, Olympia Brown certainly afflicted the comfortable in Baltimore society during what were ostensibly her sunset years.

When Olympia Brown was ninety-one years old, she traveled to Europe with her daughter, touring the continent for several months. A few months later, she died peacefully and was buried next to her husband in Racine, Wisconsin. An elementary school there has been named in her honor, and in recent years, the place in which she served as minister was renamed the Olympia Brown Unitarian Universalist Church.

*Biographical Sketch by* JUNE EDWARDS and LAURIE CARTER NOBLE

## ✦ Writings of Olympia Brown

*Acquaintances, Old and New, Among Reformers.* Milwaukee: S. E. Tate, 1911.

"Crime, Capital Punishment and Intemperance." Papers and addresses, Columbian Congress of the Universalist Church, Chicago, 1893.

*Democratic Ideals; A Memorial Sketch of Clara B. Colby.* Federal Suffrage Association, 1917.

"Hand of Fellowship" and "Installation Sermon." Services for the Ordination of the Reverend Phebe A. Hanaford as Pastor of the First Universalist Church in Hingham, MA, Feb. 19, 1868. Boston: C. C. Roberts, 1870.

"The Higher Education of Women." *The Ladies' Repository, A Universalist Monthly Magazine for the Home Circle* 51 (1874): 85.

"Olympia Brown: An Autobiography." Edited and completed by Gwendolyn Brown Willis. Racine, WI, 1960 (Typewritten). Reprinted in *The Annual Journal of the Universalist Historical Society* 4 (1963): 4–76.

"Olympia Brown: Two Sermons: But to Us There Is One God and Man Does Not Live by Bread Alone." Introduction by Ralph N. Schmidt. *The Annual Journal of the Universalist Historical Society* 4 (1963): 93–110.

*Suffrage and Religious Principle: Speeches and Writings of Olympia Brown.* Edited by Dana Greene. Metuchen, NJ: Scarecrow Press, 1988.

## ✦ Biographical Resources

Brown, E. Larkin. "Autobiographical Notes," edited by A. Ada Brown. *Michigan Pioneer and Historical Collections* 30 (1905): 424–494.

Cote, Charlotte. *Olympia Brown: The Battle for Equality.* Racine, WI: Mother Courage Press, 1988.

*Famous Wisconsin Women*. Vol. 3. Madison: Women's Auxiliary State Historical Society of Wisconsin, 1973.

Isenberg, Nancy Gale. "Victory for Truth: The Feminist Ministry of Olympia Brown." Master's thesis, University of Wisconsin at Madison, 1983.

Neu, Charles E. "Olympia Brown and the Woman's Suffrage Movement." *Wisconsin Magazine of History* 43 (Summer 1960): 277–287.

Nichols, Claudia. "Olympia Brown: Minister of Social Reform." Occasional Paper #4. Malden, MA: Unitarian Universalist Women's Heritage Society, 1992.

*Olympia Brown. A Centennial Volume Celebrating Her Ordination and Graduation in 1863*. Boston: Universalist Historical Society, 1963.

## ✦ Archives

The collected papers, letters, and sermons of Olympia Brown are at the Arthur and Elizabeth Schlesinger Library on the History of Women in America at Radcliffe College, Cambridge, MA.

# The Influence of Women in the Profession of Medicine

## Lecture at Opening of Winter Session, London School of Medicine for Women, October 1889

*With the help of her sister Emily and another woman, both of whom had now also finished medical school,* ELIZABETH BLACKWELL (1821–1910) *opened an infirmary in New York, began the first nurses' training school in the United States, and established a women's medical college with a rigorous curriculum. Later, leaving the very capable Emily Blackwell in charge of these American institutions, Elizabeth moved back to England, where she founded another medical school for women and served as professor of gynecology.*

*In the following lecture, given twenty years after her permanent return to England, Dr. Elizabeth Blackwell argued that women make exceptionally good doctors because of their nurturing natures, their joy in creating life, and their inborn opposition to social as well as physical suffering. She also cautioned, however, that women must guard against their tendency to believe whatever male professors and scientists said and must have the courage to question authority and trust their own wisdom.*

See the Biographical Sketch on pages 195–198.

Now, there is no career nobler than that of the physician. The progress and welfare of society is more intimately bound up with the prevailing tone and influence of the medical profession than with the status of any other class of men. This exceptional influence is not only due to the great importance of dealing with the issues of life and death in health and disease, but it is still more owing to the fact that the body and the mind are so inseparably blended in the human constitution that we cannot deal with one portion of this compound nature without in more or less degree affecting the other. Our ministrations to body and soul cannot be separated by a sharply defined line. The arbitrary distinction between the physician of the body and the physician of the soul—doctor and priest—tends to disappear as science advances. Every branch of medicine involves moral considerations, both as regards the practitioner and the patient. Even the amputation of a limb, the care of a case of fever, the birth of a child, all contain a moral element which is evident to the clear understanding and which cannot be neglected without injury to the doctor, to the individual, and to society. But probably it will be generally agreed that the hope of gaining money must not be the primary motive for choosing a medical career; but that interest in the line of study and kind of life, with a perception of the wide and beneficent influence which it can exert, should form the determining motive for becoming a physician.

If, then, we recognize that, although just reward for honest labor is fair, we must not enter upon medicine as a trade for getting money but from a higher motive, this motive, as it influences conduct, becomes on that account a moral motive or an ideal which should guide our future practical life as physicians. Now, this ideal necessitates a distinct conception of what is right or wrong for us, in medicine, both as human beings and as women.

Simply sensuous life, without an ideal or without higher principles of action than the limited needs of every day, tends to degrade the individual and all who surround him.

✦ ✦ ✦

You will see in the course of your medical studies—particularly if you study abroad—much to shock your enlightened intellect and revolt your moral sense. In practice also you will be subjected to strong temptations of the most varied character. But just for the reason that as women we ought to see more clearly the broken bridge or approaching danger in the onward rush of the male intellect, I now dwell on our special responsibility and shall endeavour to give the reasons for it.

My object is not to limit but to enlarge our work in medicine, when I seek to define our ideal. It is true that the great object of this human life of ours is essentially one for every human being, man or woman, barbarous or civilized. It is to become a nobler creature and to help all others to a higher human status during this brief span of earthly life. But as variety in unity is a law of creation, so there are infinite methods of progress, producing harmony instead of monotony, when the individual or classes of individuals are true to the guiding principles of their own nature.

For the ideal of every creature must be found in the relation of its own nature to the universe around it. Right and wrong are based upon the sound understanding of this positive foundation. It is this fact of variety in unity, in the progress of the race, which justifies the hope that the entrance of women into the medical profession will advance that profession. In order to carry out this noble aspiration, we must understand what the special contribution is that women may make to medicine, what the aspect of morality which they are called upon to emphasize.

It is not blind imitation of men, nor thoughtless acceptance of whatever may be taught by them that is required, for this would be to endorse the widespread error that the race is men. Our duty is loyalty to right and opposition to wrong, in accordance with the essential principles of our own nature.

✦ ✦ ✦

It is a noteworthy feature of the present day that some of our best men, witnessing the failure of so many panaceas for the intolerable evils that afflict society, are longing for that untried force—the action and cooperation of good women. "Our only hope is in women!" is a cry that may sometimes be heard from the enlightened male conscience. But still more significant is the awakening of an increasing number of women themselves. They begin to realize that truth comes to us through imperfect human media and is thus rendered imperfect; that every human teacher must be accepted for his suggestiveness only, not as absolute authority. Women are thus rising above the errors of the past, above blind acceptance of imperfect authority, and are earnestly striving to learn the will of the Creator and walk solely according to what they themselves, diligently seeking, can learn of that Divine will.

There is no line of practical work outside domestic life so eminently suited to these noble aspirations as the legitimate study and practice of medicine. The legitimate study requires the preservation in full force of those beneficent moral qualities—tenderness, sympathy, guardianship—which form an indispensable spiritual element of maternity; whilst, at the same time, the progress of the race demands that the intellectual horizon be enlarged and the understanding strengthened by the observation and reasoning which will give increased efficiency to those moral qualities.

The true physician must possess the essential qualities of maternity. The sick are as helpless in his hands as the infant. They depend absolutely upon the insight and judgment, the honesty and hopefulness, of the doctor.

The fact also that every human being we are called on to treat is, like the infant and the child, soul as well as body, must never be forgotten. Successful treatment requires the insight which comes from recognition of these facts and the sympathy that they demand. In the infinite variety of human ailments, the physician will find that she must often be the confessor of her patient, and the consulting-room should have the sacredness of the Confessional, and she must always be the counsellor and guide.

✦ ✦ ✦

Again, in the treatment of the poor, an immense demand is made upon our pity, patience, and courage. These poor victims of our social stupidity are often extremely trying. The faulty arrangements which compel us to see thirty, fifty even, in an hour exhaust the nervous system of the doctor. It requires faith and courage to recognize the real human soul under the terrible mask of squalor and disease in these crowded masses of poverty and to resist the temptation to regard them as "clinical material." The attitude of the student and doctor to the sick poor is a real test of the true physician.

✦ ✦ ✦

The freedom of entrance now accorded to women into the medical profession lays a very heavy responsibility upon us to prove that this new and increasing movement will be a future blessing to society.

We are happy in drawing into our schools a large number of capable women—women who may not only be a gain as physicians but who may exert a most beneficial influence on the profession itself, if they bring into it fresh and independent life.

✦ ✦ ✦

The two special dangers against which I would warn our students are:

*First*, the blind acceptance of what is called "authority" in medicine.

*Second*, the narrow and superficial materialism which prevails so widely amongst scientific man.

In relation to the first point—viz., distrust of authority—although I fully recognize the respect which is always due to the position of the teacher and the consideration to be shown to all who are called "heads of the profession"—I would very strongly urge you to remember that medicine is necessarily an uncertain science.

Life in its essence we cannot grasp. We understand it only through its effects, and all human judgement is fallible. Careful and wise observation bring us ever nearer to a knowledge of the conditions which are necessary for human well-being; but experience compels us to recognize the constant failure of theory or dogmatism in dealing with any of the infinitely varied phases of life. In medicine we are forced to recognize the errors in diagnosis committed even by distinguished men and suffer grievous disappointment from the failure of remedies supposed to cure the sick. We cannot fail to note the contradictory results of experiments, the same facts differing according to the observer—one fact upsetting another, and one theory driven out by a later one. . . .

Our women students especially need caution as to the blind acceptance of authority. Young women come into such a new and stimulating intellectual atmosphere when entering upon medical study that they breathe it with keen delight; they are inclined to accept with enthusiasm the brilliant theory or statement which the active intellect of a clever teacher lays before them. They are accustomed to accept the government and instruction of men as final, and it hardly occurs to them to question it. It is not the custom to realize the positive fact that methods and conclusions formed by one-half of the race only must necessarily require revision as the other half of humanity rises into conscious responsibility.

It is a difficult lesson also fully to recognize the limitations of the human intellect, which recognition, nevertheless, is necessary before we can grasp this important and positive fact in human experience—viz., that the Moral must guide the Intellectual, or there is no halting-place in the rapid incline to error. The brilliant professor will always exercise an undue influence over the inexperienced student and particularly over the woman student. I therefore strongly urge the necessity of cherishing a mild skepticism respecting the dicta of so-called medical science during the period of student life—skepticism not in relation to truth—that noble object which we hope to approach even more nearly—but skepticism in relation to the imperfect or erroneous statement of what is often presented as truth.

Of this one guiding fact, as a basis of judgment, we may be quite sure—viz., that whatever revolts our moral sense as earnest women is not in accordance with steady progress; it cannot be permanently true, and no amount of clever or logical sophistry can make it true. It will be a real service that we, as medical women, may render to the profession if we search out—calmly, patiently, but resolutely—why what revolts our enlightened sense of right and wrong is not true. We shall thus bring to light the profound reason why the moral faculties are antecedent or superior to the intellectual faculties and why the sense of right and wrong must govern medical research and practice, as well as all other lines of human effort.

As experience enlarges, we observe the immense separation in lines of conduct which gradually results from an initial divergence between right and wrong—a divergence almost imperceptible at first. We are thus compelled to come to the conclusion, in relation to our own profession, that the worship of the intellect, or so-called knowledge, as an end in itself, entirely regardless of the character of the means by which we seek to gain it, is the most dangerous error that science can make. This false principle, if adopted by the medical profession, will degrade it and inevitably produce distrust and contempt in the popular mind.

The second danger against which the student of medicine must guard is the materialism which seems to arise from undue absorption in the physical aspect of nature and which spreads like a blight in our profession.

The basis of materialism is the assertion that only sense is real.

Our medical studies necessarily begin with minute and prolonged study of what we term "dead matter." If this study be carried on without reverence, it appears to blind the student to any reality except the material under his scalpel or in his crucible—*i.e.,* the facts that the senses reveal. Proceeding logically from this false premise, that only sense is real, mind is looked upon as an outcome of the brain and life as the result of organization of matter, which is destroyed when the organization of the material body is broken up.

✦ ✦ ✦

Love, Hope, Reverence are realities of a different order from the senses, but they are positive and constant facts, always active, always working out mighty changes in human life.

# The Intellectual Progress of Colored Women

## Address to World's Congress of Representative Women, May 1893

FANNIE BARRIER WILLIAMS (1855–1944) *was a noted lecturer, musician, and clubwoman. Active in All Souls Church (Unitarian) in Chicago, she fought against employment discrimination and segregated housing. She worked for recognition of African Americans at the various conferences of the 1893 Columbian Exposition and then was asked to speak at two of them. In the following speech, "The Intellectual Progress of the Colored Women of the United States Since the Emancipation Proclamation," given at the World's Congress of Representative Women,*[36] *she praised the intelligence, morality, and cheerful optimism of those women freed from slavery less than thirty years before. Noting the many obstacles they still faced, she called for freedom from prejudice and the right of all women to receive the education needed to pursue their happiness and develop their innate abilities.*

See the Biographical Sketch on pages 275–278.

Less than thirty years ago the term progress as applied to colored women of African descent in the United States would have been an anomaly. The recognition of that term today as appropriate is a fact full of interesting significance. That the discussion of progressive womanhood in this great assemblage of the representative women of the world is considered incomplete without some account of the colored women's status is a most noteworthy evidence that we have not failed to impress ourselves on the higher side of American life.

Less is known of our women than of any other class of Americans. No organization of far-reaching influence for their special advancement, no conventions of women to take note of their progress, and no special literature reciting the incidents, the events, and all things interesting and instructive concerning them are to be found among the agencies directing their career. There has been no special interest in their peculiar condition as native-born American women. Their power to affect the social life of America, either for good or for ill, has excited not even a speculative interest.

Though there is much that is sorrowful, much that is wonderfully heroic, and much that is romantic in a peculiar way in their history, none of it has as yet been told as evidence of what is possible for these women. How few of the happy, prosperous, and eager living Americans can appreciate what it all means to be suddenly changed from irresponsible bondage to the responsibility of freedom and citizenship!

The distress of it all can never be told, and the pain of it all can never be felt except by the victims, and by those saintly women of the white race who for thirty years have been consecrated to the uplifting of a whole race of women from a long-enforced degradation.

The American people have always been impatient of ignorance and poverty. They believe with Emerson that "America is another word for opportunity," and for that reason success is a virtue and poverty and ignorance are inexcusable. This may account for the fact that our women have excited no general sympathy in the struggle to emancipate themselves from the demoralization of slavery. This new life of freedom, with its far-reaching responsibilities, had to be learned by these children of darkness mostly without a guide, a teacher, or a friend. In the mean vocabulary of slavery there was no definition of any of the virtues of life. The meaning of such precious terms as marriage, wife, family, and home could not be learned in a schoolhouse. The blue-back speller, the arithmetic, and the copybook contain no magical cures for inherited inaptitudes for the moralities. Yet it must ever be counted as one of the most wonderful things in human history how promptly and eagerly these suddenly liberated women tried to lay hold upon all that there is in human excellence. There is a touching pathos in the eagerness of these millions of new homemakers to taste the blessedness of intelligent womanhood. The path of progress in the picture is enlarged so as to bring to view these trustful and zealous students of freedom and civilization striving to overtake and keep pace with women whose emancipation has been a slow and painful process for a thousand years. The longing to be something better than they were when freedom found them has been the most notable characteristic in the development of these women. This constant striving for equality has given an upward direction to all the activities of colored women.

Freedom at once widened their vision beyond the mean cabin life of their bondage. Their native gentleness, good cheer, and hopefulness made them susceptible to those teachings that make for intelligence and righteousness. Sullenness of disposition, hatefulness, and revenge against the master class because of two centuries of ill treatment are not in the nature of our women.

✦ ✦ ✦

Evidence of growing intelligence is a sense of religious discrimination among our women. Like the nineteenth-century woman generally, our women find congeniality in all the creeds, from the Catholic creed to the no-creed of Emerson. There is a constant increase of this interesting variety in the religious life of our women.

Closely allied to this religious development is their progress in the work of education in schools and colleges. For thirty years education has been the magic word among the colored people of this country. That their greatest need was education in its broadest sense was understood by these people more strongly than it could be taught to them. It is the unvarying testimony of every teacher in the South that the mental development of the colored women as well as men has been little less than phenomenal. In twenty-five years, and under conditions discouraging in the extreme, thousands of our women have been educated as teachers. They have adapted themselves to the work of mentally lifting a whole race of people so eagerly and readily that they afford an apt illustration of the power of self-help. Not only have these women become good teachers in less than twenty-five years, but many of them are the prize teachers in the mixed schools of nearly every Northern city.

These women have also so fired the hearts of the race for education that colleges, normal schools, industrial schools, and universities have been reared by a generous public to meet the requirements of these eager students of intelligent citizenship. As American women generally are fighting against the nineteenth-century narrowness that still keeps women out of the higher institutions of learning, so our women are eagerly demanding the best of education open to their race. . . .

Today they feel strong enough to ask for but one thing, and that is the same opportunity for the acquisition of all kinds of knowledge that may be accorded to other women. This granted, in the next generation these progressive women will be found successfully occupying every field where the highest intelligence alone is admissible. In less than another generation American literature, American art, and American music will be enriched by productions having new and peculiar features of interest and excellence.

✦ ✦ ✦

The great problems of social reform that are now so engaging the highest intelligence of American women will soon need for their solution the reinforcement of that new intelligence which our women are developing. In short, our women are ambitious to be contributors to all the great moral and intellectual forces that make for the greater weal of our common country.

If this hope seems too extravagant to those of you who know these women only in their humbler capacities, I would remind you that all that we hope for and will certainly achieve in authorship and practical intelligence is more than prophesied by what has already been done, and more that can be done, by hundreds of Afro-American women whose talents are now being expended in the struggle against race resistance.

✦ ✦ ✦

The hearts of Afro-American women are too warm and too large for race hatred. Long suffering has so chastened them that they are developing a special sense of sympathy for all who suffer and fail of justice. All the associated interests of church, temperance, and social reform in which American women are winning distinction can be wonderfully advanced when our women shall be welcomed as co-workers and estimated solely by what they are worth to the moral elevation of all the people.

✦ ✦ ✦

The question of the moral progress of colored women in the United States has force and meaning in this discussion only so far as it tells the story of how the once-enslaved women have been struggling for twenty-five years to emancipate themselves from the demoralization of their enslavement.

While I duly appreciate the offensiveness of all references to American slavery, it is unavoidable to charge to that system every moral imperfection that mars the character of the colored American. The whole life and power of slavery depended upon an enforced degradation of everything human in the slaves. The slave code recognized only animal distinctions between the sexes and ruthlessly ignored those ordinary separations that belong to the social state.

It is a great wonder that two centuries of such demoralization did not work a complete extinction of all the moral instincts. But the recuperative power of these women to regain their moral instincts and to establish a respectable relationship to American womanhood is among the earlier evidences of their moral ability to rise above their conditions.

✦ ✦ ✦

[T]he daughters of women who thirty years ago were not allowed to be modest, not allowed to follow the instincts of moral rectitude, who could cry for protection to no living man, have so elevated the moral tone of their social life that new and purer standards of personal worth have been created, and new ideals of womanhood, instinct with grace and delicacy are everywhere recognized and emulated.

✦ ✦ ✦

In the item of employment colored women bear a distressing burden of mean and unreasonable discrimination. . . .

It is almost literally true that, except teaching in colored schools and menial work, colored women can find no employment in this free America. They are the only women in the country for whom real ability, virtue, and special talents count for nothing when they become applicants for respectable employment. Taught everywhere in ethics and social economy that merit always wins, colored women carefully prepare themselves for all kinds of occupation only to meet with stern refusal, rebuff, and disappointment.

✦ ✦ ✦

Can the people of this country afford to single out the women of a whole race of people as objects of their special contempt? Do these women not belong to a race that has never faltered in its support of the country's flag in every war since Attucks fell in Boston's streets?

Are they not the daughters of men who have always been true as steel against treason to everything fundamental and splendid in the republic? In short, are these women not as thoroughly American in all the circumstances of citizenship as the best citizens of our country?

If it be so, are we not justified in a feeling of desperation against that peculiar form of Americanism that shows respect for our women as servants and contempt for them when they become women of culture? We have never been taught to understand why the unwritten law of chivalry, protection, and fair play that are everywhere the conservators of women's welfare must exclude every woman of a dark complexion.

We believe that the world always needs the influence of every good and capable woman, and this rule recognizes no exceptions based on complexion. In their complaint against hindrances to their employment colored women ask for no special favors. . . .

✦ ✦ ✦

Everywhere the public mind has been filled with constant alarm lest in some way our women shall approach the social sphere of the dominant race in this country. Men and women, wise and perfectly sane in all things else, become instantly unwise and foolish at the remotest suggestion of social contact with colored men and women. At every turn in our lives we meet this fear and are humiliated by its aggressiveness and meanness. If we seek the sanctities of religion, the enlightenment of the university, the honors of politics, and the natural recreations of our common country, the social equality alarm is instantly given, and our aspirations are insulted. "Beware of social equality with the colored American" is thus written on all places, sacred or profane, in this blessed land of liberty. The most discouraging and demoralizing effect of this false sentiment concerning us is that it utterly ignores individual merit and discredits the sensibilities of intelligent womanhood. The sorrows and heartaches of a whole race of women seem to be matters of no concern to the people who so dread the social possibilities of these colored women.

✦ ✦ ✦

Our chief concern in this false social sentiment is that it attempts to hinder our further progress toward the higher spheres of womanhood. On account of it, young colored women of ambition and means are compelled in many instances to leave the country for training and education in the salons and studios of Europe. On many of the railroads of this country women of refinement and culture are driven like cattle into human cattle-cars lest the occupying of an individual seat paid for in a first-class car may result in social equality. This social quarantine on all means of travel in certain parts of the country is guarded and enforced more rigidly against us than the quarantine regulations against cholera.

Without further particularizing as to how this social question opposes our advancement, it may be stated that the contentions of colored women are in kind like those of other American women for greater freedom of development. Liberty to be all that we can be, without artificial hindrances, is a thing no less precious to us than to women generally.

✦ ✦ ✦

[T]he inalienable right to life, liberty, and the pursuit of happiness is a maxim that will become more blessed in its significance when the hand of woman shall take it from its sepulture in books and make it the gospel of everyday life and the unerring guide in the relations of all men, women, and children.

✦ ✦ ✦

# The Club Movement Among Colored Women of America

### From *A New Negro for a New Century,* 1900

*Although she had gained wide recognition as a speaker at national and international conferences,* FANNIE BARRIER WILLIAMS (1855–1944) *was initially barred from membership in the prominent and in other ways progressive Chicago Woman's Club. After her eventual acceptance, she focused her efforts on helping establish the African American women's club movement. In this article, she outlined the importance of the club movement as a major factor in raising the aspirations and esteem of black women of all socioeconomic classes as well as a vehicle for battling racial bigotry and barriers to employment, housing, and education.*

See the Biographical Sketch on pages 275–278.

The training which first enabled colored women to organize and successfully carry on club work was originally obtained in church work. These churches have been and still are the great preparatory schools in which the primary lessons of social order, mutual trustfulness, and united effort have been sustained, enlarged and beautified principally through the organized efforts of their women members. The meaning of unity of effort for the common good, the development of social sympathies grew into woman's consciousness through the privileges of church work.

Still another school of preparation for colored women has been their secret societies. "The ritual of these secret societies is not without a certain social value." They demand a higher order of intelligence than is required for church membership. Care for the sick, provisions for the decent burial of the indigent dead, the care for orphans, and the enlarging sense of sisterhood all contributed to the development of the very conditions of heart that qualify women for the more inclusive work of those social reforms that are the aim of women's clubs. The churches and secret societies have helped to make colored women acquainted with the general social condition of the race and the possibilities of social improvement.

With this training the more intelligent women of the race could not fail to follow the example and be inspired by the larger club movement of the white women. The need of social reconstruction became more and more apparent as they studied the results of women's organizations. Better homes, better schools, better protection for girls of scant home training, better sanitary conditions, better opportunities for competent young women to gain employment, and the need of being better known to the American people appealed to the conscience of progressive colored women from many communities.

The clubs and leagues organized among colored women have all been more or less in direct response to these appeals. Seriousness of purpose has thus been the main characteristic of all these organizations. While the National Federation of Woman's Clubs has served as a guide and inspiration to colored women, the club movement among them is something deeper than a mere imitation of white women. It is nothing less than the organized anxiety of women who have become intelligent enough to recognize their own low social condition and strong enough to initiate the forces of reform.

The club movement as a race influence among the colored women of the country may be fittingly said to date from July, 1895, when the first national conference of colored women was held in Boston, Massachusetts. Prior to this time there were a number of strong clubs in some of the larger cities of the country, but they were not affiliated and the larger idea of effecting the social regeneration of the race was scarcely conceived of.

Among the earlier clubs the Woman's League of Washington, D.C., organized in 1892, and the Woman's Era Club of Boston, organized in January, 1893, were and are still the most thorough and influential organizations of the kind in the country.

✦ ✦ ✦

The various activities [of the Washington League] include sewing schools, kindergartens, well-conducted night schools, and mother's meetings, all of which have been developed and made a prominent part of the educational and social forces of the colored people of the capital. . . .

The league is also especially strong in the personnel of its membership, being made up largely of teachers, many of whom are recognized as among the most cultured and influential women of the negro race in this country.

✦ ✦ ✦

The New Era Club of Boston was organized in the month of February, 1893. The desire of the cultured and public-spirited colored women of that city to do something in the way of promoting a more favorable public opinion in behalf of the negro race was the immediate incentive to this organization. The club began its work of agitation by collecting data and issuing leaflets and tracts containing well edited matter in reference to Afro-American progress. Its most conspicuous work has been the publication of the Woman's Era, the first newspaper ever published by colored women in this country. This paper gained a wide circulation and did more than any other single agency to nationalize the club idea among the colored women of the country. The New Era Club has sustained its reputation as the most representative organization of colored people in New England. It has taken the initiative in many reforms and helpful movements that have had a wide influence on race development. This club has been especially useful and influential in all local affairs that in any way affect the colored people. Deserving young men and women struggling to obtain an education and defenseless young women in distress have always been able to find substantial assistance in the New Era Club.

✦ ✦ ✦

It will thus be seen that from 1890 to 1895 the character of Afro-American womanhood began to assert itself in definite purposes and efforts in club work. . . . The incentive in most cases was quite simple and direct. How to help and protect some defenseless and tempted young woman; how to aid some poor boy to complete a much coveted education; how to lengthen the short school term in some impoverished school district; how to instruct and interest deficient mothers in the difficulties of child training are some of the motives that led to the formation of the great majority of these clubs. These were the first outreachings of sympathy and fellowship felt by women whose lives had been narrowed by the petty concerns of the struggle for existence and removed by human cruelty from all the harmonies of freedom, love, and aspirations. . . .

If the question be asked: "What do these clubs do; what do they stand for in their respective communities, and what have they actually accomplished?" satisfactory answer will be found by studying them a little at short range.

The first thing to be noted is that these club women are students of their own social condition, and the clubs themselves are schools in which are taught and learned, more or less thoroughly, the near lessons of life and living. All these clubs have a program for study. In some of the more ambitious clubs literature, music, and art are studied more or less seriously, but in all of them race problems and sociological questions directly related to the condition of the negro race in America are the principal subjects for study and discussion.

Many of the clubs, in their programs for study, plan to invite from time to time prominent men and women to address them on questions of vital interest. In this way club members not only become wide awake and interested in questions of importance to themselves and their community, but men and women who help to make and shape public opinion have an opportunity to see and know the better side of the colored race.

✦ ✦ ✦

The lessons learned in these women's organizations of the country all have a direct bearing on the social conditions of the negro race. They are such lessons that are not taught in the schools or preached from the pulpits. Homemaking has been new business to the great majority of the women whom the women's clubs aim to reach and influence. For this reason the principal object of club studies is to teach that homes are something better and dearer than rooms, furniture, comforts, and food. How to make the homes of the race the shrines of all the domestic virtues, rather than a mere shelter, is the important thing that colored women are trying to learn and teach through their club organizations.

Take for example one club in Chicago, known as the "Colored Woman's Conference," and it will be found that its aims and efforts are typical of the best purposes of club life among colored women. The special activities and aims of this particular club are the establishment of kindergartens, mothers' meetings, sewing schools for girls, day nurseries, employment bureau; promoting the cause of education by establishing a direct line of interest between the teacher and the home life of every child; friendly visiting and protection to friendless and homeless girls; and a penny savings bank as a practical lesson in frugality and economy. The special thing to be noted in this program is that colored women are not afraid to set for themselves hard and serious tasks and to make whatever sacrifices necessary to realize their high purposes.

A lack of kindergarten teachers more than a lack of money has retarded the work of establishing kindergartens, especially in the South, where they are specially needed. The progressive woman feels that an increased number of kindergartens would have a determining influence in shaping and molding the character of thousands of colored children whose home lives are scant and meager. . . .

The mothers' meetings established in connection with almost every club have probably had a more direct and beneficial influence on the everyday problems of motherhood and home-making than any other activity. Meetings of this sort have been the chief feature of the women's clubs organized by the Tuskegee teachers among the women of the hard plantation life, within reach of the Tuskegee Institute. Thousands of these women in the rural life of the South continue to live under the shadow of bondaged conditions. There has come to them scarcely a ray of light as to a better way of how to live for themselves and their offspring. . . .

In this connection especial word ought to be said in behalf of these clubs as agencies of rescue and protection to the many unprotected and defenseless colored girls to be found in every large city. No race of young women in this country have so little done for them as the young colored woman. She is unknown, she is not believed in, and in respect to favors that direct and uplift, she is an alien and unheeded. They have been literally shut out from the love, favor, and protection that chivalry and a common pride have built up around the personality and character of the young women of almost every other race. The colored women's clubs have had heart enough and intelligence enough to recognize their opportunity and duty toward their own young women, and in numerous instances have been the very salvation of unfortunate colored girls.

✦ ✦ ✦

What has been said of the earnestness and practical aim of colored women's clubs in behalf of kindergartens for the children and salvation for the girls may also be said of the practical way in which they have established and sustained sewing schools, mending schools and friendly visitations in behalf of neighborhood respectability and decency, and of their various committees that visit reformatory institutions and jails in search of opportunities to be useful. Numerous and interesting instances might be given to show to what extent these women are realizing their desire to be useful in the social regeneration of their race.

This chapter on the club movement among colored women would be incomplete without some notice of the leaders of the movement. Nothing that these club women have done or aimed to do is more interesting than themselves. What a variety of accomplishments, talents, successes, and ambitions have been brought into view and notice by these hitherto obscure women of a ransomed race! Educated? Yes, besides the thousands educated in the common schools, hundreds of them have been trained in the best colleges and universities in the country, and some of them have spent several years in the noted schools of Europe.

The women thus trained and educated are busily pursuing every kind of avocation not prohibited by American prejudices. As educators, fully twenty thousand of them are at work in the schools, colleges, and universities of the country, and some of them teach everything required to be taught from the kindergarten to the university. Among these educators and leaders of Afro-American womanhood are to be found linguists, mathematicians, musicians, artists, authors, newspaper writers, lecturers, and reform agitators, with varying degrees of excellence and success. There are women in the professions of law, medicine, dentistry, preaching, trained nursing, managers of successful business enterprises, and women of small independent fortunes made and saved within the past twenty-five years.

There are women plain, beautiful, charming, bright conversationalists, fluent, resourceful in ideas, forceful in execution, and women of all sorts of temperament and idiosyncrasies and force and delicacy of character.

All this of course is simply amazing to people trained in the habit of rating colored women too low and knowing only the menial type. To such people she is a revelation.

✦ ✦ ✦

[S]he has come to bring new hope and fresh assurances to the hapless young women of her own race. Life is not a failure. All avenues are not closed. Womanly worth of whatever race or complexion is appreciated. Love, sympathy, opportunity, and helpfulness are within the reach of those who can deserve them. The world is still yearning for pure hearts, willing hands, and bright minds. This and much more is the message brought by this new woman to the hearts of thousands of discouraged and hopeless young colored women.

It is a real message of courage, a real inspiration that has touched more sides of the Afro-American race than any other message or thing since the dawn of freedom.

✦ ✦ ✦

Young women, thus aroused to courage, to hope and self-assertion toward better things, can find inspiring examples of success and achievements in the women of their own race. They have begun to feel something of the exaltation of race pride and race ideals. They have been brought face to face with standards of living that are high and ennobling and have been made conscious of the severe penalties of social misdoings.

Around them has been created a sentiment of care, pride, protection, and chivalry that is every day deepening and widening the distinctions between right and wrong in woman's relationship to man, child, and society.

✦ ✦ ✦

Colored women organized have succeeded in touching the heart of the race, and for the first time the thrill of unity has been felt. They have set in motion moral forces that are beginning to socialize interests that have been kept apart by ignorance and the spirit of dependence.

They have begun to make the virtues as well as the wants of the colored women known to the American people. They are striving to put a new social value on themselves. Yet their work has just begun. It takes more than five or ten years to effect the social uplift of a whole race of people.

The club movement is well purposed. There is in it a strong faith, an enthusiasm born of love and sympathy, and an ever increasing intelligence in the ways and means of effecting noble results. It is not a fad. It is not an imitation. It is not a passing sentiment. It is not an expedient or an experiment. It is rather the force of a new intelligence against the old ignorance. The struggle of an enlightened conscience against the whole brood of social miseries born out of the stress and pain of a hated past.

## ✦ *Biographical Sketch*

**Born:** *February 12, 1855, Brockport, New York*

**Died:** *March 4, 1944, Brockport, New York, age 89*

**Buried:** *Barrier family plot, High Street Cemetery, Brockport, New York*

Though African American, Fannie Barrier's parents and grandparents were all free people, educated in public schools in the North. For many years, the Barriers were the only black family in the western New York town of Brockport, where Fannie was born. Well respected in the community, her parents belonged to the Baptist church, the largest church in the village, and her father, a successful businessman, served every important office open to a layman.

Fannie and her two siblings did well in school and associated freely with their white classmates, visiting each others' homes and attending social events together. As a result of this comradeship and equality, Fannie was unaware of the prejudice and discrimination that prevailed in other parts of the United States. Wanting to expand her horizons after graduation, she obtained a teaching position in a Southern ex-slave state and, for the first time, experienced the daily degradations suffered by those of African descent.

At first, Fannie tried to adapt to the dreadful conditions but later said: "I had missed the training that would have made this continued humiliation possible." Upon moving to Boston to study at the New England Conservatory of Music, she again encountered racial bias and reported that she "never quite recovered from the shock and pain of my first bitter realization that to be a colored woman is to be discredited, mistrusted and often meanly hated."[37]

In 1887, Fannie married S. Laing Williams, a lawyer and native of Georgia. They settled in Chicago, where she not only worked for justice on behalf of African Americans but also worked with white women on many other reform projects. Again, she was warmly accepted by her companions and respected for her abilities. However, in her efforts to help competent, responsible young women of color find employment and living quarters, she confronted blatant racism in the business world and starkly segregated housing.

Like her parents, Williams was strongly religious. An active member of All Souls (Unitarian) Church in Chicago, where Jenkin Lloyd Jones was minister, she gained local and national recognition by speaking at the World Parliament of Religions as well as at the World's Congress of Representative Women, two important congresses held at the World's Fair in Chicago in 1893. Through the church she met and began a forty-year friendship with Celia Parker Woolley.[38]

Accepting an invitation from Woolley and others to join the Chicago Woman's Club, a prominent progressive group with over eight hundred members, Williams was shocked to find her application fought by those who believed one black member would defile the organization. She resisted the pressure to withdraw, not wanting to offend those friends who remained loyal supporters; after a lengthy battle, she was voted in by a decisive majority.

Williams was highly involved in helping to establish the club movement for African American women. As she pointed out: "Among white women, clubs mean the forward movement of the best women in the interest of the best womanhood." For the black women, the clubs meant much more. Having no status, no role models, no concept of freedom, and little schooling, "no protection against the libelous attacks upon their characters, and no chivalry generous enough to guarantee their safety against man's inhumanity to woman,"[39] African American women desperately needed to band together to uplift their spirits and develop their competencies for homemaking and motherhood as well as employment. Under slavery, domestic arts were as untaught and unvalued as education and economic skills. The clubs, then, became the prime educational institutions, in the broadest sense, for those many women whom white society had relegated to the lowest social condition.

Active in social work in Chicago, Williams helped found two interracial benevolent institutions. In 1891, she was a founder of the Provident Hospital and Training School for Nurses. In 1905, she and the Reverend Celia Parker Woolley founded the Frederick Douglass Center, a predecessor of the NAACP (National Association for the Advancement of Colored People) and the Urban League. This innovative project brought people together across the color line for educational, cultural, and social programs.

Throughout her life, Williams fought for the rights and dignity of African American women in both the North and the South. A talented musician, speaker, and writer, she was often in demand and welcomed in cultured society. Nonetheless, she remained loyal to people of color, recognizing that the opportunities she enjoyed were not given to others of her race. And even for herself, she knew "whether I live in the North or the South, I cannot be counted for my full value."[40]

Because of her light skin, educated manner, and self-confident defiance, Williams escaped the so-called Jim Crow laws on a lecture tour through the South. She sat in first-class cars, spoke French to train conductors, and quieted her conscience by reminding herself that the laws were unjust and that she did indeed have French blood in her ancestry. Her heart ached for all the black women who lived continually under such oppression, and she dedicated her life to confronting the legal and social barriers, bigotry, and inhumanity that kept African American women from using their talents and experiencing the real meaning of freedom.

*Biographical Sketch by* JUNE EDWARDS

## ✦ Writings of Fannie Barrier Williams

"After Many Days, A Christmas Story." 1902. *Centers of the Self: Stories by Black American Women from the 19th Century to the Present,* edited by Judith A. Hamer and Martin J. Hamer, 31–45. New York: Hill & Wang, 1994.

"The Club Movement Among Colored Women of America." *A New Negro for a New Century,* edited by Booker T. Washington. Chicago: American Publishing House, 1900; Reprint, New York: Arno Press, 1969.

"The Intellectual Progress of the Colored Women of the United States since the Emancipation Proclamation." *World's Congress of Representative Women,* edited by May Wright Sewall, 696–711. Philadelphia: W. W. Houston, 1893; Reprinted in *Black Women in Nineteenth-Century Life,* edited by James Loewenberg and Ruth Bogin, 270–278. University Park: Pennsylvania State University Press, 1976.

"A Northern Negro's Autobiography." *Independent*, July 14, 1904. Reprinted in *Bearing Witness, Selections from African-American Autobiographies in the 20th Century*, edited by Henry Louis Gates, Jr., 11–22. New York: Pantheon Books, 1991.
"Religious Duty to the Negro." In *Neely's History of the Parliament of Religions*, edited by Walter H. Houghton, 631–636. Chicago: Neely, 1894.

### Other Writings in:

*Afro-American Encyclopedia*. Edited by John T. Haley. 1895.
*Charities*. Oct. 7, 1905.
*Colored American*. July 1904.
*Southern Workman*. June 1908.

## ✦ Biographical Resources

Gibson, John and William Crogman, eds. *Progress of a Race*. Cincinnati: W. H. Ferguson, 1902. Reprint, Miami: Mnemosyne, 1969.
Hine, Darlene Clark. *Black Women In America: An Historical Encyclopedia*. Brooklyn, NY: Carlson, 1993.
Loewenberg, Bert J., and Ruth Bogin, eds. *Black Women in 19th Century American Life*. University Park: Pennsylvania State University Press, 1976.

# The Struggle for Racial Justice

**by Dorothy May Emerson**

✦ ✦ ✦

MANY IMPORTANT WOMEN participated as leaders in the abolitionist movement, and a significant number of them were Unitarians and Universalists. Their speeches and writings helped spread the ideas of abolition, and their organizing and fundraising contributed practical strength to the movement. During the Civil War (1861–1865), they joined with other women and entire communities to support the troops, often raising money and collecting supplies through the Sanitary Commission, a precursor of the Red Cross, which was founded after the war by Universalist Clara Barton. Some even provided direct aid by working as nurses on the battlefield and at home. After the war, many of these women continued to work for racial justice by going to the South and establishing schools or by working in settlement houses in the North. Others worked to raise awareness of the need for continuing the struggle to combat racism and ensure justice for people of all colors. In many cases, women's work before and during the war led to the formation of ongoing women's organizations after the war, as women had learned the value and empowerment of working together.

The Reverend Samuel May, a Unitarian minister and abolitionist leader, once commented on the importance of women in the abolitionist movement, referring particularly to Lydia Maria Child and Maria Weston Chapman, with whom he worked in the New England and Massachusetts Anti-Slavery Societies: "[These two women have] in a private way been the presiding geniuses in all our councils and public meetings, often proposing the wisest measures and suggesting the most weighty thoughts, pertinent facts [and] apt illustrations."[1] In her essay "The Political Activities of Antislavery Women," Gerda Lerner points out that women provided most of the financial support for the movement.[2] This is indeed remarkable considering that at the time, women did not have property rights and most of those from the upper and middle strata did not hold jobs. Utilizing common women's activities such as sewing, making handicrafts, and cooking, they raised money through annual fairs. They also solicited poems and stories from prominent writers (even some nonabolitionists), which they published, together with their own work, in small, attractive volumes. They sold these *gift books* as a way to fund this movement for radical social change.

The first antislavery fair was organized in 1834 by Lydia Maria Child and Louisa Loring. Later fairs were organized by Maria Weston Chapman and her sisters. By the 1850s, the fairs were netting $4,000 per year. As Catherine Clinton suggests, the money raised by these fairs was much more than some sort of auxiliary aid; rather, it provided major funding for the movement and often saved the radical abolitionists from financial ruin.[3] The fairs served the dual purpose of publicizing the abolitionist cause and enlisting the support of a broad range of people.

A number of abolitionist women were influenced by the liberal religious ideas of William Ellery Channing, and he, in turn, was influenced to speak out against slavery by Lydia Maria Child's *Appeal in Favor of That Class of Americans Called Africans*, published in 1833.[4] Her biographer, Deborah Clifford, offers the following interpretation of the Reverend Channing's influence on Lydia Maria Child's religious views and how those views contributed to her dedication to abolitionism:

> *To be truly virtuous, Channing believed, all that was needed was a rejuvenated conscience and a commitment to a life of Christian benevolence. Church, government, and other external controls would vanish in the millennium. Such views accorded perfectly with Maria's own. Impatient with sectarian constraints and impelled by a fierce love of freedom, she shared this radical vision. She longed to rid the world of tyranny and oppression; and what better way than by abolishing slavery.*[5]

Numerous expressions of religious zeal can be found in the writings of abolitionist women. For some, the cause of abolition became their primary religion for a time. At the end of her life, Lydia Maria Child reflected on her experience during the early antislavery days in a letter to Theodore Weld:

> *The Holy Spirit* did *actually descend upon men and women in tongues of flame. . . .* All *suppression of selfishness makes the moment great; and mortals were never more sublimely forgetful of self than were the abolitionists in those early days, before the moral force which emanated from them had become available as a political power. Ah, my friend, that is the* only *true church organization, when heads and hearts unite in working for the welfare of the human race.*[6]

In her analysis of Maria Weston Chapman, Catherine Clinton finds that she "devoted herself to the antislavery cause with a religious fervor. Believing in the absolute existence of a right and wrong path, she felt antislavery was her only choice. . . . She believed her individual freedom was to do the greatest good for society and she pegged slavery as the ultimate evil."[7]

One of Maria Chapman's hymns, "Devotion to the Cause of Christ,"[8] makes use of probably the most common biblical reference in the abolitionist movement: "Remember them that are in bonds as bound with them." This quotation (from Hebrews 13:3) appeared on the cover of Lydia Maria Child's *Authentic Anecdotes of American Slavery* (1838) as part of an emblem showing a black woman kneeling and chained with a white woman representing Justice standing above her, about to break her chains.[9] In the hymn, Maria Chapman exhorted: "Stand up! and breathe your fearless prayer/ For those in bonds as bound with them."

The use of this symbol provides one example of what we might today interpret as unconscious racism among white abolitionists. As we seek to learn from the accomplishments of women of the past, we can also learn from their failures. Clearly, these women were sincere in their efforts to end slavery, yet their attitudes sometimes reveal more than a hint of paternalism (or maternalism). While it is important to judge the past on its own terms, we would be remiss if we failed to note underlying themes that may still influence us today in our own work for racial justice.

Despite their possible shortcomings, the women who worked for abolition did so out of great conviction and concern. They refused to sit idly by while people suffered, and they developed their skills as activists in the process. Because of their activist approach, they often found themselves crossing the boundaries between religion and social action. In fact, their actions were a concrete demonstration of their religious values. In seeking to live their religion, they were challenged to create new structures for organizations, fundraising, publications, and so on. Had they remained bound by the past, they would have stayed at home and waited for the world to change, at best providing influence through their roles as moral guardians of their husbands and children. Instead, they improvised, moved beyond thinking about what needed to happen and acted themselves to make it happen. Thus, they provide an excellent example of lived religion.

As women became active in their work for abolition, they necessarily found themselves in confrontation with societal norms regarding their role as women. Their religious zeal for the cause often forced them to move beyond the so-called women's sphere, although they dealt with this challenge in different ways. In writing about Maria Weston Chapman, Catherine Clinton concludes: "She believed men and women were identical in a spiritual realm—rendering their souls and intellects equal, yet Maria Chapman maintained that the sexes were, by necessity, separate and distinct in a temporal realm."[10] Perhaps because of her belief in the essential difference between the sexes, she was a strong advocate of women's organizations within the abolitionist movement. On a practical level, women needed to have their own organizations because of the reluctance or even outright refusal of many men to allow women to participate in their organizations. William Lloyd Garrison and the New England Anti-Slavery Society were exceptions, and Maria Chapman worked closely with both, wielding considerable influence and responsibility.

Later in her life, Maria Chapman lamented the fact that she had been so active outside the home during her children's growing-up years; she wished the abolitionist movement had come later in their lives, so that she could have better fulfilled her role as a mother. Her leadership in the abolitionist movement and its personal cost for her show that, in spite of her expressed belief in separate spheres, she clearly moved beyond such confinement in practice.

Lydia Maria Child experienced a deep conflict between her desire to express and fulfill women's role and her movement out and beyond that realm. On one hand, she provided most of the financial support for her husband and herself throughout her life, thus stepping outside women's sphere for her daily existence. Yet much of her writing for profit was aimed at an audience that remained within that sphere, for example, giving advice on making housekeeping more efficient, although she hated housekeeping and resented the time it took away from her writing. Lydia Maria Child's personal attitude toward the limitations placed on women were expressed in letters, such as this comment to her childhood friend Lucy Osgood:

> *I had much rather tramp through forests to the sound of a tambourine, with my baby strapped on my strong shoulders, than to live amid the constrained elegance of Beacon St. . . . Why should not a* woman *likewise pass through strange fires, and come out with her inmost nature unscathed? Is the question too bold?*[11]

Lydia Maria Child ultimately came to the conclusion that providing full equality for men and women was the only way society could continue to grow and develop. In a letter to Sarah Parsons, written toward the end of her life, she wrote: "The civilization of any country may always be measured by the degree of equality between men and women; and society will never come truly into order until there is perfect equality and copartnership between them in every department of life."[12]

Mary Livermore also moved from a position relatively within women's sphere to one advocating full equality for women and men. As a young wife, she struggled to learn the skills of housekeeping. Some of the most humorous parts of her autobiography deal with such topics as her attempts to interpret the directions in cookbooks and the night she and her husband buried her failed chowder in the garden. Although she eventually mastered the basic skills and was quite proud of her accomplishments (especially when her work saved the family money), her husband later encouraged her to give up housekeeping responsibilities so she could embark on her career as a public speaker on the Lyceum circuit.

Mary Livermore's conversion to women's suffrage came as a result of her work for the Sanitary Commission during the Civil War. Before that, she had expressed doubts as to whether women needed to vote to have influence, since they could always take their requests to men and expect to be heard. But after the war, she became clear in her conviction that suffrage was necessary. As with her conversion to abolition, she based her new view on direct experience:

> *I saw how women are degraded by disenfranchisement, and, in the eyes of men, are lowered to the level of the pauper, the convict, the idiot, and the lunatic and are put in the same category with them and with their own infant children. Under a republican form of government, the possession of the ballot by woman alone can make her the legal equal of man, and without this legal equality, she is robbed of her natural rights.*[13]

Once her doubt of the need for suffrage was resolved, Mary Livermore became one of the strongest advocates for women's rights in all areas of life. Her speeches influenced many others, as she outgrew the boundaries of women's sphere.

If pushing the limits of women's sphere was difficult for white women, it was even more so for black women. As slaves, African American women had been forced to work. Most of those who escaped from slavery had to work to survive. When their finances were sufficiently secure that they could afford not to work, some chose to live within what had previously been defined as women's sphere. Others who found their work outside this sphere often suffered public censure because of their choices. When Frances Watkins Harper began appearing on the lecture circuit, people questioned whether she was really a woman or, if a woman, whether she was really black. As a widow with a young child, she had to deal with the challenge of child care on the road. Yet lecturing and writing were the ways she could best support herself and her family.

Later in the nineteenth century, the women's club movement provided an important way for African American women to gather for self-empowerment. However, they had to respond to criticism, such as that from John Jacks, white editor of a Missouri town newspaper, who in 1895 charged that "the Negroes in this country are wholly devoid of morality; secondly that the women are prostitutes and natural liars and thieves."[14] The National Conference of Colored Women resolved that he had "not only slandered the women of Negro extraction but the mothers of American morality, on a question that not only involves the good respect of the present generation, but generations to come."[15] By relating their defense of African American womanhood to that of all women, they universalized the issue and drew support from those who believed in a separate women's sphere and were willing to defend its sanctity.

Thus, women who had battled for the cause of the slave and women who had fought for their own release from oppression found their voices and began to articulate their individuality. Whether consciously or not, they acted beyond women's sphere and entered the world of action and influence.

The writings in this section demonstrate women's commitment to racial justice over a period of ninety-four years, from 1833 to 1927. The authors are Unitarian and Universalist women primarily from the United States, as the focus of this section is on American slavery and its aftermath. The writings begin with white women's experiences with slavery and with the participation of both black and white women in the abolitionist and antislavery movements.

The Civil War left the South in chaos and ruin. Women who had been committed to the ideals of antislavery before the war sought to offer assistance to establish a new society based on equal justice for all. One of the primary means at their disposal was education. In this section, three white Unitarian women from the North describe their experiences working with schools in the South at the end and after the Civil War. All three, as well as those who supported their work, had to fight Southern prejudice against Yankees. Those who established schools for blacks suffered additional ostracism from Southern whites. It is interesting to note that the two women who established schools for blacks did so together with female friends. Such relationships, judged by today's standards, would undoubtedly be seen as lesbian; however, at the time, they were understood only as life-long companions.[16]

Although we have discovered only a small number of African American women who were active in Unitarian and Universalist circles, those we know of made significant contributions. The two women in this section, both Unitarians, express their awareness that the struggle is not over, along with their faith that clarifying the issues at hand will make racial justice possible.

Together, these writings reveal the broad range of ways Universalist and Unitarian women chose to work for racial justice. As they struggled to understand their role in this major social change, they articulated a vision of a world that they hoped would someday provide equity for all people.

# Appeal to End Slavery

## From *An Appeal in Favor of That Class of Americans Called Africans,* 1833

LYDIA MARIA FRANCIS CHILD (1802–1880) *was a prolific writer and articulate communicator for social reform, particularly abolition. She became a Unitarian in her teens and continued this affiliation throughout her life, although she also explored Swedenborgianism and spiritualism. Already popular as a novelist and writer/editor for women and children, she nearly destroyed her literary career when she turned her efforts to argue for abolition by writing one of the earliest and most influential abolitionist documents,* An Appeal in Favor of That Class of Americans Called Africans. *This groundbreaking piece described in detail the history and reality of slavery and presented a series of logical arguments for its abolition. By carefully considering and then rejecting alternative proposals then under public discussion, such as the possibility of relocating African Americans to Africa, she demonstrated that only complete and immediate abolition would satisfy the standards of American democracy. Her arguments persuaded many public figures, including a number of prominent Unitarians, to adopt the cause of abolition.*

See the Biographical Sketch on pages 295–298.

Reader, I beseech you not to throw down this volume as soon as you have glanced at the title. Read it, if your prejudices will allow, for the very truth's sake: If I have the most trifling claims upon your good will, for an hour's amusement to yourself, or benefit to your children, read it for my sake: Read it, if it be merely to find fresh occasion to sneer at the vulgarity of the cause: Read it, from sheer curiosity to see what a woman (who had much better attend to her household concerns) will say upon such a subject: Read it, on any terms, and my purpose will be gained.

✦ ✦ ✦

I am fully aware of the unpopularity of the task I have undertaken; but though I *expect* ridicule and censure, it is not in my nature to *fear* them.

A few years hence, the opinion of the world will be a matter in which I have not even the most transient interest; but this book will be abroad on its mission of humanity long after the hand that wrote it is mingling with the dust.

Should it be the means of advancing, even one single hour, the inevitable progress of truth and justice, I would not exchange the consciousness for all Rothchild's wealth or Sir Walter's fame.

## The Effect of Slavery on All Concerned in It

From the moment the slave is kidnapped to the last hour he draws his miserable breath, the white man's influence directly cherishes ignorance, fraud, treachery, theft, licentiousness, revenge, hatred, and murder. It cannot be denied that human nature thus operated upon must necessarily yield, more or less, to all these evils. And thus do we dare to treat beings, who, like ourselves, are heirs of immortality!

✦ ✦ ✦

In a community where all the labor is done by one class there must of course be another class who live in indolence; and we all know how much people that have nothing to do are tempted by what the world calls pleasures; the result is that slaveholding states and colonies are proverbial for dissipation. Hence, too, the contempt for industry, which prevails in such a state of society. Where none work but slaves, usefulness becomes degradation. The wife of a respectable mechanic, who accompanied her husband from Massachusetts to the South, gave great offense to her new neighbors by performing her usual household avocations; they begged her to desist from it (offering the services of their own blacks), because the sight of a white person engaged in any labor was extremely injurious to the slaves; they deemed it very important that the negroes should be taught, both by precept and example, that they alone were made to work!

✦ ✦ ✦

There is another view of this system, which I cannot unveil so completely as it ought to be. I shall be called bold for saying so much; but the facts are so important that it is a matter of conscience not to be fastidious.

The negro woman is unprotected either by law or public opinion. She is the property of her master, and her daughters are his property.

They are allowed to have no conscientious scruples, no sense of shame, no regard for the feelings of husband, or parent; they must be entirely subservient to the will of their owner, on pain of being whipped as near unto death, as will comport with his interest, or quite to death, if it suit his pleasure.

Those who know human nature would be able to conjecture the unavoidable result, even if it were not betrayed by the amount of mixed population. Think for a moment what a degrading effect must be produced on the morals of both blacks and whites by customs like these!

✦ ✦ ✦

I have more than once heard people, who had just returned from the South, speak of seeing a number of mulattos in attendance where they visited, whose resemblance to the head of the family was too striking not to be immediately observed. What sort of feeling must be excited in the minds of those slaves by being constantly exposed to the tyranny or caprice of their own brothers and sisters and by the knowledge that these near relations will on a division of the estate have power to sell them off with the cattle?

But the vices of white men eventually provide a scourge for themselves. They increase the negro race, but the negro can never increase theirs; and this is one great reason why the proportion of colored population is always so large in slaveholding countries. As the ratio increases more and more every year, the colored people must eventually be the stronger party; and when this result happens, slavery must either be abolished or government must furnish troops, of whose wages the free states must pay their proportion.

✦ ✦ ✦

The ladies who remove from the free States into the slaveholding ones almost invariably write that the sight of slavery was at first exceedingly painful; but that they soon become habituated to it; and, after a while, they are very apt to vindicate the system, upon the ground that it is extremely convenient to have such submissive servants. This reason was actually given by a lady of my acquaintance, who is considered an unusually fervent Christian. Yet Christianity expressly teaches us to love our neighbor as ourselves. This shows how dangerous it is, for even the best of us, to become *accustomed* to what is wrong.

✦ ✦ ✦

Among other apologies for slavery, it has been asserted that the Bible does not forbid it. Neither does it forbid the counterfeiting of a bank-bill. It is the *spirit* of the Holy Word, not its particular *expressions,* which must be a rule for our conduct. How can slavery be reconciled with the maxim "Do unto others, as ye would that others should unto you?" Does not the command "Thou shalt not *steal,*" prohibit *kidnapping?* And how does whipping men to death agree with the injunction "Thou shall do no *murder?*" Are we not told "to loose the band of wickedness, to undo the heavy burdens, to let the oppressed go free, and to break every yoke"?

✦ ✦ ✦

I shall perhaps be asked why I have said so much about the slave-*trade,* since it was long ago abolished in this country? There are several good reasons for it. In the first place, it is a part of the system; for if there were no slaves, there could be no slave-trade; and while there are slaves, the slave-trade *will* continue. In the next place, the trade is still briskly carried on in Africa, and slaves are smuggled into these States through the Spanish colonies. In the third place, a very extensive internal slave-trade is carried on in this country. The breeding of negro-cattle for the foreign markets (of Louisiana, Georgia, Alabama, Arkansas, and Missouri) is a very lucrative branch of business. Whole coffles of them, chained and manacled, are driven through our Capital on their way to auction. Foreigners, particularly those who come here with enthusiastic ideas of American freedom, are amazed and disgusted at the sight. A troop of slaves once passed through Washington on the Fourth of July, while drums were beating and standards flying. One of the captive negroes raised his hand, loaded with irons, and waving it toward the starry flag, sung with a smile of bitter irony, "Hail Columbia! *happy* land!"

✦ ✦ ✦

It may indeed be said, in palliation of the internal slave-trade, that the horrors of the *middle passage* are avoided. But still the amount of misery is very great. Husbands and wives, parents and children, are rudely torn from each other. There can be no doubt of this fact: advertisements are very common, in which a mother and her children are offered either in a lot, or separately, as may suit the purchaser. In one of these advertisements, I observed it stated that the youngest child was about a year old.

The captives are driven by the whip, through toilsome journeys, under a burning sun; their limbs fettered; with nothing before them but the prospect of toil more severe than that to which they have been accustomed.

The disgrace of such scenes in the capital of our republic cannot be otherwise than painful to every patriotic mind; while they furnish materials for the most pungent satire to other nations. A United States senator declared that the sight of a drove of slaves was so insupportable that he always avoided it when he could; and an intelligent Scotchman said, when he first entered Chesapeake Bay and cast his eye along our coast, the sight of the slaves brought his heart into his throat. How can we help feeling a sense of shame, when we read Moore's contemptuous couplet,

> "The fustian flag that proudly waves,
> In splendid mockery, o'er a land of slaves?"

The lines would be harmless enough if they were false; the sting lies in their truth.

Finally, I have described some of the horrors of the slave-trade, because when our constitution was formed, the government pledged itself not to abolish this traffic until 1808. We began our career of freedom by granting a twenty years' lease of iniquity—twenty years of allowed invasion of other men's rights—twenty years of bloodshed, violence, and fraud! And this will be told in our annals—this will be heard of to the end of time!

✦ ✦ ✦

## Possibility of Safe Emancipation

The slaveholders try to stop all the efforts of benevolence, by vociferous complaints about infringing upon their *property;* and justice is so subordinate to self-interest that the unrighteous claim is silently allowed, and even openly supported, by those who ought to blush for themselves, as Christians and as republicans. Let men *simplify* their arguments—let them confine themselves to one single question, "What right can a man have to compel his neighbor to toil without reward, and leave the same hopeless inheritance to his children, in order that *he* may live in luxury and indolence?" Let the doctrines of *expediency* return to the Father of Lies, who invented them and gave them power to turn every way for evil. The Christian knows no appeal from the decisions of God, plainly uttered in his conscience.

The laws of Venice allowed *property* in human beings; and upon this ground Shylock demanded his pound of flesh, cut nearest to the heart. Those who advertise mothers to be sold separately from their children likewise claim a right to human flesh; and they too cut it nearest to the heart.

The personal liberty of one man can never be the property of another. All ideas of property are founded upon the mutual agreement of the human race and are regulated by such laws as are deemed most conducive to the general good. In slavery there is no *mutual* agreement; for in that case it would not be slavery. The negro has no voice in the matter—no alternative is presented to him—no bargain is made. The beginning of his bondage is the triumph of power over weakness; its continuation is the tyranny of knowledge over ignorance. One man may as well claim an exclusive right to the air another man breathes, as to the possession of his limbs and faculties. Personal freedom is the birthright of every human being. God himself made it the first great law of creation; and no human enactment can render it null and void. "If," says, Price, "you have a right to make another man a slave, he has a right to make you a slave"; and Ramsay says, "If we have in the beginning no right to sell a man, no person has a right to buy him."

Am I reminded that the *laws* acknowledge these vested rights in human flesh? I answer the laws themselves were made by individuals who wished to justify the wrong and profit by it. We ought never to have recognized a claim which cannot exist according to the laws of God; it is our duty to atone for the error; and the sooner we make a beginning, the better will it be for us all.

✦ ✦ ✦

To enlighten public opinion is the best way that has yet been discovered for the removal of national evils; and slavery is certainly a *national* evil.

The Southern States, according to their own evidence, are impoverished by it; a great amount of wretchedness and crime inevitably follows in its train; the prosperity of the North is continually checked by it; it promotes feelings of rivalry between the States; it separates our interests; makes our councils discordant; threatens the destruction of our government; and disgraces us in the eyes of the world. I have often heard Americans who have been abroad declare that nothing embarrassed them so much as being questioned about our slaves; and that nothing was so mortifying as to have the pictures of runaway negroes pointed at in the newspapers of this republic. . . .

Now a common evil certainly implies a common right to remedy; and where is the remedy to be found, if the South in all their speeches and writings repeat that slavery *must* exist . . . and if public opinion here brands everybody as a fanatic and madman, who wishes to *inquire* what can be done? The supineness of New England on this subject reminds me of the man who being asked to work at the pump, because the vessel was going down, answered, "I am only a passenger."

✦ ✦ ✦

## Prejudices Against People of Color and Our Duties in Relation to This Subject

Our prejudice against the blacks is founded in sheer pride; and it originates in the circumstance that people of their color only are universally allowed to be slaves. We made slavery, and slavery makes the prejudice. No Christian, who questions his own conscience, can justify himself in indulging the feeling. The removal of this prejudice is not a matter of opinion—it is a matter of *duty*. We have no right to palliate a feeling, sinful in itself and highly injurious to a large number of our fellow-beings. Let us no longer act upon the narrow-minded idea that we must always continue to do wrong because we have so long been in the habit of doing it.

✦ ✦ ✦

Ought we to be called Christians if we allow a prejudice so absurd to prevent the improvement of a large portion of the human race and interfere with what all civilized nations consider the most common rights of mankind? It cannot be that my enlightened and generous countrymen will sanction anything so narrow-minded and so selfish.

✦ ✦ ✦

While we bestow our earnest disapprobation on the system of slavery, let us not flatter ourselves that we are in reality any better than our brethren of the South. Thanks to our soil and climate, and the early exertions of the excellent Society of Friends, the *form* of slavery does not exist among us; but the very *spirit* of the hateful and mischievous thing is here in all its strength. The manner in which we use what power we have gives us ample reason to be grateful that the nature of our institutions does not entrust us with more. Our prejudice against colored people is even more inveterate than it is at the South. The planter is often attached to his negroes and lavishes caresses and kind words upon them, as he would on a favorite hound: but our cold-hearted, ignoble prejudice admits of no exception—no intermission.

The Southerners have long continued habit, apparent interest, and dreaded danger to palliate the wrong they do but we stand without excuse. They tell us that Northern ships and Northern capital have been engaged in this wicked business; and the reproach is true. Several fortunes in this city have been made by the sale of negro blood. If these criminal transactions are still carried on, they are done in silence and secrecy, because public opinion has made them disgraceful. But if the free States wished to cherish the system of slavery forever, they could not take a more direct course than they now do. Those who are kind and liberal on all other subjects unite with the selfish and the proud in their unrelenting efforts to keep the colored population in the lowest state of degradation; and the influence they unconsciously exert over children early infuses into their innocent minds the same strong feelings of contempt.

✦ ✦ ✦

Is it asked what can be done? I answer, much, very much, can be effected, if each individual will try to deserve the commendation bestowed by our Savior on the woman of old—"She hath done what she could."

✦ ✦ ✦

Our preachers can speak of slavery, as they do of other evils. Our poets can find in this subject abundant room for sentiment and pathos. Our orators (provided they do not want office) may venture an allusion to our *in*-"glorious institutions."

The union of individual influence produces a vast amount of moral force, which is not the less powerful because it is often unperceived. A mere change in the *direction* of our efforts, without any increased exertion, would in the course of a few years produce an entire revolution of public feeling. This slow but sure way of doing good is almost the only means by which benevolence can effect its purpose.

✦ ✦ ✦

By publishing this book I have put my mite into the treasury. The expectation of displeasing all classes has not been unaccompanied with pain. But it has been strongly impressed upon my mind that it was a duty to fulfill this task; and worldly considerations should never stifle the voice of conscience.

## ✦ *Biographical Sketch*

**Born:** *February 11, 1802, Medford, Massachusetts*

**Died:** *October 20, 1880, Wayland, Massachusetts, age 78*

**Buried:** *Wayland, Massachusetts*

Lydia Maria Francis Child was an ardent activist and writer for racial justice who felt that she had "the heart of a man imprisoned within a woman's destiny."[17] Her works included popular novels, essays on domestic issues, and religious writings.

The youngest of seven surviving children born to Medford baker Convers Francis and his wife Susannah, Lydia was raised in a hardworking, Calvinist household. Convers Francis, Jr., her elder brother by six years, was the only member of the family who sympathized with her early interest in books. He guided her reading, even after the two were separated when he attended Harvard College and she lived with a married sister in Maine.

With little formal education, Lydia began teaching at age nineteen in Gardiner, Maine. Soon, however, she was able to join her favorite brother, Convers Francis, now installed as the minister in Watertown, Massachusetts, and to enjoy his extensive library. Lydia became a Unitarian and joined his church but was also attracted by the works of Sampson Reed to Swedenborgianism, where she experienced religion more fully than among rationalist Unitarians.

At the age of twenty-four, Lydia published the first American historical novel, *Hobomok*, the story of a romance between a white woman and a Native American. An instantaneous success, the book swept its young author into the literary circles of Boston and Cambridge. At the same time, she also became editor of *The Juvenile Miscellany*, a popular children's magazine.

On October 19, 1828, Lydia (or Maria, as she preferred to be called) married an idealistic, affectionate, but improvident young lawyer, David Child. Throughout their forty-six years of marriage, David moved from one unsuccessful venture to another, his debts a constant drain on his wife's earnings. Early in her married life, Maria published her best-selling *The Frugal Housewife* (1829) and other household manuals, which helped pay her husband's debts and bring in a small but steady stream of royalties.

In the early 1830s, abolitionist William Lloyd Garrison, as Maria wrote later, "got hold of the strings of my conscience and pulled me into Reforms."[18] The Swedenborgians had disappointed her with their disinterest in the issue of slavery, and she had turned to William Ellery Channing, who stressed the importance of Christian conscience and benevolence. Even Channing fell short of full enthusiasm for the abolition of slavery, however, so Maria helped persuade him to make his controversial public antislavery statement. In August 1833, she published *An Appeal in Favor of That Class of Americans Called Africans.* Beginning with a history of slavery and a description of its evils, the book strongly advocated immediate emancipation, challenged the conventional thinking that African Americans were a naturally inferior race, and implicated the North as well as the South in supporting the institution of slavery. Although *An Appeal* was later credited with converting more people to the abolition cause than any other publication, its immediate effect was to devastate Maria's literary career. The sentiments it expressed were so unpopular that she lost the editorship of *The Juvenile Miscellany.* Sales of her other publications also fell off dramatically, and publishers refused to look at anything new she wrote.

Determined to remain true to her cause, Maria worked with the Boston Female Anti-Slavery Society and, in 1837, was elected vice president of the Women's Anti-Slavery Convention of New York. From 1841–1843, she served as editor of the *National Anti-Slavery Standard,* published in New York in competition with Boston's *Liberator,* edited by Garrison. In her hands, the *Standard* became extremely successful, not only as an expression of abolitionist views but as a widely read family newspaper. After she resigned her editorship, due to the conflicting demands of various splinter groups within the movement, she published a collection of her popular columns, *Letters from New York,* in 1843. It was an immediate success and helped re-establish her literary career.

Having cut her ties with the antislavery organizations, Lydia Maria Child began to study world religions in preparation for writing *The Progress of Religious Ideas through Successive Ages,* which was published in several volumes in 1854. She concluded that no single religion held exclusive claim to the truth, but each had served the particular needs of its own time and place.

Upset by the passage of the Fugitive Slave Law, the uprisings against the free-soil pioneers in Kansas, and the vicious physical attack on Massachusetts Senator Charles Sumner for his antislavery position in the 1850s, Child returned to her abolitionist interests and antislavery writings. During the Civil War, she devoted herself to writing pamphlets as well as sewing and gathering educational materials. These were later published as *The Freedmen's Book* for the so-called contraband slaves who had escaped to Union lines.

After the war, Maria turned her attention to other reforms. Like many abolitionists, she believed that suffrage for black men should be granted before suffrage for women, if the stranglehold of the slave culture were ever to be broken. Even so, she became more active in the suffrage movement. She also took up the cause of Native Americans, believing that they should not be denied their own languages and religions.

When the Unitarians met in 1867 to form the Free Religious Association, Lydia Maria Child discovered with delight that the new movement held the same principles as her *Progress of Religious Ideas.* She attended the group's meetings regularly when she was in Boston. In 1878, she published *Aspirations of the World,* her own "eclectic Bible" of quotations from the world's religions.

Only during the last six years of her life, after David Child's death in 1874, was Lydia Maria Child free of the anxiety and hard physical labor of caring for her husband. Thanks to receipts from her publications and an unexpected bequest, she finally was free of financial difficulties and able to make substantial gifts to a number of her favorite causes. When she died at the age of seventy-eight, Wendell Phillips traveled to Wayland to deliver her eulogy. Speaking for her friends in the antislavery movement, he said, "We felt that neither fame, nor gain, nor danger, nor calumny had any weight with her." He added that she was "ready to die for a principle and starve for an idea."[19]

*Biographical Sketch by* JOAN W. GOODWIN

## ✦ Writings of Lydia Maria Francis Child

*An Appeal in Favor of That Class of Americans Called Africans.* Boston: Allen & Ticknor, 1833.

*Anti-Slavery Catechism.* Newburyport, MA: Charles Whipple, 1836.

*The Collected Correspondence of Lydia Maria Child.* Edited by Patricia G. Holland, Milton Meltzer, and Francine Krasno. Millwood, NY: Kraus Microform, 1980. Microfiche.

*Correspondence between Lydia Maria Child and Gov. Wise and Mrs. Mason of Virginia.* Boston: American Anti-Slavery Society, 1860.

*The Duty of Disobedience to the Fugitive Slave Act.* Boston: American Anti-Slavery Society, 1860.

*The Evils of Slavery, and the Cure of Slavery.* Newburyport, MA: Charles Whipple, 1836.

*The Freedmen's Book.* Edited and with contributions by Lydia Maria Child. Boston: Ticknor and Fields, 1865.

*Hobomok: A Tale of Early Times.* n.p., 1824; Reprinted in *Hobomok & Other Writings on Indians by Lydia Maria Child,* edited by Carolyn L. Karcher. New Brunswick, NJ: Rutgers University Press, 1986.

*Isaac T. Hopper: A True Life.* Boston: John P. Jewett, 1853.

*Letters from New York.* 1st series, New York: C. S. Francis, 1843; 2nd series, New York: C. S. Francis, 1845.

*Letters of Lydia Maria Child.* With a biographical introduction by John G. Whittier. Boston: Houghton, Mifflin, 1882.

*Lydia Maria Child: Selected Letters, 1817–1880.* Edited by Milton Meltzer and Patricia G. Holland. Amherst: University of Massachusetts Press, 1982.

*The Patriarchal Institution, as Described by Members of its Own Family.* Comp. by Lydia Maria Child. New York: American Anti-Slavery Society, 1860.

*The Right Way, The Safe Way, Proved by Emancipation in the British West Indies, and Elsewhere.* New York: American Anti-Slavery Society, 1860.

## ✦ Biographical Resources

Baer, Helene G. *The Heart Is Like Heaven: The Life of Lydia Maria Child.* Philadelphia: University of Pennsylvania Press, 1964.

Clifford, Deborah Pickman. *Crusader for Freedom: A Life of Lydia Maria Child.* Boston: Beacon Press, 1992.

Karcher, Carolyn L. *The First Woman in the Republic: A Cultural Biography of Lydia Maria Child.* Durham, NC: Duke University Press, 1995.

Meltzer, Milton. *Tongue of Flame: The Life of Lydia Maria Child.* New York: Thomas Y. Crowell, 1965.

Osborne, William S. *Lydia Maria Child.* Boston: Twayne, 1980.

## ✦ Archives

Major collections of Lydia Maria Francis Child's papers are available at the American Antiquarian Society, Worcester, Massachusetts; Boston Public Library; Cornell University Library; Library of Congress; Massachusetts Historical Society; Medford Historical Society, Medford, Massachusetts; Schlesinger Library, Radcliffe College; Society for the Preservation of New England Antiquities, Boston; and Wayland Historical Society, Wayland, Massachusetts.

# Hymns of Freedom

## Hymn Texts, Published 1836

*Antislavery hymns and songs became popular means of piercing the reluctance of Northerners to address the seriousness of the situation of slavery and their own complicity in it. Throughout the 1830s to 1850s, concerts and worship services were held regularly in Boston and elsewhere to arouse public sentiment and enthusiasm for the cause.*

MARIA WESTON CHAPMAN (1806–1885) *was the primary organizer of the Boston Female Anti-Slavery Society and a central figure in the Boston abolitionist movement, led by William Lloyd Garrison. Raised in a prominent Boston family, she was also a close friend of William Ellery Channing and a member of Federal Street Church (Unitarian). Her hymn texts illustrated her ability to translate and apply religious principles and imagery to the contemporary cause of abolition. They offered a clear challenge to people of faith to apply Christian principles to the realities of a social system based on oppression.*

See the Biographical Sketch on pages 15–18.

### Hymn for the Boston* Monthly Concert

Through all the three-hilled city now,
    Swell high the voice of prayer and praise!
Though 'the perpetual hills do bow,'
    Yet everlasting are Thy ways.

Oh! yet, as in thine ancient day,
    Thy word is truth, Thy will is love;
Thy law is FREEDOM—to obey
    That glorious gospel from above!

✦ ✦ ✦

*Originally called *Trimountain.*

## Monthly Concert of Prayer for Emancipation

Oh, God of Freedom! bless, this night,*
  The steadfast hearts that toil as one,
Till thy sure law of truth and right,
  Alike in heaven and earth, be done.

A piercing voice of grief and wrong,
  Goes upward from the groaning earth!
Oh true and holy Lord! how long?
  In majesty and might come forth!

Yet, Lord, remembering mercy too,
  Behold the oppressor in his sin;
Make all his actions just and true,
  Renew his wayward heart within.

From thee let righteous purpose flow,
  And find in every heart its home
Till truth and judgment reign below,
  And here, on earth, thy kingdom come.

✦ ✦ ✦

## The Modern Pharisees

There are who hate God's truth and laws:—
  There are who plead the oppressor's cause;
There are whose base degenerate souls,
  The breath of wealth and power controls.

✦ ✦ ✦

*The last Monday night of every month.

## Devotion to the Cause of Christ*

The memory of the faithful dead
    Be on their children's hearts this day!
Your father's God, their host that led,
    Will shield you through the stormy way.

Your Saviour bids you seek and save
    The trampled and the oppressed of earth,
At his command the storm to brave,
    Faithful and true! come boldly forth!

Their suffering though your souls must share—
    Though pride oppress and hate condemn,
Stand up! and breathe your fearless prayer
    For those in bonds as bound with them.

Unheeded fall the fierce command
    That bids the struggling soul be dumb!
Shout with a voice to rouse a land!
    Bid the free martyr spirit come!

*The present times will be but imperfectly understood by those who shall come after us; none but those *now* living, and possessing an opportunity of *seeing* the play or the machinery set in motion by the controllers of the clergy, can appreciate the strength of soul it now requires to "pray publicly" for master and slave.

# Antislavery Hymns and Songs

## Hymn Texts, Published 1836 and 1855

ELIZA LEE CABOT FOLLEN (1787–1860), *who was from a less than wealthy branch of one of Boston's foremost families, was primarily known as an author and editor of children's stories and periodicals. She and her German husband, Charles Follen—a Harvard professor and later a Unitarian minister—are often credited with introducing the Christmas tree to New England. They were also dedicated abolitionists. Eliza Follen's antislavery hymns and songs were designed to move the heart as well as prick the conscience. Her settings often involved children and mothers to demonstrate the effects of slavery on the people it harmed most.*

See the Biographical Sketch on pages 307–309.

### Where Is Thy Brother?

*"What mean ye that ye beat my people to pieces, and grind the faces of the poor? saith the Lord God of hosts."*

—Isaiah

What mean ye that ye bruise and bind
My people, saith the Lord,
And starve your craving brother's mind,
That asks to hear my word?

What mean ye that ye make them toil
Through long and dreary years,
And shed like rain upon your soil
Their blood and bitter tears?

What mean ye that ye dare to rend
The tender mother's heart;
Brothers from sisters, friend from friend,
How dare you bid them part?

What mean ye, when God's bounteous hand
To you so much has given,
That from the slave who tills your land
You keep both earth and heaven?

When at the judgment God shall call,
Where is thy brother? say,
What mean ye to the Judge of all,
To answer on that day?

✦ ✦ ✦

## On Hearing of the Sadness of the Slave-Children from the Fear of Being Sold

When children play the livelong day,
Like birds and butterflies;
As free and gay, sport time away,
And know not care or sighs
Then all the air seems fresh and fair
Around us and above.
Life's flowers are there; and everywhere
Is innocence and love.

When children pray with fear all day,
A blight must be at hand.
Then joys decay, and birds of prey
Are hovering o'er the land.
When young hearts weep as they go to sleep,
Then all the world is sad.
The flesh must creep, and woes are deep,
When children are not glad.

✦ ✦ ✦

## Remember the Slave!

Mother, when around your child
You clasp your arms in love,
And when with grateful joy you raise
Your eyes to God above;

Think of the negro-mother when
Her child is torn away,—
Sold for a little slave,—oh then
For that poor mother pray!

Father, when your happy boys
You look upon with pride,
And pray to see them, when you're old,
All blooming by your side;

Think of the man who lives to be
The father of a slave;
And asks a pitying God to give
His little son a grave!

Brothers and sisters who with joy
Meet round the social hearth,
And talk of home and happy days,
And laugh in careless mirth;

Remember then the poor young slave
Who never felt your joy,
Who, early old, has never known
The bliss to be a boy!

Ye Christian ministers of Him
Who came to make men free,
When at the Almighty Maker's throne
You bend the suppliant knee;

From the deep fountains of your soul,
Then let your prayers ascend
For the poor slave who hardly knows
That God is still his friend!

Let all who know that God is just,
That Jesus came to save
Unite in the most holy cause
Of the forsaken slave!

✦ ✦ ✦

## Auld Lang Syne

How hopeful were the early days
Our brave forefathers knew!
How beautiful their simple ways,
Their doings good and true!

CHORUS: Our early days, our early days,
With all their light, are o'er;
The mighty men and good old ways
That we shall see no more.

The glowing history we read
Of acts too great for praise;
And learn by heart each noble deed
Of those bright early days.
CHORUS

Alas, that hour of deepest gloom!
Those men so good and true
Have signed and sealed the negro's doom.
"They know not what they do."
CHORUS

To give their children peace and wealth,
Their brother's right they stole.
God sent the nation's body health,
But "leanness to its soul."
CHORUS

A prophet speaks the word today
'For erring sires atone!
That fatal Union shall ye lay
Upon the altar-stone.'
CHORUS

And from that sacrifice sublime
Shall rise the sacred fire;
The spirit of the olden time
Our people shall inspire.
CHORUS

✦ ✦ ✦

## And the Days of Thy Mourning Shall Be Ended

Lift up a voice of gladness,
Ye lowly waiting throng!
O, dry your tears of sadness,
And raise a cheerful song!

Hope on! A glorious morrow
Your aching hearts shall see;
And quench their burning sorrow
In freedom's jubilee.

The word of doom is spoken.
Your chains are loosening fast.
Ere long, they shall be broken;
And Justice reign at last.

Nation to nation calling,
Cries—liberty for all!
The tyrant's power is falling,
Is quailing at that call.

From mountain back to mountain,
Its echoes shall be heard;
And maidens at the fountain
Shall pass the holy word.

O'er mighty lake and river
Shall go the great decree,
The tyrant's chain to sever,
And set the captive free.

O'er many a flowery prairie,
Like breath from Heaven, it sighs;
And bids the sad and weary
Lift up their tearful eyes.

Ocean to ocean swelling,
With loud exulting waves,
The joyful word is telling—
There shall be no more slaves.

## ✦ *Biographical Sketch*

**Born:** *August 15, 1787, Boston, Massachusetts*
**Died:** *January 26, 1860, Brookline, Massachusetts, age 73*
**Buried:** *Mount Auburn Cemetery, Cambridge, Massachusetts*

In 1853, Harriet Beecher Stowe wrote to Eliza Lee Cabot Follen: "I have long been acquainted with you, and during all the nursery part of my life made daily use of your poems for children. I used to think sometime in those days that I would write to you and tell you how much I was obliged to you for the pleasure they gave to all of us." Today, almost 150 years later, children and parents still enjoy the "Three Little Kittens Who Lost Their Mittens," published in 1832 in *Little Songs for Boys and Girls.*

Born in 1784, Eliza was one of the thirteen children of well-educated parents, Samuel and Sarah Cabot. Theirs was a cultivated and well-connected household, closely related to several prominent families of Boston and Cambridge. What they lacked in worldly wealth was well compensated by the rich cultural atmosphere in which they lived.

After her parents' death, Eliza and two sisters lived within walking distance of the Federal Street Church, where the founder of American Unitarianism, the Reverend William Ellery Channing, was embarking on a new venture—religious education for children. Eliza began a close and life-long friendship with the Reverend Channing at this time, as she volunteered to be one of his Sunday school teachers.

Another close and life-long friend was novelist Catherine Sedgwick. She introduced Eliza to a young political refugee from Germany, Dr. Charles Theodore Christian Follen. In the course of introducing him to people in his new surroundings, Eliza discovered that they had many mutual interests, which deepened into a sincere and long-lasting love. They were married in 1828 and built a small house in Cambridge on what is now known as Follen Street. Known for their warm hospitality, the Follens' home became a popular gathering place. Their son Charles was born there in 1830.

All who have written about Charles and Eliza Follen have mentioned their gentleness of spirit and appearance. Yet the two were not popular with the "proper Bostonians," whose lucrative investments in the local textile mills depended on the slave labor that picked the cotton on Southern plantations. Coupled with the Follens' natural gentleness was a shared courageousness and adamant dedication to the abolition of slavery. Because of Dr. Follen's unwillingness to compromise or mute his convictions, his German professorship at Harvard was not re-funded, and his promising ministry at New York's All Souls Church ended with his resignation.

Yet the Follens were welcomed by the small group of rural churchgoers in Lexington, Massachusetts, who were struggling to organize what was eventually named the Free Christian Church of East Lexington (now known as the Follen Church Society). Drawing from his previous architectural studies, Charles designed the attractive octagonal church building, reminiscent of many in Germany, and was its first minister even before the building's completion. The Reverend Ralph Waldo Emerson then provided two years of interim preaching (1835–1837) to the congregation while Dr. Follen tended to other duties. It was a tragic irony that Dr. Follen died in January 1840 (at the age of forty-four), as he was returning home from New York for the dedication of his beautiful little church. The steamship *Lexington,* on which he was a passenger, caught fire and burned to the waterline.

Eliza Follen, now a fifty-three-year-old widow with a ten-year-old son, had to face life not only without her beloved companion but with little income. Her home became a small school where, along with young Charles, she prepared boys for college. She also turned again to her writing, producing a score of books for young and old. Along with the demands of providing for herself and her son, Eliza managed to remain an active participant in the abolitionist movement, serving on committees of both the Boston and Cambridge societies. She wrote, lectured, and raised funds.

Beloved by her contemporaries, Eliza Lee Follen was a rare combination of gentleness and determination. She and her husband are well remembered today by the congregation of the church they founded, which now proudly bears their name.

*Biographical Sketch by* BARBARA MARSHMAN

## ✦ Writings of Eliza Lee Cabot Follen

Anti-Slavery Hymns and Songs. *Anti-Slavery Tracts* 12 (1855).
*The Child's Friend* (a monthly periodical edited by Eliza Lee Follen, 1844–1850). Boston: L. C. Bowles, 1843–1858.

*Hymns, Songs, and Fables for Young People.* Boston: W. M. Crosby and H. P. Nichols, 1851.
"A Letter to Mothers in the Free States." *Anti-Slavery Tracts* 8 (1855): 1–4.
*The Liberty Cap.* Boston: L. C. Bowles, 1846.
"Picnic at Dedham." *Child's Friend: Designed for Families and Sunday Schools* 1 (October 1843): 21–25.
*Poems.* Boston: Wm. Crosby, 1839.
*Sketches of Married Life.* Boston: Hilliard, Gray, 1838.
*The Well-Spent Hour.* Boston: Horace B. Fuller, 1827.
*Works of Charles Follen, with a Memoir of His Life.* Edited by Eliza Follen. 5 vols. Boston: Hilliard, Gray, 1841–1842.

## ✦ Biographical Resources

*Mrs. Follen's Twilight Stories.* Special reprint ed. Lexington, MA: Follen Church Society, c. 1980.
Schlesinger, Elizabeth Bancroft. "Two Early Harvard Wives: Eliza Farrar and Eliza Follen." *New England Quarterly* (June 1965): 147–167.

# Life on a Georgia Plantation

## From *Journal of a Residence on a Georgian Plantation,* 1838–1839

FRANCES ANNE KEMBLE (1809–1893), *known as Fanny, was an actress born in London to a celebrated theatrical family. After a promising early career, including an appearance in her own play, she married Pierce Butler, a Unitarian and a slave owner. Although she had been active in Unitarian antislavery circles in England and the United States, Fanny apparently did not confront her husband's involvement with slavery until, after several years of married life in the North, they went to his two large plantations in Georgia.*

*Fannie Kemble's horror at the realities of slavery was poured into her journal, which she disguised as a series of letters to her abolitionist friend, Elizabeth Sedgwick. Because of family considerations,* Journal of a Residence on a Georgian Plantation, 1838–1839, *was not published until the middle of the Civil War, thus limiting its influence. However, Southerners claimed that its publication convinced England not to recognize the Confederate government.*

See the Biographical Sketch on pages 316–319.

Dear Elizabeth,

Such of these dwellings as I visited today were filthy and wretched in the extreme and exhibited that most deplorable consequence of ignorance and an abject condition.

✦ ✦ ✦

They must learn, and who can tell the fruit of that knowledge alone, that there are beings in the world, even with skins of a different color from their own, who have sympathy for their misfortunes, love for their virtues, and respect for their common nature—but oh! my heart is full almost to bursting as I walk among these most poor creatures.

✦ ✦ ✦

The infirmary is a large two-story building, terminating the broad orange-planted space between the two rows of houses which form the first settlement; it is built of whitewashed wood and contains four large-sized rooms. But how shall I describe to you the spectacle which was presented to me on entering the first of these? But half the casements, of which there were six, were glazed, and these were obscured with dirt, almost as much as the other windowless ones were darkened by the dingy shutters, which the shivering inmates had fastened to in order to protect themselves from the cold. In the enormous chimney glimmered the powerless embers of a few sticks of wood, round which, however, as many of the sick women as could approach were cowering, some on wooden settles, most of them on the ground, excluding those who were too ill to rise; and these last poor wretches lay prostrate on the floor, without bed, mattress, or pillow, buried in tattered and filthy blankets, which, huddled round them as they lay strewed about, left hardly space to move upon the floor. And here, in their hour of sickness and suffering, lay those whose health and strength are spent in unrequited labor for us—those who, perhaps even yesterday, were being urged on to their unpaid task—those whose husbands, fathers, brothers, and sons were even at that hour sweating over the earth, whose produce was to buy for us all the luxuries which health can revel in, all the comforts which can alleviate sickness. I stood in the midst of them, perfectly unable to speak, the tears pouring from my eyes at this sad spectacle of their misery, myself and my emotion alike strange and incomprehensible to them. Here lay women expecting every hour the terrors and agonies of childbirth, others who had just brought their doomed offspring into the world, others who were groaning over the anguish and bitter disappointment of miscarriages—here lay some burning with fever, others chilled with cold and aching with rheumatism, upon the hard cold ground, the draughts and dampness of the atmosphere increasing their sufferings, and dirt, noise, and stench, and every aggravation of which sickness is capable. . . .

Now pray take notice that this is the hospital of an estate where the owners are supposed to be humane, the overseer efficient and kind, and the Negroes remarkably well cared for and comfortable.

✦ ✦ ✦

Labor being here the especial portion of slaves, it is thenceforth degraded and considered unworthy of all but slaves. No white man, therefore, of any class puts hand to work of any kind soever. This is an exceedingly dignified way of proving their gentility for the lazy planters who prefer an idle life of semistarvation and barbarism to the degradation of doing anything themselves but the effect on the poorer whites of the country is terrible. I speak now of the scattered white population, who, too poor to possess land or slaves and having no means of living in the towns, squat (most appropriately is it so termed) either on other men's land or government districts—always here swamp or pine barren—and claim masterdom over the place they invade till ejected by the rightful proprietors. These wretched creatures will not, for they are whites (and labor belongs to blacks and slaves alone here), labor for their own subsistence. They are hardly protected from the weather by the rude shelters they frame for themselves in the midst of these dreary woods. Their food is chiefly supplied by shooting the wildfowl and venison and stealing from the cultivated patches of the plantations nearest at hand. Their clothes hang about them in filthy tatters, and the combined squalor and fierceness of their appearance is really frightful.

This population is the direct growth of slavery. The planters are loud in their execrations of these miserable vagabonds; yet they do not see that so long as labor is considered the disgraceful portion of slaves, these free men will hold it nobler to starve or steal than till the earth, with none but the despised blacks for fellow laborers. The blacks themselves—such is the infinite power of custom—acquiesce in this notion, and, as I have told you, consider it the lowest degradation in a white to use any exertion. I wonder, considering the burdens they have seen me lift, the digging, the planting, the rowing, and the walking I do, that they do not utterly condemn me, and, indeed, they seem lost in amazement at it.

✦ ✦ ✦

Judge from the details I now send you; and never forget, while reading them, that the people on this plantation are well off and consider themselves well off in comparison with the slaves on some of the neighboring estates.

## Louisa

She told it very simply, and it was most pathetic. She had not finished her task one day, when she said she felt ill, and unable to do so, and had been severely flogged by driver Bran, in whose "gang" she then was. The next day, in spite of this encouragement to labor, she had again been unable to complete her appointed work; and Bran having told her that he'd tie her up and flog her if she did not get it done, she had left the field and run into the swamp.

"Tie you up, Louisa!" said I; "what is that?"

She then described to me that they were fastened up by their wrists to a beam or a branch of a tree, their feet barely touching the ground, so as to allow them no purchase for resistance or evasion of the lash, their clothes turned over their heads, and their backs scored with a leather thong, either by the driver himself, or, if he pleases to inflict their punishment by deputy, any of the men he may choose to summon to the office; it might be father, brother, husband, or lover, if the overseer so ordered it. I turned sick, and my blood curdled listening to these details from the slender young slip of a lassie, with her poor piteous face and murmuring, pleading voice.

"Oh," said I, "Louisa; but the rattlesnakes—the dreadful rattlesnakes in the swamps; were you not afraid of those horrible creatures?"

"Oh, missis," said the poor child, "me no tink of dem; me forget all 'bout dem for de fretting."

"Why did you come home at last?"

"Oh, missis, me starve with hunger, me most dead with hunger before me come back."

"And were you flogged, Louisa?" said I, with a shudder at what the answer might be.

"No, missis, me go to hospital; me almost dead and sick so long, 'spec driver Bran him forgot 'bout de flogging."

## Old House Molly

She named to me all her children, an immense tribe; and, by-the-by, E[lizabeth], it has occurred to me that whereas the increase of this ill-fated race is frequently adduced as a proof of their good treatment and well-being, it really and truly is no such thing. . . .

They enjoy, by means of numerous children, certain positive advantages. In the first place, every woman who is pregnant, as soon as she chooses to make the fact known to the overseer, is relieved of a certain portion of her work in the field, which lightening of labor continues, of course, as long as she is so burdened. On the birth of a child certain additions of clothing and an additional weekly ration are bestowed on the family; and these matters, small as they may seem, act as powerful inducements. . . .

Moreover, they have all of them a most distinct and perfect knowledge of their value to their owners as property; and a woman thinks, and not much amiss, that the more frequently she adds to the number of her master's livestock by bringing new slaves into the world, the more claims she will have upon his consideration and good will. This was perfectly evident to me from the meritorious air with which the women always made haste to inform me of the number of children they had borne and the frequent occasions on which the older slaves would direct my attention to their children, exclaiming: "Look, missis! little niggers for you and massa; plenty little niggers for you and little missis!" A very agreeable apostrophe to me indeed, as you will believe. . . .

## Joan

In complimenting a woman called Joan upon the tidy condition of her house, she answered, with that cruel humility that it is so bad an element in their character: "Missis no 'spect to find colored folks' house clean as white folks'." The mode in which they have learned to accept the idea of their own degradation and unalterable inferiority as the most serious impediment that I see in the way of their progress, since assuredly "self-love is not so vile a sin as self-neglecting."

## Nancy

In one of the huts I went to leave some flannel, and rice, and sugar for a poor old creature called Nancy, to whom I had promised such indulgences: she is exceedingly infirm and miserable, suffering from sore limbs and an ulcerated leg so cruelly that she can hardly find rest in any position from the constant pain she endures and is quite unable to lie on her hard bed at night. As I bent over her today, trying to prop her into some posture where she might find some ease, she took hold of my hand, and with the tears streaming over her face, said: "I have worked every day through dew and damp, and sand and heat, and done good work; but oh, missis, me old and broken now; no tongue can tell how much I suffer."

## Dice

In the next cabin, which consisted of an enclosure called by courtesy a room, certainly not ten feet square, and owned by a woman called Dice—that is, not owned, of course, but inhabited by her—three grown-up human beings and eight children stow themselves by day and night. . . .

## Sophy

Sophy . . . came to beg for some rice. In asking her about her husband and children, she said she had never had any husband; that she had had two children by a white man of the name of Walker, who was employed at the mill on the rice island; she was in the hospital after the birth of the second child she bore this man, and at the same time two women, Judy and Scylla, of whose children Mr. K[ing] was the father, were recovering from their confinements. It was not a month since any of them had been delivered, when Mrs. K[ing] came to the hospital, had them all three severely flogged, a process which *she* personally superintended, and then sent them to Five Pound . . . with further orders to the drivers to flog them every day for a week. Now, E[lizabeth], if I make you sick with these disgusting stories, I cannot help it; they are the life itself here; hitherto I have thought these details intolerable enough, but this apparition of a female fiend in the middle of this hell I confess adds an element of cruelty which seems to me to surpass all the rest. Jealousy is not an uncommon quality in the feminine temperament; and just conceive the fate of these unfortunate women between the passions of their masters and mistresses, each alike armed with power to oppress and torture them.

Sophy went on to say that Isaac was her son by driver Morris, who had forced her while she was in her miserable exile at Five Pound. Almost beyond my patience with this string of detestable details, I exclaimed—foolishly enough, heaven knows: "Ah! but don't you know—did nobody ever tell or teach any of you that it is a sin to live with men who are not your husbands?"

Alas! E[lizabeth], what could the poor creature answer but what she did, seizing me at the same time vehemently by the wrist: "Oh yes, missis, we know—we know all about dat well enough; but we do anything to get our poor flesh some rest from de whip; when he made me follow him into de bush, what use me tell him no? He have strength to make me."

✦ ✦ ✦

My dearest E[lizabeth],

I write to you today in great depression and distress. I have had a most painful conversation with Mr. [Butler], who has declined receiving any of the people's petitions through me. . . .

[I am] condemned to hear and see so much wretchedness, not only without the means of alleviating it but without permission even to represent it for alleviation: this is no place for me, since I was not born among slaves and cannot bear to live among them.

Perhaps, after all, what he says is true: when I am gone they will fall back into the desperate uncomplaining habit of suffering, from which my coming among them, willing to hear and ready to help, has tempted them. He says that bringing their complaints to me, and the sight of my credulous commiseration, only tends to make them discontented and idle and brings renewed chastisement upon them; and that so, instead of really befriending them, I am only preparing more suffering for them whenever I leave the place, and they can no more cry to me for help. And so I see nothing for it but to go and leave them to their fate; perhaps, too, he is afraid of the mere contagion of freedom which breathes from the very existence of those who are free; my way of speaking to the people, of treating them, or living with them, the appeals I make to their sense of truth, of duty, of self-respect, the infinite compassion and the human consideration I feel for them—all this, of course, makes my intercourse with them dangerously suggestive of relations far different from anything they have ever known; and, as Mr. O— once almost hinted to me, my existence among slaves was an element of danger to the "institution." If I should go away, the human sympathy that I have felt for them will certainly never come near them again.

I was too unhappy to write any more, my dear friend. . . .

## ✦ *Biographical Sketch*

**Born:** *November 27, 1809, London, England*

**Died:** *January 15, 1893, London, England, age 83*

**Buried:** *Kensal Green Cemetery, London, England*

Writer and actor Frances Anne Kemble was born in London into England's most celebrated family of actors. Her mother, Maria Theresa Decamp, was a dancer, actress, and dramatic writer, and Sarah Siddons, the famous tragedian of the age, was her aunt. Fanny, as she was known, was educated at boarding schools in Bath, Boulogne, and Paris. By her late teens, she was playing opposite her father in major stage roles, some written expressly for her. Her debut as Juliet in *Romeo and Juliet* saved the Covent Garden theater, which her father managed, from forced sale.

Although Fanny actually disliked acting, she attracted huge audiences, substantially recouping her father's faltering finances. In 1834, she married Philadelphia socialite Pierce Butler, in spite of the forebodings of family and friends. His fortune came from cotton and rice plantations in Georgia, where he and his brother were absentee owners of nearly one thousand slaves. Fanny, in contrast, had been on the edge of the antislavery movements in England and the United States. Fanny moved in Unitarian circles and was a close friend of the Sedgwick family, which included popular writer Catherine Sedgwick. She admired the theological writings of William Ellery Channing; he presented her with a copy of his new work *Slavery* in 1835. Clearly, Fanny and her husband were on opposite sides of the slavery issue.

At the end of December 1838, four years into an already tumultuous marriage and with two toddler daughters, the Butler family traveled to Georgia because Pierce had to attend to some plantation business in person. He reluctantly gave in to his wife's pleading that he take her too. For three months, she remained on the plantations at Butler Island and St. Simon's. Fanny kept a journal there, formatted as letters to her friend Elizabeth Sedgwick.

The marriage deteriorated in Georgia, where Fanny saw firsthand the horrors of slavery and began to suspect Pierce of profligacy. By 1840, she had separated from him and returned to England. In 1849, when he sued her for divorce over desertion, she did not provide sufficient evidence for a countersuit. In addition, the battle for custody of their two children was long and bitter.

Valuing independence of mind and body, Fanny Kemble renounced her ineffective divorce agreement and purchased a house in a literary enclave in the Berkshires near the Sedgwicks. They, Lydia Maria Child,[20] and other abolitionists who knew about Fanny's Georgia plantation journals hoped that she would publish them. But she withheld publication, at first to save her marriage and then to protect the chance of seeing her children.

Fanny finally published her *Journal of a Residence on a Georgian Plantation, 1838–1839* during the Civil War because she was shocked at the degree of sympathy expressed in the British press and Parliament for the proslavery South. She had hoped her account would help persuade the English *not* to support the Confederacy. Although many abolitionists felt the publication came too late to have maximum impact, her account of the lives of slaves, particularly slave women, gave and still gives the world a vivid, heart-breaking record of people who could not write their own history.

After Pierce Butler died in 1867, Fanny divided much of her time between the homes of her daughters. Returning to live in England in 1877, she wrote books that featured anecdotal stories of the theater interspersed with witty and evaluative reminiscences of her life. She influenced the development of flamboyant characters portrayed in the works of Nathaniel Hawthorne, Herman Melville, and Walt Whitman. While in her late seventies, she summered in the Swiss Alps and was visited frequently by Henry James, who found her memories fascinating. He wrote *Washington Square* and three short stories based on Fanny's tales.

*Biographical Sketch by* MARJORIE CUSHMAN-HYBELS *and* SUSAN SWAN

## ✦ Writings of Frances Anne Kemble

*Adventures of John Timothy Homespun in Switzerland. A Play.* London: R. Bentley, 1889.

*Francis the First, An Historical Drama.* London: John Murray, 1832.

*Further Records, 1848–83.* New York: Henry Holt, 1891.

*Journal of a Residence in America.* Paris: A. and W. Galigani, 1835.

*Journal of a Residence on a Georgian Plantation in 1838–1839.* New York: Harper and Brothers, 1863; Reprint edited and with an Introduction by John A. Scott. Athens: University of Georgia Press, 1984.

*Notes upon Some of Shakespeare's Plays.* London: Bentley & Son, 1882.

*Poems.* Philadelphia: John Penington, 1844.

*Records of a Girlhood.* New York: Henry Holt, 1877.

*Records of Later Life.* New York: Henry Holt, 1882.

*The Star of Seville, a Drama in Five Acts.* London: Saunders & Otley, 1837.

## ✦ Biographical Resources

Armstrong, Margaret. *Fanny Kemble, A Passionate Victorian.* New York: Macmillan, 1938.

Bell, Malcolm, Jr. *Major Butler's Legacy: Five Generations of a Slaveholding Family.* Athens: University of Georgia Press, 1987.

Bobbe, Dorothie. *Fanny Kemble.* New York: Menten, Baleh, 1931.

Dewey, Mary. *Life and Letters of Catharine M. Sedgwick.* Boston: Harper & Brothers, 1871.

Driver, Leota S. *Fanny Kemble.* n. p., 1933; Reprint New York: Negro University Press, 1969.

Egbert, Oliver S. "Melville's Goneril and Fanny Kemble." *New England Quarterly* 18 (December 1945): 489–500.

Furnas, J. C. *Fanny Kemble: Leading Lady of the Nineteenth-Century Stage.* New York: Dial Press, 1982.

Geffen, Elizabeth M. *Philadelphia Unitarianism 1796–1861.* Philadelphia: University of Pennsylvania Press, 1961.

James, Henry. *Essays in London and Elsewhere.* New York: Harper and Brothers, 1893.

Kemble, Frances A. and Frances A. Butler Leigh, eds. *Principles and Privilege: Two Women's Lives on a Georgia Plantation,* with introduction by Dana D. Nelson. Ann Arbor: University of Michigan Press, 1995.

Marshall, Dorothy. *Fanny Kemble.* New York: St. Martin's Press, 1977.

Pope-Hennessy, Una. *Three English Women in America.* London: E. Benn, 1929; Reprint, London: Century, 1987.

Rushmore, Robert. *Fanny Kemble.* London: Crowell-Collier Press, 1970.

Tharp, Louise Hall. *The Appletons of Beacon Hill.* Boston: Little, Brown, 1975.

Wister, Fanny Kemble, ed. *The American Kemble: Her Journals and Unpublished Letters.* Tallahassee, FL: South Pass Press, 1972.

Wright, Constance. *Fanny Kemble and the Lovely Land.* New York: Dodd, Mead, 1972.

MARY ASHTON RICE LIVERMORE

# How I Learned the Truth about Slavery

## From Her Autobiography, 1839–1842

MARY ASHTON RICE LIVERMORE (1820–1905) *was a noted reformer active in many fields, including abolition, temperance, and slavery. One of the era's most popular lecturers, she began her career as a teacher, serving for three years as tutor to six children on a large plantation in southern Virginia. Because of her young age (she began this position as a teenager) and out of respect for the family she was serving, she went out of her way to try to understand the system of slavery. But what she observed, over the course of many months, convinced her to become a confirmed abolitionist.*

*Upon her return North, she converted to Universalism and married Universalist minister Daniel Livermore, with whom she shared the struggle to end slavery and other efforts at social reform. Her impressions of slavery, supposedly under the most humane conditions, stayed with her throughout her life, and she devoted one-third of her autobiography,* The Story of My Life, *published in 1899, to these memories.*

See the Biographical Sketch on pages 240–242.

The day was waning; the trees were casting long shadows; there was a slight chillness in the air, and it was time to return to the house. . . .

Dick and Jenny were to lead the straggling procession homeward, and just as the former was about to mount Old Rock, Pete appeared and said something to the boy in a low voice. The angry blood surged to Dick's face, his eyes flashed fire, and in a twinkling he gave the negro blow upon blow with his fist, hitting him squarely in the face. I was astounded, and when I saw the blood flowing from Peter's mouth and nostrils, I reproved Dick severely. The boy reined in his horse and turned his face toward me, white with astonishment and wrath.

"I aint gwine to take none o' Pete's sass," he said haughtily. "In the South we don't 'low niggers to sass white folks. . . ."

"But if Peter has done wrong, you should report him to your father and not punish him yourself. You are only a boy, Dick."

"Lor' me!" said Dick in surprise." Pa'd la'af at that. Why, Jim licks his black Jeff like blazes, when Jeff don't do nothin', an' Pa never meddles. You haf t' lick niggers, or they'd run over you. You don't know the South yit."

I agreed with him; I did not know the South, but I was in a fair way to learn.

✦ ✦ ✦

When the children had left us for the night and Mr. Henderson could speak with me alone, he inquired concerning Dick's punishment of Pete, which had been reported to him; and I gave him the circumstances. As I expected, he endorsed Dick's action unqualifiedly.

"The boy had the right of it," he said; "in dealing with niggers,"—this was the universal pronunciation,—"the punishment must always follow swift upon the offense, as when dealing with horses, so that they shall know what it means, or you will soon lose control of them. If you have slaves, you must first, last, and always keep them in their place."

I argued that "if he were right in his position, it was a bad thing to give a boy like Dick such unlimited power over servants; it made him judge, jury, and executioner, and there was danger he might grow to manhood tyrannical and cruel."

A long conversation followed, in which Mrs. Henderson took part. "Slave masters cannot escape becoming tyrannical and cruel," was Mr. Henderson's reply. "They are the most absolute despots in the world and can commit any outrage on their servants without fear of the law; for a black man in the South can never testify against a white man. Hard as slavery is for the blacks, it is worse for the whites and is demoralizing and debasing to our young men. We cannot help ourselves. We are not to blame for slavery, for we have inherited it as we have our land. We cannot pauperize ourselves by freeing our slaves, for our land would then be valueless with no one to cultivate it; and if we could, it would be an overwhelming disaster to them, for the negroes are only grown-up children and cannot take care of themselves. As long as we own slaves, therefore, they must be kept in order like other cattle. I won't have my slaves whipped, however, as other masters do. There are other punishments better than whipping and more effectual; and my wife will tell you that my servants are the laziest, most profitless, and most independent niggers in the county."

I believed Mr. Henderson's assertion, that his slaves were never whipped, and, as the months went by, and the abject and hopeless condition of the poor creatures, many of whom I came to know and to regard with friendly feelings, sank deeper and deeper into my heart, it was my hourly solace that their lot was a little less terrible than that of slaves on other plantations—for they were never whipped. But there came a day, the horrible experience of which haunted me for years, and the memory of which an eternity can never efface, when I learned to the contrary.

✦ ✦ ✦

One morning in early May, I had walked farther than usual, beyond High Rock, and was retracing my steps in haste, that I might not be late for breakfast. I had ascended halfway the little hill that overlooked The Mills, the cooper's shop, and blacksmith's forge, when my ears were smitten by the sound of loud and angry voices as of men in furious altercation. Savage threats and brutal curses with fierce commands were shrieked into the ear of the morning with indescribable fury, and there was a sound as of preparations for some impending event. I heard the tread of hurrying feet, the guttural tones of subordinates directing one another, a rapid movement of carts and wagons, the pounding of hammers, the rasping of saws, and the expostulations in negro *patois,* of servants criticizing each other's work. All the while the fiendish outpouring of blasphemous imprecations continued, and mingling with it I heard a most pitiful appeal for mercy and an earnest declaration of innocence.

"Oh, Massa! 'scuse me dis one time! Please Massa, jess dis one time! I sartin didn't go for t' do it! . . . Oh, Massa, please! fo' de Lawd's sake, 'scuse me! 'scuse me an' doan whip me!"

This agonized appeal for mercy seemed only to call forth a more fiendish outburst of wrath, in which I recognized the voice of Bryson, Mr. Henderson's overseer, a most repulsive man, grim-visaged and evil-eyed, who managed the field hands on the plantation. I had once seen this man in an insane paroxysm of rage over some trivial affair. A premonition of fearful ill made me sick at heart; but I was powerless to flee, and petrified with terror, I stood rooted to the spot.

As I looked, two negroes, one of gigantic size and both belonging to the plantation, dragged a light mulatto into the open space between the cooper's shop and the forge, where there was no obstruction to my vision, and began to strip him. His heartbreaking appeals for mercy and forgiveness rose on the morning air in an awful cry of anguish. It was Matt, the cooper, a most intelligent and manly fellow, a great favorite with the children and myself, and of whom Mr. Henderson often spoke as a "three-thousand dollar nigger."

"O Massa, doan have me whipped! 'Scuse me only dis yere one time! Fo' de Lawd's sake, doan whip me!" and the piteous cry rang out again and again on the morning air.

A rope was roughly tied around the man's wrists and thrown over a beam projecting from the roof of the shop, by which he was drawn up with jerks, until his toes barely touched the ground. The swish of a long whip that flashed through the air fell upon my ears. The lash sank with a cutting sound into Matt's quivering flesh. An appalling shriek of torture rose above the steady outpour of frenzied curses and demoniac taunts. Blow after blow fell upon the ensanguined body of the suffering man, while the overseer stood by urging on the terrible flagellation, in the most brutal and fiendish manner conceivable. Shriek after shriek pierced the very skies, laden with immitigable suffering, until they died into moans. At last the moans ceased; the head fell forward upon the breast, and the lacerated body hung limp and seemingly lifeless. I stood immovable, sick and faint, and heard and saw it all, paralyzed with horror and fear.

I weep now, after more than fifty years, as I write of the dreadful spectacle which met my eyes on that beautiful spring morning. I did not weep then, for I was dazed by the awful tragedy I had witnessed. I was young, had been reared in tenderness, if in asceticism, and knew nothing of deeds of cruelty. What had poor Matt done? Would he die? Would they harm me if I should go to his cabin and help his wife take care of him and comfort him? Was there danger that this overseer, if he caught me rendering service to Matt, would tie me to that beam and whip me as he had whipped him? Oh, my gracious God! How could I live longer on this plantation!

✦ ✦ ✦

How clearly I realized that the people at the North knew nothing of the institution of slavery. I had heard them defend it—and depict it as a humane organization. How utterly they failed to comprehend its brutalizing influence on the finest characters or dreamed of the outrages inflicted on the poor blacks.

✦ ✦ ✦

Since I could do nothing to change or ameliorate the condition of the slave people, I protected myself from further suffering during the remainder of my stay. I determined to know nothing more of Bryson's "discipline," nor of the sales of "unmanageable" slaves. I had seen enough of slavery to believe that any deed of cruelty or darkness was possible under its regime—enough to enable me to detect instantly the realism of *Uncle Tom's Cabin,* as I read the weekly chapters in the columns of the *New Era,* in which it was first published. "The whole system is wrong, and some time, please God, it will be abolished." Such was my thought. But I no more dreamed, than did Mr. Henderson, that a conflict was even then impending between the civilizations of the North and South that would shake the continent, abolish slavery, drench the land in fraternal blood, wrench the plantation from the ownership of his children, and leave his youngest son dead on the battlefield. And yet the strife was not a quarter of a century distant.

✦ ✦ ✦

My three years' life at the South was of great value to me in many ways and gave me an education I could not have received in any school of the time.

✦ ✦ ✦

I had always regarded the Southern people as greater sinners than those of the North, because the former clung to the institution of slavery. But in listening to Mr. Henderson's history of slavery, I learned for the first time that in the beginning of the nineteenth century, every nation of Europe owned slaves and traded in them, but had gradually freed themselves from this colossal evil, and that our republic was indebted to Great Britain for the existence of slavery on this continent. That when the American colonists shook off their allegiance to the mother country, and became independent, the different hereditary traits of the early colonists, North and South, the difference in the two sections, in climate, agricultural products, and methods of industry freed the North from slavery and fastened it on the South, so that the latter did not choose slavery but found it fastened on them and were therefore less blamable than I had believed.

# Abolitionists in Boston

## From Her Autobiography, 1845–1860

JULIA WARD HOWE (1819–1910), *born into a prominent New York family, became a Unitarian after she married Samuel Gridley Howe from Boston. A prominent leader both in women's clubs and the suffrage movement, she was one of the most popular lecturers of her time.*

*This selection is from her autobiography,* Reminiscences, *published in 1900. In it, she described her first encounters with abolitionists in Boston. Although she was initially prejudiced against these serious and committed folk, she later enthusiastically embraced both the movement and its leaders. Her transition from a reluctant participant to an active and willing participant came at least partially as a result of personal relationships. As a leader in Boston society and an advocate of the Unitarian rationalist approach, she expressed the wish that those who disagree would do so with civility and equanimity. But when forced to choose sides, she cast her lot with the abolitionists.*

See the Biographical Sketch on pages 327–331.

I had supposed the abolitionists to be men and women of rather coarse fibre, abounding in cheap and easy denunciation and seeking to lay rash hands on the complex machinery of government and of society. My husband, who largely shared their opinions, had no great sympathy with some of their methods. Theodore Parker held them in great esteem, and it was through him that one of my strongest imaginary dislikes vanished as though it had never been. The object of this dislike was William Lloyd Garrison, whom I had never seen but of whose malignity of disposition I entertained not the smallest doubt.

It happened that I met him at one of Parker's Sunday evenings at home. I soon felt that this was not the man for whom I had cherished so great a distaste. Gentle and unassuming in manner, with a pleasant voice, a benevolent countenance, and a sort of glory of sincerity in his ways and words, I could only wonder at the falsehoods that I had heard and believed concerning him.

The Parkers had then recently received the gift of a piano from members of their congregation. A friend began to play hymn tunes upon it, and those of us who could sing gathered in little groups to read from the few hymn-books which were within reach. Dr. Howe presently looked up and saw me singing from the same book with Mr. Garrison. He told me afterward that few things in the course of his life had surprised him more. From this time forth the imaginary Garrison ceased to exist for me. I learned to respect and honor the real one more and more, though as yet little foreseeing how glad I should be one day to work with and under him. The persons most frequently named as prominent abolitionists, in connection with Mr. Garrison, were Maria Weston Chapman[21] and Wendell Phillips.

Mrs. Chapman presided with much energy and grace over the antislavery bazaars which were held annually in Boston through a long space of years. For this labor of love she was somewhat decried, and the *sobriquet* of "Captain Chapman" was given her in derision. She was handsome and rather commanding in person, endowed also with an excellent taste in dress. I cannot remember that she ever spoke in public, but her presence often adorned the platform at antislavery meetings. She was the editor of the *Liberty Bell,* and was a valued friend and ally of Wendell Phillips.

✦ ✦ ✦

I recall now a scene in Tremont Temple just before the breaking out of our civil war. An anti-slavery meeting had been announced, and a scheme had been devised to break it up. As I entered I met Mrs. Chapman who said, "These are times in which antislavery people must stand by each other." On the platform were seated a number of the prominent abolitionists. Mr. Phillips was to be the second speaker, but when he stepped forward to address the meeting a perfect hubbub arose in the gallery. Shrieks, howls, and catcalls resounded. Again and again the great orator essayed to speak. Again and again his voice was drowned by the general uproar. I sat near enough to hear him say, with a smile, "Those boys in the gallery will soon tire themselves out." And so, indeed, it befell. After a delay which appeared to some of us endless, the noise subsided, and Wendell Phillips, still in the glory of his strength and manly beauty, stood up before the house, and soon held all present spellbound by the magic of his speech. The clear silver ring of his voice carried conviction with it. From head to foot, he seemed aflame with the passion of his convictions. He used the simplest English and spoke with such distinctness that his lowest tones, almost a whisper, could be heard throughout the large hall. Yerrinton, the only man who could report Wendell Phillips's speeches, once told my husband that it was like reporting chain lightning.

On the occasion of which I speak, the unruly element was quieted once for all, and the further proceedings of the meeting suffered no interruption. The mob, however, did not at once abandon its intention of doing violence to the great advocate. Soon after the time just mentioned Dr. Howe attended an evening meeting, at the close of which a crowd of rough men gathered outside the public entrance, waiting for Phillips to appear, with ugly threats of the treatment which he should receive at their hands. The doors presently opened, and Phillips came forth, walking calmly between Mrs. Chapman and Lydia Maria Child.[22] Not a hand was raised; not a threat was uttered. The crowd gave way in silence, and the two brave women parted from Phillips at the door of his own house. My husband spoke of this as one of the most impressive sights that he had ever witnessed. His report of it moved me to send word to Mr. Phillips that, in case of any recurrence of such a disturbance, I should be proud to join his bodyguard.

## ✦ *Biographical Sketch*

**Born:** *May 27, 1819, New York, New York*

**Died:** *October 17, 1910, Newport, Rhode Island, age 91*

**Buried:** *Mount Auburn Cemetery, Cambridge, Massachusetts*

Born in New York City, Julia Ward Howe was the fourth of seven children born to Julia Rush (Cutler) Ward and Samuel Ward, Jr. Her father's ancestors immigrated from England after the Restoration and became a distinguished Rhode Island family. He was a partner in the Wall Street banking firm of Prime, Ward and King. Her mother's family was from South Carolina and claimed Revolutionary War hero General Francis Marion, the "Swamp Fox," as part of its clan.

The Ward family had considerable financial resources, and none were spared in Julia's education. She was taught by a number of governesses and special tutors. She learned French, Italian, and Spanish in her early years and later studied Greek and Hebrew. Piano and voice training were also part of her education. She deeply envied her brothers, who were learning chemistry, mathematics, and other such subjects at their boarding schools, and begged them to teach her everything they learned.

Julia's mother died when she was five, and an aunt, Eliza Cutler, became the mistress of the household. She was witty, poetic, and socially active and encouraged Julia's growth in these areas. Julia's father, a devout Episcopalian, was strict, condemned all frivolity, and firmly believed in the torments of hell. He died in 1839, leaving Julia a small inheritance. When her older brother Sam married Emily Astor in 1838, the entire family gained access to high society.

Although never considered a beauty, Julia was attractive, with auburn hair and a lively personality. She was intrigued with New York society but torn by her father's disapproval. In addition, she had very real intellectual gifts, which led her into serious studies of poetry, philosophy, and languages. She published essays in the *New York Review* and *Theological Review.* She was a complex and talented woman at a time when women were expected to be mostly decorative.

While visiting Boston in 1841, Julia met Samuel Gridley Howe, a man of forty who had earlier won international acclaim as a hero for his dashing exploits in the Greek revolution. When they met, Samuel was head of the Perkins Institute for the Blind and was highly regarded for his work with children who were impaired, both blind and deaf. Julia and Samuel were married in 1843 and immediately set sail for England, where they began a year-long tour of Europe. Their first child, Julia Romana, was born in Rome.

Upon their return to the States, the Howes settled in a home near the Perkins Institute, where Julia felt acutely isolated from the life she had previously known. Moreover, she had neither the aptitude nor the training to be a housewife and found it unfulfilling. Her husband was busy with other philanthropies and causes—prison reform, Horace Mann's school reforms, education of the handicapped, and abolition of slavery—which took him away from home frequently. However, Samuel's connections with the liberal community in Boston led Julia to friendships with Theodore Parker and James Freeman Clarke. As a result, she abandoned her Episcopal upbringing and became a Unitarian.

Although Samuel was politically and religiously liberal, he disapproved of Julia's writing and forbade her to publish further articles, cutting off an area of her life that was rewarding for her. Julia bore five more children, further channeling her time and energy into domestic concerns; she thrived on motherhood and was deeply devoted to the family as it grew and eventually produced grandchildren.

Julia turned inward and began reading extensively, establishing a program of self-education that continued for the rest of her life. She read the philosophers and poets and was soon writing her own commentary and poetry. Her first published work was *Passion Flowers* (1854) followed by *Words for the Hour* (1857). Both were collections of poetry and published anonymously, though the authorship of both volumes was soon revealed. Samuel's disapproval of Julia's having any kind of public life continued and led to long periods in which the couple lived apart. In 1850, Julia spent a year in Rome with two of her children while Samuel remained in Boston.

In 1859, the Howes journeyed to Cuba. Upon their return, Julia wrote articles about the trip, which were first printed in the *Atlantic Monthly* and later collected as a book, *A Trip to Cuba.*

In November 1861, the year the Civil War began, Julia was invited to attend a review of troops near Washington, D.C., with her minister, the Reverend James Freeman Clarke. This is where she first spoke in public, to the Army of the Potomac, although she ran away twice and hid in the hospital tents to avoid the invitation.[23] Familiar with Julia's gifts as a poet and writer, the Reverend Clarke suggested that she write new, inspiring lyrics to a popular army song of the time, which had a stirring tune but depressing lyrics about the martyrdom of John Brown. Having already had the same idea, she awoke at dawn the next morning and wrote the words to "The Battle Hymn of the Republic."[24] After the words were published in the *Atlantic Monthly* in 1862, the hymn swept the North, becoming the mobilizing song of the war. The popularity of the hymn brought its author fame that grew steadily the rest of her life.

Julia also began offering lectures, with some modest success. She later began organizing what she hoped would be an international network of women working for peace but was only partially successful. Her real involvement came with the growing women's movement. In 1868, she was a founding member of the New England Women's Club, and she became its president in 1871, serving in that capacity almost continuously until her death in 1910. With Lucy Stone,[25] she founded the New England Woman Suffrage Association. When the national suffrage movement split, she and Lucy Stone became leaders of the American Woman Suffrage Association. Julia later played a crucial role in reuniting the movement into the National American Woman Suffrage Association.

In 1873, responding to a call from women in New York, Julia participated in founding the Association for the Advancement of Women, which organized congresses of women from various professions for the exchange of knowledge, ideas, and visions for the future. She became its president in 1881, and her addresses were the highlight of the annual conferences.

In 1876, Samuel Howe died, bringing the difficult marriage to an end. Shortly after his death, Julia made her first extended lecture tour into the midwestern states. Then she sailed to Europe and spent two years traveling there and in the Middle East.

In 1884, Julia directed the Women's Department of the New Orleans Cotton Exposition. Her second lecture tour took place in 1884, when she ventured to the Pacific coast, helping found women's clubs wherever she went. She was a founding member of the General Federation of Women's Clubs in 1890 and served as a director from 1893–1898. She was the first president of the Massachusetts Federation of Women's Clubs, which was organized in 1893. She preached frequently, usually from Unitarian pulpits.

In spite of her success, Julia often suffered deep depressions and struggled with feelings of unworthiness. She continued to write articles, poems, and reminiscences, and nearly every noteworthy occasion brought a request for her to compose a few commemorative words. She was famous for her salons, where distinguished people of all persuasions mingled. She became a sort of national institution, and reporters loved to interview her, printing her witty comments and recording her many activities. In 1908, Julia was the first woman elected to the American Academy of Arts and Letters.

In 1910, at the age of ninety-one, Julia Ward Howe died of pneumonia at her Newport, Rhode Island, cottage. Her funeral service was conducted at the Church of the Disciples (Unitarian), but a public memorial service was also held at Boston's Symphony Hall, at which hundreds of people were turned away. More than four thousand attendees sang "The Battle Hymn of the Republic" in her honor. A brass nameplate enscribed "Julia Ward Howe" still adorns the pew where she worshipped at Channing Memorial Church in Newport.

*Biographical Sketch by* DOROTHY BOROUSH

## ✦ Writings of Julia Ward Howe

*At Sunset.* Boston: Houghton, Mifflin, 1910.
*From the Oak to the Olive.* Boston: Lee and Shepard, 1868.
*From Sunset Ridge.* Boston: Houghton, Mifflin, 1898.

*Is Polite Society Polite? and Other Essays.* Boston: Lamson Wolffe, 1895.
*Later Lyrics.* Boston: J. E. Tilton & Col, 1866.
*Lenora or The World's Own.* Boston: Ticknor & Fields, 1857.
*Memoir of Dr. Samuel Gridley Howe.* Boston: A. J. Wright, 1876.
*Mother Goose Songs and Dances for Children.* Boston: White-Smith Music, 1931.
*Original Poems and Other Verse Set to Music as Songs.* Boston: Boston Music, 1908.
*Passion Flowers.* Boston: Ticknor, Reid & Fields, 1854.
*Reminiscences—1819 to 1899.* Boston: Houghton, Mifflin, 1899.
*Sex and Education.* Boston: Roberts Bros., 1874.
*Sketches of Representative Women of New England.* Edited by Julia Ward Howe. Boston: New England Historical Publishing, 1904.
*A Trip to Cuba.* Boston: Ticknor & Fields, 1860.
*Words for the Hour.* n.p. 1857.

## ✦ Biographical Resources

Many of the above works are autobiographical in nature, particularly *A Trip to Cuba, Later Lyrics,* and *Reminiscences.*
Hall, Florence Howe. *Julia Ward Howe and the Woman Suffrage Movement: A Selection from her Speeches and Essays with Introduction and Notes by her Daughter.* New York: Amo, 1969.
Richards, Laura E., ed. *The Walk with God.* New York: E. P. Dutton, 1919.
Richards, Laura E., and Maud Howe Elliott. *Julia Ward Howe.* 2 vols. Boston: Houghton, Mifflin, 1916.
Tharp, Louise Hall. *Three Saints and a Sinner.* Boston: Little, Brown, 1956.
Williams, Gary. *Hungry Heart: The Literary Emergence of Julia Ward Howe.* Amherst: University of Massachusetts Press, 1999.

## ✦ Archives

Julia Ward Howe's papers, journals, and scrapbooks are in Harvard University's Houghton Library and in the Schlesinger Library, Radcliffe College, Cambridge, Massachusetts.

# My Work with the Anti-Slavery Society

## From Letters, 1850–1861

SALLIE HOLLEY (1818–1893), *a Unitarian from upstate New York, was a writer, lecturer, and educator. As an agent for the American Anti-Slavery Association, she traveled extensively giving public speeches. Her letters, many of which are addressed to her life-long friend Caroline Putnam, described her life on the road in the service of abolition. They provide an insider's view of this important work for racial justice and also detail the realities of daily life and social interaction in the mid nineteenth century.*

See the Biographical Sketch on pages 339–342.

### To Miss Putnam

Rochester, New York, January, 1850

I have had a charming visit with Mr. May. He is a truly lovely person. Abby Kelley Foster has been here; she urges me very hard to go right into the antislavery lecture field.

✦ ✦ ✦

### To Miss Putnam

Oberlin, [no date]

I am to give an antislavery address in the Chapel, some time in August. I am collecting thoughts for it as I can. My subject is to be something like this: The duty of antislavery women to keep informed as to the progress and mode of the antislavery reform in our nation, to be ready to counteract the pernicious influence of such speeches as Clay's and Webster's on the plastic minds of all our young men and women.

✦ ✦ ✦

## To the Porters

Huntington, New York, September 30, 1851

You are aware that I have already entered upon my work of antislavery lecturer. My love and interest in the great cause increases and swells and brightens every hour.

It does seem to me that I have at last found out my "sphere." Miss Putnam, Mr. and Mrs. Griffing, Parker Pillsbury, and myself compose our travelling party, in one carriage. Every few days Sojourner Truth joins us and aids in our meetings. She travels in a buggy by herself. An antislavery friend loaned her a pony and buggy for the entire summer. She is quite a strong character and shows what a great intellect slavery has crushed. She talks like one who has not only *heard* of American slavery but has *seen* and *felt* it.

✦ ✦ ✦

## To Miss Putnam

South Bridgewater, August 19, 1852

My adventures and experiences as a lecturer are not very dissimilar to ours of last winter. Sometimes, the people where I go are extremely warm and cordial; they evidently feel it a pleasure and privilege to entertain the antislavery lecturers. . . .

It is very grateful when we go to a family where the woman is cut off from her neighbors' sympathy on account of her antislavery position, and to see and talk with us is a rare and rich treat. Oh, the lighting up of the face, the kindling warmth of the whole expression which I have seen on such an occasion is a whole year's refreshment.

✦ ✦ ✦

## To Miss Putnam

Abington, Massachusetts, August 26, 1852

You see how I flit from place to place. An antislavery lecturer's life has something apostolic in it, if it only be in going from town to town to preach the everlasting gospel. Today I was entertaining myself making out a memorandum of all the places and times I had lectured. I made out one hundred and fifty-six times.

September 2d—Day before yesterday Lewis Ford took us in his carriage from this place to Duxbury. The weather was delightful. We rode twenty miles through beautiful woods. We alighted at a large, old-fashioned mansion a little before six o'clock and were cordially welcomed by two maiden sisters who ushered us into a plain, old-fashioned parlor. The chairs, sofa, and table looking so quaint, as if belonging to a bygone generation. Then the mother made her appearance, a lady eighty years old, but, in spirit and conversation and manners, more like eighteen than eighty. Indeed she proved to be a most charming old lady. I was quite captivated with her, so fresh, so youthful, so beautiful. She seems to have read almost everything. Was delighted with *David Copperfield* and *Dombey and Son* and spoke of Theodore Parker with glowing enthusiasm. (He makes their house his home when he goes to Duxbury.) She admires Andrew Jackson Davis's writings, particularly his views of death. She loves Mr. Garrison and Stephen and Abby Foster; knows Lydia Maria Child.[26] Mrs. Child used to spend a great deal of time next door. Laughed when she told me Mrs. Child wrote a cook-book when she had been housekeeper and cook only a month or so. I told her it reminded me of Mrs. Swisshelm, who has been married a great many years but never had a baby until last winter, and when the child was three weeks old began a series of "Letters to Mothers."

Here I met with a sister-in-law of Mrs. Child—Mrs. Francis, wife of Professor Convers Francis of Harvard Divinity School. I told her of my great desire to see Mrs. Child. Mrs. Francis said she thought Mrs. Child would be glad to see me, though she sees very few people now-a-days; lives in a retired, quiet way; does her own work. Mrs. Francis politely said she would offer to accompany me but she thought I should be more successful alone. We both agreed that Lydia Maria Child belonged to the public and that she ought not to shut herself up so. Mrs. Child is preparing a memoir of Isaac T. Hopper.

✦ ✦ ✦

## To Miss Putnam

Lyons, January 12, 1854

The people have expressed themselves surprised and delighted with my lecture of Wednesday evening. An audience of nearly six hundred. As I usually do, I felt anxious before the lecture.

This apprehensive state of mind, which almost always attacks me just before the lecture, is a great plague, a devil that I long to cast out but as yet have not the power. I believe it is one of the kind that "goeth not out except by prayer and fasting." To a person full of composure and Christian sympathy, the perplexity I suffer about accepting or declining the invitation to Albany would be astonishing. Last evening I was asked if I would actually associate with blacks. When I said that I had done it for years, the astonishment was extreme. Oh, this antislavery movement is revealing the spirit of Christianity with new power!

✦ ✦ ✦

## To Mrs. Porter

Feltonville, September 21, 1855

The last evening Ralph Waldo Emerson addressed the convention. Mr. Phillips exalted me. Mr. Emerson entertained me. The convention closed with a poem by Mrs. E. Oakes Smith. She is a lady of fifty. She was dressed in a very thin white muslin, with four embroidered flounces edged with pink taste; low neck and bare arms, a very thin white scarf pinned on the shoulders with gold arrows. Two bracelets on each arm, an immense pin on her bosom, and her hands glistening with rings. Her head rigged in the latest fashion. There was a perceptible shock of surprise when she made her appearance. She seemed like a picture out of an old novel. Some of the women-reformers almost wept at this conclusion of the grave and important deliberations and discussions. "She is a self-intoxicated woman," said Elizabeth Peabody[27] to me as we left the hall. I laughed myself nearly into fits over it.

The last day of the convention we dined at Mrs. Garrison's with Mrs. Follen[28] and her son Charles. She is a lovely old lady.

After Dr. Channing's beautiful speech, Miss Peabody said she felt moved to rise and make a speech. She was very glad a son of Dr. Channing had spoken. This was a cause she had drunk in with her mother's milk.

Miss Putnam and I left Boston Saturday and came to these kind antislavery people, who make us fully at home in their comfortable farmhouse. Here is a peach orchard with thirty varieties. Apples, tomatoes, and grapes and not a pig on the premises. A woodchuck is being cooked for dinner!—the first meat cooked in the house since we came.

They are almost purely vegetarians, which quite suits us. We have been sitting before an open fire, with bright brass andirons, which was very pleasant as well as very comfortable. With kind love for you all.

✦ ✦ ✦

### To Mr. Porter

Farmersville, New York, September 3, 1857

The other Sunday afternoon we happened to arrive at the meeting-house before the Methodist Class Meeting was over. The minister asked me to "express my feelings." I said, My feelings were that the Methodist Church could not be a Christian church while holding, as she does, many thousands of God's dear children as property—keeping them on a level with the brute beast. The whole manner of the minister was as much as to say, If anybody had such unreasonable feelings as these, it would be more convenient for him if she would keep them to herself. He only said, however, that we had not time to discuss the administration of the church. To which I insisted, "But it is the gospel of Christ."

A week or two ago at a common-school celebration in this village, the County Superintendent invited me to address the children. Accordingly I told them of the slave-children of this country, who are not allowed to learn to read or write or spell or commit to memory the multiplication table which they had just repeated so well. Whereupon two Buchanan men rose up and left in high indignation that "an abolition lecture was poked on them." I am very sorry to even seem rude and "fanatical" but know not how to avoid it and be faithful to the cause of the slave. In fact, nothing else is so important and proper for all occasions, to be talked of, as the slave and his cause.

It would be most fitting in every sermon, every oration, every prayer, to remember earnestly the astounding fact, that *Christian* America today holds four million men, women, and children in slavery!

✦ ✦ ✦

### To the Porters

Boston, Massachusetts, January 31, 1861

Friday afternoon Miss Putnam and I had a very interesting call on Mrs. Theodore Parker. While she was showing us the library she took from a very small, old-fashioned bureau the *first book* Mr. Parker ever owned—the Latin dictionary he bought with money earned by picking huckleberries. It used to be on the shelves with the other books, but when so many people were anxious to see and handle this nucleus of the fine library, and hear its story, Mr. Parker found the binding was being torn and put it carefully away in the little bureau. The bureau is one that Theodore kept his clothes in when a boy. Such was his attachment for it that he obtained it a few years ago although it had gone out of the family. On the fly-leaf of the old dictionary was written "Theodore Parker, 1822." He was then about eleven years old. I could not but look with reverence on this token of the boy's eager thirst for knowledge and thought of the hopes that stimulated his hands to pick the huckleberries that he might buy a treasure which would never perish. All the books (except this one) "are to be removed to the public library in the spring, being given to the city by Mr. Parker's will and with Mrs. Parker's consent." "This," she said, "was Theodore's darling wish."

These dreadful times of mobs are thought to be the last struggle of the slave-power in the North, and it remains for time to prove whether such a precious life as that of Wendell Phillips is to be given up to satisfy the minions of slavery. God grant that such a costly sacrifice may be spared. I wish you could have been with us on that sublime occasion when the hosts of abolitionists sat looking danger and violence in the face as serenely as if the light of Eternity's morning had dawned on their souls. I think it was worth living a great many years to be present at the meeting in Tremont Temple last Thursday morning. I may never live to witness another day so great as that was in courage, devotion, and fidelity to principle.

The platform was crowded with the faithful and true—many a tried soldier in Freedom's long battle: Francis Jackson to preside, Edmund Quincy to aid; Mr. Phillips, like a conquering angel, with wit and wisdom on his tongue and beauty and honour on his head; James Freeman Clarke, glorious in speech and action; Ralph Waldo Emerson, serene as the sphinx of six thousand years ago; Samuel J. May, reading the Ninety-fourth Psalm, that seemed to come from the prophet's pen of today; Mrs. Lydia Maria Child, as full of enthusiasm as she could express by flashing eye, glowing cheek, and waving handkerchief, as she sat by the organ on the highest seat of the platform, making everybody glad by her presence; Mrs. Maria Chapman, sitting with the calm dignity of a queen, her sister and daughter beside her; T. W. Higginson, ready with brilliant eloquence of tongue or with the revolver's bullet—so it was said—to do battle for free speech that day; William I. Bowditch, with his venerable and dignified mien, looked quite distinguished among them all. Once when he took his place at the front of the platform, the mob called out, "There comes the old bald eagle!" and well may the little insignificant mice and weasels look out when such a glance is abroad.

✦ ✦ ✦

## To Miss Putnam

Elmira, New York, September 7, 1861

You see by Mr. May's letter and Mrs. Garrison's and the *Liberator* and *Standard,* the "old guard" thinks this is no time for abolitionists to stop working.

Personally, I should not object to remaining in one spot all winter, rather than have again the dreadful cold and fatigue and hard work of another lecturing campaign; but I confess my conscience and heart would not be satisfied with doing nothing for the noble cause, and now of all times, to give up seems to me weak and wrong. I have no doubt we could advance the cause as we have hitherto done, even if we only get a few subscribers and small collections and donations. I think we ought to work. What do you think? You know my hope and faith of old. Not many years longer can we work. You and I will be too feeble to go on many years more as we have done. Let us work while we can.

✦ ✦ ✦

November 12th—I have been in my room nearly all day writing anti-slavery letters and hope I have done my duty. At least I think I should not feel so happy as I do if I had not.

✦ ✦ ✦

## To Miss Putnam

Elmira, New York, November 18, 1861

Oh, my heart yearns toward you this morning, and the heaviest disappointment of my life would fall if *you* should die. Again and again I thank you for all your love to me. I wish I were more deserving of it. Please God I may be some day. How I should love to put my arms around your neck and kiss you!

Nov. 23d—Colored Sarah has just left my room after my hearing her lessons. What a cruel thing it is that every being should not be taught to read whilc yct a child! Sarah tries hard but makes what seems to me slow headway.

Nov. 27th—Do not forget to give me the names of some abolitionists to whom I can write for aid. I am determined to be faithful and fulfill my promise to Mrs. Garrison in this point; and may God in mercy grant that I be more faithful to meet all the obligations of coming life!

Your letter, noble, kind-hearted, and full of dear-to-me love, is here. I am inadequate to express my appreciation of your goodness and kindness; and, as the best and most comprehensive of all thanks and grateful affection possible to offer, pray *God bless you.* "Be still and know that I am God," has a deeper, fuller significance than ever before.

## ✦ *Biographical Sketch*

**Born:** *February 17, 1818, Canandaigua, New York*

**Died:** *January 12, 1893, New York, New York, age 74*

**Buried:** *Mount Hope Cemetery, Rochester, New York*

Sallie Holley worked for racial justice before the Civil War as an antislavery lecturer and after the war as an educator of African Americans. Her father, Myron Holley, was a Unitarian abolitionist and one of the founders of the Liberty Party, which later became the Free Soil and then the Republican Party. In 1841, after her father died, Holley went to live with one of her sisters in Buffalo. There she first attended a Unitarian church and was baptized by the Reverend G. W. Hosmer. During her time in Buffalo, she also began attending antislavery meetings and lectures, including a meeting in 1843 at which Frederick Douglass spoke. Holley was trying to decide what to do with her life. In 1847, on the advice of Frederick W. Holland, minister of the Rochester Unitarian church, she went to Oberlin, a coeducational and racially integrated college, to pursue a formal education.

As the only Unitarian at Oberlin, Holley found herself defending her faith to other students. When she disagreed with the preachers at the college, she would follow them home to discuss their sermons. In 1850, she wrote: "My life falls far short of my ideal, yet I think I can apprehend something of the beauty and glory of a truly Christian life. Whenever these visions come up before me, then do I yearn most to be in immediate communion with some of my dear Unitarian friends. It seems to me they have a hold, an insight into the spiritual life, that I do not find in others."[29]

Holley's religion and her politics were intertwined. She felt that supporting abolitionism was the only stance any true Christian could take. When Millard Fillmore, a member of the Unitarian church in Buffalo, signed the Fugitive Slave Act into law and was not rebuked for it, Holley refused to take communion there again: "I think I cannot consent that my name shall stand on the books of a church which will countenance voting for any pro-slavery presidential candidate. Think of a woman-whipper and a baby-stealer being countenanced as a Christian! My antislavery sympathies burn stronger and stronger."[30]

Holley's career as an antislavery lecturer began while she was still at Oberlin with speeches she made at the college. In her next-to-last year, she decided to lecture with the American Anti-Slavery Society to "plead the cause of the slave-woman." In her last year at Oberlin, she declined an offer from Frederick Douglass to write for his newspaper, the *North Star,* because of her commitment to lecturing.

Through her antislavery work at Oberlin, Holley met Caroline Putnam, who became her life-long friend and partner. The two were drawn together as the only Garrisonian abolitionists, "the only ultra radicals there," as Putnam put it.[31] Putnam traveled with Holley during much of the ten years following her graduation from Oberlin. During those years, Holley worked with the American Anti-Slavery Society and was paid $10 a week.

At the time Holley undertook this work, there was a stigma against women speaking in public. Some former friends shunned her for choosing such an unorthodox career. Even so, the lecturers traveled extensively, staying with abolitionist families. Because the antislavery stance was so unpopular, it was difficult to find places to hold meetings. Holley and Putnam lectured mostly in churches and particularly often in Quaker meetinghouses. Occasionally, proslavery protesters would walk out of the lectures. Despite the hardships she faced, Holley wrote to Mrs. Porter, of a Rochester abolitionist family, "Oh, . . . you cannot know how richly rewarded I feel, how full my enjoyment is, in going about with these anti-slavery friends."[32]

Holley avoided speaking in front of large groups and never spoke in Boston because of her fear of lecturing in front of movement leaders, whom she considered better lecturers than she was. But William Lloyd

Garrison, whom she greatly admired, said of her in 1853: "Sallie Holley has recently lectured here, to very general acceptance, as she does everywhere,—her addresses being of a religious character, without dealing with persons, churches, and parties in a way to probe them to the quick, yet doing good work for the cause."[33] Finally, in March 1854, she was prevailed upon to speak to a group assembled to hear Frederick Douglass.

Holley lectured on abolitionism from 1851 until the Civil War. The work of the abolitionists continued during the war, pushing the doctrine of immediate emancipation. The *Liberator* and the *Anti-Slavery Standard,* two abolitionist newspapers, kept publishing during the war, and Holley worked to get subscriptions for them. She also wrote fundraising letters for the American Anti-Slavery Society.

Once the Emancipation Proclamation was issued, Holley began to work for the freed slaves, continuing to raise funds and lecture. After the war, in 1865, the *Liberator* was discontinued, but the *Anti-Slavery Standard* and the American Anti-Slavery Society remained active. Holley continued to travel with the society, now speaking for the rights of the freed blacks, especially for their right to vote. She also sent clothing and money to the society and solicited new subscribers to the *Standard.* A dedicated Republican, she wrote of the Thirteenth Amendment (prohibiting slavery): "So it seems the Constitution *was* a 'covenant with death and an agreement with hell.'"[34]

After the *Standard* was discontinued and the American Anti-Slavery Society was disbanded in 1870, Holley joined Putnam, who had been teaching black students in Lottsburgh, Virginia, for two years. This work would occupy the women for the rest of their lives. They volunteered their services year-round, teaching the local black people at what came to be known as the Holley School. Their work was supported completely by donations from the North.

In the course of their work, Holley and Putnam built a new schoolhouse in Lottsburgh and brought in a number of assistant teachers, including two black women. They faced a lot of opposition from local white people, including threats of burning the schoolhouse and shooting the teachers. Certainly, the political meetings Holley regularly held to encourage black men to vote Republican did not increase her popularity among white people. In 1892, she wrote: "One of the most bitter [ex-slave holders] told a white woman that 'The old Yankee,' meaning me, 'has ruined these Lottsburgh niggers, making them think they are as good as anybody.' An ex-slave-holding lady said to me, 'I am as great a rebel as I ever was.' I do not for a moment believe any Virginian has met with a change of heart."[35]

Whether or not Sallie Holley changed the opinions of any white Virginians during her years at the Holley School, she and Caroline Putnam certainly changed the lives of many black Virginians for the better. Her educational work was a continuation of her lecturing for abolition. Sallie Holley dedicated her life to improving the lives of black Americans.

*Biographical Sketch by* MARGARET HARRELSON

## ✦ Writings of Sallie Holley

*A Life for Liberty: Anti-Slavery and Other Letters of Sallie Holley.* Edited by John White Chadwick. New York: G. P. Putnam's Sons, 1899.

## ✦ Biographical Resource

*A Life for Liberty,* cited above, also contains biographical information.

## ✦ Archives

Letters and summaries of Sallie Holley's speeches can be found in *The Liberator,* April 16, 1852–December 22, 1865.

Substantial groups of letters are located at Syracuse University in the Gerrit Smith papers and at the Massachusetts Historical Society in the antislavery collection.

# The Colored People in America

## Essay or Speech, Published 1854

FRANCES ELLEN WATKINS [HARPER] (1825–1911) *was a prolific writer, lecturer, and reformer as well as one of the most prominent African American Unitarians of her day. Born free, she grew up in Maryland; however, when the Fugitive Slave Act became law in 1850, putting free black people at risk of being taken into slavery if they remained in the South, she moved to Ohio to begin her career as a teacher and writer. In 1852, she published several poems in response to the publication of* Uncle Tom's Cabin. *In 1854, she resolved to work directly for the antislavery cause, moving to Philadelphia, where she lived at one of the stopping points along the Underground Railroad. She then moved to New England, where she launched her career as an abolitionist lecturer for the Maine Anti-Slavery Society.*

*"The Colored People of America," published in 1854 in* Poems on Miscellaneous Subjects, *may well have been one of Francis Watkins's early speeches.*[36] *In this short piece, she dramatically described the circumstances of oppression caused by centuries of slavery, which would make people of any race feel inferior, and then provided examples of the success those who have survived this system enjoy when provided access to education and other advantages.*

See the Biographical Sketch on pages 102–105.

Having been placed by a dominant race in circumstances over which we have had no control, we have been the butt of ridicule and the mark of oppression. Identified with a people over whom weary ages of degradation have passed, whatever concerns them, as a race, concerns me. I have noticed among our people a disposition to censure and upbraid each other, a disposition which has its foundation rather, perhaps, in a want of common sympathy and consideration than mutual hatred or other unholy passions. Born to an inheritance of misery, nurtured in degradation, and cradled in oppression, with the scorn of the white man upon their souls, his fetters upon their limbs, his scourge upon their flesh, what can be expected from their offspring but a mournful reaction of that cursed system which spreads its baneful influence over body and soul; which dwarfs the intellect, stunts its development, debases the spirit, and degrades the soul? Place any nation in the same condition which has been our hapless lot, fetter their limbs and degrade their souls, debase their sons and corrupt their daughters, and when the restless yearnings for liberty shall burn through heart and brain—when, tortured by wrong and goaded by oppression, the hearts that would madden with misery, or break in despair, resolve to break their thrall and escape from bondage, then let the bay of the bloodhound and the scent of the human tiger be upon their track; let them feel that, from the ceaseless murmur of the Atlantic to the sullen roar of the Pacific, from the thunders of the rainbow-crowned Niagara to the swollen waters of the Mexican gulf, they have no shelter for their bleeding feet or resting place for their defenseless heads; let them, when nominally free, feel that they have only exchanged the iron yoke of oppression for the galling fetters of a vitiated public opinion; let prejudice assign them the lowest places and the humblest positions and make them "hewers of wood and drawers of water;" let their income be so small that they must from necessity bequeath to their children an inheritance of poverty and a limited education—and tell me, reviler of our race! censurer of our people! if there is a nation in whose veins runs the purest Caucasian blood, upon whom the same causes would not produce the same effects; whose social condition, intellectual and moral character, would present a more favorable aspect than ours? But there is hope; yes, blessed be God! for our downtrodden and despised race. Public and private schools accommodate our children; and in my own southern home, I see women, whose lot is unremitted labor, saving a pittance from their scanty wages to defray the expense of learning to read. We have papers edited by colored editors, which we may consider it an honor to possess and a credit to sustain. We have a church that is extending itself from east to west, from north to south, through poverty and reproach, persecution and pain. We have our faults, our want of union and concentration of purpose; but are there not extenuating circumstances around our darkest faults—palliating excuses for our most egregious errors? And shall we not hope that the mental and moral aspect which we present is but the first step of a mighty advancement, the faintest corruscations of the day that will dawn with unclouded splendor upon our downtrodden and benighted race, and that ere long we may present to the admiring gaze of those who wish us well, a people to whom knowledge has given power, and righteousness exaltation?

# The Death of the Slave Lewis

## Poem, Published 1854

JULIA WARD HOWE (1819–1910) *was deeply affected and changed by her abolitionist friends. In the following poem, she articulated a spiritual rationale for holding accountable white masters who murdered slaves. This poem appeared in her first book of poetry,* Passion Flowers, *published anonymously in 1854.*

See the Biographical Sketch on pages 327–331.

In the deep sanctuary of sheltering night,
Kept by the angels of the stars serene,
The meanest hireling holds his vested right—
Mourner, slave, culprit, lose from thought and sight
The weight of grief that shall be, or hath been.

Within its walls young lovers tune their strings,
And ravished saints breathe adoration deep;
But softly prayer and song unfold their wings,
Lest ev'n the full heart's upward murmurings
Too rudely cross the silver spell of sleep.

From out that holy realm of night, a shriek,
As of a soul in Hades, rent the veil
Of silence—then a prophet seemed to speak,
To anger roused—not "Turn the unsmitten cheek,"
But, "Blood for blood," answered the dismal wail.

And then I heard a piteous creature lift
His agonizing pleadings, where he stood
Bound, naked, marked with many a bloody rift,
While blows urged out, in torture cries, his shrift
To one with drunken fury in his blood.

The brute but flogged the harder for his cry;
  It gave the horrid sport a keener zest:
It is appointed once for man to die,
But what the crime, the agony, say I,
  When twenty murders tear one bleeding breast?

"They beat him with a broad, flat thong,"—'t is urged,—
  "For all security of life and limb";
Brethren, was He by whom men's sins are purged,
Ev'n thus with a broad leather merely scourged,
  Why waste our womanish hearts their throbs on him?

Blows rained upon him, till his yielding brain
  Had fashioned out the tale they wished to learn,
In dreadful inspiration of his pain,—
They left him, gibbet-wise, within his chain,
  To scourge a brother victim, and return.

They set a man to watch him, they aver,
  Who, as men will, forsook his misery;
But while he staid, unless his statement err,
Not rest nor healing craved the sufferer,
  But, 'Can you lend me any help to die?'

Blind Nature has an instinct to be free;
  Despair is mighty, though her hands be tied;
Howe'er he bowed his head and bent the knee,
(The action has a dark sublimity,)
  The black man gathered up his strength, and died.

They left thee, Lewis, with thy wounds all warm,
  But when they came, to heap thy measure o'er,
Free in the fetters hung thy passive form.
Oh! theirs the crime, if in hate's wildest storm,
  Thy soul, unbidden, sought th' eternal shore.

Priests tell us of the guilt of suicide—
  Let the word pause upon the untried tongue!

They stormed life's citadel, ill-fortified,—
Till the vexed soul fled, powerless to abide,
    And Death's pale flag of truce aloft was flung.

Death was thy champion; 'neath his icy shield
    Thy rescued body laughed the whip to scorn,
While by those wound-mouths, never to be sealed,
Thy soul unto the Ever Just appealed,
    Cried out to God, 'Remember what I've borne!'

Where stays avenging Justice? Why compel
    Our hearts to seek her in th' abyss below?
Shuddering, our eyes look downwards for a hell,
Since Judge and Jury's fiat flatly fell:
    "A slave the victim? Let the white man go!"

It is no murder, when unsanctioned force
    Wastes a poor negro's life beneath the thong
In your brave South. Where freer law has course,
A man who toys too rudely with his horse
    Is held a culprit, and acquits the wrong.

But there must be a hell, as thou shalt know
    By all its furies loosed within thy breast.
Remorse shall feed on thee his hunger slow;
Or, art thou for her craving sunk too low,
    Spectres of fear shall scare thee from thy rest.

The curse of Cain shall hunt thy wandering thought,
    To frantic haste, to fainting weariness.
Lookest thou earthward, blood is there unsought;
Skyward, the clouds th' avenging hue have caught,
    And mock, like crimson monsters, thy distress.

Scourging for scourging, but in keener kind,
    And death for death, but in a living grave;
While, from th' uneasy torment of thy mind,
Thou shalt behold and envy, peace enshrined,
    The placid phantom of thy murdered slave.

Ev'n though thou babble from the mystic book,
   And taste the sacred symbols of thy creed,
Let Christ's black brother from the altar look,
Faint, falter, 'neath his withering rebuke—
   The heavenly food can poison too, at need.

I pause, unwilling further to rehearse
   Thy meeds,[37] or shut thee from God's clemency.
Rather I'll weep, and wish thee nothing worse
Than that, returning blessing for thy curse,
   Thy victim's soul may plead with God for thee.

ELIZA LEE CABOT FOLLEN

# To Mothers in the Free States

## Open Letter from *Anti-Slavery Tracts,* 1855

*Among the writings of Unitarian* ELIZA LEE CABOT FOLLEN (1787–1860) *were numerous stories and poems intended to make children aware of the injustice of slavery and the unfairness of racial prejudice. Eliza Follen also appealed to mothers to use their influence to raise antiracist children. Her widely distributed tract addressed "To Mothers in the Free States" was a response to the expansion of slavery into the western states. In it, she explained how mothers could change the system of slavery by raising sons who would not tolerate it and would fight to end it.*

See the Biographical Sketch on pages 307–309.

I speak to mothers. The mothers in the Free States could abolish slavery; American mothers are responsible for American slavery.

My countrywomen, let me ask you a few questions. Have you, to whom the holy fountain of a mother's love has been opened—when that day-star of your life, a living child, was first set in the eternal firmament of your being—solemnly consecrated this immortal soul to the service of justice, of truth, of God? to the imitation of Christ? I will take it for granted that you have performed this high and holy duty; your son, perhaps, is now a man; he is the pride of your life, the joy of your heart; you have, perhaps, some cherished picture of him when he was a boy, and you love to compare the manly face, filling and brightening daily with the record of a good and happy life, with the innocent child-face that you love for its very childishness and for the dawning prophecy you read there of what now is a happy reality. Do you, when you so look at the child and the man, and bring home to your heart the memory of this happy darling boy playing at your feet or laughing in your lap, your heart running over with love and joy, do you sometimes think what would have been your desolation of soul at his being snatched from you and sold for a slave, condemned to life-long ignorance, hard labor, and brutal treatment—bereft, both of childhood and manhood—and you, left with a breaking heart, forced to submit in silence or endure the lash should you murmur? And now when you rejoice in the manhood of your grown-up son, and his possible happy future, and find your waning existence brightened by the sunshine of his early days, do you remember the slave that has no childhood, no youth, no manhood and his poor mother who can never know your joy?

There is even a more painful picture than this for American mothers to see and one that God and man call upon them to look at and remember. You have a daughter; you are a proud, tender, virtuous mother. She is your heart's choicest treasure. You would bid the winds of Heaven to blow gently upon her; you guard her with the most sensitive care; she is as the flower of your existence. Imagine her exposed to ill usage, often cruelty, always to the lowest passions of humanity; her womanly feelings trampled upon—if possible, obliterated; her pure affections laughed at and scorned; her person desecrated; and her whole nature brought down to the level of the vileness of a licentious man. I ask you whether, when you look upon your beloved daughter, you remember the poor slave-mother and her child? Is the picture overdrawn? If you will not believe authentic statements, like those in the Key to *Uncle Tom's Cabin,* and many others never disproved, use your own reason and yourself judge whether it is improbable. The slaveholder has, by law, the same power over his slaves as he has over his cattle. He puts them up on the auction-block to be examined by slave-traders, just as cattle are examined by a butcher. The poor girl whom he owns may not refuse to do his bidding, let the act he commands be what it will; if she disobey him, he may punish her in any way he pleases; if she forcibly resists, he may flog her to death. The law of the land and the customs of society give her to him. She is his slave.

Do you not—I address every mother in the land—do you not know that such irresponsible power must be abused? Would you trust your own husbands or sons with such power? Would you dare accept it yourselves? In spite of the restraints of law and public opinion, do you not see enough of injustice, licentiousness, and cruelty to show you what a hell on earth life must be where all restraints are taken away? For my part, I only wonder that, in the South, the enormities of the Slave System are not multiplied tenfold. It speaks well for human nature that so much love and tender care and justice are practiced towards these poor helpless creatures who have nothing to protect them—nothing, save the unquenchable pity still left in the hearts of men and the fear which even the worst masters have, lying at the bottom of their hearts, of the retribution laid up for them in the world where they and their victims will soon stand side by side before the Great Judge of all. But though it doubtless is true that excessive cruelty is the exception, not the rule, yet the story of the actual treatment of the slaves is too frightful to relate. Every honest and intelligent man and woman in the land must know that Uncle Tom and Ida May owe much of their power to the ghastly truths they reveal.

But if it were proved that no cruelty was exercised towards the slaves, the case would be no better. A slaveholder calls himself the owner of that to which he has no lawful claim. He who pretends to own a human soul usurps the prerogative of the Almighty. The right of a man to himself is his first and dearest right; and there is no robbery so monstrous as that which takes it from him, thereby stripping its victim of all that is worth having in life and putting out of his power all redress save by death or crime. It is as mean as it is cruel.

You will, perhaps, say to me: "These things may be as you state them, but what can women—what can we mothers do? Why make ourselves miserable at the thought of these terrible facts, when we can do the poor sufferers no good? What can we do?" I answer, you can do everything; I repeat, you can abolish slavery. Let every mother take the subject to heart, as one in which she has a personal concern. In the silence of night, let her listen to the slave-mothers crying to her for help. Let her prayer for them be her "Soul's sincere desire." Let her promise before God to do all she can for their redemption. Let her be faithful to her vow, "in season and out of season," and watch every opportunity and means of doing, or saying, or suffering anything she can for these poor, dumb, and helpless creatures. Let her seek for light how she can best serve their cause. Let the desire to serve them go with her where she goes and dwell a perpetual presence in her home. Let her heart, her understanding, her thoughts, be ever on the alert in their cause. While she must ask for heavenly wisdom to guide her, she must take no council from her fears; she must call no man master. She must, in all things, be "true as truth, uncompromising as justice." Let no worldly favor win her, no flattery deceive her, no danger deter her. Her children will see in her every act a respect for the rights of all. They will see that neither position, nor color, nor any circumstances of life can ever make her forget that God made us all of one blood. They will grow up in an atmosphere of true Christian love. When they are of an age to understand and hear the sad story, she will tell them of the wrongs done by the white man to the poor slave. She has kindled in the hearts of her children a love of justice, a hatred of tyranny, a passionate desire to take the part of the oppressed which shall enlist them for life as the champions of their sorely-injured, downtrodden, colored brethren. Such a mother is as an abiding inspiration to her children. Her son will not vote for the

Fugitive Slave Law or the Nebraska Bill, nor become a kidnapping United States Commissioner! If he be opposed, persecuted for fidelity to the "higher law," if all his worldly prospects be destroyed, he will not waver for a moment. Should he be fined and imprisoned, or, as some faithful ones have been, called upon to die unless he will bow to the hideous idol of American slavery, he will still hold fast his faith. Like the young Hebrew, in the story of the Maccabbees, who refused to obey the tyrant, he will be ready to say:—"even in death, in the last gasp; 'thou, like a fury, takest me out of this present life; but the King of this world shall raise us up, who have died for his Laws, unto everlasting life.'" And the heroic mother will, with God's help, support him and say as the noble Hebrew mother said:—"I beseech thee my son to look upon the Heavens and the earth, and all that is therein, and consider that God made them of things that were not, and so was mankind made likewise. Fear not this tormenter; take thy death, that I may receive thee again in mercy." In the early days of our country, we had such mothers; and they had such sons. Let them of the present day emulate their example. Let them so consecrate themselves, to dedicate their children; and, ere long, the chains will fall from our three millions of captives, and the jubilee be heard in our land.

Many will say, "Suppose all our sons were sincerely devoted, what could they do? What steps can they take? The Free States have no power to abolish slavery. Show us some practical way." It is an old but true saying, "A will finds a way." But who does not know that the votes from the Free States made the Fugitive Slave Law and passed the Nebraska Bill? The Free States support Slavery. The Southerners are the *Slave-Owners*, we are the *Slave-Holders*. Put an end to the immoral participation of the Free States, and their almost as criminal indifference, and American Slavery could no longer exist. We are the greater sinners, for we have the baser motives for our share in this iniquity. A selfish fear of harm to ourselves keeps us quiet, while we see our Republic scorned or mourned over by the lovers of Justice throughout all the world. No old sacred remembrances, no time-honored prejudices, no tender associations of early and childish attachments, none of all these things can be pleaded in extenuation of our conduct. Not one of us thinks slavery right; nay, we declare it to be a sin; out of our own mouths we are condemned.

I say, then, to mothers in the Free States, you have before you a solemn duty, a glorious work. Shall the noble Florence Nightingale spend eight hours in the day upon her knees, by the bedside of her wounded and suffering fellow-men, both countrymen and enemies, and will not you listen to the cry of the millions of sufferers in your native land? Her mission is one of love and mercy only; yours is a work of love and mercy and justice. Shall she and other heroic women, taking no counsel from fear of ridicule, or that shrinking fastidious delicacy in which they have been nurtured, nor from fear of hardship, disease, or death, leave comfort, luxury, home, in pity for bodily suffering; and can our American women do nothing, risk nothing, for those in their native land who are bereft of everything that is desirable in life? Shall not the broken spirit, the bruised body, the wounded affections, the cramped and distorted intellect, the crushed aspirations of the slave be remembered by his happy and favored countrywomen? Will you not listen to his cry for help? Will you not hasten to his relief, and, "on the knees of your spirit," pray and labor for him, till his wrongs are redressed and he is set free? Can you not find the skill and the courage to apply efficient remedies to the moral contagion that is slowly but surely poisoning our very atmosphere, sapping the foundations of our existence as a Republic, so that liberty and love of justice are fast dying out in our land?

Mothers in the Free States, I tell you no idle dream; I present no visionary, impracticable idea. I tell you the simple truth when I say you can, if you will, abolish slavery. The tender heart of the boy is in the hands of the mother. From her he receives his first impressions of right and wrong—impressions which remain to him through life, mingled with the memory of his first and happiest hours. When he is tempted to abandon the highest right, to make a compromise with wrong, to adopt a time-serving policy dignified by the name of prudence and defended on the plea of necessity; then shall the memory of his mother and her faithful words come back to him—the angel of his early days. In that presence, the tempter shall stand rebuked and take his true shape of cowardice and sin. Therefore, O my countrywomen, I call upon you, I plead with you to take up this cause with a heroic faith, a martyr-like fidelity, an unquenchable courage!

I am myself a mother. I am bound with the same ties that you are. I have counted the cost and know what I demand of you. But the time has come when woman must come to the rescue in this land. As women, our all is at stake. We have, above every other motive, that especial call for our devotion—our children. They are, at once, the pledges of our sincerity and the tests of our courage. Let us not be found wanting.

# Counsels to the Newly Converted

## From *Anti-Slavery Tracts,* 1855

MARIA WESTON CHAPMAN (1806–1885) *found in abolitionism an opportunity for that kind of community action that her Unitarian church did not provide for women. An active organizer of projects and events, she was one of the leading fundraisers for the abolitionist movement. Her "Counsels to the Newly Converted" was filled with religious zeal and fervor for the cause.*[38] *She even claimed that abolition was the modern equivalent of salvation. She asked for nothing less than total commitment from those who wished to support the movement to end slavery.*

See the Biographical Sketch on pages 15–18.

Lavish your time, your money, your labors, your prayers, in that field, which is the world, and you will reap a thousand fold, now and hereafter. This movement *moves.* It is alive. Hear how everything mean and selfish struggles, hisses, and dies under its influence. Never, since the world was, has any effort been so clear, so strong, so uncompromising, so ennobling so holy, and, let me add, so successful. It is "the bright consummate flower" of the Christianity of the nineteenth century. Look at those who "have not resisted the heavenly vision" it presented them of a nation overcoming its evil propensities and doing right at all risks; ask *them* whether it has not saved their souls alive; ask *them* if it has not made them worshippers of the beauty and sublimity of high character, till they are ready to "know nothing on earth but Jesus Christ and him crucified." For this they give all—wealth, youth, health, strength, life. Worldly success, obtained by slackening their labors against slavery (and it is easy to have it on those terms at any moment, so placable a monster is the world), strikes them like failure and disgrace. They have "scorned delights, and lived laborious days," till at length they feel it no sacrifice but the highest joy. All this the American Anti-Slavery Society demands of *you.* DO IT! and be most grateful for the opportunity of fulfilling a work which is its own exceeding great reward. DO IT, and find yourself the chosen of God, to keep alive in this nation, degraded and corrupted by slavery, the noble flame of Christian faith, the sentiment of honor and fidelity, the instinct of high-mindedness, the sense of absolute, immutable duty, the charm of chivalrous and poetic feeling, which would make of the poorest Americans the Christian gentlemen of the world.

> "Cherish all these high feelings that become
> A giver of the gift of liberty."

You will find yourself under the necessity of doing it in *this* noble company or *alone.* Try it. Strive to be perfect, as God is perfect—to act up to your own highest idea, in connection with church or state in this land corrupted by slavery, and see if you are helped or hindered. . . . Secure the blessing of union for good, and be delivered from the curse of union in evil, by acting with the AMERICAN ANTI-SLAVERY SOCIETY, its members and friends.

I use this mode of expression advisedly, for I am not speaking of a mere form of association. Many are in harmonious cooperation with it who have neither signed the constitution nor subscribed the annual half dollar. Hence it is neither a formality nor a ceremony but a united, onward-flowing current of noble lives.

If, then, you feel that devotedness of heart which I verily think your question indicates, I feel free to counsel you to go *immediately* to the nearest office of the American Anti-Slavery Society, by letter, if not in person, subscribe what money can afford—the first fruits of a life-long liberality, and *study* the cause like a science, while promoting it like a gospel, under the cheering helpful sympathy of some of the best company on earth; *but not unless;* for *this* company despises what politicians, ecclesiastical and other, call "getting people committed." They have a horror of this selfish invasion of another's freedom, as of the encumbrance of selfish help. They warn you not to touch the ark with unhallowed hands.

One consideration more—the thought of what you owe to your forerunners in what you feel to be the truth. It is to follow meekly after and be baptized with the baptism that they are baptized with. "Thus it *becometh* us to fulfill all righteousness"; and the more your talents, gifts, and graces may, in your own judgment, be superior to the theirs, the more *becoming* it will be to seek their fellowship; for in the whole land they, and *they alone, are right.* It is not eulogy but fact that theirs is the path of the just, shining more and more unto the perfect day—denied only by the besotted with injustice, the committed to crime. Consider, then, not only what you owe to your slavery-cursed country, your enslaving as well as enslaved countrymen, your fathers' memory, your remotest posterity, the Christian religion, which forbids the sacrifice of one man's rights to another man's interests, and which knows no distinction of caste, color, or condition,—but consider, also, what you owe to those individuals and to that brotherhood who have battled twenty years in the breach for *your* freedom, involved with that of the meanest slave.

Imagine how the case stood with those who perished by suffocation in the Black Hole at Calcutta. Suppose that some of their number had felt the sublime impulse to place their bodies in the door and the high devoted hearts to stand the crushing till dawn awoke the tyrant; the *rest* of that doomed band might have passed out alive. This is what the American Anti-Slavery Society has been unflinchingly doing for you, and for the rest of the nation, amid torture, insult, and curses, through a long night of terror and despair. The life of the land, its precious moral sense, has been thus kept from suffocation. The free agitating air of faithful speech has saved it. The soul of the United States is not dead, thanks, under Providence, to that noble fellowship of resolute souls, to find whom the nation has been winnowed. Do your duty by them, in the name of self-respect. Such companionship is an honor accorded to but few, and of that worthy few, I would fain count you one. Strike, then, with them at the existence of slavery, and you will see individual slaves made free, antislavery leaven introduced into parties and churches, instruction diffused, the products of free labor multiplied, and fugitives protected, in exact proportion to the energy of the grand onset against the civil system.

# Letters to Heroes

## From Letters, 1859

*In 1859, white abolitionist John Brown led a racially mixed band of eighteen men in an abortive attempt to seize the federal arsenal at Harper's Ferry, Virginia. Although his use of force was denounced by some Northern abolitionists, the raid and subsequent martyrdom of John Brown and his men provided a clear indication of the violence to come. During the month between his sentencing and execution, African American Unitarian* FRANCES ELLEN WATKINS [HARPER] (1825–1911) *wrote to both John and his wife Mary to express her support.*[39] *Her letter to John was published the following year by James Redpath in his collection of reflections on the effect of the incident at Harper's Ferry. Her letter to Mary, with whom she visited while awaiting the execution, was published in 1872 by William Still in his documentation of the Underground Railroad.*

See the Biographical Sketch on pages 102–105.

### To Mary Brown

Farmer Centre, Ohio, November 14, 1859

My Dear Madam:

In an hour like this the common words of sympathy may seem like idle words, and yet I want to say something to you, the noble wife of the hero of the nineteenth century. Belonging to the race your dear husband reached forth his hand to assist, I need not tell you that my sympathies are with you. I thank you for the brave words you have spoken. A republic that produces such a wife and mother may hope for better days. Our heart may grow more hopeful for humanity when it sees the sublime sacrifice it is about to receive from his hands. Not in vain has your dear husband periled all, if the martyrdom of one hero is worth more than the life of a million cowards. From the prison comes forth a shout of triumph over that power whose ethics are robbery of the feeble and oppression of the weak, the trophies of whose chivalry are a plundered cradle and a scourged and bleeding woman. Dear sister, I thank you for the brave and noble words that you have spoken. Enclosed I send you a few dollars as a token of my gratitude, reverence and love.

Yours respectfully,
Frances Ellen Watkins

May God, our own God, sustain you in the hour of trial. If there is one thing on Earth I can do for you or yours, let me be apprised. I am at your service.

✦ ✦ ✦

## To John Brown

Kendalville, Indiana, November 25, 1859

Dear Friend:

Although the hands of Slavery throw a barrier between you and me, and it may not be my privilege to see you in your prison-house, Virginia has no bolts or bars through which I dread to send you my sympathy. In the name of the young girl sold from the warm clasp of a mother's arms to the clutches of a libertine or a profligate—in the name of the slave mother, her heart rocked to and fro by the agony of her mournful separations—I thank you, that you have been brave enough to reach out your hands to the crushed and blighted of my race. You have rocked the bloody Bastille; and I hope that from your sad fate great good may arise to the cause of freedom. Already from your prison has come a shout of triumph against the giant sin of our country. The hemlock is distilled with victory when it is pressed to the lips of Socrates. The Cross becomes a glorious ensign when Calvary's page-browed sufferer yields up his life upon it. And, if Universal Freedom is ever to be the dominant power of the land, your bodies may be only her first stepping stones to dominion. I would prefer to see Slavery go down peaceably by men breaking off their sins by righteousness and their iniquities by showing justice and mercy to the poor; but we cannot tell what the future may bring forth. God writes national judgments upon national sins; and what may be slumbering in the storehouse of divine justice we do not know. We may earnestly hope that your fate will not be a vain lesson, that it will intensify our hatred of

Slavery and love of freedom, and that your martyr grave will be a sacred altar upon which men will record their vows of undying hatred to that system which tramples on man and bids defiance to God. I have written to your dear wife and sent her a few dollars, and I pledge myself to you that I will continue to assist her. May the ever-blessed God shield you and your fellow prisoners in the darkest hour. Send my sympathy to your fellow prisoners; tell them to be of good courage; to seek a refuge in the Eternal God and lean upon His everlasting arms for a sure support. If any of them, like you, have a wife or children that I can help, let them send me word.

# Pioneer Work on the Sea Islands

## Article about Penn School, 1862–1901

LAURA MATILDA TOWNE (1825–1901), *a Unitarian from Pennsylvania, along with her life-long companion, Ellen Murray, founded one of the best-known schools for former slaves on the sea islands off the coast of South Carolina. The Penn School was established during the Civil War when plantation owners fled, abandoning their land and slaves, after the Confederacy lost the area known as Port Royal. Eventually, the school expanded to include both secondary education and teacher training. In the following article, written only a few days before her death, Laura Matilda Towne described the history of the Port Royal Colony, the founding of Penn School during the Civil War, and the school's success in sharing culture and education.*

See the Biographical Sketch on pages 367–370.

St. Helena Island lies southeast of Ladies Island, which is east of Port Royal Island. Between St. Helena and the Atlantic Ocean lie the Hunting Islands, uninhabited save by deer and the lighthouse keepers. They are merely narrow strips of sandy land, forming a breaker between St. Helena and danger. On still nights the roar of the angry ocean can be distinctly heard, as it dashes itself on the sandy barrier. St. Helena is fifteen miles long by seven broad and so indented by the sea that it is all points—Coffin' Point, Tripp's Point, Eding's Point.

It contains about fifty-six square miles and supports six thousand inhabitants, most of whom are Negroes and who were, previous to 1861, considered the very lowest slaves in South Carolina. They were ruled by black drivers, who were accountable to the owners of the plantations or to their white overseers. In old times the island grew indigo; later the crop was cotton, of the finest, longest fibre, called silk cotton and Sea Island cotton. This is a very imperious crop, demanding a whole year's hard labor to perfect and put it on the market. No holidays were allowed the slaves except Christmas and Sundays, no rest but a short night in the twenty-four hours, and that curtailed on Saturday by the necessity of grinding, on a hand-mill, the weekly ration of one peck of corn, each taking his or her turn till daylight.

Their drivers were, of necessity, severe. Uncle Robert of the Oaks, a man of kindly disposition, was ordered to whip little Lucy, the waiting-maid. He took her, with many threats, to the gin-house, and as she sank sobbing on the floor, he, a broad six-footer, lashed an upright beam with his cowhide, whispering between the strokes,

"Holler harder, chile, holler harder."

But her master, happening to glance between the chinks, saw the whole performance and immediately deposed him from his office as driver in favor of a younger, sterner man.

In 1860–1861, the owners of plantations, seeing the conflict approaching, determined to be well prepared for it. So the Negroes were worked as hard as possible, early and late, even on moonlight nights, a thing unheard of before.

"The whip rapid too much," said one.

That crop was taken from the abandoned estates by the United States Government and devoted to the education of the Negroes, though, I believe, the owners have since been compensated.

The forts at Bay Point and Hilton Head were taken by Dupont, in November, 1861, and the Confederate soldiers retreated to the mainland. In pursuance of a prearranged plan, an island vigilance committee rode from plantation to plantation, giving warning of the coming of the Federals and assisting the white families in their hurried flight, in some cases the dinner table being left all set. They carried with them a few of the house servants, especially the nurses. Every horse and vehicle was utilized, and on St. Helena, Morgan, Port Royal, Paris, and Ladies Islands, scarcely a white person remained.

The Negroes waited with the patience of their race for what would come. There were uneasy whispers about whether the Yankees came to help them or, as their owners said, to sell them to Cuba. But the question was settled by the first detachment of soldiers that, led by a Negro from Frogmore, Columbus Brown, marched up the island, telling the Negroes that they were sent by their friend, "Uncle Sam," and there was no need of fear. The government sent agents to collect the cotton crop and the army took the year's produce of corn to feed the horses.

Meanwhile the question rose, "What shall be done with these thousands of Negroes?"

The government, or rather the treasury department, organized a force of young men, some of the very highest and best of the North, placed over them Mr. Edward L. Pierce, of Milton, Mass., and sent them down to superintend the plantations. Mr. Edward Hooper was one of the principal men. Then great meetings were held in Boston, New

York, and Philadelphia, and societies were formed to send teachers to the Negroes and also much-needed clothing. In March, 1862, the Negroes set to work willingly enough on provision crops but reluctantly upon the cotton, as the superintendents had no money to offer as wages, and they themselves scarcely believed their own promises that the government would pay for the work.

In April, 1862, I landed on St. Helena as the first teacher from Pennsylvania and was followed in June by my friend, Miss Ellen Murray, an English lady, both of us being sent by the Freedmen's Aid Society of Pennsylvania. When this society closed its work, an auxiliary, the Benezet of Germantown, supported the school. After some years of varying fortune, during a part of which time we had only our own funds to depend upon, my family adopted and generously assisted the school.

The first work in 1862 was to visit the people in their homes. We found the older ones worn down with hard work and very ignorant. They counted in this fashion, "one, two, five, eight, ten"; further they knew nothing. The drivers, however, were accustomed to report upon the number of rows and tasks worked by their "gangs."

The houses were frame, clapboarded, with small windows, shuttered, not glazed; some of the chimneys were of brick, some of mud and sticks. The floors were sand and lime, beaten hard and worn in hollows. At one side was the open hearth and wide chimney, but the fires were small, the woods being carefully preserved by the owners. Large cracks under the doors let in a rush of keen air in winter. There were two or three bunks in each cabin for the grown people, but the younger ones slept on heaps of filthy rags on the floor with a blanket for cover. The household utensils consisted of one pot, in which they cooked their hominy or peas with salt pork. Occasionally a frying pan was seen. I speak of the field Negroes, not the house servants.

In such houses, spoons there were none, but long, well-worn oyster shells served the purpose. The elders first helped themselves from the hominy pot; then it was given to the children, who finished all that could be easily scraped out. Then the dogs worked at it for hours and left it clean for the next meal! Cleanliness, neatness, home-life were impossible; everything spoke of discomfort and misery. Yet a happier, jollier set of people was never seen; song and laughter prevailed, night and day.

The children mostly went entirely naked in summer, and at one plantation we visited we saw a flight of what looked like South Sea Islanders, boys and girls of full size, nude, and flying from white people's sight.

A child, in its mother's arms, screamed itself almost into convulsions as I approached the cabin door.

"What is the matter with the poor child?" I asked.

"Him aint neber shum white face, missus. Him scared."

They were rationed the first year because the corn crop had been taken to feed the horses of the troops. On my saying to one old man that after this I hoped they would raise enough to feed themselves, he answered placidly.

"Oh yes, missus, ain't we all done raise corn enough to feed ole Massa and Missus 'side we all uns, all de years?"

We opened the Penn School in September, 1862, in the Brick Church, with about eighty scholars, some of whom we had already taught in a room on the Oaks Plantation. Miss Murray had taught some to read a little. They had learned to love her and to have some sense of propriety. I had been too busy with distributing, as case after case of goods from Philadelphia was sent to my charge, visiting and above all, giving medicines and advice, and my class was made up chiefly of untrained youngsters, with five or six mothers of families.

They had no idea of sitting still, of giving attention, of ceasing to talk aloud. They lay down and went to sleep; they scuffled and struck each other. They got up by the dozen, made their curtsies and walked off to the neighboring fields for blackberries, coming back to their seats with a curtsy when they were ready. They evidently did not understand me, and I could not understand them, and after two hours and a half of effort, I was thoroughly exhausted.

We had agreed that no corporal punishment should ever be used, and to institute moral government among children used to no persuasion but that of the lash was no easy task. But they did want to learn and I resorted to a potent factor—emulation.

"There now, James is the first to know which is 'o.' James, come up here and show them."

James, proud and happy, stood before the blackboard and every eye was on his hand as he slowly made an a "o." Every child knew an "o" henceforth. With praise, emulation, and their quickly won affection, I found I could rule and teach, without the whip.

There were some amusing incidents.

A little girl, who came to school every day with a baby in her arms, or more usually on her back, asked to go home.

"But why? " I demanded.

"Dis baby—missus—him cry all de time. Me must a lef him spirit to ma house, hab for go get him."

I let her go and after some questioning learned that when a child is taken from its home, its spirit must be called to come with it, else the child will cry till its spirit is found and the two are brought together.

I afterwards noticed that never did a woman, having a child in her arms, leave my door without looking back over her shoulder and calling;

"Come chile, come Jane! I'se gwine now. Come along, darter."

So, for some years, between teaching, doctoring, and a smallpox epidemic, changes in the ruling powers, in societies, in funds, we teachers led a life of stress, labor, and anxiety. Now, teaching the children and grandchildren of our first pupils, we have no more trouble than if we were teaching a Northern white school. When a stranger comes to address them, they give the closest, most courteous attention and are ready with intelligent answers to his questions. In fact, the islanders generally long to gain knowledge and glean from every field open to them. In their lowest state, they could always do one thing well—sing. At first they sang melody alone, but after having once been given an idea of harmony, they instantly adopted it and take the different parts, soprano, contralto, tenor, and bass by nature, it seems. Their time and tone are always true.

We have grown old so happily among them. Sometimes a colored speaker from another part of the state will begin a speech on the hardness and oppression of the white people to the Negroes, but he is sure to be interrupted with;

"It's different here, brother. The white people here is our teachers and friends. They show us light and are our good friends."

✦ ✦ ✦

# Reflections on Life at Penn School

### From Letters, 1864–1884

*The letters of* LAURA MATILDA TOWNE (1825–1901) *reveal her efforts to share the details of her life at Penn School with her Northern friends. Despite their isolation from the rest of the world, the people of Port Royal were keenly aware of the outside world and its potential impact on them. Yet they had something of value both black people and white people sought to maintain. They had become friends.*

See the Biographical Sketch on pages 367–370.

Evening, December, 1864

Miss Lynch and a colored teacher from the North, Mr. Freeman, dined here and seemed well satisfied. They have just gone. I suppose it would seem strange to you to sit down with two colored people, but to us it is the most natural thing in the world. I actually forget these people are black, and it is only when I see them at a distance and cannot recognize their features that I remember it. The conversation at dinner flowed just as naturally as if we were Northern whites. Both Mr. Freeman and Miss Lynch have education and talk well. General Sherman at Hilton Head received General Saxton with flattering honor and General Foster more coolly. General Sherman is quartered in Savannah. That evacuation is a blessing if it leaves the country as this has been left for freedmen under Northern influence. I wish the Southerners would all evacuate their whole territory.

✦ ✦ ✦

October 15, 1865

The people receive the rebels better than we expected, but the reason is that they believe Johnson [President Andrew Johnson] is going to put them in their old masters' power again, and they feel that they must conciliate or be crushed. They no longer pray for the President—*our* President, as they used to call Lincoln—in the church. They keep an ominous silence and are very sad and troubled.

However, one of the best and most powerful of the old rebels returned awhile ago and has been living in his old home on sufferance. His people all went to tell him "huddy," and he was convinced of their toleration. So he told them he should get back his land and wanted to know how many would be willing to work for him for wages. They said none. "Why," he said, "hadn't you as lief work for me as for these Yankees?" "No, sir," they answered through their foreman; "even if you pay as well, sir, we had rather work for the Yankees who have been our friends."

On the mainland it is so dangerous for a negro to go about, especially with the United States Uniform on, that orders are out that no more will be allowed to go to recover their families and bring them here as they have been doing. Some of the happiest reunions have come under our observation. But now people well-to-do here have to leave wives, old mothers, and children (sold away) to starve on the mainland, when they are anxious to bring them here and provide for them. It is not true that the negro soldiers do not behave well. Here, at least, they have always been patterns, as every commander of the post will testify. These stories about them are manufactured for a purpose.

✦ ✦ ✦

August 19, 1877

I wonder what view N. takes of the facts, that for non-payment of the poll-tax, and of the fine for not doing so, a man can be put into the penitentiary and sold out of it as a slave for the time of his sentence. That is why Mr. Gleaves, Sally Fassitt's connection, fled to Canada, because he would, without perhaps even a show of trial or justice, have been condemned to the penitentiary and from that hired out on a nice plantation, subject to rules made by three directors, regarding "the quality of his food and clothing," the time of his labor per day (ten hours unless in agriculture, and then at the pleasure of the hirer), and "the nature of his punishments." There was an item in the Beaufort paper, too, which shows which way the wind blows. It was to the effect that a man *charged* with hog stealing—not convicted nor taken in the act but only charged with it—was taken by a party and severely whipped, "so saving the expense of a trial," the Beaufort *Tribune* said. If that doesn't look like slavery times, what could?

✦ ✦ ✦

October 28, 1877

The colored people here are all ardent and settled Baptists, with a little sprinkling of Methodists.

Our school is a delight. It rained one day last week, but through the pelting showers came nearly every blessed child. Some of them walk six miles and back, besides doing their task of cotton picking. Their steady eagerness to learn is just something amazing. To be deprived of a lesson is a severe punishment. "I got no reading today," or no writing, or no sums, is cause for bitter tears. This race is going to rise. It is biding its time.

✦ ✦ ✦

Beaufort, July 10, 1884

That old plague, the North Penn conductor, came and talked to me a long time at Yemassee. He says the Reading has bought the Newtown and is going to make a connection between Fern Rock and Bethaires which will cut off nine miles of the distance to New York. He said the whole race of niggers ought to be swept away, and I told him my business was with that race and that they would never be swept away, so he was disgusted and went away, leaving me to read in peace.

## ✦ *Biographical Sketch*

**Born:** *May 3, 1825, Pittsburgh, Pennsylvania*

**Died:** *February 22, 1901, St. Helena, South Carolina, age 75*

**Buried:** *Laurel Hill Cemetery, Philadelphia, Pennsylvania*

In times of crisis, individuals sometimes find a purpose that carries them through the rest of their lives. For Laura Matilda Towne, the Civil War was such a crisis and being the advocate for a group of former slaves became her purpose.

The series of events that set the stage for Towne's work began with the blockade of the Confederate coast, the capture of isolated Port Royal Sound in November 1861, and the abandonment by wealthy cotton growers of their lands and slaves. Because slaves were seen as property, there was much speculation as to their capacities. And because sea island blacks were perceived to be particularly backward in custom and speech, their Gullah dialect a mix of English and African languages, questions as to their intellectual capabilities and usefulness as workers abounded.

Abolitionists saw this situation as the perfect opportunity to demonstrate the capabilities of blacks, once and for all. In what came to be known as the Port Royal Experiment, Northern teachers, superintendents, and missionaries were called to the sea islands to help the former slaves create lives as free men and women. Laura Matilda Towne was among the first group of fifty educators who responded to the call early that next spring (1862).

Born of wealthy and resourceful parents, the middle child in a family of seven, Towne was well educated and prepared for the task. Her education included studies under Dr. Constantine Hering, the famed homeopathist. Towne's family also had a social conscience. As members of First Unitarian Church in Philadelphia, they were stirred by the antislavery sermons of William Henry Furness to become abolitionists.

Towne was thirty-six years old when she arrived on St. Helena in April 1862. She was soon joined by her life-long companion, Ellen Murray. Confronting them were nearly insurmountable obstacles: resentful, jeering Union troops; a sweltering, inhospitable climate; threatening insects; devastating epidemics; and occasional skirmishes of warfare from Confederate forces nearby. Nevertheless, Towne confidently described their work as "noble" and wished other more faint-hearted abolitionists were as proud.

Towne's homeopathic efforts were heroic. When malaria, yellow fever, smallpox, dysentery, cholera, and other illnesses swept through the islands, she was able to apply her knowledge of homeopathy and medicine to vaccinate, medicate, and nurse the sick. Her diary reveals her despair, loneliness, and exhaustion, as she was often the only hope the people had.

Murray began holding classes in June 1862, and Towne soon joined her. Teaching became their major activity, though Towne was influential in the lives of the former slaves in other ways. She served as a bridge between the government and those people it was to serve, often as an advocate for their needs and wages. She opposed speculators' attempts to buy lands that had become delinquent through nonpayment of taxes, eventually making it possible for people to own the land they had worked on all of their lives. In St. Helena, African Americans came to own seventy-five percent of the land in Beaufort County, a circumstance that greatly distinguished them from black people elsewhere in the South.

Teaching, however, was Towne's true calling, her "greatest enjoyment and privilege." Though the students were unaccustomed to classroom discipline, they made great strides and went to great efforts to learn, often walking miles to school after doing their morning chores. The first class was held at The Oaks, where Towne and Murray lived; eight students attended. Shortly thereafter, when more than eighty students began attending, classes were moved to the Brick Church, a Baptist church. A problem arose when the Baptist minister expressed shock upon learning of Towne's Unitarianism and would not serve Towne or Murray communion at church. The solution was provided by the Commission of Philadelphia's offer of a schoolhouse, which Towne immediately accepted. The new school building, shipped in sections, arrived in the fall of 1864. Towne named it Penn School in honor of William Penn and the Pennsylvania Freedmen's Aid Society, which had funded the school's first years. After that funding was exhausted, Towne, her family, other prominent Unitarians, and abolitionists of other faiths continued to support the school.

Penn School became the only school in South Carolina to provide secondary education to freed men and women, and after 1870, it also functioned as a normal school, offering teacher training. The school was unique in that Towne and Murray included African American teachers on staff. Charlotte Fortune, a free woman from the North, became a friend and co-founder of the school along with Towne and Murray. Just as important, both women welcomed African American teachers into their home.

Laura Matilda Towne was a quiet revolutionary who broke several social barriers at once: She attacked the assigned social place of African Americans by breaking entrenched patterns of subservience, enabling black people to develop independence, responsibility, and leadership, and she rejected gender expectations by eschewing domesticity and choosing to live away from home and with another woman.

Laura Matilda Towne died of influenza in 1901 at the age of seventy-five. Several hundred of her sea island neighbors followed the simple mule cart that carried her body to the Port Royal ferry, singing the spirituals she had so loved. Her body was taken to the family gravesite in Philadelphia.

While no longer a school, Penn continues as an institution to this day. Now called Penn Center, it serves as a cultural resource center for the Gullah language and heritage.

*Biographical Sketch by* AUDREY W. VINCENT

## ✦ Writings of Laura Matilda Towne

"Diary of Laura M. Towne, April 1862–May, 1864." Trans. and ed. by Elizabeth Pratt Jenks. Penn Center, St. Helena, SC.

*Letters and Diary of Laura Matilda Towne.* Edited by Rupert Sargent Holland. n.p., 1912. Reprint, New York: Negro Universities Press, 1969.

"Pioneer Work on the Sea Islands." *Southern Workman,* July 1901.

Other letters and papers can be found in the Penn School Papers, 1862–1976. Southern Historical Collection, Wilson Library, Chapel Hill, University of North Carolina.

## ✦ Biographical Resources[40]

Billington, Ray Allen, ed. *The Journal of Charlotte Forten: A Free Negro in the Slave Era.* New York: Collier Books, 1967.

Currie-McDaniel, Ruth. "Northern Women in the South, 1860–1880." *The Georgia Historical Quarterly* 86 (1992): 284–312.

Johnson, Guion G. *A Social History of the Sea Islands.* Chapel Hill: University of North Carolina Press, 1930.

Robbins, Gerald. "Laura Towne: White Pioneer in Negro Education, 1862–1901." *Journal of Education* (April 1961): 40–54.

Rose, Willie Lee. "'Iconoclasm Has Had Its Day': Abolitionists and Freedmen in South Carolina." In *The Anti-Slavery Vanguard: New Essays on the Abolitionists,* edited by Martin Duberman. New Haven, CT: Princeton University Press, 1965.

———. *Rehearsal for Reconstruction: The Port Royal Experiment.* New York: Bobbs-Merrill, 1964.

Swint, Henry Lee. *The Northern Teacher in the South, 1862–1870.* New York: Octagon Books, 1967.

# Bury Me in a Free Land

## Poem Sent to One of John Brown's Men, 1864

*Later in the Civil War,* FRANCES ELLEN WATKINS [HARPER] (1825–1911) *described her yearning for freedom in "Bury Me in a Free Land," a poem published in* The Liberator *in 1864. She sent a copy of this poem to one of John Brown's men, who was still awaiting execution.*[41] *Her vivid imagery of the horrors of slavery undoubtedly served as testimony that the prize of freedom was worth the terrible destruction of war.*

See the Biographical Sketch on pages 102–105.

Make me a grave where'er you will,
In a lowly plain, or a lofty hill,
Make it among earth's humblest graves,
But not in a land where men are slaves.

I could not rest if around my grave
I heard the steps of a trembling slave:
His shadow above my silent tomb
Would make it a place of fearful gloom.

I could not rest if I heard the tread
Of a coffle gang to the shambles led,
And the mother's shriek of wild despair
Rise like a curse on the trembling air.

I could not sleep if I saw the lash
Drinking her blood at each fearful gash,
And I saw her babes torn from her breast,
Like trembling doves from their parent nest.

I'd shudder and start if I heard the bay
Of blood-hounds seizing their human prey,
And I heard the captive plead in vain
As they bound afresh his galling chain.

If I saw young girls from their mother's arms
Bartered and sold for their youthful charms,
My eye would flash with a mournful flame
My death-paled cheek grow red with shame.

I would sleep, dear friends, where bloated might
Can rob no man of his dearest right;
My rest shall be calm in any grave
Where none can call his brother a slave.

I ask no monument, proud and high
To arrest the gaze of the passers-by;
All that my yearning spirit craves,
Is bury me not in a land of slaves.

✦ ✦ ✦

# We Are All Bound Up Together

## Speech to Eleventh National Women's Rights Convention, New York, May 1866

*When the Civil War ended,* FRANCES ELLEN WATKINS HARPER (1825–1911) *returned to her dual campaign for women's suffrage and civil rights. One of the most articulate speakers of the day, she bridged the widening gap between black and white women, never losing sight of the relationship between different oppressions. In her 1866 speech to the National Women's Rights Convention, she shared her experiences of oppression both as a woman and as an African American, claiming that when society tramples on the rights of its members, the result is a "curse in its own soul."*

See the Biographical Sketch on pages 102–105.

I feel I am something of a novice upon this platform. Born of a race whose inheritance has been outrage and wrong, most of my life had been spent in battling against those wrongs. But I did not feel as keenly as others that I had these rights in common with other women, which are now demanded. About two years ago, I stood within the shadows of my home. A great sorrow had fallen upon my life. My husband had died suddenly, leaving me a widow, with four children, one my own and the others stepchildren. I tried to keep my children together. But my husband died in debt; and before he had been in his grave three months, the administrator had swept the very milk-crocks and wash tubs from my hands. I was a farmer's wife and made butter for the Columbus market; but what could I do, when they had swept all away? They left me one thing—and that was a looking-glass! Had I died instead of my husband, how different would have been the result! By this time he would have had another wife, it is likely; and no administrator would have gone into his house, broken up his home, and sold his bed, and taken away his means of support.

I took my children in my arms and went out to seek my living. While I was gone; a neighbor to whom I had once lent five dollars went before a magistrate and swore that he believed I was a non-resident and laid an attachment on my very bed. And I went back to Ohio with my orphan children in my arms, without a single feather bed in this wide world that was not in the custody of the law. I say, then, that justice is not fulfilled so long as woman is unequal before the law.

We are all bound up together in one great bundle of humanity, and society cannot trample on the weakest and feeblest of its members without receiving the curse in its own soul. You tried that in the case of the negro. You pressed him down for two centuries; and in so doing you crippled the moral strength and paralyzed the spiritual energies of the white men of the country. When the hands of the black were fettered, white men were deprived of the liberty of speech and the freedom of the press. Society cannot afford to neglect the enlightenment of any class of its members. At the South, the legislation of the country was in behalf of the rich slaveholders, while the poor white man was neglected. What is the consequence today? From that very class of neglected poor white men comes the man who stands today with his hand upon the helm of the nation. He fails to catch the watchword of the hour and throws himself, the incarnation of meanness, across the pathway of the nation. My objection to Andrew Johnson is not that he has been a poor white man; my objection is that he keeps "poor whites" all the way through. *[Applause.]* That is the trouble with him.

This grand and glorious revolution which has commenced will fail to reach its climax of success until throughout the length and breadth of the American Republic the nation shall be so color-blind as to know no man by the color of his skin or the curl of his hair. It will then have no privileged class, trampling upon and outraging the unprivileged classes, but will be then one great privileged nation, whose privilege will be to produce the loftiest manhood and womanhood that humanity can attain.

I do not believe that giving the woman the ballot is immediately going to cure all the ills of life. I do not believe that white women are dew drops just exhaled from the skies. I think that like men they may be divided into three classes, the good, the bad, and the indifferent. The good would vote according to their convictions and principles; the bad, as dictated by prejudice or malice; and the indifferent will vote on the strongest side of the question, with the winning party.

You white women speak here of rights. I speak of wrongs. I, as a colored woman, have had in this country an education which has made me feel as if I were in the situation of Ishmael, my hand against every man and every man's hand against me. Let me go tomorrow morning and take my seat in one of your street cars—I do not know that they will do it in New York, but they will in Philadelphia—and the conductor will put up his hand and stop the car rather than let me ride.

*A Lady*—They will not do that here.

*Mrs. Harper*—They do in Philadelphia. Going from Washington to Baltimore this Spring, they put me in the smoking car. *[Loud Voices—"Shame."]* Aye, in the capital of the nation, where the black man consecrated himself to the nation's defense, faithful when the white man was faithless, they put me in the smoking car! They did it once; but the next time they tried it, they failed; for I would not go in. I felt the fight in me; but I don't want to have to fight all the time. Today I am puzzled where to make my home. I would like to make it in Philadelphia, near my own friends and relations. But if I want to ride in the streets of Philadelphia, they send me to ride on the platform with the driver. *[Cries of "Shame."]* Have women nothing to do with this? Not long since, a colored woman took her seat in an Eleventh Street car in Philadelphia, and the conductor stopped the car, and told the rest of the passengers to get out, and left the car with her in it alone, when they took it back to the station. One day I took my seat in a car, and the conductor came to me and told me to take another seat. I just screamed "murder." The man said if I was black I ought to behave myself. I knew that if he was white he was not behaving himself. Are there not wrongs to be righted?

# Establishing Schools in Wilmington

## From Diary and Letters, 1867–1871

AMY MORRIS BRADLEY (1823–1904) *served as a nurse during the Civil War. After the war, she was asked to serve as a missionary worker for the American Unitarian Association (AUA) and the Soldiers' Memorial Society, founded by the AUA to honor Unitarian soldiers who had died fighting for the Union cause. Her assignment was to open and manage a mission in Wilmington, North Carolina. Since other missionary organizations had already established schools for former slaves and schools for white children had been destroyed or deserted, she determined that the greatest need was for a school for poor white children. For the next thirty-eight years she developed and ran several schools, including a teacher-training institute. Her diary entries and letters reveal the hard work and dedication required to sustain this effort as well as her commitment to raising a generation of white children who would respect people of all races.*

See the Biographical Sketch on pages 379–381.

### Diary, 4-14-1867

Now if I can only create an energetic spirit—a spirit that desires to lift itself out of this miserable state in which slavery has kept the poor white so long—in the children of these people, I shall feel that my mission is not in vain. If I can teach them how to become good citizens and good Christians—followers of the Savior—then I shall know that the angels of our Father have guarded and guided me aright! . . . Two years ago I was . . . in Virginia laboring among Soldiers who were fighting for our glorious Union. Now I am in Wilmington, NC, teaching the orphans of Rebel soldiers to become thorough Union men and women, so that Peace and Harmony may be restored when the rising generation may come into the field of action. God grant that war and its fearful influences may never again be known in our beloved land! Mine is a mission, a great power. If I work aright! Father, give me light!

✦ ✦ ✦

## Fundraising Appeal, 5-18-69

The undersigned, Committee of the Free Schools established in the City of Wilmington by Miss Amy M. Bradley, take pleasure in reporting the progress made and work done through her instrumentality, aided by benevolent Societies and individuals—for the information of such as have interested themselves in her work and with the hope as a continuance of favor, until such time as the State and City may be able to maintain a system of public schools adequate to the wants of the public. Miss Bradley arrived in this city on the 30th of December, 1866, commissioned by the Soldiers Memorial Society and the American Unitarian Association of Boston to establish free schools for white children. . . . We know the good done by them cannot be measured by numbers or stated by words. These children are nearly all of them in such circumstances as deprive them entirely of school privileges, being unable to attend pay schools and we had no other. They are poor white children, whose parents in many cases are ignorant, with little appreciation of the benefits of education. Many of the children were poorly clad and poorly fed. Their wants in this respect are supplied, and today the improved mental and physical condition of these pupils attests more eloquently than words to the good work done. Miss Bradley has established Sabbath Schools, obtained a Library, instructed the elder girls to sew and has given much valuable instruction to the young men whose occupations prevent their attendance at the daily school. We feel certain that of the pupils attending Miss Bradley's Schools, but a very small number of these could have attended any other; they would have been thrown upon the streets uncared for, growing up in idleness and crime—instead of this sad calamity we fearlessly assert that the schools are orderly, well disciplined, well instructed and give promise of a most gratifying future. Our State free schools are not yet established; it will require time, perhaps years, to place them upon a sure basis. The end of the present term of Miss Bradley's schools is near at hand. We feel it is an imperative necessity that her schools be maintained through the session of 1869 and 1870. In view of the importance of the work we have urged Miss Bradley to go out and call upon the charitable everywhere to come to our aid. We appeal to the good and liberal with confidence that an object so deserving will be sustained.

✦ ✦ ✦

5-20-1870

My dear Mrs. Leowe,

Your letter came this morning as a benediction from the Father comes sometimes in hours of trial. Verily, He will reward you for the kind words of sympathy which it contains. Next Sunday night Misters Kidder, Martin, Chadbourn and Heat meet at my room for a final decision. I have told them, first, a proper home must be provided for myself and teachers as it would be useless to attempt keeping up without it! I will tell you candidly, my good friend, that the pressure is almost unendurable. The County Commissioners have not decided to give me the position of County Examiner, as the gentlemen told you would be done, and the five ministers are hard at work sometimes preaching, and oftener visiting my parishioners giving them information that Miss Bradley does not believe in Christ. Mr. Ashley, I have been told, says Miss B. shall not have the position of Co. Ex. [County Examiner]. So you will perceive, Mrs. Leowe, that evidently I am scared on all sides. Don't you begin to think that Amy is a powerful woman? Sectarians—Politicians, Rebels and Carpetbaggers would drive her from their midst. The first because she is a Unitarian, the second because she minds her own business and they cannot make a fool of her. The Rebels because they fear her power every way as her influence extends in the City, and the Carpetbaggers because she is so popular. . . . God reigns yet and if I but trust Him—He will protect me and give me success.

✦ ✦ ✦

## Diary, 6-16-1870

My first Sunday School—sixty present. Since the close of last term, during vacation, the numbers of different churches have been working to induce the children to leave my Sunday School and the Episcopalians have started two free schools, one near the Hemenway, the other near the Union school, and taken quite a large number from the Union day school. Sectarianism and opposition to the free school system are the obstacles in our way this year. I cannot tell the end—I shall try to work faithfully as a disciple of the Savior should work, remembering He said Blessed are they who are persecuted for righteousness sake. May I endeavor to obey His teachings ever—He will triumph in the end. And though I may not live to see the day when a Unitarian Church will be established, I firmly believe the foundation has been laid.

✦ ✦ ✦

10-22-1870

My dear Mrs. Hemenway,
I have been so hard at work since my return that I have found little leisure for correspondence, except of a business character or that relating to my office as Examiner (County school examiner). And now I am only going to say my schools have opened finally, with my new corps of teachers—new organ in the Hemenway School—new song books and many new scholars. During my absence the Episcopalians started two new free schools (sectarian) and the Lutherans also started a sectarian school—of course they have drawn away all who were of their persuasion. Still we have in the Union School 137 and in the Hemenway 115—the Roman Catholic Bishop calls my schools "Godless Schools" and warns his people about allowing their children to attend them—Still they come. Our Sunday School opened with 60—the second Sunday over 100—so the prospect is cheering all.

✦ ✦ ✦

1-10-1871

To the Reverend Charles Leowe,
Although I have not written to you during the last three months I have not been idle—the schools opened 10-10-70 and the first quarter closed Dec. 22, 1870. I have sold the Hemenway school house to the county for $3000.00. My schools have been adopted by the Committee of Wilmington Township and were opened Jan. 2, 1871 as State Schools; the State will pay $1000 and the Peabody Fund $1000. . . . "Proud"? No—not a bit—but so happy to think that her [Amy's] efforts have been so wonderfully blest. . . . She feels truly that Our Father has given His angels charge over her—Our Sunday School is still a bright spot in the Mission, and numbers 76. The persecution on the part of the Churches is greater this year than any before. I cannot hinder it . . . but when I remember that my Savior said "Blessed are ye when men shall revile you and persecute you and say all manner of evil against you falsely, for my sake." God will care for all found to be faithful and Right must triumph! Our Father reigns.

✦ ✦ ✦

1-13-1871

My dear Mrs. Hemenway,
Your [letter] of the 23rd came to me Sunday morning Dec. 25th. A Christmas offering like those of the wise men of the East some eighteen

hundred years ago—to the blessed Savior! I cannot describe my feelings on reading that portion of your letter—"And dear Amy's dream of the upper room will be realized" [an addition to the school]. It was as if Our Father had accepted the efforts which had been made to elevate this people—as from those who had heard the sayings of His Son and tried to obey them—and the reward? One of His messengers proclaimed in the letter, Christmas morning!

## ✦ *Biographical Sketch*

**Born:** *September 12, 1823, East Vassalboro, Maine*

**Died:** *January 15, 1904, Wilmington, North Carolina, age 80*

**Buried:** *Oakdale Cemetery, Wilmington, North Carolina*

"'Tis the eve of my twenty-first birthday! Thus far, mine has not been a very eventful life."[42] So begins the first entry in the first extant diary of Amy Morris Bradley, dated September 12, 1844. Amy was one of four daughters. After her mother died when she was six, she lived with her sisters in Maine. She began a teaching career at fifteen. Amy Bradley's life was not to stay uneventful, however. During the next twenty years, she taught in Maine, Massachusetts, and South Carolina; lived in Central America for several years; and was the matron (head nurse) of a hospital for Union soldiers in Washington, D.C., during the Civil War.

Amy Morris Bradley's reputation as a capable administrator during the Civil War was known to several influential people associated with the American Unitarian Association (AUA) and the Soldiers' Memorial Society (SMS). In November 1866, she was asked to open and manage the mission in Wilmington, North Carolina. When Amy arrived in Wilmington in December, she planned to open an integrated school. However, she found other denominational mission organizations had already opened schools for former slaves. The antebellum schools for white children had been destroyed or deserted.

Given these circumstances, Amy decided the greatest service the SMS and AUA could provide was to establish schools for the poor white children of New Hanover County, many of whom were the sons and daughters of Confederate soldiers. On January 9, 1867, she opened the Dry Pond School House with just three students present. By January

15, fifty students were attending. Soon, Amy was teaching day and evening schools. Due to her success, the SMS soon hired Claribel Garrish of Dover, New Hampshire, to join Amy in the mission work.

Most Southerners, black and white, were devastated in the wake of slavery and the Civil War. Poverty, disease, and illiteracy were common in most parts of the South. In addition to providing education, this combined effort of the AUA and SMS tended to Southerners' immediate needs for food, clothing, and household items. Another major goal was to achieve racial fairness and harmony in the former Confederate States. Toward this goal, Amy organized a Ladies Benevolent Society. A forerunner of today's Department of Social Services, this group rendered educational, financial, vocational, and medical aid to people who were poor and those in prisons. Amy also founded the first Unitarian congregation and Sunday school in the region.

Not everyone in Wilmington was happy to have these Northerners in New Hanover County. On March 9, 1867, the *Wilmington Journal* spoke for a segment of the community in an article which read:

> *Equally obnoxious and pernicious is it to have Yankee teachers in our midst, forming the minds and shaping the instincts of our youth—alienating them, in fact, from the principles of their fathers, and sewing the seed of their poisonous doctrine upon the unfurrowed soil. The South has heretofore been free from the puritanical schisms and isms of New England, and we regret to see the slightest indication of the establishment here of a foothold by their societies professing the doctrines of Free Loveism, Communism, Universalism, Unitarianism, and all the multiplicity of evil teachings that corrupt society and overthrow religion.*[43]

Despite some local opposition, the mission grew. In order to accommodate all the families who wanted to send their children to SMS/AUA schools, Amy opened the Hemenway School in 1868 and the Pioneer School in 1869. Given this growth, the need to train local teachers soon became apparent. Amy's last major educational gift to New Hanover County was to establish a teacher-training institute, the Tileston School, in Wilmington in 1872.

Despite her successes, Amy's work had taken its toll on her. She reflected in her diary: "My work is finished in Wilmington, for one year at least, so say the authorities and I have to yield. . . . September 12, 1873 I was fifty years old, health gone. It seems hard, but I have overworked, and the result is a worn out body and brain."[44]

After a period of rest in the North and travel in Europe, Amy returned to Wilmington and resumed the principalship of Tileston in 1876. She presided over her schools until retiring in 1891 at age sixty-eight. Amy continued to live in a teacherage on the Tileston property until her death in 1904. The words "Amy Bradley, Our School Mother" are carved on her tombstone in Oakdale Cemetery in Wilmington, paying eternal honor to this woman who did so much for the cause of education.

*Biographical Sketch by* PHOEBE POLLITT

## ✦ Writings of Amy Morris Bradley

"Diaries." Bradley Papers, Perkins Library, University of North Carolina, Durham, NC.

## ✦ Biographical Resources

Brockett, L. P., and Mary C. Vaughan. *Woman's Work in the Civil War: A Record of Heroism, Patriotism and Patience.* Philadelphia: Zeigler, McCurdy, 1867; Reprinted as *Women at War.* Stamford, CT: Longmeadow Press, 1993.

Cashman, D. *Headstrong, the Biography of Amy Morris Bradley 1832–1904.* Wilmington, NC: Broadfoot, 1990.

Sellars, Dy. *Miss Amy Bradley.* Privately printed, 1970 (available at the New Hanover Historical Society, Wilmington, NC).

## ✦ Archives

The Amy Morris Bradley papers are located in the Special Collections Library, Duke University, Durham, North Carolina.

# My Work with the Freedman's School

## From Letters, 1870–1888

*After the Civil War, Unitarian* SALLIE HOLLEY (1818–1893) *joined her friend and life partner, Caroline Putnam, in founding a school for former slaves in Lottsburgh, Virginia. They devoted twenty years of their lives to developing this school, built with donations from Northern supporters and the labor of local African Americans. Because their work ostracized them from Southern white society, they maintained strong social connections with friends in the North. Holley's letters reveal her commitment to continuing the work of racial justice beyond ending slavery and her ongoing struggle to carry out this commitment to a specific group of people for whom she accepted responsibility.*

See the Biographical Sketch on pages 339–342.

### To Miss Putnam

Boston, Massachusetts, February 17, 1870

It seems to me a sad mistake to discontinue the organization of the Anti-Slavery Society or the *Standard*. The mere fact that the colored race has such friends and guardians is a strong defense and high tower of deliverance from more wrongs and insults. The American Nation is not good enough to be trusted with the care of the black race. The blacks still need their long-tried and faithful friends of the American Anti-Slavery Society, which is a very different individual from the Nation. To discontinue our earnest defense and guard will be the signal for a volley of abuse and scorn let loose upon their defenseless heads, which Mr. Phillips should still cover with his strong and loving wing.

Does not the simple fact of the existence of such a Society in the nation's midst, such a watchful, wise friend, save the poor black race from much neglect, contumely, and wrong? Does not such a fact guarantee a respect and aid they cannot afford to relinquish?

✦ ✦ ✦

## From a Printed Letter

Lottsburgh, Virginia, August 3, 1875

It is nearly seven years since we established this Freedmen's school in Virginia. We came from our great love and pity for the poor colored people. We are not the agents of any society, we have no salary, but give purely volunteer service. Nothing could be more bare, and blank, and hopeless than our material surroundings were to begin with. But upon a two-acre strip of this desolate land, exhausted a hundred years ago with miserable tobacco raising, we have succeeded in building a cheerful Teacher's Home and a spacious, airy, pleasant new schoolhouse. We have made flower borders, strawberry-beds, melon-patches, grape-arbors, and fruit trees to blossom and flourish, to the admiration of all around us. There are seven hundred colored people in this town. Our school keeps from Christmas to Christmas, without vacation, the year round. The tides of its blessings reach every soul. The all-absorbing business of the country is corn-raising. Most of our scholars are intermittents, for they have to work nearly all summer in these immense cornfields. But by keeping the doors of our school ever open, hundreds have learned to read and write. When we first came, they did not know a letter of the alphabet or the names of the days of the week; could not count on ten fingers or name the State they lived in. And the ignorance of these white Virginians, too, is appalling—a striking illustration of the truth of what the great Wilberforce said: "No man can put a chain around his brother's neck and God not put the other end of the chain about his own."—These slaveholders, in shutting out the light of knowledge from the blacks, also shrouded themselves in the gloom of wretched ignorance.

✦ ✦ ✦

As we have no salary ourselves, we can offer others none. So their aid must ever be a labor of love. One great compensation for living in Virginia is the climate, the most delightful I ever knew. The winters are short and mild. In summer we have a refreshing breeze from off Chesapeake Bay and Potomac River. We never know a hot night. "The Evening Wind" is to us all that Bryant sings it. After having been out to play upon the wild, blue waves, it comes to cool the twilight of our summer day.

We have no white society except when our Northern friends visit us. The poor colored people come to our door every day and almost every hour. Every want in life is theirs. We are glad to help clothe them from the boxes and barrels sent down from the North. In return they weed our gardens—cut our firewood, "tote" water from the spring, etc. Sometimes their joy at seeing us is highly amusing. One day an old colored lady came to see me. She seemed greatly satisfied with the interview; when she rose to take leave she seemed to think she ought to apologize for such exuberance of spirits, and she dropped a very low curtsey, saying, "Please 'scuse me ma'am, Ise so proud when I gets 'long side of de Norf population! I knowed you was Norf population as quick as I seen you."

✦ ✦ ✦

## To Robert Morville

Lottsburgh, Virginia, November 19, 1888

Twenty years ago this very month, out of pity, commiseration, and sorrow for the poverty and ignorance of these people, I came down to Virginia to lighten their burdens and kindle their souls to a better life. To-day I cannot but believe this school and its influences have accomplished a solid and enduring blessing, good for time and good for eternity. We have taught hundreds and hundreds to read and write and cipher, besides some knowledge of geography, history—especially that of the United States—the story of our own Government, the eloquent biography of its reformers and martyrs, saints, and apostles.

As ours is a free school—no tuition exacted—and we have no salary, it is only by such interested and largehearted people as yourself, who donate the means to keep up our work, that we can continue this mission year after year.

Some of our old pupils are now teaching public colored schools in this part of the state, earning, every month, twenty-five dollars. Many of our boys and girls are in service in Baltimore and New York. A few of the older scholars have married here and are now in homes of their own.

Not one of our colored men failed to vote the Republican ticket on the sixth of November last.

This month our school counts seventy scholars and the Sunday school adds a score or two more. Our mild November days favor many little young beginners coming, who for the first time have a slate and pencil to work out the profound mystery of writing their own names.

We now have two young ladies from Massachusetts, who are mobilizing this little army of students after the pattern of Boston. It is touching to see these little dark faces light up with new thought as expressively as the pale-complexioned Saxon children's ever do. Again and again I thank you for your generous donation.

✦ ✦ ✦

## To Miss Tyler

Lottsburgh, Virginia, October 23, 1890

We have a continual struggle to keep up the school and this mission in Virginia. We have to pinch and scrimp all the time. But this work is more and more of a success every year, and I want to persevere a few years longer. Then I shall be worn out in body and shall have to give it up,—though I think old age is the loveliest part of human life, infinitely beyond any youth I ever saw or knew.

# It Is Over

## Speech to Grand Army of the Republic, Memorial Day, Dansville, New York, 1879

CLARA BARTON (1821–1912), *raised in a Universalist family, became the first woman to work in the U.S. Patent Office. Known as "heroine of the battlefield" during the Civil War, she brought much-needed supplies to the front, cared for the wounded, and even cooked for the Union army. After the war, she helped search for missing soldiers and reunited many families. She later became one of the principle founders of the American Red Cross.*

*In this Memorial Day speech, delivered fourteen years after the Civil War finally ended, Clara Barton reflected on the war and its terrible cost. She stressed the importance of remembering the dead and declared that the work of women during the war should eliminate all doubts about their right to full citizenship.*

See the Biographical Sketch on pages 387–390.

Yes, it is over. The calls are answered, the marches are ended, the nation saved, and with the glory of gladness in her eyes, the shekinah of victory on her brow, she covers her tear-stained face, and with grief-bowed head, sits humbly down in the ashes of her woe to mourn her loss—to weep her dead.

✦ ✦ ✦

Decorated graves—white May blossoms of '79. Who lays a flower on those little lost graves today, who on the thousands and thousands like them all through the land?

"Far down by the yellow rivers,
  In their oozy graves they rot;
Strange vines, and strange flowers grow o'er them
  And their far homes know them not."

Thirteen thousand dead in one prison! Three hundred thousand dead in one war! Dead everywhere! On every battlefield they lie, in the crowded yards of every prison ground, in the dark ravines of the tangled forest, in the miry poison swamps where the slimy serpent crawls by day and the will o' the wisp dances vigils at night, "in the beds of the mighty rivers, under the waves of the salt sea," in the drifting sands of the desert islands; "on the lonely picket line and by the wayside, where the weary soldier laid down with his knapsack and his gun, and his march of life was ended." There on their strange beds they sleep, till the "morning of the great reveille."

They sleep, and you remember.

✦ ✦ ✦

American women, how proud I am of you; how proud I have always been since those days to have been a woman. Abraham Lincoln said that without the help of the women the rebellion could not have been put down nor the country saved. Since that time I have counted all women citizens.

## ✦ *Biographical Sketch*

**Born:** *December 25, 1821, North Oxford, Massachusetts*

**Died:** *April 12, 1912, Glen Echo, Maryland, age 90*

**Buried:** *North Cemetery, Oxford, Massachusetts*

Clara Barton was youngest, by several years, of the five children of Stephen and Sarah Stone Barton. Originally named Clarissa Harlowe, she became known simply as Clara. Her early schooling was provided by her siblings and parents, and she was later educated in local schools. She suffered greatly from shyness during her youth and was troubled with periods of depression in her adult life. Yet despite these difficulties, by the 1870s she had founded a progressive school for disadvantaged urban children, served as an effective Civil War activist for the wounded, and was on her way to founding the American Red Cross.

Clara Barton started her career as a teacher while still in her teens, and she was very successful. But realizing that she needed more education than that provided by her local school, she enrolled in 1850 at the Universalists' Liberal Institute in Clinton, New York. Her time at the institute was stimulating and profitable, and she formed lasting friendships there. Barton was to have a life-long attachment to Universalism.

While visiting a classmate in Bordentown, New Jersey, Barton noted the number of idle children on the streets. In response, she started the town's first free school, volunteering her services as a teacher. The school grew from six pupils to six hundred in one year, and Barton recruited friends to help with the teaching. In 1853, the townspeople built a fine new school and, predictably for the times, hired a young man to be the principal and Barton's superior. Her frustration caused her to lose her voice, a problem that would recur throughout her life. Barton resigned in protest and put her teaching career behind her, moving to Washington, D.C., in February 1854.

In Washington, she obtained a job copying secret documents in the U.S. Patent Office, reputedly the first woman to work there. Her fine copperplate handwriting, her integrity, and her ability to keep secrets allowed her to overcome male prejudice and saved her from being dismissed just because she was a woman.

When the fall of Fort Sumter signaled the beginning of the Civil War, Barton, only eight months short of her fortieth birthday, wrote, "I'm well and strong and young—young enough to go to the front. If I can't be a soldier, I'll help soldiers."[45] She intended to provide supplies for the woefully ill-equipped medical personnel and to do whatever was urgent, whether it was applying bandages or cutting through bureaucratic red tape. She had great success in her campaign to obtain supplies from citizens in the North. But it was Barton's special genius to marshall the goods and transport them to the strategic place at the right moment. She was calm under fire, good at improvising, and could literally cook for an army. Like many other women caring for the wounded in both the South and the North, she brought gentleness and pragmatism to her work. Her ability to ride any horse with or without a saddle allowed her to stay until the last of her charges were evacuated from dangerous positions.

At the war's end, Clara Barton accepted a request from President Lincoln to search for missing soldiers. After having done that successfully, she embarked on a lecture tour that covered over three hundred sites. However, the stress of doing so caused her to lose her voice again. A recuperative trip to Europe provided her with new acquaintances and new opportunity. She learned of the work of the International Red Cross and observed it firsthand, helping with refugees and the wounded of the Franco-Prussian War.

Upon her return to the United States in 1873, Barton took up the major challenge of her life—the long and difficult struggle to win the hearts and conscience of the American people to become a part of the Red Cross. She faced a disinterested government, a nation bent on material gains, and a number of rival relief organizations, which extended the arduous task for nearly ten years. But finally, in 1882, she was able to write, "We are today . . . not only in full accord with the International Treaty of Geneva, but are considered one of the strongest pledged nations within it."[46]

Barton's problems with illness and despair were in the past. She was sixty-one, and years of active organizational and administrative work lay ahead. Her vision of the Red Cross as an agency providing help in peacetime disasters as well as in war was ultimately implemented. This new worldwide direction made the Red Cross the humanitarian institution that has won the gratitude of people everywhere.

Clara Barton led the new American Red Cross until 1904, though not without dissent and difficulty. After being exonerated of a series of charges and accusations of mismanagement, she resigned. She spent her last years, suitably dignified with recognition and honor, at her home in Glen Echo, Maryland, often engaged in routine domestic tasks as well as correspondence and other writing. She died there of pneumonia on Good Friday, April 12, 1912.

*Biographical Sketch by* JANET BOWERING

## ✦ Writings of Clara Barton

*The Red Cross.* Washington, DC: American National Red Cross, 1898.
*The Story of My Childhood.* New Haven, CT: Francis Atwater, 1924.
*A Story of the Red Cross: Glimpses of Fieldwork.* New York: Appleton, 1934.

## ✦ Biographical Resources

Brockett, L. P., and Mary C. Vaughan. *Woman's Work in the Civil War: A Record of Heroism, Patriotism and Patience.* Philadelphia: Zeigler, McCurdy, 1867; Reprinted as *Women at War.* Stamford, CT: Longmeadow Press, 1993.
Burton, David Henry. *Clara Barton: In the Service of Humanity.* Westport, CT: Greenwood Press, 1995.
Epher, Percy Harold. *The Life of Clara Barton.* New York: Macmillan, 1915.

Fishwick, Marshall William. *Clara Barton.* Morristown, NJ: Silver Burdett, 1966.

Oates, Stephen B. *A Woman of Valor: Clara Barton and the Civil War.* New York: Free Press, 1994.

Pryor, Elizabeth Brown. *Clara Barton: Professional Angel.* Philadelphia: University of Pennsylvania, 1987.

Ross, Isabel. *Angel of the Battlefield: The Life of Clara Barton.* New York: Harper, 1956.

Williams, Blance Colton. *Clara Barton: Daughter of Destiny.* Philadephia: J. B. Lippincott, 1941.

# Two Gentlemen of Boston

## Story in *Opportunity,* January 1926

FLORIDA YATES RUFFIN RIDLEY (1861–1943), *born in Boston the year the Civil War began, exemplifies the postwar generation, which continued to fight prejudice and worked to establish justice for all people. A well-educated Unitarian, she joined her mother, Josephine St. Pierre Ruffin, in establishing and chronicling the African American women's club movement. Florida Ridley's work as a journalist, short-story writer, and historian helped people recognize both the contributions of African Americans to Massachusetts life and culture and the continued existence of prejudice in Boston, the city of the abolitionists. Her short story "Two Gentlemen of Boston" provided important insight into the life of an African American family in the early twentieth century in a primarily white, Northern neighborhood. With wit and sensitivity, she described the subtleties of racism and the response of one young boy to "deal it the 'knock out' blow."*

See the Biographical Sketch on pages 402–404.

Usually homeward journey from school was a dignified process; it was decidedly fitting that thirteen-year-old ranking scholars of the eighth grade graduating class should have occasion for serious conversation. The closing half-hour of school, devoted to the consideration of "Gems from History and Literature," always left Arthur and Morton in a contemplative mood and ready for serious debates on the lives and deeds of Napoleon and King Arthur and Marmion and all the others.

From my shaded seat on the porch I could see them from the time they left the school yard all the way up the tree-bordered street, and as I watched the straight, manly little figures, I took delight in imagining the course of their absorbed conversation and in observing the companionship which seemed to promise so much in the way of mutual benefit and pleasure.

They were so markedly different in outward characteristics! There was always something happening to separate Arthur's blouse and trousers or to snap his garters, and in the midst of the most intense discussion even of so vital a question as to "which you'd rather be the greatest orator in the world or the greatest football player in the world"—it was always necessary for him to make some clothing adjustment; to Arthur, clothes at best, were only necessary accompaniments, and at worst, impediments to the pursuit of happiness; but these lapses from dignity and solemnity in the daily conversational intercourse of the two boys were more than redeemed by Morton, who at thirteen years of age, reflected an indelible impress of three years' contact with foreign salons—the reaction of an only child, accompanying parents of social and literary aspirations in their old-world journeyings. No intriguing considerations of "Horatius at the Bridge" could be great enough to upset the poise with which Morton would at once readjust a garter which dared to begin a false move.

Today, however, the approach of the boys was distinctly out of form—it was not that there [were] attendants to the number of eight or ten; very often their debates were extended to include followers, who gave more life and vigor to the scene and the occasions by supplementing their points with side whacks to shrubbery and high leaps at curbs. I was used to this variation from the usual, but today the formation was entirely out of the ordinary, one striking feature being that the comrades walked apart and silent, the followers compact and in earnest conversation. As the group drew near, I was startled by the sudden realization of what the scene meant. Without doubt Morton, the dilletante, and Arthur, the dreamer, had disagreed, had gone so far in the disagreement as to fight and had had a bloody fight at that! There was no sign of belligerency in their attitudes; they walked quietly and apart; characteristically, Morton had restored his clothes to some order—his Norfolk jacket was tightly buttoned to hide the dust and mud left on the blouse from its contact with the earth, but his scratched and bleeding knuckles couldn't be hidden in his efforts to cover a blackening eye with a very grimy handkerchief. Arthur was frankly dishevelled and seemed utterly indifferent to the fact that he was without hat or tie; his face carried some slight intensification of its inclination toward griminess, which for racial reasons was never as readily discernible as upon his friend Morton; his lack of bruises and general bearing indicated quite clearly that he had been the victor in the fray.

I was rather sorry that I had disclosed myself by an involuntary move toward the approaching group, for it at once became evident to me that Morton had intended to pass without stopping (what more natural); on seeing me, however, he stopped and, with the courtesy that was so charming and so marked an attribute, he tried to drag his cap from his disfigured head. "It's all right, Mrs. Allen," he said, "*merely* a little difference of opinion," and replacing his cap, he swung down the road alone, leaving me to recover, before turning to those who were left, the poise which the approach and his speech had rather upset.

I turned to my son who was evidently suffering under the disadvantage of having a "smooth talker" get in his work first. "I'll fight anybody that attacks my good name," he volunteered, with great emphasis, and then with the evident desires to level up intellectually in the eyes of the cortege, "he who steals my purse," he began, and stopped short, whether from some budding sense of good taste or from the realization that a hint to his meaning was all that was necessary to his followers, it was not clear, but he began to edge toward the screen door in silence.

It was plain that he had decided to say no more—Morton had offered no explanation, made no accusations—attempted no defense should he, Arthur, take advantage of the absence of his companion to make out a case for himself. I read in a flash their code and was convinced that any explanation of the affair would have to come from others. I was clearly out of it, how force the confidence of these gentlemen? How was it possible to chide a man for defending his good name? How call to order men who are adjusting "a mere difference of opinion" in their own way? The dignity of thirteen years must be sustained, its obligations respected, its ethics acknowledged. I accepted my evident limitations and confined myself to a meek suggestion to Arthur that it would be well to "bathe his hands in sulphur-naphthal solution." The round-eyed caravan dissolved, as Arthur passed through the screen door. I settled myself with more complacency than I felt to think over the situation. It was all so unlooked for! The companionship had been so smooth, so complementary, and then too boys now-a-days were not in the habit of disfiguring each other as in the old days—what could have ruffled Arthur's good temper and thrown Morton out of his natural poise sufficiently to bring about a bloody row?

Only the day before, Morton had graciously accepted an invitation to stay to lunch, being largely influenced, I have no doubt, by the sight of the hot biscuits which were being taken from the oven as he came through the kitchen; he had conditioned his acceptance, however, upon the loan of a clean collar. We had sat at the table in the peace and contentment that accompany a satisfactory meal, eaten in congenial company. We had dallied over the meal even longer than it took the boys to demolish two large pans of biscuits with accompaniments; the day was warm and Morton was waiting for a telephone call. He began talking of France, his parents were going over again in a few weeks. "You ought to go to Paris, Art," he said. "Why couldn't you send him over to join us, Mrs. Allen?"" He tossed this remark casually, as he gracefully broke open another biscuit. "I'd rather go to Canada and raise silver foxes," Arthur had turned to say. "Well if you came to Paris you would see where Napoleon lived—will you excuse me Mrs. Allen if I see what time it is; you know I have my violin lesson at two o'clock."

After so large and cordial an invitation, and so intimate an afternoon, it gave me some surprise to find that the friends at their very next meeting had engaged in battle.

The growth of their intimacy had been of great interest to me. In the big American public schools, democracy is most truly demonstrated in the freedom with which children make and develop friendships; even the guiding hands of parents cannot always be effective here. Arthur and Morton were neighbors, but the fact of their difference in race kept the families apart as far as social contact is concerned; Arthur being the only one of his kind in the neighborhood, the children generally had played in and out of each other's houses. Not being dependent on close social contact, and entirely unconcerned about it, the limiting of social recognitions to courteous outdoor exchanges between us parents was entirely acceptable to me.

I had at first hesitated at encouraging the close companionship between Arthur and Morton which loomed inevitable. American standards of simplicity had been too strongly bred in me to accept wholeheartedly the polish with which Morton literally shone; still Arthur with his inherited indifference to externals could stand quite a little working upon, and I not only realized the benefits that Morton would bring Arthur but also those that Morton would receive; in fact, I felt sure Morton had the advantage. Morton was never, as Arthur, so absorbed in a book that he overlooked offering a chair when necessary, but, although I worried and grieved over my young barbarian, who would bring to the table along with his immaculate young guest a pair of hands that never should have left the cellar, yet I could not but warm to the fact that he had forgotten himself in seeing that his pets received their daily attention and on time.

In the days that followed the battle, I kept "a weather eye" open for any hint or suggestion that would enlighten me as to its cause. There was some estrangement; Morton's missionary zeal had received a setback; the two boys did not walk together on the homeward journey; neither were there any interchange of visits—it was impossible for them to keep entirely apart; their interests were too close—but there was a barrier, and as I watched them in the week that followed, I became convinced that the barrier had been raised principally from the outside.

The time was drawing near for Morton's family to start upon the European trip, and I was still in the dark. My enlightenment came suddenly, however.

I was at my kitchen window making out a batch of cookies that were great favorites with the young literati; two classmates of the duelling pair were lying upon the grass beneath the window and their voices came up to me. "Art and Mort had a fight last week, when you were absent." "Gee, I never saw Mort get into a fight." "Naw, he didn't want to this time, but Art made him!" "Who licked?" "O, Art." "Did he make his nose bleed?" "Yes, and blacked his eye!" "Gee, wish I'd been there," and, after a pause, "What'd they fight about?" "Well," with deliberation, "Mort attacked Art's good name. I'd fight for my good name, wouldn't you—Mort tried to talk out of it but all the fellas were on Art's side!"

"Sure, I'd fight for my good name—did he call him a liar?"

"Worse than that, he went to the guild and he had to report his good deed, and he said he had been 'elevating a little colored boy!'"

"'Elevating a little colored boy!' Gee, wish I'd been there—is that your dog—come on" and two pair of legs went scurrying across the lawn.

A little later, Morton came in with Arthur. "We're leaving tonight, Mrs. Allen, and I came to bid you good-bye and to wish you a very pleasant summer," and the little hand was extended with its usual grace. Our young Chesterfield sailed for Europe three days later, leaving more questions in my mind than before. What had been his reaction from the fight? In his relations with Arthur, how much had he been influenced by adults? What were the parents' reactions? Were they possibly those of the rebuffed missionaries who only feel pity that the heathen do not know what is good for them? As for my little son—I never discussed the matter with him; I felt he had shown himself wiser than I.

With instinctive wisdom, he had sensed a situation to which I was blind and had met that situation adequately. I had not recognized the "patronizing pose," neither would I have had the directness and courage to reduce it to its lowest terms and deal it the "knock out" blow.

✦ ✦ ✦

# The Negro in Boston

## Article in *Our Boston,* January 1927

FLORIDA YATES RUFFIN RIDLEY (1861–1943) *helped found the Society for the Collection of Negro Folklore in Boston in 1890. Years later, she founded and served as the first president of the Society of Descendants, Early New England Negroes, from 1931–1940. Her goal was to restore and preserve the early history of African American life and culture in New England as well as to demonstrate the complexities of race relations throughout the years.*

*This 1927 article from the journal* Our Boston, *published by the Women's Municipal League of Boston, documented the long history of African Americans in this Northern city. It revealed both the successes and the struggles of being black in a white-dominated social system, along with Florida Ridley's faith that African Americans would eventually be accorded their rightful place in society.*

See the Biographical Sketch on pages 402–404.

Negroes have been identified with the history of Boston almost from the earliest days of the town and even as slaves made outstanding contributions. Phyllis Wheatley adds a compelling note to Boston's claim to literary distinction; her poems were published in London in 1773. Copps Hill, The Granary, and King's Chapel Burying Ground all hold the bodies of Negroes who served in one way or another in American wars, beginning with the American Revolution.

Mt. Auburn Cemetery accepted the work of a colored girl sculptor done in the sixties, and a Boston publisher put out, in 1865, a medical work by a colored woman doctor of the city, and the list of incorporators of the Massachusetts State Federation of Clubs carries the name of a colored woman. This notation is simply an indication of the Negroes' relation to Boston life, but an elaboration in numbers and detail, interesting as it might prove, would not seem to have place here.

In 1830, there were over seventeen hundred Negroes in Boston. Today there are approximately nineteen thousand, the increase coming through emigration from southern states, particularly Virginia and Georgia, and latterly from the West Indian Islands. The 1830 Boston Negroes, and in fact all New England Negroes, carried Indian blood much oftener than is commonly supposed. This is recorded in family traditions, as are the many escapes from African ships into the woods along the New England coast and the subsequent intermarriages with Indians.

The year 1830 has been selected by Dr. Carter Woods, as standing halfway between the war for Independence and the war for the abolition of slavery, and as representing a certain stability of conditions which makes a good reckoning point; but from 1630 to the present day, the Negro has been persistently a definite part of Boston's population. A study of his life here in those 300 years, here in the home of Liberty, the breeding spot of liberal ideas and of abounding philanthropy, is one of great psychological interest and is absolutely necessary in understanding why, after 300 years of New England environment, the Negroes in Boston have today neither political nor industrial standing of any great rating. Such a review is impossible here, but one feature of the situation should be more generally known and accepted—that it is only comparatively recently that Boston Negroes have accepted the "develop race consciousness" program. For many years they, along with thousands of the best thinkers, believed that their highest duty was to discourage race peculiarities, to cultivate a common Americanism. It was thought by many that there was danger in fostering separate groups, with separate interests, and possible individual bitterness. On this theory, leading Negroes discouraged racial enterprises, some even going so far as to denounce Negro newspapers and churches and to do it from the highest motives! The years from 1830 to 1860 saw the development of small businesses among the middle classes, white and black, of Boston. On Brattle and Union Streets there were clothing shops, "new and second hand," run by Negroes; the city was dotted with well-patronized Negro barber shops; towards the end of the century began the growth of their competent catering service, all three then supported by white patronage. When, toward the end of the century, the "race pride" slogan began to be sounded, it was the death knell of the then-existing Negro businesses; the slogan worked in more ways than one. Negroes began concentrating on Negro enterprises; liberal whites withdrew patronage, thinking it a wise movement; antagonistic whites welcomed the opportunity to crowd out competition.

A big real estate business, headed by a Negro, started on the downgrade which ended in its complete collapse; the heads of the fine and dignified old catering establishments never got a chance in the readjustment that followed; white patronage fell off from the flourishing and profitable dressmaking and tailoring establishments; colored choir singers were not replaced in white churches; and most unexpected of all, the new movement had the effect of withdrawing the backing of white voters from colored political candidates.

It can be seen that, with all its possibilities, the immediate effects of "race consolidation" was a "setback."

It was at this time, about the beginning of the century, that a general movement of colored people from the West End, which had always been their home, to the South End began, and for the first time in the history of the Negro in Boston, a colored business section began to develop, this section being in the region between Northampton and Ruggles Streets, and chiefly on Tremont St.

The first efforts were small and meager. Boston's colored population increased very slowly; Boston's educational and cultural advantages, its liberal atmosphere, and unlimited philanthropy could not outbalance its lack of industrial opportunity for the Negro. Not only did desirable emigrants go elsewhere but ambitious natives did the same. Negro business development was handicapped by the small following which, under the new order, was confined to Negroes, and which had to compete with highly financed and organized business. In late years the population has been reinforced to a degree by immigration from the West Indian islands. In general, these men and women are progressive and present a new group—a group of those trained in the trades, who have had industrial opportunities which are denied Boston Negroes. This increase in numbers has given a slight stimulus to business activity, and today, there are in the business region cooperative banks, drug stores, printing and publishing companies (one of the two newspapers is published here), and restaurants which with general patronage would be able to expand. The stores dealing in necessities cannot hope to overcome their handicaps.

Although Boston's colored population spreads itself over many sections of the city and suburbs, it is in this South End district that it is most generally massed. It is here that there are established not only the businesses but most of the churches and social and welfare organizations. In the main it is a fair region, with great possibilities for comfort and even beauty; it has wide streets, good yards, and many trees; and with the many small houses, there are unusual opportunities to avoid flat life.

It is in this section—from Northampton to Ruggles Street—that most of the civic problems of the Negro present themselves. The region houses most of the poor and unfortunate of the race, although on its fringe, and often within its border live many leaders—doctors, ministers, lawyers, etc. Naturally it is the center of civic work, but it is only within the last seven or eight years that colored people themselves have taken a leading hand in the direction of work for social and civic improvement. Not that the district had been neglected; all the large agencies have sent their conscientious workers here, but the problems needed the interpretation of colored people. It was the expectation of the early colored Bostonians that it was only a question of time and preparation when colored workers would be included upon the staff of such agencies. Feeling the urge and need of more knowledge and direct contact with social conditions, and chafing at the delay in appointing colored workers, a most decided movement was made a half dozen years ago when the League of Women for Community Service and the Women's Service Club opened commodious houses on Massachusetts Ave., from which colored women could direct certain lines of social service work. This gave an impetus to work along this line, stimulated old organizations, and encouraged new ones. There is now in the district an efficient cooperative Committee, stabilizing and centralizing the work by bringing all the large social service groups into cooperation. This Committee includes not only the organizations named but also the Boston Urban League, the Robert Gould Shaw House, the Harriet Tubman House, St. Mark's Center, and the Cooper Settlement; it also has affiliation with the Minister's Interdenominational Alliance and the Bay State Pharmaceutical and Medical Association, all organizations directly concerning themselves with the problems of colored people and all save one directly under the executive control of Negroes.

The above named agencies are cooperating with general city agencies but concentrate on the particular problems which these fail in solving—the problems of housing, recreation, and industrial opportunity. The Cooperative Committee is using its combined force also on other problems, particularly that of health (the district carries a mortality record and it is petitioning for a Health Center), but it realizes that its great field of work is that of proper housing, adequate recreation, and opportunities for making a living.

Boston's determined attitude toward the Negro in industry seems to be that he, the Negro, should be self-sufficient and his labor called upon only for certain definitely unprogressive and badly remunerated jobs; Boston's attitude is one of pure color discrimination, and it draws a dead line. Patronizing Negro businesses is practically a thing of the past for white Boston; admitting the Negro into trades and general business is simply not done. As has been shown, the Negro's own group is not large or rich enough to make the needed openings for its own members. The result of these combined conditions is that Boston offers a greater industrial handicap to the Negro than any other city in the United States. This situation leads to great and grave problems; and both the community and the Negro suffer.

Ambitious youths who elect to stay in Boston and fight it out find some opportunities in real estate, but the majority of such youth turns to the professions, which offer a fair field; lawyers, doctors, dentists, ministers, teachers, and social workers successfully practice their professions, often with a mixed clientele.

Harvard Law School has been graduating colored lawyers since 1869, and degrees in medicine have been obtained since an earlier date than that. In 1867, two colored doctors were graduated from Harvard Medical School. Not only has there been a steady stream from the Harvard Dental School, but for several years a colored man was instructor in that School.

There are indications of good work being done by the young colored people of Boston in the arts. How far their efforts will be encouraged to flourish remains to be seen—unusual gifts force recognition. A great spiritual tenor will be heard, but whether the girl who at the age of nineteen gets her name included in Mr. O'Brien's "Best Short Stories"; and another whose poems are copied by the big dailies; and the boys and girls who are getting scholarships in the art schools; whether these will be able to get the financial encouragement without which even art must die is a question. The probable answer is that this promising material which might and should enrich Boston life will find its maturing in some more favorable environment than that of Boston, whose characteristic attitude is that of giving to Negroes opportunities along every line except that of making money.

This then is the great problem of Boston Negroes, one that is no nearer satisfactory solution than it was 25 years ago when the change in industrial conditions began. Of course there have been reactions; people always "find ways out;" but reactions from arbitrary and unnatural conditions never correct the condition which, in the end, must be corrected, if the best results are to be obtained.

The social and religious life of the Negroes is that of any other average American group, except that both are more accentuated, have more flavor, and apparently give more satisfaction than the same activities of the other groups. Considering the congestion of the district criminality is not marked (according to Judge Cabot "there are comparatively few juvenile delinquents and Negroes are not conspicuous in the crime wave"). Church buildings are many and large, with congregations and Sunday Schools that tax capacity. Besides the church influence upon social life, young people come under the influence of numerous Forums and Lyceums which deal directly with their own peculiar problems. Fraternal organizations, of course, will have influence. Not only do they carry large relief benefits and philanthropy, but they own the buildings which contain most of the halls used for social purposes.

A new and promising social force is the movement of the students. Negro sororities and fraternities are gathering all college students into a solid group united for the best interests of the race. This is a national movement which is already making a deep impression and creating a large enthusiasm; every city, every town is feeling the effect of its activities. It is a young movement as yet; it is preeminently the movement of the New Negro. It is most significant in that it shows that the ideal of Negro youth is education and that it is also his ideal to use that education for high purposes.

Three hundred years of residence would seem to give the Negro a reasonable claim to be known as American. Unlike other groups, which come under separate nationality classifications and considerations, the Negro (with the exception of those who come from the West Indies) has no spot outside of America which he can claim as "homeland." The Christian birth is his religious guide; the Constitution of the United States and the American flag receive his unswerving allegiance; his spiritual and emotional development have been influenced by his special relations to American life; but his ideals are those which obtain with the average American.

## ✦ *Biographical Sketch*

**Born:** *January 29, 1861, Boston, Massachusetts*
**Died:** *February 25, 1943, Toledo, Ohio, age 82*
**Buried:** *Forest Cemetery, Toledo, Ohio*

"It is surprising to find how definite a part of accepted technique has been the closing of eyes and ears and minds to phases of Negro life and character"[47] wrote Florida Ruffin Ridley, who demanded acknowledgment of and respect for the multiethnic heritage of the United States. According to her daughter, Constance, Florida Ridley was an exceptional example of the skill and dedication of the African American intellect and accomplishment.

Florida Yates Ruffin Ridley,[48] born and educated in Boston, Massachusetts, was one of four children born to Josephine St. Pierre, a Bostonian, and George L. Ruffin, a native of Richmond, Virginia. Immediately after their marriage, Florida's parents took up residence in Liverpool, England, in order to avoid rearing a family in a slave-owning country. They returned to the United States at the outbreak of the Civil War to join in the work of ending slavery.[49]

Florida's mother, Josephine, was an abolitionist, antilynching crusader, club leader, editor, feminist, orator, and suffragist. She was inducted into the National Women's Hall of Fame in Seneca Falls, New York, in 1995. Florida's father, George, graduated from Harvard Law School in 1869, the first African American to do so; he was also one of the first African Americans admitted to practice law in Boston and the first African American judge in the Northeast.

Florida graduated from the Boston Normal School and Boston Teachers College in 1880 and became the second African American teacher in the Boston Public Schools, teaching at the Grant School from 1880–1888. "In the American public schools," she wrote, "democracy is most truly demonstrated in the freedom with which children make and develop friendships, even guiding hands of parents cannot always be effective here."[50]

On October 13, 1888, Florida married Ulysses A. Ridley, who owned a tailoring establishment in downtown Boston. Phillips Brooks, rector of Trinity Episcopal Church, to which Mrs. Ruffin belonged, married the couple at the Ruffin residence. The Ridleys then moved to

Brookline, where they raised two children and became members of Second Unitarian Church.

Florida Ridley was one of the first advocates of black history and literature. She was particularly interested in preserving the history of African Americans in the Boston area. Thus, in 1890, she became one of the founders of the Society for the Collection of Negro Folklore. She later founded the Society of Descendants, Early New England Negroes, and was its president from 1931–1940. She compiled her family history, tracing its English, French, African, and Native American roots.

Florida often worked closely with her mother, Josephine St. Pierre Ruffin, particularly in the founding of women's clubs. In 1893, this mother/daughter team—joined by Maria Baldwin (also a Unitarian), the highly esteemed principal of the Agassiz School in Cambridge, Massachusetts—organized the Woman's Era Club. The club was open to all women, but African American women provided its leadership.

Mother and daughter went on to help organize the national black women's club movement, hosting a national conference in Boston in 1895. Out of this gathering came the founding of the National Federation of Afro-American Women, for which Florida Ridley served as recording secretary. When this group merged with the Colored Women's League the following year and became the National Association of Colored Women, she served as one of the editors (from 1896–1900) of its official journal, *Women's Era*—the first newspaper in the country to be owned, managed, and published by black women.[51]

As an active and involved woman, Florida Ridley was a strong advocate of women's right to vote. She was a member of the Brookline Equal Suffrage Association from 1894–1898. In 1924, she joined with other African American women to support John W. Davis, the Democratic candidate for president of the United States.

In 1920, Josephine and Florida joined Maria Baldwin in founding the League of Women for Community Service. Florida Ridley served as executive secretary for the league from 1920–1925. The club women raised enough funds for the purchase of Boston's Farwell Mansion for their clubhouse. The clubhouse—with its massive African mahogany stairways, marble mantels, gold leaf chandeliers, and huge mirrors from Venice—provided housing for women workers from the South and college students unable to obtain dormitory accommodations on local campuses. The clubhouse is now on the National Register of Historic Places.

Florida Ridley also loved to write and succeeded in having both her fiction and nonfiction published. Her stories and articles described African American life and race relations in New England, providing valuable insight into African American life in the North.

*Biographical Sketch by* MAUDE JENKINS

## ✦ Writings of Florida Yates Ruffin Ridley

"He Must Think It Out." *Saturday Evening Quill* 1 (June 1928): 5–8.
"Maria Peters." *Saturday Evening Quill* 2 (April 1929): 12–13.
"The Negro in Boston." *Our Boston* (January 1927): 15–20.
"Opportunities and Privileges of Club Life." *The Woman's Era* 23 (October–November 1896).
"Preface: Other Bostonians." *Saturday Evening Quill* 1 (June 1928): 54–56.
"Two Gentlemen of Boston." *Opportunity* 3 (January 1926): 12–13.

## ✦ Biographical Resources

Cash, Floris Barnett. "Florida Ruffin Ridley." In *Notable Black American Women,* edited by Jessie Carney Smith. Detroit: Gale Research, 1992–1996.
Dorman, Franklin A. *Twenty Families of Color in Massachusetts 1742–1998.* Boston: New England Historic Genealogical Society, 1998.
Jenkins, Maude T. "The History of the Black Woman's Club Movement in America." Ed.D. diss., Columbia University, New York, 1984.
Roses, Lorraine Elena, and Ruth Elizabeth Randolph. *Harlem Renaissance and Beyond.* New York: G. K. Hall, 1990.

# Reform in Religion

## by Helene Knox

✦ ✦ ✦

FROM THE PERIOD of the American Revolution to the 1930s, Universalist and Unitarian women made many innovative contributions to the religious thought and practice of their respective denominations. The two traditions of liberal Christianity—by affirming both human reasoning ability and proactive initiatives to work toward personal salvation and the betterment of this world—helped these women take themselves seriously as religious thinkers. Unlike many other women of their times, the Universalists and Unitarians represented here deeply believed they had the right, the ability, and even the obligation to use their full intelligence in freedom of thought. Moreover, they applied both reason and conviction in speaking up not only in personal letters and journals but also in more public forums, publishing stories, poems, and essays and even giving speeches.

What made these women's Christianity liberal was its acceptance of certain ideas from the Enlightenment, the Age of Reason. Indeed, as the historian Ernest Cassara points out in *Universalism in America:*

> *At the risk of oversimplification, it may be said that both Unitarianism and Universalism are compromises between Christianity (especially in its Calvinistic form) and Deism. . . . They did not reject the scriptures as did the Deists, but they insisted on subjecting them to the analysis of reason, eschewing the long-standing Christian attitude that what cannot be understood must be accepted on faith. . . . Finally, like the Deists they took a vastly more optimistic view of the nature of man.*[1]

These authors' acceptance of this world view and determination to apply it to the nature and condition of women, as well as men, empowered them to challenge the normally overwhelming social stigma against any woman who dared interfere in the public sphere, especially in matters so sacrosanct as religion, theology, and the church. Results varied. Some of their attempts were ignored or forgotten; others were attacked or ridiculed. But some eventually proved so persuasive that the ideas and the writers were regarded with respect. Those who were rejected were a loss to liberal religion. They are included here, however, to acknowledge that these women's efforts were worthy gifts to the Unitarian Universalist heritage, regardless of whether they were understood and accepted in their own times.

Each writer in this section tested the thought and practice of her religion against her sense of what both of those should be for the religion to be true to its own promises. From their life experiences, they were able to see that important things were missing from religious denominations constructed primarily by male ministers, however devout and well meaning. These women understood that the overweening patriarchy that saturated their society was also embedded in their churches, contradicting the ideals of freedom, reason, tolerance, hope, and social justice preached therein. Usually in a spirit of loving admonition, they presented their alternative ideas, programs, and incarnations of reform.

Each of the two historical denominations was a social world largely unto itself. According to the stereotype, the urbane, Harvard-educated Bostonian Unitarians simply did not pay much attention to the Universalists, whom they regarded as uneducated and of a lower class than themselves. For their part, the Universalists, who preached the gospel of universal love, preferred not to associate with the reserved, unemotional Unitarians, who seemed such elitist snobs. This social division alone was enough to postpone the merger of the two liberal denominations for a century and a half. The two groups did not start to feel comfortable in each other's company until the second half of the nineteenth century, when the Reverend Thomas Starr King, for example, born a Universalist, was accepted by the Unitarians to serve in their ministry[2] and the "prophetic sisterhood" of Universalist and Unitarian women ministers supported each other's efforts to serve new churches in the Midwest, then a frontier.[3]

There were also noteworthy theological distinctions between the two denominations, as evidenced by the different subjects they discussed and debated in the late eighteenth and early nineteenth centuries. David Robinson, in his denominational history *The Unitarians and the Universalists,* summarizes these differences:

> *Universalism was more closely identified with one theological position, universal salvation. Although that was a radical position for the time, in many other respects Universalism was more conservative theologically, insisting on biblical authority and the centrality of Jesus and his atonement. The drift of Unitarianism, however, was away from biblicism and the divinity of Jesus, and throughout the nineteenth century the denomination was in the leadership of the general Protestant movement away from orthodoxy and toward modernism.*[4]

This Unitarian tendency toward modernism was evident in the disruptive Transcendentalist movement, later in the Western Unitarian Conference "Unity" group and the Free Religious Association, and ultimately in the acceptance of the agnostic and humanist stance within Unitarianism.

The texts in this section on religious reform are presented chronologically but in two parts. Those by Universalist writers are first because the history of their church as an officially independent denomination begins earlier, in 1793. The American Unitarian Association was founded only in 1825, by chance the same year that the British Unitarian denomination was instituted. Thus, the writings of Unitarian women appear in the second part of this section.

## Universalism

One of the earliest contributors to Universalism as an American movement was a European mystical pietist, Dr. George De Benneville, who came to Pennsylvania in 1741.[5] The Reverend John Murray is generally credited with the major role in institutionalizing Universalism, however. Upon arriving in the United States from England in 1770, he found to his amazement that many other believers in universal salvation were already settled in what are now the northeastern states.

These people were converts from many denominations but especially the Baptist church.[6]

Although John Murray was a passionate preacher and an effective denominational leader, he was not an original thinker in theology. His feminist wife, however, was. Thus, Judith Sargent Murray is the earliest Universalist writer presented here. Both Murrays were trinitarian, liberal Christians whose primary theological heresy was the refusal to believe in hell, the eternal torture for sinful souls after death. The Murrays reasoned that God, more loving than any human father, would not decree or permit even one of his children to suffer such a cruel fate, no matter what he or she had done. Instead, God had devised a way to save them all, through the sacrifice of Jesus Christ. This great blessing was sufficient cause for gratitude, joy, optimism, love for God and all humanity, and willing obedience to God's just and moral laws, which brought order and happiness to human lives. With these beliefs as a foundation, Judith Sargent Murray wrote and published many documents eloquently defending the human dignity and rights of women against the entrenched misogyny of the time, particularly that justified by appealing to biblical texts. Staying within the patriarchal premises of her opponents, she used a devastating reasoning ability and an elegant, formal writing style to argue her points.

A more personal kind of writing included here is that of Lucy Barns, a young trinitarian Universalist whose letters and poems about her faith were so treasured by their recipients that they were gathered and published after her untimely death in 1809. She seems not to have been influenced by the Reverend Hosea Ballou's momentous work *A Treatise on Atonement* (1805), evaluated by Robinson as "the most significant theological work in the history of American Universalism."[7] This book shifted the conceptual base of Universalism from Calvinist theology to Enlightenment rationality and persuaded many thousands of Universalists to shift their Christology from trinitarian (i.e., God in three persons—the Father, the Son, and the Holy Ghost) to unitarian (i.e., Jesus as a son of God but not God the Son, identical in substance with God the Father).

Because Universalism offered a joyful, loving, liberal Christianity mercifully free of the terrors of hell, it grew in popularity (in spite of its blatant heresy) to become the sixth-largest denomination in the United States, as one statistician reported in 1832.[8] Membership declined later in the nineteenth century, after Universalism had won its point theologically and the mainstream Protestant denominations had become sufficiently liberal that people were willing to stay in them instead of converting. The industrialization and urbanization of the Unites States at that time also depopulated many rural Universalist churches.

In 1833, the Universalists started publishing a periodical, *The Ladies' Repository,* which appealed to women and offered them the opportunity to share their thoughts in writing. The article in this section by Lucia Fidelia Wooley Gillette appeared there in 1870, proclaiming the spiritual strength the Universalist faith gave women so that they could continue to minister as lay people to everyone around them—even the men who thought of religion as "weak superstitions" best left to women. It is difficult to overlook the contradiction that professional clergy had always been men. The Universalists can be justly proud of the fact that they were the first Christians in the modern world to accept women officially into the fellowship of their ministry. There is some debate, however, as to which woman was the first minister. Olympia Brown, who was ordained by the St. Lawrence Association of Universalists in Malone, New York, in June 1863, has been generally accepted as the first woman ordained by full denominational authority. But this honor may belong to Lydia Ann Moulton Jenkins, who was apparently granted a letter of fellowship in 1858 and ordained with her husband by the Ontario Association of Universalists in Geneva, New York, in 1860.[9]

The remaining Universalist selections were all written by women ministers. The Reverend Augusta Jane Chapin, during the 1870 centennial celebration of John Murray's arrival in the United States, praised Universalist women for the many kinds of work they had been able to do and allowed to do for their church. In 1893, at the World's Parliament of Religions in Chicago, she praised women preachers and scholars of all denominations for being ready to participate fully in the momentous international, interfaith gathering. The Reverend Phebe Ann Coffin Hanaford made several contributions to Elizabeth Cady Stanton's radical project of publishing *The Woman's Bible* (1895, 1898), a collection of commentaries by women about biblical passages involving women.

In 1914, the Reverend Florence Kollock Crooker, president of the Women's Ministerial Conference of Boston, published an article in a local newspaper answering again the age-old question "Why Women Ministers?" She noted that in the churches of many denominations, the increased emphasis on meeting people's social and educational needs, as well as their spiritual ones, made the special gifts and skills of women ministers ever more valuable. The final Universalist text is a sermon preached by the Reverend Olympia Brown a few days after women, including herself, first voted in 1920. Looking back over the decades, she acknowledged that many of the gates that had once barred women from their rights had finally given way.

## Unitarianism

By the early nineteenth century, the American Unitarians had emerged from a long but nearly imperceptible drift within one wing of the Massachusetts Standing Order, the established (i.e., tax-supported) churches of the Congregationalist descendants of the Calvinist Puritans. As liberals, the Unitarians prized the use of reason in interpreting scripture and valued upright character over agreement in the details of doctrine. They were not rebels, only freer thinkers. But acrimonious public accusations from the orthodox, questioning both their doctrine and their character, forced them to defend their position and split off in 1819, when the Reverend William Ellery Channing delivered his celebrated Baltimore sermon, "Unitarian Christianity." Given congregational polity, each congregation in the denomination had to determine whether to declare itself Unitarian, and about one-third of them did.

The rationalism and doctrinal tolerance of the early liberal Congregationalists are well incarnated in the selections from the lifework of independent scholar Hannah Adams. Her circle of like-minded friends made it possible for her to compile what would now be considered an objective encyclopedia of all the religious beliefs then known. The impulse to improve the Unitarian churches is evident in the next selection, from the British Unitarian widely known as *Mrs. Barbauld,* who in 1824 offered many suggestions to counteract the "gloom" and "tremendous horrors of the calvinistic faith" that still characterized British Unitarian churches at the time.

Instrumental in the reform of Unitarian churches in the midwest was a group of women ministers known as the *Iowa Sisterhood,* who served churches in Iowa and the surrounding states from 1880–1910.

These women revived dying churches and built new ones, developing the practice of so-called full-service churches, which provided a wide range of social, educational, and service opportunities. Those churches are described by the Reverend Celia Parker Woolley in her 1889 address "The Ideal Unitarian Church." The ministers of the Iowa Sisterhood promoted social justice by inspiring their parishoners to go out into the world and work for the common good. The Reverend Mary Safford, in a popular sermon delivered to various congregations, "Obedience to the Heavenly Vision," issued such a call to action. The Iowa Sisterhood also challenged the denomination to put their values into action, as in the 1897 address by the Reverend Caroline Bartlett Crane to the Western Unitarian Conference, "The Church and Poverty." These women were critical of Unitarian and other churches for their shortcomings and lack of vision, as indicated by the Reverend Marie Jenney Howe in her article "The Young Women and the Church."[10] They were determined that Unitarian churches put their professed principles into practice through concrete actions promoting social reform.

Interspersed among these calls to action are several about the value of having good examples to follow on the spiritual path. At the 1893 World Parliament of Religions, the Reverend Marian Murdoch called attention to St. Paul's co-worker Phebe as a model to justify and encourage women's work in the church, and Fannie Barrier Williams prophesied that improving race relations in the United States would depend on how well white Christians could practice the ideals of love and compassion found in their own religion. Queen Victoria of Great Britain was praised upon the occasion of her Diamond Jubilee in Ednah Dow Cheney's 1897 address for her public example of benign virtue in a woman of authority. In her feminist theology *His Religion and Hers,* published in 1923, Charlotte Perkins Gilman imagined what a religion coming solely out of women's experience and values would be like. And in 1936, Aurelia Henry Reinhardt reaffirmed in a report for the denomination the power of Unitarian public worship for vitalizing faith and courage and providing the wellspring of the spirit of life in people's lives.

As these writings from Universalist and Unitarian women clearly demonstrate, women participated in the formation and development of theology, ethics, and practical applications of faith from the earliest days of their respective religious movements. They challenged men to apply their principles not only to themselves but also to women, to people of color, and to those forced to live in poverty. Women challenged men's religious organizations to make structural changes based on women's ways of thinking, knowing, and acting. In the process, they envisioned and helped bring into being a more inclusive and just Unitarian Universalism.

JUDITH SARGENT STEVENS [MURRAY]

# Theological Reflections

## From Letters, 1777–1778

*In 1984, Unitarian Universalist minister Gordon Gibson discovered a treasure trove of* JUDITH SARGENT STEVENS [MURRAY'S] (1751–1820) *letterbooks, in which she copied her correspondence from 1765–1818. Marianne Dunlop, an independent scholar who transcribed the first one hundred of these letters, described the theology expressed therein: "In an age in which orthodox moral discourse placed women in the same category as lunatics and children, Judith reversed the theological arguments of "the Fall" used to oppress womankind by adding impeccable logic to patriarchal premises and thereby proving that women are the moral, spiritual and rational equals of men."*[11]

*The two selections that follow are examples of the revolutionary thinking of Judith Sargent Stevens [Murray]. In a 1777 letter to her cousin Catherine Goldthwaite, Judith allowed her "pen to wander" in "levity," playing with the Adam and Eve myth as seen in Milton's* Paradise Lost. *She asked, "What woman wouldn't rather talk to an angel than to her husband?" In 1780, however, she undertook the "arduous tasks of endeavouring to combat that vulgar error," the assumed superiority of the male sex, in a well-argued letter to her friend Universalist minister Samuel Parker of Portsmouth, New Hampshire. She later printed it publicly after her essay "On the Equality of the Sexes" (see pages 149–155). In another letter, written in 1778, Judith showed her Universalist world view, simply explained, as a gift of guidance for her youngest brother, Fitz William, then age nine.*

See the Biographical Sketch on pages 156–159.

Gloucester, June 6, 1777

To [Miss Goldthwaite],

Do you not know, my dear Girl, that every Man is not an Adam? "True" you reply "but surely they ought to be unto their own Eves." Perhaps they ought—yet I must confess that my aspiring soul would hang with more rapturous delight upon the seraphic sounds which we may suppose . . . would be attained by an angel of the Most High than upon the tongue of any mortal, however dignified, however beloved, and this, I imagine, would more especially be my choice, were my senses divested of that density, in which our first Parents, by their heedless wandering, hath so wrapped them about. It is a delicate hint of the inferiority of our sex, given by Milton in the passage to which you refer—but had it been more severely described, it could no more than unveil the opinion of the Poet, as it respects the inferiority of our sex but by no means established his hypothesis—The compliment upon the conjugal affection of our general Mother, is, I confess, pretty—Yet, by your leave, most profound Bard, it appears to me, we may justly question her taste. I fancy, however, that the next to divine female, recently passing from the hands of her creating God, considering the many opportunities which she hourly enjoyed with her Cara Sposa would, upon the occasion supposed by Milton, [have] preferred the conversation of the bright Celestial—But be this as it may, surely, if indeed she were so humble, so meek, so docile her good Man might easily have resisted her blandishments when she so successfully solicited leave to quit his protecting side, and thus the wretched progeny of this deluded pair had been saved from the countless evils which have encompassed them—That Eve was indeed the weaker Vessel, I boldly take upon me to deny—Nay, it should seem she was abundantly the stronger vessel since all the deep laid Art, of the most subtle fiend that inhabited the infernal regions, was requisite to draw her from his allegiance, while Adam was overcome by the influence of the softer passions, merely by his attachment to a female—a fallen female—in whose cheek "Distemper flushing glowed" and you know, my dear, that by resisting the aberrating Fair One, Adam would have given the highest proof of manly firmness—But forgive this levity, it is seldom I allow my pen thus to wander. . . .

✦ ✦ ✦

Gloucester, July 18, 1778

To my youngest Brother,

It was with much pleasure I observed the other afternoon, in my charming child, the dawnings of a disposition, sweetly social—you recollect the conversation which passed in the chamber of our dear Parents—It was during your late illness and it originated upon my proposing to return home—you wished, while the tear glittered in your fine eye, that the apartments of our Parents were sufficiently numerous, and spacious, to accommodate all you loved, that so you might never be separated from your kindred. Our dear Mother replied, "Well, My dear, we shall eventually occupy such a house"—your rejoinder greatly affected me—These were your words—"I am not sure Mama, that I shall live in this large house—for I cannot think the wicked go to heaven—you would be angry with me were I to lie, and is not God better than you Mama? Besides, I have heard that the wicked will stay in hell, for a season, although they may go to the good place at last, and," you added, while the tears streamed upon your lovely cheek, "I am sure, I am very unhappy." This declaration from a child, not yet ten years of age, surprised and grieved me. I regret that the glooms of religion are already obtruded upon your opening Mind. I impute these melancholy, these traditionary suggestions, to the premature instructions of the Bigot, to whom the rudiments of your education hath been entrusted—your Reason, yet in its infancy, is too tender to struggle with such deep and important speculations as those by which you are at present exercised. It is astonishing that a Mind good and unadulterated as I had hoped yours was, should already have given birth to a doubt of the certainty [of] our inhabiting that house, not made with hands, to which our Mother alluded, and in which there are many Mansions—but, I repeat, ideas so erroneous, can [only] have been derived from your Preceptor. It is, my dear Boy, an irrefragible truth that Almighty God, the supreme Architect of Heaven and Earth, is your Father—God is the Father of all Mankind, and He wills that, where He is, His children should also be. Now you are to know that there is no power superior to that which is inherent in the Omnipotent Creator of the Universe, that none can withstand His sovereign decrees, and that He must, of necessity, obtain His every desire. Yet you must not conceive that the wicked will inherit heaven. No, my young Objector nothing which defileth can enter the pure and spotless dwellings of Paradise. But the children of Men stripped of every imperfection shall be clothed in undeviating Rectitude, when they shall become denizens of Elysium. Moreover the King your Father hath so declared an aversion from every thing opposite to holiness that he positively assures us if any of his children should keep his whole clean, offending in the whole course of their lives, but in one point, He will, nevertheless, for that one false step, esteem them, impure, and rank them with the number of Transgressors! Now no Man can live, in this imperfect state, without being guilty of that, which, in the sight of God, is sin. For, my dear, the very heavens which appear to us as perfect are not clean before Him. God is possessed of such infinite dignity, and such spotless equity, that even His holy angels will while in His presence, and as He chose the Race of Man should live before Him, it became necessary that every individual should possess an immaculate Nature, to [effectuate] which, God Himself bowed the Heavens and came down among us, and by a connection, which we cannot fully comprehend but which nevertheless, as intimate as your head and members, endowed us with the essence of every virtue accosted as ours, the mark of His every action, and thus wrought [for] us, a righteousness which is altogether complete, which assemblage of perfection is in [plain] language denominated a Robe—a Robe suited to the various exigencies of every human Being—and after presenting our Nature to the eye of Divinity pure and without blemish, the Savior of a lost World died to make atonement for our crimes and upon the third day arose from the dead, greatly Triumphant, re-entered the realms of blessedness, where He now reigns, constantly making intercessions for us and calling us home as best suits our interest and His Glory. Now we do not suppose the Transgressor will be assigned his place in local fire for any specified length of time, for in that case, all must be tormented—since we have all broken the Laws of our God—but we know that although the Robe of salvation covers all, yet all do not possess a consciousness that they are thus enwrapped about—and hence, a conviction of sin renders them miserable—They remain in the dark. The literal signification of the term Hell is Darkness. But the Father of our spirit positively assures us that every eye shall see the Redeemer and that Jesus Christ is the true light, which enlighteneth every Man who cometh into the World. . . . As you believe that all Mankind are the offspring of God, you will not injure those with whom you expect to spend an eternity, in the presence of Him, at whose right hand are pleasures for evermore—On the contrary, you will always as far as you are able, seek to relieve the necessities of your fellow creatures—and, in proportion as you thus act—in proportion as you follow after virtue, you will obtain the esteem and love of all who know you. . . .

✦ ✦ ✦

# Universalist Catechism

## From *Some Deductions from the System Promulgated in the Page of Divine Revelation,* 1782

JUDITH SARGENT STEVENS [MURRAY] (1751–1820), *who later married John Murray—one of the principal founders of institutionalized American Universalism—was among the first women in the United States to publish statements in support of women's rights (1790). She was also one of the earliest American writers to articulate Universalist beliefs. In the preface to her privately printed catechism for children (1782), she anticipated being attacked for "arrogance, heresy, licentiousness, &c" and tried to defuse it by saying she and her friends just wanted to be good Christian mothers. With this evidence of such conditions for women who dared to publish even private devotional writings, it is remarkable that any primary texts exist for this book.*

See the Biographical Sketch on pages 156–159.

When a female steps without the line which custom hath circumscribed, she naturally becomes an object of speculation: the public eye is very incompatible with the native modesty in which our sex are inshrined: the genial voice of applause is requisite to bring us into life, while censure will damp the timid ardor, and either extinguish or confine it to the breast, where, however, it may glow with holy energy. Such the sentiments of my soul a very obvious question arises, from whence proceeds my temerity, in thus appearing before a tribunal, where it is more than probable, I shall be accused of arrogance, heresy, licentiousness &c. &c. &c? To candid minds only I wish to address myself: Such (the feelings of my own heart assures me) will accept my apology, by way of answer to the above query. If there is any thing that ought for a moment to take place of those exquisite sensations, which we boastingly term peculiarly feminine, it is surely a sacred attention to those interests that are crowned with immortality. Whatever is *essential* to the ethereal spark which animates these transient tenements will exist when the distinction of male and female shall be forever absorbed. This thought stimulating hath banished that diffidence excited by reflections merely sexual. Yet I do not mean to insinuate that natural inferiority incapacitates the female world for any effort or progress of genius. Admitting, however, the door of science barred to us, the path of truth notwithstanding in the page of *revelation* lies open before us. There, clothed with becoming reverence, we may freely expatiate; it is this walk, aspiring as *I am;* I have presumed with trembling awe to enter: my situation in some sort impelled the arduous attempt. Many obvious questions naturally arise in the minds of children as reason begins to bud, and the young idea perforce will shoot. Placed at the head of a little family, I beheld the minds of my young folks hastening towards maturity; while I was sedulous in preparing them to act their parts upon the inferior stage of this globe, I could not but be solicitous to give them proper conceptions of the Father of their spirits, their expectations from, and obligations to, the parent Deity. To that code digested by the Assembly of Divines, *conscience* would not let me apply: happily enlightened, through the instrumentality of a favored servant of the Most High, I wished to convey the instruction I had received from the fountain of life, through this channel, to those under my care; retention would not, at all times, favor me with a harmony of ideas; as a help to my memory, I sat about methodizing the evangelical views of facted texts, which had often been inculcated upon my mind. When they appeared in the form of the following essay, they were shown to several friends, who signified their approbation by earnestly requesting copies; to avoid the trouble of furnishing which, I have consented it should be published: and this I the rather do, as I am sensible those who wish not to peruse are still at liberty; and those who do are hereby presented with an opportunity. I am well aware, there are many places in which I might have expatiated; but it was my study to curtail, recollecting it was for the emolument of children the piece was intended. Insignificant, however, as it may appear, the cry of heterodoxy may raise it up an adversary; but as I presume not to enter the lists as a disputant, should such an event take place, I shall endeavor to soothe myself, by retiring into my own family and observing the salubrious effects springing from the principles disclosed by genuine, by divine Philanthropy.

✦ ✦ ✦

**Q.** And yet I have been told that this atonement was made but for a few. Do the scriptures say it was satisfactory for the sins of all mankind?

**A.** The sacred writings abound with positive declarations to this effect; the consolatory promise was made to Adam, before he was expelled from the garden of God: it was afterwards repeated to many, chosen for that purpose. God said to Abraham, *in thee shall all the families of the earth be blessed,* and again, *in thy seed shall all the nations of the earth be blessed.* He is called by God the desire of all nations. The apostle to the Galations informs us, *that this seed was Christ.* We are told that MESSIAH *should be cut off, but not for himself.* The *restitution of all things* is preached by the mouth of all God's holy Prophets, ever since the world began. It is said *that he died for all—that he was raised again for our justification;* and an apostle thus expresses himself, *he is the propitiation for our sins; and not for ours only, but also for the sins of the whole world!* We are called upon, to *behold the Lamb of God, who* *taketh away the sin of the world.* Indeed the pages of revelation are filled with this important truth, which speaks *glory to God in the highest, peace upon earth, and goodwill towards men.*

Q. But are there not many persons who proclaim eternal damnation to the greater part of mankind?

A. There are many; the veil is yet upon the hearts of the multitude, their eyes are holden that they cannot see the things which belong to their peace; but observe my child, *there are things which do belong to their peace;* now as the day cometh, when everything that is hid shall be made manifest, for *every eye shall see,* they shall all behold him who is their peace, for thus runs the text, *they shall all know me from the least of them unto the greatest of them,* and to *know God is life eternal.*

Q. Yet doth not the word of God speak of an elect?

A. It does of the *elect precious,* which is Jesus.

Q. Are there not other Ideas given of election? Doth not Paul say, *the election hath obtained it, and the rest were blinded?*

A. It cannot be denied that the doctrine of election is to be found in the word of God, even respecting individuals, but then this is never to the exclusion of the rest of the world from future felicity—even when Paul says, *the election hath obtained it,* &c. in the very same chapter he adds, with respect to those who were blinded, *I say then, have they stumbled that they should fall? God forbid:* he declares *that all Israel shall be saved* and that for this purpose, *God hath concluded them all in unbelief.*

Q. How ought I to conceive of election according to the scriptures?

A. I think the most consistent idea is that there is [sic] a few chosen out of the world to bear witness to the truth, with whom the secret of the Lord is, from the rest, for wise reasons, it is hid; but there is a day coming when the veil shall be taken from all hearts, and in the mountain of the Lord of hosts, the feast of fat things shall be made for all people.

# In Defense of Universalism

## *Letters, Poems, and Reflections,* 1807–1809

LUCY BARNS (1780–1809), *daughter of a Universalist minister, died at age twenty-nine after a life-long affliction with asthma. From her sickbed, she wrote many letters and verses so highly esteemed for the comfort and conviction of the truth of Universalism they offered that a collection of them was soon gathered and printed as* The Female Christian: Letters and Poems Principally on Friendship and Religion. *The reprint edition of 1904 quotes the Reverend Hosea Ballou, the most prominent Universalist minister after John Murray, as having said "that the first writings by a female on Universalism published in the United States were written by Miss Lucy Barns."*[12] *Ballou respected the Murrays and probably would have given Judith Sargent Murray*[13] *credit for publishing her catechism (1782) first, if he had known of it. These writings by the frail, bedridden Lucy Barns*[14] *are notable for their energy of faith, hope, and love inspired by her trinitarian Universalist religion.*

See the Biographical Sketch on pages 428–430.

### To a Friend Professing Faith in the Gospel

March 21, 1807

Respected Friend and Sister,
Your very agreeable favor came as welcome as unexpected to my hand and prompted by friendship, rather than the flattering idea of answering your expectations, I readily comply with your request.

✦ ✦ ✦

Tho' sickness blast my hopes of earthly bliss,
And sinks my feeble frame extremely low
My soul on high ascends and mounts the throne,
Where joys unnumbered from our Maker flow.

O boundless love! O fount of every joy,
That does the fainting hearts of mortals cheer;
Which mild descends like refreshing shower,
And blesses all within this lowly sphere.

Who that beholds such goodness in a God,
Whose mighty power is equally as great,
Can say in woe he'll leave our precious soul,
To mourn eternally its wretched state?

Who that believe millions of human souls
Must groan and pine in endless misery,
(Tho' of his own eternal bliss secure)
Has enter'd into rest and liberty?

Tho' rest like this thousands may satisfy;
My soul such happiness disdains to love,
And fain would share that mis'ry with my friends,
Than share without them, endless bliss above.

✦ ✦ ✦

Is heaven a place of unalloyed bliss,
Then all mankind must have a seat therein,
Be blest in Christ, and reconcil'd to God,
And not one soul be doom'd to endless pain.

I have not a convenient opportunity to furnish you with any more of my ideas at present, but if kind Providence will permit, I will ere long, write to you again. Rejoicing that you are blest with a view of the gospel light; and praying that this blessing may ever be continued to you, which is the best consolation and support amidst the various trying scenes of this life, and the surest foundation of our hopes of immortal happiness in the next; I close this letter and bid you adieu for the present.

Your Friend and Sister,
*Lucy Barns*

✦ ✦ ✦

May 23d, 1807

Respected Friend,
I have received your very welcome letter, bearing date 24th of April. Your generous approbation of mine of the 21st of March was very gratifying; but however much you were pleased with the ideas exhibited in mine, you may be assured that yours were no less pleasing to me. . . .

You judged right concerning those few lines of poetry you transcribed in your letter; for I never before saw them. I think them very excellent; the ideas contained in them most sensibly touched my mind, and occasioned the following reflections, which I have endeavored to put into metre, as you profess to be fond of my poetical scribblings.

Could we, by works, salvation gain,
We should not then a Savior need,
Thus God, to free our souls from pain,
Would ne'er have doom'd his Son to bleed.

When once men sought eternal life,
By strictly keeping God's command;
Alas, how vain was all their strife,
For by his law not one could stand.

✦ ✦ ✦

I greatly rejoice to hear of your returning health and hope this great blessing may long be continued to you. I have no hopes of ever enjoying it myself. The asthmatic complaint, which I have ever been afflicted with from infancy, has very much impaired my constitution and therefore renders vain all hopes of relief. It has been my lot to pass through many distressing scenes of sickness, yet it has pleased God, who watches over his tender offspring with kind paternal care, to favor me with that fortitude of mind, by which I have been enabled, for the most part, to endure my afflictions with patience. I think I have great cause to rejoice that he has not suffered me to sink, totally depressed, beneath the weight of my calamity; and that while I entertain an idea that my stay is short in this present world, it has given me a firm and consolatory hope that I shall find a better and more glorious one in the next.

I should be exceeding happy to receive another letter from you, tho' 'tis uncertain whether I shall be able to write to you again very soon if ever. That you may ever remain steadfast in the faith, and continue to walk in the "straight and narrow way," is the fervent prayer of your affectionate friend and sister,

*Lucy Barns*

✦ ✦ ✦

## To a Friend Who Could Not Believe in the Final Holiness and Happiness of All Mankind

April, 1809

Honored madam,

I must humbly beg your pardon for thus presuming to address you by letter; which I hope and trust your goodness will not fail to grant. As I have not a convenient opportunity for verbal conversation and have long wished to converse with you on a subject of the greatest importance that ever occupied the human mind: which is the doctrine of endless misery. As we do not understand the scriptures alike, and being too feeble to write lengthy, I shall not attempt to quote much scripture but will endeavor to take reason for my guide. I suppose it appears very strange and mysterious to you that I should believe all mankind, without exceptions, are equally the objects of God's tender love and kind paternal care; and that they will continue to share the unbounded love and goodness of their Maker as long as they have an existence, when the scriptures abound with so many bitter curses and severe judgments (which you suppose implies a state of endless misery) pronounced against the wicked and disobedient part of mankind. But when you are truly informed of my reasons for believing thus, possibly you may entertain a more favorable opinion of my sentiments.

The scriptures declare that God is love, that he is a good Being, that he is no respecter of persons, but is good to all, and that his tender mercies are over all his works; and that he has all power in his own hand and worketh all things after the counsel of his own will. All nature, likewise, proclaims aloud this blessed and divine truth and also bespeaks his wisdom to be infinite. He kindly condescends to call us his children and permits us to address him by the endearing appellation of Father! Is it possible that so good, so kind and loving a Father can punish his tender and beloved offspring with the most exquisite misery, to the endless ages of eternity for their disobedience to him, and even for the most trivial faults? Can it be supposed that so wise and powerful a Being is under the necessity of punishing with endless misery, in order to secure the peace and honor of his government? If the infinite goodness of our heavenly Father is sufficient to inspire him with a wish to make all his children perfectly and eternally holy and happy, is not his infinite wisdom sufficient to form a plan for the completion of his wishes? and his infinite power sufficient to execute that divine purpose:

that he might not be eternally disappointed and frustrated in so benevolent a wish? I suppose you are now ready to tell me it is time to drop this subject and to speak of the justice, severity and vengeance of our heavenly Father; and to consider his right and his power to punish us as he pleases. But I do not dispute his power nor his right to punish the disobedient with endless misery, but it is his will or inclination to do it which I dispute. Neither do I think there is a single passage of scripture which represents a state of endless woe. Though I know the chastisements of the Almighty are very severe, "vengeance is mine, I will repay," saith the Lord, and the curses and judgments threatened against the disobedient are great indeed—therefore it behooves us all to be good and obedient children lest they fall upon us. For I think it is not inconsistent with the divine love of our universal Parent to chastise the transgressors of his law sufficiently to subdue their hardened hearts and stubborn will and to subject them to his holy government. But can justice require more? Certainly not. But on the contrary, whatever punishment is inflicted, after they are completely humbled and subdued, in my estimation, may justly be termed cruelty and revenge. And shall we presume to impute those hateful passions to the Almighty, which he himself has taught us to despise in each other and which we absolutely abhor even in a savage, who is not contented merely with the death of his enemy but puts him to the most cruel death which malice and revenge can possibly invent, roasting him alive in such a moderate manner as to prolong his life and misery to the utmost extent of his power? But what is that when compared with endless misery? You are a mother and doubtless possessed of as tender feelings as ever warmed the heart of a parent: and was I to say that you could with pleasure behold your children punished with such exquisite misery, even for an age, you would think that I was either beside myself or entertained a most unjust opinion of you. But if you could not endure the sight but for one age, what reason have you to suppose that the tenderest, most loving and best of fathers could endure the shocking scene to endless ages of eternity? But perhaps you will say that those who are to suffer thus are not the offspring of God but the children of the devil. I know the wicked on account of their disobedience are called the children of the wicked one; but if they are so in reality, we cannot reasonably expect they will be punished so severely for being too obedient to their father Satan, as children are in duty bound to honor and obey their parents, even by a command from the great Eternal himself. It is said that sinners justly merit endless punishment, because they sin against an infinite law, &c. But surely the Almighty knew, before he created them, that they would sin against him and likewise what punishment they would merit. Then was it an act of love, justice, or wisdom in him to force into existence millions of human beings, whom he absolutely knew would transgress his law, and thereby incur his displeasure, and necessitate him to make them eternally miserable? Had he provided a thousand Saviors for them and given them a thousand times better chance to escape that dreadful place of misery, what would it avail them? For is it possible for them to avoid what the all wise God absolutely knows will happen to them? Now if a Being of infinite love, justice, and tender mercy and a kind benevolent father could do such a thing, is it possible for us to conceive what a being of infinite hatred and revenge would do? It is believed by many that the parable of the rich man and Lazarus is a real description of heaven and hell and that it evidently sets forth the misery of those who are damned, roasting in flames of fire and begging for water, even for one drop to mitigate their sufferings, whilst those in heaven must incessantly behold their distress and hear their groans and cries and dreadful lamentations to all eternity without having the power to relieve them. If that is really the case, what person is there who possesses any real love for his fellow creatures, who would not much rather be annihilated, and be as though he never had been, than go to such a heaven?

> What would avail to me the joy of heaven,
> and all the splendor of the golden coast:
> If I must know millions of human souls
> In mis'ry groan, and are forever lost.

But I cannot believe that such a place of misery ever did exist, or ever will, until there is a change wrought in the Almighty himself and we behold the great wheel of nature rolling backwards! We are told that when we go to heaven, we shall there behold the justice of God so plain in the eternal condemnation of the ungodly that we shall finally rejoice in their misery; if so, why are not the saints here on earth now rejoicing in it, who profess to be born of the spirit of the ever living and true God, and to know their Master's will, and to obey it? And who fancy they have met with all the change they ever shall see, as they suppose no one will ever be changed after death, but surely they must meet with a much greater change than they ever yet have experienced, to *endure* much more to behold with pleasure, such a shocking scene to all eternity. Various indeed are all the arguments which might be produced from scripture, as well as reason, to prove the final restitution of all mankind to their former state of purity and holiness, since the Lord hath spoken of it by the mouth of all his holy Prophets since the world began. But I have already written more than I intended. I therefore conclude, and am, with the utmost respect and esteem,

Your Friend and very Humble Servant,
*Lucy Barns*

✦ ✦ ✦

## Reply to a Satyrical Poem Entitled "Universalism Indeed"

*"Answer a fool not according to his folly, lest thou also be like unto him."*

—Proverbs 36:4

Behold the vanity of foolishness,
Which are in these vain arguments express'd,
That children must their parents disregard,
Because from them they hope a rich reward.

How inconsistent would it be to say
I will my parents mock and disobey;
Because to me they have been kind and good,
Providing for me clothing, wealth and food.

Tho' I am e'er so wicked, base and vile,
They will be merciful and on me smile;
Therefore I'll cause them all the grief indeed,
That can from base ingratitude proceed.

✦ ✦ ✦

The mighty God who reigns in heav'n above,
Displays to all his tenderness and love,
He wills that we his precepts should obey,
Walk in a righteous and a godly way.

’Tis not for his, but for our sake alone,
He has commanded us all vice to shun,
To bless our foes and love our enemies,
And walk in paths of virtue, truth and peace.

Whenever we his precepts disobey,
A heavy judgment follows us straightaway;
Thus peace we can’t enjoy while in this land,
For sin and misery go hand in hand.

Then shall we strive on earth to build a hell,
Go on in vice, against our God rebel?
Be chain’d to Satan, strife and misery,
Because in future worlds we shall be free?

✦ ✦ ✦

Wherein, vain man, are you more just than those
Who riot, drink, game, cheat and fight their foes,
Since you confess, all this you’d freely do,
Were you not fearful vengeance would pursue.

✦ ✦ ✦

O may we from a better motive keep,
God’s holy law and walk in mildness meek;
May purest love for God our actions sway,
Guide us to serve him, and his will obey.

✦ ✦ ✦

## Serious Reflections

Amongst the various evils mankind are doomed to experience in this life, I think the doctrine of endless misery may be considered as not the least. For when I behold the disagreeable effects it has on the minds of those who believe it, I cannot but view it as a great evil. It produces a great distrust of the mercies of God; doubts, fears, and misery; and on the minds of some, it brings that horror, anguish, and despair, which totally deprives them of reason and which has caused many to put an end to their own wretched lives.

✦ ✦ ✦

I have been led more particularly to these observations, on reading a pamphlet entitled "Universal Salvation Refuted," wherein the Author has asserted that "Universalism diminishes or takes away the motive to virtue and religion." If the motive is fear of endless misery, 'tis true it takes that away. But if Universalists are led by that spirit of love, which casteth out fear, to the exercise of charity, benevolence, and goodwill towards their fellow creatures and to serve, praise, and adore their beneficent Creator, why need they fear a state of endless misery, allowing it is true?

## ✦ *Biographical Sketch*

**Born:** *March 6, 1780, Jaffrey, New Hampshire*

**Died:** *August 29, 1809, Poland, Maine, age 29*

Lucy Barns is a luminous example of both women and men of independent mind and spirit. She charted her personal and religious course by her own God-given light. She did not believe any opinion or conviction was right simply because it had always been held or attested to by others, no matter what their credentials. She needed to think things through for herself.

Lucy Barns was the eldest of three daughters born in New Hampshire to the Reverend Thomas Barnes.[15] Her father moved to Poland, Maine, at the dawning of the Second Great Awakening and in the midst of a hot Methodist revival there. With utmost simplicity and sincerity, she attended the meetings and listened to the dire warnings and comforting blandishments of the preacher. "If their explanations are correct," she affirmed, "and this singular work is sanctioned by divine authority, I am perfectly willing and ready to embrace Methodism."[16] She then turned to her Bible and carefully read verse by verse, again and again the proof texts of the revivalist. Her struggle to understand Jesus led her to the same convictions reached by Caleb Rich and Hosea Ballou.

Once convinced, Lucy felt she should openly declare her faith in Universalism. Her arguments—carefully studied and written in a crisp, clear, logical style—brought many, including her own father and sisters, to the same convictions. Wherever people would listen, she spoke of her heartfelt belief in God's universal love for humankind. Her life and forceful faith were so exemplary that even theological opponents spoke of her as a "real Christian."[17] But with the revival spirit at its peak, they could hardly leave her in her "errors and sins," as the popular theology labeled Universalist beliefs such as hers. Friends and neighbors besieged nineteen-year-old Lucy with arguments and dire tales of the harsh fate that waited unbelievers. She was not turned from her convictions, however. She read not only the Bible but all of the pamphlets opponents handed her.

When Lucy examined the censorious religious spirit of those who harassed her, she noted its "disagreeable effects . . . on the minds of those who believe it." She declared, "I cannot but believe it as a great evil. It produces a great distrust of the mercies of God; doubts, fears and misery; and on the minds of some, it brings that horror, anguish and despair, which totally deprives them of reason and which has caused many to put an end to their own wretched lives."[18] These were not idle observations, for the revival spirit of that era of interdenominational, no-holds-barred religious warfare brought casualties. The sensational press was full of examples of vulnerable and troubled people being driven to madness and death. Orthodoxy saw such despair as the tragic outcome that awaited many who would not accept the ordinances of proper faith.

Lucy saw orthodox faith quite differently. She maintained that a bitter and bleak faith—which offered little love, grace, or hope—needed to threaten its followers with dire eternal warnings to command good behavior. She rejected the notion of faith as burdensome, reasoning that people of every faith and none experience hard and hurtful times. She found the joy and hope of her own life in the easy yoke and light burden of Christ.[19]

This was no naive affirmation. Lucy had a very serious and disabling asthma, which affected her every day of her adult life and ultimately ended that life at age twenty-nine. But rather than give in to the depression and fear that consumed many severe asthmatics, she poured her energy into spreading her faith and joy. "I have," she said, "a good home, and am blessed with the kindest of parents . . . [and] an affectionate brother and two kind sisters."[20]

Following her death, some of Lucy Barns's letters, papers, poems, and sermons were gathered into a small volume titled *The Female Christian.* It circulated through Universalist circles for many years and was eventually reprinted early in the twentieth century as *Familiar Letters and Poems, Principally on Friendship and Religion,* by Lucinda W. "Aunty" Brown in Akron, Ohio. It was the first recorded work by an American woman in defense of Universalism.

*Biographical Sketch by* DAVID JOHNSON

## ✦ Writings of Lucy Barns

*Familiar Letters and Poems, Principally on Friendship and Religion.* Edited by Lucinda W. Brown. Akron, OH: Aunty Brown, 1904. Orig. pub. as *The Female Christian.* c. 1809.

## ✦ Biographical Resource

Hanson, Eliza Rice. *Our Women Workers.* Chicago: Star and Covenant, 1882.

LUCIA FIDELIA WOOLEY GILLETTE

# Woman and Religion

## Article in *The Ladies' Repository,* November 1870

LUCIA FIDELIA WOOLEY GILLETTE (1827–1905) *was the daughter of a Universalist minister and grew up to become one herself. When she came to the Bloomfield, Ontario, Universalist Church from Rochester, Minnesota, in 1888, she was probably the first ordained woman of any denomination in the province. Her ministry was highly successful. She published several books as well as many articles and poems in national and denominational newspapers and magazines.*

*The brief article that follows is reprinted in full from the Universalist journal* The Ladies' Repository. *Gillette points out that while society leaves what men consider the "weak superstitions" of religion to women, women are so sustained by their faith that they minister spiritually to men when life overcomes them. Gillette cannot imagine how "an irreligious woman" can find the strength to live without such faith.*

See the Biographical Sketch on pages 433–435.

I do not wonder that man, in his great physical strength—his activity of life—his hurry of business—his building of steamships, and railroads, and telegraphs—his leveling of mountains, and filling up of valleys—his hewing down of forests, and his building of cities out of the wilderness,—I do not wonder, I say, that he manifests so little of the religious elements in his nature. Seeing mostly through the intellect, and not having grown wise enough to believe that the strongest reasons are the reasons of the heart, he works mostly with his brain and hand and leaves the richer graces of the spirit to cluster around the character of some saintly mother, or sister, or wife, or friend. And while he finds little leisure, and perhaps less inclination, to listen to the voice of the Christ, this woman whom he trusts, and whom he vainly thinks has a brain far inferior to his own, walks in spirit along the shore of Galilee, and upon the banks of the Jordan, and up the Mount of Olives, gathering those beautiful blossoms of love and faith that always adorn the noblest and the sweetest womanhood; and he never suspects in his work of self-help, and his work of helping others also, where she has been or what she has gained, until, it may be, storms burst upon the waters, and his ships go down one after another under the heaving billows, or his railroad stock sinks; or his telegraphic shares become entangled, or his bank goes with a crash, or his business breaks up—or a mortgage takes away his farm, or death casts his bleak pall over his hearthstone, or sadder and darker still, some great temptation assails him, and he goes down before it like a mighty ship with broken masts and shattered sail, without pilot or anchor. Then he learns, strangely and slowly and yet surely, how firm and strong those "weak superstitions," as he called them, make the frail hand of that faithful friend to lift him up. Then he sees how that little hand, with nothing in it but the love of the infinite Father, leads him not back where he dwelt before—but over beyond it, to a manhood that is full of the spirit that suffered in Gethsemane and went away in the breathing of love from Calvary.

I do not wonder that man should wander so long before he finds the one best thing of earth,—but that woman, whose life is always lived through the affections, be it only that boundless affection that loves and consequently sorrows and suffers with all the world—that she can go firmly forward in the winding path that "leads to our Father's door," without a religious trust that never falters, is to me, an inexplainable mystery. That she can go forward at all fills me with astonishment. All around her are so many fearful and unseen forces, that can in a moment dash her happiness to atoms, that I keep asking myself "What will she do then?" If in days of Joy, she has only gratitude for human tenderness, what will she do when human tenderness turns away or is withdrawn? In the hour of trial, of struggle, and perhaps defeat, how can she order her life without the helpful spirit of the blessed command to "Forgive those who injure her, and to pray for those who despitefully use her, and persecute her"? Seeing never the helping FACE that smiles upon Mary and Martha—hearing never the tender, encouraging VOICE that spoke for the beauty and growth of woman's soul—feeling never the throb of that great LOVE that reaches down from heaven, where can she cling in her weakness? Upon whom can she lean in her weariness? Where can she turn in her utter desolation? When some dear one, for whom she would give every earthly hope, goes away into the darkness of death, and she cannot follow, in her unshrinking faith, to evergreen islands, and to a love and joy greater than her wish could bestow, how does the blood still course healthily through her veins or her heart continue its pulsations? Why does her reason not go out in eternal night? Verily, an irreligious woman is an unfathomable mystery.

## ✦ *Biographical Sketch*

**Born:** *April 8, 1827, Nelson Flats, New York*

**Died:** *October 14, 1905, Standing Stone, Pennsylvania, age 78*

Lucia Fidelia Wooley[21] was born in Nelson Flats, New York, the first of seven children of Edward Mott Woolley and his wife Laura, daughter of Luther and Chloe Smith. The Woolleys were Quaker farmers, but young Edward joined the Presbyterian church at age twenty and became active in theological debates with local Universalists. He was finally won over and began to sing at Universalist services until, surprised by an invitation to preach one Sunday, he proved himself an able speaker. Moving to East Hamilton in 1834, he began preaching regularly in nearby Universalist churches.[22]

His daughter was to follow in his footsteps. "Naturally slight and fragile," Fidelia (as she was called) wrote of herself:

> *I preferred, even in childhood, a seat by his side, in his shop, listening to the sound of his hammer, or the sweet cheerful tones of his voice in song, to the sports of my little companions. And a few years later, when he exchanged the labor of the hands for the toil of the study, I was always on my low seat at his feet when I could be released from the care of my young brothers and sisters, and he would explain to my childish mind the sentences he read or wrote and teach me, in his own glowing words, those great and beautiful truths that must yet redeem the world.*[23]

Fidelia's mother was in poor health and, in 1836, was seriously injuried in a carriage accident. Then in 1837, when Fidelia was ten, her father almost died of tuberculosis. He was forced to give up his posts in Hamilton and Lebanon and move his family to his parents' farm in Cazenovia, New York. However, he continued to preach in nearby towns. Too weak to drive the carriage, he entrusted the reins to small Fidelia, who rode beside him, holding an umbrella to shield him from the summer sun.[24]

As a girl, Fidelia was "slender, intellectual looking, . . . very fair, with large, friendly blue eyes, . . . light brown, wavy hair, put back plainly but loosely."[25] Her father noticed that she always carried pencil and paper with her, though she composed poetry by first singing the lines. Overhearing one of her songs, her father insisted on sending the poem to the Reverend Dolphus Skinner, editor of the *Universalist Mag-*

*azine and Advocate;* it appeared under the pen name of *Lyra,* which she continued to use until her marriage. Fidelia's father also mentioned her writing to Horace Greeley and suggested that she send something to his *New York Tribune.* Just fourteen and uncertain of the quality of her work, she put it to the test by sending a poem, "Prairie Grave," under the name of *Carrie Russell.* She was surprised when it soon appeared in the *Tribune,* and her father instantly recognized it as hers. Both he and Horace Greeley continued to encourage her, and she became a regular contributor to newspapers and magazines.

In 1847, the family moved to Michigan for Mr. Woolley's health; he preached in Pontiac, Farmington, Livonia, and Waterford until his death in 1853.[26] Fidelia's parents were divorced after her mother deserted the family, and her father remarried late in life. The children were said to have supported him throughout the domestic difficulties.

On December 23, 1850, Fidelia married Hortson Gillette in Bloomfield, Michigan, and continued to live within two miles of her father's home. A daughter, Florence, born the following October, became a close companion and assisted her mother with her writing.[27] In 1870, after her daughter was grown, Fidelia began her speaking career with a lecture on the popular writer Fanny Forrester, whose home was near Fidelia's birthplace. The lecture was praised in the local newspaper as "full of poetic fire and tender pathos."[28] Other lectures followed on topics such as "Boys and Girls" and "Margaret Fuller," as well as temperance and women's suffrage, delivered to a wide variety of audiences.

After much urging on the part of her friends, Fidelia was licensed to preach by the Michigan Universalist Convention in 1873. She was so well known and respected in the church that she could have been ordained at once. However, remembering her father's example and taking the ministerial call most seriously, she continued to work as a licentiate for four years. Finally sure that she was ready, she agreed to be ordained in Manchester, Michigan, in 1877. "God bless the Universalist ministry of Michigan for its full, free grace to women," she wrote.[29] She was to find some audiences less welcoming than the Universalists. In Hillsdale, Michigan, she found all the church doors closed against her and was forced to hold her meeting in the courthouse.[30]

Both before and after her ordination, Fidelia served as state missionary for Michigan and as an agent for the Northwestern Universalist Publishing House. Preferring missionary work to an established pastorate, she traveled extensively and preached in New Sharon and Knoxville, Iowa, and in Concordia and Delphos, Kansas. She often gave three sermons on a Sunday in addition to preaching and lecturing on secular topics during the week.

Fidelia maintained a home in Rochester, Michigan, until 1901, when she spent a year in Pomona, California, before moving to the Universalist home in Philadelphia. She died in 1905 while visiting a former parish in Pennsylvania. A life-long friend wrote this of her:

> *Circumstances combined to push her into public labor, and I know that only because love stood behind her and held her up, did she have strength to fight out successfully the battle, with her tender sensitiveness, that enabled her to make her first attempt before the public. While she is still successful, I must believe the place native to her, and in which she is happiest, and where her life manifests its greatest beauty, is with her books and her pen.*[31]

*Biographical Sketch by* JOAN W. GOODWIN

## ✦ Writings of Lucia Fidelia Wooley Gillette

*Editorial and Other Waifs.* n.p., 1889.
*Memoir of Rev. Edward Mott Woolley.* Boston: Abel Tomkins, 1855.
*Pebbles from Shore.* n.p., 1879.

## ✦ Biographical Resources

Hanson, Eliza Rice. *Our Woman Workers.* Chicago: Star and Covenant, 1882.
Hitchings, Catherine F. *Universalist and Unitarian Women Ministers* (Journal of the Universalist Historical Society) 10 (1975): 72–73.
Obituary of Lucia Fidelia Woolley Gillette. *Universalist Leader,* 25 September 1905.
Kapp, Max A. "Edward Mott Woolley." *Universalist Leader* 74 (August 1957).

## ✦ Archives

Scrapbook. Helen D. Lyman papers. Schlesinger Library, Radcliffe College, Cambridge, Massachusetts.

AUGUSTA JANE CHAPIN

# Women's Work in the Church

## From Address at Universalist Centennial, Gloucester, Massachusetts, September 1870

*The year 1870 was the centennial of John Murray's arrival in the United States, and Universalists came from far and wide to celebrate this occasion at his and the denomination's first church, in Gloucester, Massachusetts. On this gala occasion, the Reverend* AUGUSTA JANE CHAPIN (1836–1905) *praised Universalist women, the work they had done for the church, and the gospel principle of equality of male and female that had raised woman from "barbarism" to "the proud position that she occupies today." Though American women were gaining better access to higher education, they still lacked the right to vote and endured legal and economic conditions that left them few viable options other than to marry and be treated as the property of their husbands. But this was a congratulatory anniversary party, so "the glass" was seen as "half full."*

See the Biographical Sketch on pages 437–440.

I am delighted with the work that woman has found it her privilege and within the scope of her ability to do during this jubilee year of our great church. It is peculiarly fitting that women should work with enthusiasm and with zeal, that we may bless the church with our abundant offerings upon the altar of truth. Universalism, the great principles of truth that we received with the doctrine of the great redemption, has made woman what she is; has done for woman all that has brought her up from the realms of barbarism, I might say, to the proud position that she occupies today. The great principle of the Gospel, "There is neither male nor female, bond nor free, Jew nor Gentile, but ye are all one in Christ Jesus," is the uplifting principle that has blessed the world and brought woman up from the condition of slavery and ignorance to her present position; when multitudes of our best schools open wide their doors to her, and when she no longer ignorantly looks on that which is happening under the sun but looks over the world with comprehensive views and sees with clear vision all that is done. She sees what the errors of the past have been; she sees what the needs of the future are, and she sees that one of the great needs of the time is that she shall come up to a perfect comprehension of her own influence in the world.

We have been told what that influence is. Let us, sisters, use our influence in its widest power. To this gospel of the great salvation which has done so much for us, which comforts every mother's heart in the hour of bereavement, which blesses the world, and comes to every needy heart with a benediction which to the poor, the suffering, and the tempted is just what they need, and which glorifies all the blessings of our prosperous hours—to this faith, it is peculiarly proper that woman should consecrate herself.

When, after long struggles, through ways of darkness, with no one to counsel, a child in a school of an opposite faith, I came to a knowledge of this great truth, it seemed to me a foregone conclusion that there could be nothing in this world for me to do but to give my powers and my life to the promulgation of the great, the glorious truth, which is the one thing which this world needs to bring to us the dawn of the millennium morning, when upon every tented field that can be found upon the face of this whole earth there shall come forth, not conquering hosts, sweeping over the earth, and bringing bloodshed, suffering and ruin in their train, but the armies of the Prince of Peace, as they come from this tented field. And I look to the influence of woman in the future, added to the influence of our brother man, who has so long and so grandly worked—I look to her influence and to her work, as she shall wisely use the abilities which God has given her. . . .

## ✦ *Biographical Sketch*

**Born:** *July 16, 1836, Lakeville, Livingston County, New York*

**Died:** *June 30, 1905, New York, New York, age 68*

**Buried:** *Maple Grove Cemetery, Mason, Michigan*

Augusta Jane Chapin was the first woman in the world to receive an honorary doctor of divinity degree and the second woman to be ordained as a Universalist minister. She served not only as the minister to several congregations but also as a teacher, writer, lecturer, suffragist, and champion of women's rights.

Chapin began school at the age of three. She was a precocious child whose desire to learn was fostered by her father, who brought a large library along when the family moved to Vevey, Michigan, from Lakeville, New York, when she was six. Her childhood was lonely, and she spent many hours reading the New Testament, *Pilgrim's Progress,* and *Robinson Crusoe.* She committed large portions of them to memory, and they greatly influenced her life. She became a teacher at age fourteen.

At sixteen, she entered Olivet College in Olivet, Michigan; she had been denied admission at the University of Michigan because women were not admitted in 1852. Olivet was Congregational and rigorous in its religious training. The teenage Chapin had never been exposed to such strict religious doctrine. While there, she experienced a painful metamorphosis. For months, she was tormented as to whether the doctrine of eternal punishment was true or false. She isolated herself and took no advice except from orthodox commentaries. At age seventeen, she emerged from this period with the belief that all souls will eventually find salvation in the grace of God—the Universalist doctrine.

Chapin knew she was destined to be a minister. She said: "I have no recollection of ever considering the question of whether I would preach or not. . . . From the moment I believed in Universalism it was a matter of course that I was to preach it."[32] She gave her first sermon in Portland, Michigan, in 1859, and was ordained in Lansing, Michigan, on December 3, 1863. She worked as an itinerant minister for her first four years in the ministry, riding a circuit of appointments that she filled while maintaining a regular preaching schedule. She then served as minister in various towns and cities in Michigan, Wisconsin, Pennsylvania, California, Nebraska, Massachusetts, and New York.

In Iowa City (1869–1873), she rebuilt both a discouraged congregation and a church building that had burned. She felt a liberal church was needed in Iowa City to influence the potential leaders of the state who would be educated at the university there. Her ministry set the standard of excellence followed by other Iowa women ministers. Her ministry in Oak Park, Illinois, began on a temporary basis, but she was found to be such a competent minister that she was installed as pastor in 1886. During that time, she provided a home to her close friend Anna Lloyd Wright and her son Frank. She established a youth group, a junior high school group, and the Ladies Social Union "to promote the interests of the church both socially and financially, to aid the poor and to assist in any other work for which there may be occasion."[33]

Augusta Chapin also lectured on English literature for several years at Lombard University and delivered an address on the importance of a liberal education for women at Lombard's first commencement in 1856. In 1868, the trustees of the university awarded her the honorary degree of Master of Arts. In 1893, Lombard University conferred upon her the honorary degree of doctor of divinity at the Chicago World's Fair, where she was chairman of the World's Parliament of Religions.

The Reverend Chapin was among the first women to gain recognition in the denomination. As ministerial delegate for Iowa to the Universalist Centennial convention in 1870, she offered an amendment during the discussion of the proposed "law for securing a uniform system of Fellowship, Government and Discipline." She proposed that the word *candidate* be substituted for *brethren* in the article concerning letters of license to preach; her suggestion was adopted and the article passed.

Augusta Chapin was active in both the women's suffrage and temperance movements. She was a charter member of the American Woman Suffrage Association, formed in 1869 to unite local groups and promote suffrage on a national level. She was also a member of the famed Sorosis Society. In 1873, she delivered an address entitled "Women in the Ministry" at the Association for the Advancement of Women, for which she served on the first executive committee. She also served on the revising committee for Elizabeth Cady Stanton's *The Woman's Bible.*

Dr. Chapin accompanied literary parties on European tours for twelve summers. Her observations and studies resulted in instructive and highly entertaining lectures. In 1895, she taught American literature for the University Extension Division of the University of Chicago. A syllabus for her course included Women in Fiction, Women Distinguished in the Field of Literature, Voices of Women, Phillis Wheatley, Margaret Fuller, and the Cary Sisters in addition to the traditional authors of the period.

Augusta Chapin died in Brooklyn, New York, in 1905, on the eve of a European tour. The *Universalist Leader* (July 15, 1905) noted her passing with high praise: "Thus passes one of the earliest and most conspicuous of our women preachers; one who by her ability and consecration and her broad-minded sympathies with every good cause, commanded universal respect and won enduring friendships."

*Biographical Sketch by* MARY ANN PORUCZNIK *and* GLORY SOUTHWIND

## ✦ Writings of Augusta Jane Chapin

"Christmas through Women's Eyes." *Universalist Leader,* 24 December 1898.
"The Day of Salvation." *The Repository,* 1874.
"Discourse on Garfield Assasination." Speech at the Church of Our Saviour, Lapeer, MI, September 26, 1881.
"The Duty of the Hour." *The Repository,* November 1873.
"Music and Education." *The Repository,* June 1874.
"The Pulpit and the Word." *The Star in the West,* 23 December 1865.
"Success in Church Work." *The Repository,* 1874.
"University Extension." "On Behalf of Women." Speeches at the World Parliament of Religion at the Columbian Exposition, September 1893.
"What Is Christianity Doing for Woman?" *Universalist Leader,* 5 November 1898.
"Women in the Ministry." *The Repository,* February 1874.
Series of Sunday school lessons. *New Covenant.* Chicago: n.p., 1878.

## ✦ Biographical Resources

Baker, Marion. *Augusta Chapin: Pioneer Minister* [play]. Private printing, 1982.
*Centenary Voices: or A Part of the Work of the Women of the Universalist Church.* Philadelphia: Woman's Centenary Association, 1886.
Chapin, Gilbert W. *The Chapin Book of Genealogical Data.* Private printing, 1924.
Chulak, Thomas A. *A People Moving through Time: A History of the Unitarian/Universalist Church in Oak Park.* Private printing, 1979.
Fields, Jeanette. "First Woman Minister Brought Wright to Village." *Wednesday Journal,* 27 March 1991.
Hansen, Eliza Rice. *Our Woman Workers.* Chicago: Star and Covenant, 1882.
Hitchings, Catherine F. *Universalist and Unitarian Women Ministers.* (Journal of the Universalist Historical Society) 10 (1975).
Obituary: Augusta Jane Chapin. *Universalist Leader,* 15 July 1905.
Willard, Frances E., and Mary A. Livermore, eds. *A Woman of the Century.* Buffalo, NY: Charles W. Moulton, 1893.

# The Question Answered

## Poem, Published 1871

PHEBE ANN COFFIN HANAFORD (1829–1921), *a Universalist, was the first woman ordained a minister in New England, an activist for women's rights, and a prolific writer. The following poem was suggested by an incident in the lives of Lucy Stone and Antoinette Brown while they were students at Oberlin in the 1840s. Lucy Stone chose the path of political and social leadership, while Antoinette Brown [Blackwell] became the first woman ordained to the ministry.*[34]

See the Biographical Sketch on pages 442–446.

The evening hour with soothing quiet came;
The silver moon rose slowly up the sky;
Crowned with young womanhood, two friends walked forth,
Communing gladly of Life's purpose high.

The queenly step of one, the taller, ceased:
She turned, and looked full in her friend's clear eye.
"Can woman reach the pulpit?" then she asked.
And waited, with a full heart, the reply.

The answer came; but not a hope was born,
As fell those words upon the querist's heart:
"Woman may labor in full many a field,
But may not hope to act the preacher's part."

She asked of God—that woman brave and pure:
God gave the answer in the wish inspired.
The seed contained the germ; and in God's time
There came the fruitage which the words desired.

Years passed: and she who answered stood full oft
Beneath the shelter of our State-House domes;
And legislators heard her soul-full tones,
Pleading for equal rights in states and homes.

The querist stood in many a pulpit too,
Proclaiming Christ with hope to bless and save;
Her young heart glad with more than human joy,
As there she told of bliss beyond the grave.

Both have wrought nobly where few women toil,
Been pioneers in that cause, pure and high,
Which gives her place to woman by man's side,
With him to lead immortals to the sky.

Their lives have shown that naught can stay the tide
Of God's great purpose in its onward flow;
That where man nobly labors for the race,
There, too, may woman, at God's summons, go.

A quarter-century now hath passed away,
And many a woman in the pulpit stands,
Ordained to do the pastor's noble work
By more than laying on of human hands.

O God! we'll trust thee for the days to come,
Thou who hast guided woman in the Past;
And with a grateful heart thine handmaids sing,
"The day of righteous freedom dawns at last."

## ✦ *Biographical Sketch*

**Born:** *May 6, 1829, Nantucket Island, Massachusetts*

**Died:** *June 2, 1921, Rochester, New York, age 92*

**Buried:** *Orleans, New York*

A descendant of the pilot of the Mayflower, Phebe Ann Coffin was born into a Quaker family on the island of Nantucket, a true New Englander whose lineage was thoroughly American. The Quaker culture and religious practices of her childhood and adolescence became the source of her religious authority as an adult. The experience of spiritual equality within her family and within the larger community of Quakers on Nantucket allowed her self-authorizing religious and intellectual development to flourish.

Phebe's education was continuous; she remembered being carried home from school on her father's shoulders as a three-year-old. Writing and speaking were among Phebe's original gifts and thus were an integral part of her education. She took the temperance pledge at eight. At thirteen, her response to hearing antislavery speakers was her first published poem, "America." Her grandmothers were her first teachers of Scripture, personal piety, and political conscience.

At sixteen, Phebe began teaching. She married Joseph Hanaford, a teacher, homeopathic physician, and Calvinist-Baptist, when she was twenty. The usefulness of Phebe's writing helped support her son and daughter in the early years of marriage, and she would eventually publish fourteen books. Phebe remained active in her Quaker community while teaching at the Baptist church. With Quaker preacher Mary Farnum, Phebe founded the First Nantucket Female Praying Circle.

The Hanafords moved from Nantucket to Beverly, Massachusetts, in 1857. There, Phebe's friendship with two other poets brought her into close contact with Universalists, including Lucy Larcom and Mary Trask Webber. Phebe Hanaford and Mary Webber published *Chimes of Freedom and Union* in 1861.

The Hanafords moved to Reading, Massachusetts, in 1864. As Phebe chose Universalism, her father, George Coffin, asked her to come back to Nantucket to preach to her family and friends (1865). Following her daughter Florence, Phebe joined the Reading Universalist Association of Liberal Ladies for Benevolent and Useful Work (1866). In response to the Hanafords' Calvinist-Baptist minister's inquiry about which of the three faiths—Quaker, Calvinist-Baptist, or Universalist—was truly hers, she signed the membership book of the Reading Universalist Church two weeks later.

Working as an editor for two Universalist publications increased Phebe's financial contributions to the education of her son Howard and daughter Florence. Olympia Brown,[35] the Universalist minister in Weymouth, became a friend and mentor, suggesting that Phebe be licensed to preach. She became a licensed Universalist preacher, and, at Olympia Brown's request, preached to congregations in Hingham, Waltham, and other churches in need of ministerial services. Her ordination by the Hingham Universalist Church took place on February 19,

1868, making her the first woman ordained to the Universalist ministry in New England. Waltham called Phebe to their pulpit on alternate Sundays in 1869. Accepting a call to New Haven in 1870, she separated from her husband, taking Ellen Miles with her as her companion.

The public and political life of Phebe Hanaford provided a rich context for her ministry, as she moved from the causes of temperance and abolition to the support of women's suffrage. Her organizing skills found many uses, from early membership in Sorosis, one of the first women's organizations, to the suffrage platform. Julia Ward Howe[36] convened the Woman's Ministerial Conference, which benefited from Phebe's active participation.

Phebe's energetic and productive participation in all aspects of life—professional, political, and personal—reflected her comfort and effectiveness in working in groups of other women. Called to Jersey City to the Church of the Good Shepherd in 1874, she would confront and experience the limitations of her particular kind of feminine competence. Challenged by the church board to fire Ellen Miles as organist, Phebe resigned instead. A substantial part of the congregation left with Phebe and Ellen, establishing Second Universalist across the street in Library Hall. This congregation was not accepted by the Universalist convention, however.

Phebe remained in Jersey City for another seven years, lecturing, preaching, and doing itinerant ministry. In 1876, she published her most useful book, *Women of the Century,* which was republished in 1882 as *Daughters of America.* Called back to New Haven to a congregation divided by disagreement over gambling, Phebe formed the Second Universalist Church there in 1884. Her final preaching settlement was at the Christian Sabbath Society Meeting House, in Portsmouth, Rhode Island.

Phebe Hanaford retired from the settled ministry in 1891 to begin thirty years of an active educational and public ministry in a constellation of women's clubs, living in New York City with Ellen Miles. When Elizabeth Cady Stanton called together her suffrage colleagues to edit and publish *The Woman's Bible,* Phebe served on both revising committees.

After Ellen Miles's death, Phebe moved to New York state to live on a farm with a granddaughter. Such rural isolation made Phebe miss her lively urban life and devoted friends. She cast her first vote in Basom, New York, in 1918. The last years of her life were spent with her granddaughter, who moved to Rochester, New York, where they lived under difficult financial circumstances.

Phebe Ann Coffin Hanaford's long, productive life is carefully chronicled and written into the history of women's suffrage, in Universalist history, and in *Daughters of America.* Hers was truly a life lived practicing spiritual equality.

*Biographical Sketch by* SARAH BARBER-BRAUN

## ✦ Writings of Phebe Ann Coffin Hanaford

*Daughters of America; or Women of the Century.* Augusta, ME: True, 1882.

"The Finished Work; or Four Years in New Haven, A Farewell Sermon." *Daily Evening Union* (New Haven, CT), 30 March 1874.

*From Shore to Shore, and Other Poems.* Boston: B. B. Russell, 1871.

"A Glimpse of Whittier." *New York Times Saturday Review,* 4 January 1902.

"Introduction." In *Harvest Gleanings,* by Anna Gardner. New York: Fowler & Wells, 1881.

*Lucretia, The Quakeress, or Principal Triumphant.* Boston: J. Buffum, 1853.

*Ordination and Installation of Rev. Phebe A. Hanaford,* with John G. Adams. Boston: C. C. Roberts, 1870.

"Twenty Years in the Pulpit." *Woman's Journal* (27 December 1890): 1, 8.

## ✦ Biographical Resources

Gitlin-Emmer, Susan. *Roots of Our Strength.* Boston: Unitarian Universalist Women's Federation, 1980.

McCleary, Helen Cartwright. "Phebe Ann (Coffin) Hanaford. The 100th Anniversary of Her Birth." *Proceedings of the Nantucket Historical Association.* 35th Annual Meeting, 24 July 1929.

McCray, Florine Thayer. "Rev. Phoebe A. Hanaford. A Woman Minister of the Gospel." *Ladies' Home Journal,* February 1888, 3.

"Obituary: Miss Ellen E. Miles." *Daily Free Press-Tribune* (Waltham, MA), 23 March 1914.

"Obituary: Mrs. Hanaford Was Minister, Noted Writer." *Rochester (New York) Herald,* 2 June 1921.

"Phebe Ann Hanaford, A Mighty Social Force in Civil War Times and First Woman Ordained in New England, Approaches 92 Birthday." *Rochester (New York) Herald,* 17 April 1921.

"The Rev. Phebe A. Hanaford, 89 Today, Minister, Lecturer, Author and Poet, Observing Birth Anniversary at Basom." *The Daily News* (Batavia, NY), 6 May 1918.

## ✦ Archives

Anthony Family Papers, Una Winter Collection. Huntington Library, San Marino, CA.

Beverly Historical Society, Beverly, MA.

First Unitarian Universalist Society Records. Yale Divinity School, Manuscripts and Archives, New Haven, CT.

Hanaford Family Papers, private collection.

Phebe Ann Coffin Hanaford Collection, 1848–1929; Unpublished manuscripts by Barbara R. Hopkins and P. G. Toalson. Nantucket Historical Association, Nantucket, MA.

Schlesinger Library, Radcliffe College, Cambridge, MA.

Sorosis Papers. Smith College Library, Northampton, MA.

Women's Ministerial Conference, Unitarian Universalist Association. Andover-Harvard Library, Cambridge, MA.

# The Fulfillment of Prophecy

## Remarks at World's Parliament of Religions, Chicago, 1893

AUGUSTA JANE CHAPIN (1836–1905) *served on the board of managers for the historic World's Parliament of Religions held in Chicago in 1893. As one of the conference planners, she had the honor of speaking at both the opening and the closing of the gathering. In her welcoming remarks, she noted that women even one generation before would have been neither "thought of nor tolerated" for such a gathering nor indeed ready for such an opportunity. She praised the women preachers and scholars whose "new gospel of freedom and gentleness . . . has come to bless mankind."*

See the Biographical Sketch on pages 437–440.

Welcome.

I am strangely moved as I stand upon this platform and attempt to realize what it means that you all are here from so many lands representing so many and widely differing phases of religious thought and life and what it means that I am here in the midst of this unique assemblage to represent womanhood and woman's part of it all. The parliament which assembles in Chicago this morning is the grandest and most significant convocation ever gathered in the name of religion on the face of the earth.

The old world, which has rolled on through countless stages and phases of physical progress, until it is an ideal home for the human family, has, through a process of evolution or growth, reached an era of intellectual and spiritual attainment where there is malice toward none and charity for all; where, without prejudice, without fear and with perfect fidelity to personal convictions, we may clasp hands across the chasm of our indifferences and cheer each other in all that is good and true.

The World's first Parliament of Religions could not have been called sooner and have gathered the religionists of all these lands together. We had to wait for the hour to strike, until the steamship, the railway and the telegraph had brought men together, leveled their walls of separation and made them acquainted with each other; until scholars had broken the way through the pathless wilderness of ignorance, superstition and falsehood and compelled them to respect each other's honesty, devotion and intelligence. A hundred years ago the world was not ready for this parliament. Fifty years ago it could not have been convened, and had it been called but a single generation ago, one-half of the religious world could not have been directly represented.

Woman could not have had part in it in her own right for two reasons: One, that her presence would not have been thought of nor tolerated; and the other was that she, herself, was still too weak, too timid and too unschooled to avail herself of such an opportunity had it been offered. Few indeed, were they a quarter of a century ago who talked about the Divine Fatherhood and Human Brotherhood, and fewer still were they who realized the practical religious power of these conceptions. Now few are found to question them.

I am not an old woman, yet my memory runs easily back to the time when, in all the modern world, there was not one well-equipped college or university open to women students, and when, in all the modern world, no woman had been ordained, or even acknowledged, as a preacher outside the denomination of Friends. Now the doors are thrown open in our own and many other lands. Women are becoming masters of the languages in which the great sacred literatures of the world are written. They are winning the highest honors that the great universities have to bestow, and already in the field of religion hundreds have been ordained and thousands are freely speaking and teaching this new Gospel of freedom and gentleness that has come to bless mankind.

We are still at the dawn of this new era. Its grand possibilities are all before us, and its heights are ours to reach. We are assembled in this great parliament to look for the first time in each other's faces and to speak to each other our best and truest words. I can only add my heartfelt word of greeting to those you already heard. I welcome you my brothers, of every name and land, who have wrought so long and so well in accordance with the wisdom high heaven has given to you; and I welcome you, sisters, who have come with beating hearts and earnest purpose to this great feast, to participate not only in this parliament but in the great congresses associated with it. Isabella, the Catholic, had not only the perception of a new world but of an enlightened and emancipated womanhood, which should strengthen religion and bless mankind. I welcome you to the fulfillment of her prophetic vision.

✦ ✦ ✦

## Closing Remarks

The last seventeen days have seemed to many of us the fulfillment of a dream; nay, the fulfillment of a long cherished prophecy. The seers of ancient time foretold a day when there should be concord, something like what we have seen, among elements before-time discordant.

We have heard of the Fatherhood of God, the brotherhood of man, and the solidarity of the human race until these great words and truths have penetrated our minds and sunken into our hearts as never before. They will henceforth have larger meaning. No one of us all but has been intellectually strengthened and spiritually uplifted.

The last moments of the great parliament are passing. We who welcomed now speed the parting guests. We are glad you came, Oh wise men of the East, with your wise words, your large, tolerant spirit, and your gentle ways. We have been glad to sit at your feet and learn of you in these things. We are glad to have seen you face to face, and we shall count you henceforth more than ever our friends and co-workers in the great things of religion.

# Feminist Biblical Critique

## From *The Woman's Bible,* 1895

PHEBE ANN COFFIN HANAFORD (1829–1921) *courageously contributed short but incisive commentaries on several biblical passages related to women to* The Woman's Bible *(Vol. I, 1895), a project coordinated by Elizabeth Cady Stanton that attracted a firestorm of criticism followed by abysmal neglect. Stanton, having rejected biblical revelation, was too radical to be either a Unitarian or a Universalist and by her old age was utterly persuaded that the biggest barrier between women and their rights was nothing other than the Bible, which was quoted by men in powerful positions everywhere to keep women down. Her life-long friend, Susan B. Anthony,*[37] *agreed but was against undertaking this project, knowing that it would be so controversial that it would risk dividing the women's suffrage movement. When this in fact happened, Anthony nevertheless stoutly defended Stanton, to no avail.*

*In this early feminist bibilical critique, the Reverend Hanaford lamented the bloodshed recorded in the book of Judges but pointed out that the text noted that the women were not inferior to the men in such matters and were "occasionally their superior." Hanaford also indicated her disapproval of the laws in the book of Numbers that deprive women of responsibility for their own vows, unless they have no father or husband to answer for them; it is noteworthy that she named God "the Infinite Father and Mother," an idea that thrilled the Unitarian Julia Ward Howe*[38] *and many others when they heard it in Boston from Unitarian minister Theodore Parker. These two excerpts from* The Woman's Bible *are preceeded by one of the letters Stanton included in the appendix to explain the purpose of this unusual volume.*

See the Biographical Sketch on pages 442–446.

*"Ignorance is the mother of devotion."*

The following letters and comments are in answer to these questions:

1. Have the teachings of the Bible advanced or retarded the emancipation of women?
2. Have they dignified or degraded the Mothers of the Race?

DEAR MRS. STANTON: I believe, as you said in your birthday address, that women ought to demand that the Canon law, the Mosaic code, the Scriptures, prayer-books and liturgies be purged of all invidious distinctions of sex, of all false teaching as to woman's origin, character and destiny. I believe that the Bible needs explanation and comment on many statements therein which tend to degrade woman. Christ taught the equality of the sexes, and Paul said: There is neither male nor female; ye are all one in Christ Jesus; hence I welcome *The Woman's Bible* as a needed commentary in regard to woman's position.

*Phebe A. Hanaford*

✦ ✦ ✦

## Comments on Judges

Colonial days is the felicitous term given by Rev. Dr. Lyman Abbott to the period of nearly three centuries following the campaign against the inhabitants of Canaan, when the Israelites took possession of their land. The Book of Judges is a record of those colonial days, and they are described also in the first part of the book which bears the name of the prophet Samuel. During those Hebrew colonial days, as Dr. Abbott states, there was no true Capital; indeed, no true Nation. There were a variety of separate provinces, having almost as little common life as had the American colonies before the formation of the Constitution of the United States. In war these colonies united; in peace they separated from each other again.

But in one thing they were united. They clung to the teachings of their great law-giver, Moses, and emphasized a belief in one righteous God. Whether expressed by priestly ritual or in prophetic declaration, the truth was clearly revealed that the Jews were people who worshipped one God and that they accorded to Him the attribute of righteousness. He was sovereign but a just one. And to this belief they clung tenaciously, believing themselves justified in conquering the nations about them, because their God was the only ruler.

The Book of Judges contains the record of many harrowing events; but what besides savagery can be expected of a warring people whose Deity is invoked as the God of battles and who believed themselves Divinely commissioned to drive other tribes from off the face of the earth? The book is as sensational as are our newspapers; and if each chapter and verse were illustrated as are the papers of what is termed the New Journalism, they would present an appearance of striking and painful similarity.

The fate of Adoni-besek, an example of retributive justice; the treacherous act of the left-handed Ehud, causing the death of the fat King Eglon of Moab; the inhospitable cruelty and cruel inhospitality of Jael, the wife of Heber, whose hammer and nail are welded fast in historical narration with the brow of the sleeping guest, Sisera, the captain of Jabin's army; the famous exploits of Gideon, who, if he was superior strategist and warrior, gave little evidence, by his seventy sons, of his morality according to Christian standards; the death of Abimelech, which was half suicidal lest it should be said that a woman's hand had slain him; these, and more also of the same sort, leave the impression on the mind that those colonial days of the Hebrew nation were far from days of peace or of high morality; and the record of them is certainly as unfit for the minds of children and of youth as are illustrated and graphic accounts of many unholy acts which are to be found in our daily newspapers.

General Weyler, in his Cuban warfare, has, in many respects, a prototype in General Gideon, and also in General Jephthah, a mighty man of valor and the son of a harlot, as the author of the Book of Judges declares him to have been. We deprecate the savage butchery of the one—what ought we to say of the renown of the others? War is everywhere terrible, and deeds of violence and of blood are sad reminders of the imperfections of mankind. The men of those colonial days were far from being patterns of excellence; and the women matched the men, in most instances. Deborah, as a mother in Israel, won deserved renown, so that her song of victory is even now rehearsed, but it is a query that can have but one answer, whether her anthem of triumph is not a musical rehearsal of treacherous and warlike deeds, unworthy of a woman's praise?

In the Book of Judges Delilah appears, and if the mother of her strong lover, Samson, was not a perfect woman, in the modern sense, she has helped to make some readers feel that the law of heredity is a revealer of secrets and that the story of the angel of the Lord may be received with due caution. The name Delilah has become a synonym for a woman tempting to sin, and the moral weakness and physical strength of Samson show the power of heredity. But whether the stories should be in the hands of our youth, without sufficient explanation and wise commentaries, is a question which coming days will solve to the extent of a wise elimination. Solemn lessons, and those of moral import, are given in the Book of Judges; yet, as a whole, the book does not leave one with an exalted opinion of either the men or the women of those days. But it certainly gives no evidence that in shrewdness, in a wise adaptation of means to ends, in a persistent effort after desired objects, in a successful accomplishment of plans and purposes, the women were the inferiors of the men in that age. They appear to have been their equals and occasionally their superiors.

## Comments on Numbers

Numbers xx

3. *If a woman also vow a vow unto the Lord, and bind herself by a bond, being in her father's house in her youth; . . .*
5. *But if her father disallow her in the day that he heareth, not any of her vows, or of her bonds wherewith she had bound her soul, shall stand; and the Lord shall forgive her, because her father disallowed her. . . .*
9. *But every vow of a widow, and of her that is divorced, wherewith they have bound their souls, shall stand against her. . . .*
13. *Every vow, and every binding oath to afflict the soul, her husband may establish it, or her husband may make it void. . . .*

Woman is here taught that she is irresponsible. The father or the husband is all. They are wisdom, power, responsibility, but woman is a nonentity if still in her father's house or if she has a husband. I object to this teaching. It is unjust to man that he should have the added responsibility of his daughter's or wife's word, and it is cruel to woman because the irresponsibility is enslaving in its influence. It is contrary to true Gospel teaching, for only in freedom to do right can a soul dwell in that love which is the fulfilling of the law.

The whole import of this chapter is that a woman's word is worthless, unless she is a widow or divorced. While an unmarried daughter, her father is her surety; when married, the husband allows or disallows what she promises, and the promise is kept or broken according to his will. The whole Mosaic law in this respect seems based upon the idea that a woman is an irresponsible being; and that it is supposed each daughter will marry at some time and thus be continually under the control of some male, the father or the husband. Unjust, arbitrary and debasing are such ideas and the laws based upon them. Could the Infinite Father and Mother have given them to Moses? I think not.

# Why Women Ministers?

## Article in *Sunday Post,* January 11, 1914

FLORENCE ELLEN KOLLOCK CROOKER (1848–1925) *was influenced in her career choice by the Reverend Augusta Chapin and by Mary Livermore,*[39] *who was never ordained but spoke from numerous Universalist and Unitarian pulpits. She earned a doctor of divinity degree in 1875 and became a Universalist minister with many highly successful pastorates. In 1914, she was president of the Women's Ministerial Conference*[40] *of Boston.*

*In her newspaper essay "Why Women Ministers?" which follows in full, Crooker asserted that St. Paul would approve of women ministers at that time, instead of telling them to keep silent in church. She claimed that the shift in emphasis from creedal theology to "social uplift" made the gifts of women ministers ever more valuable to churches of many denominations.*

See the Biographical Sketch on pages 457–459.

The question is sometimes asked: "Why should there be women ministers?"

The answer is plain: "For the same good reasons that there is a male ministry."

That is to spread the gospel; to give religious instruction; to train the young in the ways of virtue and righteousness—in brief to help the world through the ministry of religion, as men and women are helping it through the many splendid agencies now employed in the great uplift of humanity.

St. Paul's argument is often used to oppose the entering of women into the ministerial fields, but St. Paul had his say long before the days of Sunday schools, prayer meetings, choir singing, women's missionary societies, orders of deaconesses and many other agencies through which women are carrying forward the work of the Master.

St. Paul's declaration came before the day of church halls, church suppers and the tragedy of the annual bazaar, now thought to be necessary by those members in good and regular standing, who reckon the "wimmin's work" as the chief and as the easiest way of providing for the yearly expenses.

Were St. Paul among us today, we would have in him a most sympathetic and helpful friend as we have in certain men of the Pauline temperament.

But what special claim has this part of the feminist movement upon the consideration of society, and why invade this historic field so completely and honorably occupied by men?

Because many women, like many men, have yielded to the high and holy aspirations to serve God and their fellowmen in the way they could best serve the Christian ministry.

**Now Many Women Ministers**

Is their ministry acceptable?

The reply to this is geographical. Acceptable, yes, from the Mississippi Valley West to the Pacific coast.

Let New England speak for herself.

Those who proudly call themselves pioneers in the ministry have watched, in growing interest, the trend of the movement with a clearer understanding of the apparent slow progress it has made than do the superficial and unsympathetic observers.

In 1853, 60 years ago, Antoinette Brown Blackwell was ordained to the Christian ministry by a body of Congregational ministers. The year book of that great denomination now has the names of 84 women.

That distinguished and gifted woman minister, the Rev. Olympia Brown, was graduated from the St. Lawrence Divinity School and ordained to the Christian ministry in the Universalist denomination 50 years ago. The year book of that church carries the names of 75 women in its list of ministers out of a total of 640.

The Unitarian church has found room in its ministerial ranks for 17 women.[41]

The Free Baptist before merging with the regular Baptist had upwards of 50 women. The Christian church and some branches of the Methodist church, in one of which the Rev. Anna Howard Shaw was ordained, welcome to the service of the ministry their devoted and capable women.

Not at all a discouraging outlook for the women ministry when we remember that the Christian church moves slowly in all great reforms.

Intemperance, slavery, white slaves and many other evils have been and are permitted to thrive in the most churchly communities, when the earnest, united and determined efforts of the Christian people could and would abolish them.

Great reform movements are not indigenous to the church; hence it is not strange that many denominations have been and still are slow to see the justice and wisdom of endorsing the woman ministry.

But the change now going on in the church in its usual slow, conservative way, but going on nevertheless, is the changing of the emphasis from theology to sociology, from creed to "what can I do to save others?" and will take into account the gifts peculiar to women in the work that is commonly called "the social uplift."

**Are More Sympathetic**

With the establishing of this line of work in the church the position of the woman minister will be most valuable, since she is more intuitive, more sympathetic and more tactful in meeting and ministering to those with whom the church must deal along these lines.

But her ministry in the past has wrought more for the best welfare of the church than is really known.

Always holding creeds secondary to religion pure and simple, and Christian fellowship the real test of Christian character, the woman minister has gone about in the community as a messenger of non-sectarianism and a missionary of "church unity."

As a woman she has mingled with the most devout and intellectual women of the community representing the members of all churches and no particular church.

In the women's clubs, temperance meetings, mothers' meetings and gatherings of a similar character, the woman minister has constituted an active member.

She has joined hands with Catholic and Protestant and has with them taken counsel and worked for the object that has enlisted their interest and sympathy.

A woman minister is first and always a woman; a companion of women, a friend and confidant of young people, and a lover of children.

As a woman she easily passes into the sick chamber, and her gentle ministry there is even more effective than when her parishioner is in the pew before her.

The young people easily recognize her as a friend and counselor. The children in a beautiful sense are her children, and to instruct and guide them becomes an inspiration.

With a woman's intuition, consideration and sympathy she is equal to the most delicate tasks that the domestic and social life of her parishioners may make necessary to be met and adjusted.

To the mother, sister and daughter she carries with her a peculiar favor and irresistible influence of the authority of a high priestess, and through this she leads and guides, she comforts and consoles, and thus the community and individual comes to realize "Why a woman minister."

## ✦ *Biographical Sketch*

**Born:** *January 19, 1848, near Waukesha, Wisconsin*

**Died:** *April 21, 1925, Elgin, Illinois, age 77*

Florence Ellen Kollock was born in a log cabin in rural Wisconsin. She was strongly influenced by her Universalist father, who believed in equal rights and education for women. When Florence was seventeen, she began to work as a teacher because her family's financial needs required that she earn the money to support herself in college. In that position, she came face to face with her unequal status as a woman of the nineteenth century when she realized she was being paid considerably less than male teachers. These early experiences would help prepare her to meet such opposition later in life, when, as a minister, she encountered strong prejudice against a woman in the pulpit.

Florence went on to study at the University of Wisconsin. When she read in a newspaper about a woman minister, she told her sister, "I wish I could be a preacher!" Her sister's reply was characteristic of the family's empowering attitude: "You can be, if you wish."[42] Florence wrote to Mary Livermore, then co-editor of the *New Covenant*, who advised her to enroll at St. Lawrence University in Canton, New York, one of the first theological schools open to women.[43] Florence graduated with high honors in 1875 and was ordained in Waverly, Iowa, on February 15, 1877. Augusta Chapin preached the ordination sermon.[44]

One of Florence's first settlements was in Englewood, Illinois. She helped the congregation grow from fifteen to four hundred and build two new buildings in the process. Her success established her on a par with the best preachers in Chicago. One of her projects was to establish the State Street Mission out of her suburban congregation to serve inner-city families and children. She was also active in the Congress of Liberal Religions, where she met a Unitarian minister, Joseph Henry Crooker, who a decade later would become her husband.

In 1892, Florence took a much needed sabbatical in England and Europe to travel and study social conditions abroad; she hoped to learn how men and women there were responding to the problems of poverty, crime, and disease. She saw firsthand the methods and results of the Salvation Army and the Social Settlements of Toynbee Hall.

Florence considered returning to the United States and joining the lecture circuit to promote suffrage, temperance, and other social reforms. Instead, she answered a call from a congregation in Pasadena, California, where, in three years, she brought the church out of debt and made it a self-sustaining organization. The church's financial secretary acknowledged her organizational abilities: "She, a *woman,* showed our prosperous business men how to do church business successfully."[45]

Florence next took a very different position as associate minister of the Every Day Church in the slums of Boston's South End. She struggled to apply what she had learned in England about dealing with poverty, seeking to offer practical aid as well as fostering spiritual development in the face of overwhelming physical deprivation. On Sundays, she preached all over New England to publicize and raise money to support the work of this new experiment in religion.

In 1896, at age forty-eight, she married Joseph Crooker and moved with him to Helena, Montana. Florence and Joseph's dual-ministry marriage brought them constant changes. In Ann Arbor, Michigan, Joseph served as pastor of the Unitarian Church, while Florence was commissioned to do missionary work throughout the state for both the Universalists and the Unitarians. Their marriage brought the two denominations together for the first time in such work.

Florence's work with women's organizations was another important aspect of her life. In 1902–1903, she served as president of the Women's Centenary Association (later the Association of Universalist Women). Under her leadership, the Church Building and Loan Fund was established to make interest-free loans available to responsible parishes for building and repair work. From 1910–1914, she served as president of the Women's Ministerial Conference, established years earlier by Julia Ward Howe.[46] Florence was often called upon as a spokeswoman for women in ministry. Her various speeches and writings give insight as to her understanding of her role as a woman and a minister. In 1893, she spoke at the World's Congress of Representative Women in Chicago.

In 1904, Florence and Joseph decided to move to Boston, hoping to find a small society or two to serve in their later years. She was called to St. Paul's Church in Jamaica Plain; her husband found a position in nearby West Roxbury. Despite her success in making the church self-supporting and bringing back many former parishioners, she was asked to leave after six years because some people objected to having a woman minister. After all her fine work there, this was a crushing blow that would remain a source of pain for many years.

Florence and Joseph established a home in Lexington, Massachusetts, that was their pride and joy. Before leaving there in October 1921, they performed an unfortunate ritual. They built an altar behind their house and piled on it all the notes and clippings they had accumulated over the years along with their manuscripts and personal journals. They had both been doing research and writing, hoping to publish books, but had decided that the existing book trade was such that their books, if printed, would have little impact. Unfortunately, they burned it all!

Florence deserves to be remembered for her long and successful career in ministry. Among the early women who served in this capacity, her record for strengthening churches is one of the best. In addition, her efforts to bring social reform directly into the church context make her one of the most innovative ministers of any era.

*Biographical Sketch by* DOROTHY MAY EMERSON

## ✦ Writings of Florence Ellen Kollock Crooker

"Woman in the Pulpit." Speech to the World Congress of Representative Women, Chicago, 1893 (Microfiche #235, Andover-Harvard Library).

"Why Women Ministers?" *Sunday Post,* 11 January 1914.

## ✦ Biographical Resources

Crooker, Joseph Henry. "Romance of a Pioneer." *Christian Leader,* February 6–May 8, 1926.

Emerson, Dorothy. "Representative Women." Occasional Paper #2. Malden, MA: Unitarian Universalist Women's Heritage Society, 1992.

# The Opening Doors

## Sermon Preached in Universalist Church, Racine, Wisconsin, September 12, 1920

OLYMPIA BROWN (1835–1926) *has long been acclaimed as the first woman ordained by full denominational authority in 1863.*[47] *Undeterred by the multiple barriers faced by women in her time, she was a pioneer in opening the doors of theological schools to women. She entered the Universalist ministry to fight for women's liberation and later left it for the same reason.*

*In "The Opening Doors," a sermon preached a few days after women first voted in 1920, Brown looks back over the decades and says, "The grandest thing has been the lifting up of the gates and the opening of the doors to the women of America." She appeals to her fellow Universalists to keep and spread their hopeful faith to a world exhausted and depressed by World War I.*

See the Biographical Sketch on pages 251–255.

> *"Lift up your heads O ye gates and be ye lifted up ye everlasting doors."*
>
> —Psalm 24, Verse 7

It is now nearly thirty years since I resigned my pastorate in this church. That is a long time and many things have happened, but the grandest thing has been the lifting up of the gates and the opening of the doors to the women of America, giving liberty to twenty-seven million women, thus opening to them a new and larger life and a higher ideal. The future opens before them, fraught with great possibilities of noble achievement. It is worth a lifetime to behold the victory. Then there have been other changes; Racine has grown larger and richer and the population has changed; many have come and some have gone. The everlasting doors have opened to some of our dearest, and they have been permitted to behold the mysteries that lie beyond. We see them no more. We miss their ready cooperation and sympathy and love, but we know that wherever they are, they are in God's universe and they are safe and all is well with them. We have had our struggles and our triumphs, our labors and our victories, our sorrows and our joys and some of us are growing old, but I would say in the words of Browning,

> Grow old along with me
> The best is yet to be,
> The last of life, for which the first was made;
> Our times are in His hand
> Who saith "A whole I planned,
> Youth shows but half; trust God, see all
> Nor be afraid."

Meantime, new proofs of the truths which we advocate have been accumulating, sustaining the faith in which we have lived, for which we have worked, and which has bound us together as a church. New and wonderful evidences of the truth of Universalism have come to us. We formerly were glad to be able to point to texts of Scripture as proof of our doctrines, showing to the people the impossibility of an endless hell, telling them of the one God "who will have all men to be saved and to come to the knowledge of the truth" and assuring them that "As in Adam all die even so in Christ shall all be made alive."

We relied on the promises of revelation and we still cherish these grand old texts. They are dear to our hearts and they will ever remain in our memories a precious possession.

But now they are fortified and confirmed by the promises that come to us from nature "new every morning and fresh every evening." Today we are not dependent upon any text or the letter of any book. It is the spirit that giveth life and the spirit speaks to our souls with every breath that blows. Science has been unravelling the mysteries of the universe and has brought to light new examples of the Divine power and purpose. Burbank and Edison and Madame Curie have lifted up the everlasting doors and revealed the Father's countenance, all radiant with love. Madame Curie, by working long in the laboratory has unlocked the rocks and released radium, a substance fraught with incalculable benefit to humanity. Creative chemistry has been at work and by its reactions and combinations has brought to light new powers in the earth and in the air for the use of men. We have not half measured or understood the capabilities of this planet. William Henry Perkins, a young boy of thirteen, became so much interested in chemistry that he voluntarily gave up his dinner and his noon hour to attend lectures on the subject. He went on with his researches until he had discoveries invaluable to the manufacturer, among them that of aniline dyes, and other things which have added wealth to the people. Thus earth and air are filled with proofs of Divine love, goodness and power. The mountains and the hills have spoken and the rocks and the soils have added their testimony. "The dynamic symmetries revealed in nature such as the form of the fern leaf; the nautilus; and those vegetable products in which the regular pentagon occurred or where we find a geometrical arrangement of leaves about a stalk" all show the skillful handwork of the Divine, and all these wonderful scientific discoveries and revelations are proofs of God's unfailing love. The Opening Doors lead to no dark dungeons, open upon no burning lake, give no evidence of everlasting punishment. But all gladden us with assurances of Divine Goodness and indicate the final triumph of the good. "A charmed life old goodness, hath. The tares may perish, but the grain is not for death."

Not only by the researches of science are we shown the glories of creation, but the scenes of beauty which daily greet our eyes, the song of birds, fragrance of flowers, the moonlight shining on the waves all tell the same story of divine love. "The heavens declare the glory of God and the firmament showeth his handiwork." I have here a poem written by my mother in extreme old age in which the contemplation of the natural world seems to have lifted her above the weaknesses and pains of old age and enabled her to rise, in the entire confidence, into an atmosphere of Divine Love.

**Morning Hymn**

From shades of night the morning woke;
Nature her hymn of praise began;
From all her keys the chorus broke,
Through all her chords the echoes ran.
  "Praise God" the roaring billow cried,
  The thunder's awful bass replied.
In dulcet tones of music sweet
Each lowly flower its fragrance lent;
Birds sang, the morning light to greet,
And every bough in homage bent.
  The sun arose in majesty;
  Nature in worship bent the knee.

Roll on, sweet harmonies of love.
Through all earth's blooming valleys, roll;
Above the world, the stars above,
Soars upward my enraptured soul.
  Borne on devotion's wing of fire,
  To Nature's God my thoughts aspire.

But more significant than even the voices of the natural world is the evidence of Divine life which we see in man himself. When a great heroic deed is done, humanity is lifted up and ennobled and we have the assurance that there is a spirit in man and the Lord God giveth him understanding. Oh, what grand acts of self-sacrifice and high courage, what heroism, have we seen in innumerable instances during the last few sorrowful years, all showing that there is a soul in man partaking of the Divine life. A thousand instances of depravity are forgotten in our admiration of one great heroic action by which human nature is lifted to a higher level, by which we know that man has a soul which is immortal and which enables him to utilize and make his own the wonderful resources with which the earth with all its glories is fitted up for his uses.

When the other day I saw crowds of women of all conditions coming into the polling booth all filled with great enthusiasm, forgetting old prejudices, old associations and former interest, only seeking to know how to serve the state, ready to leave their usual amusements and associations and give themselves to new subjects of study, not to serve any particular party, but only to learn to help the world I said, they are grander than I thought. They have "meat to eat that the world knows not of," there is a Divine Life in them which this new experience is revealing.

The greatness of men, the grand capabilities of women attest the worth of the human being fashioned in the image of God.

It is true that the ignorance of men and the awful mistakes they make, the wrongs they do and the sins they commit, bringing with them, even here, terrible punishment and embittering life, might cause us to doubt were it not that we see that there is a pardoning power in the spiritual world as there is healing in nature.

The river rock soon covers itself with moss and becomes a thing of beauty. The tree deformed and disfigured puts out new twigs and branches and covers itself with verdure and so the warped and travel-stained, sorrow-stricken souls of men shall at last put on the garments of Holiness. Men shall find remedies for their weakness, enlightenment for their ignorance and so rise out of their degradation and their sin.

One of our noted political prisoners said the other day in an interview, "I have never been more hopeful and more confident in the future than I am today. Nor have I ever had so great a faith in the moral order of the universe as I have today."

"There is a kinship of misery that generates the true sweetness of human nature, the very milk of human kindness." Thus the sins of men and their sorrows come at last to confirm the great truths revealed in the natural world.

And so Science: the beauties of nature and the grand possibilities of humanity furnish overwhelming proofs of the final victory of the good and the ultimate purification of every human soul.

And this is Universalism: the grandest system of religious truth that has ever been revealed to man. The doctrine for which the world waits.

A short time ago a correspondent of the *Nation* wrote to the editor begging him to publish something hopeful. He said he was so tired of being discouraged; he longed for something hopeful. And he spoke for thousands who in this time of uncertainty and chaos and confusion are longing for a ray of light, something to relieve the discouragements of the hour.

Mothers all over this land who have heard the solemn tidings that their sons have been slaughtered on the battle field; wives who have been robbed of everything—companionship, support, all the joys of life; multitudes whom the terrible pictures of suffering and torture have filled with horror, he spoke for all of these.

**All Need More Hope, Eternal Hope**

Hope! When I mourn, with sympathizing mind,
The wrongs of fate, the woes of human kind,
Thy blissful omens bid my spirit see
The boundless fields of rapture yet to be;
I watch the wheels of Nature's mazy plan,
And learn the future by the past of man.

He spoke for the whole world that is longing for hope, and Universalism is the answer to that cry, for this the world waits.

Oh Lift up your heads, O ye gates, even lift them up ye everlasting doors, that the King of Glory may come in. The Lord mighty in love, rich in tender mercies, abundant in pardoning power. He comes to bring consolation to the sorrowful, inspiration to the toiler, hope for the sinner. He comes to bless the world and to help humanity to rise out of its selfishness and ignorance.

We talk of reforms. We have hoped to make the world safe for democracy; to establish a league of peace; but the very first necessity in reform work is the recognition of Divine capabilities in man. The foundation of democracy is the realization that every human being is a child of God, entitled to the opportunities of life, worthy of respect, and requiring an atmosphere of justice and liberty for his development.

We can never make the world safe for democracy by fighting. Rather by showing the power of Justice done to each humble individual shall we be able to create a firm basis for the state. We can establish a league of peace only by teaching the nations the great lesson of the Fatherhood of God and the Brotherhood of Man.

Every nation must learn that all the people of the nations are children of God and must all share the wealth of the world. You may say that this is impracticable, far away, and can never be accomplished. But this is the work which Universalists are appointed to do. Universalists sometimes, somehow, somewhere, must ever teach this great lesson.

We are not alone. There is always an unseen power working for righteousness. The Infinite is behind us. The eternal years of God are ours.

And that is the message which I bring you today. Stand by this great faith which the world needs and which you are called to proclaim.

It is not necessary to go far away to tell the story of God's love or even to win the nations. God has given us the heathen for an inheritance. Here they come to our own city from far away countries and from the islands of the ocean. And here in Racine we may illustrate the great principles of our faith by our charity, by our kindliness and consideration for all. We shall speak the language of Universal love, and it will be heard and the message will be carried far and wide.

What signifies that your numbers are few today when you are inspired by truths that are everlasting and have before you ever the vision of final victory, the assurance of the salvation of all souls?

Universalism shall at last win the world.

Dear Friends, stand by this faith. Work for it and sacrifice for it. There is nothing in all the world so important to you as to be loyal to this faith which has placed before you the loftiest ideals, which has comforted you in sorrow, strengthened you for noble duty, and made the world beautiful for you. Do not demand immediate results but rejoice that you are worthy to be entrusted with this great message and that you are strong enough to work for a great true principle without counting the cost. Go on finding ever new applications of these truths and new enjoyments in their contemplation, always trusting in the one God which ever lives and loves. "One God, one law, one element, and one far-off divine event to which the whole creation moves."

# Religions of the World

## From Various Writings, 1784, 1817, 1832

HANNAH ADAMS (1755–1831) *was a remarkable independent scholar who, in the late eighteenth century, was recognized by her fellow liberal Congregationalists as a person who would be teaching at Harvard if such a thing had been possible for a woman. At the urging of many, especially the women among them, some prominent families subscribed to a private fund to support Hannah Adams's simple mode of life while she worked on compiling an objective description of all the religious beliefs then known. While this project began out of her simple curiosity, it soon became energized by her dismay at the biased sectarianism that contaminated so many of the sources she consulted.*

*The first excerpt included here is a statement from Hannah Adams's memoir recounting how she came to believe that respectful objectivity was both possible and desirable in describing various religious beliefs along with an explanation of what impeded her progress on this project. It is important to remember that this work appeared nearly a century before a professorship was established in the United States for what we now know as the academic study of religions.*

*The second excerpt is the "Advertisement," explaining her "nonjudgmental" approach, from the first edition of* Alphabetical Compendium of the Various Sects, *published in 1784. Her practice of this new approach is illustrated by her definitions of Universalists and Unitarians, Antitrinitarians, Arians, and Socinians, each listed in a separate entry. Her description of Unitarians in 1784 is only a few lines long, reprinted here in full. By this time, however, Universalism had already attracted a significant following and was thus given a ten-page description, of which several excerpts follow.*

*Hannah Adams also applied her method to write entries on non–Judeo/Christian religions, such as Islam, Confucianism, and even Tibetan Buddhism, which were surprisingly accurate for the time. In an appendix on "Religions of America," she included a statement of the religious beliefs of the "natives of New England" (excerpted here), who lived there before white settlement and were by 1784 almost wholly extinct.*

*Hannah Adams published her dictionary of comparative religions in four different editions, revising it each time to include current developments. Three editions were also published in London. By the publication of the final edition in 1817, entitled* A Dictionary of all Religions and Religious Denominations, *the Unitarian perspective, to which she subscribed, had developed sufficiently to warrant almost eight pages, of which several excerpts follow.*

See the Biographical Sketch on pages 472–475.

## From Her Memoir

While I was engaged in learning Latin and Greek, one of the gentlemen who taught me had by him a small manuscript from Broughton's Dictionary, giving an account of Arminians, Calvinists, and several other denominations which were most common. This awakened my curiosity, and I assiduously engaged myself in perusing all the books which I could obtain, which gave an account of the various sentiments described. I soon became disgusted with the want of candor in the authors I consulted, in giving the most unfavorable descriptions of the denominations they disliked and applying to them the names of heretics, fanatics, enthusiasts, &c. I therefore formed a plan for myself, made a blank book, and wrote rules for transcribing, and adding to, my compilation. But as I was stimulated to proceed only by curiosity and never had an idea of deriving any profit from it, the compilation went on but slowly, though I was pressed by necessity to make every exertion in my power for my immediate support. During the American revolutionary war, I learned to weave bobbin lace, which was then saleable, and much more profitable to me than spinning, sewing or knitting, which had previously been my employment. At this period I found but little time for literary pursuits.

## From the 1784 Edition

### Advertisement

The reader will please to observe that the following rules have been carefully adhered to through the whole of this performance.

1. To avoid giving the least preference of one denomination above another: omitting those passages in the authors cited, where they pass their judgment on the sentiments of which they give an account: consequently the making use of any such appelations as *Heriticks, Scismaticks, Enthusiasts, Fanaticks,* &c. is carefully avoided.

2. To give a few of the arguments of the principal sects, from their own authors, where they could be obtained.
3. To endeavor to give the sentiments of every sect in the general collective sense of that denomination.
4. To give the whole as much as possible in the words of the authors from which the compilation is made, and where that could not be done without too great prolixity, to take the utmost care not to misrepresent the ideas.

✦ ✦ ✦

UNITARIANS. A name given to the *Antitrinitarians;* the *Socinians* are also so called. The term is very comprehensive, and is applicable to a great variety of persons, who, notwithstanding, agree in this common principle, that there is *no distinction in the Divine Nature.*

✦ ✦ ✦

UNIVERSALISTS. The sentiment which has acquired its professors this appellation, was embraced by *Origen* in the third century.

✦ ✦ ✦

This title also distinguishes those who embrace the sentiments of *Mr. Relley,* a modern preacher of universal salvation, in *England,* and *Mr. Murray,* in *America.* This denomination built their scheme upon the following foundation, viz.

That Christ as *Mediator* was so united to mankind that his actions were theirs, his obedience and sufferings theirs, and consequently he has as fully restored the whole human race to the divine favour, as if all had obeyed and suffered in their own persons. The divine law now has no demands upon them nor condemning power over them. Their salvation depends upon their *union* to *Christ,* which God constituted and established before the world began. And by virtue of this *union,* they will all be admitted to Heaven at the *last day;* not one of *Christ's* members, not one of *Adam's* race will be finally lost. Christ having taken on him the seed of Abraham, he in them, and they in him, fulfilled all righteousness, obeyed the law, and underwent the penalty for the past transgressions, being all made *perfect in one.* According to this union, or being in him, *as branches in the vine, as members in the body,* &c. the people are considered together with him through all the circumstances of his *birth, life, death, resurrection, and glory.* And thus considering the whole law fulfilled in *Jesus,* and apprehending ourselves united to him, his condition and state is ours. And thus standing in him we can read the law or the doctrine of rewards and punishments without fear; because all the threatenings in the law of God have been executed upon us (as sinners and law-breakers) in him. And this sacrifice of Jesus is *all-sufficient* without any act of ours, *mental* or *external.*

✦ ✦ ✦

To prove that the atonement was satisfactory for the whole *human race,* they alledge, that the scriptures abound with positive declarations to this effect: "*The restitution of all things is preached by the mouth of all God's holy prophets ever since the world began.*" It is said that "*Christ died for all,*" that "*he is the propitiation for our sins, and not for ours only, but for the sins of the whole world.*"

This denomination admit no punishment for sin but what *Christ* suffered; but speak of a punishment which is consequent upon sin, as *darkness, distress, and misery,* which, they assert, are ever atttendant upon *transgression.* But as the scriptures assure us, *the blood of Jesus cleanseth from all sin,* "*that misery of iniquity,*" which is so predominant at present in the human heart will finally "*be consumed by the spirit of his mouth and be destroyed by the brightness of his coming.*" As "*to know the true God, and Jesus Christ is life eternal;*" and as "*all shall know him from the least to the greatest.*" That knowledge, or belief, will consequently dispel or save from all that *darkness, distress,* and *fear* which is ever attendant on *guilt* and *unbelief:* and being perfectly holy we shall consequently be perfectly and eternally happy.

✦ ✦ ✦

## Native Religion of New England

*Previous to an account of the present denominations in this part of America, a short sketch of the Aborigines will not perhaps, be unentertaining to some readers.*

The natives of *New England* believed not only a plurality of *Gods,* who made and govern the several nations of the world, but they made Deities of every thing they imagined to be great, powerful, beneficial, or hurtful to mankind: yet, they conceived one Almighty Being, who dwells in the *southwest* region of the Heavens, to be superior to all the rest: this Almighty Being they called *Kichtan,* who at first, according to their tradition, made a man and a woman out of a stone but upon some dislike destroyed them again; and then made another couple out of a tree, from whom descended all the nations of the earth; but how they came to be scattered and dispersed into countries so remote from one another they cannot tell. They believed their supreme God to be a *good Being* and paid a sort of acknowledgement to him for plenty, victory, and other benefits.

But there is another power which they called *Hobbanocko,* in English the *Devil,* of whom they stood in greater awe and worshipped merely from a principle of terror.

The immortality of the soul was universally believed among them; when good men die they said their souls went to *Kichtan,* where they meet their friends and enjoy all manner of pleasures; when wicked men die, they went to *Kichtan* also but are commanded to walk away and to wander about in restless discontent and darkness forever.

At present the Indians in *New England* are almost wholly extinct.

✦ ✦ ✦

## From the 1817 Edition

UNITARIANS, a comprehensive term, including all who believe the Deity to subsist in *one person only.* The Socinians have claimed an exclusive right to this title but unjustly, as Arians, Humanitarians, and all Antitrinitarians have an equal right to the denomination. . . . Unitarian is not opposed to Tritheist or Polytheist: it does not denote a believer in *one God* only; but a believer in God in *one person* only, in opposition to the Trinitarians.

The chief article in the religious system of the class of Unitarian Socinians is that Christ was a mere man. But they consider him as the great instrument in the hands of God of reversing all the effects of the fall; as the object of all the prophecies from Moses to his own time; as the great bond of union to virtuous and good men, who, as Christians, make one body in a peculiar sense; as introduced into the world without a human father; as having communications with God, and speaking and acting from God in such a manner as no other man ever did and, therefore, having the *form of God* and being the *Son of God* in a manner peculiar to himself: as the means of spreading divine and saving knowledge to all the world of mankind; as, under God, the head of all things to his church: and as the *Lord of life,* having power and authority from God to raise the dead and judge the world at the last day. They suppose that the great scheme of revelation was to teach men how to live *here* so as to be happy *hereafter:* and that the particular doctrines there taught, as having a connection with this great object, are those of the unity of God, his universal presence and inspection, his placability to repenting sinners, and the certainty of a life of retribution after death.

✦ ✦ ✦

This denomination maintain that repentance and a good life are of themselves sufficient to recommend us to the divine favor; and that nothing is necessary to make us in all situations the objects of his favor but such moral conduct as he has made us capable of; that Christ did nothing by his death, or in any other way, to render God merciful to sinners; but that God is, of his own accord, disposed to forgive men their sins, without any other condition than the sinner's repentance. Isaiah iv. 7. Ezek. xviii. 27. Above all, the beautiful and affecting parable of the prodigal son, (Luke xv.) is thought most decisive, that repentance is all our heavenly Father requires to restore us to his favor.

The Unitarians of all ages have adopted the sentiments of Pelagius, with respect to human nature.

The name Unitarian is also claimed by all those Christians who believe there is but one God and that this one God is the Father only, and not a trinity, consisting of Father, Son, and Holy Ghost. They may or may not believe in Christ's pre-existence.

## ✦ *Biographical Sketch*

**Born:** *October 2, 1755, Medfield, Massachusetts*

**Died:** *December 15, 1831, Brookline, Massachusetts, age 76*

**Buried:** *Mount Auburn Cemetery, Cambridge, Massachusetts*

Hannah Adams, a distant cousin of John Adams, the second president of the United States, was the first woman in this country to earn her living as a writer as well as a pioneer in comparative religion. Although discrimination against women's employment prevented her from salaried academic teaching, she influenced an entire generation of ministers, philosophers, and learned persons. Her publications included several editions of *A Dictionary of Religion,* an *Abridged History of New England,* a *History of the Jews,* and several studies of the Christian religion.

Hannah, the second daughter of five children, was born in 1755 in the village of Medfield, outside Boston, to Thomas and Elizabeth Clark Adams. Her father was an unsuccessful farmer and storekeeper who supplemented his income by boarding and teaching boys preparing for Harvard College. Hannah was allowed to educate herself with the boarders and eventually took part in the family teaching duties.

During the Revolutionary War, one of the boarders gave Hannah a dictionary of religions, which categorized the various denominations and faiths as true or false, according to the author's Christian views. Hannah resolved to recreate the resource without such prejudice and spent long hours copying the bulk of the texts. Word of her project circulated in the area, which resulted in a publishing deal arranged by her local minister.

The financial terms of this first edition benefited the broker, rather than the author, so Hannah Adams used the new copyright laws to protect her investment by seeking another publisher and producing a second edition. During three years of negotiations and revisions, she kept a country school; however, the success of the 1791 edition enabled her to leave her teaching position. Guided by the Reverend James Freeman of King's Chapel, she now made published writings the foundation of her support. From 1791–1813, her dictionary was so well received that prominent families and their sons who were students at Harvard College sought private conversations, in which she discoursed at length on her research. Thus, despite Harvard's all-male character, Hannah Adams was able to influence its students.

By the mid-1790s, Hannah felt sufficiently confident of her scholarly reputation that she prepared for use in the schools her *History of New England,* published in 1799. This volume had the misfortune of attracting the rancor of the Reverend Jedediah Morse, who had already written a lengthy treatment of the subject. Morse pursued Hannah through the courts until 1814, when her lawyer (of the Unitarian Channing family) was finally able to make him pay damages. Hannah went on to concentrate her efforts in religious studies, publishing *The Truth and Excellence of the Christian Religion Exhibited* in 1804 and the

*History of the Jews* in 1812. *Letters on the Gospels* appeared in 1824, and her final work, her *Memoir,* was published posthumously to raise money for an ailing younger sister.

James Freeman introduced Hannah Adams to Boston's Unitarian elite circles, which gave her personal and professional advantages. As a single woman, she had traveled with her widowed father, but she often lived temporarily with families who allowed her to peruse their libraries and bring to their households a raised level of family discourse. Prominent among these were President John Adams and the Reverend Joseph Stevens Buckminster, with whom Hannah resided almost until his untimely death in 1812. In addition, the gentlemen of the Boston Athenaeum allowed Hannah full use of the facility, from which women were otherwise excluded. Toward the end of her life, several prominent Bostonians established an annuity by which she was guaranteed basic support for life. Friends and family cared for her during lengthy bouts of ill health and eye problems, and after her death, their private subscriptions made Hannah Adams the first adult to be buried in the new Mount Auburn Cemetery in Cambridge.

Although her testimonial writings remained standard Unitarian Sunday School texts for two generations, Hannah Adams's scholarly reputation evaporated shortly after her death. In the 1820s and 1830s, the introduction of new theological concepts eclipsed the ideas of most of the prominent theologians of the late 1700s. Along with those of Charles Chauncey and Henry Ware, Sr., Hannah Adams's message was eclipsed by Transcendentalism and spreading Unitarianism. Her most widely recognized title has been as the first woman to support herself with her pen, but historians of religion are now beginning to recognize that her *Compendia* laid a foundation for the very theologians whose work then eclipsed her own.

Scholars are still grappling with Hannah Adams's position in women's history. Although they did not allow her to teach or preach in an institutional position, the leading men of her time supported her research, published her books, and disseminated her scholarship. These opportunities contrasted sharply with those of many women of the time, who were excluded from respectable employment and society for want of a husband, father, or brother. Hannah Adams clearly held a special place in early American society and scholarship.

*Biographical Sketch by* ELIZABETH CURTISS

## ✦ Writings of Hannah Adams

*An Alphabetical Compendium of the Various Sects Which Have Appeared in the World from the Beginning of the Christian Era to the Present Day.* Boston: Edes, 1784.

*A Dictionary of All Religions and Religious Denominations, Jewish, Heathen, Mahometan, Christian, Ancient and Modern.* Boston: Cummings and Hilliard, 1817.

*History of the Jews.* Boston: John Eliot, Junior, 1812.

*Letters on the Gospels.* Cambridge, MA: Hilliard and Metcalf, 1824.

*Memoir of Miss Hannah Adams.* Boston: Gray and Bowen, 1832.

*A Summary History of New England.* Dedham, MA: Printed for the author by H. Mann and G. H. Adams, 1799.

*The Truth and Excellence of the Christian Religion Exhibited.* Boston: Printed by David Carlisle for John West, 1804.

## ✦ Biographical Resources

Tweed, Thomas. "Introduction: Hannah Adams' Survey of the Religious Landscape." In *A Dictionary of All Religions and Religious Denominations Jewish, Heathen, Mahometan, Christian, Ancient and Modern,* Classics in Religious Studies, No. 8, edited by Carl A. Raschke. Atlanta: Scholars Press, 1992.

Wright, C. Conrad. "Adams, Hannah." *Notable American Women 1607–1950 A Biographical Dictionary,* Vol. 1, edited by Edward T. James, Janet Wilson James, and Paul S. Boyer. Cambridge: Belknap Press, 1971.

# Improving Public Worship

## From "Mrs. Barbauld's Thoughts on Public Worship," 1824

ANNA LAETITIA AIKIN BARBAULD (1743–1825) *represents British Unitarianism in a selection from an 1824 work on improving public worship. A prolific writer, poet, hymnodist, editor, critic, and social activist, she came from a family of radical dissenters. She married Unitarian minister Rochemont Barbauld and helped run a nonconformist boarding school.*

*Mrs. Barbauld (as she was generally known) recommended that the ministers be given an architecture that would allow them to be better seen and heard, without all those little boxes that separate the families of the congregation from each other. She wanted more music and more lay participation in services; more systematic teaching of doctrine, scripture, and moral duty; and less gloom and fear. She argued as passionately as any Universalist against the "heart-withering perspectives of never-ending punishments."*

See the Biographical Sketch on pages 482–485.

It must, however, be acknowledged, that, in order to give Public Worship all the grace and efficacy of which it is susceptible, much alteration is necessary. It is necessary here, as in every other concern, that timely reformation should prevent neglect. Much might be done by judgment, taste, and a devotional spirit united to improve the plan of our religious assemblies. Should a genius arise amongst us qualified for such a task, and in circumstances favorable to his being listened to, he would probably remark first on the construction of our churches, so ill adapted are a great part of them to the purposes either of hearing or seeing. He would reprobate those little gloomy solitary cells, planned by the spirit of aristocracy, which deform the building no less to the eye of taste than to the eye of benevolence, and insulating each family within its separate enclosure, favor at once the pride of rank and the laziness of indulgence. He might choose for these structures something of the amphitheatrical form, where the minister, on a raised platform, should be beheld with ease by the whole wave of people, at once bend-ing together in deep humiliation or spreading forth their hands in the earnestness of petition.

It would certainly be found desirable that the people should themselves have a large share in the performance of the service, as the intermixture of their voices would both introduce more variety and greater animation, provided pains were taken by proper teaching to enable them to bear their part with a decorum and propriety, which, it must be confessed, we do not see at present amongst those whose public services possess the advantage of responses. The explaining, and teaching them to recite such hymns and collects, as it might be thought proper they should bear a part in, would form a pleasing and useful branch of the instruction of young people and of the lower classes; it would give them an interest in the public service and might fill up agreeably a vacant hour either on the Sunday or on some other leisure day, especially if they were likewise regularly instructed in singing for the same purpose.

As we have never seen, perhaps we can hardly conceive the effect which the united voices of a whole congregation, all in the lively expression of one feeling, would have upon the mind. We should then perceive not only that we were doing the same thing in the same place but that we were doing it with one accord. The deep silence of listening expectation, the burst of united praises, the solemn pauses that invite reflection, the varied tones of humiliation, gratitude, or persuasion, would swell and melt the heart by turns; nor would there be any reason to guard against the wandering eye, when every object it rested on must forcibly recall it to the duties of the place. Possibly it might be found expedient to separate worship from instruction; the learned teacher from the leader of the public devotions, in whom voice, and popular talents, might perhaps be allowed to supersede a more deep and critical acquaintance with the doctrines of theology. One consequence, at least, would follow such a separation, that instruction would be given more systematically.

Nothing that is taught at all is taught in so vague and desultory a manner as the doctrines of religion. A congregation may attend for years, even a good preacher, and never hear the evidences of either natural or revealed religion regularly explained to them: they may attend for years and never hear a connected system of moral duties extending to the different situations and relations of life; they may attend for years and not even gain any clear idea of the history and chronology of the Old and New Testament, which are read to them every Sunday. They will hear abundance of excellent doctrine and will often feel their hearts warmed and their minds edified; but their ideas upon these subjects will be confused and imperfect, because they are treated on in a manner so totally different from everything else which bears the name of instruction. This is probably owing, to a great measure, to the custom of prefixing to every pulpit discourse a sentence, taken indiscriminately from any part of the Scriptures, under the name of a text, which at first implying an exposition, was afterwards used to suggest a subject, and is now, by degrees, dwindling into a motto. Still, however, the custom subsists, and while it serves to supersede a more methodical course of instruction, tends to keep up in the minds of the generality of hearers a very superstitious idea, not now entertained, it is to be presumed, by the generality of those who teach, of the equal sacredness and importance of every part of so miscellaneous a collection.

If these insulated discourses, of which each is complete in itself and therefore can have but little compass, were digested into a regular plan of lectures, supported by a course of reading, to which the audience might be directed, it would have the further advantage of rousing the inattentive and restraining the rambling hearer by the interest which would be created by such a connected series of information. They would occupy a larger space in the mind; they would more frequently be the subject of recollection and meditation; there would be a fear of missing one link in such a chain of truths, and the more intelligent part of a congregation might find a useful and interesting employment, in assisting the teacher in the instruction of those, who were not able to comprehend instruction with the same facility as themselves.

When such a course of instruction had been delivered, it would not be expected that discourses, into which men of genius and learning had digested their best thoughts, should be thrown by, or brought forward again, as it were, by stealth; but they would be regularly and avowedly repeated at proper intervals. It is usual upon the continent for a set of sermons to be delivered in several churches, each of which has its officiating minister for the stated public worship; and thus a whole district partakes the advantage of the labors of a man eminent for composition. Perhaps it might be desirable to join to religious information some instruction in the laws of our country, which are, or ought to be, founded upon morals, and which, by a strange solecism, are obligatory upon all, and scarcely promulgated, much less explained. Many ideas will offer themselves to a thinking man who wishes not to abolish but to improve the public worship of his country. These are only hints, offered with diffidence and respect, to those who are able to judge of and carry them into effect.

Above all, it would be desirable to separate from religion that idea of gloom, which in this country has but too generally accompanied it. The fact cannot be denied; the cause must be sought, partly in our national character, which I am afraid is not naturally either very cheerful or very social and which we shall do well to meliorate by every possible attention to our habits of life and partly to the color of our religious systems. No one who embraces the common idea of future torments, together with the doctrine of election and reprobation, the insufficiency of virtue to escape the *wrath* of God, and the strange absurdity which, it should seem, through similarity or sound alone has been admitted as an axiom, that sins committed against an Infinite Being do therefore deserve infinite punishment, no one, I will venture to assert, can believe such tenets, and have them often in his thoughts, and yet be cheerful.

Whence a system has arisen so incompatible with that justice and benevolence, which in the discourses of our Savior are represented as the most essential attributes of the Divine Being, is not easy to trace. It is probable, however, that *power,* being the most prominent feature in our conceptions of the Creator, and that of which we see the most striking image here on earth (there being a greater portion of uncontrolled power, than of unmixed wisdom or goodness to be found amongst human beings), the Deity would naturally be likened to an absolute monarch;—and most absolute monarchs having been tyrants, jealous of their sovereignty, averse to freedom of investigation, ordering affairs not with a view to the happiness of their subjects but to the advancement of their own glory; not to be approached but with rich gifts and offerings; bestowing favors not in proportion to merit but from the pure influence of caprice and blind partiality; to those who have offended them severe, and unforgiving, except induced to pardon by the importunate intercession of some favorite; confining their enemies, when they had overcome them, after a contest, in deep, dark dungeons under ground, or putting them to death in the prolonged misery of excruciating tortures—these features of human depravity have been most faithfully transferred to the Supreme Being; and men have imaged to themselves how a Nero or a Domitian would have acted, if, from the extent of their dominion there had been no escape and to the duration of it no period.

These ideas of the vulgar belief, terrible but as yet vague and undefined, passed into the speculations of the schoolmen, by whom they were combined with the metaphysical idea of eternity, arranged in specific propositions, fixed in creeds, and elaborated into systems, till at length they have been sublimed into all the tremendous horrors of the calvinistic faith. These doctrines, it is true, among thinking people, are losing ground; but there is still apparent, in that class called serious Christians, a tenderness in exposing them; a sort of leaning towards them, as in walking over a precipice one should lean to the safest side; an idea that they are, if not true, at least good to be believed, and that a salutary error is better than a dangerous truth. But that error can neither be salutary nor harmless, which attributes to the Deity injustice and cruelty; and that religion must have the worst of tendencies, which renders it dangerous for man to imitate the being whom he worships.

Let those who hold such tenets consider that the invisible Creator has no name and is identified only by his character; and they will tremble to think *what* being they are worshipping when they invoke a power capable of producing existence in order to continue it in never-ending torments. The God of the Assembly's Catechism is not the *same* God with the Deity of Thomson's Seasons and of Hutcheson's Ethics. Unity of character, in what we adore, is much more essential than unity of person. We often boast, and with reason, of the purity of our religion, as opposed to the grossness of the theology of the Greeks and Romans; but we should remember that cruelty is as much worse than licentiousness, as a Moloch is worse than a satyr.

When will Christians permit themselves to believe that the same conduct which gains them the approbation of good men here will secure the favor of heaven hereafter? When will they cease making their court to their Maker by the same servile debasement, and affectation of lowliness, by which the vain potentates of the earth are flattered? When a harmless and well-meaning man, in the exaggerated figures of theological rhetoric, calls himself the vilest of sinners, it is in precisely the same spirit of false humility, in which the courtier uses degrading and disqualifying expressions when he speaks of himself in his adulatory addresses to his sovereign. When a good man draws near the close of a life, not free indeed from faults, but pure from crime, a life spent in the habitual exercise of all those virtues which adorn and dignify human nature, and in the uniform approach to that perfection, which is confessedly unattainable in this imperfect state,—when a man, perhaps like Dr. Price, whose name will be ever pronounced with affectionate veneration and deep regard by all the friends of philosophy, virtue, and mankind, is about to resign his soul into the hands of his Maker, he ought to do it not only with a reliance on his mercy but his justice; a generous confidence and pious resignation should be blended in his deportment. It does not become him to pay the blasphemous homage of deprecating the wrath of God when he ought to throw himself into the arms of his love. He is not to think that virtue is one thing here and another in heaven or that he on whom blessings and eulogiums are ready to burst from all honest tongues can be an object of punishment with him, who is infinitely more benevolent than any of his creatures.

These remarks may be thought foreign to the subject in question; but in fact they are not so. Public Worship will be tinctured with gloom, while our ideas of its object are darkened by superstition; it will be infected with hypocrisy, while its professions and tenets run counter to the genuine, unperverted moral sense of mankind; it will not meet the countenance of philosophers, so long as we are obliged to unlearn our ethics, in order to learn divinity. Let it be considered that these opinions greatly favor immorality. The doctrine that all are vile and equally merit a state of punishment is an idea as consolatory to the profligate as it is humiliating to the saint, and that is one reason why it has always been a favorite doctrine. The indecent confidence of a Dodd,* and the debasing terrors of a Johnson or of more blameless men than he spring from one and the same source. It prevents the genuine workings of real penitence by enjoining confessions of imaginary demerit; it quenches religious gratitude, because conceiving only of two states of retribution, both in the extreme, and feeling that our crimes, whatever they may be, cannot have deserved the one, we are not sufficiently thankful for the prospect of the other, which we look upon as only a necessary alternative. Lastly, it dissolves the connection between religion and common life by introducing a set of phrases and a standard of moral feeling, totally different from those ideas of praise and blame, merit and demerit, upon which we do and must act in our commerce with our fellow creatures.

There are periods in which the human mind seems to slumber, but this is not one of them. A keen spirit of research is now abroad and de-

*"And admitted, as I trust I shall be, to the realms of bliss before you, I shall hail your arrival there with transport, and rejoice to acknowledge that you was my comforter, my advocate, and my friend."—Letter from Dr. Dodd to Dr. Johnson. See Boswell's *Life of Johnson*, Vol. II, p. 140.

mands reform. Perhaps in none of the nations of Europe will their articles of faith, or their church establishments, or their modes of worship be able to maintain their ground for many years in exactly the same position in which they stand at present. Religion and manners reciprocally act upon one another. As religion, well understood, is a most powerful agent in meliorating and softening our manners; so, on the other hand, manners, as they advance in cultivation, tend to correct and refine our religion. Thus, to a nation in any degree acquainted with the social feelings, human sacrifices, and sanguinary rites could never long appear obligatory.

The mild spirit of Christianity has, no doubt, had its influence in softening the ferocity of the Gothic times; and the increasing humanity of the present period will, in its turn, produce juster ideas of Christianity and diffuse through the solemnities of our worship the celebration of our sabbaths, and every observance connected with religion, that air of amenity and sweetness, which is the offspring of literature and the peaceful intercourses of society. The age which has demolished dungeons, rejected torture, and given so fair a prospect of abolishing the iniquity of the slave trade cannot long retain among its articles of belief the gloomy perplexities of Calvinism, and the heart-withering perspective of cruel and never-ending punishments.

## ✦ *Biographical Sketch*

**Born:** *June 20, 1743, Kibworth Harcort, Leicestershire, England*

**Died:** *March 9, 1825, London, England, age 81*

**Buried:** *Stoke Newington Cemetery, London, England*

Anna Laetitia Aikin Barbauld was the eldest child and only daughter of Mary and John Aikin, a teacher at Warrington Academy, a college for nonconformists. (At the time, university education was otherwise restricted to candidates for ordination in the Church of England.) At Warrington Academy from the ages of fifteen to thirty, Anna's wit and intelligence were encouraged and developed in the give and take of discussion with students and tutors. Notable people with whom she interacted at Warrington included Thomas Malthus, Joseph Priestley, and many future leaders of the French and American Revolutions, including Jean Paul Marat. Anna learned English, French, Italian, and even Latin and Greek at a time when it was widely believed that women were incapable of learning classical languages.

Anna wrote essays and poems but did not feel that she, as a woman, could have them published. Her brother John finally convinced her to let some of her writings be published by mixing them in with his own. It was Anna's poetry and prose that made the books instant successes. Critics, learning the poems were by a woman, expressed horror that there were none about love and complained bitterly about her wit.

Despite the popularity of her essays and poems, Anna considered a career in writing unlikely for a woman. In 1774, at the age of thirty, she accepted a suitor. Rochemont Barbauld was a nonconformist Unitarian preacher, grandson of emigre Huguenots. Anna Laetitia Barbauld accompanied her husband to his suburban London church. Parsons of the day supplemented their salaries by taking in scholars. Rochemont left that to Anna, and so began her work as an educator. On finding they could have no children of their own, Anna and Rochemont adopted a nephew conceived especially for them to adopt.

Anna's urge to write soon returned, however. She arranged for the publication of a series of fifty novels by a variety of authors, and she wrote an introduction to each one. She also wrote what seem now to be surprisingly modern and clear essays on issues of the day, from the love of terror stories to monasteries, religious tolerance, the French Revolution, theories of education, and the antislavery campaign. When she formed a book society, she shocked everybody by admitting Jews to full membership.

Anna and her brother joined the sugar boycott (to protest its production by slave labor) and suffered persecution by the neighbors for taking this stand. She wrote a letter/poem on slavery to William Wilberforce (Evangelical leader of the movement to abolish the slave trade). When it was published, Horace Walpole responded with a letter to "that virago Barbauld."[48] Anna also opposed war. She wrote: "We should do well to translate this word war into language more intelligible to us. When we pay our army and navy taxes, let us set down: so much for maiming, so much for making widows and orphans, so much for bringing famine upon a district."[49]

All these actions stemmed from Anna's Unitarian faith, which she found in everything around her. For instance, as she looked out at country fields, she wrote: "How deep the silence, yet how loud the praise."[50] Anna worshipped regularly at the chapels her husband served in Hampstead and Newington Green, where to this day there is a brass marker identifying her regular pew.

Anna wanted to see Unitarianism become an even deeper faith. She distrusted those who claimed to believe truths they could not feel. Nonconformists of the day were in love with reason and viewed as suspect even the word *enthusiasm,* which represented for them the worst of low-class evangelism. Anna challenged this. "In prayer," she wrote, "from an over-anxious fear of admitting any expression that is not strictly proper, we are apt to reject all warm imagery and in short everything that strikes upon the heart and the senses."[51] This perspective made noted Unitarian leader Joseph Priestley furious because it seemed to contradict his strong Enlightenment perspective.

It was precisely her naturalistic religion of both thought and feeling that led Anna Laetitia Barbauld to her educational innovations. She took her students to see things for themselves: to the country, to the Houses of Parliament, to the homes of famous people. And she taught them to express themselves in their native English, not Latin or Greek. Her students also shared household chores, wrote plays, and published a weekly newsletter with puzzles and games. Discipline was by student-elected captains. Hers was a whole new vision of education.

Anna was no naive idealist, however. In her children's books, the hounds catch the hares and the cats devour the birds. These books were translated into many languages and loved by generations. William Ellery Channing read these books and appreciated their natural theology. During his famous visit to Europe, he spent three days with Anna, who was, by then, quite elderly.

All this educational innovation was created while Anna supported a husband who grew increasingly insane and violent. He tried once to poison her. And on another accasion, he chased her with a knife, forcing her to jump out a window to save herself. Anna stayed against family wishes because she could not bear to commit her husband to an asylum. In the end, Rochemont Barbauld committed suicide.

After a time, Anna returned to writing, but her idea that Europe would decline and the United States become a world power was reviled. She allowed nothing more to be published.

Anna's last days were brightened by many visitors, among them William Wordsworth, Sir Walter Scott (whom she had convinced to try writing), and William Ellery Channing. She encouraged others to found the University of London. In her eighty-second year, she slipped peacefully away. At the time, her death was much noted. Since then, however, except in educational archives, she has been nearly forgotten.

*Biographical Sketch by* JUDITH WALKER-RIGGS

## ✦ Writings of Anna Laetitia Aikin Barbauld

*Devotional Pieces.* London: n.p., 1775.

*Hymns in Prose for Children.* Dublin, Ireland: M. Mills, 1798.

*Miscellaneous Pieces in Prose.* Edited by J. and A. L. Aikin. London: J. Johnson, 1773.

*Poems.* New York: Woodstock Books, 1993.

*The Poems of Anna Laetitia Barbauld.* Edited by William McCarthy and Elizabeth Kraft. Athens: The University of Georgia Press, 1994.

*A Selection from the Poems and Prose Writings of Anna Laetitia Barbauld.* Boston: Osgood, 1874.

*The Works of Anna Laetitia Barbauld with a Memoir by Lucy Aikin.* 2 vols. London: Longman, Hurst, Rees, 1825.

## ✦ Biographical Resources

Oliver, Grace. *The Story of the Life of Anna Laetitia Barbauld, with Many of Her Letters.* Boston: Cupples, Upham, 1886.

Rodgers, Betsy Aikin-Sneath. *Georgian Chronicle: Mrs. Barbauld and Her Family.* London: Methuen, 1958.

# The Ideal Unitarian Church

## From Paper Read at Western Unitarian Conference, Chicago, May 16, 1889

CELIA PARKER WOOLLEY (1848–1918) *was a Unitarian minister, educator, editor, lecturer, and reformer. She was closely associated with the publication* Unity *and was a director of the Western Unitarian Conference. In 1889, the Reverend Woolley read before the Western Unitarian Conference in Chicago a long address on "The Ideal Unitarian Church"; the main line of her argument is presented in the following excerpt. She prized reason and judgment in religion, continual spiritual growth in freedom, and character, or "practical righteousness," as more important than creed. She believed the rational church should be more than ethical; in addition, it should be reverent, inspiring, and uplifting with music and prayer. But it should be "a working church," too, one that seeks to educate and stimulate intellectual growth as well as comfort and help people while treating them in such a way as to increase their self-respect. She noted that all denominations saw this ideal and that the Unitarians would have to practice the tolerance they preached in order to become such a church.*

See the Biographical Sketch on pages 492–495.

The subject of the ideal Unitarian church must be considered from two points of view: the thought side, or that of its main principles and beliefs, and the practical side, or its relation to active life and its duties. In considering the first we must take into account two things, viz., the beliefs and doctrines usually taught in the Unitarian name and the principle or method of thought by which these beliefs have been reached. Unitarianism is not so much an organized system of religious belief as a religious movement. It is more a method of thought than an outcome. Not that the outcome of Unitarian thought is unimportant. On the contrary, the main beliefs described by that name are of that wide philosophical import, and moral necessity to man, which assure their permanent abiding-place among the world's treasures of thought. . . .

Dearly, therefore, as he may prize and profit by those beliefs which define his conception of the universe and his relation to it, the Unitarian should not hold them more dear than those faculties of reason and judgment which have enabled him to reach such beliefs.

✦ ✦ ✦

The instinct of growth in man—of spiritual growth—that is the fact that lies at the bottom of every other connected with the world's religious history. Unitarianism was the first form of religious faith frankly to recognize this fact. . . .

From the beginning Unitarianism has been a religious growth and seeking. Its first definitive utterance in this country dates from the ordination sermon of Jared Sparks by the revered leader of our faith, William E. Channing. This sermon was entitled "Unitarian Christianity." It is pervaded with the spirit of a pure rationalism throughout and is a plea for spiritual freedom. . . . Channing brought the right method to the study of religious discussions, an open and reverent mind, but could not make it yield today's results. He knew nothing of the new mental outlook obtained through the teachings of evolution nor of that new conception of the Bible which we hold today. . . . Channing sincerely believed in man's need of both reason and religion. It is reason, he tells us, which demonstrates the need of another guide, superior to itself—revelation; as it is reason which must determine the merits of different revelations, so claimed. . . . "Channing's entire life and all his written and spoken thoughts show that with him the gospel of practical righteousness was paramount to every form of opinion," says Mr. Shorey in his pamphlet on "Channing and the Unitarian Movement in the United States." . . . Theodore Parker's sermon on "The Transient and Permanent in Christianity" set forth the then novel and startling doctrine that the truth and value of Christianity were not dependent on the miracles. Christianity means a pure life, he said, belief in the overruling goodness of God and the brotherhood of man. Channing had taught that religion was not concerned with questions of the trinity and the mediatorial sacrifice but stood for just and noble living, the free exercise of all man's higher faculties. . . . Channing had taught that the old conception of Jesus and his death hindered not helped the cause of true religion; and Parker added that the miracles hindered not helped the work of Christianity. Everybody was alarmed—everybody but Channing.

✦ ✦ ✦

Unitarians can consistently have no other basis than a basis of fellowship; for this is the only one that recognizes the worth of human character, irrespective of the varying creeds and beliefs of men; that puts the performance of duty before all professions of faith and theories about duty. . . . The ideal Unitarian church can rest on no policy of exclusion.

As Channing was neither troubled nor alarmed over Parker's defection from some of the old beliefs, so I firmly believe, had he lived to a later age, he would have been as little afraid of the still more advanced opinions of Frothingham and Potter, nearly thirty years ago, or of the so-called "ethical tendencies" of Western Unitarianism today. Those of our liberal household who, with just pride, but not always with the broadest sympathy or understanding, call themselves "Channing Unitarians" should pause to ask themselves what it is to be a "Channing Unitarian." Is it to make Channing's beliefs, limited by his age and the thought conditions of that early day, ours, or to possess ourselves of his spirit? Is it to think as he did, or act as he did; to copy his opinions or to cultivate his virtues?

✦ ✦ ✦

The inevitable conclusion reached by this review of the past is that this ideal church must rest on the broadest possible basis of fellowship, welcoming to its communion all thoughtful, truth-seeking minds: that any basis of fellowship founded on belief, no matter how wide or rational, is a logical inconsistency in an organization that recognizes the necessity of religious change and progress and makes character, not creed, the test of the religious life.

With this distinctly ethical aim, an ideal church will yet be something more than ethical, using the term in the sense of those who sometimes seem to divorce it from religion. It will be a church, not simply a society or congregation. . . . Worship and aspiration will serve as factors of its spiritual life along with the work of practical duty and benevolence. The hymn and prayer will find as natural a place in its ritual as the sermon; the hymn because the voice must utter the feelings of praise and gratitude that rise in the heart; and prayer because not all the learning of the ages can prevent the instinctive turning of the soul of man to its source. . . . The ideal Unitarian church, then, will have its religious service, one that has no dwarfing or stultifying effect on the intellect of the worshiper; a service at once rational and reverent, uplifting to the heart, strengthening the understanding and consecrating the spirit to continued service in well-doing. . . . The Unitarian especially attached to the Christian name and associations can with entire consistency take part in certain services, which another, following a severer line of thought, feels bound to dispense with. Unitarianism, having the two-fold aspect of belief and method of belief, standing wholly and primarily for this method of belief, and generally, though not necessarily for some form of belief, will always attract two classes of believers: those who lay chief stress on the prevailing doctrine and those who, though they may accept the doctrine, care more for the principle or method of thought by which the doctrine is reached. Thus we shall always have with us the radical Unitarian, meaning generally the rationalist; and the conservative Unitarian, meaning generally the distinctively Christian Unitarian. I use these terms broadly, for as a matter of fact a Christian Unitarian may be as much of a rationalist as any other, so far as mental method is concerned, while many rationalists still claim the Christian name.

We come now to the practical side of our subject. The ideal church will be above everything else a working church. . . . That is, the highest church-fellowship aims to bring solace to the heart and strength to the understanding. . . .

The ideal church will be essentially modern, not only in its spirit and object but so far as possible in the exterior means and appliances with which it seeks to carry on its work. An obsolete medievalism will be as much out of place as architecture as in its form of worship. . . . We need not return to the bare, plain models preserved in the traditions of the Puritan meetinghouse, but use and simplicity should be the main motives of the modern church builder. The real use of the church of today is that of a religious workshop with club and classrooms, library, parlors, and complete domestic arrangements to further the social life of the church. There is no objection to the painted windows and the illuminated texts on the walls, provided these and other similar devices be enlarged from a simply decorative purpose, and made to further the true spirit and objects of the church, to embody a rational and living purpose. A recently constructed liberal church retains the painted window but in a way that makes a noteworthy innovation in church decoration; the lesson it seeks to illustrate being drawn, not from any of the old theological fables, but from that story of deep religious consecration and trust found in Millet's Sower. We shall always honor Correggio . . . but it is equally to our loss and our discredit when we overlook the work of artists near and of our own day. . . .

Among the working features of this church, none will be of greater worth and interest than the literary society or study class, coming to be known among us as the Unity Club. Among the orthodox sects a growing appreciation of the intellectual life and its relation to the religious is seen in the work of the Chautauquan Circle. The ideal church will be a recognized agency in the work of modern culture, the center of the neighborhood. . . . Only as the church itself becomes a leader in the world of thought can it command the respect of thinking men and women. . . .

In its relation to the social questions of the hour the ideal is the type of a helpful and progressive humanity, made intelligent through culture and the experience of life. Its office is to help the needy and comfort the afflicted but in ways that shall increase, not diminish the general sum of self-respect. . . . Believing that man is not a fallen but rising creature, the ideal church believes also in the whole man, and in the development of all his faculties, setting its hand to the accomplishment of the great high task of human perfection.

Having gone thus far in the discussion of the ideal church, a church based on a principle of thought as distinguished from any theological doctrine growing out of that principle, I pause now to raise a question which may seem to bear a contradictory purpose yet which I cannot avoid. Will this ideal church be Unitarian? That it will exist, is already taking shape, there can be no doubt; but there is room for very grave doubt as to whether it will call itself by the name of any of the historic sects of the past, even by the noble title Unitarian. There are two reasons for this doubt: first, the larger thought of religion which is beginning to obtain today, making the term include the best that has been thought and done in the world in the past, as well as its highest hope and faith for the future—this thought of religion is too broad and too securely allied to the very nature of things to need the support of any particular name. It lives in and from itself, unaided by human convention and dictum, like the divine love enclothing the universe of which, indeed, it is a part.

Another reason for this doubt, one touching us more closely, lies in the weakness of the Unitarian position—brought about by the contradictory acts of its own history and in the consequent confused popular misapprehension and indifference to the term. The few great controversies which have marked the history of Unitarianism, while they have accelerated the rate of religious progress in general, have had a weakening effect on the pride and enthusiasm of Unitarians themselves and on the missionary power of their faith. A religious body that begins by disclaiming the saving merit of any special belief and places life above doctrine as the test of a man's religious quality, yet whose history is marked by its refusal to exchange pulpits with a Parker, the public withdrawal of its support from men like Potter and Frothingham, and the kind of criticism the representatives of Western Unitarianism have received during the last three years, behaves with a human fallibility that threatens not only its own security but its future need and usefulness to the world. I do not mean to indulge in captious criticism on these points which are the sensitive spots in the Unitarian consciousness. As has been said before, it was not to be expected that the leaders in the rational religious movement of twenty-five or fifty years ago should see the full effects and bearings of the principles they had espoused. . . .

But the excuse that seems to explain and condone the mistakes of a generation or two ago can with difficulty be made to cover the shortcomings of the present. The unredeeming quality in our Unitarian mistake is seen in the fact that it has been repeated anew whenever the emphasis of our religious statement has fallen on the letter rather than the spirit, showing an unwillingness to abide the logical results of our chosen principles. Another source of weakness to the Unitarian cause is seen in the unnecessary delay and loss of golden opportunity resulting from this weak and shifting policy. . . . For one thing is certain: if this be not the ideal *Unitarian* church my words have tried to describe, at least they have described a recognized religious movement of the age, at work both in and out of all existing denominations. We see signs of it everywhere, in the independent churches springing up here and there, in the Broad church movement that has divided the English church into two parties and is making itself felt in this country in the preaching of men like Phillips Brooks and Heber Newton; in that movement towards the better understanding of man's spiritual nature and possibilities called Psychical Research, and in that new form of consecrated labor for the establishment of a higher moral ideal seen in the Ethical Culture societies. These are but a few of the signs which show how potent and universal is the spirit of model religious progress. Small matter to *it* whether it be called Unitarian or not; matter only to us who would preserve that name to other and higher uses than it has yet attained.

Certainly we should make a great mistake to insist on calling this church Unitarian in any sense of vain proprietorship. Rather should Unitarians strive to make the church of their selection as nearly ideal as possible. And ideality, it should be remembered, is nowhere attained in outward results, only in the conception of some great and lasting truth, the adoption of some high, pure motive that time cannot lose nor daily use outwear.

Our ideal church—what is it then? Primarily this: a religious organization whose basis of spiritual union lies deeper than any statement of belief can possibly reach in the natural emotions of love, awe, and gratitude common to all men, emotions that rise with the contemplation of the great mysteries of nature and being. A simple, natural piety pervades the hearts of all the worshipers in this church—men and women of faulty human lives but with a glowing conviction and inspiring purpose that keeps their faces set in the right direction.

There will be plenty of belief in this church, religious belief, devout, tender, and strong; but not the belief that constrains assent from opposing minds or likes to shape itself in words; rather the belief that takes the form of a continually expanding sense of trust—trust in that which is above and beyond us, the source of things from which we came; trust in that which is near and around us, the natural universe, with its wide and everlasting laws; in each other as friends and fellow workers; and in that wonderful system of social order and progress to which we belong. There will be plenty of believing in this church, but it will be of that glad, spontaneous kind which needs no coercion from another; plenty of the belief that springs, as Rev. J. V. Blake somewhere says, from *credo*—I believe; but nothing of that which owes its origin to *crede*—thou shalt believe. With such a plenitude of belief, fresh, constant, upspringing in the heart like any other natural emotion, like love or the sentiment of goodness—in belief so supplied and so indestructible in source and quality will be found ample motive for a life full of aspiration and busy well-doing.

Will this church ever be? It already is. For that matter, in so far as it includes every struggling attempt of man to realize it, it always has been. Only now at last we are beginning strictly to recognize its true character and purpose.

## ✦ *Biographical Sketch*

**Born:** *June 14, 1848, Toledo, Ohio*

**Died:** *March 9, 1918, Chicago, Illinois, age 69*

**Buried:** *Ashes scattered in Oak Woods Cemetery, Chicago, Illinois*

Though few today remember her or her work, Celia Parker Woolley was a prominent and effective Chicago reformer and Unitarian minister. Her reform efforts focused on women's rights, religious freedom, and racial justice.

Celia was the only surviving child of middle-class, liberal religious abolitionists Marcellus Harris and Harriet Marie (Sage) Parker. She spent her childhood and early adult years during the Civil War in Coldwater, Michigan, a Union stronghold and a stop on the Underground Railroad. Celia received an excellent education, graduating from the Coldwater Female Seminary in 1867. In 1868, she married J. H. Woolley, a dentist. In him, she found a life partner who not only shared her interest in reform and liberal religion but also wholeheartedly supported her desire to be more than a doctor's wife.

Attracted especially by Chicago's growing liberal religious community, the Woolleys moved there in 1876. They were intensely involved in the local Unitarian community as members of All Souls Church, where Jenkin Lloyd Jones was minister, and the Western Unitarian Conference, where Woolley held a number of positions on the boards of the general conference and the Women's Western Unitarian Conference. In 1893, she was pleasantly surprised when the Unitarian Society of Geneva (Illinois) called her to its pulpit, where she was ordained in 1894. The Reverend Woolley served Geneva until 1896, when she returned to Chicago to pastor the Independent Liberal Church of Lakeview. In 1898, she retired from the pulpit and resumed writing full time.

Woolley had begun writing in Coldwater, and by the 1890s, she had a long list of publications to her credit. These included three novels, *Love and Theology, Roger Hunt,* and *A Girl Graduate;* two pamphlets, *George Eliot: Suggestions for Clubs and Private Reading* and *The Ideal Unitarian Church;* an adult religious education curriculum; and hundreds of poems and essays. Her return to Chicago produced two more major works: a play, *The Angel at the Gate: An Easter Fantasy* and an autobiographical memoir, *The Western Slope.* For thirty-four years, she also published regularly in the Unitarian publication *Unity.* Woolley was drawn to themes of theological reflection and social, political, and racial justice. She demanded that her readers examine their role in the treatment of women, of African Americans, and of the working class as a corollary to their relationship to the divine.

A life-long clubwoman, Woolley ascended to the presidency of Chicago's most exclusive women's clubs, the Fortnightly and the Chicago Woman's Club, whose members included prominent settlement workers Jane Addams and Florence Kelly. Together with African American lecturer and clubwoman Fannie Barrier Williams,[52] they successfully integrated the Chicago Woman's Club. Woolley and Williams had become friends at All Souls Church, and their forty-year friendship had a formative effect on both their lives.

In 1904, Woolley's final reform effort began with the founding of the Frederick Douglass Center, Chicago's first interracial social center, with Fannie Barrier Williams. A precursor to the National Association for the Advancement of Colored People (NAACP), the Frederick Douglass Center was modeled after Hull House and offered many of the same types of community services, including educational programs and employment opportunities. The center was also Woolley's pulpit from which, every Sunday afternoon, leading religious speakers raised questions about the human condition and its relationship to the divine.

As a minister, Woolley was acutely aware of her part in expanding the traditional role of women. Through her active participation in the Western Unitarian Conference, she became part of the network of women ministers known as the *Iowa Sisterhood.*[53] In her book *The Western Slope,* she commented on the greater acceptance of women ministers in the Midwest than in the East:

> *The woman minister is doing good work, and the work is a kind that is fitted to the woman's nature. . . . She lives and carries on her work for the most part in the West, somewhere on the broad, hospitable plains of Iowa or Kansas, where she feels more at home, and is made to feel more at home, than in the convention-loving East.*[54]

As founder and head resident of the Frederick Douglass Center and founding member of the NAACP and the Chicago Urban League, Celia Parker Woolley spent the remaining years of her life fighting for African Americans' rights, privileges, and economic opportunities.

*Biographical Sketch by* KOBY LEE

## ✦ Writings of Celia Parker Woolley

*The Angel at the Gate: An Easter Fantasy.* Chicago: The Celia Parker Woolley Memorial Committee of the Chicago Woman's Club, 1919.

"Democracy and the Race Problem." *Quarterly Bulletin of the Meadville Theological School* 10 (October 1915): 3–12.

"The Frederick Douglass Center, Chicago." *The Commons* 9 (July 1904): 328–329.

*George Eliot: Suggestions for Clubs and Private Reading.* Chicago: Charles H. Kerr, 1890.

*A Girl Graduate.* New York: Houghton, Mifflin, 1889.

*The Ideal Unitarian Church.* Chicago: Charles H. Kerr, 1889. Also published in *Unity Mission* 1 (May 1889): 3–11.

*Love and Theology.* Boston: Ticknor, 1887.

"The Relation of Woman to Church and State." *The Index* 31 (January 1878): 50–52.
*Roger Hunt.* New York: Houghton, Mifflin, 1892.
*The Western Slope.* Evanston, IL: William S. Lord, 1903.

## ✦ Biographical Resources

Helvie, Clara Cook. "Unitarian Women Ministers." Bound typescript presented to the Historical Society of the American Unitarian Association, 1928. Meadville-Lombard Theological School, Chicago.
Lee, Koby. "Friendship across the Color Line: Celia Parker Woolley and Fannie Barrier Williams." Occasional Paper #15. Malden, MA: Unitarian Universalist Women's Heritage Society, 1997.
Lee-Forman, Koby. "The Simple Love of Truth: The Racial Justice Activism of Celia Parker Woolley." Ph.D. diss., Northwestern University, Evanston, IL, 1995.
Robinson, David. *The Unitarians and the Universalists.* Westport, CT: Greenwood Press, 1985.
Tucker, Cynthia Grant. *Prophetic Sisterhood: Liberal Women Ministers of the Frontier, 1880–1930.* Boston: Beacon Press, 1990.
Unitarian-Universalist Society (Geneva, IL). *Pulpit and Pew Tales.* Geneva, IL: Unitarian-Universalist Society, 1992.
Willard, Frances E., and Mary A. Livermore, eds. *A Woman of the Century.* Chicago: Charles Wells Moulton, 1893.

# Obedience to the Heavenly Vision

## Sermon Delivered at Least Twenty-Eight Times, 1889–1908

MARY AUGUSTA SAFFORD (1851–1927) *was the driving force of the Iowa Sisterhood of Unitarian ministers in the Midwest. She founded or organized six Unitarian congregations in Iowa and one in Florida, and she helped coordinate the efforts of this important group of women ministers in organizing nine other congregations. She also served as a director of the American Unitarian Association, occasional chaplain of the Iowa state legislature, and president of the Iowa Suffrage Association.*

*Because she was so busy being a minister and administrator, Mary Safford had little time to write, except for sermons and editorials in* Old & New, *the monthly journal of the Iowa Unitarian Conference. Probably the most representative of her writings is a sermon she first gave at a gathering of the Western Unitarian Conference in Chicago (October 27, 1889) and then repeated at least twenty-eight times in many places in Iowa between 1889 and 1908. This excerpt combines several versions: The beginning is from her 1899 conference sermon in Omaha, Nebraska, and the remainder is from two versions preached in Cherokee, Iowa, in 1892 and 1900. This sermon clearly demonstrates her ability to inspire her listeners to "carry forward our noble enterprise to larger and yet larger results."*

See the Biographical Sketch on pages 500–503.

> *"I saw a light from heaven and I heard a voice saying unto me, I have appeared unto thee for this purpose to make thee a minister and a witness both of these things which thou hast seen and of those things which I will appear unto thee.*
>
> *Wherefore, O King Agrippa, I was not disobedient unto the heavenly vision but shewed first unto them of Damascus and at Jerusalem and throughout all the coasts of Judea and then to the Gentiles that they should repent and turn to God and do works meet for repentance."*
>
> —Acts XXVI

Among the great souls of the ages, the apostle Paul justly takes high marks. Because he united, in that rare combination, breadth of view with intensity of purpose, his plans were lofty in conception, bold in execution, and far reaching in their results. . . .

What was the secret of his power? . . . What was it I say which gave the world a man so broad in his thought, so inclusive in his sympathy yet so mature in his devotion? Let Paul himself make answer. "Wherefore, O King Agrippa, I was not disobedient unto the heavenly vision." In these words we find the key which unlocks the wealth of that great soul whose ardor culture did not quench, which made a world its debtor. When new light came it was welcomed and used. It matters little just how, and when, and where great truths dawn upon the soul; it matters more than words can tell whether these truths are welcomed and obeyed. And Paul was not disobedient unto the heavenly vision— We cannot tell just how this vision came to him. . . . Doubtless this vision came to him in a natural not a miraculous way, was an inner experience not an external event, but it was nonetheless real. For God speaks to us as clearly in high thoughts and noble feelings as through the voiced commands in tones of thunder from the skies. What the eye of reason and conscience perceive surely is not less sacred than what the external eye beholds; hence whatever may have been the real nature of Paul's experience, that which most concerns us is the great fact that he was not disobedient unto the heavenly vision, that the truth revealed to him was wrought into his life, received his persistent ever loyal support.

For if such devotion ennobled the life of Paul not less will it exalt our lives. To us there has come a heavenly vision of eternal power and goodness which claims our obedience just as strongly as the truth made known to Paul demanded his unfaltering devotion. Aye, as the years of time speed on, as knowledge and wisdom increase and we see more clearly than our fathers saw, yet stronger and stronger grows our obligation to be true that we may not prove ungrateful for all we have received, for that heavenly vision which has slowly been prepared for us by the toil and struggle of the centuries. And so beautiful is the vision which gleams upon our sight as men and women of the liberal faith that we marvel that any are indifferent to its worth. For consider what it is as compared with what our fathers saw.

Gone is the frowning tyrant, the endless hell that cast a pall upon the days of our childhood, and instead we see a universe where law and love are one, where "nothing walks with aimless feet," where "not a worm is cloven in vain" but where all things slowly but surely and sublimely move toward "one far off divine event." In and through this majestic, orderly universe we find a Power divine, the mighty yet all loving one who guides the circling planets that go singing on their way yet stoops to "hold a human heart that it break not too far."

And this Eternal One who truly speaks in every law that plays upon our being comes near to us not only in the brave true life of Jesus but in every noble life. For we see man, not fallen from a high estate and utterly depraved but slowly climbing from better up to best, revealing more and more of the eternal love as he leaves behind him selfishness and low desires and reaches out the generous helping hand to those about him. We see him envisioned by laws which do not change, hence reaping always what he sows, saved from sin and the punishment of sin not by the merits of another but only through brave, persistent efforts to build up truth and love in his own being.

Hence we see as Paul saw that men ought everywhere to repent and turn to God doing works worthy of repentance. We see that it is not the naming of a name but the doing of the Father's will which gives entrance to that kingdom of truth and love, that real heaven of the soul which fadeth not away, that heaven which is joy and strength and peace. This is the heavenly vision our eyes behold today. Are we obedient to it? As individuals and as a church do we have that moral earnestness which Paul had, that intensive desire to share with others the great truths which gleam like stars upon our way? Thousands are still held in bondage by ignorance, by cruel views of God and man, by their own selfishness. Are we eager to give to them of the good we have received? Do we strive to show to them how beautiful it is to live when life is gladdened by a noble faith in God and man and duty? When is one sure that all things are rooted in unchanging love? We have organized this church, but are we doing all we have the power to do to help it grow, to make it a center of light and warmth in this community? A center from which there will constantly radiate the truth that liberates and lifts, the love that strengthens and consoles? Do we realize the obligation that rests upon us to carry forward our noble enterprise to larger and yet larger results?

Are we alive to the fact that as "eternal vigilance is the price of liberty" so eternal activity is the price of growth? That neither as individuals nor as a church can we make progress without effort and sacrifice? O, friends, if we would only be obedient to the heavenly vision that we enjoy today, would only proclaim most earnestly in words and deeds the glad gospel of eternal love, what might we not accomplish during the next few years!

I know men need food and clothing, but I know they also need the saving power of high thoughts and unselfish love, of that soul culture which gives to life new meaning and glory. Surely it should be our joy to give what thus has power to bless. And the world is ready now to receive the truth which once it feared or scorned, if this truth is rightly presented, if it shines in the face and glows in the life as well as speaks on the tongue. For the leaven of liberal thought has been and still is working in thoughtful minds everywhere. Witness the giving up of the doctrine of endless punishment by thousands in orthodox churches and the growth of what our congregational friends are pleased to call the New Theology—a theology that is really the Unitarianism of fifty years ago.

We are entering upon a new era of religious thought. A greater reformation is now in progress than was that of the sixteenth century. Science and the Higher Biblical Criticism are fast making it impossible for rational human beings longer to hold views that once were deemed essential to salvation. The old creeds are rapidly being outgrown. But there is danger that in the strong reaction from many old time beliefs, men and women may lose sight of those saving truths, those eternal principles of morality, without which life is not worth the living. There is danger that in throwing aside the superstitions of the past, they may also lose that reverence and moral earnestness that are indispensable to real progress. Intellectual emancipation from error without moral education is not less dangerous than bigotry. The knowledge that increases our power to do good, if we are so inclined, also enables us to do more harm if we lack the moral training that would inspire us to use this knowledge worthily.

Hence the work of the liberal church today is to be obedient to its heavenly vision. Not only must we proclaim the saving truths we hold, we must also strive to build up these truths in our own lives and in the lives of others. As Paul endured perils by land and by sea, as he gave time and energy to the work of proclaiming at Damascus and Jerusalem and throughout all the coasts of Judea that men should turn to God and do works worthy of repentance, so ought we to endure and work and freely give of our best selves in striving to promote the gospel of character that has untold power to bless the world. We may not go as Paul went on missionary tours to faraway places, but here in Cherokee, we may increase our influence for good tenfold if we will but put forth our best efforts and earnestly use the means at our command.

But for the loyalty to truth, the heroic self-sacrifice, the unfaltering devotion of those who in loneliness and anguish of soul were true to their convictions in times past, you and I would not enjoy today that religious liberty which is our priceless heritage. . . . We must realize our debt to the past, a debt that we cannot pay save by being brave and true and helpful in the present. And we must also think how much we owe to God who has given us reason, conscience, love, all the wonderful powers of being not to rust in us unused but to be employed for the helping of our brothers and sisters. Surely in view of all we have received we are most ungrateful unless we are doing the very best we can to make some noble return for it. And if there are any here today who rejoice in the great truths of the liberal faith but are doing nothing to support this faith, let me urge you for your own sake as well as for the sake of others no longer to be disobedient unto the heavenly vision. If you have money to give, give it freely, give it gladly. If silver and gold you have none, give time, give thought, give work, give anything you have the power to give that will strengthen this church and help to make it a beacon light to storm tossed souls. If you can do nothing more than simply come to church, be sure to come each Sunday. Come not merely for your own sake but also for the sake of the noble cause that is strengthened by your presence and your interest. Stay not outside. Ask not, is it a fashionable church? Is it a popular church? Is it a wealthy church? Ask only, is it a church of the living God? A church that proves the right to be by the grand truths that it proclaims, the good work that it does, the noble lives it helps create. Heed no ignoble questionings about popularity, wealth, or fashion, but obey your heavenly vision, be loyal to the truth you see, bravely stand by your convictions, and work for the human good. Then life will grow divine.

## ✦ *Biographical Sketch*

**Born:** *December 23, 1851, near Quincy, Illinois*

**Died:** *October 25, 1927, Orlando, Florida, age 75*

**Buried:** *Oakwood Cemetery, Hamilton, Illinois*

Around 1900, a joke was making the rounds in Unitarian circles in Iowa: “What do the Catholics and the Unitarians have in common?” Answer: “They both worship the virgin Mary.” Mary Safford was the reason for this joke, as she was nearly worshipped by the Unitarians in Iowa.

Mary Augusta Safford was one of three women from the town of Hamilton, Illinois, who entered the Unitarian ministry and became part of the Iowa Sisterhood.[55] Mary's family moved to Hamilton in 1855. She grew to womanhood under difficult pioneer circumstances, which prepared her for some of the hardships she would encounter later. Although in somewhat fragile health, she was full of life. Her friends said she always cherished those beautiful ideals that make strong men and women.

Mary was educated both at home and in the public schools and entered Iowa State University at the age of seventeen. Due to circumstances at home, she had to leave college and never graduated. However, she was an ardent student and continued her education on her own. When she felt qualified, she became a teacher and taught in Oakwood and Hamilton.

With some friends, Mary founded the Hawthorne Literary Society and held most of the offices in this organization. The years of leadership and practice in speaking that she gained from doing so prepared her for preaching, lecturing, and organizing churches. It was also through the Literary Society that she became acquainted with Unitarianism (although her childhood friend Eleanor Gordon came from a family with Unitarian roots, and they had discussed religion often[56]). The Reverend Oscar Clute, a Unitarian minister in Keokuk, Iowa, was a member and favorite speaker of the society, and Mary asked him to be her teacher and mentor in preparing herself for the ministry.

Although Mary's family strongly objected to her becoming a minister, as well as a Unitarian, she persisted. Under the Reverend Clute's tutelage, she began preaching in Oakwood and in the town hall in Hamilton; she also organized a Unitarian church there in 1878, the first of many she would organize, serve, or revitalize. In 1880, she was ordained at the meeting of the Iowa Unitarian Association in Humboldt, Iowa, and invited to become minister of the Humboldt church, while also serving a small group in Algona. Her friend Eleanor Gordon accompanied her and served as the high school principal in Humboldt in addition to performing many duties in the two churches.

Over the next five years, the Humboldt church was built into a large and successful congregation. Mary and Eleanor moved on to Sioux City, where a group of businesspeople were starting a church. Again, the church was soon in a new building, with a large and enthusiastic congregation and many social, literary, educational, service, and philanthropic activities. Jenkin Lloyd Jones called it "the best pastored church in the West" in 1893. Eleanor left in 1897, and two years later, Mary

Safford and her new assistant, Marie Jenney, moved to Des Moines.[57] There, Mary divided her time between the then-struggling Des Moines church and the Iowa Unitarian Association, for which she was field secretary and editor of its publication *Old & New.* She served as president of the Iowa Unitarian Association for seven years and as field secretary (missionary) for six. She was also a director of the Western Unitarian Conference and the American Unitarian Association.

In 1900, Mary exchanged pulpits with a woman minister and ardent suffragist from England, Gertrude von Petzhold. This arrangement allowed her to preach and lecture throughout England and Scotland. She also spoke at the World's Fair in Chicago and is credited with being the first woman to preach in a Jewish synagogue.

By 1910, the strain of traveling throughout the state to speak, to cajole, and to support the small congregations who could not find permanent ministers had taken its toll on Mary's health, so she retired to Orlando, Florida. There, she bought a home and an orange grove, which she managed herself, profitably. Her missionary zeal was still active, however, and she soon started a Unitarian church in Orlando.

Throughout her life, Mary Safford was a suffragist. Her approach to this, as well as other social justice issues, was to educate and inspire others so they would become involved, rather than to remain in the spotlight herself (although she did lobby Congress for the Women's Suffrage Amendment). She also served for a time as president of both the Iowa and Florida Equal Suffrage Associations and was on the board of directors of the National American Suffrage Association.

Mary's death was probably hastened by a serious fall, which fractured her hip and confined her to a wheelchair. Her last public appearance was at the dedication of the high school auditorium in Hamilton, Illinois, which she financed and donated to the town in memory of her mother and all pioneer women. Two weeks later, she died in Orlando. Her body was removed to the home of Eleanor Gordon, who had then retired in Hamilton, and a memorial service in her honor was held in the new school auditorium. Mary left her home in Orlando to the city to be used as an art museum.

An obituary in the *Des Moines Tribune* provided the following tribute to the life-work of this outstanding woman minister:

> *No death could possibly stir kindlier memories in Iowa than that of the Rev. Mary Safford. . . . She helped to shape the thinking and living of everybody who knew her, and always on a higher level. When the world has*

*reached the plane she would have put it on, and struggled to put it on, we shall have a much kindlier, a much more hopeful, a much more livable world.*[58]

*Biographical Sketch by* SARAH OELBERG

## ✦ Writings of Mary Augusta Safford

### Sermons Published in *Old & New*

"The Entry into Life." 5 (July 1896).
"The Power of Our Easter Faith." 9 (1902).
"Prayer." (July 1907).
"Ships That Pass in the Night." 4 (May 1895).
"They Shall Call His Name Immanuel." 10 (Dec. 1901).
"What Is Worthwhile." 12 (Oct. 1904).
"Your Work and Mine." 5 (March 1896).

### Speeches Published in *Old & New*

"Our Work in the Central West in Cooperation with the State Conferences." 5 (June 1896).
"Yearly Report to the Iowa Unitarian Association." 9 (Dec. 1902).

### Letters

To the *Des Moines Register and Leader* re misrepresentation of her sermon "Shall We Worship God or Jesus?" Iowa Historical Society, Iowa City.
To the Ministerial Association of Des Moines re vote to exclude Unitarians, Jews, and Catholics from membership. Reprinted in *Old & New* 12 (January 1904).
To the *Christian Register* re Harvard Divinity School's proposal for classes to train young women as parish assistants rather than ministers. Reprinted in *Old & New* (March 1907).

## ✦ Biographical Resources

Hitchings, Catherine F. *Universalist and Unitarian Women Ministers* (Journal of the Universalist Historical Society) 10 (1975).
Tucker, Cynthia Grant. *Prophetic Sisterhood: Liberal Woman Ministers on the Frontier, 1880–1930.* Boston: Beacon Press, 1990.
Vestal, Pearl Avis Gordon. "Rev. Mary Augusta Safford: Unitarian Minister." Typescript. Iowa State Historical Society, Iowa City, n.d.

## ✦ Archives

Iowa State Historical Society, Iowa City.

# A New Testament Woman

## Address to World's Parliament of Religions, Chicago, 1893

MARION MURDOCH (1848–1943), *whose mother was a Universalist, became one of the key members of the* Iowa Sisterhood, *a group of Unitarian women ministers whose missionary work helped found and organize liberal religious societies in the Midwest, still considered somewhat of a frontier, particularly by the male-dominated, Boston-based heirarchy of the denomination. Her sermons were often on reform issues, and she was known for her excellent prayers, full of poetic language and imagery.*

*At the 1893 World's Parliament of Religions, the Reverend Murdoch spoke on "A New Testament Woman." This was Phebe, deaconess of Paul's church at Cenchrea, in Corinth, whom Paul commended to the Roman church for having "been a succorer of many, and of mine own self also." Paul trusted Phebe with great responsibilities, Murdoch said, and she served the church with love, energy, and efficiency.*

See the Biographical Sketch on pages 508–511.

*"I commend unto you Phebe, our sister, who is a servant (or deaconess) of the church that is at Cenchrea; that ye receive her in the Lord as becometh saints, and that ye assist her in whatsoever business she hath need of you; for she hath been a succorer of many, and of mine own self also."*

—Romans 16:1, 2.

It is not surprising, that this passage in Paul's epistle to the Romans should be of peculiar interest. Paul's reputation as an opponent of the public work of women is well known. For many centuries he has been considered as the chief opposer of any activity, official or otherwise, by women in the churches. They were to keep silence, he said. They were not to teach, or to talk, or to preach. They were to ask no questions except in the privacy of their homes. Paul merely shared the popular opinion of his time when he exclaimed with all his customary logic,

"Man is the glory of God, but woman is the glory of the man." Either proposition standing by itself meets our hearty approval. "Man is the glory of God." "Woman is," we are told, "the glory of man." But combining them with that adversative particle we feel that Paul's doctrine of the divine humanity with reference to woman is not quite sound according to the present standard. We have come to feel that woman may also be the glory of God.

But here in this sixteenth chapter of Romans we notice a digression from the general doctrines of Paul in this direction. "I commend unto you Phebe, our sister, who is a servant (or deaconess) of the church which is at Cenchrea." I use the word deaconess or deacon because the Greek term is the same as that translated deacon elsewhere, and the committee on the new version have courageously put "or deaconess" into the margin.

By Paul's own statement, then, Phebe was deaconess of Paul's church at Cenchrea. Cenchrea was one of the ports of Corinth, in Northern Greece. This epistle to the Romans was written at Corinth and sent to Rome by Phebe. It was nearly a thousand miles by sea from Cenchrea to Rome, and this was one of the most important and one of the ablest of all Paul's letters. Yet he sent it over to Rome by this woman official of the church and said, "I commend unto you Phebe. Receive her in the Lord as becometh saints, and assist her in whatsoever business she hath need of you; for she hath been a succorer of many, and of myself also."

I have thought therefore that it might be interesting to ask ourselves the question, What did Phebe do? supplementing it with some reference to the Phebes of today. What was it that so overcame this prejudice of Paul's that he gave her a hearty testimonial and sent her over on important business to the church at Rome? It is evident that notwithstanding all the obstacles which custom had placed about her, she had been actively at work. It is doubtful whether she even asked if popular opinion would permit her service to the church. She saw that help was needed, and she went eagerly to work. She was, we may imagine, a worker full of enthusiasm for the faith, active and eager to lend a hand in the direction in which she thought her service was most needed. Knowing the prejudice of her time, she doubtless acted in advance of custom rather than in defiance of it. She was wise enough to know that if she quietly made herself useful and necessary to the church, custom would stand back and Paul would come forward to recognize her. We may suppose that she felt a deep interest in sustaining this church at

Cenchrea. She knew without doubt the great aspirations of Paul for these churches.

Something like a dream of a church universal had entered the mind of this apostle to the Gentiles. His speech at Mars Hill was a prophecy of a Parliament of Religions. And his earnest, reproving question, "Is God not the God of Gentiles also?" has taken nearly two thousand years for its affirmative answer by Christendom in America. Yes, Paul recognized that all the world he knew had some perception of the Infinite. But he knew that this perception must have its effect upon the moral life, or it would be a mockery indeed. And there was much wickedness all about. We see by the letters of Paul as well as by history how corrupt and lawless were many of the customs both in Greece and Rome. Much service was needed. And here was a woman in Cenchrea who could not sit silent and inactive and see all this. She too must work for a Universal Church. She too must bring religion into the life of humanity. Realizing that it was her duty to help she entered into this beautiful service, we doubt not, as if it were the most natural thing in the world to do.

"She hath been a succorer of many," said Paul. In what ways she aided them we need not definitely inquire. It may have been by kind encouragement or sympathy; it may have been in wise words of warning; it may have been by pecuniary assistance or active social or executive plans for the struggling church. Whatever it was, Phebe possessed the secret. "She has been a succorer of many, and of myself also," said Paul. To Phebe therefore has been accorded the honor of aiding and sustaining this heroic man who, we have dreamed, was strong enough to endure alone perils by land and sea, poverty, pain, temptation, for the cause he loved.

And when Paul had entrusted her with this letter to the Romans, how cordial must have been her reception by the church at Rome, bearing as she did not only this epistle but this hearty recognition of her services by their beloved leader. Yet with what a smile of perplexity and incredulity must the grave elders of the church have looked upon this woman-deacon whom Paul requested them to assist in whatsoever business she had in hand. This business transacted by the aid of the society at Rome, Phebe went home full of suggestions and plans, we may imagine, for her cherished Grecian Church.

In spite of all restrictions and social obstacles, in the face of unyielding custom and prejudice, she worked earnestly for her church, transacted its business, extended its influence, and was recognized as one of its most efficient servants.

Yet, notwithstanding this public work of a woman, and Paul's plain encouragement of it, the letter of his hand was the rule of the churches for many centuries, and it forbade the sisters from uttering their moral or religious word in the sanctuaries or doing public service of any sort for their own or their brother's cause. But here and there arose the Phebes who asked no favors of custom but insisted on giving the service they could in every way they could; giving it with such zeal and spirit that people forgot that there was sex in sainthood and whispered that perhaps they also were called of God.

But not until the inauguration of a radically new movement in religion were the official barriers in some degree removed. Not until the emphasis was put upon that divine love of God which would save all creatures, upon that mother heart of Deity which would enfold all its children; not until the emphasis was put upon the spirit rather than the letter of Bible literature, upon the free rather than the restricted revelations of God, upon the Holy Spirit in the human soul, without regard to sex or time or place; not until all this was proclaimed and emphasized did the Phebes ask or receive official recognition in the ministry. And it was better so. Under the old dispensation they would have been strangely out of place; under the new, it is most fitting that they should be called and chosen. Our modern Pauls are now gladly ordaining them, and the brethren are receiving them in the Lord, as becometh saints. Now may they also be the glory of God and partakers of the Spirit; now may the words of Joel be at last fulfilled: "And it shall come to pass afterward, that I will pour out my Spirit upon all flesh, and your sons and your daughters shall prophesy."

Still there are limitations and restrictions in words. Reforms in words always move more slowly than reforms in ideas. It is wonderful how we fear innovations in language. Even in appellations of the all spirit that John reverently named Love, including in that moment of his inspiration the All-Human in the All-Divine Heart, even here we are often sternly limited to a certain gender. Dr. Bartol, of Boston, says reprovingly: "Many hold that the simple name of Father is enough. They seem unconscious that there is in their moral idea of Deity any desideratum or lack. But does this figure drawn from a single human relation cover the whole ground? Is there no Motherhood in God?"

But, thank heaven, it is no longer heresy, as it was in Boston less than a century ago, to say with Theodore Parker, "God is our Infinite Mother. She will hold us in her arms of blessedness and beauty forever and ever."

But what matter the name so we cling to the idea? What matter, so we remember that it is not man or woman in the Lord, not man or woman in the spirit, nor in the ministry of the spirit? It is divine, it is human unity.

## ✦ *Biographical Sketch*

**Born:** *October 9, probably 1848,*[59] *Garnavillo, Iowa*

**Died:** *January 28, 1943, Santa Monica, California, age 95*

**Burial:** *Private cremation*

Although she was born and raised on the prairies of Iowa, Marion Murdoch enjoyed many social and educational advantages not typically available to women of the era. Her father, Judge Samuel Murdoch, was born in Pittsburgh of Presbyterian Scotch-Irish parentage. Her mother, Louisa Patch Murdoch, was from a Universalist family and was known as a woman of strong individuality. What prompted the Murdochs to move to Iowa is unknown, but Samuel quickly became a political leader. He served in the territorial legislature before Iowa achieved statehood and later in the state legislature. He was a judge of the district court and well known throughout the state.

Marion clearly inherited the vigorous mental and moral characteristics of her parents. Her upbringing emphasized the pioneer spirit. She spent her childhood in outdoor pursuits and developed a love of nature that was evident throughout her life. Preferring to work with the horses and cattle, she adamantly refused to learn the more domestic skills of cooking and sewing. This outdoor spirit was further manifested in her love of freedom and her life-long dedication to the cause of freedom for women. At eight years of age, she announced that she was going to become a minister and began preparing for that career.

Marion's education was extensive for the times. She attended Northwestern Ladies College, in Evanston, Illinois, and Fayette College in Iowa. In 1868–1869, she was enrolled at the University of Wisconsin at Madison. She graduated from the Boston School of Oratory and Literature in 1875; afterward, she accepted a teaching position in Dubuque, Iowa, and one later in Omaha, Nebraska.

Marion Murdoch finally made the decision to begin formal study for the Unitarian ministry and enrolled in the School of Liberal Theology at Meadville, Pennsylvania, in 1882. In 1885, she was the first woman to receive the degree of bachelor of divinity there. On September 1, 1885, she was ordained at the Unity Church of Humboldt, Iowa, where she had been called as the successor to Mary A. Safford[60] and brought with her, as parish assistant, her sister Amelia. These women were part of the group of women ministers known as the Iowa Sisterhood, who founded and developed numerous Unitarian churches in the Midwest during the latter part of the nineteenth century. Their efforts were extraordinary because of the frontier conditions they worked in. Their prominence as women in the ministry was also of symbolic importance to the growing women's rights movement.

Marion Murdoch served the Humboldt church for five years, posting an impressive record of effectiveness. Each year, her congregation voted a special resolution of praise and formally presented it to her. In 1890, she resigned from the Humboldt church to take a position at First Unitarian Church of Kalamazoo, Michigan, and work with the Reverend Caroline Bartlett Crane.[61] Again, she was highly praised for being "scholarly, deep and original in thought."[62]

In Kalamazoo, Marion Murdoch met Florence Buck, who was headmistress of a school there, and the two became close, life-long friends. Under Marion's persuasion, Florence became a Unitarian and decided to study for the ministry. The two moved to Meadville, where Marion did a year of graduate work while Florence began her theological studies. For Florence's final year of studies, the two went to England, where they both studied at Manchester College and Oxford University. Marion Murdoch participated in Florence's ordination in Chicago at All Souls Church during the time of the World's Parliament of Religions in 1893 and was one of the few women to speak at the Chicago congress. Her address "A New Testament Woman" discussed the possibilities and opportunities for women in the ministry at the time. Throughout her life, Marion was deeply interested in attracting talented young women to the ministry, and she encouraged that pursuit in many of the young people she worked with.

After the World's Parliament, Marion Murdoch and Florence Buck were called as co-pastors to the Unity Church in Cleveland, Ohio, where they served for six years, sharing the tasks of ministry. Marion preached and Florence conducted the service on their first Sunday in

Cleveland; they alternated that order each Sunday afterward. When asked by a male member of the Cleveland church if it took two women to make one man, Marion answered: "No, I do not think it takes two women to make one man, but I think it takes two persons to make one good pastor."

In 1899 and part of 1900, the two traveled and studied in Europe. On their return, Florence was called to Kenosha, Wisconsin, and Marion accepted a call to the church in Geneva, Illinois; they continued to live together, however, while ministering to separate parishes. Active in many other areas beside parish work, Marion Murdoch taught art and literature and public speaking. She had a low, rich speaking voice that enhanced her pulpit presence, and she spoke with passion, often on subjects of social reform. Her love of nature and her spiritual depth led her to develop her poetic gift. Her poems were published in many magazines, and she produced one book of verse, *The Hermit Thrush.* Marion was also recording secretary for the Women's Ministerial Conference (a group organized by Julia Ward Howe[63] in 1875 to support all women in the liberal ministry of any denomination), and she served on the board of trustees of the Meadville Theological School for fourteen years.

Marion's declining physical strength forced her resignation in 1906, and Florence resigned from Kenosha in 1910. Together, they went to California, where they acted as missionaries of the Unitarian faith, doing supply preaching and teaching for about a year. In 1912, Florence was appointed associate director of the Department of Religious Education for the American Unitarian Association. The pair moved to Cambridge, Massachusetts, where they lived until Florence's death in 1925. After four years alone, Marion moved back to California and lived with her younger sister until her own death in 1943.

Marion Murdoch's theology is well expressed in this quotation from her sermon entitled "Helpfulness, or How the World Moves":

> *The Divine Spirit manifested in every leaf and flower and blade of grass, in every pebble under our feet, and every star over our head, and best of all in every high and pure aspiration of each individual soul! What a revelation is this! This is the message of good tidings that I bring you today,—that the voice of the Spirit may be as audible to you as to the lawgiver of Israel if you will but open your ears to hear, and your hearts to receive.*[64]

*Biographical Sketch by* DOROTHY BOROUSH

## ✦ Writings of Marion Murdoch

"The Growth of the Hebrew People." Humboldt, IA: Unity Church, 1889.

"Helpfulness, or How the World Moves: A Sermon by Rev. Marion Murdock." Humboldt, IA: Unity Church, 1888.

*The Hermit Thrush and Other Verses.* Boston: Beacon Press, 1924.

"A New Testament Woman, or What Did Phoebe Do?" Address to the World's Parliament of Religions, Chicago, 1893.

"Women as Students and Preachers." Address at Meadville Theological School Semi-Centennial, June 1894, Meadville, Pennsylvania.

## ✦ Biographical Resources

Helvie, Clara Cook. "Unitarian Women Ministers." Bound typescript presented to the Historical Society of the American Unitarian Association, 1928.

Hitchings, Catherine F. *Unitarian Universalist Women Ministers.* 2nd ed. Boston: Unitarian Universalist Historical Society, 1985.

Tucker, Cynthia Grant. *Prophetic Sisterhood: Liberal Women Ministers of the Frontier, 1880–1930.* Boston: Beacon Press, 1990.

Willard, Frances E., and Mary A. Livermore. *A Woman of the Century.* Buffalo, NY: Charles Wells Moulton, 1893. Reprint, Detroit: Gale Research, 1967.

FANNIE BARRIER WILLIAMS

# Religious Duty to the Negro

## From Address to World's Parliament of Religions, Chicago, 1893

FANNIE BARRIER WILLIAMS (1855–1944) *was an African American Unitarian, a talented musician, public lecturer, social reform activist, and active member of All Souls Church (Unitarian) in Chicago. She spoke at the 1893 World's Parliament of Religions on "The Condition of the American Negro." After fearlessly presenting the facts on American slavery and racism, she concluded: "The hope of the negro and other dark races in America depends upon how far the white Christians can assimilate their own religion. . . . What we need is such a reinforcement of the gentle power of religion that all souls, of whatever color, shall be included within the blessed circle of its influence."*

See the Biographical Sketch on pages 275–278.

The strength and weakness of the Christian religion as believed, preached, and practiced in the United States is aptly illustrated in its influence as a civilizing and educational force among the colored people of this country. The negro was brought to this country by Christians for the use of Christians, and he has ever since been treated, estimated, and gauged by what are called Christian ideas of right and wrong.

The negro has been in America so long and has been so completely isolated from everything that is foreign to American notions as to what is compatible with Christianity that he may be fittingly said to be entirely the product of Christian influences. . . .

All attempts to Christianize the negro were limited by the important fact that he was property of a valuable and peculiar sort and that the property value must not be disturbed, even if his soul were lost. If Christianity could make the negro docile, domestic, and less an independent and fighting savage, let it be preached to that extent and no further. Do not open the Bible too wide.

Such was the false, pernicious, and demoralizing gospel preached to the American slave for two hundred years. But, bad as this teaching was, it was scarcely so demoralizing as the Christian ideals held up for the negro's emulation. When mothers saw their babes sold by Christians on the auction block in order to raise money to send missionaries to foreign lands; when black Christians saw white Christians openly do everything forbidden in the Decalogue; when, indeed, they saw, as no one else could see, hypocrisy in all things triumphant everywhere, is it not remarkable if such people have any religious sense of the purities of Christianity? . . .

That there is something higher and better in the Christian religion than rewards and punishments is a new lesson to thousands of colored people who are still worshipping under the old dispensation of the slave Bible. But it is not any easy task to unlearn religious conceptions. "Servants obey your masters" was preached and enforced by all the cruel instrumentalities of slavery in the world. . . .

Knowing full well that the religion offered to the negro was first stripped of moral instruction and suggestion, there are thousands of white church members even who charge or are ready to believe that the colored people are a race of moral reprobates. Fortunately the negro's career in America is radiant with evidence showing that he has always known the difference between courage and lawlessness of all forms, and anarchy in this country is not of negro origin nor a part of his history.

There was a notable period in the history of this country when the moral force of the negro character was tested to an extraordinary extent, and he was not found wanting. When the country was torn asunder by the passions of Civil War and everybody thirsted for blood and revenge in every violent form, when to ravage and to kill was the all-controlling passion of the hour, the negro's opportunity for retribution was ripe and at hand.

The [white] men who degraded the [black] race and were risking everything to continue that degradation left their widows, their daughters, their mothers, wealth, and all the precious interest of home in the keeping of a race who had received no lessons of moral restraint. It seems but tame to say that the negro race was loyal to that trust and responsibility. Nowhere in Christendom has such nobleness of heart and moral fortitude been exampled among any people, and a recollection of the negro's conduct under this extraordinary test should save the race from the charge of being lacking in moral instincts.

There is yet another notable example of the moral heroism of the colored American, in spite of his lack of real religious instruction. . . .

The colored churches of all denominations in this country are not evidences of our unfitness for religious equality, but they are so many evidences of the negro's religious heroism and self-respect that would not brook the canting assertion of mastery and superiority of those who could see the negro only as a slave, whether on earth or in heaven.

There is another and brighter side to the question as to how far the Christian religion has helped the colored people of America to realize their positions as citizens of this proud Republic. . . . Though the Bible was not an open book to the negro before emancipation, thousands of the enslaved men and women of the negro race learned more than was taught to them. Thousands of them realized the deeper meanings, the sweeter consolations, and the spiritual awakenings that are a part of the religious experiences of all Christians. These thousands were the nucleus out of which was to grow the correct religious life of the millions.

In justification of the church it must be said that there has always been a goodly number of heroic men and saintly women who believed in the manhood and womanhood of the negro race and at all times gave the benefit of the best religious teachings of the times. The colored people gladly acknowledge that, since emancipation, the churches of the country have almost redeemed themselves from their former sin of complicity with slavery.

The churches saw these people come into the domain of citizenship stripped of all possessions, unfurnished with intelligence [education], untrained in the school of self-sacrifice and moral restraint, with no way out of the wilderness of their ignorance of all things, and no leadership. They saw these people with no home or household organizations, no social order, no churches, no schools, and in the midst of people who, by training and instinct, could not recognize the manhood of the race. They saw the government give these people the certificate of freedom and citizenship without telling them what it meant. They saw politicians count these people as so many votes and laugh at them when they were pleading for schools of learning for their children.

They saw all the great business and industrial organizations of the country ignoring these people as having any possible relationship to the producing and consuming forces of the nation. They saw the whole white population looking with distrust and contempt upon the men and women, new and untried in the responsibilities of civil life. While the colored people of America were thus friendless and without status of any kind, the Christian churches came instantly, heroically, and powerfully to the rescue. They began at once not only to create a sentiment favorable to the uprising of these people but began the all-important work of building schools and churches. . . .

Going into states that knew nothing of public-school systems, they have created a passion for education among both races. States that have been hostile to the idea of universal intelligence, and that at one time made it a criminal offense to teach black men and women to read and write, have, under the blessed influence of the missionary work of the churches, been wonderfully converted and are now making appropriations for the education of colored children and founding and maintaining institutions that rank as normal schools, colleges, and industrial schools.

Whatever may be our just grievances in the Southern States, it is fitting that we acknowledge that, considering their poverty and past relationship to the negro race, they have done remarkably well for the cause of education among us. . . .

We are grateful to the American church for this significant change of sentiment, as we are grateful to it for making our cause and needs popular at the fireside of thousands of the best homes in the country. . . . Bearing in mind all this good work done by the churches since emancipation, it is proper to ask, What can religion further do for the colored people? This question is itself significant of the important fact that colored people are beginning to think for themselves and to feel restive and conscious of every limitation to their development.

At the risk of underestimating church work in the South, I must say that religion in its more blessed influences, in its wider and higher reaches of good in humanity, had made less progress in refining the life and character of the white and colored people of the South than the activity of the church interests of the South would warrant us in believing. That there is more profession than religion, more so-called church work than religious zeal, is characteristic of the American people generally and of the Southern people particularly.

More religion and less church may be accepted as a general answer to the question, What can religion further do to advance the condition of the colored people of the South? It is not difficult to specify wherein church interests have failed and wherein religion could have helped to improve these people. . . . With a due regard for the highly capable colored ministers of the country, I feel no hesitancy in saying that the advancement of our condition is more hindered by a large part of the ministry intrusted with leadership than by any other single cause.

Only men of moral mental force, of a patriotic regard for the relationship of the two races, can be of real service as ministers in the South. Less theology and more of human brotherhood, less declamation and more common sense and love for truth, must be the qualifications of the new ministry that shall yet save the race from the evils of false teachings. With this new and better ministry will come the reign of that religion which ministers to the heart and gives to all our soul functions an impulse to righteousness. . . .

The home and social life of these people is in urgent need of the purifying power of religion. We do not yet sufficiently appreciate the fact that the heart of every social evil and disorder among the colored people, especially of the rural South, is the lack of those inherent moral potencies of home and family that are the well-springs of all the good in human society.

In nothing was slavery so savage and so relentless as in its attempted destruction of the family instincts of the negro race in America. Individuals, not families; shelters, not home; herding, not marriages, were the cardinal sins in that system of horrors. Who can ever express in song or story the pathetic history of this race of unfortunate people when freedom came, groping about for their scattered offspring with only instinct to guide them, trying to knit together the broken ties of family kinship? It was right at this point of rehabilitation of the home-life of these people that the philanthropic efforts of America should have begun. It was right here that religion in its humanitarian tendencies of love, in its moral direction and purifying force, was most needed and still is most needed. Every preacher and every teacher in the South will tell us that preaching from the pulpit and teaching in the school-house are but half done so long as the homes are uninstructed in that practical religion that can make pure and sacred every relationship it touches of man, woman, and child.

Religion should not leave these people alone to learn from birds and beasts those blessed meanings of marriage, motherhood, and family. Religion should not utter itself only once or twice a week through a minister from a pulpit but should open every cabin door and get immediate contact with those who have not yet learned to translate into terms of conduct the promptings of religion.

How ardently do we all hope that the heart of American womanhood will yet be aroused and touched by this opportunity to elevate and broaden the home-life of these unfortunate women in black. It ought never to be said that a whole race of teachable women are permitted to grope their way unassisted toward a realization of those domestic virtues, moral impulses, and standards of family and social life that alone are badges to responsibility. There needs no evidence to show that these unfortunate people are readily susceptible to these higher and purifying influences of religion. Come from what source they may, Jew or Gentile, Protestant or Catholic, or from those who profess no religion but who indeed are often the most religious, the colored people are eager to learn and know those lessons that make men and women morally strong and responsible.

In pleading for some organized effort to improve the home life of these people we are asking for nothing but what is recognized everywhere as the necessary protection to the homes of all civilized people. Witness how beautifully and grandly the women of Christendom are organized to protect the homes against the invasions of intemperance. The Woman's Christian Temperance Union has gathered up the religious impulse of American womanhood for God, home, and native land. Again, to this union of pure hearts against the sin of intemperance is that other union in behalf of pure homes—"The Social Purity Society"; in fact, good women and brave men continually stand guard at the entrance of American homes, except that of the negro. Our homes need in a special degree those moral helps, promptings, inspirations, and protections that are now and everywhere the necessary safeguards even to the homes of those people who are cultured in all things spiritual and mental.

There is still another and important need of religion in behalf of our advancement. In nothing do the American people so contradict the spirit of their institutions, the high sentiments of their civilization, and the maxims of their religion as they do in denying to our men and women the full rights to life, liberty, and the pursuit of happiness.

The colored people have appealed to every source of power and authority for reliefs, but in vain. For the last twenty-five years we have gone to Legislatures, to political parties, and even to churches for some cure for prejudice, but we have at last learned that helps from these are merely palliative. It is a monstrous thing that nearly one-half of the so-called evangelical churches of this country repudiate and haughtily deny fellowship to every Christian lady and gentleman happening to be of African descent. It is a shameful thing to say of the Christian religion as practiced in one part of our country that a young colored man susceptible of spiritual enlightenment will find a readier welcome in a saloon or any other place than he will in any evangelical church.

The fact is that the heart of America is fearfully wrong in its understanding and sentiment concerning the colored race. The golden rule of fellowship taught in the Christian Bible becomes in practice the iron rule of race hatred. That distinguished representative from Japan who startled this parliament the other day by arraigning Christendom for its many hypocrisies must have had in mind the irreligious conduct of white American Christians toward black American Christians.

The hope of the negro and other dark races in America depends upon how far the white Christians can assimilate their own religion. At present there seems to be no ethical attitude in public opinion toward our colored citizens. White men and women are careless and meanly indifferent about the merits and rights of colored men and women. The white man who swears and the white man who prays are alike contemptuous about the claims of colored men.

In every profession, in every trade and occupation of men there is a code of ethics that governs the relationship and fosters the spirit of fraternity among its members. This is the religious sense of the people applied to the details of practical life. Yet, even these religious promptings to deal rightly too often stop short of reaching the man or woman who happens to be black. What we need is such a re-enforcement of the gentle power of religion that all souls, of whatever color, shall be included within the blessed circle of its influence. The American negro in his meager environment needs the moral helpfulness and contact of men and women whose lives are larger, sweeter, and stronger than his. It should be the mission of religion to give him this help.

CAROLINE JULIA BARTLETT CRANE

# The Church and Poverty

## From Speech Delivered at Western Unitarian Conference, 1897

*In this speech, Unitarian* CAROLINE JULIA BARTLETT CRANE (1858–1935) *put forth with grace and power the philosophy of philanthropy that guided the women ministers of the Iowa Sisterhood: "not so often to give unto him that asks as to contrive that he shall not need to ask." She suggested that religion cannot be content with merely giving alms to people who are poor but that it has an obligation to attack the basic structures that cause and perpetuate poverty, calling for a marriage of love and action. After thirteen years as a parish minister, she entered the emerging field of urban sanitation in order to be more directly involved in alleviating human suffering through work in meat-packing plants and other areas of public health.*

See the Biographical Sketch on pages 127–130.

Mr. Gannett, in one of his searching and illuminating essays, describes "The Three Stages of the Bible's Growth." First, we have the Bible as loved and revered literature; second, we have it petrified into a quarry of dogma, and, third, we have it as loved and revered literature again, only loved and revered with all the ethical discrimination and the refinement of feeling which have accrued unto us in more than a millennium of human life.

Someone might write an analogous history of "The Church and Charity." While the inspiration of the church was an ideal life, the life of Jesus, but yesterday lived in the midst of men and tomorrow to return unto them again—a life of human tenderness which exemplified the teaching, "By this shall all men know that ye are my disciples, if ye have love one to another"—the members of this church were attached not alone by the bonds of a common spiritual experience and a common expectation of a future heavenly society; they felt intensely the social bond of their common humanity and became willing stewards over one another's wants and weaknesses. The initial impulse toward generosity and self-sacrifice given by Jesus' teaching and example was, it must be admitted, to a great extent, relieved of natural obstacles by the early doctrine that the present world-society was soon to end, and what, then, could it profit a man to be seeking preferment and laying up treasure in this perishable world? However, the primitive Christian communism was a quite natural outcome of the influences that were strongest and best in the early Christian Church. "For we are members of one another"; "if eating meat maketh my brother to offend, I will eat no meat while the world stands"; "if I have all faith so that I could remove mountains, and have not love, it profiteth me nothing"—these are quite natural expressions of the feeling of oneness among the members of the primitive church. And the exclamation of the Pagans—"See how these Christians love one another!"—was a tribute to the genuineness of that exceptional manifestation of the truly religious life.

In those times and among those people, poverty was not regarded as it is today. The Ebionite doctrines, which gloried in poverty for its own sake, had still weight, the early converts were most of them poor, and the very genius of their religion was to share with each other all they had—need being the title to help. As long as the Christian brotherhood was real—vitalized by the Spirit of Him who said, "He that hath two coats, let him impart to him that hath none"—the church had no problem of poverty in the modern sense within its borders. And the attitude toward poverty and misfortune without is disclosed by the Emperor Julian's efforts to inaugurate a Pagan charitable movement, "because," he said, "it is a scandal that the Galileeans should support the destitute not only of their religion but of ours."

But when the Christian Church, released from persecution, had acquired the power to persecute; when, abandoning the hope of Christ's early return to establish the Messianic kingdom, it conceived the new motive of building up a temporal kingdom for him and his chosen ones; . . . when the compassionate Man of Galilee was apotheosized into an inhuman god, commanding, "Depart from me, ye cursed, into the everlasting fire prepared for the Devil and his angels," then the Church took thought of the saving quality of charity, of such words as, "Whoever giveth a cup of cold water only shall in no wise lose his reward," and, "Inasmuch as ye have done it unto the least of these, ye have done it unto me," and "He that hath pity on the poor lendeth to the Lord." The giving to the poor went on, but it was largely divorced from the spirit of love and brotherhood which made Paul exclaim, "Though I bestow all my goods to feed the poor, and though I give my body to be burned, and have not charity, it profiteth me nothing!"

The Church's literal following of the precepts of Jesus, divorced from Jesus' spirit, has been one of the most fruitful sources of the curse of poverty and pauperism upon the world today. "Give unto him that asketh, and from him that would borrow turn not thou away!" Whatever is to be said of the wisdom of such an injunction, this much is certain, that the man who obeys it is bound also to obey that other primary command, "love thy neighbor as thyself," which would mean to give also much brotherliness and personal solicitude to the pensioner. But to divorce the precept of giving from the principle of loving is to make charity like papier mâché fruit stuck upon a barren and death-stricken tree—it may look well at a distance, but, as Paul says, "It is nothing." As the modern, scientific philanthropists would say, "It is a great deal worse than nothing!"

✦ ✦ ✦

The Lady Bountiful, dispensing loaves to all who come, "no questions asked," or those two duchesses who went about craving the privilege of performing the most menial and loathsome tasks for sick paupers (merely as a means of spiritual grace unto themselves), these are the conspicuous types of Christian charity through many centuries, though we cannot doubt that the real charity, which is love and which vaunteth not itself and seeketh not its own, lived on in the heart and life of many a devout follower of the religion of Jesus, and so the torch was handed down.

Today we are entering upon what Miss Jane Addams has happily named "the renaissance of Christianity." Beginning with the worship in spirit, then continuing for long in the worship of the letter, the text, the dogma, Christianity is now swinging back again into the spirit of its founders; just as the Bible has passed from literature through dogma back to literature again.

But, as our estimation of the Bible has added to it all the insight and ethical discrimination of many hundreds of years, so modern Christian charity, at its best is a return upon a spiral, back to, but yet far above that of the earliest time.

Today there is some zeal, according to knowledge dearly bought. Today the Church realizes that she has been through centuries contributing to create the poverty that now confronts her, and the more enlightened members of that church no longer contend for a distinction between Christian charity and human charity; no longer kindly apply first century precepts to nineteenth century problems. All true philanthropists, whatever their names or antecedents, rest back upon that fundamental principle, which was laid down by Jesus and others, that men should love and serve each other; and Christian charity and scientific charity are becoming one.

Today the Church, in so far as it is wise, seeks the causes of evils it would remedy. Not so often to give unto him that asks as to contrive that he shall not need to ask. Regarding poverty as a symptom of physical, mental, moral, or industrial disorder or disease, the problem is how to find and apply the remedy. A few churches of today (and it will be many churches of the future) engage in this high and holy task—a task so great that it overflows Sunday and fills every day of every week. Preaching from the pulpit those eternal principles of human right and brotherhood which are at war with every form of oppression and slavery and slothfulness and those truths of self-reverence and worship of the highest which would lift men out of mean and ignoble ways of life; seldom seeking to commit the church as a church to specific schemes of Reform, but seeking to so enlighten the minds and touch the hearts of the people that they, as business men or lawyers or doctors or editors or legislators or aldermen or laborers, as women in public or domestic life, shall commit themselves, according to their several consciences, to whatsoever things make for the common good.

✦ ✦ ✦

O, but to help the worthy is not so hard! To make a loan, to find employment, to give cheer in times of hardship and discouragement—this will do.

But the unworthy! Here is the task of the Church and of the world. To relieve poverty of manhood, of motive, of hope; to sting into life the deadened purpose; to cure locomotor ataxia of the spirit; to lift upright the cringing pauper soul (whether these problems are associated with physical destitution or not), here is the task of church and state, of man and God! To give food and clothing—what avail? Nay, it is dire need like this which demands the costliest gift in human power.

Out of the chasm that opened in the Roman Forum, so the legend reads, came forth an awful voice, demanding that the most precious thing in Rome be cast thereon ere the fearful hollow would be closed. And men brought their stores of gold, and women their jewels, and cast them in. And still the chasm yawned, till the noblest Roman youth of them all came to the brink and looked in and cast himself into that pit, and it was closed.

And here and there a man, a woman, has read and understood this parable and has cast a pure, true, rightly-yearning life into the yawning gulf of direst human need; has lived or died, as need might be, for others' weal. And whether it has been Father Damien on the leper island, or Clara Barton ministering to the outraged Armenians, or Booker T. Washington among the benighted negroes of the Black Belt of the South, or Arnold Toynbee or Jane Addams, or the Salvation Army lassie amid the forsaken ones in the slums of a great city, or the humblest father and mother making sacrifices that their children may enter into a richer life, or the countless mother, father-hearts that yearn over the unmothered, unfathered little ones, all these testify that here in the self-forgetting life is the more excellent way; and they hear the voice of one who greatly loved, saying:

"Children, love one another, love one another! for love is of God!"

EDNAH DOW LITTLEHALE CHENEY

# The Reign of Womanhood

## From Address at Unitarian Service in Commemoration of Queen Victoria's Diamond Jubilee, June 20, 1897

EDNAH DOW LITTLEHALE CHENEY (1824–1904), *whose father was a Universalist, stated in her memoirs that she considered herself a Unitarian. A member of the Free Religious Association, she was its president from 1903–1904.*

*Ednah Dow Littlehale Cheney's 1897 address to Unitarians on the occasion of the Diamond Jubilee of Great Britain's Queen Victoria praised Victoria for her benign and steady virtue and also for her public example of a woman of authority incarnating the ideal of "divine womanhood," expressed by Goethe's Faust as "Das Ewig Weibliche zieht uns hinan" ("The Eternal Womanly leadeth us on"). Honoring and imitating such female virtues could only bless humanity.*

See the Biographical Sketch on pages 531–535.

*So God created man in His own image, in the image of God created He him; male and female created He them.*

—Genesis 1:27.

This one verse contains a condensed statement of the great beginning of creation. First, God created man in His own image, and this is repeated, in the image of God created He him; then as duality begins to appear, male and female created He them, and the history of mankind in its struggle begins to be related.

The problem of our age is womanhood; and therefore on this day when we celebrate the longest, the most prosperous and peaceful reign which England has ever known, and under the beneficent guiding hand of a true woman, it is becoming for us to consider this great problem, not so much in its outward and practical form, which it will take our next century to work out, as in its inner meaning and in reference to the eternal principles which alone will lead us to its final and triumphant solution.

For the true meaning of this primal question of sex does not consist alone of the outward form, which envelops the human spirit, but in its essential spirit. We are seeking to fathom the secret of life and to enter into the purposes of creation. We are trying, if not to comprehend, at least to apprehend the thought of God, when out of the peaceful unity of being He brought all this complex, warring, jarring life of creation, in which the two forces ever tending to reunion and mutual action are the necessary condition of all life. Sex as the most universal manifestation of the first step in creation is traceable throughout all life. . . . This great mystery, how out of the One comes first the two, and out of the twain again come the many, confronts us everywhere, in science, in life, in metaphysics, in religion.

We, as Unitarians, may rightfully give up the narrow form of a Trinity which saw the incarnation of God in one mystic Being alone, and not in all the wondrous world of life, but we cannot get away from the philosophic Trinity which recognizes the One, the All, the two through which unity acts, and the resulting third which is the Spirit of Life, making possible all this universe of infinite variety and yet underlying harmony.

✦ ✦ ✦

In the most ancient religions known to us the human mind has recognized that the duality which it finds in life has its origin in the divine nature.

✦ ✦ ✦

[This thought] becomes somewhat obscured in Christian theology, because of the tendency to dogma, . . . but it has still always existed there in the essential thought of the Trinity and in the very inadequate, though beautiful, symbolism which accepted the Virgin Mary, the mother of Jesus, as the Divine Mother of mankind. And so necessary is this recognition to the human heart that the honor and love due to the primal Infinite God, or to His representative in humanity, the Divine Son, was almost obscured by the tenderer trust and affection given to the Queen of Heaven. In our own day this great thought has again found expression from the deep heart of Theodore Parker, whose reverent invocation to the Source of all good, as "our Father and Mother, too," will never be forgotten by those who were wont to hear it.

✦ ✦ ✦

In his greatest poem, Faust, the German Goethe, the leading thinker and poet of our age, has given immortal expression to the thought of the divine womanhood, in the line which is spoken by the chorus Mysticus at the close of the man's life-long struggle and which opens the way to his redemption:

"Das Ewig Weibliche zieht uns hinan."
(The Eternal Womanly leadeth us on.)

The word "eternal" makes the grand thought of this line. Woman is not an accident of creation, a necessity of earthly life, a second thought of God, who found man too lonely if left to himself and who therefore made for him a pleasing toy to charm his leisure hours and soothe him when ill or weary. It is not woman as a minister to earthly pleasure that leadeth us on. It is the eternally womanly, as truly divine, as essential to the order of being as the manly, who is to lead the soul upward and onward, into that entire oneness with God which is redemption and Heaven. . . . What leadeth us on? The attractive principle, the love which receives impulse and becomes creative. It is at once attraction which stimulates action and the centripetal power which holds action true to its centre. While the degradation of womanhood is the most terrible evil of all time, . . . there remains yet one Pole Star of Faith which shines through the gloomiest darkness and gives us hope that humanity can never wholly lose its way. . . . The lowest, vilest man does not willingly lose his ideal of woman, does somehow cherish some feeling of motherhood, some belief in an unselfish love, some little gleam of romance in his heart, some sense that a woman's prayers are more powerful than his curses, some thought of the child that might have clung about his knees, some recognition that there is a power of love, an "eternally womanly" that may yet lead him upward and on to redeemed life out of the very jaws of death and hell. Hence, men judge actual women so severely as not answering to their ideal. You remember when the miners of California, living for months and years their wild, half-savage life, heard that an emigrant train was coming, bringing women in their company, they exclaimed: "Thank God, the women are coming to make us better." They knew not who they were; they might be the very refuse of the slums of the cities, driven out by dishonor and vice, but the men did not think of that; they recognized the "eternally womanly." . . .

Man's relation to woman is the great fact of his moral life. If he fails in it, no matter how the world may condone his fault, it saps the very strength of his manhood. . . . When it is claimed that women should take their share of the active work and vital responsibility of the world's life, we often hear men say, "Oh, we do not want woman brought down from her lofty pedestal; we want our ideal kept high and pure." Do you ever think that woman, too, must have her ideal of man kept pure and holy? Can she touch pitch and not be defiled? Her ideal of man must match her own standard of spiritual purity and truth, or instead of leading him on she is dragged down to the dust with him. The whole meaning of sex is mutual relation and the one sex must be fit to mate the other.

✦ ✦ ✦

If the human heart was not satisfied in its earliest efforts to draw near to the secrets of life without the recognition of the woman, the mother, in God, whence came then the debasing views of woman which have had such sway in the world and have produced such corruption and misery that we shrink from any effort to portray it? Even the effort to express this dual thought of God, mingled with an anthropomorphism which, "making of God even such a one as themselves," has enlarged the selfish, narrow passions of humanity into universal proportions, until the great fact of evil and sin covered the whole sphere of thought and religion. This tremendous problem of the existence of evil demanded a solution. Man must have been wholly divine, pure in his origin; what could have separated him from God? It must be a power almost equal to God that could thus strive against and often seemingly overcome him; and, as this power was subtle and wise after its kind, and knew that when the best is turned to evil it becomes the worst, so the evil power sought his instrument in woman, the embodiment of love, and she came to express in the popular theology not the upward, redeeming source of good but the arch temptress to sin and evil. Thus woman in many mythologies is both the tempter and savior. She represents attractive love, and that love is capable of being the greatest incentive to good or the most fearful impulse to evil, as it is received and developed. So in Hebrew thought woman is the tempter; yet the pure mother bringing forth the son, that is, restoring the whole, the harmony brings also salvation. So even the thought of fatherhood and motherhood became tainted with sin, and the monstrous doctrine, which lies like a heavy pall over the sweet region of theology, the doctrine of innate depravity and total alienation from God, being conceived and born in sin, has carried its message of doubt, despair, and hate into the fairest regions of life. Against it the doctrine of the divine motherhood is perpetually striving, and it is to the recognition of the holiness of the feminine principle that we must look for the regeneration of the world. Jesus set a little child in the midst of them and said, "Of such is the kingdom of heaven." Could He have been thinking of him as the offspring of the devil? In the Christian church the two opposite conceptions of woman have remained side by side struggling with each other; but where in the words of Jesus Himself, even when He speaks to one who calls herself a sinner, is there ever a want of recognition of the love to which all will be forgiven? There was a time when woman was the type of all evil and when the deepest and holiest of human relations could not be consecrated within the walls of a church. It was a great step in the recognition of her nature when marriage was recognized as a sacrament, a symbol of that divine union which can alone promote harmony and life. Even now it is felt that the presence of woman desecrates many of the holy places of the church, and, while the Virgin is honored, and saints and martyrs are objects of prayer and devotion, the human, living mother is not received into the active service and honors of the church. Nor are our Protestant skirts free from this reproach, while large bodies of religious men refuse to hear the divine message if it come from the lips of a woman. Yet in all religions and all mythologies woman has had direct reception from divinity and become the inspired prophetess. There is one aspect of the religious veneration for woman which, while it has its deep meaning and beautiful expression, has yet worked great mischief, because it is partial and not the whole truth. In the ancient religions we find that it is mainly as the human mother that woman is honored. As a wife she is loved indeed, but loved as a possession, and this love, so often selfish and exacting, allied so closely to selfish enjoyment and the lust of power, has thus become the greatest of dangers, the worst of foes to woman. It is only the mother who has always claimed a certain independent value and secured a measure of pure honor and respect, and even this feeling is vitiated by the selfish superstition that, as the father of sons whom she has brought to him the lasting glory of the man is secure. Thus even in the deepest corruption of womanhood something of purity and nobility and truth has lingered about the idea of motherhood, and its power to restore purity to the soul, and hope to the life, is acknowledged even in those whom the world counts as lost. . . . But sin, falsehood, misery come in whenever we separate one function, however important, from the whole of life. Wholeness is holiness, and when we assume to cut off one part we destroy the harmony, we vitiate the purity of the whole. Fatherhood, too, is great and holy, so holy that we have transferred its name to the One, the Author of all good, but fatherhood is not the only duty of humanity. . . . Woman is a mother; but she is more than a mother. She is a living, immortal soul. She is a child of God and she is bound to fulfill all life and all righteousness as much as man is.

✦ ✦ ✦

So woman has too often accepted a fancied duty, a romantic virtue, instead of recognizing her whole relation to God and humanity, which demands of her the full development of her nature and the employment of every God-given faculty. . . . With the exclusive acceptance of special function has grown the idea of woman as an accident of creation, an adjunct to the masculine type of humanity, created for his enjoyment and help, and having no right to seek her own fullness of life and action. . . .

Woman is constantly tending towards relation, and her happiness is not complete, her life is not fulfilled except in recognition of the life of others, in perpetual receiving from and giving out to others.

You will tell me and tell me correctly that this is also true of man and that the highest man is no more self-dependent than the most loving woman.

But this truth of relation which has been emphasized and developed, though often in the poorest way, as regards woman, has been obscured in man, as he has so largely taken the material aggressive part of the life of the world, and as woman, in so far truly his worst enemy, has yielded to his exactions and fostered his pride of authority and self-love.

But woman's ideal of man is as truly that of a nobly, grandly, unselfish self-forgetfulness as his of her. . . .

True manhood and true womanhood are ever appearing in various forms, for the two are one. I know not whether Coleridge is right in asserting, or Theodore Parker was wrong in denying, that there is sex in souls. . . . I believe that, as we rise higher and higher in the scale of spiritual being, the differing qualities which we find expressed in sex are blended into a more perfect harmony and that out of the differentiation, out of the duality which is necessary for creation and life, we come ever and ever nearer to a restored harmony and unity of being.

So when we consider the highest representatives of masculine humanity, Philip Sydney, Fenelon, St. Francis, Channing, and above all the great founders of religions, Buddha and our own blessed Jesus, we cannot but recognize in them the perfect blending of the finest womanly traits with the strength and power which we attribute to man. And so in woman, Joan of Arc, the girl warrior; Elizabeth of Hungary; Catherine of Sienna; Louise of Prussia; Florence Nightingale—hold our reverence by their firm, manly courage and endurance, as much as they win our hearts by their feminine beauty and tenderness. . . .

[W]e hear the echoes of her onward tread, and those who fear its victory are helping it on by the interest and discussion they excite. Everywhere there is new recognition of her rights and her duties. . . . The young woman no longer prides herself on the delicacy of her constitution and the nervous weakness which screams at the sight of a spider, but guards her health as a precious possession, not to preserve her personal beauty, but to give her strength to do her work.

Everywhere there is a fresh inquiry in woman's essential nature.

✦ ✦ ✦

While pessimism has been rampant in our day and the degeneration of society has been the theme of philosophers, . . . there are gleams of hope and promise which show us that "the eternal womanly is still leading us on" and that man's noblest nature is asserting itself and struggling up to the same high aims.

In our own day we are blessed with the reign of womanhood (long may it continue), which is enough to cheer our hearts and confirm our faith in its ultimate power in the kingdom of man.

✦ ✦ ✦

For sixty years a woman has sat upon the throne of the foremost nation of Europe. Her name is known, beloved, and honored all around the earth, for the sun does not set upon the world that owns her sway. We do not claim her as an exceptional woman but as a true woman. Not gifted with the dangerously fascinating beauty of Mary of Scotland, the genius of Elizabeth of England, or the daring of Catherine of Russia, she is a typical woman, clear in her perceptions of right, entire in her devotion to duty, loving and tender in her heart, holy and pure in her life. She has accepted the high position to which she was called by inheritance, with its heavy responsibilities, but has done so not that the nation be governed by her personal will but that the whole wisdom of the past, as embodied in law and the best intelligence of the whole people, might find expression in her action.

✦ ✦ ✦

We are thankful today for the noble life of the Queen of these realms; we are thankful for it as a history of human progress towards more and better national life; but more than all do we prize it and thank God for it, as a prophecy of the finer, broader development of womanhood and of the time when all the strength of manhood and all the love of womanhood shall be so blended in life that they shall bring us nearer to the kingdom of God, the reign of truth and peace.

## ✦ *Biographical Sketch*

**Born:** *June 27, 1824, Boston, Massachusetts*

**Died:** *November 19, 1904, Jamaica Plain, Massachusetts, age 80*

**Buried:** *South Manchester, Connecticut*

As a reformer, philanthropist, lecturer, and writer, Ednah Dow Littlehale Cheney traveled in Transcendentalist circles and actively participated in the movements for women's rights and the education of freed slaves. She was known as an effective speaker and organizer as well as a poet, essayist, and biographer.

Ednah was born in Boston, the third daughter of Ednah Parker Dow and Sargent Smith Littlehale. Of her eight siblings, five died in infancy. She particularly remembered the death of one baby sister. Then eight years old, Ednah earnestly prayed God to spare the baby and was shocked when she awoke to find her sister dead. In later years, she reflected on this incident as it affected her faith development.

Her father, a successful wholesale grocer, had grown up in a Gloucester Universalist family and was "not very strict in religious regulations," according to Ednah. She remembered his reading the Bible to the children on Sunday afternoons. When she heard the story of God's commanding the escaping Israelites to "borrow" jewels from their Egyptian neighbors, she looked into her father's face and asked, "Father, was that right?" Not hesitating between the claims of biblical authority and his daughter's sense of justice, he answered, "No, my child, it was not."[65] Politically as well as religiously liberal, Sargent Smith Littlehale supported the women's rights and antislavery movements.

Ednah's mother's family in Exeter, New Hampshire, was orthodox, and Ednah experienced severe Calvinist restrictions on Sundays when she visited there. In Boston, she went with her family to church and Sunday school on Church Green and, in her early teens, began to take a real interest in the services. About the same time, she spent summers with an aunt and uncle in Maine. Her uncle was a Unitarian, and she went with him to services in Dover. Ednah attended various schools in Boston, but her education seems to have prospered best at home, where both parents were avid readers, or in Maine, where she could explore her uncle's library.

In 1851, Ednah's beloved father died, leaving his family in comfortable circumstances. Ednah, then twenty-seven, turned her energies to forming a design school for women, similar to one she had discovered during a stay in Philadelphia. The school was not successful, but the supervisory committee included Harriot Kezia Hunt, Abby W. May, and Julia Ward Howe[66] in addition to Ednah and such distinguished gentlemen as James Russell Lowell and Charles Eliot Norton. Ednah enjoyed committee meetings "as lively and entertaining as a literary club."[67]

In 1853, Ednah married Seth Wells Cheney, a prominent portrait artist from a silk-manufacturing family in South Manchester, Connecticut. His poor health took them to Europe during the winter of 1854–1855. They returned to South Manchester, where a daughter, Margaret Swan Cheney, was born on September 8, 1855. A year later, Seth Cheney died, and Ednah returned to Boston with Margaret.

After a visit from Dr. Marie Zakrzewska of New York, Ednah became interested in medical education for women. She was instrumental in founding the New England Hospital for Women and Children in connection with the New England Female Medical College and served as secretary of the hospital board until 1887, when she became president; she kept that post until 1902.

Ednah was also active in the antislavery movement and knew Harriet Tubman and Harriet Jacobs, an escaped slave who lived with the family of N. P. Willis, a Boston poet. Her acquaintance with these remarkable women led to her interest in education for former slaves. When the Civil War began, she became secretary of a committee to provide supplies to the black regiment of Colonel Robert Gould Shaw and was one of the teachers sent by the Freedmen's Society to the regiment's encampment, where they taught the men to read using the New Testament as text. After the war, Ednah became secretary of the Teachers' Committee of the New England Freedmen's Aid Society, which sent teachers to work with former slaves in the South. The schools received both moral and monetary support from Ednah, who made several trips from 1867 to 1875 to visit and encourage the teachers.

Ednah also turned to the women's rights movement and became vice president of the Massachusetts Woman Suffrage Association from 1870 to 1872, although she was not an advocate of immediate suffrage. As a founder and financial backer of the New England Women's Club in 1868, she hoped to provide members with the experience in organization and decision making they would need as responsible voters of the future. She led the successful movement to elect women to the Boston School Committee in 1873 and, six years later, helped women gain the right to vote in school elections. With her old friend Abby May, she organized the Massachusetts School Suffrage Association and served as vice president and then president until 1901. With another old friend, Julia Ward Howe, Ednah worked with the American Association for the Advancement of Women.

As writer and editor, Ednah Dow Cheney was responsible for several volumes of poetry and stories for children as well as articles for the *North American Review.* She had written stories as a schoolgirl, with ministers and artists as heroes; once, she even portrayed family friend Bronson Alcott as a character. Her first book was *The Hand Book for American Citizens* (1866), written for the freedmen's schools. Next, she published *Patience* (1871), a popular collection of solitaire card games. Turning to biography, she wrote memoirs of Louisa May Alcott, surgeon Susan Dimock, Abby May, and sculptor Christian Daniel Rauch. Always interested in art, Ednah wrote *Gleanings in the Fields of Art* (1881) and lectured on art and literature at the Concord School of Philosophy founded by Bronson Alcott. Her *Memoir of Seth W. Cheney* was published in 1881, and her own *Reminiscences,* in 1902. Her novel *Nora's Return* (1890) was a sequel to Henrik Ibsen's play *A Doll's House.*

Early in life, Ednah fell under the influence of Transcendentalism. She attended Ralph Waldo Emerson's lectures with her father and "always felt very close to him," though she "never had any intimacy with him." She absorbed the life and thought of Margaret Fuller[68] and was "astonished to find how large a part of 'what I am when I am most myself' I have derived from her."[69] She attended Fuller's series of Conversations and later gave a lecture about Fuller to the Congress of American Advancement of Women, tracing her significance to her advocacy of individual freedom and development as well as equal political rights.

It was Theodore Parker, however, who most influenced Ednah Dow Cheney's religious thinking. In 1842, she read the sermon on "The Transient and Permanent in Christianity," for which Parker was severely criticized. "It took hold of me like the voice of Truth itself," she wrote. For this young woman, not yet twenty, Parker "threw new light on the life and thought of Jesus." When Ednah's youngest sister died in 1845, Parker came, talked with her, and left her "changed in mind," able to feel the sister's continuing presence. "It was Mr. Parker's wonderful trust that gave him such power to comfort and strengthen the hearts of others," she wrote.[70] When her husband died, Parker came to Connecticut to perform the service.

In 1867, Ednah discovered the Free Religious Association. She became a director, spoke often at the Sunday afternoon meetings, and continued to be actively involved for the rest of her life. The 1893 Parliament of Religions impressed her with "the importance, not only of unity, but of difference,"[71] including the Eastern religions, among others, and even raising her hopes that the rift between Trinitarians and Unitarians might be closed.

Ednah Dow Littlehale Cheney died of pneumonia in Jamaica Plain, Massachusetts, where she had lived since 1864. She had no heirs, as her daughter Margaret had died of typhoid fever some years earlier. Despite her many personal losses, Ednah remained optimistic and idealistic to the end of her life.

*Biographical Sketch by* JOAN W. GOODWIN

## ✦ Writings of Ednah Dow Littlehale Cheney

"Emerson and Boston." In *The Genius and Character of Emerson: Lectures at the Concord School of Philosophy.* Boston: JR Osgood, 1885.

*Faithful to the Light.* Boston: American Unitarian Association, 1884.

*Gleanings in the Field of Art.* Boston: Lee and Shepard, 1881.

*Louisa May Alcott: Her Life, Letters, and Journals.* Edited by Ednah Dow Cheney. Boston: Roberts Brothers, 1889. Reprint, with an introduction by Ann Douglas. New York: Chelsea House, 1980.

*Memoir of Seth W. Cheney.* Boston: Lee and Shepard, 1881.

*Nora's Return: A Sequel to "The Doll's House" of Henrik Ibsen.* Boston: Lee and Shepard, 1890.
*Patience: A Series of Games with Cards.* Boston: Lee and Shepard, 1870.
*Reminiscences of Ednah Dow Cheney.* Boston: Lee and Shepard, 1902.

## ✦ Biographical Resources

New England Women's Club. *Ednah Dow Cheney, 1824–1904.* Memorial meeting, February 20, 1905.
Howe, Julia Ward, ed. *Sketches of Representative Women of New England.* Boston: New England Historical Publishing, 1904.
Willard, Frances E. and Mary A. Livermore, eds. *A Woman of the Century.* Buffalo, NY: Moulton, 1893.

## ✦ Archives

The papers of Ednah Dow Littlehale Cheney are at the Boston Public Library, the Massachusetts Historical Society, the Sophia Smith Collection at Smith College, and the Schlesinger Library at Radcliffe College.

# The Young Women and the Church

## Article in *Old & New,* September 1905

MARIE HOFFENDAHL JENNEY HOWE (1870–1934), *one of the younger members of the Iowa Sisterhood, served five years as a minister in Unitarian churches in Iowa, eventually moving on to become a public lecturer and writer and a founder of the Heterodoxy Club in New York City. She found the culture within churches stifling, which led her to feel that her vision of true equality and new opportunities for women could not be realized within organized churches, even liberal ones.*

*In this selection, Marie Jenney Howe expressed the sentiments of several women who left the ministry to become speakers, activists, and philanthropists because they felt the church was too constraining. The forcefulness of her writing borders on anger that may seem uncharacteristic of women ministers but undoubtedly reveals why she left the ministry.*[72]

See the Biographical Sketch on pages 542–544.

The young women and the church seem to be getting along pretty well together. There are plenty of churches for the young women; there are plenty of young women for the church. The church loves the young women; the young women love the church. They are attached. You cannot possibly detach them. At first glance, there seems to be no problem, and nothing to discuss.

There are ways and ways of loving. In especial, there are two ways of loving. To love unselfishly, what does that mean? It means to study a friend's needs and respond to them. It means to consider her development and contribute toward it. To love selfishly, what does that mean? If I love a friend selfishly, I see her disabilities and limitations. I do not help her to overcome the disability or rise above the limitation. I take advantage of her weakness and her ignorance, and I use her for my own ends. There are just two ways of treating a friend. One way is to ask:

"What can you do for me?" The other way is to ask: "What can I do for you?" The latter question, the church does not ask of its women.

The church says to its men: "What can we do for you?" It says to its women: "What can you do for us?" The church loves its women, but it loves them with a selfish love.

Let me illustrate by quoting a typical case. A certain young woman had an older brother and a younger brother. All three went to college. In due course of time they returned. The young men went to church—sometimes, and the young woman always. When it became necessary to nominate a trustee, men asked the older brother to serve. They said that they wanted young blood, and that it would interest him in the church, and that it would hold him. It did hold him until his term of office expired when he slipped back into his former indifference. It became necessary to nominate an usher. They asked the younger brother to serve. They said it would hold him. It did hold him until his term of office expired when he also slipped back into his former indifference. And all this time the young woman continued to attend church. But she desired a more vital, a more substantive part in the church life. She went to the minister and put the question to him: "What can I do for the church?" He thought a long time and then replied: "There is the sewing society." She told him she was not fond of sewing; girls aren't now-a-days, you know, especially college girls. The minister said he would think it over. He thought and thought as much as two minutes and then dismissed the subject from his mind. In many churches we are confronted by this situation. There is no use for any young woman unless she sews.

The minister was a bachelor. He had never had a sister. He once told me how he wished he had a sister. I thought it was so nice of him to wish he had a sister. Yes! he said he always wished he had a sister, so that there would be someone to sit 'round and sew with his mother. That was his idea of women. They were beings who sat 'round and sewed. This seems to be the theological idea. Perhaps it is bred in Divinity Schools.

There was a society for men in this minister's church, and there was a gymnasium—for men. There was a boy's reading room, a young men's debating society, a boy's military club. And everybody said: "How perfectly splendid it is the way our minister works with the men and boys." And all the while the women of the church sat 'round and sewed.

I once overheard a conversation between a husband and wife, in which the wife was reproaching her husband in all the earnestness of jest because he used to be more attentive to her before marriage.

"My dear," he defended himself, "When I want a car, I stand in the middle of the street and wave my umbrella. When the car stops, I get aboard and take my seat, but I do not go on waving the umbrella."

That is exactly the attitude of the church toward its women. It has them all aboard. There is nothing for them to fuss about. But this is the attitude of the coquette who never wastes attention on those she is sure of. Also, it is the attitude of the politician; but should it be the attitude of the church, the institution that is supposed to minister the souls? Way back in the fourth century, A.D., a certain church council decided that women had no souls. But now-a-days, we do not doubt their souls. What is it that we doubt? Their pocket books?

I wish to limit my subject to women. I do not care to analyze the position of men. I use them only as a standard of comparison. You cannot see a thing alone and see it truly. The truth about a subject is its relation to other subjects. In order to prove the truth about my assertion of woman's position in the church, let us compare woman's work with man's work in the church. What is man's share in church work? Man's share is to put his hand in his pocket and contribute toward expenses, and no especial credit is due him for his effort unless some sacrifice is entailed. As for the men who put their hands deep down in their pockets, verily they have their reward.

What else do men do for the church? I have thought, and thought, and thought of the other things that men do for the church. I can remember one thing more: They hold office. They do it thoroughly. They hold every office there is to be had.

What is the women's share in church work? They sew; they bake; they wait on table and wash dishes. They hold fairs, give entertainments and raise money in every way. They contribute all the drudgery. Don't you consider it drudgery? These things are not drudgery, it is true, when someone else does them. You would consider it drudgery if it devolved upon you instead of only on your wife, mother, and daughter. To sum it up, men's share of church work is receiving the honor and the glory. Women's share is giving drudgery and devotion.

To bring it home still closer, let us contrast the men's club with the women's club. Say that the men's club meets tonight—you are a man; you go. You are seated at the table and told that some one will wait on you soon. You are dined and entertained. You are told to smoke. And as a culminating attraction, you are assured that no women are admitted unless, of course, for purposes of cooking, waiting on table and washing dishes. There they are needed still.

The women's club meets this afternoon. You are a woman; you go. Didn't you bring your thimble? they ask, or didn't you bake a cake? If it is a supper they will say: "Will you wait on table or wash dishes? You are given your choice of these two alternatives. No generalization can be made universal in its application, but as a generalization who can deny that the manual work of a church is largely done by the women and that the honors are largely carried by the men!

✦ ✦ ✦

But we could not have fairs unless we sewed! The time has come to give up church fairs totally and forever. Turn them over to the children. They do nicely for them. Most women hate fairs. There is only one thing they hate worse, and that is, to say so. It behooves us to pay more attention to the brightest and best of our modern women, or we lose them from the activities of the church life. . . .

I have sketched what is: Now let me sketch what ought to be. All sewing should be delegated to a committee who enjoy it. Church fairs should be given to children for whom they are appropriate. The church supper should be put in the hands of caterers. Or, if it is to be a sort of jollification, the men and women should take part together. I once witnessed a men's supper undertaken for the sake of sport. It was uncommonly successful. And after seeing the ease and celerity with which the men put it through, and comparing this with the difficulty and exhaustion of women undertaking the same work, the unprejudiced observer must conclude that if the Almighty intended church suppers to be the function of one sex, natural fitness determines in favor of the men.

To utilize our women for church work is to use them as church assets. Nothing but exceeding poverty should drive a church to such extremes. Women who never cook or wash dishes in their own homes are compelled to do this work in the parlors of the church and, after toiling for hours at this unaccustomed labor, will reach their homes in a state of exhaustion, a condition which their husbands would not permit them to suffer from in pursuance of their own domestic necessities. And this is done to save a couple of dollars, which is what it would cost to hire a substitute in some woman who makes dish washing her business.

Every minister should study the special needs of the women of his church and should give them what they need for their development—not what the church requires for its organization. It is time we decided to economize in some other way than through the women in our churches. The special needs of women in this day and generation are self-reliance, mental independence and more self-respect. What does the church contribute toward this end? The progress of women and their self-development is gained outside of the church. The women's club gives to them; the church takes from them. Is it any wonder that the stronger, more forceful of our modern women are foresaking the life of the church for the life of the club? If the church gave them the opportunity to speak in public, to hold office and to gain the confidence that comes from large responsibility, it would retain these most desirable women, instead of driving them to more congenial channels of work. The only opportunity the church gives its women is the opportunity to look on and listen and admire, while others perform.

The church offices should be open to all. The trustees, ushers, chairmen of committees should represent women as well as men. Women should be encouraged to enter the ministry. Just as men in the pulpits mean women in the pews, so also women in the pulpits mean men in the pews.

Another example of the preference accorded to men in the church is seen in the substance of the sermon. It is addressed to men, illustrated from the lives and occupations of men. Notice the next sermon that you hear. I should be surprised if a single expression or illustration takes any cognizance whatever of the facts that women comprise three-fourths of the congregation. One would think in listening to the average sermon that not one woman is noticed in the audience. The woman listens and as far as her needs and necessities are concerned, the sermon might as well be preached in Greek or Hebrew.

Go to the dedication of a church or attend the services of the laying of the corner stone. Not a woman's name will be mentioned; not a woman's service acknowledged. Go to a church club or adult class; you will seldom find that its leader is a woman. Go to the church conference, you will find the speakers are men. In our most progressive churches there may be a women's afternoon into which all the women's interests are crowded and at which the entire audience is comprised of women. They are regarded as an auxiliary, a side issue, a help mate to the main organization of men. They are not accorded a place in the main body or an individuality as one-half of the whole.

Until sermons are directed toward women as much as toward men, until important offices are given as largely to women as to men, until their services are remembered at dedications and cornerstone celebrations, as well as these occasions serve to remind us of the services of men, until pulpits are filled with women as well as men and classes are led by women as well as by men, let us not claim an equality that does not exist in our churches or pretend that the churches accord an equal treatment to its women and its men.

The duty of the church toward its women is to lift them where the men stand, is to help and not discourage their effort toward self-development.

Drive this question to its logical conclusion, and we have an answer to the problem—Why men do not go to church. The reason why men do not go to church is because women do. The reason why men do not go to church is because women are there in the majority. There may be many other reasons why men remain at home, but the main reason, the determining factor is, because the women predominate. In a solution of this problem let us not imagine that the mere presence of women constitutes the objectionable feature. Not women's presence but their inferior position is the determining factor. A majority of equals would not influence men to stay at home. It is the predominance of inferiors that frightens them away. . . .

What are we going to do about it? We must prove that religion is manly. There are two ways of doing it. One way, and this is the usual and popular way, is to give all dominance and leadership to men, even to the extent of holding meetings that exclude women. That proves that these meetings at least are manly, that men need not be ashamed to attend. The Young Men's Christian Association has a greater hold upon men than the church because it excludes women from its meetings. Men who will not attend church on Sunday morning will go to the YMCA meetings in the afternoon. The afternoon meetings are for men only and therefore manly.

The other way of solving this question is by putting the two social groups on the same plane of equality. If the women are not inferior, there is no need to exclude them. What do I mean by the plane of equality? I mean giving to women the same privileges and offices that we extend to men. When all do the same thing, there is nothing left to be ashamed of.

✦ ✦ ✦

But if there is only one group there is no danger of inferiors driving out superiors, because no inferiors are there. It is far easier to get rid of inferiority than to drive out inferiors.

## ✦ *Biographical Sketch*

**Born:** *December 26, 1870, Syracuse, New York*
**Died:** *February 28, 1934, Harmon-on-Hudson, New York, age 63*

Marie Hoffendahl Jenney was born in Syracuse, New York, on December 26, 1870. Her parents were members of the May Memorial Unitarian Church, and her mother was a pioneer suffragist in New York. Marie received her early training at a preparatory school in Dobbs Ferry, New York, and then went to Meadville Theological School to become a Unitarian minister. While there, she wrote her thesis on the social settlement movement. Her belief that ministry must go beyond prophecy and character building and become committed to social progress through direct involvement often unsettled her professors and peers. She challenged them with her understanding of ministry as the "prophet in action."[73] Graduating in 1897, Marie returned to Syracuse to be ordained at May Memorial on June 28, 1898. Mary Safford, Florence Buck, and Marion E. Murdoch participated in the service.[74]

Before graduation, in October 1896, Marie Jenney went to Sioux City, Iowa, where she served as an assistant to the Reverend Mary Safford. When Safford's associate, Eleanor Gordon, left in 1897, Marie stayed on in Sioux City.[75] When Mary relocated to Des Moines in June 1899, Marie went along as her associate. The agreement was that Safford would preach twice a month and do whatever else she could while also serving as field secretary of the Iowa Unitarian Association, and Marie would serve as the full-time minister at the salary of $800.

During Marie's tenure in Des Moines, the church flourished, and by the time of its twenty-fifth anniversary in 1902, a "largely increased and very joyful and enthusiastic parish" celebrated its success.[76] Marie also reorganized the women's club in the church, making it more intellectual and more focused on social justice issues. In 1901, she gave a series of eight programs on English poet Robert Browning. As time passed, however, she became increasingly dissatisfied with the role of the church and its inability to empower women.

Influenced by the radical proposals of Charlotte Perkins Stetson [Gilman] in *Women and Economics,* Marie Jenney introduced herself to the author through a letter and the two became friends. In 1900, Marie presented a series of pulpit papers on "Reform, Leadership, and Christian Socialism," in which she advocated socialist strategies as the best hope for a just world. She stressed that women needed to develop more individuality and become self-supporting and economically free, while men needed to practice the spirit of Christianity. She suggested home industries as a way for women to gain financial independence.

In the summer of 1901, Marie took a trip abroad, partly to learn more about socialism. Then, in 1903, she resigned her position in Des Moines to pursue her ideals of suffrage and radical feminism and never returned to ministry.

The next year, Marie married an old friend who shared many of her radical social views, Frederic C. Howe. He was an idealistic attorney, an ardent champion of people who were poor and downtrodden, and a supporter of labor reforms. He wrote nine books, lectured, ran Chatauquas, and worked as an economist and attorney. He served in the Ohio senate and as U.S. Commissioner of Immigration at the Port of New York. All of this kept him very busy, and at times, Marie felt abandoned at home.

At this time, Marie took to the lecture circuit; her highly developed intellect and keen insight made her a popular speaker on social and literary themes. She also produced two popular books on the Frenchwoman who wrote novels under the pen name *George Sand*. Marie wanted to present the character of this greatly misunderstood woman in a more kindly light to the English-speaking world. Perhaps she saw some parallels in her own life.

While Frederic was in the Ohio senate and they lived in Cleveland, Marie was active in the Consumer's League and a leader in the feminist movement until World War I. When the Howes moved to New York, where they lived for many years, Marie met Rose Young, with whom she formed a close and emotionally satisfying relationship. Together, they founded the Heterodoxy Club, in which controversial issues of the day were discussed. (They defined as *heterodox* ideas that were not in agreement with accepted beliefs, especially those that departed from church doctrine or dogma.) There, Marie was nurtured by the companionship of women, making up for what she was missing in her marriage.

After losing her first and only baby, an infant son, Marie found consolation in the club and her friend Rose Young. Even so, she grew more and more disillusioned by the events of her time. Her health failed, and she died at home in 1934. A memorial service was held in her honor by the Heterodoxy Club on March 25; it was attended by many of the leading men and women of New York City.

*Biographical Sketch by* SARAH OELBERG

## ✦ Writings of Marie Hoffendahl Jenney Howe

"American League for Civic Improvement." *Old & New* 11 (September 1902).

*George Sand: The Search for Love.* New York: John Day, 1927.

"Unselfishness and Resignation: In What Way Are They the Will of God?" *Old & New* 8 (February 1900).

"The Young Women and the Church." *Old & New* (September 1905).

## ✦ Biographical Resources

Phillips, Charles W. "History of First Unitarian Church." Typescript, Unitarian Church archives, Des Moines, IA, n.d.

*Fifty Years of Unity Church, 1885–1935.* Sioux City, IA: Historical Committee, n.d.

Hitchings, Catherine F. *Universalist and Unitarian Women Ministers* (Journal of the Universalist Historical Society) 10 (1975).

Tucker, Cynthia Grant. *Prophetic Sisterhood: Liberal Women Ministers of the Frontier, 1880–1930.* Boston: Beacon Press, 1990.

# Effects of Her Religion

**From *His Religion and Hers,* 1923**

CHARLOTTE PERKINS STETSON GILMAN (1860–1935) *came from a family full of Unitarians and is thus considered to have strong Unitarian connections. Though she was neither a minister nor active in a Unitarian church, her poems were among the favorite pulpit readings of Unitarian ministers. Best known as the author of the feminist classics* Women and Economics *(1898) and* Herland *(1915), she also wrote one of the first books of feminist theology,* His Religion and Hers: A Study of the Faith of Our Fathers and the Work of Our Mothers.

*The following excerpt shows what Gilman imagined a female religion would be like—one based on life and growth instead of the combativeness and competition that seemed so attractive to men. The ordinary activities of nurturing and caring for children and creating useful and beautiful domestic objects would lead a woman to imagine the "Power under all this pouring flood of Life" to be the first Mother.*

See the Biographical Sketch on pages 551–554.

Sweeping from our minds every misleading ancient legend, let us see clearly what has been happening on earth; where women come in, their special nature, power, and purpose, and particularly the work of motherhood. We see the long process of physical evolution leading up to the human animal; the stream of life pouring like a river, modified by conditions, struggling where struggle was necessary, changing in sudden mutations from some inner urge, and rising in proportion as it produced new powers.

We see the mother, the race type,[77] manifesting new faculties, transmitting her faculties to her young, and devising more and more efficacious means to promote that great process. We see the father, reaching race equality at length, contributing more and more of service to the young. Finally we come to humanity and the stage of social evolution. In this we find new powers in action.

In lower forms there is no vehicle of life but the physical body. Whatever progress is attained is shown only in the creature itself, is transmitted only from parent to young. Humanity enters upon a superior and wholly different process of development. Our progress is attained through interpersonal qualities and activities and embodied in the works of our hands; we make things, and our forward movement is to be measured by the things we make. This gain is transmitted far and wide and down all the ages, quite outside of physical heredity. Our human progress is cumulative, continuous, entered upon by generation after generation, each standing on the attainments of those before and adding to them.

Humanity is a living form which is virtually "immortal" on earth and subject to constant improvement.

What constitute the forces promoting human improvement?

The major force is that of evolution itself, the law of growth; to that, with us, is added conscious effort; and to that, again, our supreme function of humaniculture, education, wherein we see a conscious society gathering up its best achievements and so applying them to the young as enormously to facilitate the natural processes of growth.

✦ ✦ ✦

Thus we see in humanity a form of life collective, organic, as natural as any others, as open to unconscious progress as those behind it, but richer far in power of action, able to recognize and promote its own evolution. . . .

But when at last the perception of evolution did reach mankind, it came to minds already so heavily masculized that they were unable to see this universal process as one of growth; all they could see was their own process—combat. "The struggle for existence" is the popular idea of evolution. Evolution is what makes an egg hatch. It does not have to fight with anything; it just grows. . . .

Growth is the natural law, and the human being adds to growth the new power of culture.

Improvement through heredity is a reproductive process, most powerfully promoted by the female.

Improvement through culture is a race process, which has no relation to sex, except as we may claim it to be a higher extension of work originating in motherhood.

Improvement through combat is a sex process proper to males, by which the victor transmits his superior strength to the young.

On that male tendency to combat, on his instinctive delight in it rests our later doctrine that there is some virtue inherent in effort, that hard things are good for us, that it is not good to make things easy. It is true that at times it is necessary to do difficult things but not true that their advantage lies in their difficulty.

The natural law is to reduce difficulties, to make every present activity easier in order that we may undertake higher ones, and this is clearly proved in every cultural process. Our wealth and power rest on cultural processes, not on combative ones. By taking care of plant life and animal life we have raised all the food of the world. We develop nothing by combat, unless it is the game-cock, a useless creature kept to amuse men.

Now, if we can see the position of the normal human mother in her responsibility to human life, to human progress, there begins to appear some shining dawn of what the world may expect when she does her duty, some foreshadowing of her effect upon religion and of the wide new hope which such changed religion would open to us.

First and deepest is the conscious recognition of that great fact of reproduction which is unconsciously submitted to by lower mothers—that life inheres in the race, which is undying, rather than in the individual, which dies. In uncounted millions mothers have bowed to this law, caring nothing for their own lives so that their young might live. This we have foolishly called "the maternal sacrifice." It is not a sacrifice at all; it is a life process, as natural as any other. When the time arrived that the mother was of more use to the young by staying alive, she stayed alive. She, in those early forms, had no more consciousness of virtue or of power than had her mate; but she, human and conscious, can visualize her duty, her first duty as a female, to maintain and to improve the human race.

This she has never recognized until now, still hardly sees.

For all the ages she has been taught that her first, last, and only duty was to man. Her very children were for him; indeed, he fondly supposed that he alone gave them life, she being but the soil in which to plant the seed. All the laws and all the religions worked to the same end—that embodied in our Pauline instruction, "Wives submit yourselves to your husbands,"—so she submitted to our racial degradation or rebelled and was destroyed.

The new motherhood will submit to nothing but its own great governing law—to maintain and improve the human race. It will recognize that its whole duty is to the race through the child and that all the loveliness of love, all the happiness of kind association, every beautiful higher growth which has come to the relation of the sexes in humanity are subsequent to the primal duty. They assist, promote, and beautify the human sex relation, but they must not contravert its reason for being. The human mother will see down the ages. Her children will not end with one generation, nor with two. She can consciously and effectively build a better race as naturally as some poor insect lays her eggs and dies. We have not yet had the human mother in her freedom and power, only the subject mother, helpless and oversexed. In normal motherhood, sex use will be measured by its service to the young, not its enjoyment by the individual.

In the third chapter was briefly indicated the essential difference in approach of the awakening mind of woman, as religious ideas began to form. From her great function, birth, with its long period of prevision, its climactic expression in bringing forth the child, its years of unselfish service with rich results, she would have apprehended God in a widely different view from that of man—as a power promoting endless growth.

When, now and later, she boldly brings to bear on existing religions this life-based view, this view so wholly in consonance with all the laws we know, and so plainly adapted to bettering human conduct, we may look for large results. It is naturally difficult for us, so long trained in death-based theories, with the concept of a personal God trying to rescue a pitiful few from a ruined world, to face the absolute reverse—the thought of God as a successfully acting power engaged in improving the world, with ourselves as conscious helpers in the process.

In place of cringing away from our responsibility and shouldering it off on some principle of evil, some devil, or some woman, we shall frankly admit that there is nothing the matter with the world but our own behavior. Able at last to see what it is that is doing the mischief, we are able also to stop it.

Our primitive ideas of God, which we insist on maintaining as immovably as possible, have left us in strange difficulties as to human trouble. To a personalized and masculinized deity we attributed all knowledge and all power; to ourselves we attributed nothing but "poor human nature"; and then, having to face the obvious miseries of life, the explanation was sought in some "inscrutable" purpose of God or in some malicious anti-god of awful power. Of late years the somewhat clearer and less reverent mind of man has postulated a god good enough as far as he went but incomplete, a young half-grown deity, doing his best with his world, and likely to improve.

But thought of God aroused by birth leads along a different road, to a different conclusion. The primitive woman had no more knowledge than the primitive man, but she had impulses and feelings quite other than his and utterly different experiences. Early religion was not built on knowledge but on impulses, feelings, and experiences.

From hers would naturally arise such thoughts as these:

"Here is Life. It comes in installments, not all at once. The old ones die; the new ones come. They do not come ready-made; they are not finished; they have to be taken care of. It is a pleasure to take care of them, to make new people. Everywhere we see the same process, motherhood carrying on life. The mother tree has seeds which make new trees; the mother birds lay eggs which make new birds; the mother beast brings forth her little one to take her place in time and carry on the line. . . .

"What a wonderful thing is Life! Life everlasting, going on continuously, in steps, the evercoming new ones taking the place of the old worn-out ones—how beautiful! And we cannot stop it if we would; nothing stops it; after the flood has fallen, after the ice is melted, after the forest fire has burnt out, year after year when winter is over, rises Life, always young, re-born—how glorious! . . .

"This grain is large and fine, it grows best in this kind of soil; I will pull out the other things around so that it will grow better. I will get some more and plant it here where it grows best. . . . This seed which I planted and took care of is better than what grew without help. I can make things better by taking care of them. . . .

"I have taught my child all I knew. He is wiser than that other whose mother died, who grew up, indeed, but is not so wise. Teaching is a help in living. Care and teaching makes things better. . . .

"I can make things! I can make pots of clay. I can make baskets of reeds. I can make clothes of skins. I can build a shelter for my little ones. I can soften food with fire—it keeps longer if it is cooked. . . .

"Not only can I make things but I can make them beautiful! With colors, with stitches, with lines on the soft clay, with patterns in the woven reeds, I can make beauty! Beauty! What a pleasure it is to be skillful and make things and to make them beautiful! I will teach my daughter. . . .

"She has thought of a new pattern, more beautiful than mine. Ah! Life is not only in the animals: it is in the things we make; they grow too! Life, always coming, through motherhood, always growing, always improving through care and teaching! And this new product of life—not babies but things, useful things, made beautiful—what a joy life is! . . .

"What does it all? What is behind it all? Who is the first Mother, Teacher, Server, Maker? What Power under all this pouring flood of Life? What Love behind this ceaseless mother-love? What Goodness to make Life so good, so full of growing joy?" . . .

Thus would the woman's mind have reached the thought of God.

✦ ✦ ✦

The new premises for our religious thought will as inevitably lead to right conduct as the old premises have led to wrong. Where the older religions left life on earth neglected, the new will find its place of action here. Where the old saw human labor as a curse, the new will find in it joyful and natural expression of power. Where the old demanded belief in the unprovable and supernatural, the new will develop understanding of clear natural law. Where the old issued commands, the new will show cause and effect. Where the old drove the unwilling by threats of punishment or lured them by promise of reward, the new will cultivate the natural powers which lead and push us on. Where the old saw life as evil and humanity as a broken, feeble thing, the new will see life as a glory and humanity as its highest crown, rich with untested powers.

✦ ✦ ✦

The "newness" of religion here discussed does not involve any contradiction of the previous truths taught in past ages. It does involve the discarding of various beliefs and the apprehension of some new ones. The new ones offered are not strange to any well-informed modern mind: that evolution means growth, not mere combat; that the human race is young and growing and open to measureless improvement; that the female is the race type and her natural impulses are more in accordance with the laws of growth than those of the male; that the race lives immortally on earth, recreated through birth, and so, through love and service, may rise continually; that social development as a conscious process is our chief duty; that God is the Life within us, the Life of the world, to be worshiped in fruition; that religion is the strongest help in modifying our conscious behavior, but that it cannot so help in social evolution without teaching these truths.

✦ ✦ ✦

Missionaries the world over find it easier to teach the A, B, C's of their religion to people of some other religion, or without any, than they do to carry out their own religion in their own country.

The life-based kind works differently. Religion is not a private affair. "Believing" it is of no consequence whatever, unless it is applied, and its application requires the continuous behavior of all people for as long as the race endures.

Religion is not a skylight; it is the Front Door.

✦ ✦ ✦

Happiness is fulfillment of function. It is conscious transmission of power. It is the expression of God. It belongs to humanity in a higher degree than to any soaring lark, because we are able to express more God more fully than any other creature.

## ✦ *Biographical Sketch*

**Born:** *July 3, 1860, Hartford, Connecticut*

**Died:** *August 17, 1935, Pasadena, California, age 75*

**Buried:** *Ashes scattered*

Charlotte Perkins Gilman, as she is most commonly known, was born on July 3, 1860, to Frederick Beecher Perkins and Mary Fitch (Westcott) Perkins in Hartford, Connecticut. Only one of her three siblings, Thomas, survived infancy. Frederick Beecher Perkins left the family shortly after Charlotte's birth, providing little financial support to them. He and Mary eventually divorced. Thus, Charlotte's early years were colored primarily by economic uncertainty and constant relocation, as Mary Perkins moved the family often to escape creditors.

Charlotte's schooling was quite limited, due to the lack of a permanent place of residence; however, she did briefly attend the Rhode Island School of Design. She worked as a commercial artist, art teacher, and governess in her early adult years.

In May 1884, Charlotte married Charles Walter Stetson. The birth of their daughter, Katherine Beecher Stetson in March 1885, was followed by a severe episode of depression for Charlotte. This experience of what today would be diagnosed as postpartum depression was a second formative influence in Charlotte's life and was later used as a basis for her ground-breaking story "The Yellow Wallpaper." In 1888, she and Katherine moved to California; despite attempts at reconciliation, Charlotte and Walter divorced in 1894. He married Charlotte's friend, Grace Ellery Channing, with Charlotte's blessing. Having experienced childhood without the presence of a father, Charlotte sent Katherine back East to live with Walter and Grace.

After her move to California, Charlotte began to write short stories to support herself, her mother, and her daughter. She published a book of verse during this period and served as co-editor of *Impress,* the journal of the Pacific Coast Woman's Press Association. She also began to lecture.

In June 1900, Charlotte married lawyer George Houghton Gilman, with whom she had corresponded for many years. He was her first cousin and seven years younger than she. He encouraged her to continue writing and lecturing. After his death in 1934, Charlotte lived with her daughter's family in Pasadena, California. Suffering from breast cancer, she committed suicide in 1935. Her remains were cremated.

Charlotte Gilman moved in the same circles as many feminists and suffragists. Most notably, she worked with Sarah B. Cooper to plan the California Woman's Congresses of 1894 and 1895, and she was acquainted with Jane Addams, living briefly at Hull House in Chicago and later at another social settlement in Chicago.

Probably nothing had more influence on the intellectual life of the time than the publication of Charles Darwin's *On the Origin of Species* in 1859. The most direct influence on Charlotte came from the work of Lester Frank Ward, who attacked the social Darwinism of Herbert Spencer by suggesting that there was a conscious component to social evolution. For Charlotte, however, his most significant theory was that women were the evolutionary superiors of men, a thesis which she developed in much of her work.

Documenting Charlotte Perkins Gilman's religious connections is difficult. There is no evidence that she ever openly espoused any organized religion. However, she had many informal ties to the Unitarian church, beginning quite early in her life. Her uncle was Edward Everett Hale, a Unitarian minister, and her best friend (who later married Walter Stetson) was Grace Ellery Channing, granddaughter of William Ellery Channing. Charlotte's work influenced many members of the Unitarian clergy, some of whom quoted her poems from the pulpit.[78] She also lectured in many Protestant churches, including Unitarian and Universalist ones,[79] and "was a frequent guest preacher in liberal Protestant pulpits, most commonly Unitarian ones." Her wedding to Houghton was conducted by a Unitarian minister. (Apparently, they had a difficult time finding a minister willing to perform the ceremony because of her prior divorce.[80])

Charlotte Perkins Gilman was, however, a deeply spiritual person. She fashioned her own personal system of religious belief that was both mystical and rational—in some ways, similar to Unitarianism. One instance of how her feminism influenced her theology was that she "denounced the arrogance that falsely ascribed maleness to the deity."[81] Her view of herself as a deeply religious person and her highly developed spirituality seem similar to the kinds of personal religious journeys Unitarian Universalists often make, either alone or with the encouragement of their congregations.

Although ahead of her time in many ways, Charlotte Perkins Gilman was neglected until the resurgence of the current women's movement. She integrated in a unique way diverse ideas from many sources—the women's suffrage movement, economics, evolutionary theory, socialism, and theology—thus creating a system that was fairly consistent internally. Perhaps more importantly, she then lived according to her ideals more fully than most people. For instance, her decision to divorce and then send her daughter to live with her father and stepmother was not made lightly, and she endured extreme public criticism for it. Divorce was quite uncommon at this time, but for a mother to give up, or "abandon," her child was an unthinkable act. Charlotte recognized her own unsuitability for mothering and truly believed that her daughter would be better off living in a stable, two-parent family. Moreover, it is significant that Charlotte knew before her marriage to Houghton that he would support her career as writer and lecturer, even though this meant that they would not enjoy a traditional marital relationship.

Charlotte Perkins Gilman's decision to end her life is the final evidence of the profound effort she made to live and die in accordance with her ideals. It is also another instance in which her thinking was far ahead of that of most of her contemporaries. Part of her definition of living included having the ability to serve; when someone could no longer be useful, she should have the right to choose a quick and painless death. Not only her words but her ultimate action show once again how she truly attempted to live as she believed. Perhaps this is her most significant legacy.

*Biographical Sketch by* KIMBERLY MINER

## ✦ Writings of Charlotte Perkins Stetson Gilman

*Concerning Children.* Boston: Small, Maynard, 1900.
*Herland.* New York: Pantheon, 1979.
*His Religion and Hers.* London: T. Fisher Unwin, 1924.
*The Home: Its Work and Influence.* New York: McClure Phillips, 1903.
*Human Work.* New York: McClure, Phillips, 1904.
*In This Our World.* Boston: Small, Maynard, 1899.
*The Living of Charlotte Perkins Gilman: An Autobiography.* New York: Appleton-Century, 1935.
*The Man-Made World; or Our Androcentric Culture.* New York: Charlton, 1911.
*Moving the Mountain.* New York: Charlton, 1911.
*Suffrage Songs and Verses.* New York: Charlton, 1911.
*What Diantha Did.* New York: Charlton, 1910.
*Women and Economics: A Study of the Economic Relation between Men and Women as a Factor in Social Evolution.* Boston: Small, Maynard, 1898.
*The Yellow Wallpaper.* Boston: Small, Maynard, 1899.

## ✦ Biographical Resources

Allen, Polly Wynn. *Building Domestic Liberty: Charlotte Perkins Gilman's Architectural Feminism.* Amherst: University of Massachusetts, 1988.
Ceplair, Larry, ed. *Charlotte Perkins Gilman: A Nonfiction Reader.* New York: Columbia University, 1991.
Hill, Mary A., ed. *A Journey from Within: The Love Letters of Charlotte Perkins Gilman, 1897–1900.* Lewisburg: Bucknell University, 1995.
Knight, Denise D., ed. *Diaries of Charlotte Perkins Gilman.* Charlottesville: University Press of Virginia, 1994.
Knight, Denise D., ed. *Later Poetry of Charlotte Perkins Gilman.* Newark: University of Delaware, 1996.
Lane, Ann J., ed. *Charlotte Perkins Gilman Reader: The Yellow Wallpaper and Other Fiction.* New York: Pantheon, 1980.

# Worship: Its Fundamental Place in Liberal Religion

## From *Report of the Commission on Appraisal*, American Unitarian Association, 1936

AURELIA ISABEL HENRY REINHARDT (1877–1948) *was a Unitarian educator whose leadership as president of Mills College in Oakland, California, built the school into a women's liberal arts college with a worldwide reputation. As an important lay preacher and denominational leader, she helped bring the American Unitarian Association through a difficult period of reorganization and served from 1940–1942 as its first woman moderator. Her essay on worship helped bring the denomination together despite theological upheaval.*

*This essay was written for the* Report of the Commission on Appraisal *to the American Unitarian Association (1936). Reinhardt was a member of the commission, appointed during the crisis of the Great Depression to take a close look at the denomination's assets and liabilities as well as its future prospects. She wrote that public worship is the only activity that no other social institution can accomplish and that the church must make it happen because it unites "the worshippers in a common kinship of existence and of understanding . . . less for intellectual information and ethical direction than as a vitalizing of the whole human organism."*

See the Biographical Sketch on pages 563–566.

The Commission, in its investigations at the behest of the annual meeting, has already recorded testimony of important agreements throughout the fellowship: that Unitarians hold to the principle of religious liberalism; that they wish their church to continue as a definite, organic expression of this liberalism; and that historically they have always urged the right of the individual to intellectual freedom in theological belief and the right of the congregation to religious and aesthetic freedom in the forms of public worship.

It is the purpose of this paper to discuss the place of worship in the exercise of liberal religion, to face the charge that the dynamic of worship has largely been lost in liberal churches, to find explanations for the existing situation, and to suggest reasons and methods for reformation. To achieve this in a brief statement is not an easy task, perhaps an impossible one. It is simpler to analyze the intellectual content of a theology and to account historically for the evolution and disintegration of artistic forms and ritualistic content than to satisfy the modern man that there are spiritual values. Dissatisfied as he is with his own conclusions, he still insists in his disbelief that the psychological factors of life are as fundamental to the whole man as the biological.

✦ ✦ ✦

## Worship

Historically, worship has played a basic part in all mature religions. By whatever name it was called, religion has provided the place in temple, synagogue, or mosque and named the festivals and calendar days where men could unite in glorifying deity. The act of joining in worship or adoration united the worshippers in a common kinship of existence and of understanding.

Liberal religionists know that a final definition of God has always been beyond man's ability to conceive or to state. Such a definition grows less conceivable as creation daily widens to mortal view. The sciences that push the sky and the horizon to farther distance and open the universe of the atom but add to religion's intellectual difficulty while they clarify and emphasize its spiritual responsibility.

We do not live in an era where our souls find satisfaction in a journey to Jerusalem, to Rome, or to Canterbury. We are more and more deeply alone than St. Augustine whose cry we hear down the centuries, "Our hearts are restless 'til they find rest in Thee."

✦ ✦ ✦

## I. Contemporary Situation in Liberal Churches

It has taken little formal investigation for the writer to learn something of the condition of public worship in the congregations of our fellowship. As one might have supposed there is complete independence in the forms used. Hymnals and service books of variety and value are available at Headquarters. The metropolitan churches show successful effort in using materials and developing services of prayer and praise adequate to the large demands of liberal religion at this time. Churches in smaller towns and in rural districts are most in need of help. Lacking knowledge of materials or leadership in preparing forms of public worship, services are often sadly lacking in significance and in beauty. Inquiring as to the reason for monotony and threatened vacuity, one learns that it is the result of an effort to give a minority of the congregation due right. Criticism has eliminated the thing criticized, but the creative processes have brought into being nothing to take the place of the rejected. One church member, disliking archaic vocabulary, asks that hymns be omitted. Another, disbelieving in prayer, urges the omission of petition. A third, prejudiced against ritual, insists that responsive readings be eschewed. A fourth, convinced that the Bible is responsible for most of man's vagueness of thinking as well as his business and political failures, demands pulpit readings confined to economic and scientific statement or to poetic descriptions.

In such churches, of a possible complete and satisfying service of worship, only a sermon is left. A sermon is an honorable instrument to achieve an intellectual or moral end. In itself it is not a service of worship. . . .

As far as my investigation went, I found no congregation demanding and receiving such limitations in its public worship, where the ministers did not grant the emergence of disquieting difficulties: dissension in the congregation; heightened critical attitudes; diminution of religious participation; secularizing of interests; sometimes, the definite withdrawal of part of the membership.

A few such ministers sympathized so definitely with the members asking for educational opportunities in economics, politics, and the social problems of our industrial era that they preferred to encourage this important effort even at the expense of the service of worship. Others agreed with the writer that the Unitarian fellowship includes admirable organizations which foster the secular interests and enterprises of members and that public lectures, group study, social experimentation, etc. are best carried on in these organizations and at times other than the hours traditionally set aside for worship. . . .

## II. History Of Worship

There is visible proof that the liberal churches cannot exist unless worship remains a distinctive and fundamental exercise of the congregation. . . . Ours is the first generation to visualize history in something like totality. Even partial historic perspective makes us conscious of the unbroken continuity of human experience and within that the integral place of religion in the long march of civilization. Always where man has journeyed, religion has been with him. Always through religion has he striven to formulate the constant content of his life, the laws of his being. . . .

Out of Protestantism our Unitarian branch of the Christian faith came into being over a century ago, not as a distinctly new religion, not even as a religion to be fed by a continuous assault on the old as obsolete, but as a reinterpretation of the old in the twin lights of eternal truth and new knowledge. Protestantism was a child of the Roman church, which was itself sister to the Greek church, and both had for parents Judaism and Greek philosophy. These in turn descended from diverse and more ancient ancestors, have given to their descendants qualities which are contradictory and to be explained only by understanding the sources from which they came. Fresh interpretations of ancient truth belong to our later day. Each new day will bring its own interpretation.

The Christian church has shaped the development of our race for almost two thousand years, and "it offers the surest pledge of the individual's incorporation into the permanent experiences of the race." Through the church our intimate and highest experience becomes not the worship of God and the service of man but the worship of God for the service of man. The liberal church cannot eliminate such a spiritual inheritance. Others may reconstruct material environment, but the church must be concerned with man's inner state. Because modern man is more conscious of his biological characteristics, more confused in his economic relationships, active if not more powerful politically, he is not less in need of inner strength. Because he knows more scientific laws and applies them with more technical expertness, he is not complete master of his mind and spirit. Indeed, psychologists have been for years studying the relation of personal religion to mental stability. In Jung's *Modern Man in Search of a Soul*, p. 264, one finds this remarkable statement: "During the past thirty years, people from all the civilized countries of the earth have consulted me, . . . the larger number being Protestants, a smaller number being Jews, and not more than five or six being Catholics. Among all . . . over thirty-five there has not been one whose problem in the last resort was not that of finding a religious outlook on life. Every one of them fell ill because he had lost that which the living religions of every age have given to their followers and none of them has been really healed who did not regain his religious outlook." And again, p. 278, "Religions are systems of healing for psychic illness. . . . Man is never helped in his suffering by what he thinks for himself, but only by revelations of a wisdom greater than his own."

In a recent number of the American Medical Journal was an article calling attention to a situation in our own country more alarming than Jung's scholarly testimony. Contemporary life with much motion and little rest, with attention continuously divided, with concentration interrupted, with emotion constantly heightened, has added twenty percent in the last decade to the proportion of the population mentally unstable.

The habit of personal devotion helps to prevent such individual disaster and aids in bringing basic poise, serenity, and direction to conduct. It can be said of public worship that as men are separated into disparate, warring groups by competitive methods and egocentric pursuits, so public worship unifies them in their common search for the Ultimate Good and their obligation to that Good as brothers.

✦ ✦ ✦

What initially brought worship into the practice of the early Christians is a historic question which has often been asked. The answer points to the source in evolving Judaistic tradition and custom with the later twin commandments into which were crammed the wisdom of the law and the vision of the Prophets to love God with heart and soul and mind and one's neighbor as one's self. Then came the simple breaking of bread to be done in remembrance of a beloved Leader. Out of these grew the institution of the mass and all that is related to it.

Protestant scholars push back the explanation of Christian worship into human needs older even than Christianity's founder. The Quaker Joan Fry says, "Man has two primal needs—the need to adore and the need of power." Newman says man yearns for perfection and through worship moves toward his goal. Dean Sperry believes the passion to understand and to be saved demand recourse to Deity. Dr. Vogt makes the heartening discovery that worship meets man's yearning for unalloyed joy.

## III. Protestantism and Worship

Doubtless the founders of Protestantism did not wish to weaken or to eliminate worship when they led the people out of cathedrals and the smoke of incense to simple chapels where ornaments did not absorb attention or the gold needed for the poor. Freedom from institutional tyranny, freedom from official authority, freedom from outgrown forms and obsolete phrases—these were won by establishing a spontaneous and flexible service in the mother tongue of the worshippers.

Such an evolution was inevitable. During the centuries when the lay mind was held in leash, when questions were an impertinence and faith claimed all mystery for her own, man's creative imagination flowered into an abundance of significant and symbolic beauty. He loved God by building his aspiration into cathedrals, by weaving sacred tapestry, by embroidering altar cloths, and carving the Holy Grail. He worshipped Him in melody and sacred poem, and loving brothers together sang in chorals and marched in pageant and fought for the Holy Sepulcher.

The cataclysm that came upon Christendom before freedom of belief, of methods, and of service, was won as part of man's titanic struggle for individual freedoms. The victory clarified for all time the obligations of organized religion and limited its prerogatives and pretensions. It released the lay mind to pursue unfrightened its inquiries into the laws of nature. Man naturally became more preoccupied with the here than the hereafter. He built not a Kingdom of Heaven but a Kingdom of Earth and gave to it "the power and the glory." He remembered the intellectual freedom he had won when it came to religion and its part in his life. Part of the price paid for his release was that among the things relegated to the outworn and forgotten for generations were the two commandments and the neglect of that most precious of human privileges "the enjoyment of God forever."

✦ ✦ ✦

Dr. Vogt aptly expresses a plea for the functioning of the creative imagination in worship: "Primarily, the religious moment is not the moment of thinking, nor of action, but of joy." . . .

There are organizations in the [Unitarian] fellowship for each interest and effort, time and place for every valid undertaking to be developed and carried back usefully into the family and the community. Our reiterated belief in this is strengthened by Henry Nelson Weiman's charge "That the church has not seen that provision, for worship is the chief thing it has to do. . . . Worship is one of the sources out of which new creations in the art of living arise. It is in worship that new paths open up; worship is the only suitable preparation for the greatest creative artistry in the world, the art of reshaping the total vital process of living."

## IV. Public Worship and the Liberal Fellowship

In the search for God and for the kinship of man, liberal religion, as have all its ancestors, will continue to express its triumph in exercises of worship. These exercises we can refer to at this writing only briefly, their occasion, their content, and their form.

1. *Occasion of Public Worship*—Public worship is most satisfactorily held with regularity on the traditional Sabbath of the week. If, as the writer believes, public worship has both objective and subjective values, it should be carried on throughout all the weeks of the year, and the church edifice should be open daily for personal devotion. Since the reinterpretation of man's life is part of the gift of religion, the occasions of worship will be increased. New emphases will be made as fresh experience enriches life. Successful forms of worship are being developed in various churches to center the service on pre-arranged occasions having to do with the enduring ideals of Christianity, democracy, and humanity. The institution of the family, government by the people, the ideal of international comity, youth in its promise and responsibility, any rooted significance in individual or group life that should grow heavenward with the years—these make our modern occasions for gratitude and petition, the Saints' days in the calendar of the modern church. Dean Inge uses another metaphor to express a challenging and related thought: "It is not the office of the church to be a weathercock spinning with the vacillating spirit of the age, but rather to be the stable background for the shifting drama of civilization."

2. *Content*—The content of services presents many problems but of the kind related not to paucity but to embarrassment of riches. There is the conflict between the old and the contemporary, between the religious and the secular, between complete formality and the personal initiative and individual participation which characterizes the Protestant and democratic taste. But these problems can be solved. Our fellowship and all ministers within it must be concerned in developing services suitable to our era. They will use the Bible, the liturgies of the Greek Church, the Roman Missal, and the Book of Common Prayer. They will use the best of the literature of prayer and praise that has grown up in recent centuries. A study of this literature and its adaptation to use is a challenge to liberal religionists who have here important proof that the creative inspiration of Christianity did not end in the thirteenth century. Part of the content of modern worship must be the new science, the visions of integrated humanity, and wider concepts of

deity. Worship should be a *revelation*, not of God's message delivered finally twenty centuries ago but of his presence and inspiration in all ages and times, and especially here and now through his children and to each of them, even the humblest.

3. *Form*—For adequacy and beauty, the pattern of public worship has much to learn from worship's remarkable and wise past. Nothing that yesterday has done is without significance. It is for contemporary designers and planners of form to know their yesterdays. Was it Santayana who said that "The best prophet is he who has the best memory"?

The very building, its materials and shape are examples of hearts and hands rejoicing. So the modern church, though simple it may have to be, should first of all express its purpose in itself and so influence the worshippers, however unconsciously, by its rightness, its integrity of structure. The building should make, if possible, careful use of the symbols time has fashioned which defy the limitations of verbal vocabulary and suggest the variety and importance of that which cannot be expressed. Because worship is a deep human emotion, it is related to all the arts and needs for adequate expression all of them not only architecture but also music of instrument and human voice, poetry of exalted strain, and design, color, and rhythm of the graphic arts. The pattern of public worship is an intricate one. Like a certain type of mathematics, it requires together with the usual three dimensions of art, the unaccustomed fourth dimension of adventuring spirit. Perhaps it is also fitting to recall that the mother of Polyhymnia herself was Mnemosyne, Memory.

Modern psychology has analyzed the uses and processes of worship. It values them less for intellectual information and ethical direction than as a vitalizing of the whole human organism. Faith is revived, courage is renewed by a joyous achievement through beauty to Reality.

In his valuable contributions to the creating and living patterns for contemporary public worship, the writer must again refer to Dr. Vogt's publications on "Art and Worship" and "Modern Worship" and to the excellent chapter XIV, "The Order of Service" in Dean Sperry's *Reality in Worship*. "During its course of an hour, . . . the order of worship should compass praise, penitence, and the assurance of forgiveness, thanksgiving, petition, intercession, edification, inspiration, consecration, benediction . . . expressed through prayers, responses, hymns, anthems, chants, lectures, and sermons." . . . "A service of worship is a poem written by the lover of God, a song sung by the lover of God, and the pattern of the poem or the song is prescribed in advance by the nature of the experience."

So far into man's past goes his need of finding "rest for his soul," and so varied have been his spiritual quests, it is not strange that the form of his spiritual satisfaction is a unity out of multiplicity.

To insure the satisfying of the omnipresent need of our neighbors and brethren, let the liberal fellowship set its hand and mind to the task of reviving adequate public worship. Comprehensive of those human and spiritual needs which find articulate expression only through religion, nothing shall be included which is insignificant, insincere, or out of harmony with the high purpose of liberal religion. Nor shall there be omitted anything that long use has proved fundamental in lifting the heart of man from discontent, sorrow, and failure, rendering him glad that he has come into the House of the Lord.

## ✦ *Biographical Sketch*

**Born:** *April 1, 1877, San Francisco, California*

**Died:** *January 28, 1948, Palo Alto, California, age 70*

**Buried:** *Ashes entombed at the Columbarium, Oakland, California*

An expectant audience was not disappointed when Frederick May Eliot, the president of the American Unitarian Association, introduced the first woman moderator to them. Speaking to the assembled delegates at the 1940 May Meeting, he called Aurelia Henry Reinhardt "as distinguished a Unitarian as there is in the land."[82] Aurelia Reinhardt proved herself to be a distinguished leader of the Unitarian movement, not only through her two-year term as moderator during the bleak years of war in Europe but throughout her life. She was a scholar, an educator, an advocate for women, and a committed bibliophile.

Born in California, one of six children, Aurelia Isabel Henry began to excel in her studies while attending Boy's High in San Francisco. She pursued a degree in English literature at the University of California, Berkeley, graduating in 1898. After several years of teaching in Idaho, she returned to her studies of literature and completed a Ph.D. at Yale University in 1905. During this period, Aurelia Henry not only wrote a dissertation (on Ben Johnson's work *Epicoene*) but also translated

Dante's essay "De Monarchia" from Italian into English. Both studies were published, attesting to her strong scholarship and fine writing style. Aurelia Henry's literary pursuits in higher education were an indication of the determination that would mark all of her achievements in later life. She was, significantly, among a small group of women who undertook graduate education in the early 1900s and an even smaller number of women who would demonstrate leadership in educational administration, religious life, and civic engagement.

Aurelia Henry married Dr. George Reinhardt in 1906. Just six years later, she found herself a widow and the single parent of two small sons. She was able to secure a teaching position through the University of California's extension program. Then, in 1916, her life and that of a small, struggling women's college irreversibly changed when she assumed the presidency of Mills College in Oakland. She remained as its head for twenty-seven years, retiring in 1943 after a successful program of student and faculty expansion. Among the universities granting her honorary degrees were the University of California, the University of Southern California, and Oberlin College.

In addition to her work as an educator, Aurelia Reinhardt worked tirelessly for peace. As early as 1919, she publicly declared herself an advocate for world peace. Although a Republican Party activist, she broke ranks to stand behind President Woodrow Wilson's plan for the League of Nations. A member of more than a dozen peace organizations for the next three decades, she served as a delegate to the founding meetings of the United Nations in San Francisco in 1945. She spoke to dozens of church and community groups about the imperative of peace and the importance of international collaboration, including the value of cultural and educational exchange exemplified by UNESCO.

While engaged in these peace activities and fulfilling her responsibilities as president of Mills College, Aurelia Reinhardt also took a leadership role in civic groups, including serving as president of the American Association of University Women, as chairman of the department of education for the General Federation of Women's Clubs, and as a member of a number of local governmental commissions. Because of her belief in civil society and its responsibilities, she invariably took the side of those individuals who had no resources, who lacked adequate support, or who had in some other way been marginalized by society. She spoke on behalf of youth during the Depression and for women's equal access to education and professional recognition throughout her life.

An avid nature lover, Aurelia Reinhardt was also active in environmental preservation groups, including those concerned about the forests of California. Her persistence in warning against the threat to nature from rampant development was relentless and took many forms. This view was based on a theology she believed to be infused by Christian Unitarian understanding.

The importance of Unitarian religious identity for Aurelia Reinhardt cannot be overstated. Married in the First Unitarian Church of Berkeley, she was later to join the church to which her family had belonged, the Oakland Unitarian Church, where she even assumed interim ministerial responsibility during a short period in the 1940s. Known for her eloquence and delight in making new friends, she was asked to speak in many Unitarian churches and rarely refused the opportunity.

Aurelia Reinhardt attracted national recognition when she was invited to deliver the Ware lecture at the May Meeting of the American Unitarian Association in 1932, one year after Nobel laureate Jane Addams. Two years later, she joined a select group of religious leaders in the movement to prepare the report of the Commission on Appraisal, *Unitarians Face a New Age.* She wrote the chapter on worship, which remains a singular contribution to Unitarian understanding of liturgy and worship. In the same period, she served on the board of trustees of the Starr King School for Ministry in Berkeley. She stated this goal for professional religious leadership: "Let us not forget that the future includes more women in the ministry than we have ever known before."[83] She was enthusiastic about this prospect.

*Biographical Sketch by* CLARE B. FISCHER

## ✦ Writings of Aurelia Isabel Henry Reinhardt

"Colleges for Women and Education for Peace." In *Proceedings of the Institute of International Relations* 4 (1929): 222. Los Angeles: University of Southern California.

*The De Monarchia of Dante Aligheri,* edited with translation and notes. Boston: Houghton, Mifflin, 1904.

*Epicoene, or the Silent Woman,* by Ben Johnson. Edited with introduction, notes, and glossary. New York: Holt, 1906.

"Education of the Women of the United States." *International Education Association: Addresses and Proceedings* 59 (1921): 65–74.

*The Garden Club of America's Redwood Grove.* Oakland, CA: Mills College, Eucalyptus Press, 1935.

"What Price Peace? In *The San Francisco Conference and the United Nations: Proceedings of the Institute of World Affairs* 21 (1946): 131–139. Los Angeles: University of Southern California.

"Worship: Its Fundamental Place in Liberal Religion." In *Unitarians Face a New Age: The Report of the Commission on Appraisal,* 70–79. Boston: American Unitarian Association, 1936.

## ✦ Biographical Resources

Crompton, Arnold. *Aurelia Henry Reinhardt, A Biographical Sketch.* Berkeley, CA: Starr King School for the Ministry, 1977.

Hedley, George. *Aurelia Henry Reinhardt.* Oakland, CA: Mills College, 1961.

## ✦ Archives

Over 1,000 file folders containing invaluable data and memorabilia are available in the Mills College Archives, Oakland, CA.

# An Era of Feminine Foment

OUR UNITARIAN AND UNIVERSALIST women of the last century in both England and America have had one virtue in common. They have been pioneers. Whether the goals they pursued were in literature, science, education, the arts, or reform, with supreme courage and indefatigable will, have they marched in the van. As one biographical writer suggests in her book, *Great Women* (most of whom as in all such symposiums, were Unitarians and Universalists), they were *Ladies in Revolt.* Unwilling to subscribe with their apathetic sisters to the axiom that "progress is automatic," they insisted with Justice Holmes that, "The way the inevitable comes to pass is through effort."

These women who have literally made history were not outstanding persons who happened to be Unitarians or Universalists in their religion. Not at all. It was their dynamic religious liberalism which made them great. Theirs was a religion inspiring them to live in the real world, grim and ugly though they found it, rather than the dream world of orthodox Christianity. Little time and energy could they spend speculating on the pearly gates of heaven or the bowels of hell. There was too much to do on earth. Unitarianism and Universalism which stressed the free spirit of inquiry and criticism made them seek and speak the truth. Their religion meant to them not theological quibbling but individual and social growth. It was the "elan vital" motivating them both in their inner lives and their overt deeds. With the "divine discontent" of Emerson they felt that patience, rather than virtue, was more often another name for cowardice.

The Unitarian and Universalist religion was in short, an ethical leaven, and the result was an era of "Feminine Foment."

—RAMONA SAWYER BARTH[1]

# About This Anthology

✦ ✦ ✦

THE IDEA FOR THIS BOOK germinated at a gathering of Unitarian Universalist women at Cedar Hill Conference Center in Duxbury, Massachusetts, in October 1989. The meeting was made possible by a grant from the Unitarian Universalist Association, through what was then called the *Denominational Grants Panel.* The purpose was to create ways to bring forth the history of the women of the liberal religious traditions of Universalism and Unitarianism.

The seed for this anthology had been planted earlier in my own mind when I was a student at Harvard Divinity School. Seeking a better understanding of the foremothers of the religious tradition in which I was preparing for the ministry, I found my feminist anger aroused by the invisibility of historical Universalist and Unitarian women in my studies. I had to do something about this situation! Fortunately, the Unitarian Universalist Women's Federation agreed to sponsor a project on women's history, allowing me to obtain a grant to fund the initial meeting that outlined this anthology. I naively thought an anthology would be a fairly simple and quick way to begin recovering our long-lost "herstory."

The gathering at Cedar Hill provided the structure that remains the basis for this current anthology, but something else happened at that historic meeting that actually delayed the publication process for a number of years. The need emerged for an ongoing Unitarian Universalist women's history organization. It became clear from the energy and interests of many of the women at the gathering that something more immediate needed to be done to raise awareness within the denomination of the need for serious work on Unitarian and Universalist women's history. Proposals were made and later carried out for workshops at the Unitarian Universalist Women's Federation Biennial and at the Unitarian Universalist General Assembly. We believed we could generate interest in Unitarian Universalist women's history by providing people with tools for beginning their own historical investigations and inspiring them to become involved in recovering the herstory of our liberal religious movements.

Much of the initial work that came out of the Cedar Hill meeting focused on preparing for the denominational gathering in Milwaukee, Wisconsin, in June 1990. We circulated a brochure to introduce the new project, initially called the *Women's History Publication Project*, inviting contributions of energy and money. A worship service was developed and presented at the General Assembly, and we offered copies for sale. Since I had already begun to collect information on women whose writings might be appropriate for publication, we printed my "Compendium of Resources" and sold it as the project's working papers. Later that summer, thanks to a research fellowship from the Massachusetts Historical Society, I was able to locate many of the writings I had identified and begin compiling resources for the anthology.

In the years that followed, a women's history network developed within the denomination. In 1991, we founded the Unitarian Universalist Women's Heritage Society (UUWHS), complete with a board of directors, independent affiliate status with the Unitarian Universalist Association, and tax-exempt status with the Internal Revenue Service. We presented workshops and worship services at General Assemblies and district conferences and before local and district women's groups. We established a semiannual newsletter and a series of "Occasional Papers." Eventually, we received funding from the Unitarian Universalist Veatch Program, now at Shelter Rock. In 1992, we established an office at the Unitarian Universalist Church in Medford, Massachusetts. In 1998, the office moved to the First Parish Church in Malden, Massachusetts.

Throughout the years of development of UUWHS, work on the anthology continued in bits and pieces. Esther Kanipe had put out a call for submissions following the meeting in Duxbury. Some selections were received, including a few biographical sketches of women to be featured. As word about the anthology spread and as new society publications were developed, additional pieces of writing were discovered and submitted for the anthology.

A number of students from various institutions provided invaluable assistance in the development of this anthology. Margaret Harrelson, then an undergraduate student from Earlham College in Indiana, came for a six-month internship in 1991 to research abolitionist women. Lee Bluemel, Lisa Doege, Vicki Jenkins, Marie Norton, and Jacquelyn O'Sullivan—field education students from Harvard Divinity School and Andover-Newton in 1991–1992—read potential selections and offered feedback on their readability and impact. In 1993, Helene Knox, intern from Starr King School for the Ministry, worked with me to refine the initial outline, gathered all the material that had been collected, and began the process of actually placing texts into chapters and noting where major gaps occurred.

As the piles of potential selections grew, certain areas were represented more substantially than others. We realized more space was needed to demonstrate how ideas and practices of reform developed over time. To explore each area in depth, we needed to limit the number of sections in the anthology. The practical solution was to develop the sections for which we already had the most material. Areas of reform not included in the first volume would have to wait for succeeding ones.

As we surveyed what had been assembled, a new topic emerged that had not been in the initial outline—the idea of reform in general. Thus, we added a section exploring the origins and nature of the notion of reform. Other sections focused on education, racial justice, and religion. Still other significant areas of reform will be explored in future volumes.

In 1994, I contacted June Edwards, Laurie Carter Noble, and Jean Hoefer, all of whom had attended the initial gathering in 1989. June agreed to take responsibility for developing the section on education. Laurie and Jean agreed to read the anthology in draft form and offer editorial suggestions. Helene Knox, now back home in Oakland, agreed to continue work on the religion section. In 1996, Susan Swan joined the project as an editorial consultant on the introductions and the biographical sketches.

Other people came forth to take on additional roles. Kay Ritter volunteered to put the proposed selections on computer, so they could be more easily edited and their comparable lengths determined. Irene Baros-Johnson agreed to write biographical sketches on British Unitarian women. Anne Goodwin, administrator for the Women's Heritage

Society, worked with me on an application to the UUA Panel for Theological Education, resulting in a grant for completion of the anthology. When Lara Hoke joined the Heritage Society staff, first as a field education student and later as administrator, she took on the major task of proofreading and correcting texts. Danielle Brown, Emily Gledhill, Lynne Levine, Victoria Weinstein, Marilyn Wilson, Melissa (Sam) Sherman, and Bonnie Smith have also assisted with text preparation.

Those who had submitted biographies early on were contacted for permission to adapt them to the form now established for the anthology. As contacts were made for people to write additional biographical sketches, new ideas emerged concerning the place of the biographies in the overall scheme of the project. Originally conceived as brief introductions to the texts, the biographies began to take on lives of their own. Each woman who agreed to write a biographical sketch felt a special connection with the writer she chose. Taken together, these connections establish a sort of personal historical lineage between Unitarian and Universalist women of the past and Unitarian Universalist women and men of the present.

An important guide through much of this process was Elizabeth Nordbeck. In 1991, I entered the Doctor of Ministry program at Andover-Newton Theological School in order to gain further historical background to develop this anthology. Elizabeth Nordbeck, a scholar of Congregationalist history, was my advisor and mentor. Also serving on my doctoral committee were two UU ministers, Anita Farber-Robertson and David Johnson, who read and critiqued the anthology as it developed.

Later, Sarah Oelberg, Laurie Carter Noble, and Bonnie Smith along with UUWHS board members Dorothy Boroush, Joan Goodwin, Christine Jaronski, and David Johnson reviewed the manuscript and provided helpful suggestions. Jean Hoefer's editing suggestions were an important contribution to the readability of this book. Bonnie Smith updated the Judith Sargent Murray materials. Sarah Oelberg contributed additional selections and biographies to improve representation from midwestern women. Laurie Carter Noble provided invaluable assistance in the final editing process. Skinner House editor Mary Benard contributed many hours of careful reading and incredible patience.

Without the contributions of all of these people, this anthology would not have been created. This has truly been a collaborative effort. Thank you, one and all!

The development of this anthology would have been impossible without the support of the Unitarian Universalist Women's Heritage Society. This assistance has included financial support, historical resources, editing suggestions, and a large measure of encouragement to keep going on what sometimes seemed like an impossible project to complete. While the UUWHS has provided considerable input, any omissions or errors in scholarship are mine alone, as I am solely responsible for the final contents.

In the interests of further scholarship, please let us know what you would like to see included in future anthologies. We would like your perspectives to be represented in the next volume of what we hope will become a series of anthologies. Thank you for your participation in the recovery and development of Unitarian Universalist women's history.

—D. M. E.

# Contributors

✦ ✦ ✦

SARAH BARBER-BRAUN is a 1984 graduate of Starr King School for the Ministry. She has devoted the last seventeen years to exploring the life and ministry of Phebe Hanaford. In June 1998, with the assistance of the New York State Convention of Universalists and the Unitarian Universalist Women's Heritage Society, she dedicated a gravestone at Phebe Hanaford's previously unmarked grave in Orleans, New York.

IRENE BAROS-JOHNSON received a master of divinity degree from Drew Theological School in Madison, New Jersey. She co-wrote the sesquicentennial history of the May Memorial Unitarian Society in Syracuse, New York, *May No One Be a Stranger*. She also wrote *To Further a Freer Religious Expression* and *Some Integration Movement* about the early years of the Unitarian Universalist Church of Augusta, Georgia. In 1994, she received a Unitarian Universalist Women's Federation Feminist Theology Award to further work on the worship/study project "Urged Onward by a Longtime Friend: Lucretia Mott and the Unitarians."

PAULA BLANCHARD is the author of *Margaret Fuller: From Transcendentalism to Revolution* as well as biographies of Sarah Orne Jewett and Canadian painter and writer Emily Carr.

DOROTHY BOROUSH received her master of divinity degree from Chicago Theological Seminary. She served churches in Michigan, Connecticut, and Massachusetts before becoming district executive for the Ballou Channing District. Now retired, she serves on the board of the Unitarian Universalist Women's Heritage Society.

JANET BOWERING attended St. Lawrence University and Theological School and was ordained to the Universalist ministry in 1955. She was minister of the Universalist Unitarian Church of Haverhill, Massachusetts, from 1979 until her retirement in 1996. Meadville Lombard Theological School awarded her a doctor of divinity degree in 1998. Her past denominational involvement includes serving on the board of the Unitarian Universalist Women's Federation, as president of the Unitarian Universalist Historical Society, and as chairperson of the board of the Church of the Larger Fellowship. Currently, she is a board member of the Unitarian Universalist Women's Heritage Society.

PAULA COPESTICK earned a master's and education specalist degree from Kent State University. Paula is a retired sociology instructor and vocational rehabilitation counselor. Currently, she is pursuing her interest of eighteen years in women's history by writing articles, conducting workshops, and presenting programs on women of the nineteenth century. She is a charter member of the Unitarian Universalist Women's Heritage Society.

ELIZABETH CURTISS is a Unitarian Universalist community-based minister, specializing in denominational history. She has served as vice president of the Unitarian Universalist Historical Society and is participating in a team effort to archive the papers of George Huntston Williams. She received a master of international affairs degree from Columbia University in 1981, with a certificate in South Asian Studies, and a master of divinity degree from Harvard Divinity School in 1990.

MARJORIE CUSHMAN-HYBELS is a member of the Unitarian Universalist congregation of First Parish in Needham, Massachusetts, and retired executive director of the Needham Council on Aging. She has taught lipreading to late-deafened adults as a volunteer for over twenty-five years. She also teaches Elderhostel courses on women's history. She is particularly fascinated by foreign women's observations on the United States.

HELEN R. DEESE retired as professor of English at Tennessee Technological University in 1998, becoming professor emerita. She is the Caroline Dall Editor for the Massachusetts Historical Society. From 1998 to 1999, she was a Mellon research fellow at the American Antiquarian Society in Worcester, Massachusetts.

LISA DOEGE was ordained by the congregation of Unity Church Unitarian in St. Paul, Minnesota, in 1994. She is currently parish minister at First Unitarian Church in South Bend, Indiana. She began studying the life and work of Eleanor Gordon during her senior year at Harvard Divinity School, when she was a field education student with the Unitarian Universalist Women's Heritage Society.

MARIANNE DUNLOP teaches English as a second language under the auspices of the Laubach Literacy Council of San Diego County, Inc. She received her master of women's history degree in 1989 and serves as an advisory board member at the Sargent House Museum in Gloucester, Massachusetts.

JUNE EDWARDS is an associate professor of education at the State University of New York at Oneonta. She is the author of *Opposing Censorship in Public Schools: Religion, Morality, and Literature* and numerous articles on church and state issues regarding public education. Her areas of specialty include the history of education, the philosophy of education, and school law. Her article "The Unitarian Influence on Elizabeth Peabody and American Kindergartens" was published as an Occasional Paper by the Unitarian Universalist Women's Heritage Society. She is currently working on a book on nineteenth- and early twentieth-century women educators and their influence on modern education.

CLARE B. FISCHER is Aurelia Henry Reinhardt Professor of Religion and Culture at Starr King School for Ministry in Berkeley, California. She teaches courses in comparative sociology of religion, social thought, and feminism. Her scholarly interests include issues of civil society in the postmodern, postcolonial world; the changing role of middle-class women in Indonesia; and the scope and nature of ritual process with an emphasis on pilgrimage studies.

JOAN W. GOODWIN is an independent scholar with special interest in nineteenth-century American women. She is the author of *The Remarkable Mrs. Ripley: The Life of Sarah Alden Bradford Ripley*. For a number of years, she served Unitarian Universalist congregations as a religious educator and also worked for the Unitarian Universalist Association in the field of church extension. Now retired, she is chair of the board of directors of the Unitarian Universalist Women's Heritage Society.

MARGARET HARRELSON does information systems support in Durham, North Carolina. In 1991, she did an internship with the Unitarian Universalist Women's Heritage Society, where she researched nineteenth-century Unitarian and Universalist women who were racial justice advocates. She graduated from Earlham College in 1992 with a bachelor of arts degree in women's studies. She is a member of the Eno River Unitarian Universalist Fellowship.

COLLEEN HURST became interested in Susan B. Anthony while at First Unitarian Church in Rochester, New York. She became the church historian and a trustee of the Susan B. Anthony House and pursued the singular connections of the early women's rights movement, her church, and Susan B. Anthony. She receives great satisfaction from seeing the growing interest and scholarship in women's history and participating in it, even in the smallest way.

MAUDE JENKINS is an educator, psychiatric social worker, and Unitarian Universalist. Her dissertation at Columbia University, "The History of the Black Woman's Club Movement in America," was inspired by her affiliation with the League for Women in Community Service at 558 Massachusetts Avenue in Boston. A member of the American Historical Association, she is committed to researching the contributions of African American women.

DAVID JOHNSON has been minister of the First Parish in Brookline since 1988. He also has served as secretary of the Unitarian Universalist Historical Society and as a board member and secretary of the Unitarian Universalist Women's Heritage Society. He currently teaches a survey course in Unitarian Universalist history at Andover Newton Theological School.

ELEA KEMLER graduated from Barnard College, where she majored in women's studies. She later graduated from the Harvard Divinity School and was ordained in 1994. She is minister of the Unitarian Universalist Society of Gardner, Massachusetts, the small, central Massachusetts mill town where Lucy Stone gave her first public address.

HELENE KNOX earned a doctorate in English at the University of California at Berkeley and has taught British and American literature on the East and West Coasts and also for two years as a Fulbright Scholar in France and Germany. She has been a Unitarian Universalist since 1961 and graduated with a master of divinity degree from Starr King School for the Ministry in Berkeley, specializing in Unitarian Universalist history and theology. In 1991, she received a Unitarian Universalist Women's Federation Feminist Theology Award for her collection of poems on men and women in Unitarian Universalist history, *Among Our Chalices.*

KOBY LEE is associate director of the School of Continuing Studies and assistant professor of continuing studies at North Park University in Chicago, Illinois, where she teaches women's studies, United States history, and an occasional course in ethics. Her Biographical Sketch was drawn from a larger work she has written, which focuses on Celia Parker Woolley's racial justice activism.

BARBARA MARSHMAN graduated in 1932 from the Massachusetts School of Art, where she majored in costume design. In 1937, she joined the Follen Church Society, founded by Eliza Cabot Follen's husband, Charles. She remained a member there and was active in maintaining the Follens' presence in the church until her death from cancer in 1996.

KIMBERLY MINER graduated from Pittsburgh Theological Seminary and was ordained as a Unitarian Universalist minister in 1999. She is currently serving Thomas Unitarian Universalist Church in Smithton, Pennsylvania. She is very interested in women's writings about theology.

LAURIE CARTER NOBLE, writer and long-time Unitarian Universalist and social justice activist, has written extensively on issues affecting women and children. A founding member of the Unitarian Universalist Women's Heritage Society, she is currently working on a biographical study of Unitarian and Universalist women in the nineteenth century and the women's suffrage movement. She is also the editor of the Reverend Violet Kochendoerfer's autobiography, *A Modern Pioneer*. She teaches writing workshops and is particularly interested in helping women write the stories of their lives and those of their foremothers.

SARAH OELBERG received her doctor of ministry degree from Meadville/Lombard Theological School in 1991. Since then, she has been the minister of the Nora Unitarian Universalist Church in Hanska, Minnesota, and the Mankato Unitarian Universalist Fellowship in Mankato, Minnesota. Before becoming a minister, she was a college professor and taught at Yeshiva University, New York University, and Buena Vista College. She has had a life-long interest in Unitarian Universalist history and has written a manuscript, *Fire Across the Prairie,* the history of Unitarianism in Iowa from statehood until World War I.

PHOEBE POLLITT graduated from nursing school at the University of North Carolina in 1977 and earned a doctorate in curriculum and instruction from the University of North Carolina at Greensboro in 1994. She is currently working on a piece about the Reverend Hannah Powell, a Universalist minister.

MARY ANN PORUCZNIK is a member of the National Women's History Network and a HerStoryTeller who portrays Augusta Chapin and other women of the nineteenth century for schools, organizations, and groups. She is continually fascinated by the accomplishments and inspiration of early feminists and the message they have for contemporary women.

QIYAMAH RAHMAN, a Unitarian Universalist since 1993, assumed the role of district executive for the Thomas Jefferson District in July 1999. Formerly a member of the Thurman Hamer Ellington Unitarian Universalist Fellowship and Ministry and the Unitarian Universalist Congregation of Atlanta, Qiyamah has the honor of fellowshipping with all the congregations in the Thomas Jefferson District. She is pursuing a doctorate in African women's studies on domestic violence in South Africa at Clark Atlanta University. She self-published her first book, *Walking Toward the Light,* a collection of healing affirmations for women who have experienced violence. She is a queen mother in the village of Gomoa Achiase in Ghana.

BONNIE HURD SMITH has a bachelor of arts degree in history and communications and a master of science degree in communications management from Simmons College. She is the director of the Judith

Sargent Murray Society and the Boston Women's Heritage Trail. She has written a book about Judith Sargent Murray called *From Gloucester to Philadelphia in 1790* and is currently working on a collection of her letters.

GLORY SOUTHWIND graduated from Northeastern Illinois University with a degree in women's studies. She has been conducting research on Augusta Chapin for ten years.

SUSAN SWAN is a writer/educator with master's degrees in American studies and education. Her career has focused on furthering developmental education in high school and in the first two years of college. Her publications include articles in *American Women Writers* and in *The New Orleans Review*. She is also a musician and attends, writes, and works in the archives for Emmanuel Church in Boston. Currently, she is an administrator of special services and teaches freshmen at Suffolk University.

AUDREY W. VINCENT holds a master of education degree in English from Kent State University as well as a master of divinity degree and a doctor of ministry degree from the School of Theology at Claremont, California. Prior to her career in the ministry, she taught junior and senior high school English and film studies on the junior college level. Her interest in the story of Laura Matilda Towne began in conversations with a parishioner, Milton H. Rahn, who uncovered her lost story years ago.

JUDITH WALKER-RIGGS has been a Unitarian minister since 1964, trained at Manchester College, Oxford University (the direct descendent of Warrington Academy), and has served in England, the United States, and Belgium. She became interested in Anna Laetitia Barbauld while a student. From 1991 to 1998, she served one of the churches that Anna's husband served as minister and lived in the building where Anna Barbauld taught.

VICTORIA WEINSTEIN is a graduate of Harvard Divinity School and currently serves as minister of Channing Memorial Church in Howard County, Maryland. She was the recipient of a 1997 Feminist Theology Award from the Unitarian Universalist Women's Federation.

MARILYN CARROLL WILSON is a Unitarian Universalist living in Winchester, Massachusetts. She is a clinical psychologist by training and has read widely in the areas of health, healing, history, and spirituality. She is a freelance writer, special projects editor, and event organizer.

# Notes

✦ ✦ ✦

## The Past, the Present, and the Future

1. From Ella Lyman Cabot, *Our Part in the World* (Boston: Beacon Press, 1918). Ella Lyman Cabot (1880–1930), Unitarian, was a pioneer in education, the author of numerous books, and a member of the Massachusetts State Board of Education. These excerpts are from one of her contributions to the Beacon Course in Religious Education developed by the American Unitarian Association.

## Standing Before Us

1. Published in the songbook *Take Up the Song,* which may be ordered for $7.45 (including postage) from Sisters Unlimited, Inc., 1180 VT Route 22A, Bridport, VT 05734, Phone: (802) 758-2549, e-mail: ceagle4@aol.com. Carole Etzler Eagleheart is a Unitarian Universalist musician, workshop and worship leader, artist, and activist. This song, "Standing Before Us," has become the theme song for work to reclaim Unitarian Universalist women's heritage. Words and music copyright © 1983 by Carole Etzler Eagleheart.

## Call to Reform

1. For example, see Nancy Cott, *The Bonds of Womanhood: "Woman's Sphere" in New England, 1780–1835* (New Haven, CT: Yale University Press, 1977); Keith Melder, *The Beginnings of Sisterhood: The American Woman's Rights Movement, 1800–1850* (New York: Schocken, 1970); Robert Abzug, *Cosmos Crumbling: American Reform and the Religious Imagination* (New York: Oxford University Press, 1994).

2. Barbara Weltner, "The Cult of True Womanhood: 1820–1860," *American Quarterly* 18 (Summer 1966): 151–174; Aileen S. Kraditor, *Up from the Pedestal: Selected Writings in the History of American Feminism* (Chicago: Quadrangle Books, 1968).

3. Cott, 152–153.

4. Olive Banks, *Faces of Feminism* (London: Basil Blackwell, 1981), 63–64.

5. See Ellen DuBois, *Feminism and Suffrage: The Emergence of an Independent Women's Movement in America, 1848–1869* (Ithaca, NY: Cornell University Press, 1978); Mary P. Ryan, *The Cradle of the Middle–Class: The Family in Oneida County, New York, 1780–1865* (Cambridge: Cambridge University Press, 1981).

6. See Nancy A. Hewitt, *Women's Activism and Social Change: Rochester, New York, 1822–1872* (Ithaca, NY: Cornell University Press, 1984); Blanche Glassman Hersh, *The Slavery of Sex: Feminist-Abolitionism in America* (Chicago: University of Illinois Press, 1978).

7. Cott, 204.

8. See Raymond Holt, *The Unitarian Contribution to Social Progress in England* (London: Allen & Unwin, 1938).

9. Christine Bolt, *The Women's Movements in the United States and Britain from the 1790s to the 1920s* (Amherst: University of Massachusetts Press, 1993), 57.

10. Duncan Crow, *The Victorian Woman* (London: Allen and Unwin, 1971), 155. See also Kathryn Gleadle, *The Early Feminists: Radical Unitarians and the Emergence of the Women's Rights Movement, 1843–1851* (Basingstoke, Eng.: Macmillan, 1995), and Ruth Watts, *Gender, Power and the Unitarians in England 1760–1860* (London: Longman, 1998).

11. Banks, 29–32. David Johnson (e-mail to D. Emerson, March 26, 1997) points out that although this individualism may have characterized the early years, by the mid to late nineteenth century, American Unitarian women had created an institutional base for their work both within and beyond the denomination.

12. For example, see Eleanor Flexner, *Century of Struggle: The Woman's Rights Movement in the United States* (Cambridge: Belknap Press, 1975), 16–17; Gerda Lerner, *The Creation of Feminist Consciousness* (New York: Oxford University Press, 1993), 158–159, 213.

13. Anne Firor Scott, *Natural Allies: Women's Associations in American History* (Urbana: University of Illinois Press), 50, 75.

14. Conversation with Mary Ruthsdotter and Bonnie Eisenberg (at the office of the National Women's History Project, Windsor, CA, July 5, 1995) concerning *Women Win the Vote: A Gazette from the National Women's History Project* (1995). For another example of misidentification, see Donna Behnke, *Religious Issues in Nineteenth Century Feminism* (Troy, NY: Whitson, 1982), in which she identified Mary Livermore as the wife of a Unitarian minister (p. 19); Daniel Livermore was a *Universalist* minister.

15. February 26, 1788, in Julian Boyd, ed., *Papers of Thomas Jefferson* 12 (1955): 625.

16. March 31, 1776, *Adams Family Correspondence*, Vol. 1, 369–370.

17. February 13, 1791, Adams papers, Massachusetts Historical Society, Boston.

18. March 31, 1776, *Adams Family Correspondence,* Vol. 1, 369–370.

19. October 12, 1815, Adams papers, reel 427.

20. May 5, 1816, Adams papers, reel 431.

21. January 3, 1818, Adams papers, reel 442.

22. Louis Filler, *The Crusade Against Slavery* (New York: Harper Torchbooks, 1960), 55.

23. For an interesting contemporary reflection on these events, see John Pierce's unpublished *Memoirs,* vol. 7, manuscripts in the Massachusetts Historical Society, 52ff.

24. See the description of "Angelina Grimke's Address" in *The Concise History of Woman Suffrage: Selections from the Classic Work of Stanton, Anthony, Gage and Harper*, ed. Mari Jo and Paul Buhle, 73–77 (Urbana: University of Illinois Press, 1978).

25. See the writings and Biographical Sketch of Harriet Martineau (pages 169–178 and 188–190).

26. Quoted in Filler, 75–76.

27. *The Liberator,* May 31, 1844.

28. Maria Weston Chapman, "The Young Sailor," in *The Liberty Bell* (Boston: The Anti-Slavery Bazaar, 1853), 195–196.

29. See the writings and Biographical Sketch of Laura Matilda Towne (pages 360–370).

30. Maria Weston Chapman to Edward Atkinson, an antislavery activist (Brookline, MA, c. March 1862), in the Edward Atkinson manuscripts at the Massachusetts Historical Society. Quoted in *The Anti-Slavery Vanguard,* ed. Martin Duberman (Princeton, NJ: Princeton University Press, 1965), 194.

31. See the writings and Biographical Sketch of Lydia Maria Francis Child (pages 287–298).

32. Filler, 129.

33. Daniel D. Smith, *Universalist* 2 (2 November 1833): 184. Quoted in Russell Miller, *The Larger Hope* (Boston: Unitarian Universalist Association, 1979), 537.

34. B. Susan Brown, "The Spark Within, The Flame Without" (Term paper, Harvard Divinity School, 1995), 20.

35. Brown, 39.

36. Duncan Crow, *The Victorian Woman* (London: Allen and Unwin, 1971), 169.

37. See the writings and Biographical Sketch of Elizabeth Palmer Peabody (pages 216–224 and 243–245).

38. See the writings and Biographical Sketch of Susan B. Anthony (pages 42–53).

39. See the writings and Biographical Sketch of Elizabeth Blackwell (pages 191–198 and 256–261).

40. Quoted in Eugene B. Navias, *Singing Our History: Tales, Texts, and Tunes from Two Centuries of Unitarian and Universalist Hymns* (Boston: Unitarian Universalist Association, 1975), 55.

41. See *Singing the Living Tradition* (Boston: Beacon Press, 1993), #122, #273.

42. Quoted in Eliza Rice Hanson, *Our Women Workers* (Chicago: Star and Covenant, 1882), 62.

43. "Frances Dana Gage," in *History of Women's Suffrage,* vol. 1, ed. Elizabeth Cady Stanton, Susan B. Anthony, and Matilda J. Gage, (New York: Fowler and Wells, 1881), 110.

44. This was one of several ongoing ventures to provide educational opportunities for recently freed African Americans. Unitarian Laura Matilda Towne arrived on nearby St. Helena Island earlier that year and remained nearly forty years until her death. See Towne's writings and Biographical Sketch in this volume (pages 360–370.)

45. "Clara Barton," in *History of Women's Suffrage,* vol. 1, ed. Elizabeth Cady Stanton, Susan B. Anthony, and Matilda J. Gage (New York: Fowler and Wells, 1881), 429. Also see the writings and Biographical Sketch of Clara Barton in this volume (pages 386–390).

46. See the writings and Biographical Sketch of Elizabeth Blackwell (pages 191–198 and 256–261).

47. See the writings and Biographical Sketch of Harriot Kezia Hunt (pages 199–207).

48. "Woman Wants Bread, Not the Ballot," in *Life and Work of Susan B. Anthony,* vol. 2, ed. Ida H. Harper (Indianapolis: Hollenbeck, 1908), 1003.

49. See the writings and Biographical Sketch of Lucy Stone (pages 30–34 and 54–58).

50. See the writings and Biographical Sketch of Charlotte Perkins Stetson Gilman (pages 545–554).

51. Letter to the Reverend Anna Howard Shaw, in *Life and Work of Susan B. Anthony,* 678.

52. Quoted in Elizabeth Griffith, *In Her Own Right: The Life of Elizabeth Cady Stanton* (New York: Oxford University Press, 1984), 185.

53. Quoted in *Life and Work of Susan B. Anthony* (in order): Letter to Isabella Beecher Hooker, 899; interview with reporter "Nellie Bly," 859; speech to women's temperance crusade, 457; and last public speech, 1409.

54. See the writings and Biographical Sketch of Harriet Martineau (pages 169–178 and 188–190).

55. See the writings and Biographical Sketch of Mary Carpenter (pages 225–232).

56. See the writings and Biographical Sketch of Elizabeth Blackwell (pages 191–198 and 256–261).

57. Barbara Smith Bodichon, *Women and Work* (London: Bosworth & Harrison, 1857).

58. Barbara Leigh Smith Bodichon, *An American Diary, 1857–1858* (London: Routledge & Kegan Paul, 1972), 158.

59. Anne Firor Scott, *Natural Allies: Women's Associations in American History* (Urbana: University of Illinois, 1993), 116.

60. See the writings and Biographical Sketch of Susan B. Anthony (pages 42–53).

61. See the writings and Biographical Sketches of Susan B. Anthony (pages 42–53) and Julia Ward Howe (pages 325–331 and 345–348).

62. See the writings and Biographical Sketch of Mary Carpenter (pages 225–232).

63. See the writings and Biographical Sketch of Barbara Leigh Smith Bodichon (pages 59–68).

64. See the writings and Biographical Sketch of Mary Carpenter (pages 225–232).

65. See Fannie Barrier Williams, "Address to World's Congress of Representative Women, 1893" (pages 262–268) and Augusta Jane Chapin, "Remarks at the World's Parliament of Religions, Chicago, 1893" (pages 447–449).

66. Mary Helen Washington, *Invented Lives: Narratives of Black Women 1860–1960* (New York: Doubleday, 1987), 47.

67. See the writings and Biographical Sketch of Harriot Kezia Hunt (pages 199–207).

68. See the writings and Biographical Sketch of Elizabeth Blackwell (pages 191–198 and 256–261).

69. In Winifred and Frances Kirkland, *Girls Who Became Leaders* (New York: Ray Long and Richard R. Smith, 1932), 89.

70. This group of approximately twenty Unitarian women ministers supported each other in their studies to become ministers and also founded churches and rescued inactive ones in the central Midwest during the late nineteenth and early twentieth centuries.

71. In 1893, the four-hundredth anniversary of Columbus's landing in the Western hemisphere was celebrated with a World's Fair in Chicago. Among the related conferences held was the initial World's Parliament of Religions, which marked the first time representatives from the world's major religions had come together to share their perspectives in a nonjudgmental context. Several women were included among the speakers.

72. See the writings and Biographical Sketches of Mary Safford (pages 496–503) and Eleanor Elizabeth Elizabeth Gordon (pages 131–142).

73. See the writings and Biographical Sketches of Susan B. Anthony (pages 42–53) and Lucy Stone (pages 30–34 and 54–58).

74. Davidson Loehr, Introduction to "Life's Challenge" (sermon presented by Crane at People's Church, Kalamazoo, MI, 1898).

75. Cynthia Grant Tucker, *The Prophetic Sisterhood: Liberal Women Ministers of the Frontier, 1880–1930* (Boston: Beacon Press, 1990), 195.

76. This group of approximately twenty Unitarian women ministers supported each other in their studies to become ministers and also founded churches and rescued inactive ones in the central Midwest during the late nineteenth and early twentieth centuries. Also see the writings and Biographical Sketches of Mary Safford (pages 496–503) and Marie Hoffendahl Jenney Howe (pages 536–544) in this volume.

77. Eleanor Gordon, "A Little Bit of a Long Story" (Typescript, 1934).

78. Tucker, 17.

79. Tucker, 18.

80. Tucker, 52.

81. See the writings and Biographical Sketch of Marion Murdoch (pages 504–511).

82. Clara Cook Helvie, "Unitarian Women Ministers" (Bound typescript, 1928), 53.

## The Search for Education

1. Jean Jacques Rousseau, *facsimile,* trans. Barbara Foxley (New York: Dutton, 1966), 322, 326.

2. Cited in Dale Spender, ed., *The Education Papers: Women's Quest for Equality in Britain, 1850–1912* (London: Routledge & Kegan Paul, 1987), 11, 23.

3. Cited in Susan Phinney Conrad, *Perish the Thought* (Secaucus, NJ: Citadel Press, 1978), 18.

4. Most schools in the seventeenth and even early eighteenth centuries, both public and private, were controlled by advocates of particular faiths who did not hesitate to enforce those faiths. This was true in colleges and universities as well as in lower levels of education. These strong affiliations drove religious liberals to work for free and unsectarian education.

5. Barbara Welter, "The Cult of True Womanhood, 1820–1860," *American Quarterly* 18 (1966): 151–175.

6. Beecher is often criticized for refusing to support women's suffrage and for advocating wives' submission to their husbands. Nonetheless, she did much

to elevate the domestic life of women, worked for equal or better education for girls, and turned public school teaching into a respectable career for intelligent, educated females. She was an outspoken leader, writer, and businesswoman—not at all like the meek and mild homebody she recommended other women should be. See discussion of the influence of Beecher's *Treatise on Domestic Economy* in Barbara Goldsmith, *Other Powers: The Age of Suffrage, Spiritualism, and the Scandalous Victoria Woodhull* (New York: Knopf, 1998), 22–24.

7. Display at the Women's Rights National Historical Park, Seneca Falls, New York, Summer 1998. See also the writings and Biographical Sketch of Mary Ashton Rice Livermore (pages 233–242 and 320–324).

8. Cited in Barbara Miller Solomon, *In the Company of Educated Women* (New Haven, CT: Yale University Press, 1985), 56.

9. See Myra Sadker and David Sadker, *Failing at Fairness: How America's Schools Cheat Girls* (New York: Charles Scribner's Sons, 1994).

10. The friend was a Universalist minister, the Reverend Samuel Parker of Portsmouth, New Hampshire, who later moved to Boston. They were close friends and exchanged lengthy, intellectual letters.

11. It was formerly thought that her birthday was May 1. However, later evidence from her letters shows that May 5 is the correct date.

12. Judith Sargent Murray, "Letter 108," Judith Sargent Murray Papers (Andover, MA: Northeast Document Conservation Center for the Mississippi Department of Archives and History, Jackson, Mississippi, 1989).

13. See the writings and Biographical Sketch of Judith Sargent Murray (pages 149–159).

14. See the writings and Biographical Sketch of Margaret Fuller (pages 24–29 and 179–187).

15. See the writings and Biographical Sketch of Eliza Lee Cabot Follen (pages 302–309 and 349–353).

16. See the writings and Biographical Sketch of Maria Weston Chapman (pages 13–18, 299–301, and 354–356).

17. Susan Hoecher-Drysdale, *Harriet Martineau: First Woman Sociologist* (Oxford: Berg, 1992).

18. Elizabeth Peabody's foreign language bookstore was the first of its kind. It served as a gathering place for prominent and intellectual women and men. See the writings and Biographical Sketch of Elizabeth Palmer Peabody (pages 216–224 and 243–245).

19. A Scottish term referring to a mark made by a pen.

20. Joan Von Mehren, *Minerva and the Muse: A Life of Margaret Fuller* (Amherst: University of Massachusetts, 1994), 219.

21. See the writings and Biographical Sketch of Lucy Stone (pages 30–34 and 54–58).

22. See the writings and Biographical Sketch of Lucy Stone (pages 30–34 and 54–58).

23. See the writings and Biographical Sketches of Elizabeth Palmer Peabody (pages 216–224 and 243–245) and Margaret Fuller (pages 24–29 and 179–187).

24. Journals, April 4, 1841 (manuscript).

25. See the writings and Biographical Sketch of Margaret Fuller (pages 24–29 and 179–187).

26. See the writings and Biographical Sketch of Margaret Fuller (pages 24–29 and 179–187).

27. See Friedrich Froebel, *The Education of Man,* trans. and anno. W. N. Hailmann (New York: D. Appleton, 1907). Elizabeth Peabody used the original German edition, published in 1826.

28. *Lectures in the Training School for Kindergartners* (New York: D. C. Heath, 1886), 84.

29. See the writings and Biographical Sketch of Frances Power Cobbe (pages 85–94).

30. See the writings and Biographical Sketch of Harriet Martineau (pages 169–178 and 188–190).

31. See the writings and Biographical Sketches of Julia Ward Howe (pages 325–331 and 345–348) and Lucy Stone (pages 30–34 and 54–58).

32. This honor may actually belong to Lydia Ann Jenkins, who was apparently granted a letter of fellowship in 1858 and ordained in 1860 with her husband by the Ontario Association of Universalists in Geneva, New York. In addition, Antoinette Brown [Blackwell], who was later fellowshipped as a Unitarian minister, was ordained in 1853 by the Congregational church of South Butler, New York, but without the approval of the Congregational General Conference.

33. See note 32.

34. See the writings and Biographical Sketches of Lucy Stone (pages 30–34 and 54–58) and Susan B. Anthony (pages 42–53).

35. Quoted in *Dictionary of American Biography* (New York: Charles Scribner's Sons, 1929), 151.

36. The World's Congress of Representative Women, the opening event of the 1893 Columbian Exposition in Chicago, brought together women of the United States and around the world. It was the first great gathering of women across religious, class, racial, and national boundaries to dialogue, plan, and set a common course.

37. Fannie Barrier Williams, in *Bearing Witness, Selections from African-American Autobiographies*, ed. Henry Louis Gates, Jr. (New York: Pantheon Books, 1991), 13–14.

38. See the writings and Biographical Sketch of Celia Parker Woolley (pages 486–495).

39. Williams in *Bearing Witness,* 382.

40. Williams, 22.

## The Struggle for Racial Justice

1. Samuel May quoted in Deborah Clifford, *Crusader for Freedom: A Life of Lydia Maria Child* (Boston: Beacon Press, 1992), 110.

2. Gerda Lerner, *The Majority Finds Its Past: Placing Women in History* (New York: Oxford University Press, 1979), 114.

3. Catherine Clinton, "Maria Weston Chapman," in *Portraits of American Women,* ed. G. J. Barker-Benfield and Catherine Clinton (New York: St. Martin's Press, 1991), 151.

4. Clifford, 129. According to Perry Miller (*The Transcendentalists: An Anthology* [Cambridge, MA: Harvard University Press, 1950], 21) and Child's own correspondence *(Letters of Lydia Maria Child* [Boston: Houghton Mifflin, 1882]), Channing was so impressed with Child's *Appeal* that he walked 1.5 miles from his house to hers, despite ill health, to discuss it with her. After their three-hour conversation, he credited her with inspiring him speak out on the issue.

5. Clifford, 98.

6. Lydia Maria Child to Theodore Weld, July 10, 1880, in *Lydia Maria Child: Selected Letters,* ed. Milton Meltzer and Patricia Holland (Amherst: University of Massachusetts Press, 1982), 563.

7. Clinton, 150, 160.

8. The hymn text is reprinted on p. 301 of this volume.

9. See Jean Fagan Yellin, *Women and Sisters: The Antislavery Feminists in American Culture* (New Haven, CT: Yale University Press, 1989), 1–26. This symbol began to appear in the early 1830s. The original version showed a chained and kneeling slave woman as the only figure in the symbol, but later versions depicted Justice as a white woman about to free the slave. In an era of few visual images, this symbol—often accompanied by the saying "Am I not a woman and a sister?"—had the dramatic effect of mobilizing white women by confronting them with the reality of an African American woman in chains. However, as J. F. Yellin writes: "With the inclusion of an empowered white chain-breaking liberator, the enchained black supplicants are seen as powerless. The appearance of the chain breaker . . . makes it unnecessary for the slaves to rise and break their own chains." Nevertheless, many slaves did break their own chains.

10. Clinton, 160.

11. Lydia Maria Child to Lucy Osgood, June 28, 1846, in *Lydia Maria Child: Selected Letters,* 227.

12. Lydia Maria Child to Sarah Parsons, February 10, 1877, in *Lydia Maria Child: Selected Letters,* 539.

13. Mary Livermore, *Story of My Life* (Hartford, CT: A. D. Worthington, 1899), 480.

14. Maude Jenkins, "The History of the Black Woman's Club Movement in America,"Ed.D. Dissertation, Columbia University Teachers College, 1984, 61.

15. Jenkins, 66.

16. For a historical analysis of lesbian relationships, see Lillian Faderman, *Surpassing the Love of Men: Romantic Friendship and Love between Women from the Renaissance to the Present* (New York: Morrow, 1981).

17. Lydia Maria Child to Charles Sumner in *Lydia Maria Child: Selected Letters,* 283–284.

18. Clifford, 98.

19. Quoted in *Letters of Lydia Maria Child* (1882), 263–268.

20. See the writings and Biographical Sketch of Lydia Maria Francis Child (pages 287–298).

21. See the writings and Biographical Sketch of Maria Weston Chapman (pages 13–18, 299–301, and 354–356).

22. See the writings and Biographical Sketch of Lydia Maria Francis Child (pages 287–298).

23. Florence Howe Hall, *The Story of the Battle Hymn of the Republic* (New York: Harper and Brothers, 1916), 44–45.

24. Julia Ward Howe, *Reminiscences 1819–1899* (Boston: Houghton Mifflin, 1900), 273–277.

25. See the writings and Biographical Sketch of Lucy Stone (pages 30–34 and 54–58).

26. See the writings and Biographical Sketch of Lydia Maria Francis Child (pages 287–298).

27. See the writings and Biographical Sketch of Elizabeth Palmer Peabody (pages 216–224 and 243–245).

28. See the writings and Biographical Sketch of Eliza Lee Cabot Follen (pages 302–309 and 349–353).

29. Sallie Holley, *A Life for Liberty: Anti-Slavery and Other Letters of Sallie Holley*, ed. John White Chadwick (New York: G. P. Putnam's Sons, 1899), 69.

30. Quoted in Holley.

31. Holley, 59, 52.

32. Holley, 81.

33. Holley, 94.

34. Holley, 192. Holley is quoting William Lloyd Garrison.

35. Holley, 277–278.

36. Frances Smith Foster, ed., *A Brighter Coming Day: A Frances Ellen Watkins Harper Reader* (New York: Feminist Press at CUNY, 1990), 95.

37. The term *meeds* means "recompense; earned reward; fitting return."

38. Douglas C. Stange, *Patterns of Anti-Slavery among American Unitarians, 1831–1860* (Cranbury, NJ: Associated University Presses, 1977), 45.

39. Liberal women, especially activist abolitionist Unitarians, continued to follow the struggle of John Brown's family after his death and helped them in many ways, including providing education for his children and grandchildren.

40. Thanks to Dr. William F. Jenks—whose spouse, Elizabeth Pratt Jenks, patiently and attentively transcribed Towne's original notes—for furnishing a copy of Laura Matilda Towne's diary, recently made known. Dr. Jenks is a distant descendent of Laura Matilda Towne's family. Additional thanks to Milton H. Rahn for uncovering Towne's story and striving diligently to spread the word about her.

41. Smith Foster, 177.

42. Amy Morris Bradley, 1844, unpublished diaries.

43. *Wilmington Journal,* March 9, 1867 (no author given).

44. Amy Morris Bradley, 1873, unpublished diaries, Bradley Papers, Manuscript Department, Perkins Library, Duke University, Durham, NC.

45. Quoted in Marshall Fishwick, *Clara Barton* (Morristown, NJ: Silver Burdett, 1966), 27.

46. Quoted in Fishwick, 62.

47. Quoted in Lorraine E. Roses and Ruth E. Randolf, *Harlem Renaissance and Beyond* (New York: G. K. Hall , 1990), 283.

48. According to Franklin A. Dorman, *Twenty Families of Color in Massachusetts 1742–1998* (Boston: New England Historic Genealogical Society, 1998), Florida's birth name was Amelia (p. 411). No other source gives this information.

49. Elizabeth Fortson Arroyo, "Josephine St. Pierre Ruffin," in *Black Women in America: An Encyclopedia,* edited by Darlene Clark Hine et al. (Bloomington: Indiana University Press, 1993).

50. Florida Ruffin Ridley, "Two Gentlemen of Boston,"*Opportunity* 3 (January 1926): 13.

51. Dorman, 410.

## Reform in Religion

1. Ernest Cassara, ed., *Universalism in America: A Documentary History of a Liberal Faith,* 2nd ed. (Boston: Skinner House, 1984), 6.

2. David Robinson, *The Unitarians and the Universalists. Denominations in America,* vol. 1 (Westport, CT: Greenwood Press, 1985), 97–98.

3. Cynthia Grant Tucker, *The Prophetic Sisterhood: Liberal Women Ministers of the Frontier, 1880–1930* (Boston: Beacon Press, 1990).

4. Robinson, 5.

5. Robinson, 246.

6. Cassara, 5.

7. Robinson, 61.

8. For a thorough discussion of the controversy over the relative size and strength of Universalism in the nineteenth century, see Russell Miller, *The Larger Hope: The First Century of the Universalist Church in America, 1770–1870* (Boston: Unitarian Universalist Association, 1979), 162–165.

9. Robinson, 199, 282–283. Also Antoinette Brown [Blackwell], who was later fellowshipped as a Unitarian minister, was ordained in 1853 by the Congregational church of South Butler, New York, but without the approval of the Congregational General Conference, as this was not considered strictly necessary according to their congregational polity.

10. See also the writings and Biographical Sketches of the Reverends Eleanor Elizabeth Gordon (pages 131–142) and Caroline Julia Bartlett Crane (pages 117–130 and 519–523).

11. Marianne Dunlop, in a letter to Helene Knox, October 7, 1993.

12. Lucy Barns, *Familiar Letters and Poems* (Akron, OH: Aunty Brown, 1904).

13. See also the writings and Biographical Sketch of Judith Sargent Murray (pages 149–159).

14. In biographical materials, the family name is spelled *Barnes;* however, in the republication of her work by "Aunty" Brown, the name is spelled *Barns.* The latter will be used in this anthology.

15. See note 14.

16. Quoted in Eliza Rice Hanson, *Our Women Workers* (Chicago: Star and Covenant Office, 1882), 11.

17. Hanson, 11.

18. Barns, 50.

19. Lucy Barns, Letter "To a Respected Friend," May 23, 1807, in *Familiar Letters and Poems* (Akron, OH: Aunty Brown, 1904), 16.

20. Lucy Barns, Letter "To a Lady Confined with Illness," December 27, 1806, in *Familiar Letters and Poems,* 9.

21. Note that the Woolley family spelled their last name with two *l*'s; however, Lucia Fidelia Wooley regularly spelled her name with only one.

22. Fidelia Wooley Gillette, *Memoir of Rev. Edward Mott Woolley* (Boston: Abel Tomkins, 1855), 105.

23. Gillette, 1–2.

24. Gillette, 154.

25. Hanson, 472.

26. Max A. Kapp, "Edward Mott Woolley," *Universalist Leader* 74 (August 1957).

27. A. B. Grosh, "Introduction," in Fidelia Wooley Gillette, *Memoir of Rev. Edward Mott Woolley* (Boston: Abel Tomkins, 1855), xvi.

28. Hanson, 475.

29. Hanson, 476.

30. From a clipping in a scrapbook, April 1899 (Helen D. Lyman papers, Schlesinger Library, Radcliffe College).

31. Quoted in Catherine F. Hitchings, *Universalist and Unitarian Women Ministers* (Journal of the Universalist Historical Society) 10 (1975): 72.

32. Quoted in Hanson, 434.

33. Quoted in Thomas A. Chulak, *A People Moving through Time: A History of the Unitarian/Universalist Church in Oak Park* (Private printing, 1979).

34. Although the ordination of Antoinette Brown appears to have been the first instance of a woman receiving this honor, it was without the approval of the Congregational General Conference. Soon after her ordination, she began to doubt orthodox tenets and was later fellowshipped as a Unitarian minister. See the introduction to this section (pages 405–412) for a fuller discussion of other women who may be considered the first to have been ordained. Also see the writings and Biographical Sketch of Lucy Stone (pages 30–34 and 54–58).

35. See the writings and Biographical Sketch of Olympia Brown (pages 246–255 and 460–466).

36. See the writings and Biographical Sketch of Julia Ward Howe (pages 325–331 and 345–348).

37. See the writings and Biographical Sketch of Susan B. Anthony (pages 42–53).

38. See the writings and Biographical Sketch of Julia Ward Howe (pages 325–331 and 345–348).

39. See the writings and Biographical Sketches of Augusta Jane Chapin (pages 436–440 and 447–449) and Mary Ashton Rice Livermore (pages 233–242 and 320–324).

40. The Women's Ministerial Conference, founded by Julia Ward Howe, welcomed women of all faiths who saw their public work as ministry, regardless of whether they were ordained or otherwise recognized by institutional churches. This conference provided an essential, supportive sisterhood for many of these women, particularly those on the east coast, who felt rejected by the male-dominated religious world. Also see the writings and Biographical Sketch of Julia Ward Howe (pages 325–331 and 345–348).

41. Approximately thirty-three women were ordained to the Unitarian ministry in the nineteenth century; however, only three were ordained between 1901 and 1916, largely because women's ordination was actively discouraged by the Reverend Samuel Eliot, president of the denomination during those years.

42. Joseph Henry Crooker, "The Romance of a Pioneer," *Christian Leader* (27 February 1926): 6.

43. See the writings and Biographical Sketch of Mary Ashton Rice Livermore (pages 233–242 and 320–324).

44. See the writings and Biographical Sketch of Augusta Chapin (pages 436–440 and 447–449).

45. Joseph Henry Crooker, "The Romance of a Pioneer," *Christian Leader* (20 March 1926): 17.

46. See the writings and Biographical Sketch of Julia Ward Howe (pages 325–331 and 345–348).

47. This honor may belong to Lydia Ann Jenkins, who was apparently granted a letter of fellowship in 1858 and ordained with her husband by the Ontario Association of Universalists in Geneva, New York, in 1860. In addition, Antoinette Brown [Blackwell], who was later fellowshipped as a Unitarian minister, was ordained in 1853 by the Congregational church of South Butler, New York, but without approval of the Congregational General Conference.

48. Horace Walpole, quoted in the hundredth anniversary obituary memorial to Anna Laetitia Barbauld, *The Inquirer,* 7 March 1925.

49. Quoted in Grace Oliver, *The Story of the Life of Anna Laetitia Barbauld, with Many of Her Letters* (Boston: Cupples, Upham, 1886).

50. Anna Laetitia Barbauld, "A Summer Evening's Meditation," in *The Works of Anna Laetitia Barbauld with a Memoir by Lucy Aiken*, vol. 1 (London: Longman, Hurst, Rees, 1825).

51. Anna Laetitia Barbauld, "Thoughts on the Devotional Taste and on Sects and Establishments," in *The Works of Anna Laetitia Barbauld with a Memoir by Lucy Aiken*, vol. 2 (London: Longman, Hurst, Rees, 1825).

52. See the writings and Biographical Sketch of Fannie Barrier Williams (pages 262–278 and 512–518).

53. See Cynthia Grant Tucker, *The Prophetic Sisterhood: Liberal Women Ministers of the Frontier, 1880–1930* (Boston: Beacon Press, 1990). And in this text, see the writings and Biographical Sketches of Eleanor Elizabeth Gordon (pages 131–142), Mary Safford (pages 496–503), Marie Hoffendahl Jenney Howe (pages 536–544), and Caroline Julia Bartlett Crane (pages 117–130 and 519–523), who were also members of the Iowa Sisterhood.

54. Celia Parker Woolley, *The Western Slope* (Evanston, IL: William S. Lord, 1903).

55. The others were Eleanor Elizabeth Gordon and Caroline Julia Bartlett Crane. See their writings and Biographical Sketches on pages 131–142 (Gordon) and pages 117–130 and 519–523 (Crane).

56. See the writings and Biographical Sketch of Eleanor Elizabeth Gordon (pages 131–142).

57. See the writings and Biographical Sketch of Marie Hoffendahl Jenney Howe (pages 536–544).

58. Clipping from the Iowa State Historical Society (n.d.).

59. Different sources cite different dates for the year of Marion Murdoch's birth, ranging from 1848 to 1855. The state of Iowa did not keep birth records before 1880, so there is no official record. The program for her memorial service gives the year 1848, so that date is used in this anthology. Different sources also use different spellings of her last name: *Murdoch* (as shown here) and *Murdock.*

60. See the writings and Biographical Sketch of Mary Augusta Safford (pages 496–503).

61. See the writings and Biographical Sketch of Caroline Julia Bartlett Crane (pages 117–130 and 519–523).

62. Clara Cook Helvie, "Unitarian Women Ministers" (Typescript, 1928), 48.

63. See the writings and Biographical Sketch of Julia Ward Howe (pages 325–331 and 345–348).

64. Marion Murdock, "Helpfulness, or How the World Moves: A Sermon by Rev. Marion Murdock" (Humboldt, IA: Unity Church, 1888).

65. Ednah Dow Cheney, *Reminiscences* (Boston: Lee & Shepard, 1902), 29.

66. See the writings and Biographical Sketches of Harriot Kezia Hunt (pages 199–207) and Julia Ward Howe (pages 325–331 and 345–348).

67. Cheney, 75.

68. See the writings and Biographical Sketch of Margaret Fuller (pages 24–29 and 179–187).

69. Cheney, 99, 100–101.

70. Cheney, 102, 103.

71. Cheney, 148, 149.

72. This article originally was attributed to Elizabeth Padgham, but a subsequent issue identified the author as Marie Hoffendahl Jenney Howe.

73. Quoted in Tucker, 168.

74. See the writings and Biographical Sketches of Mary Augusta Safford (pages 496–503) and Marion Murdoch (pages 504–511).

75. See the writings and Biographical Sketch of Eleanor Elizabeth Gordon (pages 131–142).

76. Charles W. Phillips, "History of First Unitarian Church" (Typescript, Unitarian Church, Des Moines, IA, n.d.).

77. Discussion of the concept of *race type* is common in writings of the day on evolution. The term is used indicate that aspect of a species that determines the model for its evolution.

78. Polly Wynn Allen, *Building Domestic Liberty: Charlotte Perkins Gilman's Architectural Feminism* (Amherst: University of Massachusetts, 1988), 44.

79. Larry Ceplair, ed., *Charlotte Perkins Gilman: A Nonfiction Reader* (New York: Columbia University, 1991), 42.

80. Allen, 29, 45.

81. Allen, 34.

82. Quoted in Arnold Crompton, *Aurelia Henry Reinhardt, A Biographical Sketch* (Berkeley: Starr King School for the Ministry, 1997).

83. Quoted in Crompton.

## An Era of Feminine Foment

1. From Ramona Sawyer Barth, "Unitarian Women of the 19th Century," *Journal for Liberal Religion* 7 (1949): 133. Ramona Sawyer Barth (b. 1911) is a Unitarian Universalist (formerly Unitarian) writer and historian. This text was written prior to the Unitarian Universalist merger; original references to *Unitarian* have therefore been amended, with the author's permission, to include Universalist women, as well.

# References

✦ ✦ ✦

**Note:** This list of sources of anthology texts provides information about the earliest known locations of these texts. In some cases, reprint editions and other anthologies are also listed for readers who wish to learn more about these authors and texts.

## Call to Reform


Adams, Abigail. "We Are Determined to Foment a Rebellion." From *Mercy Warren,* by Alice Brown. New York: Charles Scribner's Sons, 1896.

Anthony, Susan B. "Woman's Rights and Wrongs." From notes for a speech (1854), Folder 23, Susan B. Anthony Collection. Schlesinger Library, Radcliffe College. Cambridge, MA.

Bodichon, Barbara Smith. *Reasons for the Enfranchisement of Women.* London: J. Bale, 1866.

Cary, Alice. "What Do Women Want of a Club?" From *A Memorial of Alice and Phoebe Cary, with Some of Their Later Poems* (pp. 78–82), edited by Mary Clemmer Ames. New York: Hurd and Houghton, 1873.

Chapman, Maria Weston. "The Times That Try Men's Souls." In *History of Woman Suffrage.* Vol. 1 (pp. 82–83), edited by Elizabeth Cady Stanton, Susan B. Anthony, and Matilda Jocelyn Gage. New York: Fowler and Wells, 1881.

Cobbe, Frances Power. "Woman as a Citizen of the State." In *The Duties of Women: A Course of Lectures* (pp. 172–193). London: Williams and Norgate, 1881. Reprint, Boston: Geo. H. Ellis, 1991.

[Crane], Caroline J. Bartlett. "The Individual Factor in Social Regeneration." *The New Unity* 34, new series 3 (6 August 1896): 382–384.

———. "What Women Can Do in Uniting the Culture and Relgious Forces of Society." In *Proceedings of the First American Congress of Liberal Religious Societies, Chicago, May 22–25, 1894* (pp. 18–21). Chicago: n.p., 1894.

Fuller, Margaret. "In Behalf of Woman." From *Woman in the Nineteenth Century* (pp. 24, 112, 136–137, 173–174). London: Clarke, 1845.

Gage, Frances Dana. "Male and Female Created He Them." In *History of Woman Suffrage.* Vol. 1 (pp. 112–113), edited by Elizabeth Cady Stanton, Susan B. Anthony, and Matilda Jocelyn Gage. New York: Fowler and Wells, 1881.

———. "One Hundred Years Hence." In *History of Woman Suffrage.* Vol. 3 (pp. 38–39), edited by Elizabeth Cady Stanton, Susan B. Anthony, and Matilda Jocelyn Gage. Rochester, NY: Susan B. Anthony, 1886. Reprinted in Eugene B. Navias, *Singing Our History: Tales, Texts and Tunes from Two Centuries of Unitarian and Universalist Hymns.* Boston: Unitarian Universalist Association, 1975.

Gordon, Eleanor. "Our Mission to Save by Culture." *Old & New* 9 (September 1900): 7.

———. "The Worth of Sympathy." *Old and New* 15 (June 1907): 43–44.

Harper, Frances Ellen Watkins. "The Woman's Christian Temperance Union and the Colored Woman." *African Methodist Episcopal Church Review* 4 (July 1888): 313–316. Reprinted in Frances Smith Foster, *A Brighter Coming Day: A Frances Ellen Watkins Reader.* New York: Feminist Press, 1990.

———. "Woman's Political Future." In *World's Congress of Representative Women* (pp. 435–437). Philadelphia: W. W. Houston, 1893. Reprinted in *Black Women in Nineteenth Century American Life: Their Words, Their Thoughts, Their Feelings* (pp. 244–247), edited by Bert James Loewenberg and Ruth Bogin (pp. 244–247). University Park: Pennsylvania State University Press, 1976.

[Mayo], Sarah Carter Edgarton. "A Thought on Female Culture." *Universalist and Ladies Repository* 10 (December 1841): 249.

Robinson, Harriet. "Uplifting the Sphere of Woman's Life." From *Massachusetts in the Woman Suffrage Movement.* Boston: Roberts Brothers, 1881.

Spencer, Anna Garlin. "Advantages and Disadvantages of Organization." In *World's Congress of Representative Women* (pp. 170–177). Philadelphia: W. W. Houston, 1893.

Stone, Lucy. "Disappointment Is the Lot of Women." From *History of Woman Suffrage.* Vol. 1 (pp. 165–167), edited by Elizabeth Cady Stanton, Susan B. Anthony, and Matilda Jocelyn Gage. New York: Fowler and Wells, 1881.

———. "To Labor for the Elevation of My Sex," Letter to Hannah Stone (1846). From *Lucy Stone: Pioneer of Woman's Rights* (pp. 65–67), by Alice Stone Blackwell. Boston: Little, Brown, 1930.

Stone, Lucy, and Henry Blackwell. "Protest Against the Laws of Marriage." In *History of Woman Suffrage.* Vol. 1 (pp. 260–261), edited by Elizabeth Cady Stanton, Susan B. Anthony, and Matilda Jocelyn Gage. New York: Fowler and Wells, 1881.

Stowe, Emily. "The Century of the Woman Movement." Unspecified newspaper clipping, Stowe-Gullen Collection. Victoria University. Toronto, n.d.

## The Search for Education

Blackwell, Elizabeth. "Criticism of the Physical Education of Girls." From *The Laws of Life, in Reference to the Physical Education of Girls* (pp. 122–134). New York: George Putnam, 1852.

———. "The Influence of Women in the Profession of Medicine." In *Essays in Medical Sociology.* Vol. 2 (pp. 5–27). London: Ernest Bell, 1902.

Brown, Olympia. "The Higher Education of Women." *The Repository* 51 (February 1874): 81–86.

Carpenter, Mary. "The Education of Workhouse Girls." From *On the Education of Pauper Girls.* Bristol: n.p., 1862. Reprinted in *The Education Papers* (pp. 50–57), edited by Dale Spender. New York: Routledge & Kegan Paul, 1987.

Dall, Caroline Healey. "The Educational Rights of Women." From "The Christian Demand and the Public Opinion," in *The College, the Market, and the Court; or Woman's Relation to Education, Labor, and Law* (pp. 3–10). Boston: Lee and Shepard, 1867.

Fuller, Margaret. "Conversations." From *Memoirs of Margaret Fuller Ossoli.* Vol. 1 (pp. 324–333), edited by Ralph Waldo Emerson, William Henry Channing, and James Freeman Clarke. Boston: Phillips, Sampson, 1852–1853.

———. "Profession of Teaching." From "The Wrongs of American Women. The Duty of American Women," in *Woman in the 19th Century and Kindred Papers Relating to the Sphere, Condition and Duties of Woman* (pp. 223–225), edited by Arthur B. Fuller. Boston: John P. Jewett, 1855. Reprint, New York: Source Book Press, n.d. Originally published in the *New York Tribune,* 30 September 1845.

———. "School Teaching." From *Memoirs of Margaret Fuller Ossoli.* Vol. 1 (pp. 177–180), edited by Ralph Waldo Emerson, William Henry Channing, and James Freeman Clarke. Boston: Phillips, Sampson, 1852–1853.

Hunt, Harriot Kezia. "From Educator to Physician." From *Glances and Glimpses; or 50 Years Social Including 20 Years Professional Life* (pp. 45–58, 110–117). Boston: John P. Jewett, 1856.

Livermore, Mary. "What Shall We Do with Our Daughters?" In *The Story of My Life; Or, The Sunshine and Shadow of Seventy Years* (pp. 615–629). Hartford, CT: A. D. Worthington, 1899.

Martineau, Harriet. *Household Education* (pp. 240–245). London: E. Moxon, 1848.

———. "On Female Education." *Monthly Repository* 18 (1823): 77–81.

Murray, Judith Sargent. "On the Equality of the Sexes." *Massachusetts Magazine* (March–April 1790): 132–135, 223–226.

Peabody, Elizabeth Palmer. "Spiritual Aspects of Early Childhood Education." From *Lectures in the Training Schools for Kindergartners* (pp. 14, 87–88, 158, 161, 164, 168, 170–171, 175). Boston: D. C. Heath, 1886.

———. "Thoughts on Kindergarten Education." From *Guide to the Kindergarten and Intermediate Class.* Rev. ed. (pp. 10–14, 35–37, 43–44, 56, 58–60, 104). New York: E. Steiger, 1877.

Williams, Fannie Barrier. "Club Movement among Colored Women." In *A New Negro for a New Century* (pp. 383–387, 390, 393, 416), edited by Booker T. Washington et al. Chicago: American Publishing House, 1900.

———. "The Intellectual Progress of the Colored Women of the United States since the Emancipation Proclamation." In *World's Congress of Representative Women* (pp. 696–711), edited by May Wright Sewall. Philadelphia: W. W. Houston, 1893. Reprinted in *Black Women in Nineteenth Century American Life: Their Words, Their Thoughts, Their Feelings* (pp. 270–278), edited by Bert James Loewenberg and Ruth Bogin. University Park: Pennsylvania State University Press, 1976.

Wollstonecraft, Mary. "Thoughts on the Education of Women." From *A Vindication of the Rights of Woman.* 2nd ed. 1792. Reprinted in *A Wollstonecraft Anthology* (pp. 84–112), edited by Janet Todd. New York: Columbia University, 1990.

## The Struggle for Racial Justice

Barton, Clara. "It Is Over: Speech to the Grand Army of the Republic, Memorial Day, 1879." From *Our Women Workers* (pp. 377–378), by Eliza Rice Hanson. Chicago: Star and Covenant Office, 1882.

Bradley, Amy Morris. "Establishing Schools in Wilmington." From diary and letters. Special Collections, William R. Perkins Library. Duke University, Durham, NC.

Chapman, Maria Weston. "How Can I Help Abolish Slavery? or, Counsels to the Newly Converted." *Anti-Slavery Tracts* 14 (1855): 7–9.

———. "Hymns of Freedom." In *Songs of the Free and Hymns of Christian Freedom.* Boston: Isaac Knapp, 1836.

Child, Lydia Maria. "Appeal to End Slavery." From *An Appeal in Favor of That Class of Americans Called Africans* (pp. 16, 22–24, 28–37, 99–100, 126–127, 134–135, 195–196, 210, 211, 216). New York: John S. Taylor, 1836.

Follen, Eliza Cabot. "And the Days of Thy Mourning Shall Be Ended." *Anti-Slavery Tracts* 12 (1855): 5–6.

———. "Auld Lang Syne." *Anti-Slavery Tracts* 12 (1855): 4.

———. "On Hearing of the Sadness of the Slave-Children from the Fear of Being Sold." *Anti-Slavery Tracts* 12 (1855): 8. Previously published as "Children in Slavery." In *Poems.* Boston: Wm. Crosby, 1839.

———. "Remember the Slave!" *Anti-Slavery Tracts* 12 (1855): 2–3.

———. "To Mothers in the Free States." *Anti-Slavery Tracts* 8 (1855): 1–4.

———. "Where Is Thy Brother?" In *Songs of the Free and Hymns of Christian Freedom.* Boston: Isaac Knapp, 1836.

[Harper], Frances Ellen Watkins. "Bury Me in a Free Land." *Liberator,* 14 January 1864.

———. "The Colored People in America." In *Poems on Miscellaneous Subjects.* Boston: J. B. Yerrington and Son, 1854.

———. "Letter to John Brown, November 1859." In *Echoes of Harper's Ferry* (pp. 418–419), edited by James Redpath. Boston: Thayer and Eldridge, 1860.

———. "Letter to Mary Brown, November 1859." In *The Underground Rail Road* (p. 791), edited by William Still. Philadelphia: Porters and Coates, 1872.

———. "We Are All Bound Up Together." In *Proceedings of the 11th Women's Rights Convention* (pp. 45–48). New York: n.p., May 1866.

Holley, Sallie. "My Work with the Anti-Slavery Society." From *A Life for Liberty: Anti-Slavery and Other Letters of Sallie Holley* (pp. 67–68, 80, 86–88, 99–100, 133–134, 149–150), edited by John White Chadwick. New York: G. P. Putnam's Sons, 1899.

———. “My Work with the Freedman’s School.” From *A Life for Liberty: Anti-Slavery and Other Letters of Sallie Holley* (pp. 209–213, 257–259), edited by John White Chadwick. New York: G. P. Putnam’s Sons, 1899.

Howe, Julia Ward. “Abolitionists in Boston.” From *Reminiscences 1819–1899* (pp. 152–157). Boston: Houghton, Mifflin, 1900.

———. “The Death of the Slave Lewis.” In *Passion Flowers* (pp. 161–165). Boston: Ticknor, Reed and Fields, 1854.

Kemble, Frances Anne. *Journal of a Residence on a Georgian Plantation in 1838–1839.* 1863. Reprint, edited by John A. Scott. Athens: University of Georgia Press, 1984.

Livermore, Mary. “How I Learned the Truth about Slavery.” From *The Story of My Life* (pp. 182–188, 212–217, 330, 356, 362–365). Hartford, CT: A. D. Worthington, 1899.

Ridley, Florida Ruffin. “The Negro in Boston.” *Our Boston* 2 (January 1927): 15–20.

———. “Two Gentlemen of Boston.” *Opportunity* (January 1926): 12–13.

Towne, Laura Matilda. “Pioneer Work on the Sea Islands.” *Southern Workman* (July 1901): 396–410.

———. “Reflections on Life at Penn School.” In *Letters and Diary of Laura M. Towne* (pp. 146, 167–168, 272–273, 281, 310), edited by Rupert S. Holland. Cambridge, MA: Riverside Press, 1912. Reprint, New York: Negro Universities Press, 1969.

## Reform in Religion

Adams, Hannah. “Religions of the World.” From *A Dictionary of All Religions and Religious Denominations.* 4th ed. (pp. 295–297). New York: James Eastburn, 1817; and *An Alphabetical Compendium of the Various Sects* (title page and pp. lv–lvi, 189, 190, 196–197, 199–200). Boston: B. Edes & Sons, 1784.

———. *Memoir of Miss Hannah Adams Written by Herself* (pp. 10–11). Boston: Gray & Bowen, 1832.

Barbauld, Anna Laetitia. “Improving Public Worship.” From “In What Respects Many of the Forms and Habits of Public Worship Are Susceptible of Improvement.” Section 5 of “Mrs. Barbauld’s Thoughts on Public Worship.” In *Collection of Essays and Tracts in Theology* (pp. 323–334), edited by Jared Sparks. Boston: n.p., 1824.

Barns, Lucy. “In Defense of Universalism.” From *Familiar Letters and Poems* (pp. 10–30, 46–51). Portland, ME: Printed by Francis Douglas, 1809. Reprint, Akron, OH: Aunty Brown, 1904.

Brown, Olympia. “Opening Doors.” Olympia Brown Papers, Schlesinger Library. Cambridge, MA. Reprinted in *Suffrage and Religious Principle: Speeches and Writings of Olympia Brown* (pp. 167–193), edited by Dana Greene. Metuchen, NJ: Scarecrow Press, 1983.

Chapin, Augusta J. “Women’s Work in the Church.” In *Proceedings at the Universalist Centennial* (pp. 52–53). Boston: Universalist Publishing House, 1870.

———. "The Fulfillment of Prophecy." From *The World's Congress of Religions* (pp. 25–26, 947), edited by J. W. Hanson. Boston: Gately & O'Gorman, 1894.

Cheney, Ednah Dow. "The Reign of Womanhood." In *Reminiscences* (pp. 223–236). Boston: Lee and Shephard, 1902.

Crane, Caroline Bartlett. "The Church and Poverty." *Old & New* 6 (October 1897): 255–257.

Crooker, Florence Kollock. "Why Women Ministers?" *Sunday Post* (11 January 1914).

Gillette, L. F. W. "Woman and Religion." *Ladies Repository* 44 (November 1870): 384.

Gilman, Charlotte Perkins [Stetson]. *His Religion and Hers: A Study of the Faith of Our Fathers and the Work of Our Mothers* (pp. 240–251, 260, 275, 283, 298). New York: Century, 1923. Reprint, Westport, CT: Hyperion Press, 1976.

Hanaford, Phebe. "The Question Answered." In *From Shore to Shore and Other Poems* (pp. 275–277). Boston: B. B. Russell, 1871.

———. "Feminist Biblical Critique." From *The Woman's Bible* (pp. 34–36, 116–118, 186), edited by Elizabeth Cady Stanton and the Revising Committee. New York: European, 1895. Reprint, Seattle: Coalition Task Force on Women and Religion, 1974.

Howe, Marie Jenney. "The Young Women and the Church." *Old & New* (September 1905). Originally attributed to Elizabeth Padgham.

Murdock, Marion. "A New Testament Woman." In *World's Parliament of Religions* (pp. 797–800). Chicago: Parliament, 1893.

[Murray], Judith Sargent Stevens. "Universal Catechism." From *Some Deductions from the System Promulgated in the Page of Divine Revelation: Ranged in the Order and Form of a Catechism.* Portsmouth, NH: Privately printed, 1782. Reprint, Cambridge, MA: Judith Sargent Murray Society, 1999.

———. "Theological Reflections." Letter 54, June 6, 1777. In *Judith Sargent Murray: Her First 100 Letters* (pp. 62–63), edited by Marianne Dunlop and Bonnie Smith. Gloucester, MA: Sargent House Museum, 1995.

———. "To My Youngest Brother: Letter 88." In *Judith Sargent Murray: Her First 100 Letters* (pp. 102–103), edited by Marianne Dunlop and Bonnie Smith. Gloucester, MA: Sargent House Museum, 1995.

Reinhardt, Aurelia Henry. "Worship: Its Fundamental Place in Liberal Religion." In *Unitarians Face a New Age: Report of the Commission on Appraisal* (pp. 70–78). Boston: American Unitarian Association, 1936.

Safford, Mary. "Obedience to the Heavenly Vision," transcribed by Sarah Oelberg. Mary Safford Papers. State Historical Society of Iowa, Iowa City, IA.

Williams, Fannie Barrier. "Religious Duty to the Negro." In *Neely's History of the Parliament of Religions* (pp. 631–636), edited by Walter Houghton. Chicago: Neely, 1894.

Woolley, Celia Parker. "The Ideal Unitarian Church." *Unity Mission* 1 (May 1889): 3–11.

# Index

✦ ✦ ✦

**Note:** Page numbers in **bold** indicate Biographical Sketches.

# About the Editor

✦ ✦ ✦

DOROTHY MAY EMERSON has been active for years in uncovering and communicating the contributions of historic Universalist and Unitarian women to the quest for social justice. Her search for her justice-seeking foremothers led to the development of this anthology and to the founding of the Unitarian Universalist Women's Heritage Society, which she currently serves as executive director. A Unitarian Universalist minister since 1988, she holds a master of divinity degree from Harvard Divinity School and a doctor of ministry degree from Andover Newton Theological School. She has served churches in Wakefield, Belmont, Medford, and Weymouth, Massachusetts. She has lectured on Unitarian Universalist women's history at Meadville/Lombard Theological School and is a frequent speaker and workshop leader at conferences and congregations across the United States. She lives with her partner in Medford, Massachusetts, where they share the operation of Rainbow Solutions—Financial and Educational Services for the New Millennium.